ACCA

Paper 2.2

CORPORATE AND BUSINESS LAW

For exams in December 2005 and June 2006

Study Text

In this June 2005 new edition

- A new **user-friendly format** for easy navigation
- **Exam-centred topic coverage**, directly linked to ACCA's syllabus and study guide
- **Exam focus points** showing you what the examiner will want you to do
- Regular **fast forward** summaries emphasising the key points in each chapter
- **Questions** and **quick quizzes** to test your understanding
- **Exam question bank** containing exam standard questions with answers
- **A full index** and table of cases

BPP's **i-Learn** and **i-Pass** products also support this paper.

FOR EXAMS IN DECEMBER 2005 AND JUNE 2006

SCOTTISH VARIANT CANDIDATES

BPP's FREE Scottish variant supplement enhances this Study Text and tells you what you need to know for the exam. Telephone Customer Services on 0845 0751 100 (UK callers only) or 020 8740 2211 for more information.

First edition 2001
Fifth edition June 2005

ISBN 0 7517 2317 7 (Previous edition 0 7517 1664 2)

British Library Cataloguing-in-Publication Data
A catalogue record for this book
is available from the British Library

Published by

BPP Professional Education
Aldine House, Aldine Place
London W12 8AW

www.bpp.com

Printed in Great Britain by Ashford Colour Press

We are grateful to the Association of Chartered Certified Accountants for permission to reproduce past examination questions. The suggested solutions in the exam answer bank have been prepared by BPP Professional Education.

Contents

Page

Computer-based learning products from BPP

If you want to reinforce your studies by **interactive** learning, try BPP's **i-Learn** product, covering major syllabus areas in an interactive format. For **self-testing**, try **i-Pass,** which offers a large number of **objective test questions**, particularly useful where objective test questions form part of the exam.

See the order form at the back of this text for details of these innovative learning tools.

Learn Online

Learn Online uses BPP's wealth of teaching experience to produce a fully **interactive** e-learning resource **delivered via the Internet**. The site offers comprehensive **tutor support** and features areas such as **study**, **practice**, **email service**, **revision** and **useful resources**.

Visit our website www.bpp.com/learnonline/cima to sample aspects of the campus free of charge.

Learning to Learn Accountancy

BPP's ground-breaking **Learning to Learn Accountancy** book is designed to be used both at the outset of your ACCA studies and throughout the process of learning accountancy. It challenges you to consider how you study and gives you helpful hints about how to approach the various types of paper which you will encounter. It can help you **focus your studies on the subject and exam**, enabling you to **acquire knowledge**, **practise and revise efficiently and effectively**.

The BPP Study Text

Aims of this Study Text

To provide you with the knowledge and understanding, skills and application techniques that you need if you are to be successful in your exams

This Study Text has been written around the **Corporate and Business Law** syllabus.

- It is **comprehensive**. It covers the syllabus content. No more, no less.
- It is written at the **right level**. Each chapter is written with ACCA's syllabus and study guide in mind
- It is targeted to the **exam**. We have taken account of the pilot paper, guidance the examiner has given and the assessment methodology.

To allow you to study in the way that best suits your learning style and the time you have available, by following your personal Study Plan (see page (viii))

You may be studying at home on your own until the date of the exam, or you may be attending a full-time course. You may like to (and have time to) read every word, or you may prefer to (or only have time to) skim-read and devote the remainder of your time to question practice. Wherever you fall in the spectrum, you will find the BPP Study Text meets your needs in designing and following your personal Study Plan.

To tie in with the other components of the BPP Effective Study Package to ensure you have the best possible chance of passing the exam (see page (vi))

The BPP Effective Study Package

Recommended period of use	The BPP Effective Study Package
From the outset and throughout	**Learning to Learn Accountancy** Read this invaluable book as you begin your studies and refer to it as you work through the various elements of the BPP Effective Study Package. It will help you to acquire knowledge, practice and revise, efficiently and effectively.
Three to twelve months before the exam	**Study Text and i-Learn** Use the Study Text to acquire knowledge, understanding, skills and the ability to apply techniques. Use BPP's **i-Learn** product to reinforce your learning.
Throughout	**Learn Online** Study, practise, revise and take advantage of other useful resources with BPP's fully interactive e-learning site with comprehensive tutor support.
Throughout	**i-Pass** **i-Pass**, our computer-based testing package, provides objective test questions in a variety of formats and is ideal for self-assessment.
One to six months before the exam	**Practice & Revision Kit** Try the numerous examination-format questions, for which there are realistic suggested solutions prepared by BPP's own authors. Then attempt the two mock exams.
From three months before the exam until the last minute	**Passcards** Work through these short, memorable notes which are focused on what is most likely to come up in the exam you will be sitting.
One to six months before the exam	**Success CDs** The CDs cover the vital elements of your syllabus in less than 90 minutes per subject. They also contain exam hints to help you fine tune your strategy.

Help yourself study for your ACCA exams

Exams for professional bodies such as ACCA are very different from those you have taken at college or university. You will be under **greater time pressure before** the exam – as you may be combining your study with work. There are many different ways of learning and so the BPP Study Text offers you a number of different tools to help you through. Here are some hints and tips: they are not plucked out of the air, but **based on research and experience**. (You don't need to know that long-term memory is in the same part of the brain as emotions and feelings - but it's a fact anyway.)

The right approach

1 **The right attitude**

Believe in yourself	Yes, there is a lot to learn. Yes, it is a challenge. But thousands have succeeded before and you can too.
Remember why you're doing it	Studying might seem a grind at times, but you are doing it for a reason: to advance your career.

2 **The right focus**

Read through the Syllabus and learning outcomes	These tell you what you are expected to know and are supplemented by Exam focus points in the text.
Study the Exam Paper section	Past papers are likely to be good guides to what you should expect in the exam.

3 **The right method**

The whole picture	You need to grasp the detail - but keeping in mind how everything fits into the whole picture will help you understand better. • The **Introduction** of each chapter puts the material in context. • The **Syllabus content, Study guide** and **Exam focus points** show you what you need to **grasp**.
In your own words	To absorb the information (and to practise your written communication skills), it helps to **put it into your own words**. • **Take notes.** • Answer the **questions** in each chapter. You will practise your written communication skills, which become increasingly important as you progress through your ACCA exams. • Draw **mindmaps**. We have an example for the whole syllabus. • Try **'teaching' a subject** to a colleague or friend.
Give yourself cues to jog your memory	The BPP Study Text uses **bold** to **highlight key points**. • Try **colour coding** with a highlighter pen. • Write **key points** on cards.

4 **The right review**

Review, review, review	It is a **fact** that regularly reviewing a topic in summary form can **fix it in your memory**. Because **review** is so important, the BPP Study Text helps you to do so in many ways. • **Chapter roundups** summarise the 'Fast forward' key points in each chapter. Use them to recap each study session. • The **Quick quiz** is another review technique you can use to ensure that you have grasped the essentials. • Go through the **Examples** in each chapter a second or third time.

Developing your personal Study Plan

BPP's **Learning to Learn Accountancy** book emphasises the need to prepare (and use) a study plan. Planning and sticking to the plan are key elements of learning success.
There are four steps you should work through.

Step 1 **How do you learn?**

First you need to be aware of your style of learning. The BPP **Learning to Learn Accountancy** book commits a chapter to this **self-discovery**. What types of intelligence do you display when learning? You might be advised to brush up on certain study skills before launching into this Study Text.

BPP's **Learning to Learn Accountancy** book helps you to identify what intelligences you show more strongly and then details how you can tailor your study process to your preferences. It also includes handy hints on how to develop intelligences you exhibit less strongly, but which might be needed as you study accountancy.

Are you a **theorist** or are you more **practical**? If you would rather get to grips with a theory before trying to apply it in practice, you should follow the study sequence on page (ix). If the reverse is true (you like to know why you are learning theory before you do so), you might be advised to flick through Study Text chapters and look at examples, case studies and questions (Steps 8, 9 and 10 in the **suggested study sequence**) before reading through the detailed theory.

Step 2 **How much time do you have?**

Work out the time you have available per week, given the following.

- The standard you have set yourself
- The time you need to set aside later for work on the Practice & Revision Kit and Passcards
- The other exam(s) you are sitting
- Very importantly, practical matters such as work, travel, exercise, sleep and social life

		Hours
Note your time available in box A.	A	

Step 3 **Allocate your time**

- Take the time you have available per week for this Study Text shown in box A, multiply it by the number of weeks available and insert the result in box B. B [ ]
- Divide the figure in box B by the number of chapters in this text and insert the result in box C. C [ ]

Remember that this is only a rough guide. Some of the chapters in this book are longer and more complicated than others, and you will find some subjects easier to understand than others.

Step 4 **Implement**

Set about studying each chapter in the time shown in box C, following the key study steps in the order suggested by your particular learning style.

This is your personal **Study Plan**. You should try and combine it with the study sequence outlined below. You may want to modify the sequence a little (as has been suggested above) to adapt it to your **personal style**.

BPP's **Learning to Learn Accountancy** gives further guidance on developing a study plan, and deciding where and when to study.

Suggested study sequence

It is likely that the best way to approach this Study Text is to tackle the chapters in the order in which you find them. Taking into account your individual learning style, you could follow this sequence.

Key study steps	Activity
Step 1 **Topic list**	Each numbered topic is a numbered section in the chapter.
Step 2 **Introduction**	This gives you the big picture in terms of the context of the chapter. The content is referenced to the Study Guide, and Exam Guidance shows how the topic is likely to be examined. In other words, it sets your objectives for study.
Step 3 **Knowledge brought forward boxes**	In these we highlight information and techniques that it is assumed you have 'brought forward' with you from your earlier studies. If there are topics which have changed recently due to legislation for example, these topics are explained in more detail.
Step 4 **Fast forward**	Fast forward boxes give you a quick summary of the content of each of the main chapter sections. They are listed together in the roundup at the end of each chapter to provide you with an overview of the contents of the whole chapter.
Step 5 **Explanations**	Proceed methodically through the chapter, reading each section thoroughly and making sure you understand.
Step 6 **Key terms and Exam focus points**	• Key terms can often earn you *easy marks* if you state them clearly and correctly in an appropriate exam answer (and they are highlighted in the index at the back of the text). • Exam focus points state how we think the examiner intends to examine certain topics.
Step 7 **Note taking**	Take brief notes, if you wish. Avoid the temptation to copy out too much. Remember that being able to put something into your own words is a sign of being able to understand it. If you find you cannot explain something you have read, read it again before you make the notes.

Key study steps	Activity
Step 8 **Examples**	Follow each through to its solution very carefully.
Step 9 **Case studies**	Study each one, and try to add flesh to them from your own experience. They are designed to show how the topics you are studying come alive (and often come unstuck) in the real world.
Step 10 **Questions**	Make a very good attempt at each one.
Step 11 **Answers**	Check yours against ours, and make sure you understand any discrepancies.
Step 12 **Chapter roundup**	Work through it carefully, to make sure you have grasped the significance of all the fast forward points.
Step 13 **Quick quiz**	When you are happy that you have covered the chapter, use the Quick quiz to check how much you have remembered of the topics covered and to practise questions in a variety of formats.
Step 14 **Question practice**	Either at this point, or later when you are thinking about revising, make a full attempt at the Question(s) suggested at the very end of the chapter. You can find these in the Exam Question Bank at the end of the Study Text, along with the answers so you can see how you did. We highlight those that are introductory, and those which are of the standard you would expect to find in an exam. If you have bought i-Pass, use this too.

Short of time: Skim study technique?

You may find you simply do not have the time available to follow all the key study steps for each chapter, however you adapt them for your particular learning style. If this is the case, follow the **skim study** technique below.

- Study the chapters in the order you find them in the Study Text.
- For each chapter:
  - Follow the key study steps 1-3
  - Skim-read through step 5, looking out for the points highlighted in the fast forward boxes (step 4)
  - Jump to step 12
  - Go back to step 6
  - Follow through steps 8 and 9
  - Prepare outline answers to questions (steps 10/11)
  - Try the Quick quiz (step 13), following up any items you can't answer
  - Do a plan for the Question (step 14), comparing it against our answers
  - You should probably still follow step 7 (note-taking), although you may decide simply to rely on the BPP Passcards for this.

Moving on...

However you study, when you are ready to embark on the practice and revision phase of the BPP Effective Study Package, you should still refer back to this Study Text, both as a source of **reference** (you should find the index particularly helpful for this) and as a way to **review** (the Fast forwards, Exam focus points, Chapter roundups and Quick quizzes help you here).

And remember to keep careful hold of this Study Text – you will find it invaluable in your work.

More advice on Study Skills can be found in BPP's **Learning to Learn Accountancy** book.

Syllabus

Aim

To develop a knowledge and understanding of the general legal framework within which an accountant operates. To develop an awareness of and an ability to understand both common law and statute in relation to specific legal areas of central importance to business.

Objectives

On completion of this paper candidates should be able to:

- Analyse and evaluate situations from a legal perspective
- Identify the essential elements of the English legal system including the main sources of law and explain its operation
- Explain and demonstrate an ability to use the essential principles relating to the formation, content and remedies for the breach of contracts
- Explain the rules of agency as they apply to sole traders, partnerships and companies
- Explain the law relating to partnerships
- Describe the different types of company and explain the rules relating to their financing, management, administration and regulation
- Explain the law relating to employment relationships with particular regard to dismissal, redundancy and discrimination

Position of the paper in the overall syllabus

There is no prerequisite knowledge for this paper although the generic skills developed in Part 1 will provide the basis for the substantive study undertaken.

Although all of the work done in other papers in Part 2 takes place within the legal framework, legal regulation is particularly relevant to Paper 2.1 *Information Systems,* Paper 2.3 *Business Taxation (UK)* and Paper 2.6 *Audit and Internal Review.* Questions in Paper 2.2 will not assume, or draw on, any knowledge from those papers.

In Part 3, Paper 3.2 *Advanced Taxation,* will require an ability to understand and apply tax law. Paper 3.6 *Advanced Corporate Reporting* will address the issue of corporate insolvency.

1 **The English legal system**

This section provides an introduction to some key features of the English legal system and will facilitate understanding of the sources of law, how law is administered and how legal rules emerge in the legal system.

(a) Court structure and the administration of justice
(b) Case law and legislation: precedent, statutory instruments, statutory interpretation
(c) Arbitration
(d) The impact of European Community legislation
(e) Human Rights

2 **General principles of the law of contract**

This section deals with major features of the formation, content and discharge of a contract and will provide an understanding of the basic nature of contractual agreements.

(a) Formation: offer, consideration, intention to create legal relations
(b) Contents: terms, exclusion clauses and their control
(c) Contracts in restraint of trade
(d) Breach of contract and remedies

3 **Agency and partnership**

This section will familiarise the student with those general rules of agency which find specific application in relation to partnerships and companies. It also examines the legal rules governing the operation of partnerships.

(a) Creation of agency
(b) Principal and agent: reciprocal rights and duties
(c) Authority of the agent
(d) Formation of partnerships
(e) Internal regulation of partnerships
(f) Partnerships and outsiders

4 **The company form**

This section deals with the nature of companies: both the private company and the public limited company, in comparison to the sole trader and the partnership.

(a) The limited company – distinguished from partnership
(b) The private company and public limited company
(c) The meaning and consequences of separate legal personality

5 **The formation and constitution of the company**

This section examines the legal requirements controlling the setting up of a company.

(a) The formalities involved in registering a company
(b) The constitutional documents of the company memorandum and articles of association
(c) The contractual capacity of a company
(d) Statutory books: records and returns

6 **Capital and financing of companies**

This section deals in outline with the capital and financing of companies, covering share and loan capital.

(a) Share capital: ordinary and preference shares
(b) Loan capital: debentures and company charges
(c) Capital maintenance and dividend law

7 **Management and administration of a company**

This section takes an overview of the legal obligations of the management in relation to the administration of the company. The role of key personnel is identified and the rights and obligations they have are explored.

(a) Directors: appointment, termination of office and disqualification; duties (especially duty of care); powers

(b) Company secretary: duties; powers

(c) Auditors: appointment, removal, resignation; duties; powers

(d) Insider dealing

8 **Company meetings**

This section deals with the function and conduct of the company meeting.

(a) Types of meetings: ordinary and extraordinary general meetings
(b) Types of resolutions: ordinary, extraordinary, special, elective and written

9 **Majority control and minority protection**

This section examines the way in which potential abuses of majority power may be prevented or remedied.

(a) Unfair prejudice
(b) Just and equitable winding up
(c) DTI investigations

10 **Insolvency**

This section will introduce students to the ways in which insolvent companies may be dealt with.

(a) Voluntary liquidation
(b) Compulsory liquidation
(c) Administration

11 **Employment**

This section focuses on the major legislative and common law principles which govern employment relationships.

(a) Contracts of service and contracts for services
(b) Unfair and wrongful dismissal
(c) Redundancy
(d) Discrimination

Excluded topics

The syllabus does not attempt to cover every aspect of the various subject areas it deals with. For example, contract does not cover misrepresentation or frustration.

Key areas of the syllabus

Company law, as set out in sections 4-10 above, is central to the syllabus and it will provide a possible 50% of the total marks allocated in any particular paper.

Paper 2.2

Corporate and Business Law (English)

Study Guide

1 ENGLISH LEGAL SYSTEM – 1

Court structure and administration of justice

- Understand how different types of cases are dealt with by different courts
- Identify the major courts and their relationship of seniority
- Explain how appeals go from one court to another

2 ENGLISH LEGAL SYSTEM – 2

Case law and legislation

- Explain what is meant by case law and precedent within the context of the hierarchy of the courts
- Explain legislation and evaluate delegated legislation
- Illustrate the rules and presumptions used by the courts in interpreting statutes
- The impact of human rights law

3 ENGLISH LEGAL SYSTEM – 3

European Union as a source of law

- Evaluate the impact of the various institutions of the European Union on UK law
- Provide examples of the impact of the EU on domestic law

Arbitration

Evaluate arbitration as an alternative to the court structure in business relationships

4 GENERAL PRINCIPLES OF THE LAW OF CONTRACT – 1

Formation

- Analyse the nature of a simple contract
- Distinguish the legal requirements for the creation of a contract
- Explain the meaning of offer and distinguish it from invitations to treat
- Explain the meaning and consequence of acceptance

5 GENERAL PRINCIPLES OF THE LAW OF CONTRACT – 2

Formation

- Explain the need for consideration
- Consider the doctrine of privity
- Distinguish the presumptions relating to intention to create legal relations

6 GENERAL PRINCIPLES OF THE LAW OF CONTRACT – 3

Contents

- Distinguish terms from mere representations
- Define the various contractual terms
- Explain the effect of exclusion clauses and evaluate their control

7 GENERAL PRINCIPLES OF THE LAW OF CONTRACT – 4

Breach of contract and remedies

- Explain the meaning and effect of breach of contract
- Explain the rules relating to the award of damages
- Consider the equitable remedies for breach of contract

8 AGENCY – 1

- Define the role of the agent and give examples of such relationships
- Explain how the agency relationship is established
- Define the authority of the agent

9 AGENCY – 2

- Analyse the reciprocal rights and duties between principal and agent
- Detail the relationship between the agent and third parties

10 PARTNERSHIP – 1

Formation of partnership

- Define and explain the role of the partnership form in the context of contemporary business organisation
- Consider how partnerships come into being
- Demonstrate a knowledge of the legislation governing the partnership, both unlimited and limited

11 PARTNERSHIP – 2

Internal regulation of partnerships

- Analyse the duties of partners to each other
- Analyse the rights of partners to each other
- Explain what is meant by partnership property

12 PARTNERSHIP – 3

Partnerships and outsiders

- Explain the authority of partners in relation to partnership activity
- Analyse the liability of various partners for partnership debts
- Explain the way in which partnerships can be brought to an end

13 COMPANY LAW – 1

The company form

- Distinguish between companies and partnerships

- Analyse different types of companies, especially private and public companies
- Explain the meaning and effect of limited liability

14 COMPANY LAW – 2

The company form

- Illustrate the effect of separate personality
- Cite instances where separate personality will be ignored

15 COMPANY LAW – 3

The formation of the company

- Describe the procedure for registering companies, both public and private
- Detail the statutory books, records and returns that companies must keep or make
- Explain the controls over the names that companies may or must use

16 COMPANY LAW – 4

The constitution of the company

- Detail the content and effect of the memorandum of association
- Describe the contents of Table A articles of association
- Analyse the effect of a company's constitutional documents
- Explain how articles of association can be changed

17 COMPANY LAW – 5

Share capital

- Examine the different meanings of capital
- Illustrate the difference between various classes of shares
- Explain the procedure for altering class rights

18 COMPANY LAW – 6

Loan capital

- Define companies' borrowing powers
- Explain the meaning of debenture
- Distinguish loan capital from share capital
- Explain the concept of a company charge and distinguish between fixed and floating charges
- Detail the need and the procedure for registering company charges

19 COMPANY LAW – 7

Capital maintenance and dividend law

- Explain the doctrine of capital maintenance
- Examine the effect of issuing shares at either discount, or premium
- Explain the rules governing the distribution of dividends in both private and public companies

20 COMPANY LAW – 8

Directors – 1

- Explain the role of directors in the operation of a company
- Detail the ways in which directors are appointed, can lose their office or be subject to a disqualification order
- Distinguish between the powers of the board of directors, the managing director and individual directors to bind their company

21 COMPANY LAW – 9

Directors – 2

- Explain the duties that directors owe to their companies
- Demonstrate an understanding of some of the ways in which the companies legislation has attempted to control directors
- Distinguish between fraudulent and wrongful trading
- Insider dealing

22 COMPANY LAW – 10

Other company officers

- Detail the appointment procedure relating to, and the duties and powers of, a company secretary
- Detail the appointment procedure relating to, and the duties and powers of, company auditors

23 COMPANY LAW – 11

Company meetings and resolutions

- Distinguish between types of meetings: ordinary and extraordinary general meetings and class meetings
- Explain the procedure for calling such meetings
- detail the procedure for conducting company meetings
- Distinguish between types of resolutions: ordinary, extraordinary, special, elective and written

24 COMPANY LAW – 12

Majority control and minority protection

- Explain the normal rule of majority control as expressed in *Foss v Harbottle*
- Consider the common law exceptions to *Foss v Harbottle*
- Evaluate the just and equitable winding up procedures as a means of protecting minority rights
- Discuss the statutory protection relating to unfairly prejudicial conduct under the companies legislation as an alternative to winding up
- Consider Department of Trade and Industry investigations as a form of minority protection

25 COMPANY INSOLVENCY – 13

- Explain the meaning of and procedure involved in voluntary liquidation
- Explain the meaning of and procedure involved in compulsory liquidation
- Consider administration as an alternative to winding up

26 EMPLOYMENT LAW – 1

Contracts of service and for services

- Distinguish between employees and the self-employed
- Explain why such a distinction is important
- Explain the nature of the contract of employment and give examples of the main duties placed on the parties to such a contract

27 EMPLOYMENT LAW – 2

Dismissal and redundancy

- Distinguish between wrongful and unfair dismissal including constructive dismissal
- Explain what is meant by redundancy
- Detail the remedies available to those who have been subject to unfair dismissal or redundancy

28 EMPLOYMENT LAW – 3

Discrimination

- Explain what is meant by discrimination in its various forms, including indirect as well as direct discrimination
- Detail the legal provisions which seek to control discrimination
- Detail the remedies available to those who have been subjected to discrimination

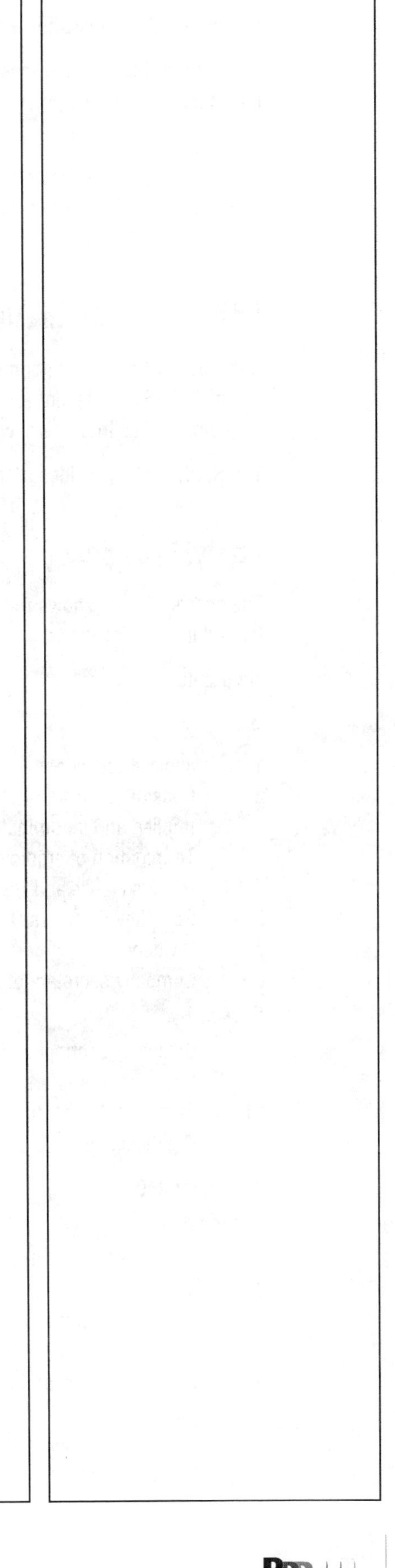

The exam paper

The examination is a three hour paper divided into two sections.

Section A will contain short knowledge-based questions.

Section B will be problem-based and will test communication skills and the ability to appraise and analyse information.

		Number of Marks
Section A:	Choice of 6 from 8 questions (10 marks each)	60
Section B:	Choice of 2 from 4 questions (20 marks each)	40
		100

Additional information

Knowledge of new legislation will not be expected until at least six months after the last day of the month in which the Royal Assent (or similar procedure in other country) is given, or six months after the specific provision comes into effect, whichever is the later.

The Study Guide provides more detailed guidance on the syllabus.

Analysis of past papers

The analysis below shows the topics which have been examined in all sittings of the current syllabus so far and in the Pilot Paper.

June 2005

Section A

1 Judicial precedent
2 Consideration
3 Implied and innominate terms
4 Termination of employment
5 Objects clause and *ultra vires*
6 Company Directors Disqualification Act 1986
7 Dividends
8 Company secretary of a plc

Section B

9 Breach of contract and remedies
10 Duties of promoters
11 Shares and debentures: types of company
12 Rights, liabilities and authority of partners

December 2004

Section A

1 ELS: Statutory interpretation
2 Contract: offers, invitation to threat and tenders
3 Contract: privity and how it can be avoided
4 Contract: remedies for breach
5 Company: types of director
6 Company: names and 'passing off'
7 Company: insider dealing
8 Company: winding up, S122IA 1986

Section B

9 Contract: formation including intention to create, consideration and acceptance
10 Employment: dismissal including rights and remedies
11 Business associations: types of business association and appropriateness
12 Company: objects clause and directors' duties

June 2004

Section A

1 English legal system: judicial precedent
2 Contract: offers and invitations to treat
3 Contract: measure and remoteness of damages
4 Employment law: redundancy
5 Company: winding up
6 Company: Articles of Association
7 Company: debentures and charges
8 Company: redemption and purchase of shares

Section B

9 Contract: exclusion clauses
10 Partnership: partnership property and dissolution
11 Company: shareholder liability and issue of shares
12 Company: directors' authority and duties; removal of directors

December 2003

Section A

1 English legal system: sources of law
2 Contract: unilateral and collateral contracts
3 Contract: contract terms
4 Agency: establishment of agency
5 Business associations: liability of partners
6 Company: memorandum of association; business names
7 Company: share capital
8 Company: appointment and removal of directors

Section B

9 Contract: offer and acceptance
10 Employment: employees and independent contractors
11 Company: director's contracts and insider dealing
12 Company: wrongful and fraudulent trading

June 2003

Section A

1 English legal system: delegated legislation
2 Contract: offer, acceptance and revocation
3 Contract: in restraint of trade
4 Contract: remedies for breach
5 Employment: fair and unfair dismissal
6 Company: veil of incorporation
7 Company: directors' powers
8 Company: auditors

Section B

9 Contract: consideration, privity
10 Partnership: rights and duties

11 Company: minority protection
12 Company: memorandum, articles, charges

December 2002

Section A

1 English legal system: civil court system and procedure
2 Contract: consideration
3 Contract: express and implied terms
4 Contract: remedies for breach
5 Business associations: termination of partnership
6 Company: promoters and pre-incorporation contracts
7 Company: class rights
8 Company: written and elective resolutions

Section B

9 Contract: existing contractual duties
10 Employment: unfair dismissal and redundancy
11 Company: alteration of share capital
12 Company: authority of company directors

June 2002

Section A

1 English legal system: EU law
2 Contract: distinction between offer and invitation to treat
3 Contract: exclusion clauses and their control
4 Employment: employer common law duties, constructive dismissal
5 Business associations: limited/unlimited companies
6 Company: directors' fiduciary duties
7 Company: dividends
8 Company: compulsory/voluntary winding up

Section B

9 Contract: breach of contract
10 Business associations: partnership and agency
11 Company: publicity and registration
12 Company: articles and directors

December 2001

Section A

1 English legal system: statutory interpretation, Human Rights Act 1998
2 Contract: privity
3 Contract: discharge
4 Employment: constructive dismissal, disability discrimination
5 Business associations: names and legal implications
6 Agency: authority
7 Company: share capital
8 Company: general meetings

Section B

1 Contract: agreement
2 Business associations: best options
3 Company: insider dealing
4 Company: minority protection

Pilot paper

Section A

1 English legal system: delegated legislation
2 Contract: intention to create legal relations
3 Contract: terms, conditions and warranties
4 Contract: damages
5 Employment: contracts of service/for service
6 Company: formation
7 Company: loan capital
8 Company: company secretary

Section B

9 Contract: formation
10 Partnership: rights and duties
11 Company: directors duties and appointment, articles
12 Company: directors duties/disqualification

Oxford Brookes BSc (Hons) in Applied Accounting

The standard required of candidates completing Part 2 is that required in the final year of a UK degree. Students completing Parts 1 and 2 will have satisfied the examination requirement for an honours degree in Applied Accounting, awarded by Oxford Brookes University.

To achieve the degree, you must also submit two pieces of work based on a **Research and Analysis Project.**

- A 5,000 word **Report** on your chosen topic, which demonstrates that you have acquired the necessary research, analytical and IT skills.
- A 1,500 word **Key Skills Statement**, indicating how you have developed your interpersonal and communication skills.

BPP was selected by the ACCA and Oxford Brookes University to produce the official text *Success in your Research and Analysis Project* to support students in this task. The book pays particular attention to key skills not covered in the professional examinations.

BPP also offers courses and mentoring services.

The Oxford Brookes project text can be ordered using the form at the end of this study text.

Oxford Institute of International Finance MBA

The Oxford Institute of International Finance (OXIIF), a joint venture between the ACCA and Oxford Brookes University, offers an MBA for finance professionals.

For this MBA, credits are awarded for your ACCA studies, and entry to the MBA course is available to those who have completed their ACCA professional stage studies. The MBA was launched in 2002 and has attracted participants from all over the world.

The qualification features an introductory module (*Foundations of Management*). Other modules include *Global Business Strategy, Managing Self Development,* and *Organisational Change & Transformation.*

Research Methods are also taught, as they underpin the **research dissertation**.

The MBA programme is delivered through the use of targeted paper study materials, developed by BPP, and taught over the Internet by OXIIF personnel using BPP's virtual campus software.

For further information, please see the Oxford Institute's website: www.oxfordinstitute.org.

Continuing professional development

ACCA introduced a new continuing professional development requirement for members from 1 January 2005. Members will be required to complete and record 40 units of CPD annually, of which 21 units must be verifiable learning or training activity.

BPP has an established professional development department which offers a range of relevant, professional courses to reflect the needs of professionals working in both industry and practice. To find out more, visit the website: www.bpp.com/pd or call the client care team on 0845 226 2422.

Syllabus mindmap

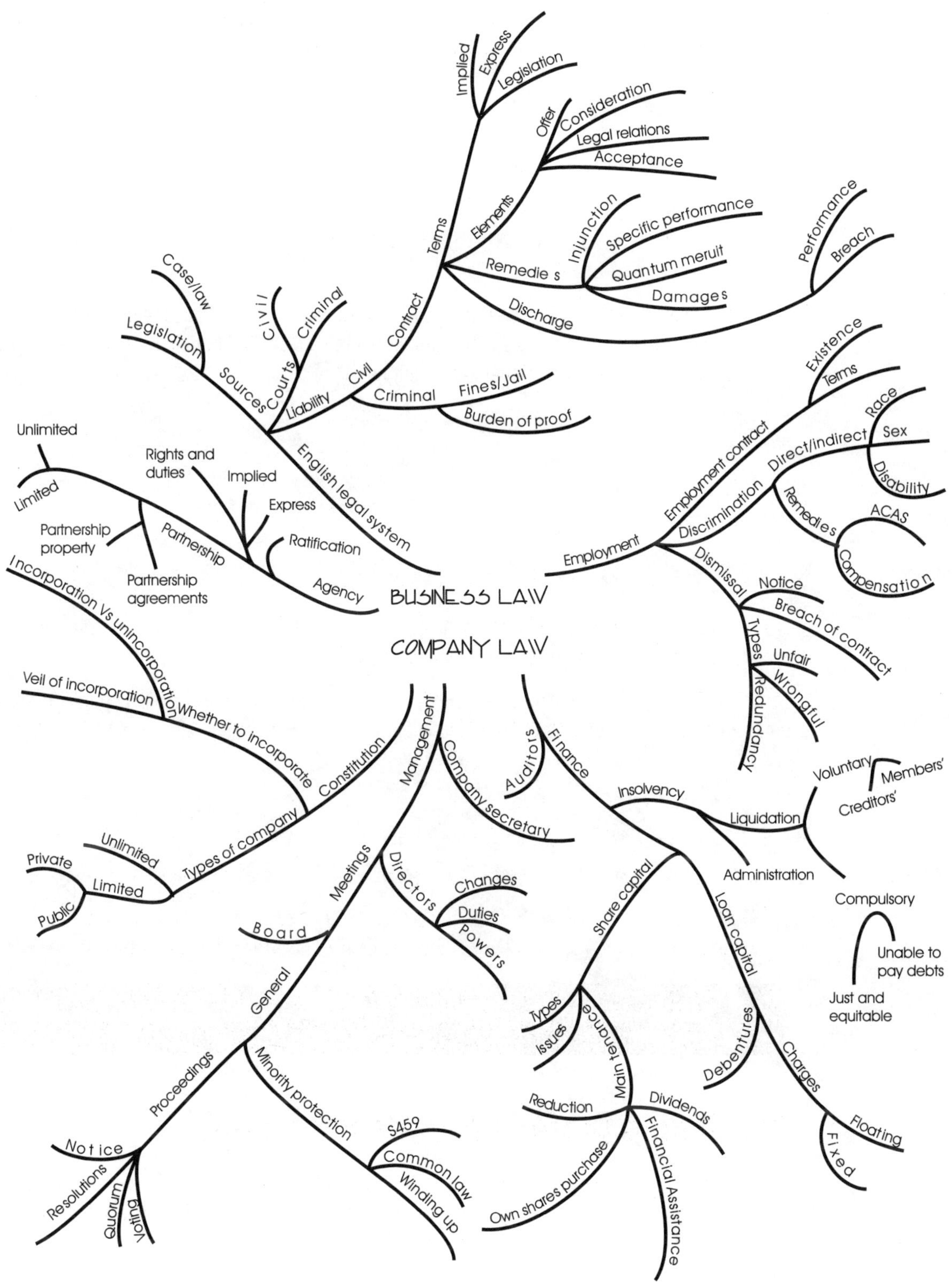

Part A
English Legal System

1

Introduction to English law

Topic list	Syllabus reference
1 Criminal and civil liability	1(a)
2 The system of courts	1(a)
3 Tribunals	1(a)
4 Arbitration	1(c)

Introduction

As an **accountant**, you are obviously not expected to be an expert **lawyer**. Why then study corporate and business law? The aim of this syllabus is to develop a knowledge and understanding of the general legal framework within which an accountant operates. Whether working in a partnership or a company (business associations), you will be in an organisation that operates within the English legal system. The organisation will make contracts in its dealings with suppliers and customers and it will be subject to employment law in 'hiring and firing' staff. These are just a couple of examples of the interaction of the law with everyday business life. As an accountant, whether involved with the purchase ledger, the sales ledger, the payroll or in some other way, what you can and cannot do will be dictated as much by the law as by your company's policies and procedures. You will not need to be an expert in legal matters, but if you at least have some awareness of the effect of the law on what you do, you will be a better accountant.

The **English legal system** consists of practical and down-to-earth sets of procedures and rules designed to provide resolutions to ordinary problems. Publicity tends to focus on the higher courts, such as the Court of Appeal and the House of Lords. However the vast majority of cases are heard in the magistrates' courts or the county courts.

Introduction (cont)

Many people, when they think of the law, have an image in their minds of judge and jury, or 'cops and robbers'. These are manifestations of **criminal** law. Business conduct is generally regulated by **civil** law. The distinction between criminal and civil law is fundamental to the English legal system. In order to understand the English legal system, it is necessary to understand the differences between criminal and civil cases.

This chapter therefore explains the difference between criminal and civil law and the **court system** which has evolved for each is described. **Alternatives** to actions in the courts are also covered.

The material in this chapter is most likely to come up as a more straightforward Section A question rather than a more complex, scenario-style Section B question.

1 Criminal and civil liability

Key term

The distinction between criminal liability and civil liability is central to the English legal system.

As stated in the introduction to this chapter, it is often the criminal law about which the general public has a clearer perception and keener interest. Some of the high profile criminal cases at London's Old Bailey are deemed extremely newsworthy. Civil law, on the other hand, receives less overt media coverage (with the exception of actions in tort, such as negligence or defamation, which are outside the scope of this syllabus, and some Human Rights cases). However, every time you buy or sell goods, or start or finish an employment contract, your actions, and those of the other party, are governed by civil law.

The distinction between criminal and civil liability is central to the English legal system and to the way the court system is structured.

1.1 Criminal law

FAST FORWARD

In criminal cases, the state prosecutes the wrongdoer.

Key term

A **crime** is conduct prohibited by the law.

In a criminal case the State is the prosecutor (in rare cases it may be a private person) because it is the community as a whole which suffers as a result of the law being broken. **Persons guilty of crime may be punished by fines payable to the State or imprisonment**, or other community-based punishment.

Generally, the **police** take the initial decision to prosecute, but this is then reviewed by the Crown Prosecution Service. Some prosecutions are started by the Director of Public Prosecutions, who is the head of the Crown Prosecution Service.

In a criminal trial, the **burden of proof** to convict the **accused** rests with the **prosecution**, which must prove its case **beyond reasonable doubt**.

A criminal case might be referred to as *R v Smith.* The prosecution is brought in the name of the Crown (R signifying *Regina,* the Queen).

1.2 Civil proceedings

FAST FORWARD

Civil law exists to regulate disputes over the rights and obligations of persons dealing with each other.

In civil proceedings, the case must be proved on the **balance of probability,** to convince the court that it is **more probable than not that the assertions are true**.

Terminology in civil cases is different from that in criminal cases. The **claimant** sues the **defendant**. A civil case would therefore be referred to as, for example, *Smith v Megacorp plc.*

One of the most important areas of civil liability for business, and accountants in particular, is the law of **contract**. The law of contract is looked at in detail in Part B of this text.

1.3 Distinction between criminal and civil cases

It is not an act or event which creates the distinction, but the legal consequences. A single event might give rise to criminal and civil proceedings.

Illustration

A broken leg caused to a pedestrian by a drunken driver is a single event which may give rise to:

- **criminal case** (prosecution by the State for the offence of driving with excess alcohol), and
- **civil case** (the pedestrian sues for compensation for pain and suffering).

The two sorts of proceedings are usually easily distinguished because three vital factors are different:

- The **courts** where the case is heard
- The **procedures**
- The **terminology**

Illustration

In criminal cases the rules of evidence are very strict. For example, a confession will be carefully examined to see if any pressure was brought to bear upon the accused, but an admission in a civil case will not be subjected to such scrutiny.

Question

Criminal and civil law

While on a sales trip, one of your employees is involved in a car accident. The other vehicle involved is damaged and it is alleged that your employee is to blame. What legal proceedings may arise as a result of this incident?

Answer

Your employee may be guilty of a driving offence such as careless driving. The police, to whom the incident should be reported, will investigate, and if the facts indicate a driving offence, will prosecute him, probably in the local magistrates' court. The owner of the damaged vehicle (or his insurers) may sue the driver at fault in civil proceedings to recover damages. A claim would probably be brought in the county court.

2 The system of courts **12/02**

The **courts** have to be organised to facilitate the working of the legal system. There are four main functional aspects of the court system which underlie its structure.

(a) **Civil and criminal law** differ so much in substance and procedure that they are best administered in separate courts.

(b) **Local courts** allow the vast bulk of small legal proceedings to be decentralised. But important civil cases begin in the High Court in London.

(c) Although the courts form a single system and many courts have a general civil jurisdiction, there is some **specialisation** both within the High Court and in other courts with separate functions.

(d) There is a system of review by **appeals** to higher courts.

2.1 The civil courts

FAST FORWARD

The **civil court structure** comprises the following.

- **Magistrates' courts** mostly deal with small domestic matters.
- **County courts** hear claims in contract and tort, equitable matters, land and probate disputes among others.
- The **Crown Court** hears appeals from magistrates' courts.
- The **High Court** is divided into three specialist divisions.
- The **Court of Appeal** hears appeals from the County Court, the High Court, the Restrictive Practices Court, and from the Employment Appeal Tribunal.
- The **House of Lords** hears appeals from the Court of Appeal and the High Court.

The diagram below sets out the English **civil** court structure.

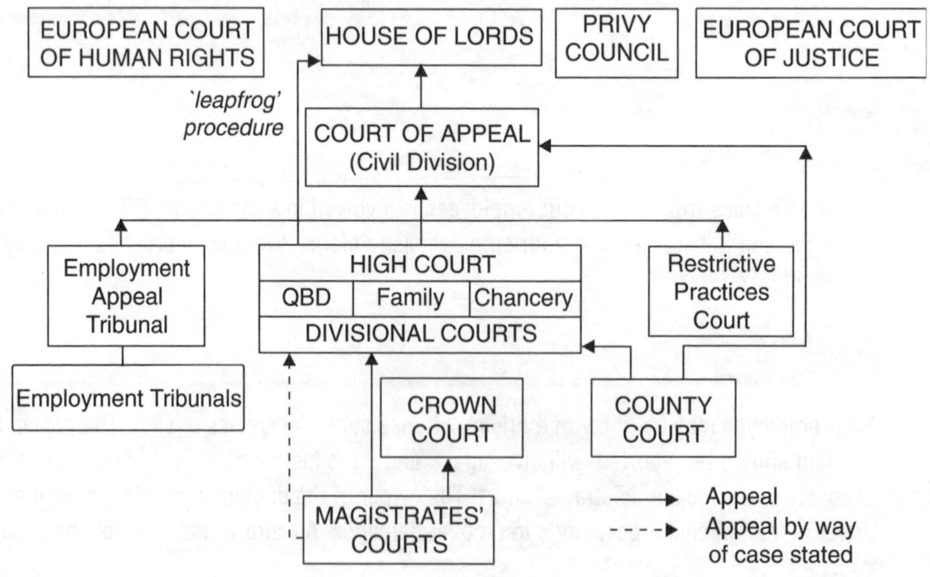

In appropriate cases it is possible to refer a case to either the European Court of Human Rights or the European Court of Justice, although they are not strictly within the English court structure.

2.2 The criminal court structure

FAST FORWARD

The **criminal court structure** comprises the following.

- **Magistrates' courts** hear summary offences and committal proceedings for indictable offences.
- The **Crown Court** tries serious criminal (indictable) offences and hears appeals from magistrates' courts.
- The **Divisional Court of QBD** hears appeals by way of case stated from magistrates' courts and the Crown Court.
- The **Court of Appeal** hears appeals from the Crown Court.
- The **House of Lords** hears appeals from the Court of Appeal or a Divisional Court of QBD.

The diagram below sets out the English **criminal** court structure.

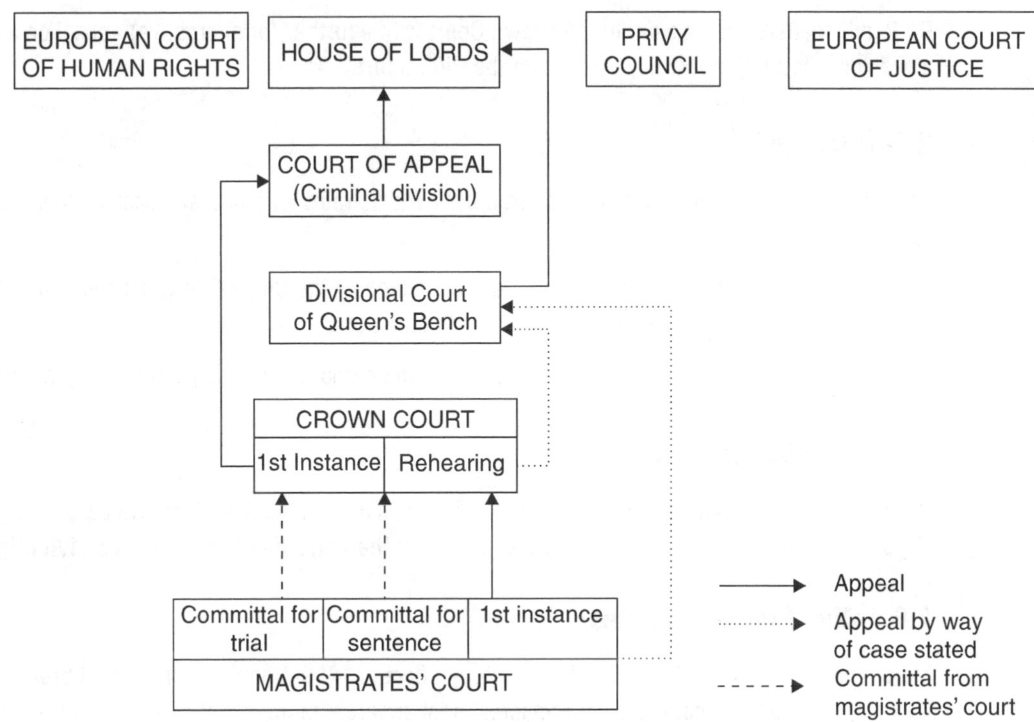

A limited number of Commonwealth countries allow appeal to the Privy Council in London, which is mostly staffed by House of Lords judges.

2.3 Magistrates' courts

Magistrates' courts are the **inferior criminal courts**.

- They try summarily (without a jury) all minor offences.
- They conduct **committal proceedings**, which are preliminary investigations of the prosecution case, when the offence is **triable** only on indictment (by a Crown Court).

Key terms

Indictable offences are more serious offences that can only be heard in a Crown Court.

Summary offences are minor crimes, only triable summarily in magistrates' courts.

Some offences are **'triable either way'**.

Magistrates also have **some civil jurisdiction** which includes the following:

- **Family proceedings** (financial provision for parties to a marriage and children, the custody or supervision of children and guardianship, and adoption orders).
- Various types of **licensing**
- Enforcement of **local authority** charges and rates

2.4 Appeals

A defendant convicted on a criminal charge in a magistrates' court has a general right to a rehearing by a Crown Court. A **'case stated' appeal** is based on the idea that magistrates or the Crown Court have wrongly interpreted the law. If not, then the case may be sent back to the lower court with instructions as to how it should be decided.

On family matters, appeals are to the Crown Court with a further (or alternative) appeal on a point of law to a divisional court of the Family Division of the High Court.

2.5 Personnel

The key personnel in the magistrates court are the magistrates who hear the cases. These fall into two categories:

- Magistrates, who are lay persons selected by the Chancellor (Justices of the Peace)
- District Judges (professional paid magistrates)

The magistrates' courts are also staffed by clerks, who can provide legal advice for lay magistrates.

2.6 The county court

County courts have **civil jurisdiction only** but deal with almost every kind of civil case. The practical importance of the county courts is that they deal with **the majority of the country's civil litigation**.

2.6.1 Civil Procedure Rules

Major changes to the system of civil justice took effect in 1999, bringing in new **civil procedure rules** which apply to all civil courts. Their impact is most apparent in the county courts and the High Court. They are commonly referred to as the **Woolf reforms**, having been masterminded by Lord Woolf, then Master of the Rolls.

The new procedures have led to lead to **quicker and less confrontational** settlement of disputes at the beginning of a case, to encourage parties to consider **alternative methods** of dispute resolution, and to avoid the excessive expense of litigation.

Under the reforms, the Court has the power to control every aspect of the litigation process, shifting responsibility away from the litigants and their advisers. This will affect a wide range of commercial disputes. The Court is intended to be a place of **last resort** and not a place of first resort.

There are two principal areas in which the civil procedure rules are relevant:

(a) Tracking
(b) Case management

2.6.2 Tracking

After a defence has been filed, the case will be allocated to one of three tracks. This is the new **three track** system.

(a) In the **small claims track**, claims of no more than £5,000 will be heard. These are cases that are to be dealt with quickly and informally, often without the need for legal representation or for a full hearing.

(b) The **fast track** is for claims of between £5,000 and £15,000 where the trial is to last no longer than one day. These are subject to a simplified court procedure and a fixed timetable designed to enable the claim to be determined within 30 weeks.

(c) Under the **multi-track**, claims of £15,000 which are to be managed by the courts will be heard.

2.6.3 Case management

After allocation, the court will give directions setting out the procedures to be followed in bringing multi-track cases to trial. These will be an initial 'case management conference' to encourage parties to settle the dispute or to consider alternative dispute resolutions (such as mediation or arbitration). Features of the procedures include the following.

(a) A **pre-action protocol**, which entails setting out the claim in full to the defendant in an attempt to negotiate a settlement. The emphasis is placed on co-operation to identify the main issues. Failure to co-operate may lead to cost penalties, regardless of the eventual outcome of the case.

(b) A strict **timetable** for exchange of evidence is set by the court, including witness statements and relevant documents. Those holding themselves out as potential expert witnesses should be prepared to arrange their affairs to meet the court's commitments (*Matthews v Tarmac Bricks and Tiles Ltd 1999; Linda Rollinson v Kimberly Clark Ltd 1999*).

(c) A three week **trial window** is allocated once the defence has been received. This does not change and the trial can fall anytime within the three week period.

(d) There are cost **penalties** for failing to meet any deadline or date set by the court.

These Civil Procedure Rules are subject to continuous review and update. A lot of legal terms previously in common usage have been replaced, for example a 'counterclaim' is now referred to as a 'part 20 claim' and a 'payment into court' is referred to as a 'part 36 claim'.

There is a new senior judge with overall responsibility for civil justice, known as the **Head of Civil Justice**. His appointment is designed to raise the status of civil justice, which has long been in the shadow of the criminal justice system.

2.6.4 The county court

The county court is involved in the following matters.

- **Contract and tort** (except defamation of character) claims.
- **Equitable matters** concerning trusts, mortgages and partnership dissolution.
- Disputes concerning **land**.
- **Undefended matrimonial** cases.
- **Probate matters**.
- **Miscellaneous matters** conferred by various statutes, for example the Consumer Credit Act 1974.
- Some **bankruptcy**, company winding-up and admiralty cases.

The county court deals with the following:

(a) All small claims track cases, and
(b) All fast track cases.

Multi-track cases are allocated either to the county court or to the High Court.

2.6.5 Appeals

From the county court there is a right of appeal direct to the Civil Division of the Court of Appeal for multi-track cases. In most other cases an appeal goes to the relevant Division of the High Court.

2.6.6 Personnel

The personnel in the county court consists of:

- Circuit judges, assisted by
- District judges

2.7 The Crown Court

The Crown Court is a single court forming part of the **Supreme Court**, but it sits in 90 different towns and cities and also at the **Central Criminal Court** (the Old Bailey) in London.

It deals with the following matters:

- **Indictable offences** with a jury.
- **Appeals** from magistrates' courts.
- **Committals for sentencing** from magistrates' courts.

The Crown Court deals with a few types of **civil cases**, for example **appeals** from the magistrates' court on matters of affiliation, betting, gaming and licensing

2.7.1 Appeals

From the Crown Court there is a right of appeal on criminal matters to the Criminal Division of the Court of Appeal. An appeal by way of 'case stated' on a point of law may also be made to a Divisional Court of the Queen's Bench Division.

2.7.2 Personnel

The Crown Court has the following personnel:

- High Court judges (for serious offences)
- Circuit judges
- Recorders

2.8 The High Court

The **High Court** is organised into three divisions:

- Queen's Bench Division
- Chancery Division
- Family Division

2.9 Queen's Bench Division

The Queen's Bench Division (QBD) deals mainly with common law matters:

- Actions based on **contract or tort**.
- Some appeals from the **County Court**
- **Appeals** by way of case stated from **magistrates' courts**.
- Some **appeals** from the **Crown Court**.

It also has a **supervisory role** over other inferior courts. It is the largest of the three divisions, having 73 judges. It includes a separate Admiralty Court to deal with shipping matters, and a Commercial Court which specialises in commercial cases. The QBD sits in London and a small number of large cities in England and Wales.

It may issue a writ of **habeas corpus**, which is an order for the release of a person wrongfully detained, and also prerogative orders against inferior courts, tribunals and other bodies such as local authorities. There are three types of **prerogative order.**

- A **mandatory order** requires the court or other body to carry out a public duty.
- A **prohibitory order** prevents a court or tribunal from exceeding its jurisdiction (before it has done so).
- A **quashing order** orders a court or tribunal which has taken action to submit the record of its proceedings to the High Court for review.

2.10 Chancery Division

This division deals with traditional equity matters.

- **Trusts** and **mortgages**
- **Revenue** matters
- **Bankruptcy** (though outside London this is a county court subject)
- Disputed **wills** and administration of estates of deceased persons
- **Partnership** and **company** matters

There is a separate **Companies Court** within the division which deals with liquidations and other company proceedings, and a Patents Court established under the Patents Act 1977.

2.11 Family Division

This division deals with:

- **Matrimonial** cases
- **Family property** cases
- **Proceedings relating to children** (wardship, guardianship, adoption, legitimacy)
- **Appeals** from magistrates' courts on family matters.
- **Appeals** from county courts on family matters

2.12 Appeals

Civil appeals from the High Court may be made to the **Court of Appeal (Civil Division)** or to the **House of Lords**, under what is known as the **'leapfrog'** procedure. This procedure is rarely used.

Criminal appeals are made direct to the House of Lords where the case has reached the High Court on appeal from a magistrates' court or from the Crown Court.

2.13 Personnel

The High Court is staffed by **High Court (puisne) judges**. The chief judges in each division are as follows:

- Queen's Bench Division: Lord Chief Justice
- Family Division: President
- Chancery Division: Lord Chancellor (nominally) in practice, Vice Chancellor.

2.14 The Court of Appeal

Key terms

A **court of first instance** is the court where the case is originally heard in full. The **appeal court** is the court to which an appeal is made against the ruling or the sentence.

If the appeal court finds in favour of the appellant the original decision is **reversed** ie the result is changed, but the law is not. This is different from **overruling** which happens when a higher court finds a lower court's decision to be wrong in law and in future the law is changed.

2.15 Civil Division

The Civil Division of the Court of Appeal can hear appeals from the High Court, county courts, and from certain other courts and special tribunals. It may uphold or reverse the earlier decision or order a new trial.

2.16 Criminal Division

The Criminal Division of the Court of Appeal hears appeals from the Crown Court. It may also be invited to review a criminal case by the Home Secretary or to consider a point of law at the request of the Attorney General.

2.17 Appeals

Appeals lie to the House of Lords.

2.18 Personnel

The Court of Appeal is staffed by the Lord Justices of Appeal. The chief judges in each division are as follows:

- Civil division: Master of the Rolls
- Criminal division: Lord Chief Justice

2.19 The House of Lords

The House of Lords is staffed by **Lords of Appeal in Ordinary** (also called **Law Lords**). It has a **judicial role**, as the highest appeal court of the legal system. Judges in the House of Lords are also made life peers so they may choose to attend sittings of the House of Lords when it is exercising its legislative function (ie as part of Parliament) but they rarely do so.

Question — Appeals

List the court (or courts) to which an appeal may be made from each of the following:

(a) The county court
(b) The High Court (civil cases)

(Refer to the court structure diagram on page 6.)

Answer

(a) The Court of Appeal (Civil Division) or the High Court (for some bankruptcy cases).
(b) The Court of Appeal (Civil Division) or the House of Lords.

3 Tribunals

FAST FORWARD

The court system is not the only way to settle disputes. There are tribunals and also the alternative procedure of arbitration.

There are a number of other courts and tribunals which feature prominently in the English legal system, either because they have a relatively important status or because they have a heavy caseload. For example tribunals deal with over 250,000 cases each year on issues ranging from employment to social security matters to land. They are supervised by the Council on Tribunals.

3.1 Employment tribunals

Employment tribunals (formerly known as industrial tribunals) are governed by the Industrial Tribunals Act 1996. This sets out their composition, competence and procedure.

Each tribunal is staffed by a legally qualified **chairman** and two other persons, one representing the interests of employers and one representing the interests of employees. They have a wide jurisdiction over most disputes between **employee and employer**.

- Disputes about **redundancy** pay
- Complaints of **unfair dismissal**
- Questions as to **terms of contracts** of employment
- **Equal pay** claims or disputes over issues such as **maternity pay**
- Appeals against health and safety notices
- Complaints about sex, race and disability **discrimination** (dealt with in Chapter 25)
- Disputes over trade union membership

There is a right of appeal to the **Employment Appeal Tribunal (EAT)**. This is a court of equal status with the High Court. It hears appeals from tribunals mainly on employment matters. A **High Court judge** and two **lay assessors** from a panel appointed on the Lord Chancellor's recommendation sit. From the EAT there is a right of appeal to the Court of Appeal.

3.2 Advantages and disadvantages of tribunals

Advantages include: speed of proceedings, cheaper costs, informality in comparison to courts, flexibility (not bound by rules of precedent) accessibility to individuals and lack of publicity.

Disadvantages include: no unified, formal appeals procedure, lack of legal aid for most parties, presentation of arguments by people who are not qualified lawyers.

Reform of the system of tribunals is ongoing. The Leggatt Review made a number of recommendations to unify the tribunals system in 2000, and the Government has announced its intention to unite the ten largest tribunals in the UK.

4 Arbitration

A dispute may be referred to arbitration either by agreement out of court, or compulsorily. In a case of arbitration, the dispute is decided by a third party (often a lawyer) rather than a court of law. This eliminates the adversarial nature of court proceedings and means that there is not a 'winner' and a 'loser' after the dispute. This means that business relationships can often continue successfully after arbitration has happened and a dispute has been resolved, whereas after a court case is won or lost there is often a sense of bitterness, and a business relationship may well break down.

4.1 Voluntary agreements

It is common practice to include in **commercial contracts** a clause providing that any dispute is to be settled by arbitration under the relevant legislation. Sometimes arbitration clauses are also contained in partnership agreements or even in the constitutions of smaller companies. The arbitration clause just forms one clause in the contract between the two parties and the partners are expected to abide by it should a dispute arise. If they do not, then arguably they are in breach of contract (covered later in this study text).

Advantages of arbitration	
Binding decisions	The decision given in an arbitration is usually final. This helps to ensure both cost and time are left to a minimum. However, no right of appeal may seem to be a disadvantage to some.
Arbitrator	In arbitration it is possible to use a **specialist** as arbitrator. Particularly in complex commercial disputes, this can be a significant advantage over litigation.
Speed and economy	In theory, arbitration is quicker and cheaper than litigation. (Although this may not be the case when matters of commercial law are involved). Proceedings are more informal.
Confidentiality	This is often perceived as the key advantage of arbitration. The public and the press have no right of entry to arbitration proceedings. This means that the public cannot obtain potentially sensitive information, and the parties are less likely to suffer damaging publicity.

Unless otherwise agreed, a hearing before an arbitrator follows the same essential procedure as in a court of law. However, following the **Arbitration Act 1996**, the arbitrators and parties can settle on the form of the arbitration. They may, for instance dispense with formal hearings and strict rules of evidence and procedure.

4.2 Compulsory arbitration

In addition to voluntary arbitration as described above, compulsory arbitration may be enforced in the following circumstances.

- Certain statutes provide for arbitration on disputes arising out of the provision of the statute.
- The High Court may order that a case of a technical nature shall be tried or investigated by an Official Referee or other arbitrator.

4.3 Procedure

The Arbitration Act 1996 aimed to introduce greater speed and flexibility into the arbitration process, in particular by conferring upon the parties the right to make their own agreement on virtually all aspects of the arbitration.

The Arbitration Act 1996 states that:

- The object of arbitration is to obtain the fair resolution of disputes by an impartial tribunal without necessary delay or expense
- The parties should be free to agree how their disputes are resolved (referred to as autonomy of the parties)
- Generally, the courts are not expected to intervene in the arbitration process

4.4 The arbitrator

There may be one arbitrator or a panel, to be decided by the parties. The parties cannot take action against the arbitrator unless the latter has acted in bad faith. There are very limited rights of appeal after arbitration, mostly relating to the jurisdiction of the panel, or the procedures followed.

Chapter roundup

- The distinction between criminal liability and civil liability is central to the English legal system.
- Crime is conduct prohibited by law.
  - The **State** is the **prosecutor**, the perpetrator is **punished** and fines are payable to the State.
  - There is an accused and a prosecution, and the case must be proved beyond reasonable doubt.
  - The courts **must be used** to settle the matter.
- **Civil law** regulates disputes over the rights and obligations of persons **dealing with each other.**
  - The State has no role, there is **no concept of punishment** and **compensation** is owed to the wronged person.
  - There is a **claimant** and a **defendant**, and the case must be proved on the **balance of probabilities.**
  - The parties are free to settle the dispute **outside the court system**.
- The **civil court structure** comprises the following.
  - **Magistrates' courts** mostly deal with small domestic matters.
  - **County courts** hear claims in contract and tort, equitable matters, land and probate disputes among others.
  - The **Crown Court** hears appeals from magistrates' courts.
  - The **High Court** is divided into three specialist divisions.
  - The **Court of Appeal** hears appeals from the County Court, the High Court, the Restrictive Practices Court, and from the Employment Appeal Tribunal.
  - The **House of Lords** hears appeals from the Court of Appeal and the High Court.
- The **criminal court structure** comprises the following.
  - **Magistrates' courts** hear summary offences and committal proceedings for indictable offences.
  - The **Crown Court** tries serious criminal (indictable) offences and hears appeals from magistrates' courts.
  - The **Divisional Court of QBD** hears appeals by way of case stated from magistrates' courts and the Crown Court.
  - The **Court of Appeal** hears appeals from the Crown Court.
  - The **House of Lords** hears appeals from the Court of Appeal or a Divisional Court of QBD.
- The court system is not the only way to settle disputes.
  - **Administrative tribunals**, such as social security appeal tribunals and employment tribunals, deal with the administration of Acts of Parliament and delegated legislation, that is, disputes between individuals and government agencies or between two individuals.
  - **Arbitration** allows parties to bring their dispute before a non-legal independent expert so that he may decide the case, although an arbitrator's award may be enforced in the same manner as a High Court judgment.

Quick quiz

1 **Fill in the blanks** in the statements below, using the words in the box.

- The distinction between (1) ……………….. and (2) ……………….. liability is central to the English legal system.
- (3) ……………….. allows parties to bring their dispute before a non-legal independent expert so that he may decide the case.

criminal	arbitration	civil

2 What is the standard of proof in civil proceedings?

3 What kind of judge sits in the House of Lords?

4 The Employment Appeal Tribunal is a court of equal status with the High Court.

True ☐

False ☐

5 All the following statements relate to criminal and civil law. Which one of the statements is correct?

A A criminal case may subsequently give rise to a civil case, but a civil case cannot subsequently give rise to a criminal case

B The main purpose of civil law is to compensate the injured party and to punish the injuring party

C A custodial sentence can be passed on the defendant in a civil case, providing the defendant is a natural person and not an incorporated body

D The main purpose of civil law is to enforce the claimant's rights rather than to punish the defendant.

6 What are the three tracks in the three track system for allocation of civil court cases?

7 Which court or courts might hear an appeal from the High Court in a civil case?

8 What is the monetary limit for a small claims case?

Answers to quick quiz

1 (1) criminal (2) civil (3) arbitration

2 The case must be proved on the balance of probability

3 Lord of Appeal in Ordinary, or Law Lord

4 True

5 D

6 (1) Small claims track (2) fast track (3) multi-track

7 (1) The Court of Appeal (Civil Division) (2) The House of Lords (under the leapfrog procedure)

8 £5,000

Now try the question below from the Exam Question Bank

Number	Level	Marks	Time
Q1	Examination	10	18 mins

Sources of English law

Topic list	Syllabus reference
1 Case law	1(b)
2 Legislation	1(b)
3 European Community law	1(d)

Introduction

There are four **current** (legal) sources of law. These are the means by which the law is currently brought into existence.

The two **historical** sources of law are **equity** and the **common law**. The development of historical sources has led to one of the main legal sources of law, **case law** and informs much of the other main source, **legislation**.

Case law is based on a system of precedent, whereby judges apply legal principles decided in previous cases to facts presented in current cases. This **doctrine of judicial precedent** has a number of associated rules to make it work, and these are considered in section 1 of this Chapter.

The law is not static but changes and develops, reflecting the values and institutions of each era. There has been an increasing flow of new laws designed, for example, to deal with social problems and to develop the national economy.

The second major current source of law, **legislation**, is created by Parliament. Since Parliament often lacks the necessary time or expertise, the fine detail of some legislation may be left for civil servants or local authorities to provide in **delegated legislation**.

Introduction (cont)

There are a number of situations which might lead to a need for laws to be **interpreted**. There are several different sources of assistance for a judge in this task of **statutory interpretation**. All these matters are considered in section 2.

By virtue of the European Communities Act 1972, **EU law** now forms part of UK law. It is probably the most important area of developing law in the UK. Some European law has direct effect in the UK and some has to be given implementation in English law by the passing of legislation.

The fourth source, custom, is of little practical importance as a source of law, but is still classified as a current source.

This chapter provides the basis for much of the law you will learn in the rest of the Study Text, particularly contract and employment which are heavily based on case law.

However, any source of law is likely to be examined in its own right as well, although it is likely that this would be as a Section A question. The pilot paper examined delegated legislation in Section A.

European law is an increasingly important source of law for the United Kingdom, and you should expect the exam to reflect this importance. This being said, it seems that it is still a topic more suited to being examined in Part A.

1 Case law 12/03

FAST FORWARD

> The first legal source of law, consisting of decisions made in the courts, is **case law,** which is judge-made law based on the underlying principle of consistency. Once a legal or equitable principle is decided by an appropriate court it is a **judicial precedent**.

1.1 Common law and equity

The earliest element of the legal system to develop was the **common law**, a system incorporating rigid rules applied by royal courts, often with harsh results. Equity was developed, two or three hundred years later, as a system of law applied by the Lord Chancellor in situations where justice did not appear to be done under common law principles.

Key terms

> **Common law** is the body of legal rules common to the whole country which is embodied in judicial decisions.
>
> **Equity** is a term which applies to a specific set of legal principles which were developed by the Court of Chancery to supplement (but not replace) the common law. It is based on fair dealings between the parties. It added to and improved on the common law by introducing the concept of fairness.

The interaction of equity and common law produced three major changes.

(a) **New rights**. Equity recognised and protected rights for which the common law gave no safeguards.

(b) **Better procedure**. Equity could be more effective than common law in bringing a disputed matter to a decision.

(c) **Better remedies**. The standard common law remedy for the successful claimant was the award of damages for his loss. The Chancellor developed remedies not available in other courts. Equity was able to make the following orders.

- That the defendant must do what he had agreed to do (**specific performance**)
- That the defendant must abstain from wrongdoing (**injunction**)
- Alteration of a document to reflect the parties' true intentions (**rectification**)
- Restoration of the pre-contract status quo (**rescission**)

Case law incorporates decisions made by judges under both historic legal systems and the expression 'common law' is often used to describe all case law whatever its historic origin. . **A court's decision** is

expected to be **consistent with previous decisions** and to provide an opinion which can be used to direct future relationships. This is the basis of the system of **judicial precedent**.

1.2 Doctrine of judicial precedent — 6/04, 6/05

The system of judicial precedent is based on a fundamental feature of English law which is that **principles of English law do not become inoperative through the lapse of time**.

Illustration

in *R v Casement 1916*, the Treason Act 1351 was consulted. This does not just apply to Acts of Parliament, but also to case law. The outcome of *Pinnel's case 1602* is still important today when examining the law of contract.

Key terms

In any later case to which that principle is relevant the same principle should (subject to certain exceptions) be applied. This doctrine of consistency, following precedent, is expressed in the maxim **stare decisis** which means 'to stand by a decision'.

A **precedent** is a previous court decision which another court is bound to follow by deciding a subsequent case in the same way.

The doctrine of **judicial precedent** means that a judge is bound to apply a decision from an earlier case to the facts of the case before him, provided, among other conditions, that there is no material difference between the cases and the previous case created a 'binding' precedent.

Judicial precedent is based on three elements.

- **Reports.** There must be adequate and reliable reports of earlier decisions.
- **Rules.** There must be rules for extracting a legal principle from a previous set of facts and applying it to current facts.
- **Classification.** Precedents must be classified into those that are **binding** and those which are merely **persuasive.**

1.3 Law reports

There are major series of law reports on general law bound as annual volumes. In addition, there are several electronic databases which include cases reported in the paper reports and other cases.

Every case has a title, usually (in a civil case) in the form *Carlill v Carbolic Smoke Ball Co.* This denotes Carlill (claimant) versus Carbolic Smoke Ball Co (defendant). In the event of an appeal, the **claimant's** name is still shown first, whether he is the **appellant** or the **respondent**. Since January 2001 all judgements of the superior courts are given a 'uniform citation' to facilitate publication on the Internet. A House of Lords judgement will be referenced [year] UKHL [unique number].

Some cases are cited by reference to the subject matter. Thus case names have included *Re Barrow Haematite Steel Co* (a company case), *Re Adams and Kensington Vestry* (a trust case) and in shipping cases the name of the ship, for example, *The Wagon Mound.*

Some older cases may be referred to by a single name, for example *Pinnel's case.* In a full citation the title of the case is followed by abbreviated particulars of the volume of the law reports in which the case is reported, for example, *Best v Samuel Fox & Co Ltd* (1952) 2 All ER 394 (the report is at p 394 of Vol. 2 of the All England Reports for 1952).

As regards content a full law report includes details of the following.

- Names of the parties
- Court in which the case was decided
- Judge or judges
- Date of the hearing
- Points of law established
- Earlier cases cited
- Previous history of the litigation
- Facts
- Names of counsel and their arguments
- Verbatim text of the judgement
- Order of the court
- Whether leave to appeal was granted
- Solicitors
- Reporting barrister

It is only decisions of the higher courts in important cases (the High Court, the Court of Appeal and the Judicial Committee of the House of Lords) which are included in the general law reports.

Exam focus point

Students are often perplexed as to how much they are expected to memorise of cases referred to in textbooks. By far the most important aspect of a case for examination purposes is what it was about; that is, **the point of law which it illustrates or establishes**. This is the knowledge that you must apply when answering exam questions.

It is not generally necessary to recite the exact details of the events behind a case. However, knowing the facts of cases is helpful, not least because exam questions may well include scenarios in which the facts are based on a well-known case.

Never make up case names! This may seem like absurd advice, but examiners have commented that markers sometimes come across references in scripts to cases which they are not familiar with, but which, upon investigation, are found to be fictitious. So, if you forget a case name, don't make a guess at it. Start your answer by saying: 'In a decided case......'.

The doctrine of judicial precedent is designed to provide **consistency** in the law. Four things must be considered when examining a precedent before it can be applied to a case.

- A decision must be based on a **proposition of law** before it can be considered as a precedent. It may **not** be a decision on a **question of fact**.
- It must form part of the **ratio decidendi** of the case.
- The **material facts** of each case must be comparable.
- The preceding court must have had a **superior (or in some cases, equal) status** to the later court, such that its decisions are binding on the later court.

1.4 Ratio decidendi

FAST FORWARD

Statements made by judges can be classified as ratio decidendi or obiter dicta.

A judgement will start with a description of the facts of the case and probably a review of earlier precedents. The judge will then make **statements of law applicable to the legal problems** raised by the material facts which, **if the basis for the decision**, are **known as the ratio decidendi** of the case, which is the **vital element which binds future judges**.

Key term

'The **ratio decidendi** of a case is any rule of law expressly or impliedly treated by the judge as a necessary step in reaching his conclusion, having regard to the line of reasoning adopted by him, or a necessary part of his direction to the jury.' (Cross: *Precedent in English Law.*)

Statements made by a judge are either classed as ratio decidendi or obiter dicta. There are two types of obiter dicta, (which means something said 'by the way').

- A judge's statements of legal principle might not form the basis of the decision.
- A judge's statements might not be based on the existing material facts but on hypothetical facts. See for example *Central London Property Trust v High Trees House*, covered in Chapter 6 section 3.

Key term

Obiter dicta are words in a judgement which are said 'by the way'.
They **do not** form part of the **ratio decidendi** and are not binding on future cases but merely persuasive.

It is not always easy to identify the ratio decidendi. In decisions of appeal courts, where there are three or even five separate judgements, the members of the court may reach the same conclusion but give different reasons. Many judges indicate in their speeches which comments are 'ratio' and which are 'obiter'.

1.5 Distinguishing the facts

Although there may arguably be a finite number of legal principles to consider when deciding a case, there is an infinite variety of facts which may be presented.

It is necessary to consider how far the facts of the previous and the latest case are similar. If the differences appear significant the court may **distinguish the earlier case on the facts** and thereby **avoid following it as a precedent**.

1.6 Status of the court

Not every decision made in every court is binding as a judicial precedent. The **court's status** has a significant effect on whether its decisions are binding, persuasive or disregarded. You may want to refer back to the court structure diagram on page 6 while you read the following table.

Court	Bound by	Decisions binding
Magistrates' Court	• High Court • The Court of Appeal • House of Lords • European Court of Justice	• No one • Not even itself
County Court	• High Court • The Court of Appeal • House of Lords • European Court of Justice	• No one • Not even itself
Crown Court	• High Court (QBD) • The Court of Appeal • House of Lords • European Court of Justice	• No one • However, its decisions are reported more widely and are more authoritative

Court	Bound by	Decisions binding
The High Court consists of divisions: • Queen's bench • Chancery • Family	(a) Judge sitting alone • The divisional court • The Court of Appeal • House of Lords • European Court of Justice	(a) Judge sitting alone • Magistrates' court • County court • Crown Court
	(b) Judges sitting together • Any divisional court • The Court of Appeal • House of Lords • European Court of Justice	(b) Judges sitting together • Magistrates' Court • County Court • Crown Court • Divisional Courts
The Court of Appeal	• Own decisions • House of Lords (subject to an exception below) • European Court of Justice	• All inferior English courts • Itself (subject to the exception)
The House of Lords	• Itself (except in exceptional cases) • European Court of Justice	• All English Courts • Itself (except in exceptional cases)
The European Court of Justice	• No one • Not even itself	• All English Courts

1.7 Court of Appeal exception

In *Young v Bristol Aeroplane Co 1944,* it was decided that the civil division of the Court of Appeal is usually bound by its own decisions and those of the House of Lords, unless:

- Two if its previous decisions conflict, when it must decide which to follow
- The previous decision conflicts with a subsequent House of Lords decision
- The previous decision was made with a lack of care (per incuriam)

Exam focus point

It is particularly important that you know the position of the Court of Appeal and the House of Lords in this hierarchy.

Question

Case law

What do you think are the advantages of case law as a source of law?

Answer

The law is decided fairly and **predictably**, so that businessmen and individuals can regulate their conduct by reference to the law. The **risk** of mistakes in individual cases is reduced by the use of precedents. Case law can **adapt** to changing circumstances in society, since it arises directly out of the actions of society. Case law, having been developed in **practical** situations, is suitable for use in other practical situations.

1.8 Persuasive precedents

Apart from binding precedents, reported decisions of any court may be treated as **persuasive precedents**. Persuasive precedents may be, but need not be, followed in a later case.

A court of higher status is not only free to disregard the decision of a court of lower status, it may also deprive it of authority and expressly **overrule** it. Remember that this does not reverse the previous decision. Overruling a decision does not affect its outcome.

Key terms

Where an earlier decision was made by a lower court, the judges can **overrule** that earlier decision if they disagree with the lower court's statement of the law. **The outcome of the earlier decision remains the same, but will not be followed**.

If the decision of a lower court is appealed to a higher one, the higher court may **reverse** the decision if they feel the lower court has wrongly interpreted the law. **When a decision is reversed, the higher court is usually also overruling the lower court's statement of the law**.

Question — Decisions

Match each of the following definitions to the correct term.

(a) A court higher up in the hierarchy overturns the decision of a lower court on appeal in the same case.

(b) A principle laid down by a lower court is overturned by a higher court in a different, later case.

(c) A judge states that the material facts of the case before him are sufficiently different from those of an earlier case as to enable the application of a different rule of law.

(1) Distinguishing
(2) Overruling
(3) Reversing

Answer

(a) (3)
(b) (2)
(c) (1)

If, in a case before the House of Lords, there is a **dispute about a point of European Community law** it must be referred to the European Court for a ruling. The European court does not create or follow precedents as such, and the provisions of EU directives should not be used to interpret UK legislation.

A case in the High Court may be taken on appeal to the Court of Appeal. If the latter reverses the former decision, that first decision cannot be a precedent. If the original decision had been reached by following precedent, then reversing that decision overrules the precedent.

1.9 Avoidance of a binding precedent

Even if a precedent appears to be binding, there are **a number of grounds on which a court may decline to follow it**.

(a) It may be able to **distinguish the facts**.

(b) It may declare the ratio decidendi **obscure**, particularly when a Court of Appeal decision by three or five judges gives as many rationes.

(c) It may declare the previous decision made **per incuriam**: without taking account of some essential point of law, such as an important precedent.

(d) It may declare it to be in **conflict with a fundamental principle of law**; for example where a court has failed to apply the doctrine of privity of contract: *Beswick v Beswick 1968*.

(e) It may declare an earlier precedent to be **too wide.** For example, the duty of care to third parties, first propounded in *Donoghue v Stevenson 1932,* has since been considerably refined.

Question

Binding precedent

Fill in the following table, then check your answer.

Name of court	Binds	Bound by
Magistrates' court		
County court		
Crown Court		
High Court (single judge)		
High Court (Divisional court)		
Court of Appeal		
House of Lords		
European Court of Justice		

1.10 The advantages and disadvantages of precedent

Many of the strengths of judicial precedent as the cornerstone of English law also indicate some of its weaknesses.

Factor	Advantage	Disadvantage
Certainty	The law is decided fairly and predictably Guidance given to judges and risk of mistake reduced.	Judges may sometimes be forced to make illogical distinctions to avoid an unfair result.
Clarity	Following the reasoning of ratio decidendi should lead to statements of general legal principles	Sometimes, judgements may appear to be inconsistent with each other or legal principles followed.
Flexibility	The system is able to change with changing circumstances	However, the system can limit judges' discretion.
Detail	Precedent states how the law applies to facts and should be flexible enough to allow for details to be different.	The detail produces a vast body of reports to take into account. Judges often distinguish on the facts to avoid a precedent.
Practicality	Case law is based on experience of actual cases brought before the courts. This is an advantage over legislation which can be found wanting when tested.	

2 Legislation 12/03

FAST FORWARD

The second major legal source of law is legislation. UK statute law may take the form of Acts of Parliament or delegated legislation under the Acts.

Statute law is made by Parliament (or in exercise of law-making powers delegated by Parliament). Until the United Kingdom entered the European Community in 1973 the UK Parliament was completely **sovereign**.

In recent years however, UK membership of the European Community has restricted the previously unfettered power of Parliament. There is an **obligation**, imposed by the Treaty of Rome, **to bring UK law into line with the Treaty itself and with directives**. Regulations, having the force of law in every member state, may be made under provisions of the Treaty of Rome.

2.1 Parliamentary sovereignty

Parliamentary sovereignty gives rise to a number of consequences. Parliament may

- **Repeal** earlier statutes
- **Overrule** or modify case law developed in the courts, or
- **Make new law** on subjects which have not been regulated by law before.

In practice, Parliament usually follows certain **conventions** which limit its freedom.

No Parliament can legislate so as to prevent a future Parliament changing the law.

The judges have to **interpret** statute law and they may find a meaning in a statutory rule which those Members of Parliament who promoted the statute did not intend.

The **validity** of an Act of Parliament cannot be questioned.

> *Cheney v Conn 1968*
> *The facts:* The claimant objected to his tax assessment under the Finance Act 1964 because some of the tax collected was used to fund the manufacture of nuclear weapons. He alleged that this was contrary to the Geneva Conventions Act 1957 and in conflict with international law.
>
> *Decision:* The 1964 Act gave clear authority to collect the taxes.

However, the judge may declare an Act to be 'incompatible' with the European Convention on Human Rights (see Chapter 3).

In addition to making new law and altering existing law, Parliament may make the law clearer by passing a **codifying** statute (such as the Sale of Goods Act 1979) to put case law on a statutory basis, or a **consolidating** statute to incorporate an original statute and its successive amendments into a single statute (such as the Employment Rights Act 1996 or the Companies Act 1985).

2.2 Parliamentary procedure

A proposal for legislation can be brought by the government or a backbench MP or a peer. A government bill may be aired in public in a **Government Green** or **White Paper**. A government bill may be introduced into either the House of Commons or the House of Lords. When the Bill has passed through one House it must then go through the same stages in the other House.

In each House the successive stages of dealing with the Bill are as follows.

Stage 1. *First reading.* Publication and introduction into the agenda. No debate.

Stage 2. *Second reading.* Debate on the general merits of the Bill. No amendments at this stage.

Stage 3. *Committee stage.* The Bill is examined by a Standing Committee of about 20 members, representing the main parties and including some members at least who specialise in the relevant subject. If the Bill is very important all or part of the Committee Stage may be taken by the House as a whole sitting as a committee.

Stage 4. *Report stage.* The Bill as amended in committee is reported to the full House for approval.

Stage 5. *Third reading.* This is the final approval stage.

When it has passed through both Houses it is submitted for the **Royal Assent** which is given on the Queen's behalf by a committee of the Lord Chancellor and two other peers. It then becomes an Act of Parliament (statute) but it does not come into operation until a commencement date is notified by statutory instrument.

2.2.1 Advantages and disadvantages of statute law

Statute law has the following advantages and disadvantages:

(a) **Advantages**

- The House of Commons is elected at intervals of not more than five years. Hence the law making process is theoretically responsive to public opinion.
- Statute law can in theory deal with any problem.
- Statutes are carefully constructed codes of law.
- A new problem in society or some unwelcome development in case law can be dealt with by passing an Act of Parliament.

(b) **Disadvantages**

- Statutes are bulky (about 70 public statutes are passed each year and the complete set of statutes runs to more than 40 volumes of several hundred pages each).
- Parliament often lacks time to consider draft legislation in sufficient detail.
- A substantial statute can take up a lot of Parliamentary time.
- Statute law is a statement of general rules. Those who draft it cannot anticipate every individual case which may arise.

2.3 Delegated legislation — Pilot paper, 6/03

To save time in Parliament, Acts usually contain a section by which power is given to a minister, or public body such as a local authority, to make **subordinate or delegated legislation**.

Key term

> **Delegated legislation** means rules of law, often of a detailed nature, made by subordinate bodies to whom the power to do so has been given by statute.

Delegated legislation appears in various forms.

- Ministerial powers are exercised by **statutory instruments.** Statutory instruments are the most common form of delegated legislation.
- **Local authorities** are given statutory powers to make **bye-laws**.
- Parliament gives power to certain **professional bodies** to regulate their members' conduct.
- **Rules of Court** may be made by the judiciary to control court procedure.

2.3.1 Control over delegated legislation

Parliament does exercise some **control** over delegated legislation by keeping the making of new delegated legislation under review.

- Some statutory instruments do not take effect until approved by **affirmative resolution** of Parliament.
- Most other statutory instruments must be laid before Parliament for 40 days before they take effect.

There are standing **Scrutiny Committees** of both Houses whose duty it is to examine statutory instruments with a view to raising objections if necessary.

A statutory instrument may be challenged in the courts on the grounds that it exceeds the prescribed limits or has been made without due compliance with the correct procedure.

Both statutes and delegated legislation under it are expressed in general terms. It is not possible to provide in the Act for each eventuality which falls within its remit. It therefore often falls to judges to interpret Acts.

Human Rights Act 1998

This is considered in detail in Chapter 3, but it has implications here. One of the consequences of the Act is that higher courts can **strike out** legislation which does not comply with the convention. This acts as another **control** over **delegated legislation.**

2.3.2 Advantages and disadvantages

Delegated legislation has the following **advantages**:

- Parliament does not have time to examine matters of detail.
- Much of the content of delegated legislation is technical and is better worked out in consultation with professional, commercial or industrial groups outside Parliament.
- If new or altered regulations are required later, they can be issued without referring back to Parliament.
- The system allows the law to be enacted quickly.

The **disadvantages** of the system are as follows.

- Because delegated legislation can be produced in large amounts, the **volume** of such law-making becomes unmanageable.
- The system is **unrepresentative** in that power is given to civil servants who are not democratically elected.
- The different sorts of delegated legislation which may be produced by virtue of one statute can greatly **confuse** users.

Exam focus point

The meaning, effect, advantages, disadvantages and control of delegated legislation were examined in the pilot paper.

2.4 Statutory interpretation 12/01

There are a number of situations which might lead to a need for statutory interpretation.

(a) **Ambiguity** might be caused by an error in drafting.

(b) **Uncertainty** may arise where the words of a statute are intended to apply to a range of factual situations and the courts must decide whether the case before them falls into any of these situations.

(c) There may be **unforeseeable developments**.

(d) The draft may use a **broad term**. Thus, the word vehicle may need to be considered in relation to the use of skateboards or bicycles.

There are a number of different sources of assistance for a judge in his task of statutory interpretation. These are the **principles of statutory interpretation** and consist of:

- Rules
- Presumptions
- Other aids (intrinsic or extrinsic)

2.4.1 Rules of statutory interpretation

In interpreting the words of a statute the courts have developed a number of well-established general rules.

2.4.2 The literal rule

Key term

The **literal rule** means that words should be given their plain, ordinary or literal meaning unless this would give rise to manifest absurdity or inconsistency with the rest of the statute.

Normally a word should be construed in the same literal sense wherever it appears throughout the statute.

Illustration

In *Whitely v Chapell 1868* a statute aimed at preventing electoral malpractice made it an offence to impersonate 'any person entitled to vote' at an election. The accused was acquitted because he impersonated a dead person, who was clearly not entitled to vote.

Until relatively recently, judges also used the 'golden' rule and 'mischief' rule of statutory interpretation. These have now been subsumed into the literal and purposive rules.

2.4.3 The purposive role

Key term

Under this approach to statutory interpretation, the words of a statute are interpreted not only in their ordinary, literal and grammatical sense, but also with reference to the context and purpose of the legislation, ie what is the legislation trying to achieve?

Illustration

This shows how the court took account of the mischief or weakness which the statute was explicitly intended to remedy.

Gardiner v Sevenoaks RDC 1950
The facts: The purpose of an Act was to provide for the safe storage of film wherever it might be stored on 'premises'. The claimant argued that 'premises' did not include a cave and so the Act had no application to his case.

Decision: The purpose of the Act was to protect the safety of persons working in all places where film was stored. If film was stored in a cave, the word 'premises' included the cave.

The key to the purposive approach is that the judge construes the statute in such a way as to **be consistent with the purpose of the statute** as he understands it, even if the wording of the statute could be applied literally without leading to manifest absurdity.

Human Rights Act 1998

UK courts are now required to interpret UK legislation in a way compatible with the convention so far as it is possible to do so. This is an example of **purposive** interpretation.

2.4.4 The contextual rule

Key term

The **contextual rule** means that a word should be construed in its context: it is permissible to look at the statute as a whole to discover the meaning of a word in it.

The courts have been paying more attention to what Parliament intended in recent times. This is in order that the courts apply the law for the purpose for which it is enacted by Parliament. A more purposive approach is also being taken because so many international and EU regulations come to be interpreted by the courts.

2.5 General rules of interpretation

2.5.1 The eiusdem generis rule

Statutes often list a number of specific things and end the list with more general words. In that case the general words are to be limited in their meaning to other things of the same kind as the specific items which precede them.

Evans v Cross 1938
The facts: E was charged with driving his car in such a way as to 'ignore a traffic sign', having crossed to the wrong side of a white line. 'Traffic sign' was defined in the Act as 'all signals, warning signposts, direction posts, signs or other devices'.

Decision: 'Other device' must be limited in its meaning to a category of such signs. A painted line was quite different from that category.

2.5.2 Expressio unius est exclusio alterius

To express one thing is by implication to exclude anything else.

2.5.3 Words must be understood in their context

A word draws meaning from the other words around it. If a statute mentioned 'children's books, children's toys and clothes' it would be reasonable to assume that 'clothes' meant children's clothes.

2.5.4 In pari materia

If the statute forms part of a series which deals with similar subject matter, the court may look to the interpretation of previous statutes on the assumption that Parliament intended the same thing.

2.6 Presumptions of statutory interpretation

Unless the statute contains express words to the contrary it is assumed that the following presumptions of statutory interpretation apply, each of which may be rebutted by contrary evidence.

- **A statute does not alter the existing common law**. If a statute is capable of two interpretations, one involving alteration of the common law and the other one not, the latter interpretation is to be preferred.
- **If a statute deprives a person of his property**, say by nationalisation, he is to be compensated for its value.
- **A statute is not intended to deprive a person of his liberty**. If it does so, clear words must be used. This is relevant in legislation covering, for example, mental health and immigration.
- **A statute does not have retrospective effect** to a date earlier than its becoming law.
- **A statute does not bind the Crown**. In certain areas, the Crown's potential liability is great and this is therefore an extremely important presumption.
- **A statute generally has effect only in the UK**. However a statute does not run counter to international law and should be interpreted so as to give effect to international obligations.
- **A statute cannot impose criminal liability** without proof of guilty intention. Many modern statutes rebut this presumption by imposing strict liability, say for dangerous driving under the Road Traffic Act.
- **A statute does not repeal other statutes**.
- Any point on which the statute leaves a gap or omission is outside the scope of the statute.

2.7 Other assistance in interpretation

The Interpretation Act 1987 defines certain terms frequently found in legislation. The Act also states that, unless a specific intention to the contrary exists, the use in a statute of masculine gender terminology also includes the feminine, and vice versa. Similarly, words in the singular include plurals, and vice versa.

Intrinsic aids to statutory interpretation consist of the following.

- The **long title** of an Act, which may give guidance as to the Act's general objective.
- The **preamble** of an Act often directs the judge as to its intentions and objects.
- **Interpretation sections** to Acts. Particularly long, complicated and wide-ranging Acts often contain self-explanations; for instance, s 207 of the Financial Services Act 1986 defines 'authorised persons' and 'recognised investment exchanges' for its purposes.
- **Sidenotes**. Statutes often have summary notes in the margin.

Key terms

Intrinsic aids are those words contained in the Queen's Printer's copy of the statute. **Extrinsic** aids are those found elsewhere.

Extrinsic aids include the following.

(a) Reports of the Law Commission, royal commissions, the Law Reform Committee and other official committees.

(b) Hansard, the official journal of UK Parliamentary debates. This follows a decision of the House of Lords in *Pepper v Hart 1992* where the House of Lords decided that it is acceptable to look at the original speech which first introduced a bill to ascertain its meaning, but only if the statute is ambiguous or obscure or its literal meaning would lead to absurdity.

3 European Community law

FAST FORWARD

The third source of law is EU law. Different types of EU law have different effects in the UK.

3.1 Introduction to EU law

The **European Economic Community** was set up by the First Treaty of Rome 1957. Its immediate aim was the integration of the economies of the member states. A more long-term aim is political integration. There are in total three individual **European Communities** to which all the member states belong.

- The **European Coal and Steel Community** (ECSC) set up in 1951
- The **European Economic Community** (EEC) set up in 1957
- The **European Atomic Energy Community** (EURATOM) set up in 1957

The term **European Union** (EU) is now used loosely to refer to the three communities together, and the same term is more correctly used when referring to more recent areas of co-operation, for example, following the Maastricht Treaty.

The term **European Community** (EC) is used as synonymous with the EEC.

There were six original signatories to the Treaty of Rome. Subsequently, Great Britain, Eire and Denmark joined in 1973, Greece in 1981 and Spain and Portugal in 1986. Membership of the EC was extended to Austria, Sweden and Finland from 1 January 1995. On 1 May 2004 Poland, Hungary, Cyprus, Malta, Czech Republic, Lithuania, Latvia, Estonia, Slovakia and Slovenia joined, bringing the total number of member states to 25.

Exam focus point

At the time of writing, there are 25 member states of the EU, with more applying. Keep an eye on the press for developments!

3.1.1 The single market

Under the Single European Act 1986, the EU heads of government committed themselves to the progressive setting up of a single market. The Act defines a single market as 'an area without internal frontiers in which the free movement of goods, persons, services and capital is ensured in accordance with the provisions of this Treaty'.

3.1.2 Community institutions

There are four main **institutions** established by the Treaties. Three are political institutions: the **Commission**, the **Council of Ministers** and the **European Parliament**. The fourth is the **European Court of Justice.**

Institution	Activities and personnel
The European Commission	The European Commission is the **executive** body of the EU. Its main activities are 'formulating proposals for new community policies, mediating between the Member States to secure the adoption of these proposals, co-ordinating national policies and overseeing the execution of existing community policies'. There are twenty Commissioners appointed by mutual agreement of the member governments. The Commission has a wide legislative function. It is responsible for drafting most EC legislation, and puts its proposals before the Council for enactment.
The Council of Ministers	The Council is the Community's **decision-making body**. It 'takes the final decision on most EC legislation, concludes agreements with foreign countries and decides on the Community budget'. The Council comprises **representatives of the member states**; each government sends a relevant minister as its delegate. Different voting arrangements apply in different situations. Sometimes a unanimous vote is required; more usually a 'qualified majority' will suffice. This involves the use of a **weighted voting system**, based on the relative population of member states.
The European Parliament	The **European Parliament** is a directly elected body. Members sit in political groupings rather than by country. The Parliament has consultative and advisory functions which are exercised through standing committees dealing with specialist topics.
The European Court of Justice	This is a court of first instance from which there is no appeal. The jurisdiction of the European Court falls under four main heads. • Legal matters arising from the acts or omissions of member states, such as failure of a member state to fulfil its treaty obligations. • Rulings on legal issues affecting persons which arise from EU law. • Actions brought against EU institutions by member states, individuals or companies. • Disputes between the Communities and their employees, although these are usually heard by the Court of First Instance. • The ECJ provides authoritative interpretations on matters of European Law to the UK courts.
The European Court of First Instance	Because of the increasing workload of the ECJ this court was created in 1989 to relieve the ECJ of certain minor types of case. Appeal on points of law is to the ECJ.

Courts

Can you remember what a 'court of first instance' is?

Answer

If not, look back to Chapter 1.

When a legal issue affecting persons which arises from EU law comes before the Judicial Committee of the House of Lords, which is the final court of appeal in the UK, the Judicial Committee is obliged to refer it to the European Court for a ruling.

Thereafter the English court (duly instructed as to the meaning) must apply the rule to the case before it.

The Court consists of judges appointed for six year periods on recommendation of member states. They are assisted by **Advocates-General** who submit reasoned argument on the issues before the Court. The Court gives a single judgment.

3.1.3 Other institutions

The four institutions described above are the main European Community institutions. There are a number of other bodies including the Economic and Social Committee, the European Investment Bank and the European Court of First Instance.

3.2 Sources of EU law 6/02

The sources of community law may be described as primary or secondary. The primary sources of law are the foundation treaties themselves.

- The **Treaty of Paris 1951**, which established the **ECSC**.
- The **First Treaty of Rome 1957**, which established **the EEC**.
- The **Second Treaty of Rome 1957**, which established the **EURATOM**.

Secondary legislation takes three forms, with the Council and Commission being empowered to do the following:

- Make **regulations**
- Issue **directives**
- Take **decisions**

They may also make recommendations and deliver opinions although these are only persuasive in authority.

3.2.1 Direct applicability and direct effect

To understand the importance of regulations, directives and decisions, it is necessary to appreciate the distinction between **direct applicability** and **direct effect**.

Community law which is directly applicable in member states comes into force without any act of implementation by member states, and it confers rights and imposes obligations directly on individuals.

Consequently, where EU law is directly applicable it can override legislation passed by the UK parliament to the extent that it is inconsistent with the EU provision. Only regulations can be directly applicable. Regulations, directives and decisions may have direct effect but only when it is unconditional and precise.

Where there is direct effect the EU provision may confer rights on an individual against the state or a state body, but not rights against others. An example of direct effect is seen in:

Marshall v Southampton and South West Hampshire Area Health Authority 1986
The facts: The claimant was dismissed at the age of 62, although she wished to continue working until the age of 65. The defendant's policy was that normal retirement age for its employees was the age when a state pension becomes payable.

Decision: A directive on equal treatment was to be interpreted as meaning that a policy based on the qualifying age for a state pension (which under national legislation was different for men and women) constituted discrimination on the grounds of sex. The policy was therefore contrary to the directive.

3.2.2 Regulations

Regulations have the force of law in every EU state without need of national legislation. In this sense regulations are described as directly applicable. Their objective is to obtain uniformity of law throughout the EU. They are formulated by the Commission but must be authorised by the Council of Ministers.

Key term

Regulations apply throughout the Community and they become part of the law of each member nation as soon as they come into force without the need for each country to make its own legislation.

Direct law-making of this type is generally restricted to matters within the basic aims of Treaty of Rome, such as the establishment of a single unrestricted market in the EC territory in manufactured goods. For example, certain types of agreement which would restrict competition are prohibited, and attract punishment by fine.

Acts of implementation are actually prohibited, in case a member state alters the scope of the regulation in question.

3.2.3 Directives

Key term

Directives are issued to the governments of the EU member states requiring them within a specified period (usually two years) to alter the national laws of the state so that they conform to the directive.

Until a directive is given effect by a UK statute it does not usually affect legal rights and obligations of individuals. The wording of a directive may be cited in legal proceedings, but generally **statutory interpretation is a matter for the UK courts**.

Van Duyn v Home Office 1974
The facts: The claimant, a Dutch national, was refused leave to enter the UK because she was intending to work for the Church of Scientology, a movement which the UK government saw as socially harmful. An EU directive required that any such restriction on the grounds of 'public policy or of public security shall be based exclusively on the personal conduct of the individual concerned'. She claimed that the refusal was not based on personal conduct.

Decision: The claimant's membership of an organisation was 'personal conduct' and so the decision to exclude her was consistent with the directive.

Attention!

Directives are the most significant and important means of importing formulated by the EU law into the UK legal system.

3.2.4 Decisions

Decisions of an administrative nature are made by the European Commission in Brussels.

Key term

A **decision** may be addressed to a state, person or a company and is immediately binding, but only on the recipient.

3.2.5 Legislative procedure

Proposals for EU legislation are drafted by the Commission. These drafts are referred to member states for comments.

These preliminary consultations between the Commission and the member states may continue over a period of years and result in extensive alteration of the draft directive. The directives are also debated in the preparatory stage by the European Parliament. The final stage is the consideration of a directive by the Council of Ministers.

If the Council approves, it authorises the issue of the directive and the member states must then alter their law accordingly.

Question — **EU secondary legislation**

Describe the three types of secondary legislation.

Answer

A **regulation** is a rule of law designed to obtain uniformity throughout the member states. It is directly applicable without the need for national legislation. A **directive** is issued to member states requiring them to make such changes to their own law as prescribed by the directive. A **decision** is binding in its entirety upon those to whom it is addressed, whether they be member states or corporate bodies. In the case of member states, a decision has direct effect.

Exam focus point

EU law is a very important topic, so do not neglect it.

3.2.6 Interpretation of EU law

EU legislation is drafted in a different way from UK legislation. The legislation states the broad principles and leaves the judges to develop the detail. EU legislation is deemed equally valid in any language in which it is originally published.

The English courts should try to follow the approach of European courts when interpreting the legislation. To do otherwise would create differences in the way in which the law is interpreted and applied in different member states.

A directive which has not been implemented into the law of a member state and is not of direct effect may still have some impact on UK law. First, a UK court can have regard to such a directive in interpreting national law (*Marleasing SA v La Commercial International de Alimentacion SA (1990)).* Secondly the failure of the UK to implement a directive may give rise to a liability in damages (*Francovich v Italy* (1991)).

In the case *Brasserie du Pecheur SA v Germany* and *R v Secretary of State for Transport ex p Factortame (No 4) Ltd (1996)* the *Francovich* decision was applied.

The facts: In *Brasserie du Pecheur* a French brewery had been forced to discontinue exports to Germany because its beer did not comply with a German purity law which was itself contrary to an EU directive which did not have direct effect. In *Factortame* (see below) Spanish fishermen had purchased British registered vessels but had been rendered ineligible to fish in UK waters because UK legislation which was inconsistent with EU directives had been upheld by the UK courts. The claimants were seeking damages from the German and UK governments respectively.

Decision: The ECJ held that the principle of state liability established in *Francovich* applied to all acts or omissions in a state whether the acts or omissions were legislative, executive or judicial. However, the ECJ went on to hold that damages are recoverable from a state by individuals who have suffered loss as a result of the state's breach of EU law only if three conditions are met:

- The law broken must have been intended to confer rights on individuals
- The breach must be serious eg a deliberate breach by the state
- There must be a causal link between the state's breach and the claimant's loss.

The House of Lords then ruled that the UK's breach was sufficiently serious to allow the claimant's action to proceed subject to proof of the link between the claimant's loss and the UK's breach of EU law.

3.3 EU law in the UK 12/03

The directives to which Parliament must ultimately conform are issued as a result of negotiation and often agreement between the UK government and the other governments of the EU.

The UK government in turn is dependent on the support of a majority of Members of Parliament to retain office. To that extent, Parliament has indirect influence on the EU law-making process.

The House of Lords acknowledged the supremacy of EU law in the Factortame litigation.

Factortame Ltd v Secretary of State for Transport (No 2) 1991
The facts: Article 52 of the Treaty of Rome prohibits discrimination against the nationals of another EC member state. The Merchant Shipping Act 1988 requires 75% of directors and shareholders in companies operating British-registered fishing vessels to be British. Certain UK companies controlled by Spanish nationals and fishing in British waters were unable to meet these conditions. They brought a claim against the UK government on the grounds that the Act was incompatible with EU law.

Decision: The ECJ laid down that EU law must be fully and uniformly applied in all member states.

Chapter roundup

- The first legal source of law, consisting of decisions made in the courts, is **case law,** which is judge-made law based on the underlying principle of consistency. Once a legal or equitable principle is decided by an appropriate court it is a **judicial precedent**.
- Case law has developed from the interaction of the common law and equity.
  - **Common law** (legal rights) is applied **automatically** and comprised a **complete system** of law. **Rights** are enforceable against anyone and everyone, regardless of their knowledge that the rights exist.
  - **Equity** (equitable rights) is applied **at the court's discretion** and does **not** comprise a **complete system** of law. **Rights** are enforceable only against those persons who know or ought to know of their existence and must be exercised without undue delay. **Remedies**, for example an injunction, are given against the person.
- In order that judicial precedent provides consistency in law, the ratio decidendi must be identified. The material facts must be the same. The status of the court which set the precedent must be such as to bind the present court. Rationes decidendi are the reasons for the decision being made – they alone are binding. Obiter dicta are comments made by the deciding judge in passing and are persuasive only.
- The House of Lords binds itself (but may depart from its own decisions) and all lower courts. The Court of Appeal binds itself and all lower courts. A Divisional Court of the High Court (two or more judges) binds itself and all lower courts. The High Court (single judge) binds all lower courts. Crown Court decisions may be of persuasive authority. The county court and magistrates' courts do not make binding precedent.
- The second major legal source of law is legislation. UK statute law may take the form of Acts of Parliament or delegated legislation under the Acts, for example statutory instruments or bye-laws.
- The third legal source of law is EU law. There are three individual European Communities. The European Coal and Steel Community was established by the Treaty of Paris 1951, the European Economic Community by the First Treaty of Rome 1957 and the European Atomic Energy Community by the Second Treaty of Rome 1957.
- The European Commission is the executive body of the Community. The Council of Ministers is the Community's decision-making body and has to approve any legislation proposed by the Commission. The European Parliament has a consultative role. The European Court of Justice is the judicial body of the Community.
- The sources of EU law may be described as primary or secondary. The primary sources of law are the Foundation treaties themselves. The secondary sources of law are legislation, which takes three forms.
  - Regulations are self-executing.
  - Directives generally require national legislation to be effective, usually within two years.
  - Decisions are immediately binding on the person to whom they are addressed.

Quick quiz

1 **Fill in the blanks** in the statements below, using the words in the box.

- In order that (1) ……………….. provides (2) ……………….. in the law, a precedent must be carefully examined before it can be applied to a particular (3) ……………….. It must be a proposition of (4) ……………….. . The (5) ……………….. must be identified. The (6) ……………….. must be the same.
- The (7) ……………….. of the court which set the precedent must be such as to (8) ……………….. the present court.

• bind	• judicial precedent
• case	• status
• ratio decidendi	• law
• material facts	• consistency

2 What is the final step in the life of a Bill?

3 Obiter dicta form part of the ratio decidendi.

True ☐

False ☐

4 Which of these decisions binds the Crown Court?

Decisions of the County Court ☐

Decisions of the High Court ☐

Decisions of the Court of Appeal ☐

Decisions of the House of Lords ☐

5 In 1989, Mr Justice Jeffries, a High Court judge sitting alone, is deciding a case which has similar material facts to one decided by the Court of Appeal in 1889. He can decline to be bound by this decision by showing that

A The status of the previous court is not such as can bind him
B The decision was taken too long ago to be of any relevance
C The decision does not accord with the rules of a statute passed in 1890
D The obiter dicta are obscure

6 Overruling a decision of a lower court affects the outcome of that earlier decision.

True ☐

False ☐

7 Match each of the following definitions to the correct term.

(a) A court higher up in the hierarchy overturns the decision of a lower court on appeal in the same case.

(b) A principle laid down by a lower court is overturned by a higher court in a different, later case.

(c) A judge states that the material facts of the case before him are sufficiently different from those of an earlier case as to enable the application of a different rule of law.

(1) Distinguishing
(2) Overruling
(3) Reversing

8 The rule that a statute should be construed to give effect to the intended outcome of the legislation is known as the .... role.

9 What type of EU legislation is directly applicable?

10 UK parliament is sovereign of the European Commission.

True ☐

False ☐

11 Link each European Body to its role

(a)	European Commission	(i)	Decision-making legislative body
(b)	Council of Ministers	(ii)	Judicial body
(c)	European Parliament	(iii)	Executive/legislative body
(d)	European Court of Justice	(iv)	Consultative role

12 List the primary sources of European Community law.

Answers to quick quiz

1 (1) judicial precedent (2) consistency (3) case (4) law (5) ratio decidendi (6) material facts (7) status (8) bind

2 The third reading (final approval stage)

3 False

4 Decisions of the High Court, Court of Appeal and House of Lords

5 C. A High Court judge is bound by decisions of the Court of Appeal

6 False

7 (a) 3
(b) 2
(c) 1

8 Purposive role

9 Regulations

10 False

11 (a), (iii)
(b), (i)
(c), (iv)
(d), (ii)

12 Treaty of Paris 1951
First Treaty of Rome 1957
Second Treaty of Rome 1957

Now try the question below from the Exam Question Bank

Number	Level	Marks	Time
Q2	Examination	10	18 mins

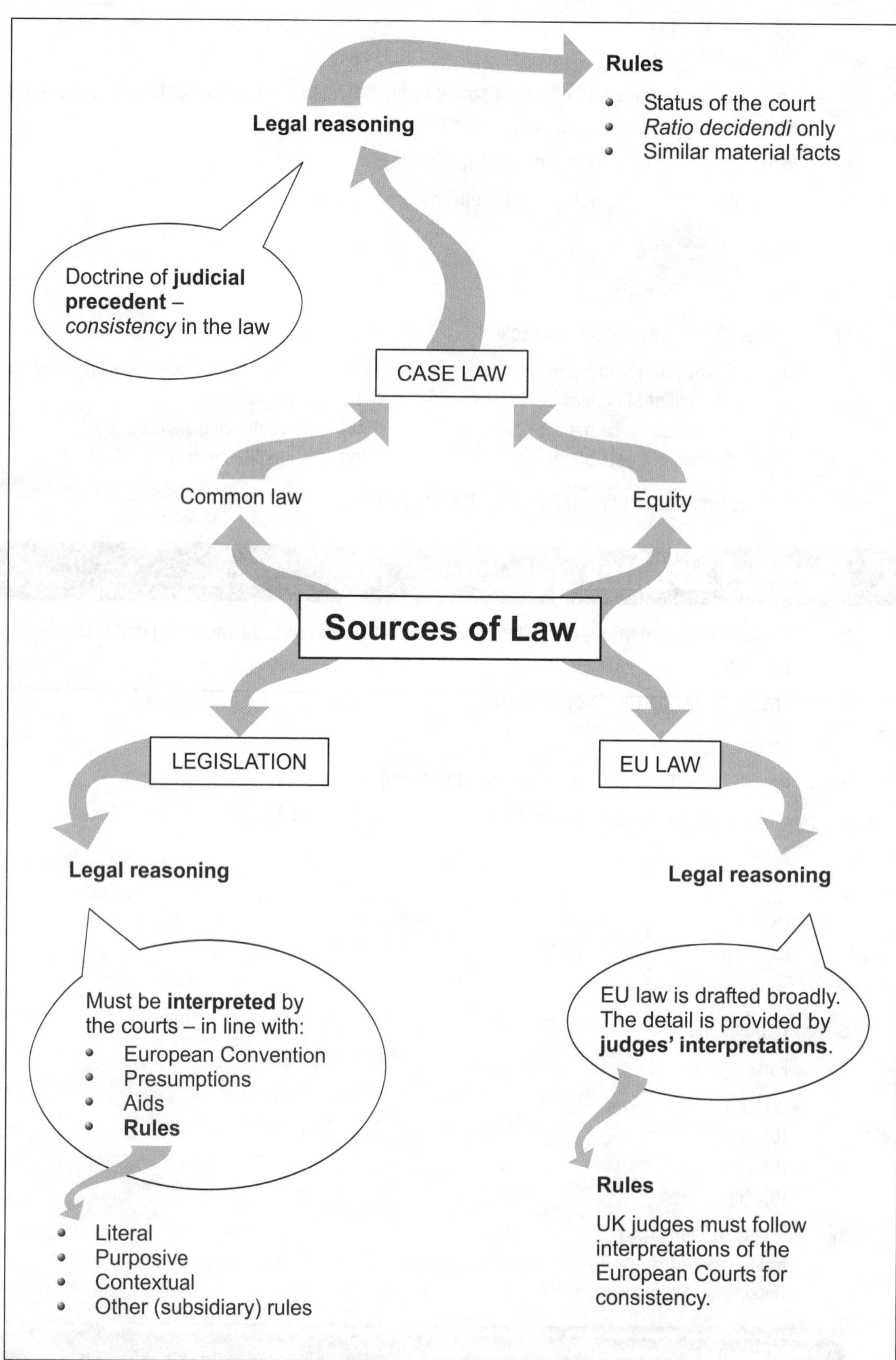
Rules
Status of the court
Ratio decidendi only
Similar material facts
Legal reasoning
Doctrine of judicial precedent – consistency in the law
CASE LAW
Common law
Equity
Sources of Law
LEGISLATION
EU LAW
Legal reasoning
Legal reasoning
Must be interpreted by the courts – in line with:
European Convention
Presumptions
Aids
Rules
EU law is drafted broadly. The detail is provided by judges' interpretations.
Literal
Purposive
Contextual
Other (subsidiary) rules
Rules
UK judges must follow interpretations of the European Courts for consistency.

3

Human rights

Topic list	Syllabus reference
1 The European Convention on Human Rights	1(e)
2 The Human Rights Act 1998	1(e)
3 Convention rights	1(e)
4 The impact of the Act	1(e)

Introduction

As outlined in Chapter 2, EU law is an increasingly important source of UK law.

However, there are significant numbers of examples of **how European law which does not derive from the European Union has affected UK law**. A recent and pervasive example is the **Human Rights legislation** which came into force in the UK in October 2000. A basic outline and history of the **Human Rights Act 1998** is given in this Chapter. The Act will be referred to throughout the Study Text, as it has the potential to affect many areas of UK law.

The Act has significant implications for '**public authorities**', which includes the courts, the police and Parliament. The key duty for the courts is the requirement to **interpret UK legislation** in a way that is **compatible** with the European Convention on Human Rights. New law drafted by Parliament must also be compatible, or the person proposing the legislation must state that it is not so.

Human rights will never form more than ten marks of a question in its own right. However, it is a pervasive issue, so may impact in a minor way in several questions in any given paper.

1 The European Convention on Human Rights

The Human Rights Act 1998 is a key example of the influence of International law in the United Kingdom.

The Act came into operation on 2 October 2000. The extent of the impact of the legislation is becoming clearer as case law develops.

The Act incorporates the 'European Convention for the Protection of Human Rights and Fundamental Freedoms' (more commonly referred to as the 'European Convention on Human Rights') into UK domestic law.

Key term

> The **European Convention on Human Rights** is an agreement on basic human rights, put together by major powers in the wake of the human rights abuses that occurred during World War Two and signed by those powers, including the United Kingdom, in 1951.

During the second half of the twentieth century, the European Convention on Human Rights was used as a guideline in the English courts. It was widely believed that UK political and legal institutions were well suited to the protection of fundamental human rights and that incorporation of the Convention into English law was not necessary. However, any individual who felt his rights had been violated could take a case to the European Court of Human Rights in Strasbourg.

Towards the end of the 1990s, it became clear that the British government was of the opinion that it was not sufficient to rely on existing law to ensure protection of human rights. The Human Rights Act was therefore developed as a means of ensuring that these fundamental rights were enshrined in the English legal system. English courts now have a statutory duty to ensure that English laws are interpreted 'as far as possible' in a manner which is compatible with the **convention rights** incorporated by the Human Rights Act.

Thus an individual can now ask the UK courts to consider his convention rights, and need not take a case to Strasbourg.

2 The Human Rights Act 1998 12/01

FAST FORWARD

> The Human Rights Act 1998 incorporates the European Convention on Human Rights into UK domestic law.
> The impact of the legislation is pervasive in many areas of UK law.

Exam focus point

> The examiner has commented that as the law relating to the Human Rights Act (HRA) is in its infancy, the knowledge of the law required for the exam is restricted. The impact of the HRA will never be more than a 10 mark question on its own and not in the near future.
>
> However, the impact of HRA will be pervasive. it has the potential to impact in many different areas of law. You should be aware of the provisions so that you can see the potential impacts throughout the *Corporate and Business law syllabus.*
>
> This text will highlight some of the early cases and some areas which might be affected by the HRA. You should ensure that your knowledge of the Convention which the law incorporates in UK law is sufficient that you can understand the impacts which are pointed out, and identify further impacts if required.

The Act binds **public authorities** (defined as bodies undertaking functions of a public nature). These include government departments, local authorities, courts and schools. These public authorities must not breach an individual's rights. In the case of proceedings against a public authority, there is a limitation period of one year from the date on which the act complained of is alleged to have occurred.

The European Court of Human Rights is now the final court of appeal after a case has been brought in the domestic courts.

This means that the final source of appeal (after the House of Lords) is the European Court of Human Rights. There is **no appeal** from the European Court of Human Rights **to the European Court of Justice.** The two courts are not linked.

2.1 The impact of the Human Rights Act

The key impact that the inclusion of the convention into the UK law has on English law is that **UK courts are now required to interpret UK law in a way compatible with the Convention** so far as it is possible to do so.

The Convention will also be incorporated into the English legal system under the Human Rights Act in the following ways.

Existing legislation must be interpreted in a way which is compatible with convention rights. This means that the courts must take into account decisions and judgements of the European Court of Human Rights. If a court feels that any provision of legislation is incompatible with the Convention, it may make a declaration of that incompatibility. However, any legislation which has been declared incompatible is still valid in domestic law until it is amended. However, a court can make it unlawful for a public authority to act in a way which is incompatible with a Convention right.

In the case of **new legislation**, it is necessary for the person responsible for a Bill to make a statement of compatibility with the Convention before the Bill's second reading. Where such a statement has been made a court can still declare the legislation to be incompatible with Convention rights.

3 Convention rights

The Human Rights Act protects a number of **Convention rights**. These are Articles which are set out in the Convention and which have now been incorporated into English law.

Exam focus point

Do not worry about learning all the details of the Convention. You should simply **be aware** of some of the major rights and freedoms.

3.1 Articles

The relevant Articles are shown below. Not all of these are of particular relevant to accountants, for example Articles 3, 4 and 12, but we show them all for the sake of interest and completeness.

THE ARTICLES

Part I – The convention

Rights and freedoms

Article 2 Right to life

1 Everyone's right to life shall be protected by law. No one shall be deprived of his life intentionally save in the execution of a sentence of a court following his conviction of a crime for which this penalty is provided by law.

2 Deprivation of life shall not be regarded as inflicted in contravention of this Article when it results from the use of force which is no more than absolutely necessary.

(a) In defence of any person from unlawful violence
(b) In order to effect a lawful arrest or to prevent the escape for a person lawfully detained
(c) In action lawfully taken for the purpose of quelling a riot or insurrection

Article 3 Prohibition of torture

No one shall be subjected to torture or to inhuman or degrading treatment or punishment.

Article 4 Prohibition of slavery and forced labour

1 No one shall be held in slavery or servitude.

2 No one shall be required to perform forced labour or compulsory labour.

3 For the purpose of the Article the term 'forced or compulsory labour' shall not include:

(a) Any work required to be done in the ordinary course of detention imposed according to the provisions of Article 5 of this Convention or during conditional release from such detention;

(b) Any service of a military character, or in the case of conscientious objectors in countries where they are recognised, service exacted instead of compulsory military service;

(c) Any work or service which forms part of normal civic obligations.

Article 5 Right to liberty and security

1 Everyone has the right to liberty and security of person. No one shall be deprived of his liberty save in the following cases and in accordance with a procedure prescribed by law:

(a) The lawful detention of a person after conviction by a competent court;

(b) The lawful arrest or detention of a person for non-compliance with the lawful order of a court or in order to secure the fulfilment of any obligation prescribed by law;

(c) The lawful arrest or detention of a person effected for the purpose of bringing him before the competent legal authority on reasonable suspicion of having committed an offence or when it is reasonably considered necessary to prevent his committing another offence or fleeing after having done so;

(d) The detention of a minor by lawful order for the purpose of educational supervision or for the purpose of bringing him before the competent legal authority;

(e) The lawful detention of persons for the prevention of the spreading of infectious diseases, of persons of unsound mind, alcoholics or drug addicts or vagrants;

(f) The lawful arrest or detention of a person to prevent his effecting an unauthorised entry into the country or of a person against whom action is being taken with a view to deportation or extradition.

2 Everyone who is arrested shall be informed promptly, in a language which he understands, of the reasons for his arrest and of any charge against him.

3 Everyone arrested or detained in accordance with the provisions of Paragraph 12(c) of this Article shall be brought promptly before a judge or other officer authorised by law to exercise judicial power and shall be entitled to trial within a reasonable time or to release pending trial. Release may be conditioned by guarantees to appear for trial.

4 Everyone who is deprived of hi liberty by arrest of detention shall be entitled to take proceedings by which the lawfulness of his detention shall be decided speedily by a court and his release ordered if the detention is not lawful.

5 Everyone who has been the victim of arrest or detention in contravention if the provisions of this Article shall have an enforceable right to compensation.

Article 6 Right to a fair trial

1 In the determination of his civil rights and obligations or of any criminal charge against him, everyone is entitled to fair and public hearing within a reasonable time by an independent and impartial tribunal established by law. Judgement shall be pronounced publicly but the press and the public may be excluded from all or part of the trial in the interest of morals, public order, or national security in a democratic society where the interest of juveniles or the protection of the private life of the parties so require, or to the extent strictly necessary in the opinion of the court in special circumstances where publicity would prejudice the interests of justice.

2 Everyone charged with a criminal offence should be presumed innocent until proven guilty according to law.

3 Everyone charged with a criminal offence has the following minimum rights:

(a) To be informed promptly, in a language which he understands and in detail, of the nature and cause of the accusation against him;

(b) To have adequate time and facilities for the preparation of his defence;

(c) To defend himself in person or through legal assistance of his own choosing, or, if he has not sufficient means to pay for legal assistance, to be given it free of charge when the interests of justice so require;

(d) To examine or have examined witnesses against him and to obtain the attendance and examination of witnesses on his behalf under the same conditions as witnesses against him;

(e) To have the free assistance of an interpreter if he cannot understand or speak the language used in court.

Article 7 No punishment without law

1 No one shall be held guilty of any criminal offence on account of any act or omission which did not constitute a criminal offence under national or international law at the time that it was committed. Nor shall a heavier penalty be imposed than the one that was applicable at the time the criminal offence was committed.

2 This Article shall not prejudice the trial and punishment of any person for any act or omission which, at the time when it was committed, was criminal according to the general principles of law recognised by civilised nations.

Article 8 Right to respect for private and family life

1 Everyone has a right to respect for his private and family life, his home and his correspondence.

2 There shall be no interference by a public authority with the exercise of his right except as is in accordance with the law and is necessary in a democratic society in the interest of national security, public safety or the economic well-being of the country, for the prevention of disorder or crime, for the protection of health or morals or for the protection of the rights and freedoms of others.

Article 9 Freedom of thought, conscience and religion

1 Everyone has the right to freedom of thought, conscience and religion; this right includes freedom to change his religion or belief and freedom, either alone or in community with others and in public or private, to manifest his religion or belief, in worship, teaching, practice and observance.

2 Freedom to manifest one's religion or beliefs shall be subject only to such limitations as are prescribed by law and are necessary in a democratic society in the interests of public safety, for the protection of the rights and freedoms of others.

Article 10 Freedom of expression

1 Everyone has the right to freedom of expression. This right shall include freedom to hold opinions and to receive and impart information and ideas without interference by public authority and regardless of frontiers. This Article shall not prevent States from requiring the licensing of broadcasting, television or cinema enterprises.

2 The exercise of these freedoms, since it carries with it duties and responsibilities, may be subject to such formalities, conditions, restrictions, or penalties as are prescribed by law and are necessary in a democratic society, in the interests of national security, territorial integrity or public safety, for the prevention of disorder and crime, for the protection of health or morals, for the protection of the reputation or rights of others, for preventing the disclosure of information received in confidence or for maintaining the authority and impartiality of the judiciary.

Article 11 Freedom of assembly and association

1 Everyone has the right to freedom and peaceful assembly and to freedom of association with others including the right to form and to join trade unions for the protection of his interests.

2 No restrictions shall be placed on the exercise of these rights other than such as are prescribed by law and are necessary in a democratic society in the interests of national security or public safety for the prevention of disorder and crime, for the protection of health or morals or the protection of the rights and freedoms of others. This Article shall not prevent the imposition of lawful restriction in the exercise of those rights by members of the armed forces, or the police or of the administration of state

Article 12 Right to marry

Men and women of marriageable age have the right to marry and to found a family, according to the national laws governing the exercise of this right.

Article 14 Prohibition of discrimination

The enjoyment of the rights and freedoms set forth in the Convention shall be secured without discrimination on any ground such as sex, race, colour, language, religion, political or other opinion, national or social origin, association with a national minority, property, birth or other status.

The rights under the Act fall into three categories.

(a) **Absolute rights** cannot be restricted in any circumstances, even in times of war or public emergency. They are **inalienable**.

(b) **Derogable rights** may be derogated by the government. This means that the government may opt out of particular rights (although not simply for reasons of public interest).

(c) **Qualified rights** are those which are subject to restriction in order to take the public interest into account.

Articles 2, 3, 4(1) and 7 set out rights which are **absolute**. Articles 4(2), 4(3), 5 and 6 set out **derogable** rights. Articles 8, 9, 10 and 11 contain **qualified** rights. These qualified rights are subject to the interests of:

- National security
- Public safety
- Prevention of disorder and crime and
- Protection of health, morals and the rights of others

3.2 Protocols

The Convention also contains a number of **protocols**, which supplement the Convention.

PROTOCOLS

Part II – The First Protocol

Article 1 Protection of property

Every natural or legal person is entitled to the peaceful enjoyment of his possessions. No one shall be deprived of his possessions except in the public interest and subject to the conditions provided for by law and by the general principles of international law.

The preceding provisions shall not, however, in any way impair the right of a State to enforce such laws as it deems necessary to control the use of property in accordance with the general interests or to secure the payment of taxes of other contributions or penalties.

Article 2 Right to education

No person shall be denied the right to education. In the exercise of any functions which it assumes in relation to education and to teaching, the State shall respect the right of parents to ensure such education and teaching in conformity with their own religious and philosophical convictions.

Article 3 Right to free elections

The High Contracting Parties undertake to hold free elections at reasonable intervals by secret ballot, under conditions which will ensure the free expression of the opinion of the people in the choice of the legislature.

Part III – The Sixth Protocol

Article 1 Abolition of the death penalty

The death penalty shall be abolished. No one shall be condemned to such a penalty or executed.

Article 2 Death penalty in time of war

A State may make provision in its law for the death penalty in respect of acts committed in time of war or of imminent threat of war; such penalty shall be applied only in the instances laid down in the law and in accordance with its provisions. The State shall communicate to the Secretary General of the council of Europe the relevant provision of that law.

4 The impact of the Act

FAST FORWARD

The impact of the Act is still in its early days, but is likely to be significant in UK law.

This Study Text highlights other areas of potential impact in relevant chapters. Some ideas of where the legislation could impact on the rest of UK law are summarised here.

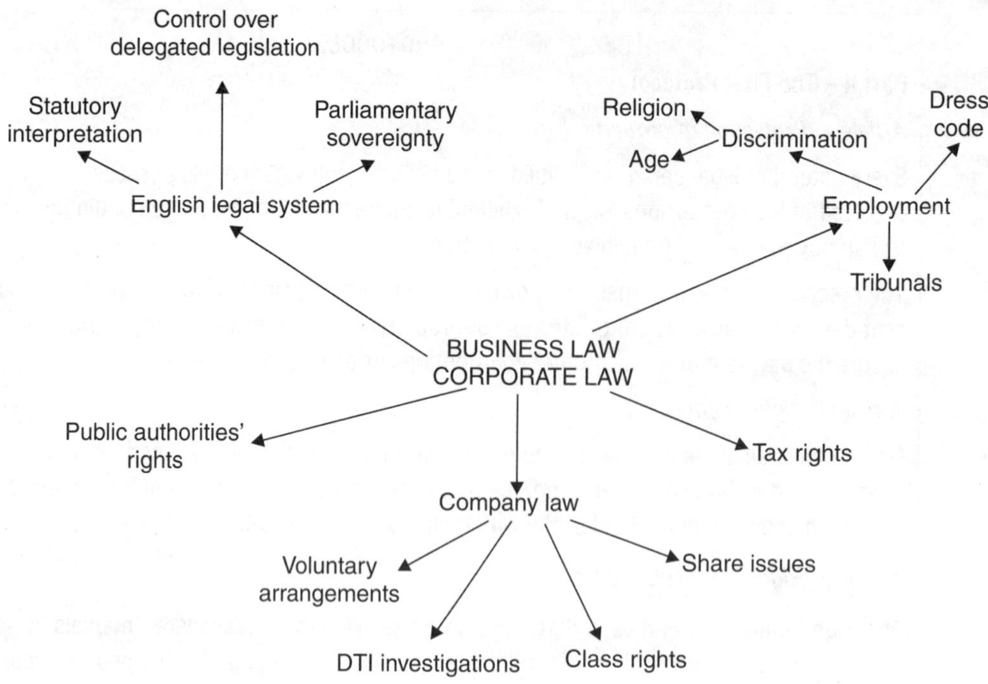

Exam focus point

There has been limited case law to date under the Human Rights Act. The examiner has indicated that candidates should be aware of high profile cases relating to the Act so you should watch out in the press for cases.

Some claims under the Act may gain much popular and media support but still fail.

> *Pretty v DPP 2001*
>
> *The facts:* The terminally ill applicant wished her husband to assist her to commit suicide at a time and in a manner of her choosing. The husband would be liable to prosecution under s2(1) Suicide Act 1961, which makes it an offence to aid, abet, counsel or procure the suicide of another. The applicant sought an undertaking from the DPP that her husband would not be prosecuted, since the offence was inconsistent with her right to life under the Convention. The DPP gave no such undertaking and the applicant contended that her rights under various Articles of the Convention, including articles 2 and 3, were being infringed.
>
> *Decision*: The right to the dignity of life was not a right to die with dignity but the right to live with as much dignity as possible until that life reached its natural end. The 1961 Act was not incompatible with the claimant's convention rights.

The impact of the Act will not be fully known until it has been further tested in the courts. For example, it is not clear exactly what is meant by the right to 'respect for private and family life' or the 'right to a fair trial'. In addition, the question of conflict between the right to respect for private and family life and the right of 'freedom of expression' has been pointed out by many commentators.

Chapter roundup

- The Human Rights Act 1998 incorporates the European Convention on Human Rights into UK domestic law.
- The impact of the legislation is likely to be pervasive in many areas of UK law.

Quick quiz

1 What is the right of appeal from the European Court of Human Rights?

2 The UK courts may interpret UK law literally as they always did prior to the Human Rights Act 1998

True ☐

False ☐

3 Match each of the following articles to the type of right which it enshrines.

(a) Everyone's right to life shall be protected by law
(b) Everyone has the right to liberty and security of person
(c) Everyone has the right to freedom of expression

(1) Derogable
(2) Absolute
(3) Qualified

Answers to quick quiz

1 There is no right of further appeal

2 False. They must interpret UK law in accordance with the Convention.

3 (a) (2), (b) (1), (c) (3)

Now try the question below from the Exam Question Bank

Number	Level	Marks	Time
Q3	Introductory	n/a	10 mins

Part B
Law of contract

Introduction to the law of contract

4

Topic list	Syllabus reference
1 Definition of contract	2
2 Factors affecting the modern contract	2
3 The essentials of a contract	2
4 Contractual capacity	2
5 Form of a contract	2

Introduction

One of the main aims of this syllabus is to give you a good understanding of the key **business and company law rules** which underpin competence in financial and management accounting.

Law is a technical subject and it is necessary that you can demonstrate good technical knowledge of legal rules and principles.

This chapter introduces the topic of the **law of contract**. The essential elements for the formation of a contract, introduced in Section 3 of the chapter, are discussed in detail in Chapters 5 and 6. Some apparently valid contracts may be void ie of no legal effect. The most important example of such a contract is one in restraint of trade, which is described in Chapter 7.

It is a prerequisite for forming a binding agreement that both parties should have the **capacity** (section 4) to enter into it.

As a general rule, a contract does not need to be made in writing but may be made in any **form**. There are three exceptions, discussed at the end of this chapter.

This section provides an introduction to the law of contract. As such, it is essential background to Chapters 5 – 8, but most of it is unlikely to be examined in isolation.

1 Definition of contract

A **valid contract is a legally binding agreement**, formed by the mutual consent of two parties.

Key term

A **contract** may be defined as an **agreement which legally binds the parties.** The underlying theory is that a contract is the outcome of 'consenting minds'. However, parties are judged by what they have said, written or done, rather then by what they were actually thinking.

'An agreement which the law will recognise and enforce which, apart from other important applications, forms the basis of most business relationships and transactions.'

2 Factors affecting the modern contract

FAST FORWARD

The law seeks to protect the idea of 'freedom of contract', although **contractual terms** may be regulated by **statute**, particularly where the parties are of unequal bargaining strength.

2.1 Inequality of bargaining power

It is almost invariably the case that the two parties to a contract bring with them differing levels of **bargaining power**. Many contracts are made between experts and ordinary consumers. The law will intervene **only** where the former takes unfair advantage of his position and not simply because one party was in an inferior bargaining position. **Freedom of contract** is a term sometimes used and can be defined as follows.

> 'The principle that parties are completely unrestricted in deciding whether or not to enter into an agreement and, if they do so, upon the terms governing that relationship. In practice, this is not always the case because one may be in a much stronger economic position, and legislation has been introduced in order to redress the balance.'

2.2 The standard form contract

Mass production and nationalisation have led to the **standard form contract**.

Key term

The **standard form contract** is a document prepared by many large organisations setting out the terms on which they contract with their customers. The individual must usually take it or leave it. For example, a customer has to accept his supply of electricity on the electricity board's terms – he is not likely to succeed in negotiating special terms, unless he represents a large consumer such as a factory.

2.3 Consumer protection

In the second half of the twentieth century, there has been a surge of interest in consumer matters. The development of a mass market for often complex goods has meant that the consumer can no longer rely on his own judgement when buying sophisticated goods or services. Consumer interests are now served by two main areas.

(a) **Consumer protection agencies**, which include government departments (the Office of Fair Trading) and independent bodies (the Consumers' Association).

(b) **Legislation**.

Public policy sometimes requires that the freedom of contract should be modified. For example, the **Consumer Credit Act 1974** and the **Unfair Contract Terms Act 1977** both regulate the extent to which contracts can contain certain terms.

Exam focus point

Contract law questions will commonly take the form of scenarios and will require you to advise one of the parties of the legal position, such as asking whether or not a contract has been formed.

2.4 The electronic contract

English law has been concerned with formulating the rules for oral and written contracts for centuries, and cases decided in the 1800s continue to be valid today. As you will see in the next chapter, there are a number of important rules which depend on the timing of the sending and receipt of letters by post. With the advent of first the telex machine and then the fax machine, the law has had to be applied to new situations. Now the development of the internet for commercial purposes has brought new challenges as new ways of doing business come into being. We look at electronic contracts further in the next chapter.

3 The essentials of a contract

FAST FORWARD

The **three essential elements** of a contract are **offer and acceptance**, **consideration** and **intention to enter into legal relations**.

The courts will usually look for evidence of **three essential elements** in any contract.

- There must be an agreement usually made by **offer and acceptance**.
- The parties must have an **intention to create legal relations** between themselves.
- There must be a bargain by which the obligations assumed by one party are supported by **consideration** (value) given by the other.

We will explore these three essential elements in the next two chapters.

3.1 Validity factors

Even if these essential elements can be shown, a contract may not necessarily be valid or may only be partially valid. The validity of a contract may also be affected by any of the following factors.

- **Capacity**. Some persons have only restricted capacity to enter into contracts.
- **Form**. Some contracts must be made in a particular form.
- **Content**. In general the parties may enter into a contract on whatever terms they choose. Some terms which the parties do not express may be **implied**, and some terms which the parties do express are **overridden** by statutory rules.
- **Genuine consent**. A mistake or misrepresentation made by one party may affect the validity of a contract. Parties may be induced to enter into a contract by **undue influence** or **duress**.
- **Legality**. The courts will not enforce a contract which is deemed to be illegal or contrary to public policy.

We will look at capacity to contract and the form of a contract towards the end of the chapter. The content of a contract, including certainty of terms, is examined in Chapter 7.

Question

Essentials of a binding contract

What are the essential elements of a binding contract?

Answer

There must be an intention to create legal relations. There must be an agreement made by offer and acceptance. There must be consideration.

A contract which does not satisfy the relevant tests may be either **void, voidable** or **unenforceable**.

Key terms

A **void contract** is not a contract at all. The parties are not bound by it and if they transfer property under it they can sometimes recover their goods even from a third party.

A **voidable contract** is a contract which one party may set aside. Property transferred before avoidance is usually irrecoverable from a third party.

An **unenforceable contract** is a valid contract and property transferred under it cannot be recovered even from the other party to the contract. But if either party refuses to perform or to complete his part of the performance of the contract, the other party cannot compel him to do so. A contract is usually unenforceable when the required evidence of its terms, for example, written evidence of a contract relating to land, is not available.

Illustration

In this syllabus the most important example of contracts which are **void** are contracts in restraint of trade. These are discussed in Chapter 7.

4 Contractual capacity

12/01

English law states that a party is only bound by a contract into which he entered if he had the capacity to contract.

4.1 Companies

Companies and other artificial legal persons, such as local authorities, do not have the same unlimited capacity as a healthy human being. Often they are limited in what they can do by their constitutions, which only give them certain powers. Actions done outside those powers are said to be **ultra vires** – literally, '**beyond the powers'**. Ultra vires contracts are void, so neither party can enforce their terms.

The ultra vires rule as it applies to companies is now of very limited effect following the Companies Act 1989, which amended relevant sections of the Companies Act 1985.

(a) Companies can adopt a general clause in their constitutions which enable them to act as a **'general commercial company'**, so they are not restricted to certain types of activity.

(b) The validity of an act done by a company cannot be questioned on the ground that the company lacked capacity; in addition, the power of the company's directors to bind it are

deemed to be **free of limitation**, provided that the third party dealing with the company acted in good faith.

4.2 Mental incapacity

If a person who is temporarily insane, under the influence of drugs, or drunk, enters into a contract it is binding, with exceptions.

- If he is at the time incapable of understanding the nature of the contract
- If the other party knows or ought to know of his disability

When goods are supplied to a person under such disability, he must pay a reasonable price for them in any event (s 3 Sale of Goods Act 1979).

4.3 Minors

Many agreements entered into by a minor are unenforceable against him by the other parties, although he may choose to ratify them within a reasonable time of reaching the age of 18. A minor **is** bound by certain types of agreement unless he chooses to avoid them. These include a contract concerning land, a purchase of shares and a partnership agreement. A minor is bound by a contact for necessary goods (eg to purchase equipment needed for school) and services, eg dentistry.

5 Form of a contract

As a general rule, **a contract may be made in any form**. It may be written, or oral, or inferred from the conduct of the parties. For example, a customer in a self-service shop may take his selected goods to the cash desk, pay for them and walk out without saying a word.

Writing is not usually necessary except in the following circumstances.

- Some contracts must be by **deed.**
- Some contracts must be in **writing.**
- Some contracts must be **evidenced in writing.**

5.1 Contracts by deed

A contract by deed must be in **writing** and it must be **signed**. Delivery must take place. Delivery is conduct indicating that the person executing the deed intends to be bound by it.

These contracts must be by deed.

- **Leases** for three years or more
- A **conveyance** or transfer of a legal estate in land (including a mortgage)
- A promise not supported by consideration (such as a **covenant** for example a promise to pay a regular sum to a charity)

Key term

A contract by deed is sometimes referred to as a **specialty contract**. Any other type of contract may be referred to as a **simple contract**.

5.2 Contracts which must be in writing

Some types of contract are required to be in the form of a written document, usually signed by at least one of the parties.

These contracts must be in writing.

- A **transfer of shares** in a limited company
- The sale or disposition of an **interest in land**
- **Bills of exchange** and **cheques**
- **Consumer credit** contracts

A contract for the sale or disposition of land promises to transfer title at a future date and must be in writing. The conveyance or transfer must be by deed and will therefore also be in writing.

In the case of consumer credit transactions, the effect of failure to make the agreement in the prescribed form is to make the agreement unenforceable against the debtor unless the creditor obtains a court order.

5.3 Contracts which must be evidenced in writing

Certain contracts may be made orally, but are not enforceable in a court of law unless there is written evidence of their terms. The most important contract of this type is the contract of **guarantee**.

Chapter roundup

- A **valid contract is a legally binding agreement**, formed by the mutual consent of two parties.
- The law seeks to protect the idea of 'freedom of contract', although **contractual terms** may be regulated by **statute**, particularly where the parties are of unequal bargaining strength.
- The **three essential elements** of a contract are **offer and acceptance**, **consideration** and **intention to enter into legal relations**.
- There are a number of factors which may affect the **validity** of a contract. For a contract to be binding it must also satisfy various tests relating to **legality**, the **form** of the agreement, **content** of the agreement, **genuineness of consent** and the **capacity** of the parties to contract.
- A contract which does not satisfy the relevant tests above may be:
  - **Void** (neither party is bound)
  - **Voidable** (the contract is binding unless and until one party chooses to avoid it)
  - **Unenforceable** (the contract is valid but its terms cannot be enforced in a legal sense (although it may be ratified)
- The most important example of a **void** contract is one in restraint of trade.
- Although most contracts may be made **in any form**, some must be made in a particular form. A number of commercial contracts must be made in writing, for example.

Quick quiz

1 Which one of the contracts below is a standard form contract?

A A document put forward for the customer's signature by a supplier of goods in which pre-printed contractual terms are set out

B A document signed by both parties to a contract in which contractual terms as negotiated between them are set down

C An oral agreement to enter into relations on the basis of terms as agreed following negotiations between the parties

D An oral agreement between two parties who have negotiated terms regarding the standards of performance to be met by each party in the main contract

2 A valid contract is a legally binding agreement. The three essential elements of a contract are (1) ………………., (2) ………………. and (3) ………………. .

3 A voidable contract is not a contract at all.

True ☐

False ☐

4 Match the term to its definition.

	Term		Definition
(a)	Voidable	(1)	The contract is valid but its terms cannot be brought to bear in a legal sense
(b)	Unenforceable	(2)	Neither party is bound
(c)	Void	(3)	The contract is binding unless and until one party chooses to avoid it

5 Match the contract type to its required form.

	Contract type		Form
(a)	Covenant to make payments to charity	(1)	In writing
(b)	Transfer of shares	(2)	Evidenced in writing
(c)	Guarantee	(3)	By deed

Answers to quick quiz

1 A

2 Offer and acceptance, consideration, intention to create legal relations

3 False

4 Voidable (3)
Unenforceable (1)
Void (2)

5 (a) (3)
(b) (1)
(c) (2)

Now try the question below from the Exam Question Bank

Number	Level	Marks	Time
Q4	Introductory	n/a	10 mins

Essentials of a valid simple contract I

Topic list	Syllabus reference
1 Offer	2(a)
2 Termination of offer	2(a)
3 Acceptance	2(a)
4 Communication of acceptance	2(a)
5 Agreement without offer and acceptance	2(a)
6 Intention to create legal relations	2(a)

Introduction

In Chapter 4 we introduced the general principles of the law of contract. In the next two chapters we consider the **three essential elements** of a contract. This chapter and the next cover important topics that will form the basis of answers to any problem questions on contract in Section B of the paper.

The first essential element of a binding contract is **agreement**. To determine whether or not an agreement has been reached, the courts will consider whether one party has made a firm **offer** which the other party has **accepted**.

In most contracts, offer and acceptance may be made orally or in writing, or they may be implied by the conduct of the parties. The person making an offer is the offeror and the person to whom an offer is made is the offeree.

An agreement is not a binding contract unless the parties **intend to create legal relations**. What matters is not what the parties have in their minds, but the inferences that reasonable people would draw from their words or conduct.

The law of contract is an important syllabus area and could be examined in either of parts A and B of the exam, or both.

If examined in Part B, a question on contract is likely to be scenario based, requiring you to apply your knowledge of contract formation to given facts.

In the pilot paper, intention was examined in Section A, while the rules surrounding offer and acceptance were considered in part of a general scenario question on contract formation.

1 Offer

Pilot paper, 12/01, 6/03, 12/03, 6/04

FAST FORWARD

The first essential element in the formation of a binding contract is **agreement**. This is usually evidenced by **offer and acceptance**. An offer is a definite promise to be bound on specific terms, and must be distinguished from the mere **supply of information** and from an **invitation to treat**.

Key term

An **offer** is a **definite promise to be bound on specific terms**. An offer may be defined as follows.

'An express or implied statement of the terms on which the maker is prepared to be contractually bound if it is accepted unconditionally. The offer may be made to one person, to a class of persons or to the world at large, and only the person or one of the persons to whom it is made may accept it.'

A definite offer does not have to be made to a particular person. It may be made to a class of persons or to the world at large.

Exam focus point

The case below is very important in the law of contract. Learn it before you learn any others. The topic of offer and acceptance is an important one.

Carlill v Carbolic Smoke Ball Co 1893

The facts: The manufacturers of a patent medicine published an advertisement by which they undertook to pay '£100 reward .... to any person who contracts .... influenza .... after having used the smoke ball three times daily for two weeks'. The advertisement added that £1,000 had been deposited at a bank 'showing our sincerity in this matter'. The claimant read the advertisement, purchased the smoke ball and used it as directed. She contracted influenza and claimed her £100 reward. In their defence the manufacturers argued against this.

(a) The offer was so vague that it could not form the basis of a contract, as no time limit was specified.

(b) It was not an offer which could be accepted since it was offered to the whole world.

Decision: The court disagreed.

(a) The smoke ball must protect the user during the period of use – the offer was not vague.

(b) Such an offer was possible, as it could be compared to reward cases.

You should note that Carlill is an unusual case in that advertisements are not usually regarded as offers, as you will see shortly.

A statement which is vague cannot be an offer but an apparently vague offer can be made certain by reference to previous dealing or customs.

Gunthing v Lynn 1831

The facts: The offeror offered to pay a further sum for a horse if it was 'lucky'.

Decision: The offer was too vague and no contract could be formed.

Hillas & Co Ltd v Arcos Ltd 1932

The facts: The claimants agreed to purchase from the defendants '22,000 standards of softwood goods of fair specification over the season 1930'. The agreement contained an option to buy a further 100,000 standards in 1931, without terms as to the kind or size of timber being specified. The 1930 transaction took place, but the sellers refused to supply any wood in 1931, saying that the agreement was too vague.

Decision: The missing terms of the agreement could be ascertained by reference to the previous transactions.

An offer must be distinguished from a statement which supplies of information, from a statement of intention and from an invitation to treat.

1.1 Supply of information

Only an offer in the proper sense may be accepted so as to form a binding contract. A statement which sets out possible terms of a contract is not an offer unless this is clearly indicated.

> *Harvey v Facey 1893*
> *The facts:* The claimant telegraphed to the defendant 'Will you sell us Bumper Hall Pen? Telegraph lowest cash price'. The defendant telegraphed in reply 'Lowest price for Bumper Hall Pen, £900'. The claimant telegraphed to accept what he regarded as an offer; the defendant made no further reply.
>
> *Decision:* The defendant's telegram was merely a statement of his minimum price if a sale were to be agreed. It was not an offer which the claimant could accept.

If in the course of negotiations for a sale, the vendor states the price at which he will sell, that statement may be an offer which can be accepted.

> *Bigg v Boyd Gibbons 1971*
> *The facts:* In the course of correspondence the defendant rejected an offer of £20,000 by the claimant and added 'for a quick sale I would accept £26,000 .... if you are not interested in this price would you please let me know immediately'. The claimant accepted this price of £26,000 and the defendant acknowledged his acceptance.
>
> *Decision:* In this context the defendant must be treated as making an offer which the claimant had accepted.

Reference to a more detailed document will not necessarily prevent a statement from being an offer.

> *Bowerman and Another v Association of British Travel Agents Ltd 1996*
> *The facts*: The case arose out of the insolvency in 1991 of a tour operator through whom a school party had booked a holiday. The party claimed a full refund under the ABTA scheme of protection. The ABTA scheme did not extend to one item, namely the holiday insurance premium and this was explained in ABTA's detailed handbook. The claimant argued that the 'ABTA promise' (to refund holiday expenses, widely advertised in the press) constituted an offer to the public at large, and that offer was accepted when the holiday was booked with the relevant tour operator.
>
> *Decision*: The public had been encouraged by ABTA to read the written 'ABTA promise' as creating a legally binding obligation to reimburse all the expenses of the holiday.

1.2 A statement of intention

Advertising that an event such as an auction will take place is not an offer to sell. Potential buyers may not sue the auctioneer if the auction does not take place: *Harris v Nickerson 1873.* This is an example of a statement of intention which is not actionable.

1.3 An invitation to treat **6/02, 6/04**

Where a party is initiating negotiations he is said to have made an invitation to treat. An **invitation to treat** cannot be accepted to form a binding contract. Examples of invitations to treat include.

- **Auction** sales
- **Advertisements** (for example, price lists or newspaper advertisements)
- **Exhibition** of goods for sale
- An **invitation** for tenders

Key terms

An **invitation to treat** can be defined as follows.

'An indication that a person is prepared to receive offers with a view to entering into a binding contract, for example, an advertisement of goods for sale or a company prospectus inviting offers for shares. It must be distinguished from an offer which requires only acceptance to conclude the contract.'

(Note that on the facts of a particular case advertisements etc may be construed as an offer: the Carlill case is an example. However in most exam questions advertisements are invitations to treat: read the facts of the question carefully.)

1.3.1 Auction sales

The bid itself is the offer, which the auctioneer is free to accept or reject: *Payne v Cave 1789.* An auction is defined as a contract for the sale of property under which offers are made by bidders stating the price at which they are prepared to buy and acceptance takes place by the fall of the auctioneer's hammer. Where an auction is stated to be 'without reserve' the auctioneer is offering goods for sale and the bid is the acceptance *Barry v Davies (2000).* A reserve is a specified minimum price.

1.3.2 Advertisements

An advertisement of goods for sale is usually an attempt to induce offers.

> *Partridge v Crittenden 1968*
>
> *The facts:* Mr Partridge placed an advertisement for 'Bramblefinch cocks, bramblefinch hens, 25s each'. The RSPCA brought a prosecution against him for offering for sale a brambling in contravention of the Protection of Birds Act 1954. The justices convicted Partridge and he appealed.
>
> *Decision:* The conviction was quashed. Although there had been a sale in contravention of the Act, the prosecution could not rely on the offence of 'offering for sale', as the advertisement only constituted an invitation to treat.

The circulation of a price list is also an invitation to treat: *Grainger v Gough 1896,* where it was noted:

'The transmission of such a price-list does not amount to an offer.... If it were so, the merchant might find himself involved in any number of contractual obligations to supply wine of a particular description which he would be quite unable to carry out, his stock of wine of that description being necessarily limited'.

1.3.3 Exhibition of goods for sale

Displaying goods in a shop window or on the open shelves of a self service shop or advertising goods for sale, is normally an invitation to treat.

> *Fisher v Bell 1961*
>
> *The facts:* A shopkeeper was prosecuted for offering for sale an offensive weapon by exhibiting a flick knife in his shop window.
>
> *Decision:* The display of an article with a price on it in a shop window is merely an invitation to treat.
>
> *Pharmaceutical Society of Great Britain v Boots Cash Chemists (Southern) 1952*
>
> *The facts:* Certain drugs could only be sold under the supervision of a registered pharmacist. The claimant claimed this rule had been broken by Boots who displayed these drugs in a self-service shop. Boots contended that there was no sale until a customer brought the goods to the cash desk and offered to buy them. A registered pharmacist was stationed at this point.
>
> *Decision:* The court found for Boots and commented that if it were true that a customer accepted an offer to sell by removing goods from the shelf, he could not then change his mind and put them back as this would constitute breach of contract.

1.3.4 Invitation for tenders

A **tender** is an estimate submitted in response to a prior request. When a person tenders for a contract he is making an offer to the person who has advertised a contract as being available. An invitation for tenders does not generally amount to an offer to contract with the person quoting the lowest price, except where the person inviting tenders actually makes it clear that he is making an offer.

Question — **Offer**

Bianca goes into a shop and sees a price label on a CD for £15. She takes the CD to the checkout, but the checkout operator tells her that the label is misprinted and should read £20. Bianca maintains that she only has to pay £15. How would you describe the price on the price label in terms of contract law?

Answer

Display of goods for sale with a price label is an invitation to treat (*Fisher v Bell 1961*), that is an invitation to the customer to make an offer which the shop can either accept or reject. But note that it can be a criminal offence to mislabel goods in this way.

2 Termination of offer

An offer may only be accepted while the offer is still open. In the absence of an acceptance, an offer may be **terminated** in any of the following ways.

- Rejection
- Counter-offer
- Lapse of time
- Revocation by the offeror
- Failure of a condition to which the offer was subject
- Death of one of the parties

2.1 Rejection

As noted earlier, outright rejection terminates an offer. A counter-offer, when the person to whom the offer was made proposes new or amended terms, also terminates the original offer.

Key term

A **counter-offer** is a final rejection of the original offer. If a counter-offer is made, the original offeror may accept it, but if he rejects it his original offer is no longer available for acceptance.

Hyde v Wrench 1840
The facts: The defendant offered to sell property to the claimant for £1,000 on 6 June. Two days later, the claimant made a counter-offer of £950 which the defendant rejected on 27 June. The claimant then informed the defendant on 29 June that he accepted the original offer of £1,000.

Decision: The original offer of £1,000 had been terminated by the counter-offer of £950.

2.2 Counter-offer

Acceptance must be unqualified agreement to the terms of the offer. A purported acceptance which introduces any new terms is a counter-offer, which has the effect of terminating the original offer.

A counter-offer may of course be accepted by the original offeror.

Butler Machine Tool Co v Ex-cell-O Corp (England) 1979
The facts: The claimant offered to sell tools to the defendant. Their quotation included details of their standard terms. The defendant 'accepted' the offer, enclosing their own standard terms. The claimant acknowledged acceptance by returning a tear-off slip from the order form.

Decision: The defendant's order was really a counter-offer. The claimant had accepted this by returning the tear-off slip.

2.2.1 Request for information

It is possible to respond to an offer by making a **request for information**. Such a request may be a request as to whether or not other terms would be acceptable – it is not a counter-offer.

Stevenson v McLean 1880
The facts: The defendant offered to sell iron at '40s net cash per ton, open till Monday'. The claimant enquired whether he would agree to delivery spread over two months. The defendant did not reply and (within the stated time limit), the claimant accepted the original offer. Meanwhile the defendant had sold the iron to a third party.

Decision: There was a contract since the claimant had merely enquired as to a variation of terms.

2.3 Lapse of time

An offer may be expressed to last for a **specified time**. If, however, there is no express time limit set, it expires after a **reasonable time**.

Ramsgate Victoria Hotel Co v Montefiore 1866
The facts: The defendant applied to the company in June for shares and paid a deposit. At the end of November the company sent him an acceptance by issue of a letter of allotment and requested payment of the balance due. The defendant contended that his offer had expired and could no longer be accepted.

Decision: The offer was for a reasonable time only and five months was much more than that. The offer had lapsed.

2.4 Revocation of an offer 6/03

The offeror may **revoke** his offer at any time before acceptance: *Payne v Cave 1789*. If he undertakes that his offer shall remain open for acceptance for a specified time he may nonetheless revoke it within that time, unless by a separate contract he has bound himself to keep it open.

Routledge v Grant 1828
The facts: The defendant offered to buy the claimant's house for a fixed sum, requiring acceptance within six weeks. Within the six weeks specified, he withdrew his offer.

Decision: The defendant could revoke his offer at any time before acceptance, even though the time limit had not expired.

Revocation may be an express statement or may be an act of the offeror. His revocation does not take effect until the revocation is communicated to the offeree. This raises two important points.

(a) The first point is that posting a letter of revocation is not a sufficient act of revocation.

Byrne v Van Tienhoven 1880
The facts: The defendants were in Cardiff; the claimants in New York. The sequence of events was as follows.

1 October	Letter posted in Cardiff, offering to sell 1,000 boxes of tinplates.
8 October	Letter of revocation of offer posted in Cardiff.
11 October	Letter of offer received in New York and telegram of acceptance sent.
15 October	Letter confirming acceptance posted in New York.
20 October	Letter of revocation received in New York. The offeree had meanwhile resold the contract goods.

Decision: The letter of revocation could not take effect until received (20 October); it could not revoke the contract made by the telegram acceptance of the offer on 11 October.

(b) The second point is that **revocation of offer may be communicated by any third party who is a sufficiently reliable informant**.

Dickinson v Dodds 1876
The facts: The defendant, on 10 June, wrote to the claimant to offer property for sale at £800, adding 'this offer to be left open until Friday 12 June, 9.00 am.' On 11 June the defendant sold the property to another buyer, A. B, who had been an intermediary between Dickinson and Dodds, informed Dickinson that the defendant had sold to someone else. On Friday 12 June, before 9.00 am, the claimant handed to the defendant a formal letter of acceptance.

Decision: The defendant was free to revoke his offer and had done so by sale to a third party; the claimant could not accept the offer after he had learnt from a reliable informant of the revocation of the offer to him.

However, this case should be treated with caution and it may be that only an agent can revoke an offer.

2.5 Failure of a condition

An offer may be conditional in that it is dependent on some event occurring or there being a change of circumstances. If the condition is not satisfied, the offer is not capable of acceptance.

Financings Ltd v Stimson 1962
The facts: The defendant wished to purchase a car, and on 16 March signed a hire-purchase form. The form, issued by the claimants, stated that the agreement would be binding only upon signature by them. On 20 March the defendant, not satisfied with the car, returned it. On 24 March the car was stolen from the premises of the dealer, and was recovered badly damaged. On 25 March the claimants signed the form. They sued the defendant for breach of contract.

Decision: The defendant was not bound to take the car. His signing of the agreement was actually an offer to contract with the claimant. There was an implied condition in this offer that the car would be in a reasonable condition.

2.6 Termination by death

The death of the offeree terminates the offer. The offeror's death terminates the offer, unless the offeree accepts the offer in ignorance of the death, and the offer is not of a personal nature.

Bradbury v Morgan 1862
The facts: X offered to guarantee payment by Y in respect of goods to be supplied by the claimant. X died and the claimant, in ignorance of his death, continued to supply goods to Y. The claimant then sued X's executors on the guarantee.

Decision: X's offer was a continuing commercial offer which the claimant had accepted by supply of goods after X's death. The guarantee stood.

3 Acceptance

Pilot paper, 12/01, 6/03, 12/03

FAST FORWARD

Acceptance must be unqualified agreement to all the terms of the offer. **Acceptance** is generally not effective until **communicated** to the offeror, the principal exception being where the **'postal rule'** applies.

Key term

Acceptance may be defined as follows.

'A positive act by a person to whom an offer has been made which, if unconditional, brings a binding contract into effect.'

Acceptance may be by **express words**, by **action** or **inferred from conduct**.

Brogden v Metropolitan Railway Co 1877
The facts: For many years the claimant supplied coal to the defendant. He suggested that they should enter into a written agreement and the defendant's agent sent a draft to him for consideration. The parties applied to their dealings the terms of the draft agreement, but they never signed a final version. The claimant later denied that there was any agreement between him and the defendant.

Decision: The conduct of the parties was only explicable on the assumption that they both agreed to the terms of the draft.

3.1 Silence

There must be some **act** on the part of the offeree to indicate his acceptance.

Felthouse v Bindley 1862
The facts: The claimant wrote to his nephew offering to buy the nephew's horse, adding 'If I hear no more about him, I consider the horse mine'. The nephew intended to accept his uncle's offer but did not reply. He instructed the defendant, an auctioneer, not to sell the horse. Owing to a misunderstanding the horse was sold to someone else. The uncle sued the auctioneer.

Decision: The action failed. The claimant had no title to the horse.

Goods which are sent or services which are rendered to a person who did not request them are not 'accepted' merely because he does not return them to the sender: Unsolicited Goods and Services Act 1971. The recipient may treat them as an unsolicited gift.

3.2 Acceptance 'subject to contract'

Acceptance **'subject to contract'** means that the offeree is agreeable to the terms of the offer but proposes that the parties should negotiate a formal contract. Neither party is bound until the formal contract is signed. Agreements for the sale of land in England are usually made 'subject to contract'.

Acceptance 'subject to contract' must be distinguished from outright acceptance made on the understanding that the parties wish to replace the preliminary contract with another at a later stage. Even if the immediate contract is described as 'provisional', it takes effect at once.

Branca v Cobarro 1947
The facts: A vendor agreed to sell a mushroom farm under a contract which was declared to be 'a provisional agreement until a fully legalised agreement is signed'.

Decision: By the use of the word 'provisional', the parties had intended their agreement to be binding until, by mutual agreement, they made another to replace it.

3.3 Letters of intent

Key term

A **letter of intent** is a means by which one party gives a strong indication to another that he is likely to place a contract with him.

Thus a building contractor tendering for a large construction contract may need to sub-contract certain (specialist) aspects of the work. The sub-contractor will be asked to provide an estimate so that the main contractor can finalise his own tender.

Usually, a letter of intent is worded so as not to create any legal obligation. However, in some cases it may be phrased so that it includes an invitation to commence preliminary work. In such circumstances, it creates an obligation to pay for that work.

British Steel Corpn v Cleveland Bridge and Engineering Co Ltd 1984
The facts: The defendants asked the claimants to supply nodes for a complex steel lattice-work frame, and sent the claimants a letter of intent, stating their intention to place an order on their standard terms. The claimants stated that they were unwilling to contract on such terms, but started work, and eventually completed and delivered all the nodes. They sued for the value of the nodes and the defendants counter-claimed for damages for late delivery.

Decision: Since the parties had not reached agreement over such matters as late delivery, there was no contract, and so there could be no question of damages for late delivery. However, since the claimants had undertaken work at the request of the defendants and the defendants had accepted this work, the claimants were entitled to a reasonable remuneration for services rendered.

3.4 Acceptance of a tender

As we saw earlier, an invitation for tenders is an invitation to treat. There are two distinct types of tender.

(a) A tender to perform one task, such as building a new hospital, is an offer which can be accepted.

(b) A tender to supply or perform a series of things, such as the supply of vegetables daily to a restaurant, is not accepted until an order is placed. It is a standing offer. Each order placed by the offeree is an individual act of acceptance creating a separate contract. Until orders are placed there is no contract and the tenderer can terminate his standing offer.

Great Northern Railways v Witham 1873
The facts: The defendant tendered successfully for the supply of stores to the claimant over a period of one year. In his tender he undertook 'to supply ... such quantities as the company may order from time to time'. After making some deliveries he refused to fulfil an order which the claimant had given.

Decision: He was in breach of contract in refusing to fulfil the order given but might revoke his tender and need not then fulfil any future orders within the remainder of the 12 month period.

3.5 Counter-offers and requests for information

As we saw in Section 2, a counter-offer does not constitute acceptance; it is the making of a new offer which may in turn be accepted or rejected. Nor is a request for further information an acceptance.

Question **Offer and acceptance**

In January Elle offered to buy Jane's boat for £3,000. Jane immediately wrote a letter to Elle saying 'For a quick sale I would accept £3,500. If not interested please let me know as soon as possible.' Elle did not see the letter until March when she returned from a business trip but then replied. 'I accept your offer. I trust that if I pay £3,000 now, you can wait until June for the remaining £500.' On receiving the letter, Jane attached a 'sold' sign on the boat but forgot to reply to Elle. Is there a contract between Elle and Jane? If so, what are its terms?

Answer

Elle's offer of £3,000 is an **offer**. Many offers are in fact made by prospective purchasers rather than by vendors. Jane's letter forms a **counter-offer**, which has the effect of terminating Elle's offer: *Hyde v Wrench 1840*. Elle may now accept or reject this counter-offer.

There is nothing to indicate that Jane's (counter) offer is not still open in March. An offer may be expressed to last for a **specified time**. It then expires at the end of that time. If, however, there is no express time limit set, it expires after a **reasonable time**.

Elle's reply, using the words 'I accept your offer' **appear conclusive. However they are not**. The enquiry as to variation of terms does not constitute acceptance or rejection: *Stevenson v McLean 1880*. The effect of Elle's reply is probably best analysed as being a **new counter-offer** including terms as to deferred payment, which **Jane purports to accept by affixing a 'sold' sign**. The court would need to decide whether, in all the circumstances, acceptance can be deemed to have been communicated.

Following *Butler Machine Tool Co v Ex-Cell-O Corp (England) 1979*, the **counter-offer introduces new terms**, that is, price. The price is therefore £3,500. As to **date of payment**, it would appear that the attachment of a 'sold' sign to the boat is confirmation that the revised terms proposed by Jane are acceptable.

4 Communication of acceptance

The general rule is that acceptance **must be communicated** to the offeror and the acceptance is not effective (and hence there is no contract) until this has been done. However this rule does not apply in all cases.

4.1 Waiver of communication

The offeror may dispense with the need for communication of acceptance. Such a waiver may be express or may be inferred from the circumstances. In *Carlill v Carbolic Smoke Ball Co 1893*, it was held that it was sufficient for the claimant to act on the offer without notifying her acceptance of it. This was an example of a **unilateral contract**, where the offer takes the form of a promise to pay money in return for an act.

4.2 Prescribed mode of communication

The offeror may call for communication of acceptance by specified means. Communication of acceptance by some other means equally expeditious generally constitutes a valid acceptance unless specified otherwise: *Tinn v Hoffmann 1873*. This would probably apply also to acceptance by fax machine or e-mail. The offeror would have to use very precise wording if a specified means of communication is to be treated as mandatory.

Yates Building Co v R J Pulleyn & Sons (York) 1975
The facts: The offer called for acceptance by registered or recorded delivery letter. The offeree sent an ordinary letter which arrived without delay.

Decision: The offeror had suffered no disadvantage and had not stipulated that acceptance must be made in this way only. The acceptance was valid.

4.3 No mode of communication prescribed

The offeree can use any method but must ensure that his **acceptance is understood** if he chooses an **instantaneous method of communication**.

Entores v Miles Far Eastern Corporation 1955
The facts: The claimants sent an offer by telex to the defendants' agent in Amsterdam and the latter sent an acceptance by telex. The claimants alleged breach of contract and wished to serve a writ.

Decision: The acceptance took effect (and the contract was made) when the telex message was printed out on the claimants' terminal in London. A writ could therefore be issued.

4.4 The postal rule

The offeror may expressly or by implication indicate that he expects acceptance by means of a letter sent through the post.

Key term

The **postal rule** states that, where the use of the post is within the contemplation of both the parties, the acceptance is complete and effective as soon as a letter is posted, even though it may be delayed or even lost altogether in the post.

Adams v Lindsell 1818
The facts: The defendants made an offer by letter to the claimant on 2 September 1817 requiring an answer 'in course of post'. It reached the claimants on 5 September; they immediately posted a letter of acceptance, which reached the defendants on 9 September. The defendants could have expected a reply by 7 September, and they assumed that the absence of a reply within the expected period indicated non-acceptance and sold the goods to another buyer on 8 September.

Decision: The acceptance was made 'in course of post' (no time limit was imposed) and was effective when posted on 5 September.

The intention to use the post for communication of acceptance may be deduced from the circumstances.

Household Fire and Carriage Accident Insurance Co v Grant 1879
The facts: The defendant handed a letter of application for shares to the claimant company's agent in Swansea for posting to the company in London. The company posted an acceptance which never arrived. The defendant was called upon to pay the amount outstanding on his shares.

Decision: The defendant had to pay. The contract had been formed when the acceptance was posted, regardless of the fact that it was lost.

Under the postal rule, the offeror may be unaware that a contract has been made. If that possibility is clearly inconsistent with the nature of the transaction the letter of acceptance takes effect only when received. In particular, if the offer stipulates a particular mode of communication, the postal rule may not apply.

Holwell Securities v Hughes 1974
The facts: Hughes granted to the claimant an option to purchase land to be exercised 'by notice in writing'. A letter giving notice of the exercise of the option was lost in the post.

Decision: The words 'notice in writing' must mean notice actually received by the vendor; hence notice had not been given to accept the offer .

Acceptance of an offer may **only** be made **by a person authorised** to do so. This will usually be the offeree or his authorised agents.

Powell v Lee 1908
The facts: The claimant was appointed to a post as a headmaster. Without authorisation, he was informed of the appointment by one of the managers. Later, it was decided to give the post to someone else. The claimant sued for breach of contract.

Decision: Since communication of acceptance was unauthorised, there was no valid agreement and hence no contract.

Exam focus point

Offer and acceptance are key areas and could be examined in problem form in Section B of the paper as they were in the pilot paper and the December 2001 paper. You must be able to both identify and explain the relevant legal rules and principles, which will allow you to present a reasoned answer.

Question — **Formation of contract**

Frank writes to Xiao-Xiao on 1 July offering to sell him his sailing dinghy for £1,200. On 8 July, having received no reply, he decides to withdraw this offer and sends a second letter. On 10 July, Xiao-Xiao receives the original offer letter and immediately telephones his acceptance to Frank's wife. He follows this up with a letter posted the same day. Frank's second letter arrives on 14 July and Xiao-Xiao learns that Mel has bought the boat the previous day. What is the legal situation?

Answer

The revocation takes effect when received on 14 July. The acceptance by Xiao-Xiao takes effect when posted on 10 July. Therefore a contract is formed on 10 July and Frank's sale of the dinghy to Mel is in breach of his contract with Xiao-Xiao.

4.5 Cross-offers

If two offers, identical in terms, cross in the post, there is no contract: *Tinn v Hoffmann 1873.*

Illustration

If A offers to sell his car to B for £1,000 and B offers to buy A's car for £1,000, there is no contract, as there is no acceptance.

4.6 Unilateral contracts 12/03, 12/04

The question arises as to whether contractual obligations arise if a party, in ignorance of an offer, performs an act which fulfils the terms of the offer. If A offers a **reward** to anyone who finds and returns his lost property and B, in ignorance of the offer, does in fact return it to him, is B entitled to the promised reward? There is agreement by conduct, but B is not accepting A's offer since he is unaware of it.

R v Clarke 1927
The facts: A reward was offered for information leading to the arrest and conviction of a murderer. If the information was provided by an accomplice, he would receive a free pardon. C claimed the reward, admitting that he had acted to save his own skin and that all thought of the reward had passed out his mind.

Decision: There could not be acceptance without knowledge of the offer.

However, acceptance may still be valid even if the offer was not the sole reason for the action.

Williams v Carwardine 1833
The facts: A reward was offered to bring criminals to book. The claimant, an accomplice in the crime, supplied the information, with knowledge of the reward.

Decision: As the information was given with knowledge, the acceptance was related to the offer.

Question

Communication of acceptance

John offers to sell his car to Ahmed for £2,000 on 1 July saying that the offer will stay open for a week. Ahmed tells his brother that he would like to accept the offer. Unknown to Ahmed, his brother informs John of this on 4 July. On 5 July John, with his girlfriend present, sells the car to Gina. John's girlfriend tells Ahmed about this later that day. The next day, Ahmed delivers a letter of acceptance to John. Is John in breach of contract?

Answer

Communication of acceptance may only be made by a person authorised to do so (*Powell v Lee 1908*), therefore Ahmed's brother's purported acceptance is not valid. Revocation of an offer may be communicated by a reliable informant (*Dickinson v Dodds 1876*), so Ahmed is made aware of the revocation on 5 July. His attempted acceptance on 6 July is therefore not valid.

As there was no consideration to support any separate agreement to keep the offer open for a week, John is free to sell the car to Gina.

As we saw above, *Carlill v Carbolic Smoke Ball Company 1893* is one example of a unilateral contract. Here the defendants advertised that they would pay £100 to anyone who caught influenza while using their product. This was held to be an offer to the world at large capable of being accepted by anyone fulfilling the necessary conditions. However, it was not necessary that anyone fulfilled the conditions, but as soon Carlill began to **use** the product, the defendants were bound by their offer.

An ordinary offer can be revoked at any time before complete acceptance and, once revoked, can no longer be accepted (*Routledge v Grant 1828*). However, in the case of a unilateral contract, the courts have held that an offer cannot be revoked once the offeree has begun to perform whatever act is necessary (*Errington v Errington 1953).*

5 Agreement without offer and acceptance

Because the courts cannot ascertain the intentions of the parties, they must rely on what the parties **say or do**. In certain cases they may go beyond what can be inferred from the words and actions of the parties and **construct** a contract.

Clarke v Dunraven 1897

The facts: The owners of two yachts entered them for a regatta. Each undertook in a letter to the Club Secretary to obey the Club's rules, which included an obligation to pay all damages caused by fouling. The defendant's yacht fouled the claimant's yacht, which sank. The claimant sued for damages. The defendant argued that his only liability was under the Merchant Shipping Act 1862 and was therefore set at £8 per ton.

Decision: A contract had been created between the parties when they entered their yachts for the regatta, at which point they had accepted the club's rules. The claimant was entitled to recover full damages.

5.1 Collateral contracts 12/03

FAST FORWARD

In certain circumstances, the courts may infer the existence of a contract without the formalities of offer and acceptance. This type of contract is a **collateral contract**.

Key term

A **collateral contract** is a contract the consideration for which is the making of some other contract. If there are two separate contracts between on the one hand A and B and on the other hand A and C, on terms which involve some concerted action between B and C, there may be a contract between B and C.

There is a contract between B and C despite the absence of direct communication between them.

Shanklin Pier Ltd v Detel Products 1951

The facts: The defendants gave assurances to the claimants that their paint would be satisfactory and durable if used in repainting the claimant's pier. The claimants in their contract with X and Co for the repainting of the pier specified that X and Co should use this paint. The paint proved very unsatisfactory. The claimants sued the defendants for breach of undertaking. The defendants argued that there was no contract between the claimants and themselves.

Decision: The contract between the claimants and X and Co requiring the use of the defendant's paint was the consideration for a contract between the claimants and the defendant.

6 Intention to create legal relations Pilot paper, 12/01, 12/04

FAST FORWARD

Various cases give us a set of rules to apply to determine whether the parties to a contract intended to be legally bound by it.

Where there is no express statement as to whether or not legal relations are intended, the courts apply one of two **rebuttable presumptions** to a case.

- **Social, domestic and family arrangements** are not usually intended to be binding.
- **Commercial agreements** are usually intended by the parties involved to be legally binding.

Key term

Intention to create legal relations can be defined as follows.

'An agreement will only become a legally binding contract if the parties intend this to be so. This will be strongly presumed in the case of business agreements but presumed otherwise if the agreement is of a friendly, social or domestic nature.'

6.1 Domestic arrangements

6.1.1 Husband and wife

The fact that the parties are husband and wife does not mean that they cannot enter into a binding contract with one another. Contrast the following two cases.

Balfour v Balfour 1919
The facts: The defendant was employed in Ceylon. He and his wife returned to the UK on leave but it was agreed that for health reasons she would not return to Ceylon with him. He promised to pay her £30 a month as maintenance. Later the marriage ended in divorce and the wife sued for the monthly allowance which the husband no longer paid.

Decision: An informal agreement of indefinite duration made between husband and wife whose marriage had not at the time broken up was not intended to be legally binding.

Merritt v Merritt 1970
The facts: The husband had left the matrimonial home, which was owned in the joint names of husband and wife, to live with another woman. The spouses met and held a discussion, in the course of which he agreed to pay her £40 a month out of which she agreed to keep up the mortgage payments. The wife made the husband sign a note of these terms and an undertaking to transfer the house into her name when the mortgage had been paid off. The wife paid off the mortgage but the husband refused to transfer the house to her.

Decision: In the circumstances, an intention to create legal relations was to be inferred and the wife could sue for breach of contract.

Where agreements between husband and wife or other relatives relate to **property matters** the courts are very ready to impute an intention to create legal relations.

6.1.2 Relatives

Agreements between other family members may also be examined by the courts.

Jones v Padavatton 1969
The facts: The claimant wanted her daughter to move to England to train as a barrister, and offered to pay her a monthly allowance. The daughter did so in 1962. In 1964 the claimant bought a house in London; part of the house was occupied by the daughter and the other part let to tenants whose rent was collected by the daughter for herself. In 1967 the claimant and her daughter quarrelled and the claimant issued a summons claiming possession of the house. The daughter sued for her allowance.

Decision: There were two agreements to consider: the daughter's agreement to read for the bar in exchange for a monthly allowance, and the agreement by which the daughter lived in her mother's house and collected the rent from tenants. Neither agreement was intended to create legal relations.

6.1.3 Other domestic arrangements

Domestic arrangements extend to those between people who are not related but who have a close relationship of some form. The nature of the agreement itself may lead to the conclusion that legal relations were intended.

Simpkins v Pays 1955

The facts: The defendant, her granddaughter and the claimant, a paying boarder, took part together each week in a competition organised by a Sunday newspaper. The arrangements over postage and other expenses were informal and the entries were made in the grandmother's name. One week they won £750; the paying boarder claimed a third share, but the defendant refused to pay on the grounds that there was no intention to create legal relations.

Decision: There was a 'mutuality in the arrangements between the parties', amounting to a contract.

Exam focus point

This is the sort of question which could be argued either way. The examiner will give you credit for valid arguments. Intention is an integral part of the formation of a contract and so should not be ignored. Its importance can be seen by its inclusion in the pilot paper.

6.2 Commercial agreements

When business people enter into commercial agreements it is presumed that there is an intention to enter into legal relations unless this is **expressly disclaimed** or the **circumstances indicates otherwise**.

Rose and Frank v Crompton 1923

The facts: A commercial agreement by which the defendants appointed the claimant to be its distributor in the USA contained a clause described as 'the Honourable Pledge Clause' which expressly stated that the arrangement was 'not subject to legal jurisdiction' in either country. The defendants terminated the agreement without giving notice as required, and refused to deliver goods ordered by the claimants although they had accepted these orders when placed.

Decision: The general agreement was not legally binding as there was no obligation to stand by any clause in it. However the orders for goods were separate and binding contracts. The claim for damages for breach of the agreement failed, but the claim for damages for non-delivery of goods ordered succeeded.

The words relied on by a party to a commercial agreement to show that legal relations are not intended are not always clear. In such cases, the **burden of proof** is **on the party seeking to escape liability**.

Edwards v Skyways Ltd 1964

The facts: In negotiations over the terms for making the claimant redundant, the defendants gave him the choice either of withdrawing his total contributions from their contributory pension fund or of receiving a paid-up pension. It was agreed that if he chose the first option, the defendants would make an ex gratia payment to him. He chose the first option; his contributions were refunded but the ex gratia payment was not made. He sued for breach of contract.

Decision: Although the defendants argued that the use of the phrase ex gratia showed no intention to create legal relations, this was a commercial arrangement and the burden of rebutting the presumption of legal relations had not been discharged by the defendants.

6.3 Statutory provisions

Procedural agreements between **employers and trade** unions for the settlement of disputes are not intended to give rise to legal relations in spite of their elaborate content: s 179 Trade Union and Labour Relations (Consolidation) Act 1992.

6.4 Letters of comfort

For many years, holding companies have given **'letters of comfort'** to creditors of subsidiaries which purport to give some comfort as to the ability of the subsidiary to pay its debts. Such letters have always been presumed in the past not to be legally binding.

Kleinwort Benson Ltd v Malaysia Mining Corpn Bhd 1989
The facts: The claimants lent money to the defendant's subsidiary, having received a letter from the defendant stating 'it is our policy to ensure that the business is at all times in a position to meet its liabilities to you.' The subsidiary went into liquidation, and the bank claimed against the holding company for the outstanding indebtedness.

Decision: The letter of comfort was a statement of existing policy and not a promise that the policy would continue in the future. Because both parties were well aware that in business parlance a 'letter of comfort' imposed moral and not legal responsibilities, it was held not to have been given with the intention of creating legal relations.

6.5 Transactions binding in honour only

If the parties state that an agreement is **'binding in honour only'**, this amounts to an express denial of intention to create legal relations.

Jones v Vernons Pools 1938
The facts: The claimant argued that he had sent to the defendant a football pools coupon on which his predictions entitled him to a dividend. The defendants denied having received the coupon. A clause on the coupon stated that the transaction should not 'give rise to any legal relationship ... but ... be binding in honour only'.

Decision: This clause was a bar to an action in court.

Exam focus point

There is a 'contract formation checklist' given in section 5 of the chapter which summarises all the important rules relating to the formation of a contract.

Chapter roundup

- The first essential element of a binding contract is **agreement**. This is usually evidenced by **offer and acceptance**. An offer is a definite promise to be bound on specific terms, and must be distinguished from the mere **supply of information** and from an **invitation to treat**.
- **Acceptance** must be unqualified agreement to all the terms of the offer. **Acceptance** is generally not effective until **communicated** to the offeror, the principal exception being where the **'postal rule'** applies in which case acceptance is complete and effective as soon as notice of it is posted.
- In certain circumstances, the courts may infer the existence of a contract without the formalities of offer and acceptance. This type of contract is a **collateral contract**.
- Both parties to a contract must **intend** the agreement to give rise to legal obligations. Their intentions as to this point may be express – 'this agreement is not subject to legal jurisdiction' – or may be inferred from the circumstances. **Social, domestic and family** arrangements are assumed not to be legally binding unless the contrary is clearly shown. **Commercial** agreements are assumed to be legally binding unless the contrary is clearly demonstrated.

Quick quiz

1 Give the name of a case in which an offer was made to the world at large.

2 How is the circulation of a price list categorised in the law of contract?

offer	tender
invitation to treat	auction

3 **Fill in the blanks** in the statements below, using the words in the box.

- As a general rule, acceptance must be (1) ……………….. to the (2) ……………….. and is not effective until this has been done.
- An (3) ……………….. is a definite promise to be bound on specific terms, and must be distinguished from a supply of (4) ……………….. and from an (5) ………………..
- A counter-offer counts as (6) ……………….. of the original offer

• information	• offer	• invitation to treat
• rejection	• communicated	• offeror

4 Advertising an auction is an offer to sell

True ☐

False ☐

5 Give four examples of situations likely to be invitation to treat

……………….. ………………..

……………….. ………………..

6 As a general rule, silence cannot constitute acceptance.

True ☐

False ☐

7 Define the postal rule.

8 Give four instances when an offer is terminated.

Answers to quick quiz

1 *Carlill v Carbolic Smoke Ball Co 1893*

2 Invitation to treat

3 (1) Communicated (2) offeror (3) offer (4) information (5) invitation to treat (6) rejection

4 False

5 Auction sales
Advertisements
Exhibition of goods for sale
Invitation to treat

6 True

7 The postal rule states that, where the use of the post is within the contemplation of both the parties, the acceptance is complete and effective as soon as a letter is posted, even though it may be delayed or even lost altogether in the post.

8 Rejection
Lapse of time
Revocation by the offeror
Failure of a condition to which the offer was subject
Death of one of the parties

Now try the questions below from the Exam Question Bank

Number	Level	Marks	Time
Q5	Examination	10	18 mins
Q6	Examination	20	36 mins

Essentials of a valid simple contract II

Topic list	Syllabus reference
1 Consideration	2(a)
2 Adequacy and sufficiency of consideration	2(a)
3 Promissory estoppel	2(a)
4 Privity of contract	2(a)
5 Contract formation checklist	2(a)
6 The electronic contract	2(a)

Introduction

The third of the three essential elements of a contract is **consideration**. The promise which a claimant seeks to enforce must be shown to be part of a bargain to which the claimant has himself contributed. Related to consideration are the doctrines of **promissory estoppel** and **privity of contract**, which are explained in this chapter. Finally there is a short section which introduces some of the issues relating to **electronic** contracts.

As was the case with Chapter 5, contract is an important topic area. Questions on contract, particularly in Section B, might draw on all aspects of the law of contract and therefore include items from all of Chapters 4 to 8. The question on contract formation in the pilot paper included aspects of consideration as well as offer and acceptance.

1 Consideration

Pilot paper, 12/01, 12/02, 6/03

FAST FORWARD

Consideration is an essential part of most contracts. It is what each party brings to the contract.

Key terms

Consideration has been defined as:

'A valuable consideration in the sense of the law may consist either in some right, interest, profit or benefit accruing to one party, or some forbearance, detriment, loss or responsibility given, suffered or undertaken by the other.' *From Currie v Misa 1875*

Another definition of consideration was given by the House of Lords in *Dunlop v Selfridge 1915.*

'An act or forbearance of one party, or the promise thereof, is the price for which the promise of the other is bought, and the promise thus given for value is enforceable.'

Using the language of purchase and sale, it could be said that one party must know that he has bought the other party's promises either by performing some act of his own or by offering a promise of his own.

1.1 Valid consideration

FAST FORWARD

Consideration may be **executed** (an act in return for a promise) or **executory** (a promise in return for a promise). It may not be **past**, unless one of three recognised exceptions applies.

There are two broad types of valid consideration – **executed** and **executory**. If consideration is **past** then it is not enforceable.

Executed consideration is an act in return for a promise. The consideration for the promise is a performed, or executed, act.

Illustration

A offers a reward for the return of lost property, his promise becomes binding when B performs the act of returning A's property to him. A is not bound to pay anything to anyone until the prescribed act is done. C's act in Carlill's case in response to the smoke ball company's promise of reward was thus executed consideration.

Key term

Executed consideration can be defined as follows.

'That which takes place at the present time. Thus in a contract for the sale of goods, the consideration is executed if the price is paid at the same time that the goods are delivered.'

Executory consideration is a promise given for a promise. The consideration in support of each promise is the other promise, not a performed act.

Illustration

If a customer orders goods which a shopkeeper undertakes to obtain from the manufacturer, the shopkeeper promises to supply the goods and the customer promises to accept and pay for them. Neither has yet done anything but each has given a promise to obtain the promise of the other. It would be breach of contract if either withdrew without the consent of the other.

Key terms

Executory consideration can be defined as follows.

'That which is to take place at some future time. The consideration for the delivery of goods would be executory if it is a promise to pay at a future date.'

1.2 Past consideration

Key term

Past consideration can be defined as follows.

'... something which has already been done at the time the promise is made. An example would be a promise to pay for work already carried out, unless there was an implied promise to pay a reasonable sum before the work began.'

Anything which has already been done before a promise in return is given is past consideration which, as a general rule, is not sufficient to make the promise binding. The following is the key case in this area:

Re McArdle 1951
The facts: Under a will the testator's children were entitled to a house after their mother's death. In the mother's lifetime one of the children and his wife lived in the house with the mother. The wife made improvements to the house. The children later agreed in writing to repay the wife 'in consideration of your carrying out certain alterations and improvements'. But at the mother's death they refused to do so.

Decision: The work on the house had all been completed before the documents were signed. At the time of the promise the improvements were past consideration and so the promise was not binding.

If there is an existing contract and one party makes a further promise no contract will arise. Even if such a promise is directly related to the previous bargain, it will be held to have been made upon past consideration.

Roscorla v Thomas 1842
The facts: The claimant agreed to buy a horse from the defendant at a given price. When negotiations were over and the contract was formed, the defendant told the claimant that the horse was 'sound and free from vice'. The horse turned out to be vicious and the claimant brought an action on the warranty.

Decision: The express promise was made after the sale was over and was unsupported by fresh consideration.

In three cases past consideration for a promise does suffice to make the promise binding.

(a) Past consideration is sufficient to create liability on a **bill of exchange** (such as a cheque) under s 27 Bills of Exchange Act 1882. Most cheques are issued to pay existing debts.

Key term

A **bill of exchange** can be defined as:

'A negotiable instrument, drawn by one party on another, for example by a supplier of goods on a customer, who by accepting (signing) the bill, acknowledges the debt, which may be payable immediately (a sight draft) or at some future date (a time draft). The holder of the bill can thereafter use an accepted time draft to pay a debt to a third party or discount it to raise cash.'

(b) After six (or in some cases twelve) years the right to sue for recovery of a debt becomes **statute barred** by the Limitation Act 1980. If, after that period, the debtor makes written acknowledgement of the creditor's claim, the claim is again enforceable at law.

(c) When a request is made for a **service** this request may imply a promise to pay for it. If, after the service has been rendered, the person who made the request promises a specific reward, this is treated as fixing the amount to be paid.

Lampleigh v Braithwaite 1615
The facts: The defendant had killed a man and had asked the claimant to obtain for him a royal pardon. The claimant did so at his own expense. The defendant then promised to pay him £100. He failed to pay it and was sued.

Decision: The defendant's request was regarded as containing an implied promise to pay, and the subsequent promise merely fixed the amount.

Both parties must have assumed throughout their negotiations that the services were ultimately to be paid for.

Re Casey's Patents 1892
The facts: A and B, joint owners of patent rights, asked their employee, C, as an extra task to find licensees to work the patents. After C had done so, A and B agreed to reward him for his past services with one third of the patent rights. A died and his executors denied that the promise was binding.

Decision: The promise to C was binding since it merely fixed the 'reasonable remuneration' which A and B by implication promised to pay before the service was given.

Question **Consideration**

Emma, a law student, is in her car, waiting for the traffic lights to change at a busy intersection. Steve steps off the pavement with a bucket and cloth and proceeds to clean the windscreen of her car. Afterwards, Emma tells him that she will pay him £5. She then drives away. Advise Steve.

Answer

Emma is not bound to pay the £5, because at the time the promise was made, Steve's actions were past consideration.

2 Adequacy and sufficiency of consideration 12/02, 6/05

FAST FORWARD

The long-established rule is that consideration need not be adequate but it must be sufficient.

The court will also seek to ensure that a particular act or promise can actually be deemed to be consideration. Learn these rules:

(a) **Consideration need not be adequate** (that is, equal in value to the consideration received in return). There is no remedy at law for someone who simply makes a poor bargain.

(b) **Consideration must be sufficient**. It must be capable in law of being regarded as consideration by the courts.

2.1 Adequacy

It is presumed that each party is capable of serving his own interests, and the courts will not seek to weigh up the comparative value of the promises or acts exchanged.

Thomas v Thomas 1842
The facts: By his will the claimant's husband expressed the wish that his widow should have the use of his house during her life. The defendants, his executors, allowed the widow to occupy the house (a) in accordance with her husband's wishes and (b) in return for her undertaking to pay a rent of £1 per annum. They later said that their promise to let her occupy the house was not supported by consideration.

Decision: Compliance with the husband's wishes was not valuable consideration (no economic value attached to it), but the nominal rent was sufficient consideration.

2.2 Sufficiency **6/03**

Consideration is sufficient if it has some identifiable value. The law only requires an element of bargain, not necessarily that it should be a good bargain.

Chappell & Co v Nestle Co 1960
The facts: As a sales promotion scheme, the defendant offered to supply a record to anyone who sent in a postal order for 1s.6d and three wrappers from 6d bars of chocolate made by them. The claimants owned the copyright of the tune. They sued for infringement of copyright. In the ensuing dispute over royalties the issue was whether the wrappers, which were thrown away when received, were part of the consideration for the promise to supply the record. The defendants offered to pay a royalty based on the price of 1s.6d per record, but the claimants rejected this, claiming that the wrappers also represented part of the consideration.

Decision: The wrappers were part of the consideration as they had commercial value to the defendants.

As stated earlier, forbearance or the promise of it may be sufficient consideration if it has some value, or amounts to giving up something of value.

Horton v Horton 1961
The facts: Under a separation agreement, the defendant agreed to pay his wife (the claimant) £30 per month. Under the deed this amount was a net payment after deduction of income tax; for nine months the husband paid it without any deduction so that the wife had to make the deductions herself. He then signed a document agreeing to pay such amount as 'after the deduction of income tax should amount to the clear sum of £30'. He paid this for three years, then stopped, pleading that the later agreement was not supported by consideration.

Decision: The later agreement was supported by consideration: the wife could have sued to have the original agreement rectified, but did not.

2.2.1 Performance of existing contractual duties

Performance of an **existing obligation imposed by statute** is no consideration for a promise of reward.

Collins v Godefroy 1831
The facts: The claimant had been subpoenaed to give evidence on behalf of the defendant in another case. He alleged that the defendant had promised to pay him six guineas for appearing.

Decision: There was no consideration for this promise.

But if some **extra service** is given that is sufficient consideration.

Glasbrook Bros v Glamorgan CC 1925
The facts: At a time of industrial unrest, colliery owners, rejecting the view of the police that a mobile force was enough, agreed to pay for a special guard on the mine. Later they repudiated liability saying that the police had done no more than perform their public duty of maintaining order, and that no consideration was given.

Decision: The police had done more than perform their general duties. The extra services given, beyond what the police in their discretion deemed necessary, were consideration for the promise to pay.

In the *Glasbrook* case the threat to law and order was not caused by either of the parties. Where one party's actions lead to the need for heightened police presence, and the police deem this presence necessary, they may also be entitled to payment.

Harris v Sheffield United F.C. Ltd 1988
The facts: The defendants argued that they did not have to pay for a large police presence at their home matches.

Decision: They had voluntarily decided to hold matches on Saturday afternoons when large attendances were likely, increasing the risk of disorder.

2.2.2 Promise of additional reward

If there is already a contract between A and B, and B promises **additional reward** to A if he (A) will perform his existing duties, there is no consideration from A to make that promise binding.

Stilk v Myrick 1809
The facts: Two members of the crew of a ship deserted in a foreign port. The master was unable to recruit substitutes and promised the rest of the crew that they would share the wages of the deserters if they would complete the voyage home short-handed. The shipowners however repudiated the promise.

Decision: In performing their existing contractual duties the crew gave no consideration for the promise of extra pay and the promise was not binding.

If a claimant does **more than perform an existing contractual duty**, this may amount to consideration.

Hartley v Ponsonby 1857
The facts: 17 men out of a crew of 36 deserted. The remainder were promised an extra £40 each to work the ship to Bombay. The claimant, one of the remaining crew-members, sued to recover this amount.

Decision: The large number of desertions made the voyage exceptionally hazardous, and this had the effect of discharging the original contract. The claimant's promise to complete the voyage formed consideration for the promise to pay an additional £40.

The courts now appear to be taking a slightly different line on the payment of additional consideration. It may be that where the party promising the additional reward has received a 'practical' benefit that will be treated as consideration even if, in law, he has received no more that he was already entitled to under the contract.

Williams v Roffey Bros & Nicholls (Contractors) Ltd 1990
The facts: The claimants agreed to do carpentry work for the defendants, who were engaged as contractors to refurbish a block of flats, at a fixed price of £20,000. The work ran late and so the defendants, concerned that the job might not be finished on time and that they would have to pay money under a penalty clause, agreed to pay the claimants an extra £10,300 to ensure the work was completed on time. They later refused to pay the extra amount.

Decision: The fact that there was no apparent consideration for the promise to pay the extra was not held to be important, as in the court's view both parties derived a practical benefit from the promise. The telling point was that the defendants' promise had not been extracted by duress or fraud: it was therefore binding. The defendant had avoided the possible penalty.

Exam focus point

Williams v Roffey Bros is important because it is a newer case than the bulk of contract cases, most of which were decided in the nineteenth century.

Re Selectmove 1994
The facts: A company which was the subject of a winding up order offered to settle its outstanding debts by instalment. An Inland Revenue inspector agreed to the proposal. The company tried to enforce it.

Decision: Despite the verdict in *Williams v Roffey Brothers* the court followed *Foakes v Beer* (see below) in holding that an agreement to pay in instalments in unenforceable. Even though the creditor may obtain some practical benefit this is not adequate consideration to render the agreement legally binding in respect of part payment of debts.

2.2.3 Performance of existing contractual duty to a third party

If A promises B a reward if B will perform his **existing contract** with C, there is consideration for A's promise since he obtains a benefit to which he previously had no right, and B assumes new obligations.

Shadwell v Shadwell 1860
The facts: The claimant, a barrister, was engaged to marry E. His uncle promised the claimant that if he (the nephew) married E (as he did), the uncle would during their joint lives pay to his nephew £150 p.a. until such time as the nephew was earning 600 guineas p.a. at the bar (which never transpired). The uncle died after eighteen years owing six annual payments. The claimant claimed the arrears from his uncle's executors, who denied that there was consideration for the promise.

Decision: There was sufficient consideration for the reasons given above.

2.2.4 Waiver of existing rights

Illustration

If X owes Y £100 but Y agrees to accept a lesser sum, say £80, in full settlement of Y's claim, that is a promise by Y to waive his entitlement to the balance of £20. The promise, like any other, should be supported by consideration.

The case below is important.

Foakes v Beer 1884
The facts: The defendant had obtained judgement against the claimant. Judgement debts bear interest from the date of the judgement. By a written agreement the defendant agreed to accept payment by instalments, no mention being made of the interest. Once the claimant had paid the amount of the debt in full, the defendant claimed interest, claiming that the agreement was not supported by consideration.

Decision: She was entitled to the debt with interest. No consideration had been given by the claimant for waiver of any part of her rights against him.

There are, however, exceptions to the rule that the debtor (denoted by 'X' in the following paragraphs) must give consideration if the waiver is to be binding.

	Exceptions
Alternative consideration *Anon 1495* *Pinnel's Case 1602*	If X offers and Y accepts anything to which Y is not already entitled, the extra thing is sufficient consideration for the waiver. • Goods instead of cash • Early payment
Bargain between the creditors *Woods v Robarts 1818*	If X arranges with creditors that they will each accept part payment in full entitlement, that is bargain between the creditors X has given no consideration but he can hold the creditors individually to the agreed terms
Third party part payment *Welby v Drake 1825*	If a third party (Z) offers part payment and Y agrees to release X from Y's claim to the balance, Y has received consideration from Z against whom he had no previous claim
Promissory estoppel	The principle of promissory estoppel may prevent Y from retracting his promise with retrospective effect.

3 Promissory estoppel

FAST FORWARD

The principle of **promissory estoppel** was developed in *Central London Property Trust v High Trees House 1947*. It means that in some cases where someone has made a promise they can be prevented from denying it.

Key term

The doctrine of **promissory estoppel** works as follows.

If a creditor (Y) makes a promise (unsupported by consideration) to the debtor (X) that Y will not insist on the full discharge of the debt, and the promise is made with the intention that X should act on it and he does so, Y is **estopped** from retracting his promise, unless X can be restored to his original position.

Central London Property Trust v High Trees House 1947
The facts: In September 1939, the claimants let a block of flats to the defendants at an annual rent of £2,500 p.a. It was difficult to let the individual flats in wartime, so in January 1940 the claimants agreed in writing to accept a reduced rent of £1,250 p.a. No time limit was set on the arrangement but it was clearly related to wartime conditions. The reduced rent was paid from 1940 to 1945 and the defendants sublet flats during the period on the basis of their expected liability to pay rent under the head lease at £1,250 only. In 1945 the flats were fully let. The claimants demanded a full rent of £2,500 p.a., both retrospectively and for the future. They tested this claim by suing for rent at the full rate for the last two quarters of 1945.

Decision: The agreement of January 1940 ceased to operate early in 1945. The claim was upheld. However, had the claimants sued for arrears for the period 1940-1945, the 1940 agreement would have served to defeat the claim. The latter statement is *obiter dicta*.

If the defendants in the *High Trees* case had sued on the promise, they would have failed for want of consideration. The principle is **'a shield not a sword**.'

Combe v Combe 1951
The facts: A wife obtained a divorce decree *nisi* against her husband. He then promised her that he would make maintenance payments of £100 per annum. The wife did not apply to the court for an order for maintenance but this forbearance was not at the husband's request. The decree was made absolute; the husband paid no maintenance; the wife sued him on his promise. In the High Court the wife obtained judgement on the basis of the principle of promissory estoppel.

Decision: (In the Court of Appeal) Promissory estoppel 'does not create new causes of action where none existed before. It only prevents a party from insisting on his strict legal rights when it would be unjust to allow him to enforce them'. The wife's claim failed.

Promissory estoppel only applies to a promise of waiver which is **entirely voluntary**.

D and C Builders v Rees 1966
The facts: The defendants owed £482 to the claimants who were in acute financial difficulties. The claimants reluctantly agreed to accept £300 in full settlement. They later claimed the balance.

Decision: The debt must be paid in full. Promissory estoppel only applies to a promise voluntarily given. The defendants had been aware of and had exploited the claimants' difficulties.

Question — **Waiver of contractual rights**

Ahmed agrees to paint Emma's dining room for £400. When the job is completed, Emma tells him she will only pay £300. He accepts reluctantly, because he needs some money quickly. Is he entitled to claim the full amount the following week?

Answer

A promise to waive an existing right is not binding unless separate consideration is given, so Ahmed is not bound to accept less. He would be bound if he had made the waiver with the intention that Emma should place reliance on it and she had actually done so. The fact that the waiver was not entirely voluntary (*D&C Builders v Rees 1966*) is not relevant, as promissory estoppel is not being claimed. Ahmed may claim the balance.

4 Privity of contract **12/01, 6/03**

FAST FORWARD

As a general rule, only a person who is a party to a contract has enforceable rights or obligations under it. This is the doctrine of **privity of contract**. The Contracts (Rights of Third Parties) Act 1999 has had a fundamental effect on the doctrine.

There is a maxim in contract law which states that **consideration must move from the promisee**. As consideration is the price of a promise, the price must be paid by the person who seeks to enforce the promise.

Illustration

A promises B that (for a consideration provided by B) A will confer a benefit on C, then C cannot as a general rule enforce A's promise since C has given no consideration for it.

Tweddle v Atkinson 1861
The facts: The claimant married the daughter of G. On the occasion of the marriage, the claimant's father and G exchanged promises that they would each pay a sum of money to the claimant. G died without making the promised payment and the claimant sued G's executor for the specified amount.

Decision: The claimant had provided no consideration for G's promise.

In *Tweddle's* case each father could have sued the other but the claimant could not sue. The rule that consideration must move from the promisee overlaps with the rule that **only a party to a contract can enforce it**. No-one may be entitled to or bound by the terms of a contract to which he is not an original party: *Price v Easton 1833.*

Key term

Privity of contract can be defined as follows.

As a general rule, only a person who is a party to a contract has enforceable rights or obligations under it. Third parties have no right of action save in certain exceptional instances.

The following is the leading case on privity of contract.

Dunlop v Selfridge 1915
The facts: The claimant supplied tyres to X, a distributor, on terms that X would not re-sell the tyres at less than the prescribed retail price. If X sold the tyres wholesale to trade customers, X must impose a similar condition on those buyers to observe minimum retail prices. X resold tyres on these conditions to the defendant. Under the terms of the contract between X and Selfridge, Selfridge was to pay to the claimant a sum of £5 per tyre if it sold tyres to customers below the minimum retail price. They sold tyres to two customers at less than the minimum price. The claimant sued to recover £5 per tyre as liquidated damages.

Decision: The claimant could not recover damages under a contract (between X and Selfridge) to which it was not a party.

The party to the contract who imposes the condition or obtains a promise of a benefit for a third party can usually enforce it, but damages cannot be recovered on the third party's behalf, since a claimant can only recover damages for a loss he has suffered. Other remedies may be sought however.

Beswick v Beswick 1968
The facts: X transferred his business to the defendant, his nephew, in consideration for a pension of £6.10s per week and, after his death, a weekly annuity to X's widow. Only one such annuity payment was made. The widow brought an action against the nephew, asking for an order of specific performance. She sued both as administratrix of her husband's estate and in her personal capacity as recipient.

Decision: As her husband's representative, the widow was successful in enforcing the contract for a third party's (her own) benefit. In her personal capacity she had no right of action.

Where the contract is one which provides something for the enjoyment of both the contracting party and third parties – such as a family holiday – the contracting party may be entitled to recover damages for his loss of the benefit: *Jackson v Horizon Holidays Ltd 1975.*

4.1 Exceptions

There are a number of exceptions to the rule of privity of contract.

	Exceptions
Implied trusts	Equity may hold that an implied trust has been created *Gregory and Parker v Willimans 1817* *The facts:* P owed money to G and W. He agreed with W to transfer his property to W if W would pay his (P's) debt to G. The property was transferred, but W refused to pay G. G could not sue on the contract between P and W. *Decision:* P could be regarded as a trustee for G, and G would therefore bring an action jointly with P.
Statutory exceptions	Road Traffic Act 1972: A person injured in a road accident may claim against the motorist's insurers. Married Woman's Property Act 1882: Permits husband and wife to insure his or her own life for the benefit of the other under a trust which the beneficiary can enforce Contracts (Rights of Third Parties) Act 1999: see below
Agency	In normal circumstances the agent discloses to a third party with whom he contracts that he is acting for a principal. The contract, when made, is between the principal and the third party. The agent has no liability under the contact and no right to enforce it. Agency is considered further in Chapter 9.
Covenants	A restrictive covenant may run with land *Tulk v Moxhay 1848* *The facts:* The claimant owned several plots of land in Leicester Square. He sold one to X, who agreed not to build on it, but to preserve it in its existing condition. It was sold on, eventually being purchased by the defendant, who, although he was aware of the restriction, proposed to build on it. The claimant sought an injunction. *Decision:* The injunction was granted.

4.2 Contracts (Rights of Third Parties) Act 1999

This Act has a fundamental effect on the rule of **privity of contract** by setting out the circumstances in which a third party has a right to enforce a contract term or have it varied or rescinded, and a right to all the remedies that are available for breach of contract. It brings the law in England, Wales and Northern Ireland into line with Scotland, most of the EU and the US.

There is a two-limbed test for the circumstances in which a third party may enforce a contract term.

- Whether the contract itself expressly so provides
- Where the term confers a benefit on the third party, unless it appears that the contracting parties did not intend him to have the right to enforce it.

The third party must be expressly identified in the contract by name, class or description, but need not be in existence when the contract is made (for example, an unborn child or a future spouse). The Act enables a third party to take advantage of exclusion clauses as well as to enforce 'positive' rights.

The Act does not confer third party rights in relation to a company's memorandum and articles (which are contracts between a company and its members under s 14 of the Companies Act 1985), or employment contracts. So, for example, a customer of an employer cannot use this Act to enforce a term of a contract of employment against an employee.

5 Contract formation checklist

Essential element	Components	Definition	Rules	Exceptions
Agreement	**Offer**	'A definite promise to be bound on specific terms'	Cannot be vague Does not have to be made to particular person Must be distinguished from invitation to treat	
	+			
	Acceptance	'A positive act by a person to whom an offer has been made which, if unconditional, brings a binding contract into effect.'	May be express words, action or inferred from action, but not silence. Must be unconditional acceptance of terms (ie not counter-offer) Must be communicated to the offeror ⇨	Unless: (1) Offeror waives the need (2) Particular means of communication prescribed (3) Under postal rule, a posted letter does not arrive acceptance remains valid.
			Offer can only be accepted when it remains open – it may lapse in the following situations: (1) Rejection (2) Lapse of time (3) Revocation (4) Failure of condition (5) Death	

Essential element	Components	Definition	Rules	Exceptions
Intention		'An agreement will only become legally binding if the parties intend that this will be so'	If the intention is expressed in the contract, that expression will be followed.	
			If there is no express intention in the agreement, the courts apply 'rebuttable presumptions:' (1) Family or social agreements not intended to be (2) Commercial agreements intended to be binding	No exceptions – but remember the presumptions are rebuttable – if you can prove otherwise, the courts will apply what you can prove.
Consideration	**Executed or Executory**	'A valuable consideration in the sense of the law may consist either in some right, interest, profit or benefit accruing to one party, or some forbearance detriment, loss or responsibility given, suffered or undertaken by the other.'	Must not be past	(1) Bills of exchange (2) Written confirmation (3) Implied promise to pay for a service
			Need not be adequate	
			Must be sufficient	
			Waiver of rights under a contract must be matched by consideration from the other party.	(1) Alternative consideration given (goods, early settlement) (2) Third party pays part – rest is cancelled (3) Doctrine of promissory estoppel
			Consideration must move from the promisee (privity of contract), only they then have rights in the contract	(1) Trusts (2) Statutory exceptions (Contracts (Rights of 3Ps Act) (3) Agency (4) Restrictive covenants

6 The electronic contract

It could be said that the case of *Byrne v van Tienhoven*, dating from 1880, is an early example of an electronic contract. In that case, the sending of an acceptance by telegram was an important action in a chain of events leading to the formation of a contract. Since then, technology has permitted such actions to become almost instantaneous. Fax messages, e-mails and use of the internet may all play a part in the communication of offers and purported acceptances.

Exam focus point

If a scenario is presented involving modern technology, you will earn marks for applying your knowledge of the basic law of contract. There may well be very little case law in some areas – or none – but as long as you work through each step of the scenario in a logical manner, you should do well.

This is a potentially wide ranging topic and the law is still in its infancy. Below is a summary of the issues which will need to be considered.

(a) **In writing**? There are two main reasons why contracts need to be in writing.

- A written contract provides evidence of the terms of the contract.
- The requirement of formality allows a weaker party to 'think twice' before entering into a transaction.

An electronic contract meets the reasoning behind the requirement for writing, and can thus be said to be in writing.

(b) **Signed?** In 2000 the UK government passed legislation to give legal effect to 'digital signatures', thereby giving an electronic contract the same status as contracts in more traditional formats.

(c) **Timing of acceptance**. A contract comes into existence when an offer is accepted; in the case of acceptance by letter, this is when the letter is posted not when it is received. Internet e-mail shares many of the qualities of conventional mail – it is not usually instantaneous and may be subject to delay. Therefore the postal rule, with any problems arising from it, probably applies, although the point has not been tested.

(d) **Consideration**. Difficulties with credit card payments have slowed the growth of electronic commerce. The Internet is largely insecure, and this may cause problems when it comes to payment.

Activities on the internet are largely **unregulated** at the moment, but this is likely to change, as governments recognise the business opportunities available and the EU seeks to **protect consumers**. **Basic legal principles** must therefore be applied.

Of course, the internet is much more than simply a means of sending and receiving messages. As the commercial applications of the world wide web have been exploited, a new 'shop front' has been developed. Some sites are highly automated and software handles ordering, stock checking, payment processing and despatch confirmation without human involvement.

There are risks associated with leaving commercial transactions to automated IT programs. Eliminating human intervention and fully automating the sales process, for example, can increase the likelihood of errors. A notable recent example is the Argos website in the UK which offered television sets for £2.99, rather than £299. The following are some of the **practical legal issues** that must be faced by a **seller** when contracting on-line.

- Websites should be constructed as shop windows, that is, **invitations to treat** rather than offers.
- **Terms and conditions** governing electronic transactions should be made explicit and clear.
- **An indication of interest** by a purchaser visiting the website should be understood by both parties to be **an offer**, not an acceptance, which the seller is then free to accept or reject.

- Sellers can continue to use **disclaimers of liability**, clearly displayed on the website, subject to the usual **consumer protection laws** on unfair terms.
- The **law and jurisdiction** governing the transaction should be made clear, for example, 'All transactions are governed by English law'.
- The seller should make sure that any **web pages do not contravene local laws** (for example, those relating to advertising standards) in the countries targeted.
- A **time limit** should be set for all offers made on the website, which should take account of potential delays in receiving emails.

Chapter roundup

- 'A valuable consideration in the sense of the law may consist either in some right, interest, profit or benefit accruing to one party, or some forbearance, detriment, loss or responsibility given, suffered or undertaken by the other'. This definition of **consideration**, the third essential element of a binding contract, was given in Currie v Misa 1875.
- Consideration may be **executed** (an act in return for a promise) or **executory** (a promise in return for a promise). It may not be **past**, unless one of three recognised exceptions applies.
- Consideration need not be **adequate**, but it must be **sufficient**. This means that what is tendered as consideration must be capable in law of being regarded as consideration, but need not necessarily be equal in value to the consideration received in return.
- The principle of **promissory estoppel** was developed in *Central London Property Trust v High Trees House 1947.*
- As a general rule, only a person who is a party to a contract has enforceable rights or obligations under it. This is the doctrine of **privity of contract**, as demonstrated in *Dunlop v Selfridge 1915.* The Contracts (Rights of Third Parties) Act 1999 has had a fundamental effect on the doctrine.

Quick quiz

1 Distinguish between executed and executory consideration.

2 Past consideration, as a general rule, is not sufficient to make a promise binding.

True ☐

False ☐

3 Consideration need not be (1) .... but it must be (2) ....

4 If Alice promises Ben that (for a consideration provided by Ben) Alice will confer a benefit on Charlotte, then .... cannot at common law enforce Alice's promise. This is the doctrine of

privity of contract
frustration

5 What is the doctrine of promissory estoppel?

6 A promise of additional reward for existing duties is not generally binding

True ☐

False ☐

Answers to quick quiz

1 Executed consideration is an *act* in return for a promise such as paying for goods when the shopkeeper hands them over. Executory consideration is a *promise* given for a promise, such as promising to pay for goods that the shopkeeper puts on order for you.

2 True

3 (1) adequate, (2) sufficient

4 Charlotte
Privity of contract

5 If a creditor (Y) makes a promise (unsupported by consideration) to the debtor (X) that Y will not insist on the full discharge of the debt, and the promise is made with the intention that X should act on it and he does so, Y is estopped from retracting his promise, unless X can be restored to his original position.

6 True (as in *Stilk v Myrick*)

Now try the question below from the Exam Question Bank

Number	Level	Marks	Time
Q27	Examination	20	36 mins

The terms of a contract

7

Topic list	Syllabus reference
1 Contract terms	2(b)
2 Express terms and implied terms	2(b)
3 Conditions and warranties	2(b)
4 Exclusion clauses	2(b)
5 The Unfair Contract Terms Act 1977	2(b)
6 The Unfair Terms in Consumer Contracts Regulations 1999	2(b)
7 Restraint of trade	2(c)

Introduction

In Chapters 5 and 6 we considered the formation of contracts. In this chapter we consider how **terms may be incorporated** into a contract. We will also consider how one party to a contract may seek to exclude his liability under a contract by the use of a specific type of contract term: the **exclusion** (or exemption) clause.

As a general principle the parties may by their offer and acceptance include in their contract whatever terms they prefer. But the law may modify these express terms in various ways.

(a) Statements made in the pre-contract negotiations may become **terms** of the contract or remain as **representations**, to which different rules attach. The distinction is explained in Section 1.

(b) The terms must be sufficiently **complete and precise** to produce an agreement which can be binding. If they are vague there may be no contract. These express terms are considered in Section 2 of this chapter. In addition to the express terms of the agreement, additional terms may be implied by law. We also consider **implied terms**.

(c) The terms of the contract are usually classified as **conditions** or as **warranties** according to their importance. This classification is described in Section 3.

Introduction (cont)

(d) To be enforceable, terms must be **validly incorporated** into the contract. Because most court decisions about valid incorporation of contract terms are made in respect of exclusion clauses, we will look at this topic in the context of exclusion clauses, in section 4.

(e) **Terms** which exclude or restrict liability for breach of contract **may be restricted** in their effect or be overridden **by common law or statute**: the law in this area is explained in sections 5 and 6.

(f) Some terms may be void, as we discussed in Chapter 4. We look at restraints of trade in section 7.

This is a large chapter, any part of which could form a Section A question or some of a Section B question. Remember that you may have to apply your knowledge to a scenario. In the pilot paper, a straightforward Section A question asked for definitions of: terms, conditions, warranties and innominate terms.

1 Contract terms **Pilot Paper**

FAST FORWARD

Statements made by the parties to a contract may be classified as **terms or representations**.

In addition to the final contract, many statements may be made during the process of negotiation that often leads to the formation of a contract. It is important to be able to establish whether what has been written or said actually amounts to a contract term or whether it is simply a representation. **Statements may be classified as terms or as representations**.

Key term

A **representation** is something which induces the formation of a contract but which does not become a **term** of the contract. The importance of the distinction is that different remedies are available depending on whether a term is broken or a representation turns out to be untrue.

If something said in negotiations proves to be untrue, the party misled can claim for **breach of contract** if the statement became a **term** of the contract. (If the pre-contract statement was merely a **representation** then the party misled can claim misrepresentation; this usually results in a lesser remedy than in cases of breach of contract.) There are a number of factors that a court may consider in determining if a statement is or is not a term.

The court will consider **when** the representation was made to assess whether it was designed as a contract term or merely as an incidental statement. The court will also look at the **importance** the recipient of the information attached to it.

Bannerman v White 1861
The facts: In negotiations for the sale of hops the buyer emphasised that it was **essential** to him that the hops should not have been treated with sulphur adding that, if they had, he would not even bother to ask the price. The seller replied explicitly that no sulphur had been used. It was later discovered that a small proportion of the hops (5 acres out of 300) had been treated with sulphur. The buyer refused to pay the price.

Decision: The representation as to the absence of sulphur was intended to be a **term** of the contract.

Routledge v McKay 1954
The facts: The defendant, in discussing the possible sale of his motorcycle to the claimant, said on 23 October that the cycle was a 1942 model; he took this information from the registration document. On 30 October the parties made a written contract which did not refer to the year of the model and the purchaser had not indicated that the age of the cycle was of critical importance to him. The actual date was 1930.

Decision: The buyer's claim for damages failed. The reference to a 1942 model was a **representation made prior** to the contract

If the statement is made by a person with **special knowledge** it is more likely to be treated as a contract term.

> *Dick Bentley Productions v Arnold Smith Motors 1965*
> *The facts:* The defendants sold the claimants a car which they stated to have done only 20,000 miles since a replacement engine and gear-box had been fitted. In fact the car had covered 100,000 miles since then and was unsatisfactory.
>
> *Decision:* The defendants' statement was a term of the contract and the claimants were entitled to damages.
>
> *Oscar Chess v Williams 1957*
> *The facts:* The defendant, when selling his car to the claimant car dealers, stated (as the registration book showed) that his car was a 1948 model and the dealers valued it at £280 in the transaction. In fact it was a 1939 model, worth only £175, and the registration book had been altered by a previous owner.
>
> *Decision:* The statement was a mere representation. The seller was not an expert and the buyer had better means of discovering the truth.

2 Express terms and implied terms 12/02

FAST FORWARD

As a general rule, the parties to a contract may include in the agreement whatever **terms** they choose. This is the principle of **freedom of contract**.

2.1 Express terms

An express term is a term expressly agreed by the parties to a contract to be a term of that contract. In examining a contract, the courts will look first at the terms expressly agreed by the parties.

An apparently binding legal agreement must be **complete in its terms** to be a valid contract.

> *Scammell v Ouston 1941*
> *The facts:* The defendants wished to buy a motor-van from the claimants on hire-purchase. They placed an order 'on the understanding that the balance of purchase price can be had on hire-purchase terms over a period of two years'. The hire-purchase terms were never specified.
>
> *Decision:* The court was unable to identify a contract which it could uphold because the language used was so vague.

It is always possible for the parties to leave an essential term to be **settled by other means**, for example by an independent third party.

Illustration

It may be agreed to sell at the open market price on the day of delivery, or to invite an arbitrator to determine a fair price. The price may be determined by the course of dealing between the parties.

Where an agreement appears vague or incomplete, the courts will seek to uphold it by looking at the **intention of the parties**: *Hillas & Co Ltd v Arcos Ltd 1932.* If the parties use standard printed conditions, some of which are inappropriate, such phrases may be disregarded.

Nicolene v Simmonds 1953
The facts: The claimant offered to buy steel bars from the defendant. A contract was made by correspondence, in which the defendant provided that 'the usual conditions of acceptance apply'. The defendant failed to deliver the goods and argued that there had been no explicit agreement.

Decision: The words should be disregarded. The contract was complete without these words; there were no usual conditions of acceptance.

2.2 Oral evidence of contract terms

Often there is no written evidence of the terms of a contract. The court must ascertain as a **question of fact** exactly what was said.

If the contract is in writing, and all the necessary terms are present, the courts will interpret the terms of the contract by reference to the written document. They will not admit oral evidence to add to, vary or contradict written terms.

Hawrish v Bank of Montreal 1969
The facts: A solicitor gave to a company's bank a personal guarantee 'of all present and future debts' of the company. He later sought to give evidence to show that the guarantee applied only to a particular overdraft existing when the guarantee was given.

Decision: Such evidence was inadmissible.

There are the following exceptions to the rule.

(a) Oral evidence may be given of trade practice or custom: *Hutton v Warren 1836*.

(b) The parties may agree orally that their written consent should not take effect until a **condition precedent** has been satisfied, for example, a written contract to buy a house subject to a verbal agreement that it would take effect only if the purchaser's surveyor gave a satisfactory report: *Pym v Campbell 1856*.

(c) Oral evidence may be given as an addition to a written contract if it can be shown that the document was not intended to comprise all the agreed terms.

SS Ardennes (Cargo Owners) v SS Ardennes (Owners) 1951
The facts: The claimants were orange-growers in Spain and the defendants were shipowners. A printed bill of lading provided that the ship might go 'by any route...directly or indirectly' to London. The shipowners' agent had given a verbal undertaking that the vessel would sail direct from Spain to London. The ship sailed via Antwerp, so that the oranges arrived late and a favourable market was missed.

Decision: Evidence might be given of the verbal undertaking as a term overriding the bill of lading.

2.3 Implied terms 6/05

FAST FORWARD

Terms may be implied by the **courts**, by **statute** or by **custom**.

There are occasions where certain terms are not **expressly** adopted by the parties. Additional terms of a contract may be **implied** by law: by custom, statute or the courts to bring efficacy to the contract.

Key term

An **implied term** can be defined as follows.

'A term deemed to form part of a contract even though not expressly mentioned. Some such terms may be implied by the courts as necessary to give effect to the presumed intentions of the parties. Other terms may be implied by statute, for example, the Sale of Goods Act.'

2.3.1 Terms implied by custom

The parties may enter into a contract subject to customs of their trade. Any express term overrides a term which might be implied by custom.

Hutton v Warren 1836
The facts: The defendant landlord gave the claimant, a tenant farmer, notice to quit the farm. He insisted that the tenant should continue to farm the land during the period of notice. The tenant asked for 'a fair allowance' for seeds and labour from which he received no benefit because he was to leave the farm.

Decision: By custom he was bound to farm the land until the end of the tenancy; but he was also entitled to a fair allowance for seeds and labour incurred.

Les Affreteurs v Walford 1919
The facts: A charter of a ship provided expressly for a 3% commission payment to be made 'on signing the charter'. There was a trade custom that it should only be paid at a later stage. The ship was requisitioned by the French government and so no hire was earned.

Decision: An express term prevails over a term otherwise implied by custom. The commission was payable on hire.

2.3.2 Terms implied by statute

Terms may be implied by statute. In some cases the statute permits the parties to contract out of the statutory terms. In other cases the statutory terms are obligatory: the protection given by the Sale of Goods Act 1979 to a consumer who buys goods from a trader cannot be taken away from him.

2.3.3 Terms implied by the courts

Terms may be implied if the court concludes that the parties intended those terms to apply to the contract.

The Moorcock 1889
The facts: The owners of a wharf agreed that a ship should be moored alongside to unload its cargo. It was well known that at low water the ship would ground on the mud at the bottom. At ebb tide the ship settled on a ridge concealed beneath the mud and suffered damage.

Decision: It was an implied term, though not expressed, that the ground alongside the wharf was safe at low tide since both parties knew that the ship must rest on it.

A term of a contract which is left to be implied and is not expressed is often something that goes without saying; so that, if while the parties were making their bargain an officious bystander were to suggest some express provision for it, they would say "why should we put that in? That's obvious" : This was put forward in *Shirlaw v Southern Foundries 1940.* The terms is required to give **efficacy** to the contract, that is, to make it work in practice.

The court may also imply terms because the court believes such a term to be a 'necessary incident' of this type of contract.

Liverpool City Council v Irwin 1977
The facts: The defendants were tenants in a tower block owned by the claimants. There was no formal tenancy agreement. The defendants withheld rent, alleging that the claimants had breached implied terms because *inter alia* the lifts did not work and the stairs were unlit.

Decision: Tenants could only occupy the building with access to stairs and/or lifts, so terms needed to be implied on these matters.

Where a term is implied as a 'necessary incident' it has precedent value and such terms will be implied into future contracts of the same type.

3 Conditions and warranties **Pilot Paper, 12/03**

FAST FORWARD

Statements which are classified as contract terms may be further categorised as **conditions** or **warranties**. A condition is a vital term going to the root of the contract, while a warranty is a term subsidiary to the main purpose of the contract. The remedies available for breach are different in each case.

Exam focus point

It is fundamental that students can explain and distinguish between conditions and warranties. The effects of their breach are different.

The terms of the contract are usually classified by their relative importance as **conditions** or **warranties**.

(a) **A condition is a vital term**, going to the root of the contract, breach of which entitles the injured party to decide to treat the contract as **discharged** and to claim damages.

Key term

A **condition** can be defined as follows.

'An important term which is vital to a contract so that its breach will destroy the basis of the agreement. It may arise from an express agreement between the parties or may be implied by law.

(b) **A warranty is a term subsidiary to the main purpose of the contract**, breach of which only entitles the injured party to claim damages.

Key term

A **warranty** can be defined as follows.

'A minor term in a contract. If broken, the injured party must continue performance but may claim damages for the loss suffered.'

Poussard v Spiers 1876
The facts: Mme Poussard agreed to sing in an opera throughout a series of performances. Owing to illness she was unable to appear on the opening night and the next few days. The producer engaged a substitute who insisted that she should be engaged for the whole run. When Mme Poussard recovered, the producer declined to accept her services for the remaining performances.

Decision: Failure to sing on the opening night was a breach of condition which entitled the producer to treat the contract for the remaining performances as discharged.

Bettini v Gye 1876
The facts: An opera singer was engaged for a series of performances under a contract by which he had to be in London for rehearsals six days before the opening performance. Owing to illness he did not arrive until the third day before the opening. The defendant refused to accept his services, treating the contract as discharged.

Decision: The rehearsal clause was subsidiary to the main purpose of the contract.

Schuler v Wickham Machine Tool Sales 1973
The facts: The claimants entered into a contract with the defendants giving them the sole right to sell panel presses in England. A clause of the contract provided that the defendants' representative should visit six named firms each week to solicit orders. The defendants' representative failed on a few occasions to do so and the claimants claimed to be entitled to repudiate the agreement.

Decision: Such minor breaches by the defendants did not entitle the claimants to repudiate.

Classification may depend on the following issues.

(a) **Statute** often identifies implied terms specifically as conditions or warranties. An example is the Sale of Goods Act 1979.

(b) **Case law** may also define particular types of clauses as conditions, for example a clause as to the date of 'expected readiness' of a ship let to a charterer: *The Mihalis Angelos 1971.*

(c) The court may construe what was the intention of the parties at the time the contract was made as to whether a broken term was to be a condition or a warranty: *Bunge Corporation v Tradax SA 1981.*

It is important to remember that if the injured party merely wants damages, there is no need to consider whether the term broken is a condition or a warranty, since either type of breach entitles the injured party to damages.

Question

Conditions and warranties

Norma, a professional singer, enters into a contract to sing throughout a series of concerts. A term in the contract states that she must attend five rehearsals before the opening night. Norma falls ill and misses the last two rehearsals and the opening night. Is she in breach of contract? Give reasons.

Answer

Norma is in breach of contract as she has failed to fulfil the condition that she would sing on the opening night (*Poussard v Spiers 1876*). Had she just failed to attend the two rehearsals, this would have amounted to breach of warranty (*Bettini v Gye 1876*).

3.1 Innominate terms **12/03, 6/05**

Traditionally, terms were either classified as conditions or warranties and the injured party could choose to end the contract only for breach of condition. Sometimes a warranty was broken with catastrophic results, yet the court could not permit the injured party to end the contract because the term broken was not a condition. More recently the courts have held that where the breach deprives the injured party of **substantially the whole benefit** of the contract the term broken can be called '**Innominate'** and the injured party can choose to end the contract even if it could not be regarded as a condition.

If the nature and effect of the breach is such as to deprive the injured party of most of his benefit from the contract then it will be treated as if the guilty party had breached a condition.

The doctrine was developed in:

Hong Kong Fir Shipping Co Ltd v Kawasaki Kisa Kaisha Ltd 1962
The facts: The defendants chartered a ship from the claimants for a period of 24 months. A term in the contract stated that the claimants would provide a ship which was 'in every way fitted for ordinary cargo service'. Because of the engine's age and the crew's lack of competence the ship's first voyage, from Liverpool to Osaka, was delayed for 5 months and further repairs were required at the end of it. The defendants purported to terminate the contract, so the claimants sued for breach of contract; the defendants claimed that the claimants were in breach of a contractual condition.

Decision: The term was innominate and could not automatically be construed as either a condition or a warranty. The obligation of 'seaworthiness' embodied in many charterparty agreements was too complex to be fitted into one of the two categories.

The ship was still available for 17 out of 24 months. The consequences of the breach were not so serious that the defendants could be justified in terminating the contract as a result.

Exam focus point

Do not over emphasise innominate terms. Being able to provide an explanation is sufficient.

Question

Breach

Phil agrees with Professional Cars plc that they are to provide a white Rolls Royce for his daughter's wedding. On the day the driver arrives in a black Ford Scorpio. Phil sends him away. What is the consequence?

Answer

Phil can sue Professional Cars plc for breach of contract. The company has not agreed to supply 'a car' but 'a white Rolls Royce'. Its failure to fulfil this term allows Phil to sue for breach if he wishes to claim damages, eg the cost of hiring another car. It does not matter if the term broken is a condition or a warranty.

Question

Consequences of breach

To what is the injured party to a contract entitled in the event of breach of:

(a) A condition by the other party?
(b) A warranty by the other party?

Answer

(a) He may choose to treat the contract as discharged and repudiate or terminate the contract, or alternatively he may go on with it and sue for damages.

(b) He may claim damages only.

4 Exclusion clauses 6/02, 6/04

FAST FORWARD

An **exclusion clause** may attempt to restrict one party's liability for breach of contract or for negligence.

To be enforceable, a term must be validly incorporated into a contract. Because most disputes about whether a term has been incorporated arise in the context of exclusion clauses, much of the relevant case law surrounds exclusion clauses. In this section, we will examine the ways in which the courts may determine:

(a) whether an exclusion clause (as a contract term) has been validly *incorporated* into the contract; and

(b) if so, how the exclusion clause should be *interpreted*

Key term

An **exclusion clause** can be defined as follows.

'A clause in a contract which purports to exclude liability altogether or to restrict it by limiting damages or by imposing other onerous conditions. They are sometimes referred to as **exemption clauses**.

There has been strong criticism of the use of exclusion clauses in contracts made between manufacturers or sellers of goods or services and private citizens as consumers. The seller puts forward standard conditions of sale which the buyer may not understand, but which he must accept if he wishes to buy. With these so-called **standard form contracts**, the presence of exclusion clauses becomes an important consideration.

For many years the courts demonstrated the hostility of the common law to exclusion clauses by developing various rules of case law designed to restrain their effect. These are described in this section of the chapter. To these must also be added the considerable statutory safeguards provided by the **Unfair Contract Terms Act 1977** (UCTA). These are considered in the next section of this chapter.

The statutory rules do permit exclusion clauses to continue in some circumstances. Hence it is necessary to consider both the **older case law** and the **newer statutory rules**.

The **courts** have generally sought to protect consumers from the harsher effects of exclusion clauses in two ways.

(a) An exclusion clause must be properly **incorporated** into a contract before it has any legal effect.

(b) Exclusion clauses are **interpreted** strictly. This may prevent the application of the clause.

4.1 Incorporation of exclusion clauses

FAST FORWARD

The courts protect customers from the harsher effects of exclusion clauses by ensuring that they are properly **incorporated** into a contract and then by **interpreting** them strictly.

Uncertainty often arises over which terms have actually been **incorporated** into a contract.

- The document containing notice of the clause must be an **integral part** of the contract.
- If the document is an integral part of the contract, a term may not usually be disputed if it is included in a document which a party has **signed**.
- The term must be put forward **before** the contract is made.
- If the contact is not signed, an exclusion clause is not a binding term unless the person whose rights it restricts was made **sufficiently aware** of it at the time of agreeing to it.
- **Onerous terms** must be sufficiently highlighted (it is doubtful whether this applies to signed contracts).

4.1.1 Contractual documents

Where the exclusion clause is contained in an unsigned document it must be shown that this document is an integral part of the contract and is one which could be expected to contain terms.

Chapelton v Barry UDC 1940
The facts: There was a pile of deck chairs and a notice stating 'Hire of chairs 2d per session of three hours'. The claimant took two chairs, paid for them and received two tickets which were headed 'receipt' which he put in his pocket. One of the chairs collapsed and he was injured. The defendant council relied on a notice on the back of the tickets by which it disclaimed liability for injury.

Decision: The notice advertising chairs for hire gave no warning of limiting conditions and it was not reasonable to communicate them on a receipt. The disclaimer of liability was not binding on the claimant.

Thompson v LMS Railway 1930
The facts: An elderly lady who could not read asked her niece to buy her a railway excursion ticket on which was printed 'Excursion: for conditions see back'. On the back it was stated that the ticket was issued subject to conditions contained in the company's timetables. These conditions excluded liability for injury.

Decision: The conditions had been adequately communicated and therefore had been accepted.

4.1.2 Signed contracts

If a person signs a document containing a term he is held to have agreed to the term even if he had not read the document. But this is not so if the party who puts forward the document for signature gives a misleading explanation of the term's legal effect.

L'Estrange v Graucob 1934
The facts: The defendant sold to the claimant, a shopkeeper, a slot machine under conditions which excluded the claimant's normal rights under the Sale of Goods Act 1893. The claimant signed the document described as a 'Sales Agreement' and including clauses in 'legible, but regrettably small print'.

Decision: The conditions were binding on the claimant since she had signed them. It was not material that the defendant had given her no information of their terms nor called her attention to them.

Curtis v Chemical Cleaning Co 1951
The facts: The claimant took her wedding dress to be cleaned. She was asked to sign a receipt on which there were conditions which she was told restricted the cleaner's liability and in particular placed on the claimant the risk of damage to beads and sequins on the dress. The document in facts contained a clause 'that the company is not liable for any damage however caused'. The dress was badly stained in the course of cleaning.

Decision: The cleaners could not rely on their disclaimer since they had misled the claimant. She was entitled to assume that she was running the risk of damage to beads and sequins only.

4.1.3 Unsigned contracts

Each party must be aware of the contract's terms before or **at the time of entering into the agreement** if they are to be binding.

Olley v Marlborough Court 1949
The facts: A husband and wife arrived at a hotel and paid for a room in advance. On reaching their bedroom they saw a notice on the wall by which the hotel disclaimed liability for loss of valuables unless handed to the management for safe keeping. The wife locked the room and handed the key in at the reception desk. A thief obtained the key and stole the wife's furs from the bedroom.

Decision: The hotel could not rely on the notice disclaiming liability since the contract had been made previously and the disclaimer was too late.

Complications can arise when it is difficult to determine at exactly **what point in time** the contract is formed so as to determine whether or not a term is validly included.

Thornton v Shoe Lane Parking Ltd 1971
The facts: The claimant wished to park his car in the defendant's automatic car park. He had seen a sign saying 'All cars parked at owner's risk' outside the car park and when he received his ticket he saw that it contained words which he did not read. In fact these made the contract subject to conditions displayed

obscurely on the premises. These not only disclaimed liability for damage but also excluded liability for injury. When he returned to collect his car there was an accident in which he was badly injured.

Decision: The reference on the ticket to conditions was received too late for the conditions to be included as contractual terms. At any rate, it was unreasonable for a term disclaiming liability for personal injury to be presented so obscurely. Note that since the Unfair Contracts Terms Act 1977 the personal injury clause would be unenforceable anyway.

An exception to the rule that there should be prior notice of the terms is where the parties have had **consistent dealings** with each other in the past, and the documents used then contained similar terms.

J Spurling Ltd v Bradshaw 1956
The facts: Having dealt with a company of warehousemen for many years, the defendant gave it eight barrels of orange juice for storage. A document he received a few days later acknowledged receipt and contained a clause excluding liability for damage caused by negligence. When he collected the barrels they were empty and he refused to pay.

Decision: It was a valid clause as it had also been present in the course of previous dealings, even though he had never read it.

If the parties have had previous dealings (not on a consistent basis) then the person to be bound by the term must be **sufficiently aware** of it at the time of making the latest contract.

Hollier v Rambler Motors 1972
The facts: On three or four occasions over a period of five years the claimant had had repairs done at a garage. On each occasion he had signed a form by which the garage disclaimed liability for damage caused by fire to customers' cars. The car was damaged by fire caused by negligence of garage employees. The garage contended that the disclaimer had by course of dealing become an established term of any contract made between them and the claimant.

Decision: The garage was liable. There was no evidence to show that the claimant knew of and agreed to the condition as a continuing term of his contracts with the garage.

4.1.4 Onerous terms

Where a term is particularly unusual and onerous it should be highlighted (although it is doubtful whether this applies to signed contracts). Failure to do so may mean that it does not become incorporated into the contract.

Interfoto Picture Library Ltd v Stiletto Visual Programmes Ltd 1988
The facts: 47 photographic transparencies were delivered to the defendant together with a delivery note with conditions on the back. Included in small type was a clause stating that for every day late each transparency was held a 'holding fee' of £5 plus VAT would be charged. They were returned 14 days late. The claimants sued for the full amount.

Decision: The term was onerous and had not been sufficiently brought to the attention of the defendant. The court reduced the fee to one tenth of the contractual figure to reflect more fairly the loss caused to the claimants by the delay.

Question

Exclusion clause

Natasha hires a care from a car rental company. On arrival at their office she is given a form, which includes terms and conditions in small print on the back, and asked to sign it. She does so and pays the hire charge. When she gets into the car, she happens to look in the glove compartment and sees a document headed 'Limitation of Liability'. This states that the hire company will not be liable for any injury caused by a defect in the car unless this is as a result of the company's negligence. While Natasha is driving on the motorway, the airbag inflates and causes her to crash. She is badly injured. Assuming that negligence is not claimed, what is the status of the exclusion clause?

Answer

There must be prior notice of the presence of an exclusion clause. The answer here will depend on whether this exclusion was included in the original terms and conditions (and therefore merely reinforced by the later document) or not. The hire company's only other possible defence will be to show a consistent course of dealings with Natasha.

4.2 Interpretation of exclusion clauses

In deciding what an exclusion clause means, the courts interpret any ambiguity against the person at fault who relies on the exclusion. This is known as the **contra proferentem rule**. Liability can only be excluded or restricted by clear words.

In the *Hollier* case above, the court decided that as a matter of interpretation the disclaimer of liability could be interpreted to apply:

- Only to accidental fire damage or
- To fire damage caused in any way including negligence.

It should therefore be interpreted against the garage in the narrower sense of (a) so that it did not give exemption from fire damage due to negligence. If a person wishes successfully to exclude or limit liability for loss caused by negligence the courts require that the word 'negligence', or an accepted synonym for it, should be included in the clause.

Alderslade v Hendon Laundry 1945
The facts: The conditions of contracts made by a laundry with its customers excluded liability for loss of or damage to customers' clothing in the possession of the laundry. By its negligence the laundry lost the claimant's handkerchief.

Decision: The exclusion clause would have no meaning unless it covered loss or damage due to negligence. It did therefore cover loss by negligence.

4.2.1 The 'main purpose' rule

When construing an exclusion clause the court will also consider the **main purpose rule**. By this, the court presumes that the clause was not intended to defeat the main purpose of the contract.

4.2.2 Fundamental breach

There is no doubt that at common law a properly drafted exclusion clause can cover any breach of contract.

Photo Productions v Securicor Transport 1980
The facts: The defendants agreed to guard the claimants' factory under a contract by which the defendant were excluded from liability for damage caused by any of their employees. One of the guards deliberately started a small fire which destroyed the factory and contents. It was contended that Securicor had entirely failed to perform their contract and so they could not rely on any exclusion clause in the contract.

Decision: There is no principle that total failure to perform a contract deprives the party at fault of any exclusion from liability provided by the contract. In this case the exclusion clause was drawn widely enough to cover the damage which had happened. As the fire occurred before the UCTA was in force, the Act could not apply here. But if it had done it would have been necessary to consider whether the exclusion clause was reasonable.

Exam focus point

The reliance on the exclusion clause is an everyday occurrence in business dealings and therefore is of great practical relevance.

5 The Unfair Contract Terms Act 1977

The Unfair Contract Terms Act 1977 aims to protect consumers (effectively individuals) when they enter contracts by stating that some exclusion clauses are void, and considering whether others are reasonable.

When considering the **validity** of exclusion clauses the courts have had to strike a balance between:

- The principle that parties should have complete **freedom to contract** on whatever terms they wish, and
- The need to **protect the public** from unfair exclusion clauses

Exclusion clauses do have a proper place in business. They can be used to allocate contractual risk, and thus to determine in advance who is to insure against that risk. Between businessmen with similar bargaining power exclusion clauses are a legitimate device. The main limitations are now contained in the Unfair Contract Terms Act 1977.

Before we consider the specific terms of UCTA, it is necessary to describe how its scope is restricted.

(a) In general the Act only applies to clauses inserted into agreements by **commercial concerns or businesses**. In principle private persons may restrict liability as much as they wish.

(b) The Act does not apply to some contracts, for example contracts of insurance or contracts relating to the transfer of an interest in land.

(c) Specifically, the Act applies to:

  (i) clauses that attempt to limit liability for negligence;
  (ii) clauses that attempt to limit liability for breach of contract.

The Act uses two techniques for controlling exclusion clauses – some types of clauses are **void**, whereas others are subject to a **test of reasonableness**.

The main provisions can be summarised as follows:

(a) Any clause that attempts to restrict liability for death or personal injury arising from negligence is **void**.

(b) Any clause that attempts to restrict liability for other loss or damage arising from negligence is void unless it can be shown to be **reasonable**.

(c) Any clause that attempts to limit liability for breach of contract, where the contract is based on standard terms or conditions, or where one of the parties is a consumer, is void unless it can be shown to be **reasonable**.

5.1 Clauses which are void

If an exclusion clause is made **void by statute** it is unnecessary to consider how other legal rules might affect it. There is simply no need to assess whether it is reasonable.

A clause is void by statute in the following circumstances.

- A clause which purports to exclude or limit liability for **death or personal injury** resulting from negligence is void: s 2(1) UCTA.
- A guarantee clause which purports to exclude or limit liability for loss or damage caused by a **defect** of the goods in **consumer use** is void: s 5 UCTA.
- In a contract for the sale or hire purchase of goods, a clause that purports to exclude the condition that the seller has a **right to sell** the goods is void: s 6(1) UCTA.
- In a contract for the sale of goods, hire purchase, supply of work or materials or exchange *with a consumer*, a clause that purports to exclude or limit liability for breach of the conditions relating to description, quality, fitness and sample implied by the Sale of Goods Act 1979 is void: s 6(2) and 7(2) UCTA.

The first of these circumstances, as set down in S2(1) UCTA, is the most important one to be aware of.

5.2 Clauses which are subject to a test of reasonableness

If a clause is not automatically void, it is subject to a test of reasonableness. The main provisions of the Act that refer to this type of clause are set out in Sections 2, 3, 6 and 7 of the Act.

5.3 Exclusion of liability for negligence (s 2)

As we saw above, a person acting in the course of a business cannot, by reference to any contract term, restrict his liability for **death or personal injury** resulting from negligence. The clause containing the term is simply void. In the case of **other loss or damage**, a person cannot introduce a clause restricting his liability for negligence unless the term is **reasonable**.

5.4 Standard term contracts and consumer contracts (s 3)

The person who uses a standard-term contract in dealing with a **consumer** cannot, unless the term is **reasonable**, restrict liability for his own breach.

> *George Mitchell Ltd v Finney Lock Seeds Ltd 1983*
> *The facts:* The claimant ordered 30 pounds of Dutch winter cabbage seeds from the defendants. The defendant's standard term contract included an exclusion clause that limited their liability to a refund of the amount paid by the claimant. The wrong type of cabbage seed was delivered. The seed was planted over 63 acres, but when the crop came up it was not fit for human consumption. The claimant claimed £61,500 damages plus £30,000 interest.
>
> *Decision:* At common law the exclusion clause would have protected the defendant, but the court decided in favour of the claimant, relying exclusively on the statutory ground of reasonableness.

5.4.1 Consumers

Where a business engages in an activity which is merely incidental to the business, the activity will not be in the course of the business unless it is an integral part and carried on with a degree of regularity.

R & B Customs Brokers Ltd v United Dominions Trust Ltd 1988
The facts: The claimants, a company owned by Mr and Mrs Bell and operating as a shipping broker, bought a second-hand Colt Shogun. The car was to be used partly for business and partly for private use.

Decision: This was a consumer sale, since the company was not in the business of buying cars.

5.5 Sale and supply of goods (ss 6-7)

Any contract (that is, consumer or non-consumer) for the sale or hire purchase of goods cannot exclude the implied condition that the seller has a **right to sell** the goods.

As we saw earlier when looking at clauses that are automatically void, a **consumer** contract for the sale of goods, hire purchase, supply of work or materials or exchange of goods cannot exclude or restrict liability for breach of the conditions relating to description, quality, fitness and sample implied by the Sale of Goods Act 1979 and the Supply of Goods and Services Act 1982. For a non-consumer contract, such exclusions are subject to a **reasonableness** test. The rules are set out in the following table.

Exemption clauses in contracts for the sale of goods or supply of work or materials			
		Consumer transaction	Non-consumer transaction
Implied terms	Title	Void	Void
	Description	Void	Subject to reasonableness test
	Quality and suitability	Void	Subject to reasonableness test
	Sample	Void	Subject to reasonableness test

5.6 The statutory test of reasonableness (s 11)

The term must be fair and reasonable having regard to all the circumstances which were, or which ought to have been, known to the parties when the contract was made. The burden of proving reasonableness lies on the person seeking to rely on the clause. Statutory guidelines have been included in the Act to assist the determination of reasonableness. For instance, the court will consider the following.

- The relative **strength** of the parties' bargaining positions.
- Whether any **inducement** (for example, a reduced price) was offered to the customer to persuade him to accept limitation of his rights.
- Whether the customer **knew or ought to have known** of the existence and extent of the exclusion clause.
- If failure to comply with a condition (for example, failure to give notice of a defect within a short period) excludes or restricts the customer's rights, whether it was reasonable to expect when the contract was made that compliance with the condition would be practicable.
- Whether the goods were made, processed or adapted to the **special order** of the customer (UCTA Sch 2).

Smith v Eric S Bush 1989
The facts: A surveyor prepared a report on a property which contained a clause disclaiming liability for the accuracy and validity of the report. In fact the survey was negligently done and the claimant had to make good a lot of defects once the property was purchased.

Decision: In the absence of special difficulties, it was unreasonable for the surveyor to disclaim liability given the cost of the report, his profession and his knowledge that it would be relied upon to make a major purchase.

St Albans City and District Council v International Computers Ltd 1994

The facts: The defendants had been hired to assess population figures on which to base community charges (local government taxation). Their standard contract contained a clause restricting liability to £100,000. The database which they supplied to the claimants was seriously inaccurate and the latter sustained a loss of £1.3 million.

Decision: The clause was unreasonable. The defendants could not justify this limitation, which was very low in relation to the potential loss. In addition, they had aggregate insurance of £50 million. The defendants had to pay full damages.

Question — UCTA

The Unfair Contract Terms Act 1977 limits the extent to which it is possible to exclude or restrict *business liability*. What do you understand by the phrase business liability?

Answer

Business liability is liability, in tort or contract, which arises from things done or to be done in the course of a business or from the occupation of premises used for business purposes of the occupier. Business includes a profession and the activities of any government department or public or local authority.

Exam focus point

A good way to look at UCTA is to write down which terms are void under UCTA and which are subject to a reasonableness test. It is vital you understand which contracts UCTA applies to.

6 The Unfair Terms in Consumer Contracts Regulations 1999

FAST FORWARD

The Unfair Terms in Consumer Contracts Regulations 1999 define what is meant by an **unfair term**. They deal with consumer contracts and terms which have not been individually negotiated.

These regulations implemented an EU directive on unfair contract terms. UCTA 1977 continues to apply. There are now three layers of relevant law.

- The **common law**, which applies to all contracts, regardless of whether or not one party is a consumer
- **UCTA 1977**, which applies to all contracts and which has specific provisions for consumer contracts
- **The Regulations** (**UTCCR 1999**), which only apply to consumer contracts and to terms which have not been individually negotiated

The new regulations apply to contracts for the supply of goods or services.

- They apply to terms in consumer contracts.

Key term

A **consumer** is defined as 'a natural person who, in making a contract to which these regulations apply, is acting for purposes which are outside his business'.

- They apply to contractual terms which have not been individually negotiated.
- There are a number of exceptions including contracts relating to family law or to the incorporation or organisation of companies and partnerships and employment contracts.

A key aspect of the regulations is the definition of an unfair term.

Key term

> An **unfair term** is any term which causes a significant imbalance in the parties' rights and obligations under the contract to the detriment of the consumer.

In making an assessment of good faith, the courts will have regard to the following.

- The **strength of the bargaining positions** of the parties
- Whether the consumer had an **inducement** to agree to the term
- Whether the goods or services were sold or supplied to the **special order** of the consumer
- The extent to which the seller or supplier has dealt **fairly and equitably** with the consumer

The effect of the regulations is to render certain terms in consumer contracts unfair.

- Excluding or limiting liability of the seller when the consumer dies or is injured, where this results from an act or omission of the seller
- Excluding or limiting liability where there is partial or incomplete performance of a contract by the seller
- Making a contract binding on the consumer where the seller can still avoid performing the contract

Two forms of redress are available.

- A consumer who has concluded a contract containing an unfair term can ask the court to find that the unfair term should not be binding.
- A complaint, for example by an individual, a consumer group or a trading standards department can be made to the Director General of Fair Trading.

7 Restraint of trade 6/03

FAST FORWARD

> Contracts including clauses in restraint of trade are usually valid except for the restraint. Restraint of trade means limiting someone's ability to do their job or carry on their business.

To complete this chapter on contract terms, we look at a specific type of term which is often encountered in two different situations:

(a) The contract of employment, and
(b) The contract for sale and purchase of a business.

A **restraint of trade** clause seeks to limit a person's freedom to carry on a trade or business. A typical example would be where a contract of employment stated that the employee on leaving his employer could not engage in a similar activity to that carried on by the employer for a number of years in a particular locality.

If a contract includes a restraint of trade clause, the restraint may be void and unenforceable but the rest of the contract is usually valid. As explained below the **general policy of the law is against upholding any restrictions on a person's freedom to work** or carry on a trade. But there are some exceptions.

Key term

> Any restriction on a person's normal freedom to carry on a trade, business or profession in such a way and with such persons as he chooses is a **restraint of trade**.

A restraint of trade is treated as contrary to public policy and therefore **void** unless it can be justified under the principles explained below. If a restraint is void the remainder of the contract by which the restraint is imposed is usually valid and binding – it is merely the restraint which is struck out as invalid.

The objection to a restraint of trade is that it denies to a community useful services which would otherwise be available. On the other hand, it is recognised that a restraint may be needed to **protect legitimate interests**. A restraint of trade **may** therefore **be justified** and be **enforceable** in the following circumstances.

- The person who imposes it has a **legitimate interest** to protect
- The restraint is **reasonable between the parties** as a protection of that interest
- It is also **reasonable from the standpoint of the community**

In principle any restraint of trade may be subject to scrutiny by reference to the tests set out in the previous paragraph. But where the parties have agreed upon it in the normal course of business and on the basis of **equal bargaining strength**, it is accepted that the restraint is justifiable and valid without detailed examination. **In practice the doctrine of restraint of trade is applicable only in two areas.**

We will look at two important areas where the doctrine of restraint of trade is applicable.

7.1 Restraints on employees

An employer may (in consideration of the payment of wages) insist that the employee's services shall be given only to him while the employment continues. But any restraint imposed on the employee's freedom to take up other employment (or to carry on business on his own account) **after** leaving the employer's service is void unless it can be justified.

A restraint may be justified if it seeks to prevent the employee using:

- Trade secrets
- Trade connections

as the employer is entitled to protect these interests.

An employee who has access to **trade secrets** such as manufacturing processes or even financial and commercial information which is confidential, may therefore be restricted to prevent his using it after leaving his present job.

In contrast to trade secrets the employer has no right to restrain an employee from exercising a **personal skill** acquired in the employer's service.

Forster & Sons v Suggett 1918
The facts: As works manager S had access to technical know-how of his employer's business of making glass bottles. His contract of employment provided that for five years after leaving his employer's service he would not carry on or be interested in the manufacture of glass bottles in the UK or other glass-making similar to that of his employer's business.

Decision: It must be shown (and in this case it had been) that the employee had access to secret manufacturing processes. The restraint was valid.

Morris v Saxelby 1916
The facts: S worked for M as an apprentice and rose to become head of a department. He had some limited knowledge of the employer's technical secrets but essentially he became a skilled draftsman in engineering design work. He undertook that for seven years after leaving his employment he would not engage in any similar business in the UK.

Decision: This was a restraint on the use by S of technical skill and knowledge acquired in the service of M. M had no right to be protected from the competition of a former employee using his own skills.

If the employer imposes the restraint to protect his **connection** with his customers or clients, he must show that the employee had something **more than a routine contact** with them.

The restraint is **only valid** if the **nature** of the employee's duties gives him an **intimate knowledge** of the affairs or requirements of customers such that, if he leaves to take up other work, they might follow him because of his knowledge (as distinct from his personal skill).

Fitch v Dewes 1921
The facts: D was successively an articled clerk and a managing clerk in the employment of F, a solicitor. D undertook never to practise as a solicitor (after leaving F) within seven miles of F's practice.

Decision: The restraint was valid since D's knowledge of the affairs of F's clients should not be used to the detriment of F. (In modern practice a restriction unlimited in time will probably be treated as excessive.)

S W Strange v Mann 1965
The facts: A bookmaker employed M to conduct business, mainly by telephone, with his clients. M's contract of service restricted his freedom to take similar employment.

Decision: The contact between M and his employer's clients was too remote to give him the required influence over them. The restraint was void.

If the employer can show that the restraint is imposed to protect his legitimate interest he must next show that it is **reasonable** between parties – **no more than is necessary to protect his interest**. Many restraints have been held void because they

- Prohibited the employee from working in a wider area than the catchment area of the employer's business *(Mason Provident Clothing & Supply Co Ltd 1973),* or
- Restricted him for an excessively long time, more than was necessary to eliminate his influence

Exam focus point

The reasonableness of the geographical extent or time limit of restraint of trade clauses will depend on the circumstances of each case. In the *Dewes* case, above, the area was predominantly rural and there was therefore a limited number of clients in the 7 mile restriction area. In the *Office Angels* case, below, in heavily populated London, a 3 kilometre restriction was unreasonable.

In the exam, you need to assess such factors as these given in the question so that you can come to justified conclusions about whether a restraint of trade clause might be considered reasonable or not.

Note that in *Dewes* case above a lifelong restraint was held valid – it depends on the nature of the employer's interest to be protected.

The modern practice is generally to restrain an employee only for a short time within an area related to the employer's business or to prohibit him only from soliciting or doing business with customers known to him.

If the restraint is too wide the entire restriction is usually void and not merely the excess which is unreasonable. The court will not rewrite an excessive restraint by limiting it to that part which might be reasonable.

Office Angels Ltd v Rainer-Thomas and O'Connor 1991
The facts: The defendants' contracts of employment included clauses stating that, for a period of six months after leaving the claimant's employ, they would neither solicit clients of the business nor engage in similar business within a radius of 3 kilometres of the branch in the City of London. The defendants left and set up their own business in a nearby location. An injunction was obtained preventing this in the High Court. The defendants appealed.

Decision: The restraint on the poaching of clients was reasonable, but the area of restraint was not. The whole restraint clause was void.

7.1.1 The blue pencil rule

In some cases however, the court has concluded that the **parties did not intend** by the words used **to adopt as wide a restraint** as the words might impose and have **struck out the words which are too wide**. This is the **'blue pencil'** rule of **simple deletion**.

Home Counties Dairies v Skilton 1970
The facts: A milk roundsman's contract of employment prohibited him, for one year after leaving his employment, from selling milk or dairy produce to customers of the employer to whom the roundsman had supplied his employer's goods during the final six months of his employment.

Decision: The words 'or dairy produce' were excessive since they would prevent the employee from engaging in a different trade, such as a grocery shop. As the object of the restraint was to protect the employer's connection with customers who purchased their milk, the restraint would be upheld in respect of milk supplied only.

A restraint (in a contract of service) which is reasonable between the parties is not, by definition, prejudicial to the public interest.

In recent years a subtle form of restriction has become popular with employers: the **'garden leave' clause**, whereby the employer insists that the employee serves out a long period of notice at home. However, if the employer does not keep up salaries and benefits, he risks a claim for breach of contract.

7.2 Restraints on vendors of businesses

A purchaser of the goodwill of a business has a right to protect what he has bought by imposing restrictions to prevent the vendor doing business with his old customers or clients. The restraint must **protect** the business sold and it **must not be excessive**.

British Reinforced Concrete Engineering Co v Schelff 1921
The facts: S carried on a small local business of making one type of road reinforcement. He sold his business to BC which carried on business throughout the UK in making a range of road reinforcements. S undertook not to compete with BC in the sale or manufacture of road reinforcements.

Decision: The restraint was void since it was widely drawn to protect BC from any competition by S. In buying the business of S, BC was only entitled to protect what they bought – a local business making one type of product and not the entire range produced by BC in the UK.

Allied Dunbar (Frank Weisinger) Ltd v Frank Weisinger 1987
The facts: The defendant had sold his business to A, for a sum which included £386,000 as consideration for F, a financial consultant who had built up his successful business from scratch, not to be employed in a similar capacity for 2 years.

Decision: The restraint was valid, since it was agreed after equal negotiation, paid for and reasonable in itself.

For goodwill to be protected it must actually exist. The courts will not allow 'protection of goodwill' to be a smokescreen for barefaced restraint of competition.

Vancouver Malt & Sake Brewing Co Ltd v Vancouver Breweries Ltd 1934
The facts: The defendant was licensed to brew beer but in fact only produced sake. It sold its business and agreed to a term restraining it from brewing beer for 15 years. It later began to produce beer and the purchaser sought to enforce the restraint.

Decision: Since the seller did not, at the time of sale, produce beer the purchaser only paid for tangible assets because there was no beer-brewing goodwill to sell. The purchaser had not provided consideration for the promise not to produce beer and so he could not enforce it.

Chapter roundup

- Statements made by the parties may be classified as **terms or representations**. Different **remedies** attach to breach of a term and to misrepresentation respectively.
- As a general rule, the parties to a contract may include in the agreement whatever **terms** they choose. This is the principle of **freedom of contract**. Terms clearly included in the contract are **express terms**. The law may complement or replace terms by **implying** terms into a contract. Terms may be implied by the **courts**, by **statute** or by **custom**.
- Statements which are classified as contract terms may be further categorised as **conditions** or **warranties**. A condition is a vital term going to the root of the contract, while a warranty is a term subsidiary to the main purpose of the contract. The remedies available for breach are different in each case. It may not be possible to determine whether a term is a condition or a warranty. Such terms are classified by the courts as **innominate terms**.
- An **exclusion clause** may attempt to restrict one party's liability for breach of contract or for negligence. Because of inequality of bargaining power, the **Unfair Contract Terms Act 1977** renders **void** certain exclusion clauses in sale of goods or supply of services contracts and any clause which purports to exclude liability for death or personal injury resulting from negligence.
- The courts protect customers from the harsher effects of exclusion clauses by ensuring that they are properly **incorporated** into a contract and then by **interpreting** them strictly.
- The general rules
  - A clause may not usually be disputed if it is in a document which has been signed.
  - The clause must be put forward before the contract is made.
  - Both parties must be aware of it.
- An exclusion clause may not be sufficiently widely drawn as to cover a **fundamental breach** of contract
- The application of UCTA 1977 depends to a great extent upon whether there is a **consumer sale**. A contract between business operations is considerably less affected by the Act. Both types often have to satisfy a statutory test of **reasonableness**.
- The Unfair Terms in Consumer Contracts Regulations 1999 define what is meant by an **unfair term**.
- Some terms in a contract can be void, for example clauses in restraint of trade.
- Contracts including clauses in restraint of trade are usually valid except for the restraint. The courts may apply a 'blue pencil' to any unreasonable aspects of the clause.

Quick quiz

1 Why is it important to distinguish between terms and representations?

2 A term may be implied into a contract by

1 Statute
2 Trade practice unless an express term overrides it
3 The court to provide for events not contemplated by the parties
4 The court to give effect to a term which the parties had agreed upon but failed to express because it was obvious
5 The court to override an express term which is contrary to normal custom

A 2 and 3 only
B 1, 2 and 4 only
C 1, 4 and 5 only
D 1, 3, 4 and 5 only

3 **Fill in the blanks** in the statements below, using the words in the box.

- A (1) .... is a vital term, going to the root of the contract, breach of which entitles the injured party to treat the contract as (2) .... and claim (3) ....
- A (4) .... is a term (5) .... to the main purpose of the contract.
- The consequence of a term being classified as innominate is that the court must decide what is the actual effect of its (6) ....

• breach	• condition	• subsidiary
• warranty	• damages	• discharged

4 Give an example of a statute which identifies implied terms specifically as conditions or warranties.

5 Terms implied by custom cannot be overridden

True ☐

False ☐

6 A contract in restraint of trade is always void.

True ☐

False ☐

7 The following definition of a consumer is contained in UCTA 77. Fill in the gaps.

(a) He neither makes the contract in course of (1) .... nor holds himself out as doing so

(b) The other (2) .... does make the contract in course of (3) ....

(c) In the case of a contract governed by the law of (4) ...., the goods are of a type ordinarily supplied for (5) ....

8 Match the layers of law to their jurisdictions in the law of contract

(a) Common law (1) All contracts with specific provisions for consumer contracts
(b) UCTA 1977 (2) Applies only to consumer contracts and to non-negotiated terms
(c) UTCCR 1999 (3) All contracts

9 What is the 'contra proferentem' rule?

Answers to quick quiz

1 The importance of the distinction is that different remedies are available depending on whether a term is broken or a representation turns out to be untrue.

2 B

3 (1) condition (2) discharged (3) damages (4) warranty (5) subsidiary (6) breach

4 Sale of Goods Act 1979

5 False

6 False

7 (1) business, (2) party, (3) business, (4) sale of goods, (5) private use or consumption

8 (a) (3)
(b) (1)
(c) (2)

9 In deciding what an exclusion clause means, the courts interpret any ambiguity against the person at fault who relies on the exclusion.

Now try the questions below from the Exam Question Bank

Number	Level	Marks	Time
Q7	Examination	20	36 mins
Q8	Examination	10	18 mins

Discharge of contract

Topic list	Syllabus reference
1 Discharge by performance	2(d)
2 Breach of contract	2(d)
3 Damages	2(d)
4 Remoteness of damage	2(d)
5 Measure of damages	2(d)
6 Liquidated damages and penalty clauses	2(d)
7 Other common law remedies	2(d)
8 Equitable remedies	2(d)
9 Limitation to actions for breach	2(d)

Introduction

In Chapters 5 and 6 we saw how a contract comes into existence and in Chapter 7 we considered some of the factors which can affect a contract. In this chapter we examine how a contract may be breached and the remedies for that.

You should, however, remember that most business contracts are discharged by **performance** as the parties intended.

If a contract is breached, a party has a number of remedies.

- **Damages** are a form of compensation for loss caused by the breach.
- An **action for the price** may be commenced where the breach is failure to pay.
- A ***quantum meruit*** is payment to the claimant for the value of what he has done.
- **Specific performance**, an equitable remedy, is a court order to the defendant to perform the contract.
- An **injunction** is a court order for the other party to observe negative restrictions.

In some cases the injured party can terminate the contract.

- **Rescission** means that the contract is cancelled or rejected and the parties restored to their pre-contract positions. It is usually applied when a contract is voidable.

Introduction (cont)

Damages and action for the price are **common law remedies** and are most frequently sought when a remedy is needed for breach of contract, since they arise as of right. The other types of remedy are **equitable remedies** which are only appropriate in specialised circumstances.

You might be required to discuss breach of contract and its remedies in a general way. However, as the examiner has emphasised the importance of application of knowledge in this paper, you should be able to suggest **specific** solutions to given problems. Section A of the pilot paper specifically examined damages.

1 Discharge by performance

FAST FORWARD

A contract is usually discharged by performance. There are a number of exceptions to the principle that the performance must be complete and exact, in order to ensure that the interests of both parties are protected.

Performance is the normal method of discharge of a contract. Each party fulfils or performs his contractual obligations and the agreement is then ended. As a general rule contractual obligations are discharged only by **complete and exact performance**.

> *Cutter v Powell 1795*
> *The facts:* The defendant employed C as second mate of a ship sailing from Jamaica to Liverpool at a wage for the complete voyage of 30 guineas. The voyage began on 2 August and C died at sea on 20 September, when the ship was still 19 days from Liverpool. C's widow sued for a proportionate part of the agreed sum.
>
> *Decision:* C was entitled to nothing unless he completed the voyage.
>
> *Bolton v Mahadeva 1972*
> *The facts:* The claimant agreed to install a central heating system in the defendant's home for £800. The work was defective: the system did not heat adequately and it gave off fumes. The defendant refused to pay for it.
>
> *Decision:* The claimant could recover nothing.

Where there is partial performance and partial non-performance (breach) the question arises as to whether the contract breaker can claim the price of the part of the work properly performed. In the above cases the defendant might appear to have profited since he obtained part of what the claimant contracted to deliver without himself having to pay anything. The courts have developed a number of exceptions to the rule to ensure that the interests of both parties are protected and the contract breaker can claim for the work completed. The exceptions are as follows:

- The doctrine of substantial performance
- Where the promisee accepts partial performance
- Where the promisee prevents performance
- Severable contracts

1.1 Substantial performance

The doctrine of substantial performance may be applied, especially in contracts for building work. If the building contractor has completed a very large part of the essential work, he may claim the contract price less a deduction for the minor work outstanding.

Sumpter v Hedges 1898
The facts: The claimant undertook to erect buildings on the land of the defendant for a price of £565. He partially erected the buildings, then abandoned the work when it was only completed to the value of £333. The defendant completed the work using materials left on his land. The claimant sued for the value of his materials used by the defendant and for the value of his work.

Decision: The defendant must pay for the materials since he had elected to use them but he had no obligation to pay the unpaid balance of the charges for work done by the claimant before abandoning it. It was not a case of substantial performance of the contract.

Hoenig v Isaacs 1952
The facts: The defendant employed the claimant to decorate and furnish his flat at a total price of £750. There were defects in the furniture which could be put right at a cost of £56. The defendant argued that the claimant was only entitled to reasonable remuneration.

Decision: The defendant must pay the balance owing of the total price of £750 less an allowance of £56, as the claimant had substantially completed the contract.

1.2 Partial performance

The promisee may accept partial performance and must then pay for it. The principle here is that although the promisor has only partially fulfilled his contractual obligations, it may sometimes be possible to infer the existence of a fresh agreement by which it is agreed that payment will be made for work already done or goods already supplied. Mere performance by the promisor is not enough; it must be open to the promisee either to accept or reject the benefit of the contract.

Question — **Partial performance**

Why could the doctrine of partial performance not be applied in *Cutter v Powell*?

Answer

Partial performance can only be accepted by the promisee when he has a choice of acceptance or rejection. In *Cutter v Powell,* performance consisted of Cutter's services as second mate. Once he had provided those services, they could not be 'returned' by the shipowners after his death.

1.3 Prevention of performance

The injured party may prevent performance. In that case the offer of performance is sufficient discharge.

If one party is prevented by the other from performing the contract completely he may sue for damages for breach of contract, or alternatively bring a quantum meruit action to claim for the amount of work done.

Planché v Colburn 1831
The facts: The claimant had agreed to write a book on costumes and armour for the defendants' 'Juvenile Library' series. He was to receive £100 on completion. He did some research and wrote part of the book. The defendants then abandoned the series.

Decision: The claimant was entitled to 50 guineas as reasonable remuneration on a *quantum meruit* basis.

1.4 Severable contracts

The contract may provide for performance by instalments with separate payment for each of them (a divisible or severable contract).

> *Taylor v Laird 1856*
> *The facts:* The claimant agreed to captain a ship up the River Niger at a rate of £50 per month. He abandoned the job before it was completed. He claimed his pay for the months completed.
>
> *Decision:* He was entitled to £50 for each complete month. Effectively this was a contract that provided for performance and payment in monthly instalments.

Question — **Substantial performance**

Carol employs Lawrence as an interior designer and decorator to do some work on her apartment. The contract price is £15,000. Lawrence completes the work within the allotted time. When inspecting the work, Carol notices that a lampshade she specified has not been supplied and that the door handles are of the wrong design. She tells Lawrence the job is incomplete and refuses to pay. Advise Lawrence.

Answer

Lawrence should be able to rely on the doctrine of substantial performance. He is entitled to receive the contract price less a reasonable deduction for the defects and omissions.

2 Breach of contract — 12/01, 6/02, 6/05

As described above, a contract is usually discharged by **complete and exact performance.**

A party is said to be in breach of contract where, without lawful excuse, he does not perform his contractual obligations precisely. A person sometimes has a lawful excuse not to perform contractual obligations.

- Performance is **impossible**, perhaps because of some unforeseeable event.
- He has tendered performance but this has been **rejected.**
- The **other party** has made it **impossible** for him to perform.
- The contract has been discharged through **frustration**.
- The parties have by **agreement** permitted **non-performance.**

Breach of contract gives rise to a secondary obligation to pay damages to the other party but, the primary obligation to perform the contract's terms remains unless the party in default has **repudiated** the contract, either before performance is due or before the contract has been fully performed, and this repudiation has been accepted by the injured party.

Key term

> **Repudiation** can be defined as a breach of contract which entitles the injured party to end the contract if he so chooses.

2.1 Repudiatory breach

> Breach of a condition in a contract or other repudiatory breach allows the injured party to terminate the contract unless the injured party elects to treat the contract as continuing and merely claim damages for his loss.

Key term

> A **repudiatory breach** occurs where a party indicates, either by words or by conduct, that he does not intend to honour his contractual obligations or commits a breach of condition or commits a breach which has very serious consequences for the injured party

It does not automatically discharge the contract – indeed the injured party has a choice.

- He can elect to treat the contract as repudiated by the other, recover damages and treat himself as being discharged from his primary obligations under the contract.
- He can elect to affirm the contract.

2.1.1 Types of repudiatory breach

Repudiatory breach giving rise to a right either to terminate or to affirm arises in the following circumstances.

(a) **Refusal to perform (renunciation).** One party renounces his contractual obligations by showing that he has no intention to perform them: *Hochster v De la Tour 1853.* (See below.)

(b) **Failure to perform an entire obligation**. An entire obligation is said to be one where complete and precise performance of it is a precondition of the other party's performance.

(c) **Incapacitation.** Where a party prevents himself from performing his contractual obligations he is treated as if he refused to perform them. For instance, where A sells a thing to C even though he promised to sell it to B he is in repudiatory breach of his contract with B.

(d) **Breach of condition** (discussed in Chapter 7)

(e) **Breach of an innominate term** which has the effect of depriving the injured party of substantially the whole benefit of the contract (discussed in Chapter 7).

2.1.2 Anticipatory breach

FAST FORWARD

> If there is **anticipatory breach** (one party declares in advance that he will not perform his side of the bargain when the time for performance arrives) the other party may treat the contract as discharged forthwith, or continue with his obligations until actual breach occurs. His claim for damages will then depend upon what he has actually lost.

Repudiation may be **explicit** or **implicit**. A party may break a condition of the contract merely by declaring in advance that he will not perform it, or by some other action which makes future performance impossible. The other party may treat this as **anticipatory breach**

- Treat the contract as discharged forthwith
- At his option may allow the contract to continue until there is an actual breach

Hochster v De La Tour 1853
The facts: The defendant engaged the claimant as a courier to accompany him on a European tour commencing on 1 June. On 11 May he wrote to the claimant to say that he no longer required his services. On 22 May the claimant commenced legal proceedings for anticipatory breach of contract. The defendant objected that there was no actionable breach until 1 June.

Decision: The claimant was entitled to sue as soon as the anticipatory breach occurred on 11 May.

Where the injured party allows the contract to continue, it may happen that the parties are discharged from their obligations without liability by some other cause which occurs later.

If the innocent party elects to treat the contract as still in force the former may continue with his preparations for performance and **recover the agreed price** for his services. Any claim for damages will be assessed on the basis of what the claimant has really lost.

White & Carter (Councils) v McGregor 1961

The facts: The claimants supplied litter bins to local councils, and were paid not by the councils but by traders who hired advertising space on the bins. The defendant contracted with them for advertising of his business. He then wrote to cancel the contract but the claimants elected to advertise as agreed, even though they had at the time of cancellation taken no steps to perform the contract. They performed the contract and claimed the agreed payment.

Decision: The contract continued in force and they were entitled to recover the agreed price for their services. Repudiation does not, of itself, bring the contract to an end. It gives the innocent party the choice of affirmation or rejection.

The Mihalis Angelos 1971

The facts: The parties entered into an agreement for the charter of a ship to be 'ready to load at Haiphong' (in Vietnam) on 1 July 1965. The charterers had the option to cancel if the ship was not ready to load by 20 July. On 17 July the charterers repudiated the contract believing (wrongly) that they were entitled to do so. The shipowners accepted the repudiation and claimed damages. On 17 July the ship was still in Hong Kong and could not have reached Haiphong by 20 July.

Decision: The shipowners were entitled only to nominal damages since they would have been unable to perform the contract and the charterers could have cancelled it without liability on 20 July.

2.1.3 Termination for repudiatory breach

To terminate for repudiatory breach the innocent party must notify the other of his decision. This may be by way of refusal to accept defects in performance, refusal to accept further performance or refusal to perform his own obligations.

- He is not bound by his future or continuing contractual obligations, and cannot be sued on them.
- He need not accept nor pay for further performance.
- He can refuse to pay for partial or defective performance already received, unless the contract is severable.
- He can reclaim money paid to a defaulter if he can and does reject defective performance.
- He is not discharged from the contractual obligations which were due at the time of termination.

The innocent party can also claim damages from the defaulter. An innocent party who began to perform his contractual obligations but who was prevented from completing them by the defaulter can claim reasonable remuneration on a quantum meruit basis.

2.1.4 Affirmation after repudiatory breach

If a person is aware of the other party's repudiatory breach and of his own right to terminate the contract as a result but still decides to treat the contract as being in existence he is said to have **affirmed the contract**. The contract remains fully in force.

3 Damages — Pilot Paper, 12/02

FAST FORWARD

Damages form the main remedy in actions for breach of contract, but there are others: injunctions and specific performance are the most important.

Key term

Damages are a common law remedy and are primarily intended to **restore the party who has suffered loss to the same position he would have been in if the contract had been performed**.

In a claim for damages the first issue is **remoteness of damage**. Here the courts consider how far down the sequence of cause and effect the consequences of breach should be traced before they should be ignored. Secondly, the court must decide how much money to award in respect of the breach and its relevant consequences. This is the **measure of damages**.

4 Remoteness of damage 6/04

Under the rule in *Hadley v Baxendale* damages may only be awarded in respect of loss as follows.

(a)
- **The loss must arise naturally** from the breach.
- The loss must arise **in a manner which the parties may reasonably be supposed to have contemplated**, in making the contract, as the probable result of the breach of it.

(b) A loss outside the natural course of events will only be compensated if the exceptional circumstances are within the defendant's knowledge when he made the contract.

Hadley v Baxendale 1854
The facts: The claimants owned a mill at Gloucester whose main crank shaft had broken. They made a contract with the defendant for the transport of the broken shaft to Greenwich to serve as a pattern for making a new shaft. Owing to neglect by the defendant delivery was delayed and the mill was out of action for a longer period. The defendant did not know that the mill would be idle during this interval. He was merely aware that he had to transport a broken millshaft. The claimants claimed for loss of profits of the mill during the period of delay.

Decision: Although the failure of the carrier to perform the contract promptly was the direct cause of the stoppage of the mill for an unnecessarily long time, the claim must fail since the defendant did not know that the mill would be idle until the new shaft was delivered. Moreover it was not a natural consequence of delay in transport of a broken shaft that the mill would be out of action. The miller might have a spare.

The defendant is liable only if he knew of the special circumstances from which the abnormal consequence of breach could arise.

Victoria Laundry (Windsor) v Newman Industries 1949
The facts: The defendants contracted to sell a large boiler to the claimants 'for immediate use' in their business of launderers and dyers. Owing to an accident in dismantling the boiler at its previous site delivery was delayed. The defendants were aware of the nature of the claimants' business and had been informed that the claimants were most anxious to put the boiler into use in the shortest possible space of time. The claimants claimed damages for normal loss of profits for the period of delay and for loss of abnormal profits from losing 'highly lucrative' dyeing contracts to be undertaken if the boiler had been delivered on time.

Decision: Damages for loss of normal profits were recoverable since in the circumstances failure to deliver major industrial equipment ordered for immediate use would be expected to prevent operation of the plant. The claim for loss of special profits failed because the defendants had no knowledge of the dyeing contracts.

Contrast this ruling with the case below.

The Heron II 1969
The facts: K entered into a contract with C for the shipment of a cargo of sugar belonging to C to Basra. He was aware that C were sugar merchants but he did not know that C intended to sell the cargo as soon as it reached Basra. The ship arrived nine days late and in that time the price of sugar on the market in Basra had fallen. C claimed damages for the loss due to the fall in market value.

Decision: The claim succeeded. It is common knowledge that market values of commodities fluctuate so that delay might cause loss.

If the type of loss caused is not too remote the defendant may be liable for serious consequences.

H Parsons (Livestock) v Uttley Ingham 1978
The facts: There was a contract for the supply and installation of a large storage hopper to hold pig foods. Owing to negligence of the defendant supplier the ventilation cowl was left closed. The pig food went mouldy. Young pigs contracted a rare intestinal disease, from which 254 died. The pig farmer claimed damages for the value of the dead pigs and loss of profits from selling the pigs when mature.

Decision: Some degree of illness of the pigs was to be expected as a natural consequence. Since illness was to be expected, death from illness was not too remote.

5 Measure of damages **6/04**

FAST FORWARD

The **measure of damages** is that which will **compensate for the loss incurred**. It is not intended that the injured party should profit from a claim. Damages may be awarded for financial and non-financial loss.

As a general rule the amount awarded as damages is what is needed to put the claimant in the position he would have achieved if the contract had been performed. This is sometimes referred to as protecting the **expectation interest** of the claimant.

A claimant may alternatively seek to have his **reliance interest** protected; this refers to the position he would have been in had he not relied on the contract. This compensates for wasted expenditure.

The onus is on the defendant to show that the expenditure would not have been recovered if the contract had been performed.

C & P Haulage v Middleton 1983
The facts: The claimants granted to the defendant a 6-month renewable licence to occupy premises as an engineering workshop. He incurred expenditure in doing up the premises, although the contract provided that he could not remove any fixtures he installed. He was ejected in breach of the licence agreement 10 weeks before the end of a 6-month term. He sued for damages.

Decision: The defendant could only recover nominal damages. He could not recover the cost of equipping the premises (as reliance loss) as he would not have been able to do so if the contract had been lawfully terminated.

If a contract is speculative, it may be unclear what profit might result.

Anglia Television Ltd v Reed 1972
The facts: The claimants engaged an actor to appear in a film they were making for television. He pulled out at the last moment and the project was abandoned. The claimants claimed the preparatory expenditure, such as hiring other actors and researching suitable locations.

Decision: Damages were awarded as claimed. It is impossible to tell whether an unmade film will be a success or a failure and, had the claimants claimed for loss of profits, they would not have succeeded.

The general principle is to compensate for **actual financial loss**.

Thompson Ltd v Robinson (Gunmakers) Ltd 1955
The facts: The defendants contracted to buy a Vanguard car from the claimants. They refused to take delivery and the claimants sued for loss of profit on the transaction. There was at the time a considerable excess of supply of such cars over demand for them and the claimants were unable to sell the car.

Decision: The market price rule, which the defendants argued should be applied, was inappropriate in the current market. The seller had lost a sale and was entitled to the profit.

Charter v Sullivan 1957
The facts: The facts were the same as in the previous case, except that the sellers were able to sell every car obtained from the manufacturers.

Decision: Only nominal damages were payable.

5.1 Non-financial loss

In some recent cases damages have been recovered for mental distress where that is the main result of the breach. It is uncertain how far the courts will develop this concept. Contrast the cases below.

Jarvis v Swan Tours 1973
The facts: The claimant entered into a contract for holiday accommodation at a winter sports centre. What was provided was much inferior to the description given in the defendant's brochure. Damages on the basis of financial loss only were assessed at £32.

Decision: The damages should be increased to £125 to compensate for disappointment and distress because this was a contract the principle purpose of which was the giving of pleasure.

Alexander v Rolls Royce Motor Cars Ltd 1995
The facts: The claimant sued for breach of contract to repair his Rolls Royce motor car and claimed damages for distress and inconvenience or loss of enjoyment of the car.

Decision: Breach of contract to repair a car did not give rise to any liability for damages for distress, inconvenience or loss of enjoyment.

5.2 Cost of cure

Where there has been a breach and the claimant is seeking to be put in the position he would have been in if the contract had been performed, by seeking a sum of money to 'cure' the defect which constituted the breach, he may be denied the cost of cure if it is wholly disproportionate to the breach.

Ruxley Electronics and Construction Ltd v Forsyth 1995
The facts: A householder discovered that the swimming pool he had ordered to be built was shallower than specified. He sued the builder for damages, including the cost of demolition of the pool and construction of a new one. Despite its shortcomings, the pool as built was perfectly serviceable and safe to dive into.

Decision: The expenditure involved in rectifying the breach was out of all proportion to the benefit of such rectification. The claimant was awarded a small sum to cover loss of amenity.

5.3 Mitigation of loss **6/03**

In assessing the amount of damages it is assumed that the claimant will take any reasonable steps to reduce or **mitigate** his loss. The burden of proof is on the defendant to show that the claimant failed to take a reasonable opportunity of mitigation.

Payzu Ltd v Saunders 1919
The facts: The parties had entered into a contract for the supply of goods to be delivered and paid for by instalments. The claimants failed to pay for the first instalment when due, one month after delivery. The defendants declined to make further deliveries unless the claimants paid cash in advance with their orders. The claimants refused to accept delivery on those terms. The price of the goods rose, and they sued for breach of contract.

Decision: The seller had no right to repudiate the original contract. But the claimants should have mitigated their loss by accepting the seller's offer of delivery against cash payment. Damages were limited to the amount of their assumed loss if they had paid in advance, which was interest over the period of pre-payment.

The injured party is not required to take discreditable or risky measures to reduce his loss since these are not 'reasonable'.

Pilkington v Wood 1953
The facts: The claimant bought a house in Hampshire, having been advised by his solicitor that title was good. The following year, he decided to sell it. A purchaser was found but it was discovered that the house was not saleable at the agreed price, as the title was not good. The defendant was negligent in his investigation of title and was liable to pay damages of £2,000, being the difference between the market value of the house with good title and its market value with defective title. The defendant argued that the claimant should have mitigated his loss by taking action against the previous vendor for conveying a defective title.

Decision: This would have involved complicated litigation and it was not clear that he would have succeeded. The claimant was under no duty to embark on such a hazardous venture 'to protect his solicitor from the consequences of his own carelessness'.

Question — **Measure of damages**

Chana agrees to buy a car which runs on LPG from Mike's Motors for £6,000. Mike paid £5,500 for the car. On the agreed day, Chana arrives at the dealers but refuses to accept or pay for the car. In the meantime, the car's market value has risen to £7,000. The following week Mike sells the car for £7,500. Mike claims against Chana for damages. How much is he likely to be awarded?

Answer

He is unlikely to be awarded damages, as he has incurred no loss.

6 Liquidated damages and penalty clauses 6/03

To avoid later complicated calculations of loss, or disputes over damages payable, the parties may include up-front in their contract a formula *(***liquidated damages***)* for determining the damages payable for breach.

Key term

Liquidated damages can be defined as 'a fixed or ascertainable sum agreed by the parties at the time of contracting, payable in the event of a breach, for example, an amount payable per day for failure to complete a building. If they are a genuine attempt to pre-estimate the likely loss the court will enforce payment.'

Dunlop Pneumatic Tyre Co Ltd v New Garage & Motor Co Ltd 1915
The facts: The contract (for the sale of tyres to a garage) imposed a minimum retail price. The contract provided that £5 per tyre should be paid by the buyer if he resold at less than the prescribed retail price or in four other possible cases of breach of contract. He did sell at a lower price and argued that £5 per tyre was a 'penalty' and not a genuine pre-estimate of loss.

Decision: As a general rule when a fixed amount is to be paid as damages for breaches of different kinds, some more serious in their consequences than others, that is not a genuine pre-estimate of loss and so it is void as a 'penalty'. In this case the formula was an honest attempt to agree on liquidated damages and would be upheld.

Ford Motor Co (England) Ltd v Armstrong 1915
The facts: The defendant had undertaken not to sell the claimant's cars below list price, not to sell Ford cars to other dealers and not to exhibit any Ford cars without permission. A £250 penalty was payable for each breach as being the agreed damage which the claimant would sustain.

Decision: Since the same sum was payable for different kinds of loss it was not a genuine pre-estimate of loss and was in the nature of a penalty. Unlike the *Dunlop* case the figure set was held to be excessive.

A contractual term designed as a **penalty clause** to discourage breach is void and not enforceable. Relief from penalty clauses is an example of the influence of equity in the law of contract, and has most frequently been seen in consumer credit cases.

Key term

A **penalty clause** can be defined as 'a clause in a contract providing for a specified sum of money to be payable in the event of a subsequent breach. If its purpose is merely to deter a potential difficulty, it will be held void and the court will proceed to assess unliquidated damages.'

Bridge v Campbell Discount Co 1962
The facts: A clause in a hire purchase contract required the debtor to pay on termination both arrears of payments due before termination and an amount which, together with payments made and due before termination, amounted to two thirds of the HP price, and additionally to return the goods.

Decision: This was a penalty clause and void since, in almost all circumstances, the creditor would receive on termination more than 100% of the value of the goods.

We have seen that if a clause for liquidated damages is included in the contract it should be highlighted as an **onerous term.** In *Interfoto Picture Library Ltd v Stiletto Visual Programmes Ltd 1988,* the defendants did not plead that the clause in question was a penalty clause and hence void, but it is probable that they could have done.

7 Other common law remedies 12/02

7.1 Action for the price

If the breach of contract arises out of one party's failure to pay the contractually agreed price due under the contract, the creditor should bring a personal action against the debtor to recover that sum. This is a fairly straightforward procedure but is subject to two specific limitations.

The first is that an **action for the price** under a contract for the sale of goods may only be brought if property has passed to the buyer, unless the price has been agreed to be payable on a specific date: s 49 Sale of Goods Act 1979.

Secondly, whilst the injured party may recover an agreed sum due at the time of an anticipatory breach, sums which become due after the anticipatory breach may not be recovered unless he affirms the contract.

7.2 Quantum meruit

In particular situations, a claim may be made on a quantum meruit basis as an alternative to an action for damages for breach of contract.

Key term

> The phrase **quantum meruit** literally means **'how much it is worth'**. It is a measure of the value of contractual work which has been performed. The aim of such an award is to restore the claimant to the position he would have been in if the contract had never been made, and is therefore known as a **restitutory** award.

Quantum meruit is likely to be sought where one party has already performed part of his obligations and the other party then repudiates the contract.

De Barnardy v Harding 1853
The facts: The claimant agreed to advertise and sell tickets for the defendant, who was erecting stands for spectators to view the funeral of the Duke of Wellington. The defendant cancelled the arrangement without justification.

Decision: The claimant might recover the value of services rendered.

In most cases, a quantum meruit claim is needed because the other party has unjustifiably prevented performance: *Planché v Colburn 1831*.

Because it is restitutory, a quantum meruit award is usually for a smaller amount than an award of damages. However where only nominal damages would be awarded (say because the claimant would not have been able to perform the contract anyway) a quantum meruit claim would still be available and would yield a higher amount.

8 Equitable remedies 12/02

8.1 Specific performance

The court may at its discretion give an equitable remedy by ordering the defendant to perform his part of the contract instead of letting him 'buy himself out of it' by paying damages for breach.

Key term

> **Specific performance** can be defined as 'an order of the court directing a person to perform an obligation. It is an equitable remedy awarded at the discretion of the court when damages would not be an adequate remedy. Its principal use is in contracts for the sale of land but may also be used to compel a sale of shares or debentures. It will never be used in the case of employment or other contracts involving personal services.'

An order will be made for specific performance of a contract for the sale of land since the claimant may need the land for a particular purpose and would not be adequately compensated by damages for the loss of his bargain.

The order will not be made if it would require performance over a period of time and the court could not ensure that the defendant did comply fully with the order. Therefore specific performance is not ordered for contracts of employment or personal service nor usually for building contracts.

8.2 Injunction

Key term

> An **injunction** is a discretionary court order and an equitable remedy, requiring the defendant to observe a negative restriction of a contract.

An injunction may be made to enforce a contract of personal service for which an order of specific performance would be refused.

Warner Bros Pictures Inc v Nelson 1937
The facts: The defendant (the film star Bette Davis) agreed to work for a year for the claimants and not during the year to work for any other producer nor 'to engage in any other occupation' without the consent of the claimants. She came to England during the year to work for a British film producer. The claimants sued for an injunction to restrain her from this work and she resisted arguing that if the restriction were enforced she must either work for them or abandon her livelihood.

Decision: The court would not make an injunction if it would have the result suggested by the defendant. But the claimants merely asked for an injunction to restrain her from working for a British film producer. This was one part of the restriction accepted by her under her contract and it was fair to hold her to it to that extent.

An injunction is limited to enforcement of contract terms which are in substance negative restraints.

Metropolitan Electric Supply Co v Ginder 1901
The facts: The defendant contracted to take all the electricity which he required from the claimants. They sued for an injunction to restrain him from obtaining electricity from another supplier.

Decision: The contract term (electricity only from the one supplier) implied a negative restriction (no supplies from any other source) and to that extent it could be enforced by injunction.

An injunction would not be made merely to restrain the defendant from acts inconsistent with his positive obligations.

Whitwood Chemical Co v Hardman 1891
The facts: The defendant agreed to give the whole of his time to his employers, the claimants. In fact he occasionally worked for others. The employers sued for an injunction to restrain him.

Decision: By his contract he merely stated what he would do. This did not imply an undertaking to abstain from doing other things .

8.2.1 Mareva or 'freezing' injunctions

The Mareva injunction is named from the case of *Mareva Compania Naviera SA v International Bulkcarriers SA 1975*, but it has now been given statutory effect by s 37 Supreme Court Act 1981. If the claimant can convince the court that he has a good case and that there is a danger of the defendant's assets being exported or dissipated, he may be awarded an injunction which restricts the defendant's dealing with the assets.

8.3 Rescission

Strictly speaking the equitable right to **rescind** an agreement is not a remedy for breach of contract – it is a right which exists in certain circumstances, such as where a contract is **voidable**.

Rescinding a contract means that it is cancelled or rejected and the parties are restored to their pre-contract condition. Four conditions must be met.

- It must be possible for each party to be returned to the pre-contract condition *(restitutio in integrum).*
- An innocent third party who has acquired rights in the subject matter of the contract will prevent the original transaction being rescinded.
- The right to rescission must be exercised within a reasonable time of it arising.
- Where a person affirms a contract expressly or by conduct it may not then be rescinded.

Exam focus point

> You may be asked for a general discussion of remedies for breach of contract. Alternatively, you may be asked whether a particular remedy, say specific performance, is appropriate in any given situation.

9 Limitation to actions for breach

The right to sue for breach of contract becomes statute-barred after six years from the date on which the cause of action accrued: s 5 Limitation Act 1980. The period is twelve years if the contract is by deed.

In three situations the six year period begins not at the date of the breach but later.

(a) If the **claimant is a minor or under some other contractual disability** (for example, of unsound mind) at the time of the breach of contract, the six year period begins to run only when his disability ceases or he dies.

(b) If the **defendant or his agent conceals the right of action by fraud** or if the action is for relief from the results of a mistake, the six year period begins to run only when the claimant discovered or could by reasonable diligence have discovered the fraud, concealment or mistake: s 32 Limitation Act 1980. An innocent third party who acquired property which is affected by these rules is protected against any action in respect of them: s 32(4).

(c) The normal period of six years can be extended where **information relevant** to the possible claims is **deliberately concealed after the period of six years has started to run**.

Where the claim can only be for specific performance or injunction, the Limitation Act 1980 does not apply. Instead, the claim may be limited by the equitable doctrine of delay or 'laches'.

Allcard v Skinner 1887
The facts: The claimant entered a Protestant convent in 1868 and, in compliance with a vow of poverty, transferred property worth about £7,000 to the Order by 1878. In 1879 she left the order and became a Roman Catholic. Six years later she demanded the return of the balance of her gift, claiming undue influence by the defendant, the Lady Superior of the Protestant sisterhood.

Decision: This was a case of undue influence for which a right of rescission may be available, since the rule of the Order forbade its members from seeking the advice of outsiders. But the claimant's delay in making her claim debarred her from recovering her property.

9.1 Extension of the limitation period

The limitation period may be extended if the debt, or any other certain monetary amount, is either acknowledged or paid in part before the original six (or twelve) years has expired: s 29. Hence if a debt accrues on 1.1.04, the original limitation period expires on 31.12.09. But if part-payment is received on 1.1.08, the debt is reinstated and does not then become 'statute-barred' until 31.12.13.

(a) The claim must be acknowledged as existing, not just as possible, but it need not be quantified. It must be in writing, signed by the debtor and addressed to the creditor: s 30.

(b) To be effective, the part payment must be identifiable with the particular debt, not just a payment on a running account.

Chapter roundup

- A contract is usually discharged by performance. There are a number of exceptions to the principle that the performance must be complete and exact, in order to ensure that the interests of both parties are protected.
- Breach of a condition in a contract or other repudiatory breach allows the injured party to terminate the contract unless the injured party elects to treat the contract as continuing and merely claim damages for his loss.
- If there is **anticipatory breach** (one party declares in advance that he will not perform his side of the bargain when the time for performance arrives) the other party may treat the contract as discharged forthwith, or continue with his obligations until actual breach occurs. His claim for damages will then depend upon what he has actually lost.
- **Damages** are a common law remedy intended to restore the party who has suffered loss to the position he would have been in had the contract been performed. The two tests applied to a claim for damages relate to **remoteness of damage** and **measure of damages**.
- Remoteness of damage is tested by the **two limbs** of the rule in **Hadley v Baxendale 1854**.
  - The first part of the rule states that the **loss must arise either naturally**, according to the usual course of things, from the breach or in a manner which the parties may reasonably be supposed to have contemplated, in making the contract, as a probate result of its breach.
  - The second part of the rule provides that a **loss outside the usual course of events** will only be compensated if the exceptional circumstances which caused it were within the defendant's **actual or constructive knowledge** when he made the contract.
- The **measure of damages** is that which will **compensate for the loss incurred**. It is not intended that the injured party should profit from a claim. Damages may be awarded for financial and non-financial loss.
- A simple **action for the price** to recover the agreed sum should be brought if breach of contract is failure to pay the price. But property must have passed from seller to buyer, and complications arise where there is anticipatory breach.
- A **quantum meruit** is a claim which is available as an alternative to damages. The injured party in a breach of a contract may claim the value of his work. The aim of such an award is to restore the claimant to the position he would have been in had the contract never been made. It is a **restitutory** award.
- An order for **specific performance** is an equitable remedy. The party in breach is ordered to perform his side of the contract. Such an order is only made where damages are inadequate compensation, such as in a sale of land, and where actual consideration has passed.
- A contract of personal performance or one which extends over a period of time are not usually subject to a decree of specific performance.
- An **injunction** is an equitable remedy which requires that a negative condition in the agreement be fulfilled.

Quick quiz

1 **Fill in the blanks** in the statements below, using the words in the box.

- (1) .... are a (2) .... remedy designed to restore the injured party to the position he would have been in had the contract been (3) ....
- A loss outside the natural course of events will only be compensated if the (4) .... circumstances are within the (5) ....'s knowledge at the time of making the contract.
- In assessing the amount of damage it is assumed that the (6) .... will (7) .... his loss.
- A contractual term designed as a (8) .... is (9) ....

• mitigate	• performed	• claimant
• penalty clause	• exceptional	• damages
• common law	• void	• defendant

2 Damages are a common law remedy

True ☐

False ☐

3 **Fill in the blanks** in the statements below.

- Performance must as a rule be (1) .... and (2) ....
- When anticipatory breach occurs, the injured party has two options. These are

  (3) ....

  (4) ....

4 What is the two-limbed rule set out in *Hadley v Baxendale*?

5 The amount awarded as damages is what is needed to put the claimant in the position he would have achieved if the contract had been performed. What interest is being protected here?

expectation
reliance

6 A court will never enforce a liquidated damages clause, as any attempt to discourage breach is void.

True ☐

False ☐

7 Are each of the following remedies based on (i) equity or (ii) common law?

(a) Quantum meruit
(b) Injunction
(c) Action for the price
(d) Rescission
(e) Specific performance

8 What are the two limitations on the creditor's right to bring an action for the price?

9 What four conditions must be met for rescission to be possible?

10 The case of *Allcard v Skinner* illustrates the doctrine of

promissory estoppel	frustration
delay or 'laches'	mitigation of loss

Answers to quick quiz

1 (1) damages (2) common law (3) performed
(4) exceptional (5) defendant (6) claimant
(7) mitigate (8) penalty clause (9) void

2 True

3 (1) complete (2) exact
(3) treat the contract as discharged forthwith
(4) allow the contract to continue until there is an actual breach

4 (i) The loss must arise naturally from the breach

(ii) The loss must arise in a manner which the parties may reasonably be supposed to have contemplated, in making the contract, as the probable result of the breach of it.

5 Expectation

6 False

7 (a) Common law
(b) Equity
(c) Common law
(d) Equity
(e) Equity

8 (i) An action for the price under a contract for the sale of goods may only be brought if property has passed (or price is payable on a specified date).

(ii) Sums which become due after an anticipatory breach may not be recovered unless the creditor has affirmed the contract.

9 (a) It must be possible for each party to be returned to the pre-contract condition *(restitutio in integrum).*

(b) An innocent third party who has acquired rights in the subject matter of the contract will prevent the original transaction being rescinded.

(c) The right to rescission must be exercised within a reasonable time of it arising.

(d) Where a person affirms a contract expressly or by conduct it may not then be rescinded.

10 Delay or 'laches'

Now try the questions below from the Exam Question Bank

Number	Level	Marks	Time
Q9	Examination	10	18 mins
Q10	Examination	20	36 mins

Part C
Agency and business associations

Agency

Topic list	Syllabus reference
1 Agents	3(a)
2 Creation of agency	3(a)
3 Duties and rights of an agent	3(b)
4 Authority of the agent	3(c)
5 Disclosed and undisclosed agency	3(c)
6 Relations between agent and third parties	3(c)
7 Termination of agency	3(c)

Introduction

Additional legal rules apply to certain specific types of contract. Agency has important business applications, particularly for those acting on behalf of companies or partnerships which are introduced in Chapter 10. In this chapter we examine how the agency relationship arises and how the agent's authority is acquired and defined.

'Agents' are employed by 'principals' to perform tasks which the principals cannot or do not wish to perform themselves, typically because the principal does not have the time or expertise to carry out the task.

If businessmen did not employ the services of factors, brokers, estate agents, *del credere* agents, bankers and auctioneers, they would be weighed down by the need to make contracts with or dispose of property to third parties and would probably achieve very little else.

In normal circumstances the agent discloses to the other party that he (the agent) is acting for a principal whose identity is also disclosed. However, this is not necessarily the case. If a person enters into a contract apparently on his own account as principal but in fact as agent on behalf of a principal, the doctrine of the undisclosed principal determines the position of the parties.

We also consider the legal position, rights and duties of the third party with whom the agent has contracted. Finally, we examine termination of agency.

Partnership is the key example of agency in this syllabus and it seems likely that questions on the two areas could be linked.

1 Agents

FAST FORWARD

Agency is a very important feature of modern commercial life. The basic principles of agency are seen in action in partnerships and they govern the way company directors and promoters behave.

Key term

Agency is a relationship which exists between two legal persons (the principal and the agent) in which the function of the agent is to form a contract between his principal and a third party.

1.1 Types of agent

FAST FORWARD

There are a number of specific types of agent. These have either evolved in particular trades or developed in response to specific commercial needs. Among the more frequently encountered types of agent are factors, brokers, estate agents, del credere agents, bankers and auctioneers.

In practice, there are many examples of agency relationships which you are probably accustomed to, although you may be aware that they are examples of the laws of agency. Some examples are listed below.

1.1.1 Partners

The **most important example** in your syllabus is that of the partnership. Partnerships will be discussed in more detail in Chapter 10. A **key feature** of partnerships is that the partners are agents of each other.

1.1.2 Promoters

Promoters will be discussed in Chapter 11. Promoters act on behalf **of an unincorporated company** (that is, one which has not yet been formed).

1.1.3 Factors

A factor (also called a 'mercantile agent') is a person whose ordinary business is to sell goods, or consign them for sale, or to buy goods, or to raise money on the security of goods: Factors Act 1889. His principal gives him implied authority to enter into such transactions and usually gives him possession of the goods.

Illustration

A motor dealer to whom the owner of a vehicle delivers the vehicle (and registration details) with authority to sell it.

1.1.4 Brokers

There are many kinds of broker in different trades. Any broker is essentially a middleman or intermediary who arranges contracts in return for commission or brokerage.

An **insurance broker** is an agent of an insurer who arranges contracts of insurance with the other party who wishes to be insured. However, in some contexts (for example, when the broker assists a car owner to complete a proposal form) he is also treated as the agent of the insured. Insurance, especially marine insurance, has complicated rules applicable to the relationship (insurer-broker-insured).

1.1.5 Estate agents

An estate agent is an intermediary who seeks to find a buyer of a house or other property belonging to his principal. This profession is regulated by the Estate Agents Act 1979 which among other things requires an estate agent to give notice of his charges to his principal and to insure against liability for loss of any deposit paid by a buyer to the agent as stakeholder etc pending completion of the sale.

1.1.6 *Del credere* agents

A *del credere* agent undertakes (in return for extra commission) responsibility for due payment of the contract price by persons whom he introduces to his principal. He undertakes that a buyer will pay for goods delivered to him but not that he will accept the goods. It is a form of financial support which is convenient where the other party and his creditworthiness is unknown to the principal.

1.1.7 Bankers

The duties owed by a bank to its customer are similar to those owed by an agent, but the **banker-customer contract** is **not** one of **agency** in the normal run of things, such as in the operation of a current account.

Banks **often do act as agents** for their customers: examples are where they undertake to arrange the buying and selling of shares or where they offer advice on other investments, such as life assurance and pensions.

1.1.8 Auctioneers

An auctioneer is an agent who is authorised to sell property at auction, usually in a room or place to which the public has access. He is the agent of the vendor. But when the sale has been completed he is also the agent of the buyer for the purpose of making a written record of the sale. This serves to provide the written evidence (against both parties) which is required to make enforceable a contract for the sale of land (although obviously auctioneers are involved in many other sales than just those of land).

1.1.9 Commercial agents

A commercial agent is an independent agent who has a continuing authority in connection with the sale or purchase of goods.

- An independent agent is not a partner, director or employee. He or she is self-employed.
- A continuing authority means that one-off transactions, such as a one-off sale at auction or a one-off sale by an estate agent, are excluded.
- An individual or a company can be a commercial agent.
- The business of the principal must be the sale or purchase of goods.

The relationship between a principal and a commercial agent is governed by the Commercial Agents (Council Directive) Regulations 1993.

2 Creation of agency 12/03

The relationship of principal and agent is usually created by mutual consent. The consent (with one exception, discussed below) need not be formal nor expressed in a written document. **It is usually an 'express' agreement**, even if it is created in an informal manner.

Illustration

Peter may ask Alan to take Peter's shoes to be repaired. Peter and Alan thereby expressly agree that Alan is to be Peter's agent in making a contract between Peter and Thomas, the shoe repairer.

Agency may be created in a number of different ways.

- Consent
- Operation of law
- Estoppel

The agent does not form contracts with third parties on his own behalf, and so it is not necessary that he has full contractual capacity. The principal must have full contractual capacity.

2.1 Agency by consent

Consent may be express or implied. When an agent is authorised by his principal to carry out a certain task or act in a certain capacity, he is said to have **actual authority.**

2.1.1 Express agency

Usually an agent is **expressly appointed** by the principal to undertake certain transactions. Very often the appointment is oral, but the informality of the appointment does not make any difference to the fact that agency is created.

In **commercial transactions** it is usual to appoint an agent **in writing**, so that the terms and extent of the relationship are set down to avoid misunderstanding. As noted above, this is not essential.

In many cases nowadays an agency agreement will be based on a **contract** between principal and agent. This will of course entail the presence of the essential elements of contract, discussed in Chapter 4, 5 and 6.

If there is no contract, for example where a person instructs an **estate agent** to sell his domestic residence for him, the estate agent is not under any **obligation** to find a buyer. If he does so, he will be entitled to remuneration, but this is not contractual consideration, rather a normal feature of the law of agency.

2.1.2 Implied agency

Two persons may by their relationship or their conduct to each other **imply** an agreement between them that one is the agent of the other.

Illustration

An employee's duties include making contracts for his employer, say by ordering goods on his account, the employee is, by implied agreement, the agent of the employer for this purpose. An agent authorised in this way is said to have implied authority.

This implied authority may fall into one of three categories.

(a) It may be **incidental** authority, which is the implied authority do whatever is necessarily or normally incidental to the agent's activities.

(b) It may be **customary** authority. Customary authority relates to the authority of agents operating in a particular market or business, such that they have the authority which an agent operating in that market or business usually has.

(c) It may be **usual** authority. This is similar to customary authority, and confers upon an agent who occupies a particular position or engages in a particular trade the authority to act in a manner usual to persons in that position or trade.

These will be examined in more detail in the section on authority of the agent below.

2.2 Agency by operation of law

The most important instance in which agency can arise by operation of law is the case of **agency of necessity**.

> 'Agency of necessity arises by operation of law in certain cases where a person is faced with an emergency in which the property or interests of another person are in imminent jeopardy and it becomes necessary, in order to preserve the property or interests, to act for that person without his authority'. *(Bowstead on Agency)*

The principle of agency of necessity is of restricted application. Its origins can be found in mercantile law, and in shipping law in particular.

A number of conditions must be satisfied for agency of necessity to arise.

(a) The agent must have **no practical way of contacting** the principal to obtain the principal's instructions.

Springer v Great Western Railway 1921
The facts: A carrier discovered that a consignment of fruit was going bad. He sold it locally instead of delivering it to its destination.

Decision: He was not an agent of necessity as he could have obtained instructions from the owner of the fruit.

(b) The actions of the agent must be as a result of some **pressing need for action**, usually an emergency of some kind, involving for example perishable goods or starving animals.

Prager v Blatspeil, Stamp and Heacock Ltd 1924
The facts: An agent bought skins on behalf of his principal, but could not send them to the principal because of the prevailing wartime conditions. Being unable to communicate with the principal, he sold the skins.

Decision: He was not an agent of necessity, as he could have stored the skins until after the war.

(c) The agent must have acted **bona fide** (in good faith). This means that he must act in the interests of the principal rather than in his own interests.

Sachs v Miklos 1948
The facts: M agreed to store furniture which belonged to S. After a considerable time had elapsed M needed the storage space for his own use. He tried to contact S to get the furniture removed but was unable to trace S. M then sold the furniture. S sued M for conversion and M pleaded agency of necessity in making the sale.

Decision: There was no agency of necessity since no emergency had arisen and M had sold the furniture for his own convenience. If M's house had been destroyed by fire and the furniture left in the open M would then have been justified in selling it.

(d) The **action** taken by the agent must have been **reasonable and prudent in the circumstances.**

Great Northern Railway v Swaffield 1874

The facts: S delivered a horse to a railway for transport to another station but failed to collect it on arrival as agreed. The railway claimed from S the cost of feeding and stabling the horse arguing that if it had delivered the horse to a stable that would have been a contract made under agency of necessity and S would be bound to pay.

Decision: The railway claim would be upheld for the reasons given.

It should be noted that cases of necessity have invariably involved carriers and circumstances where **modern day telecommunications may prevent an agent of necessity arising** very often.

2.3 Agency by estoppel

Agency by estoppel arises when the words or conduct of the principal **give to a third party** the **impression** that the agent's authority is greater than it really is and the third party, as a result, acts upon this. This introduces the concept of ostensible, or **apparent, authority**.

Illustration

If Paul leads Tina to believe that Adam is Paul's agent, and Tina deals with Adam on that basis, Paul is bound by the contract with Tina which Adam has made on his behalf. This situation may arise in the following circumstances.

- When Adam, who dealt with Tina as Paul's authorised agent, continues to do so after his authority as agent of Paul has been terminated but Tina is unaware of it
- When Adam, to Paul's knowledge, enters into transactions with Tina as if Adam were Paul's agent and Paul fails to inform Tina that Adam is not Paul's agent
- When Adam, who dealt with Tina as Paul's authorised agent, acts beyond the scope of the authority actually conferred upon him by Paul but Tina is unaware of it.

Agency by estoppel can only arise where the **conduct** of the **apparent principal** creates it. Agency does not arise by estoppel if it is the 'agent' who holds himself out as agent, not the 'principal': *Armagas Ltd v Mundogas SA, The Ocean Frost 1986*

2.4 Ratification

In certain circumstances the relationship of principal and agent can be created or extended with **retrospective effect**. If A makes a contract on behalf of P at a time when A has no authority from P, the contract may later be ratified by P and then has retrospective effect to the time when A made the contract.

Ratification only validates past acts of the purported agent. It gives no authority for the future: *Irvine v Union Bank of Australia 1877.*

2.4.1 Method of ratification

Ratification may be express or implied. Express ratification is usually fairly clear-cut. Implied ratification must be deduced from the conduct of the 'principal' and from the circumstances of the case. In particular, the principal **may only ratify if the following conditions are satisfied.**

- He does so within a **reasonable time** after the agent has made the contract for him.
- He ratifies the **whole contract** and not merely parts of it. Otherwise the effect would be that a new contract would exist which the third party had not intended to enter into.
- He **communicates a sufficiently clear intention of ratifying**, either by express words or by conduct such as refusing to return goods purchased for him by an agent who lacked authority (mere passive inactivity does not amount to ratification).
- He is either **fully informed** of the terms of the contract **or** is **prepared to ratify whatever** the agent may have **agreed** to on his behalf.

2.4.2 Who may ratify?

Only a principal may ratify the acts of the purported agent. There are **four conditions** of ratification.

2.4.3 Existence of principal

The **principal must have been in existence** at the time of the agent's act.

2.4.4 Legal capacity of the principal

In order to be able to ratify a contract, a **principal must have the legal capacity** to make the contract himself, both at the time the act was carried out and at the time of the purported ratification.

> *Boston Deep Sea Fishing and Ice Co Ltd v Farnham 1957*
> *The facts:* The appellants, a company of trawler owners, took control of a French trawler lying in an English port when France fell to the German army. The French company purported to ratify their acts.
>
> *Decision:* Since, at the time the acts were done, the French company was an alien enemy at common law, it could not have carried out the acts itself. It did not therefore have legal capacity and could not ratify.

2.4.5 Principal capable of being ascertained

An **unnamed** principal should be **capable of being ascertained**, or identified, at the time that the unauthorised actions occurred.

2.4.6 Agent acting on behalf of principal

If the agent has not revealed that he was acting as an agent, in other words that there is an **undisclosed** principal, then the **undisclosed principal will not be able to ratify**.

2.4.7 The effects of ratification

Ratification, as we have seen, has retrospective effect. Once ratification has taken place, the following situation arises.

- The principal may sue or be sued by the third party
- The agent no longer has any liability to the third party
- The agent is no longer liable for exceeding his authority
- The principal is liable to pay the agent reasonable remuneration

The principle of **ratification** does pose one particular **problem** illustrated by the following example.

Illustration

Anna purports to act as Pat's agent. Tim offers to buy goods from Anna, who accepts this offer. The question may arise as to whether or not Tim can revoke his offer before Pat ratifies the acceptance. Under the law of contract, an offer may be revoked at any time up to acceptance. However, once Pat ratifies her agent's actions, the ratification has retrospective effect. Pat is of course free to decide whether or not to ratify.

The above situation may appear strange: the third party is bound as soon as the agent acts, while the principal is not bound unless and until he ratifies.

This rule appears somewhat **unjust to the third party**, and certain **limitations** have been developed. Three are given below.

- Ratification must take place within a **reasonable time** so as to minimise uncertainty.
- The third party's offer may be made **expressly subject to ratification**.
- If the third party commits a **breach of contract** after the agent's acceptance but **before ratification**, he will **not be liable to the principal**.

3 Duties and rights of an agent

When an agent agrees to perform services for his principal for reward there is a contract between them. But even if the agent undertakes his duties without reward he has obligations to his principal. The agent's duties are listed below.

The courts have always sought to ensure that a person does not abuse the confidence of another for whom he is acting.

> 'The position of principal and agent gives rise to particular and onerous duties on the part of the agent, and the high standard of conduct required from him springs from the fiduciary relationship between his employer and himself. His position is confidential, it readily lends itself to abuse. A strict and salutary rule is required to meet the special situation. ' *Armstrong v Jackson 1917*

3.1 Duties

3.1.1 Performance

The agent who agrees to act as agent for reward has a contractual obligation to perform his agreed task. An unpaid agent is not bound to carry out his agreed duties (there is no consideration). Any agent may refuse to perform an illegal act.

3.1.2 Obedience

The agent must act strictly in accordance with his principal's instructions insofar as these are lawful and reasonable. Even if he believes disobedience to be in his principal's best interests, he may not disobey instructions. Only if he is asked to commit an illegal act may he do so.

3.1.3 Skill

A paid agent undertakes to maintain the standard of skill and care to be expected of a person in his profession.

An accountant has a duty to his client to show the skill and care of a competent accountant. An unpaid agent if he acts as agent (which he need not do) must show the skill and care which people ordinarily use in managing their own affairs.

3.1.4 Personal performance

The agent is presumably selected because of his personal qualities and owes a duty to perform his task himself and not to delegate it to another. But he may delegate in a few special circumstances, if delegation is necessary, such as a solicitor acting for a client would be obliged to instruct a stockbroker to buy or sell listed securities on the Stock Exchange.

3.1.5 Accountability

An agent must both provide full information to his principal of his agency transactions and account to him for all moneys arising from them.

3.1.6 No conflict of interest

The agent owes to his principal a duty not to put himself in a situation where his own interests conflict with those of the principal; for example, he must not sell his own property to the principal (even if the sale is at a fair price).

3.1.7 Confidence

The agent must keep in confidence what he knows of his principal's affairs even after the agency relationship has ceased.

3.1.8 Any benefit

Any benefit must be handed over to the principal unless he agrees that the agent may retain it. Although an agent is entitled to his agreed remuneration, he must account to the principal for any other benefits. If he accepts from the other party any commission or reward as an inducement to make the contract with him, it is considered to be a bribe and the contract is fraudulent.

> *Boston Deep Sea Fishing & Ice Co v Ansell 1888*
> *The facts:* A, who was managing director of the claimant company, accepted commissions from suppliers on orders which he placed with them for goods supplied to the company. He was dismissed and the company sued to recover from him the commissions.
>
> *Decision:* The company was justified in dismissing A and he must account to it for the commissions.

The principal who discovers that his agent has accepted a bribe may do the following.

- **Dismiss** the agent
- **Recover the amount** of the bribe from him (as in *Ansell's* case)
- **Refuse to pay him** his agreed remuneration, and recover amounts already paid
- **Repudiate the contract** with the third party
- **Sue** both the agent and the third party who paid the bribe to recover damages for any loss. He may not recover any more than this – so he may not, for instance, recover the bribe from the agent and compensation from the third party so as to make a profit
- **Seek prosecution** of the agent under the Prevention of Corruption Act 1916.

3.2 Rights of the agent

3.2.1 Indemnity

The agent is entitled to be repaid his expenses and to be indemnified by his principal against losses and liabilities. These rights are limited to acts of the agent done properly within the limits of his authority.

If he acts in an unauthorised manner or negligently he loses his entitlement. He may recover expenses properly paid even if he was not legally bound to pay, for example, a solicitor who pays counsel's fees (which the counsel cannot recover at law) may reclaim this expense from his client.

3.2.2 Remuneration

The agent is also entitled to be paid any agreed remuneration for his services by his principal. The amount may have been expressly agreed or be implied, for example by trade or professional practice. If it is agreed that the agent is to be remunerated but the amount has not been fixed, the agent is entitled to a reasonable amount.

Question — **Duties of a principal**

There is a degree of overlap between the *rights* of an agent and the *duties* of a principal. What do you think are the duties of a principal?

Answer

(a) Provided the agent has performed the acts he was employed to do, and has abided by his duties, the principal has a duty to pay him his agreed remuneration, even if he has derived no benefit from his acts.

(b) The principal has a duty not to prevent his agent from performing the acts for which he is to receive remuneration.

(c) If the principal agrees to pay the agent only on the occurrence of a certain event which the agent is to bring about, and then the event happens without the agent's intervention, the principal does not have to pay: *Miller, Son & Co v Radford 1903*.

(d) The principal has a duty to indemnify his agent for expenses legitimately incurred.

4 Authority of the agent — 12/01

FAST FORWARD An agent's authority may be express, implied or ostensible.

The **contract** made by the agent is **binding** on the principal and the other party **only if** the **agent was acting within the limits of his authority** from his principal. In analysing the limits of an agent's authority, three distinct sources of authority can be identified:

- Express authority
- Implied authority
- Ostensible authority

4.1 Express authority

Express authority is a matter between principal and agent. This is authority explicitly given by the principal to the agent to make a particular contract.

The extent of the agent's express authority will depend on the construction of the words used on his appointment. If the appointment is in writing, then the document will need to be examined. If it is oral, then the scope of the agent's authority will be a matter of evidence.

If the agent contracts outside the scope of his express (actual) authority, he may be liable to the principal and the third party for breach of warranty of authority.

4.2 Implied authority

Where there is no express authority, authority may be **implied** from the nature of the agent's activities or from what is usual in the circumstances.

Implied authority falls into one of three categories.

- Implied incidental authority
- Implied customary authority
- Implied usual authority

Exam focus point

> These may be considered to be rather 'fine' legal distinctions. It is important primarily that you can write about express, implied and ostensible authority. Move on to these subdivisions of implied authority only when you are confident on the basics.

The basis of **implied incidental authority** is that the principal, by appointing an agent to act in a particular capacity, gives him authority to make those contracts which are a necessary or normal incident of the agent's activities.

Commonly, incidental authority applies to subordinate acts necessary for the execution of express actual authority. It supplements the express authority, and may cover such things as the authority to advertise when given express authority to sell goods.

Implied customary authority is that which an agent operating in a particular market or business usually has.

Implied usual authority is that which an agent who occupies a particular position or engages in a particular trade usually has.

Between principal and agent the latter's express authority is paramount; the agent cannot contravene the principal's express instructions by claiming that he had implied authority for acting in the way he did.

But as far as **third parties** are concerned, they are entitled to assume that the agent has implied usual authority unless they know to the contrary.

> *Watteau v Fenwick 1893*
> *The facts:* The owner of a hotel (F) employed the previous owner H to manage it. F forbade H to buy cigars on credit but H did buy cigars from W. W sued F who argued that he was not bound by the contract, since H had no actual authority to make it, and that W believed that H still owned the hotel.
>
> *Decision:* It was within the usual authority of a manager of a hotel to buy cigars on credit and F was bound by the contract (although W did not even know that H was the agent of F) since his restriction of usual authority had not been communicated.

4.3 Actual authority

Express and implied authority are sometimes referred to together as **actual authority**. This distinguishes them from **ostensible** or **apparent authority** , which is discussed next in this section.

Key term

> Actual authority is a legal relationship between principal and agent created by a consensual agreement to which they alone are parties.

4.4 Ostensible authority

The ostensible (or apparent) authority of an agent is that which his principal represents to other persons (with whom the agent deals) that he has given to the agent. As a result an agent with limited **express** or **implied** authority can be held in practice to have a more extensive authority.

Illustration

A principal employs a stockbroker to sell shares. It is an implied term of the arrangement between them that the broker shall (unless otherwise agreed) have **actual authority** to do what is usual in practice for a broker selling shares for a client (but no more than that). Any person who deals with the broker is on his side entitled to assume (unless informed to the contrary) that the broker has, as his actual or apparent authority, the usual authority of a broker by his client. Thus far the two forms of authority are co-extensive.

Ostensible authority (unlike implied authority) is not however restricted to what is usual and incidental. The principal may expressly or by inference from his conduct confer on the agent any amount of ostensible or apparent authority.

Illustration

A partner has considerable but limited implied authority merely by virtue of being a partner. If, however, the other partners allow him to exercise a greater authority than is implied, they represent that he has it and they are bound by the contracts which he makes within the limits of this ostensible authority.

It is not necessary that the agreement is in the form of a contract.

> *Freeman & Lockyer v Buckhurst Park Properties (Mangal) Ltd 1964*
> *The facts:* K and H carried on business as property developers through a company which they owned in equal shares. Each appointed another director, making four in all, but H lived abroad and the business of the company was left entirely under the control of K. As a director K had no actual or apparent authority to enter into contracts as agent of the company but he did make contracts as if he were a managing director without authority to do so. The other directors were aware of these activities but had not authorised them. The claimants sued the company for work done on K's instructions.
>
> *Decision:* There had been a representation by the company through its board of directors that K was the authorised agent of the company. The board had authority to make such contracts and also had power to delegate authority to K by appointing him to be Managing Director. Although there had been no actual delegation to K, the company had by its mere acquiescence led the claimants to believe that A was an authorised agent and the claimants had relied on it. The company was bound

by the contract made by K under the principle of 'holding out' (or estoppel). The company was estopped from denying (that is, not permitted to deny) that K was its agent although K had no actual authority from the company.

It can be seen that it is the conduct of the 'principal' which creates ostensible authority. It does not matter whether there is a pre-existing agency relationship or not.

Exam focus point

This is important – ostensible authority arises in two distinct ways. It may arise where a person makes a representation to third parties that a particular person has the authority to act as their agent without actually appointing them as their agent. Alternatively, it may arise where a principal has previously represented to a third party that an agent has authority to act on his or her behalf.

4.4.1 Representation

The **representation must be made by the principal or an agent acting on his behalf.** It cannot be made by the agent who is claiming apparent authority: *Armagas Ltd v Mundogas SA, The Ocean Frost 1986.*

It must be a **representation of fact, not one of law**. For example, if a third party is shown a power of attorney and misunderstands its effect, he will be unable to recover from the principal. This is because the content and interpretation of such a document is a matter of law.

The representation must be **made to the third party**. This also distinguishes ostensible authority from actual authority, where the third party need know nothing of the agent's authority.

4.4.2 Reliance

It must be shown that the **third party relied on the representation**. If there is no causal link between the third party's loss and the representation, the third party will not be able to hold the principal as liable.

Illustration

If the third party did not believe that the agent had authority or positively knows the contrary, even if the agent appeared to have it, then apparent authority cannot be claimed.

4.4.3 Alteration of position

It is enough that the third party alters his position as a result of reliance on the representation. He does not have to suffer any detriment as a result, but damages would in such an event be minimal.

Where a principal has represented to a third party that an agent has authority to act, and has subsequently revoked the agent's authority, this may be insufficient to escape liability. The principal should inform third parties who have previously dealt with the agent of the change in circumstances: *Willis Faber & Co Ltd v Joyce 1911*. This is particularly relevant to partnerships and the position when a partner leaves a partnership.

Question — **Ostensible authority**

Categories of ostensible authority were discussed earlier in this chapter. Give three examples of occasions when ostensible authority may arise.

Answer

- Where a person allows another, who is not his agent, to appear as if he is.
- Where a principal allows his agent to give the impression that he has more extensive authority than is really the case.
- Where, following termination of the agency relationship, a principal allows his former agent to continue to appear as his agent.

5 Disclosed and undisclosed agency

FAST FORWARD

In normal circumstances the agent discloses to the third party that he is acting for a principal whose identity is also disclosed. The contract is between the principal and the third party. This is disclosed agency.

5.1 Disclosed

In normal circumstances the agent discloses to the other party that he (the agent) is acting for a principal whose identity is also disclosed. The contract, when made, is between the principal and the other party.

The agent has no liability under the contract and no right to enforce it. An agent may, however, be liable under the contract in some cases.

- If the agent **executes a deed** in his own name he should sign 'J Smith by his attorney H Jones' (Smith being the principal).
- If the agent signs a **negotiable instrument** without indicating that he does so in a representative character on behalf of a principal he may be liable. For instance, if a director signs a company cheque 'H Black, Director XYZ Ltd' he merely describes his position as director. To avoid liability, he should sign 'for and on behalf of XYZ Ltd'. The same rules may apply to other written contracts signed by an agent.
- Where by **trade custom** the agent is liable, for example, advertising agents are liable to the media for contracts made on behalf of their clients.
- Where the **principal is fictitious or non-existent**, the agent contracts for himself and so is liable as the true principal.

If, in making the contract, the agent discloses that he acts for an **unnamed principal** the position is also as described above. (You should note that an unnamed principal is a disclosed principal.)

5.2 Undisclosed

FAST FORWARD

If a person enters into a contract apparently on his own account as principal but he is in fact acting as agent on behalf of a principal, the doctrine of the **undisclosed principal** determines the position of the parties.

The doctrine of the undisclosed principal states that, provided that the agent acts within the scope of his authority, it is possible to put forward evidence which shows that the undisclosed principal is a party to the transactions. As a result he may sue or be sued on the contract made between agent and third party.

The undisclosed principal will usually intervene and enforce the contract on his own behalf against the other party since it is really his contract, not the agent's. Until such time as the principal takes this action, the agent himself may sue the third party (since he is treated as the other party to the contract).

The undisclosed principal's right to intervene in a contract made by his agent is limited to those contracts which the agent was authorised to make as agent – he cannot ratify an unauthorised act or seek to take over the agent's contract without the third party's consent.

The **undisclosed principal** is also **prevented** from **taking over a contract** in the following circumstances.

(a) Where the contract terms are such that **agency is implicitly denied**.

Humble v Hunter 1848
The facts: The principal (P) authorised his agent (A) to charter out his ship. A contracted with a third party for the charter of the vessel, describing himself as 'owner' of it.

Decision: The principal could not enforce the contract against the third party because the agent had implied that he was the owner and hence the principal. P's ownership contradicted the contract's terms.

(b) Where the contract terms are such that **agency is expressly denied**.

United Kingdom Mutual SS Assurance Association v Nevill 1887
The facts: The managing part-owner of a vessel became a member of the claimant mutual association and insured a ship under the rules of the association, which prescribed that only members were liable to pay premiums. The part-owner became bankrupt and the defendant, a part-owner, was approached for contributions.

Decision: As the defendant was not a member, he could not intervene as an undisclosed principal.

(c) Where the agent, when making the contract, **expressly denied that a principal was involved**.

(d) Where the **identity of the parties is material to the third party** – that is, where the third party wanted to contract with the agent and would not have contracted at all if he had known of the identity of the principal.

Said v Butt 1920
The facts: The claimant, a theatre critic, had a disagreement with the defendant, who was manager of a particular theatre and who had banned him from attending there. He wanted to see the first night of a new play, 'The Whirligig', at the theatre and so asked Pollock, whom the manager did not know to be connected with him, to obtain a ticket for him. The claimant was refused admission on the ticket and sued for breach of contract.

Decision: Said's identity was of great importance to the theatre and it would not have contracted with Pollock if it had known that the claimant was his undisclosed principal. The claimant could not enforce the ticket.

5.2.1 The legal effects of undisclosed agency

If the contract is not performed as agreed the third party may, on discovering the true facts:

- Hold the agent personally bound by the contract (as the agent appeared to be contracting on his own account)
- Elect to treat the principal as the other party to the contract.

But he must elect for one or the other within a **reasonable time** of discovering the facts, and cannot sue both principal and agent.

The third party who commences legal proceedings against either agent or principal may withdraw (before judgment is given) in order to sue the other.

If, however, he obtains judgment on the breach of contract he cannot sue the other even if the judgment is unsatisfied.

Question — **Undisclosed agency**

Why is the distinction between disclosed agency and undisclosed agency important?

Answer

(a) The personal liability of the agent will vary depending on whether or not the principal was disclosed at the time the contract was made between agent and third party.

(b) The agent's power to bind his principal will vary in a similar way.

(c) Ratification is only effective if the agent discloses that he is acting on behalf of a principal.

6 Relations between agent and third parties

An agent contracting for his principal within his actual and/or apparent authority generally has no liability on the contract and is not entitled to enforce it. However, there are **circumstances** when the **agent will be personally liable** and can enforce it.

(a) When he intended to undertake personal liability – as where he signs a contract as party to it without signifying that he is an agent. In particular, he will be liable on a cheque which he signs without indicating his agency status: s 26 Bills of Exchange Act 1882.

(b) Where the **principal was undisclosed**

(c) Where it is usual business practice or trade custom for an agent to be liable and entitled. For example, an advertising agent is liable to the media for contracts made on its client's behalf.

(d) Where the agent is acting on his own behalf even though he purports to act for a principal (see *Kelner v Baxter 1866*, where the agents thought they were acting on behalf of a company principal which was not yet in existence)

(e) Where the agent contracts by deed without having a power of attorney from the principal

Where an agent enters into a collateral contract with the third party with whom he has contracted on the principal's behalf, there is separate liability and entitlement to enforcement on that collateral contract.

It can happen that there is **joint liability** of agent and principal. This is usually the case where an agent did not disclose that he acted for a principal.

6.1 Breach of warranty of authority

An agent who **exceeds his ostensible authority** will generally have **no liability to his principal**, since the latter will not be bound by the unauthorised contract made for him. But the agent **will be liable** in such a case **to the third party** for breach of warranty of authority.

Illustration

If A purports to enter into a contract with X on behalf of P, A warrants, or guarantees, to X that P exists and has capacity to enter into the contract, and that A has authority from P to make the contract for him. If any of these implied warranties proves to be untrue, then (unless P ratifies the contract) X may claim damages from A for his loss, provided that X was unaware that A had no authority to make the contract. A is liable even though he was himself unaware that he lacked authority, eg because P had died. In *Kelner v Baxter 1866* the promoters of a company were liable since they made a contract for a non-existent principal.

7 Termination of agency

FAST FORWARD

Agency is usually terminated by agreement.

Agency is primarily terminated when the **parties agree** that the relationship should end.

It may also be terminated by **operation of law** in the following situations:

- Principal or agent dies
- Principal or agent becomes insane
- Principal becomes bankrupt, or agent becomes bankrupt and this interferes with his position as agent

Termination brings the **actual authority** of the agent to an end. However, third parties are allowed to enforce contracts made later by the 'agent' until they are actively or constructively informed of the termination of the agency relationship.

Chapter roundup

- Agency can be defined as a relationship which exists between two legal persons, the principal and the agent, in which the function of the agent is to form a contract between his principal and a third party.
- There are a number of specific types of agent. These have either evolved in particular trades or developed in response to specific commercial needs. Among the more frequently encountered types of agent are factors, brokers, estate agents, del credere agents, bankers and auctioneers.
- The relationship between principal and agent is usually created by mutual consent.
- An agent's authority may be express, implied or ostensible.
- Consent to agency need not be formal, nor, with one exception, need it be contained in a written document. An agency relationship may also be created by operation of law or by estoppel.
- In certain circumstances the relationship of principal and agent can be created, or extended, with retrospective effect. This is the doctrine of ratification.
- Ostensible, or apparent, authority is that which a principal represents to third parties (with whom the agent deals) that he has given to the agent.
- In normal circumstances the agent discloses to the third party that he is acting for a principal whose identity is also disclosed. The contract is between the principal and the third party. This is disclosed agency.
- If a person enters into a contract apparently on his own account as principal but in fact as agent on behalf of a principal, the doctrine of the undisclosed principal applies: the undisclosed principal may intervene and enforce the contract on his own behalf. There are certain situations where the undisclosed principal is prevented from taking over a contract.
- The principal is usually liable to the third party for contracts formed by his agent within the latter's actual or apparent authority. There are certain circumstances, however, where the agent will be personally liable on the contract and can enforce it.
- Agency is usually terminated by agreement.

Quick quiz

1 **Fill in the gaps** using the words in the boxes below.

.... is the......................... which exists between two .... persons, the ....and the agent, in which the function of the agent is to form a .... between his .... and a ....

(1)	relationship	(4)	principal	(6)	principal
(2)	third party	(5)	legal	(7)	agency
(3)	contract				

2 Link the definition with the type of implied authority.

(a) Incidental authority

(b) Customary authority

(c) Usual authority

(i) The authority which an agent operating in a particular market usually has
(ii) The authority to act in a manner usual to person in a particular position or trade
(iii) The implied authority to do whatever is necessary to the agent's activities.

3 Which of the following is not a necessary condition of agency of necessity?

(a) Agent has not practical way of contacting principal
(b) A pressing need for action exists
(c) The agent must have the principal's permission
(d) The agent must act bona fide in the interests of the principal
(e) The action must be reasonable and prudent in the circumstances

4 A principal may, in certain circumstances, ratify the acts of the agent which has retrospective effect

True ☐

False ☐

5 What is the best definition of ostensible authority?

(a) The authority which the principal represents to other persons that he has given to the agent.
(b) The authority implied to other persons by the agent's actions.

6 An agent may disobey the instructions of the principal if he believes disobedience to be in the best interests of the principal.

True ☐

False ☐

7 Give three instances where an undisclosed principal is prevented from taking over a contract.

(1) ....

(2) ....

(3) ....

8 A principal is bound, even if the agent's acts were fraudulent.

True ☐

False ☐

Answers to quick quiz

1 7, 1, 5, 4 (6), 3, 6 (4), 2

2 (a)(iii), (b)(i), (c)(ii)

3 (c)

4 True

5 (a)

6 False

7 Any of:

(1) Where contract terms are such that agency is implicitly denied
(2) Where contract terms are such that agency is expressly denies
(3) Where the agent expressly denied the existence of a principal
(4) Where the identity of the parties is material to the third party

8 True

Now try the question below from the Exam Question Bank

Number	Level	Marks	Time
Q11	Examination	20	36 mins

10

Business associations

Topic list	Syllabus reference
1 Partnerships	3(d)(e)(f)
2 Limited liability partnerships	3(d)(e)
3 Companies	4(a)
4 Liability	4(c)
5 Veil of incorporation	4(c)
6 Distinction between partnerships and companies	4(a)

Introduction

In this chapter we introduce two of the three most common types of business association in the United Kingdom: **partnerships** and **companies.**

It is vital that you be able to **distinguish** between these types of business association and be able to give advice in an exam situation as to which would be the most **appropriate** for a prospective business person to use when setting up their business.

The **basic concepts** and the distinguishing features are therefore set out in this chapter, while later chapters go on to outline more legal details, particularly companies, which are the main focus of the next section of the syllabus.

The key difference between partnerships and companies is a consequence of **separate legal personality**. This chapter outlines this doctrine and also, when the 'veil of incorporation' will be lifted and the members and directors identified.

Separate legal personality is a fundamental concept of company law and one which you must grasp fully, before continuing through the syllabus.

This chapter links the topic areas of agency, partnership and companies. It is important to see the links between them.

Company law has been highlighted as a key topic area for the exam and it is important to grasp the fundamental aspect of company law – separate legal personality – to be able to answer any question arising on company law.

1 Partnerships

12/01

FAST FORWARD

Partnership is 'the relation which subsists between persons carrying on a business in common with a view of profit'.

A traditional partnership is **not** a separate legal person distinct from its members, it is **merely** a 'relationship' between persons.

While the provision of a partnership is informal in theory, there may be considerable formalities to agree between the partners in practice.

Partnership is a common form of business association. It is **flexible**, because it either be a **formal** or **informal** arrangement, so can be used for large organisations or a small husband and wife operation.

Partnership is normal practice in the professions as most professions prohibit their members from carrying on practice through limited companies. Note that some professions permit members to trade as 'limited liability partnerships' which share may characteristics with companies. Businessmen are not so restricted and generally prefer to trade through a limited company for the advantages this can bring.

1.1 Definition of unlimited partnership

A partnership exists whenever the facts satisfy the statutory definition (s 1 Partnership Act 1890), which is as follows.

Key term

'**Partnership** is the relation which subsists between persons carrying on a business in common with a view of profit.'

1.1.1 The relation which subsists between persons

'Person' includes a corporation such as a registered company as well as an individual living person.

There must be at least **two** partners. If, therefore, two men are in partnership, one dies and the survivor carries on the business he is a sole trader. There is no longer a partnership.

1.1.2 Carrying on a business

Business is defined to include 'every trade, occupation or profession': s 45. But three points should be noted.

(a) A business is a **form of activity**. If two or more persons are merely the passive joint owners of revenue-producing property, such as investments or rented houses, that fact of itself does not make them partners: s 2(1).

(b) A business can consist of a **single transaction**. These situations are often described as 'joint ventures'.

(c) Carrying on a business must have a **beginning and an end**. A partnership begins when the partners agree to conduct their **business activity** together and this can be before the business actually begins to trade. Thus in *Khan v Miah 2001* the parties to a proposed venture (running a restaurant) were partners even before the restaurant opened because, on the facts, they were clearly carrying on the business. Evidence of this was provided by the leasing of premises, hiring equipment and the opening of a bank account.

1.1.3 In common

Broadly this phrase means that the partners must be associated in the business as **joint proprietors**. The evidence that this is so is found in their taking a share of the profits, especially net profits.

1.1.4 A view of profit

If persons enter into a partnership with a view to making profits but they actually suffer losses, it is still a partnership. The test to be applied is one of **intention**. Where a person engages in a business with another as a common endeavour other then with a view to sharing profits (eg to gain business experience) there is no partnership *Davies v Newman (2000)*.

1.1.5 Consequences of definition

In most cases there is no doubt about the existence of a partnership. The partners declare their intention by such steps as signing a written partnership agreement and adopting a firm name. These outward and visible signs of the existence of a partnership are not essential – a partnership can exist without them.

1.2 Terminology

The word 'firm' is correctly used to denote a partnership. It is **not** correct to apply it to a registered company (though the newspapers often do so).

The word 'company' may form part of the name of a partnership form, for example, 'Smith and Company'. But 'limited company' or 'registered company' is **only** applied to a company incorporated under the Companies Act 1985.

1.3 Formation

A partnership can be a very informal arrangement. This is reflected in the procedure to form a partnership. A partnership is **formed when two or more people agree to run a business together**.

Illustration

A husband and wife who run a shop together are partners; a shop owner and his employee are not.

In law then, the formation of a partnership is essentially straightforward. People make an agreement together to run a business, and carry that agreement out.

Question — **Formation of partnership**

Imagine that two of the 'big four' firms of accountants wanted to merge. The partners agreed on 1 June 2005 that they would merge and become a new partnership, known as the Biggest Accountancy Partnership. In law, this is straightforward.

What problems do you think they might encounter?

Answer

As we have seen in law, when the partners agree to form a new partnership, then they have a new partnership.

In practice, however, if two massive businesses such as two big five firms decided to merge, the details of the formation of the new partnership would be far more complex than that. Here is a list of just some of the things that they would have to consider.

- Profit share
- Employees
- Recruitment policy
- Future partners' policy

- Partnership property
- Partner hierarchy
- Standard partners authority to act in the new firm's name
- Fair trading and monopoly issues

In practice, the formation of such a new partnership would be an enormous enterprise.

In practice, the formalities of setting up a partnership may be more **complex** than simple agreement. Many professional people use partnerships. These business associations can be vast organisations with substantial revenue and expenditure, such as the big four accountancy firms and many City law firms.

Such organisations have so many partners that the relationships between them has to be **regulated**. Thus forming some partnerships can involve creating **detailed partnership agreements** which lay out terms and conditions of partnership. Partnership agreements are discussed below, as part of the internal regulations of a partnership.

1.4 Internal regulation — Pilot paper, 6/03, 6/05

FAST FORWARD

The internal regulation of partnerships is governed by the Partnership Act 1890. This sets out the basic rights and duties of a partner.

The rights and duties may be expressly denied in a Partnership agreement. There is no compulsion to have a partnership agreement.

Partnerships are governed by the Partnership Act 1890. It sets out basic rights and duties of partners. These **rights and duties in most cases can be expressly overruled** in a partnership agreement. However, **in the absence of any express provision**, they are **assumed**. The key provisions of the Act are set out below.

1.4.1 Rights and duties

In summary, the key rights and duties of a partner are as follows.

Rights	Duties
To be involved in decision making which affects the business	
To share in the profits	To share in any losses
To examine the accounts	
To insist on openness and honesty from fellow partners	To show utmost good faith to fellow partners
To veto new partners	
	To indemnify fellow partners against bearing more than their share of losses of expenses of the partnership

The table above shows the key rights and duties of partners. Whilst partnership agreements might vary the details of such rights and duties, for example, that junior partners share in the profits to a lesser extent than senior partners, these basic rights are likely not to be varied in detailed partnership agreements.

Many of these rights and duties are set out in the Partnership Act but one, the duty of good faith, is not and its arises from general principles of equity. Examples of the scope of the duty of good faith are numerous. For example, it is a breach of this duty to exercise a legal right, eg to expel a partner for an improper motive. It is the principle that prohibits partners from keeping profits derived for the partnership without the consent of the other partners (now also contained in S29).

1.4.2 Further terms implied by Partnership Act 1890

The table below shows the requirements of the Partnership Act 1890 in more detail.

Areas of the Partnership Act	Description
Freedom of variation	The partnership agreement may be varied with the consent of all the partners. This may be formal or informal: s.19.
Profits and losses	These are shared equally in the absence of contrary agreement. However, if the partnership agreement states that profits are to be shared in certain proportions then, losses are to be shared in the same proportions: s 24.
Interest on capital	None is paid on capital except by agreement. However, a partner is entitled to 5% interest on **advances** beyond his original capital: s 24.
Indemnity	The firm must indemnify any partner against liabilities incurred in the ordinary and proper conduct of the partnership business or in doing anything necessarily done for the preservation of the partnership property or business: s 24.
Management	Every partner is entitled to take part in managing the firm's business; ordinary management decisions can be made by a majority of partners: s 24.
Change in business	Any decision on changing the nature of the partnership's business must be unanimous: s 24.
Remuneration	No partner is entitled to remuneration such as salary for acting in the partnership business: s 24.
Records and accounts	These must be kept at the main place of business, and must be open to inspection by all partners: s 24.
New partners	New partners must only be introduced with the consent of all existing partners: s 24.
Expulsion	A partner may only be expelled by a majority of votes when the partnership agreement allows; even then, the power must only be used in good faith and for good reason: s 25.
Dissolution	The authority of the partners after dissolution continues so far as is necessary to wind up the partnership affairs and complete transactions already begun. On dissolution, any partner can insist on realisation of the firm's assets, payment of the firm's debts and distribution of the surplus.
Capital deficiency	The remaining partners share a capital deficiency (what a partner owes but cannot pay back) not as a loss but in ratio to the amounts of capital which they originally contributed to the firm. This is the rule in *Garner v Murray 1904*.

1.4.3 Partnership agreement

A written partnership agreement is **not** legally required. In practice, there are advantages in setting down in writing the terms of their association.

(a) It **fills** in the **details** which the law would not imply – the nature of the firm's business, its name, and the bank at which the firm will maintain its account.

(b) A written agreement serves to **override terms** otherwise implied by the Partnership Act 1890 which are inappropriate to the partnership. The Act, for example, implies (unless otherwise agreed) that partners share profits equally. In practice, where partners contribute unequal capital to the partnership, the partnership agreement will provide for unequal division of profits and losses.

1.4.4 Partnership property 6/04

Partners may offer property (this means any assets rather than money) of their own for use by the partnership. If, for example, one of them owned an office block then the partnership could be permitted to use it. This can lead to disputes over whether assets are owned by individual partners or by the partnership (all the partners jointly).

Key term

> **Partnership property** is assets beneficially owned by all of the partners, or the firm (as the partners are known collectively). The ownership does not have to be in equal shares.

It is important to distinguish between assets which are the property of the partnership and assets which are the property of the individual partners. This is because:

(a) partnership property does not belong to any individual partner; it must be applied exclusively for partnership purposes and in accordance with the partnership agreement;

(b) any increase in the value of partnership property belongs to the partnership and not to individual partners;

(c) partnership property is available for the partnership's creditors in the event of the partnership becoming insolvent, whereas a creditor of an individual partner can claim only the assets of that partner;

(d) on dissolution every partner can insist that partnership property is sold and the proceeds divided between them; and

(e) unless the partners agree otherwise, partnership property which consists of land is, in equity, deemed to be personal property

While the definition may seem simple, disputes often arise over whether property belongs to the partnership or the individual. Consider the following example.

Illustration

FACTS	CONSEQUENCES
A partner buys an office block which is subsequently used by the partnership	1 The partner owns the asset himself and 'lends' it to the partnership. 2 The partner, as an agent of the other partners, purchased the property, and it is owned jointly. 3 The partner purchased the property using partnership funds but it is owned by him.

Whether the property belongs to the partnership or to the partner is treated as a question of fact which is determined by reference to any partnership agreement and, in the absence of any agreement, Section 20 provides that:

(a) All property and rights and interests in property originally brought into the partnership stock, or acquired on the partnership's behalf for the purposes of (and in the course of) the partnership business, are property and must be held and applied by the partners exclusively for the purposes of the partnership and in accordance with the partnership agreement.

(b) Unless the contrary intention appears, property bought with money belonging to the partnership is deemed to have been bought for the partnership.

The best way to avoid the problem of partnership property is to expressly state in a partnership agreement what is partnership property and what is not and to make express arrangements when partners introduce assets after formation.

1.5 External relationships **Pilot paper, 6/02, 6/03**

There are two key issues in the external relationships of partners.

- The **authority** of a partner to transact with the outsider on behalf of the partnership
- The **liability** of partners as a result of one partner's actions.

1.5.1 Authority **6/05**

You learnt about agency in Chapter 9. The authority of partners to bind each other in contract is based on the principles of agency. Section 5 provides that a partner is the agent of the partnership and his co-partners.

This means that some of his acts bind the other partners, either because he has, or appears to have, authority. The **Partnership Act** 1890 **defines** the **authority** of a partner to make contracts as follows.

Every partner is an **agent** of the firm and his other partners for the purpose of the business of the partnership, and the acts of every partner who does any act for carrying on the **usual way** of business if the kind carried on by the firm of which he is a member **bind the firm** and his partners, **unless** the partner so acting has **in fact no authority** to act for the firm in the particular matter, **and the person with whom he is dealing** either **knows that he has no authority**, or does not know or believe him to be a partner.

Where on partner pledges the credit of the firm for a **purpose apparently not connected** with the firm's ordinary course of business, the **firm is not bound, unless** he is in fact **specially authorised** by the other partners: but this section does not affect any personal liability incurred by an individual.

If it has been **agreed between the partners** that any **restriction** shall be placed on the power of any one or more of them to bind the firm, **no act** done in contravention of the agreement is **binding** on the firm with respect to **persons having notice of the agreement.**

The key point to note about authority of partners is that other than when the partner has actual authority the authority often **depends on the perception of the third party**. If the third party genuinely believes that the partner has authority, the partner is likely to bind the firm.

1.5.2 Liability

Partners are jointly liable, as the firm, for contracts which the partners have made which bind the firm. The link between authority and liability can be seen in the following diagram.

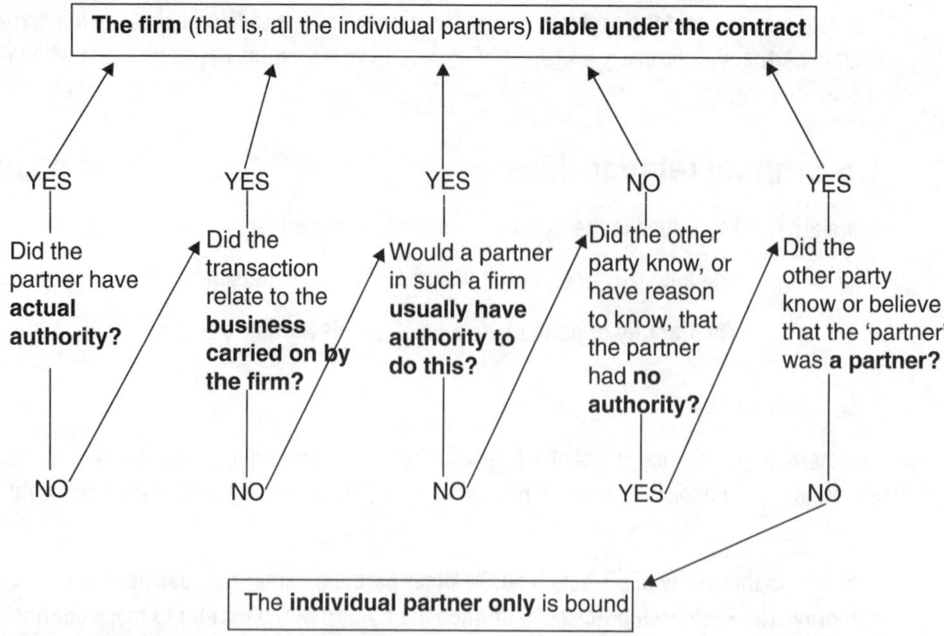

The key issue in determining whether the firm is liable is often whether the particular transaction related to 'the business carried on by the partnership'. This is a question of fact.

	Partner liability
New partners	A new partner admitted to an existing firm is liable for debts incurred only after he becomes a partner. He is not liable for debts incurred before he was a partner unless he agrees to become liable (S17).
Retiring partners	The partner who retires is still liable for any outstanding debts incurred while he was a partner, unless the creditor has agreed to release him from liability. He is also liable for debts of the firm incurred after his retirement if he creditor knew him to be a partner (before retirement) and has not had notice of his retirement (S17). Therefore, it is **vital** on retirement that a partner **gives notice** to all the creditors of the firm. However a partner who is retiring may enter into an agreement with the continuing partners that they will indemnify him against any liability for post retirement debts.

1.6 Dissolution 12/02, 6/04

FAST FORWARD

The Partnership Act states when partnership is terminated.

Dissolution is when partnership comes to an end. In this context, 'partnership' means the existing partners.

Illustration

Alison, Ben, Caroline and David are in partnership as accountants. Caroline decides to change career and become an interior designer. In her place, Alison, Ben and David invite Emily to join the partnership.

As far as third parties are concerned, a partnership offering accountancy services still exists. In fact, however, the old partnership (ABCD) has been dissolved, and a new partnership (ABDE) has replaced it.

The Partnership Act 1890 also provides that partnership is terminated in the following instances.

- **Passing of time**, if the partnership was entered into for a fixed term
- **Termination of the venture**, if entered into for a single venture
- The **death or bankruptcy** of a partner (partnership agreement may vary)
- **Subsequent illegality**
- **Notice** given by a partner if it is a partnership of indefinite duration
- **Order of the court** granted to a partner

Note that the partnership agreement may include other circumstances in which a partnership will terminate.

In the event of the termination of a partnership, the partnership's assets are realised and the proceeds applied in this order (S42):

(i) Paying off external debts
(ii) Repaying to the partners any advance made over and above their capital contribution
(iii) Repaying the partners' capital contributions
(iv) Anything left over is then repaid to the partners in the profit sharing ratio.

If a partner retires or dies the firm may continue to operate and an account occurs to determine the rights of the departing partner. A partnership may continue to trade after the partnership has been terminated, and this can give rise to difficult issues as to how the profit realised post-termination is to be divided. In *Popat v Shonchhatra 1997* the business carried on for some two years after P. left the partnership (which terminated the partnership). The partnership agreement did not deal with post-cessation profit. P. was entitled to a share of the revenue proportionate to his entitlement to partnership assets at the date he left, less an allowance to S for his efforts in carrying on the business. Capital profits made post-dissolution were divided equally between the partners.

The partnership agreement can exclude some of these provisions and can avoid dissolution in the following circumstances.

- Death of a partner
- Bankruptcy of a partner

In such cases the business will continue and the relative rights of the partners must be determined. In such cases there will be a valuation of the firm's assets and appropriate sums must be paid to the departing partner (or his estate). It is wise to make such provisions to give stability to the partnership.

1.7 Supervision

There is no formal supervision of partnerships. Their accounts need not be in prescribed form nor is audit necessary. The public has no means or legal right of inspection of the firm's accounts or other information such as companies must provide.

Partnerships are subject to some statutes which affect businesses or individuals generally, for example:

- Business Names Act
- Relevant taxation statutes

Therefore, if the partners carry on business under a firm's name which is not the surnames of them all, say, 'Smith, Jones & Co', they are required to disclose the **names** of the **partners** on their letterheads and at their places of business. They are required to make a **return** of their **profits** for income tax and **usually** to **register** for VAT.

Where it is the case that professional people are using a partnership as their business vehicle, the acts of that partnership will be regulated to an extent by their professional body. For example, the acts of a partnerships of certified chartered accountants are regulated by the ACCA.

2 Limited liability partnerships 12/03

FAST FORWARD

Limited Liability Partnerships are a hybrid of partnerships and companies. They require incorporation, and have several of the publicity requirements of companies.

There are two distinct forms of limited liability partnership.

2.1 Limited Partnership Act 1907

A limited partnership under the Limited Partnership Act 1907 is also known as a limited liability partnership. This type of partnership is very rare today and accounts for less than 1% of all partnerships in the UK. A limited partnership is formed when one or more of the partners invest capital into the business but do not participate in running and managing the business. These partners therefore have limited liability as they can only lose the amount of money that they initially invested into the business.

In a limited partnership under the 1907 Act, the law states that there must be at least one partner that has limited liability and at least one partner that has unlimited liability (a general partner).

The general partner has control of the management of the business. However, none of the limited partners are permitted to participate in the management of the business. If they do, their limited liability is lost. A limited partner cannot bind the partnership. Only the general partner can do that.

In order to take advantage of the protection afforded by limited liability, an organisation which constitutes itself as a limited partnership must comply with the requirements of the Limited Partnership Act 1907. In particular, the partnership must be registered at Companies House giving details of the partners and the extent of their liability.

2.2 Limited Liability Partnership Act 2000 12/03

A more recent development in partnership law has been the introduction of a new form of business vehicle, the limited liability partnership. These are permitted under the Limited Liability Partnership Act 2000 and have been in use since April 2001. Note that they are very different from the limited liability partnerships allowable under the 1907 Act.

Key terms

A **limited liability partnership (LLP)** formed under the 2000 Act is a corporate body which has separate legal personality from its members and therefore some of the advantages and disadvantages of a company.

An LLP combines the features of a partnership along with limited liability and creation of a legal personality more usually associated with limited companies. An LLP is not dissolved on a change of membership. At the end of the life of such a partnership, it is wound up rather like a company.

2.3 Formation

A limited liability partnership may be formed by persons associating to carry on lawful business with a view to profit, but it **must be incorporated** to be recognised.

To be incorporated, the subscribers must send the correct document to the Registrar of Companies and must sign that document. The form must state the following:

- The **name** of the LLP
- The **location** of its **registered office** (England and Wales/Wales/Scotland)
- The **address** of the registered office
- The name and address of all the **members** of the LLP
- Which of the members are to be **designated members** (see below)

There is also a registration fee.

An LLP can be incorporated wherever 'two or more persons associated with the carrying on a lawful business with a view to profit...have subscribed their names to an incorporation document...' (LLP Act 2000).

2.4 Internal regulation

The members of the LLP are those who subscribe to the original incorporation document, and those admitted afterwards in accordance with the terms of the partnership agreement.

The rights and duties of the partners will usually be set out in a **partnership agreement**. In the absence of a partnership agreement, the rights and duties are set out in regulations under the Act.

LLPs must have designated members, who must take responsibility for the publicity requirements of the LLP, see below.

2.5 External relationships

Every member is an **agent** of the LLP. As such, where the member has authority, the LLP will be bound by the acts of the member.

The **LLP will not be bound by the acts of the member where:**

- He has **no authority** and the **third party is aware** of that fact
- He has **ceased to be a member**, and the **third party is aware** of that fact

2.6 Dissolution

An LLP **does not dissolve on a member leaving** it, in the same way that a traditional partnership does. Where a member has died or (for a corporate member) been wound up, that member ceases to be a member, but the LLP continues in existence.

An **LLP must therefore be wound up** when the time has come for it to be dissolved. This is achieved under provisions **similar to company winding up** provisions.

2.7 Supervision

As can be seen in the incorporation procedures, LLPs come under the supervision of the **Registrar of Companies**.

LLPs are required to have **designated members** who are responsible for signing relevant documents and returning them to the Registrar. Each LLP must have two designated members.

Designated members are required to:

- Sign notices sent to the Registrar
- Appoint auditors (if they are required)
- Sign the accounts
- Deliver the accounts to the Registrar

The Registrar will maintain a file containing the publicised documents of the LLP at Companies House.

3 Companies

12/01

FAST FORWARD

A company has a separate legal identity from its members. This is one of the fundamental cornerstones of company law: the company is a legal entity in its own right, totally distinct from its members.

A company is another very popular form of business association in the UK. Over 150,000 companies are formed each year.

By its nature, a company is more **formal** than a partnership. There is substantially **more legislation** on the formation and procedures of companies than any other business association, hence the weighting towards company law of the rest of this text.

The key reason that the company is a popular form of business association is that the **liability of its members to contribute to the debts of the company is significantly limited**. This will be explained more later in this chapter. For many people, this benefit outweighs the disadvantage of the formality surrounding companies.

3.1 Definition of a company

Key terms

For the purposes of this study text, a **company** is an entity registered under the Companies Act 1985.

The key feature of a company is that it has a legal personality (existence) distinct from its members and directors.

3.2 Legal personality

A person possesses legal rights and is subject to legal obligations. In law, the term person is used to denote two categories of legal person.

- An individual human being is a **natural person**.
- The law also recognises **artificial persons** in the form of companies.

Key term

Corporate personality is a common law principle that grants a company a legal entity, separate from the members who comprise it. It follows that the property of a company belongs to that company, debts of the company must be satisfied from the assets of that company, and the company has perpetual succession until wound up.

A corporation is a **legal entity** separate from the natural persons connected with it, for example as members or directors. Corporations are classified in one of the following categories.

Categories	Description
Corporations sole	A corporation sole is an **official position** which is filled by one person who is replaced from time to time. The Public Trustee and the Treasury Solicitor are corporations sole.
Chartered corporations	These are usually **charities** or bodies such as the Association of Chartered Certified Accountants, formed by Royal Charter.
Statutory corporations	Statutory corporations are formed by special Acts of Parliament. This method is little used now, as it is slow and expensive. It was used in the nineteenth century to form railway and canal companies.
Community Interest Companies	A special form of company for use by 'social' enterprises in that it is pursuing purposes beneficial to the community (Companies (Audit, Investigation and Community Enterprise) Act 2004).
Registered companies	Registration under the Companies Act 1985 is the normal method of incorporating a commercial concern. Any body of this type is properly called a company.

The first case which clearly demonstrated the separate legal personality of companies is of great significance to any study of company law and is therefore set out in some detail below.

> *Salomon v Salomon & Co Ltd 1897*
> *The facts*: The claimant, S, had carried on business as a leather merchant and boot manufacturer for 30 years. He decided to form a limited company to purchase the business, he and six members of his family each subscribing for one share. The company then purchased the business from S for £38,782, the purchase price being payable to the claimant by way of the issue of 20,000 £1 shares, the issue of debentures for £10,000 (effectively making Salomon a secured creditor) and the payment of £8,782 in cash. The company did not prosper and was wound up a year later, at which point its liabilities exceeded its assets. The liquidator, representing unsecured trade creditors of the company, claimed that the company's business was in effect still the claimant's (he owned 20,001 of 20,007 shares) and that he should bear liability for its debts and that payment of the debenture debt to him should be postponed until the company's trade creditors were paid.
>
> *Decision:* At first instance, and in the Court of Appeal, that the other shareholders were 'mere puppets' and that the company had been irregularly incorporated. Salomon should indemnify the company against its liabilities. The House of Lords however held that the business was owned by, and its debts were liabilities of, the company. The claimant was under no liability to the company or its creditors, his debentures were validly issued and the security created by them over the company's assets was effective. This was because the company was a legal entity separate and distinct from S.

The principle of separate legal personality has been confirmed by more recent cases, one of which follows.

> *Lee v Lee's Air Farming Ltd 1960*
> *The facts*: Mr Lee, who owned the majority of the shares of an aerial crop-spraying business, and was the sole working director of the company, was killed while piloting the aircraft.
>
> *Decision:* Although he was the majority shareholder and sole working director of the company, he and the company were separate legal persons and therefore he could also be an employee with rights against it when killed in an accident in the course of his employment.

4 Liability

6/04

A key consequence of the fact that the company is distinct from its members is that its members therefore have **limited liability**.

4.1 Limited liability for members

Key term

Limited liability is a protection offered to members of certain types of company. In the event of business failure, the members will only be asked to contribute identifiable amounts to the assets of the business.

4.1.1 Protection offered to members

The **company** itself is **liable without limit for its own debts.** If the company buys plastic from another company, for example, it owes the other company money.

Limited liability is a benefit to members for its members (shareholders). They own the business, so might be the people who the creditors logically asked to pay the debts of the company if the company is unable to pay them itself.

Limited liability prevents this by stipulating the creditors of the company cannot demand the company's debts from members of the company, other then in the rare case when the company is formed as an 'unlimited' company.

4.1.2 Business failure

As the company is liable for all its own debts, limited liability only becomes and issue in the event of a business failure when the company is unable to pay its own debts.

This will result in the winding up of the company (see Chapter 23) which will enable the creditors to be paid from the proceeds of any assets remaining in the company. It is at winding up that limited liability becomes relevant.

4.1.3 Members asked to contribute identifiable amounts

Although the creditors of the company cannot ask the members of the company to pay the debts of the company, there are some amounts that members are required to pay, in the event of a winding up.

Type of company	Amount owed by member at winding up
Company limited by shares	Any outstanding amount from when they originally purchased their shares from the company. If the member's shares are fully paid, they do not have to contribute anything in the event of a winding up.
Company limited by guarantee	The amount they guaranteed to pay in the event of a winding up

4.2 Liability for the company

A mentioned above, the company is liable without limit for its own debts.

A company, as a separate legal entity, may also have liabilities in tort and crime. Criminal liability of companies is a topical area following recent disasters such as the Paddington and Hatfield rail disasters.

It is currently extremely difficult to prosecute a company on criminal charges, as it is necessary to show a 'mens rea', or controlling mind, if the crime requires the defendant company to have 'intended' to commit the crime.

Unless a company is very small it is difficult to show that the mind controlling the company was connected with the criminal act.

However, the Law Commission have issued proposals which include a charge of killing by gross carelessness, which it would be easier to charge companies with. There is, at present, no such criminal offence in the United Kingdom.

Question

Limitation of liability

Hattie and two friends wish to set up a small business. Hattie is concerned that, following her initial investment, she will have no access to additional funds, and is worried what might happen if anything goes wrong. Advise her on the relative merits of a company and a partnership.

Answer

The question of liability appears to be important to Hattie. As a member of a limited company, her liability would be limited – as a member at least – to the nominal value of her shareholding. If the three friends decide to form a partnership, they should be advised that they will have **unlimited** liability for the debts of the partnership. (A partnership does **not** have a legal responsibility distinct from the partners).

5 Veil of incorporation

6/03

FAST FORWARD

A 'veil of incorporation' is drawn between the members and the company protecting the members from the consequences of the company's actions. It may be lifted:

– To enforce the law
– When people are seeking to evade their obligations
– In certain group situations

To recap, the reason that members have limited liability and do not have to pay the debts of the company is that through incorporation, the company establishes a separate legal personality from the people who own or run it (the members/shareholders/directors).

This means that people can look at a company and not know who or what owns it.

The fact that members are 'hidden' in this way is sometimes referred to as the '**veil of incorporation'.** Literally, the members are 'veiled' from view.

5.1 Lifting the veil

It is sometimes necessary by law to look at who the owners of a company are. This is referred to as lifting the veil. It can be done to:

- **Identify** the **company** with its **members** and/or directors.
- Treat a **group of companies** as a **single commercial entity** (if a company is owned by another company).

The more important of these two reasons is the first one, although the second reason can sometimes be more complex. The main instances for lifting the veil are given below.

5.2 Lifting the veil by statute to enforce the law

sometimes a statute requires the court to 'lift the veil'. Examples include:

5.2.1 Liability of a sole member for a company's debts

Every public company must have a minimum membership of at least two members: s 1. If therefore a public company has two members and one dies or transfers his shares to the other. The one surviving member is made liable (with the company) for its debts if:

(a) The company **carries on business** after **six months** from the time when the membership is reduced to one, and

(b) The **surviving member knows** that it is carrying on business with himself as sole member.

The member's liability is not retrospective and extends only to debts of the company incurred **after** the **six months** have expired: s 24.

5.2.2 Liability for trading without trading certificate

A public company must, under s 117, obtain a certificate from the Registrar before it may commence to trade. Failure to do so leads to **personal liability** for the directors for any loss or damage suffered by a third party to a transaction entered into by the company in contravention of s 117.

5.2.3 Fraudulent and wrongful trading

If, when a company is wound up, it appears that its business has been carried on with **intent** to **defraud creditors** or others, the court may decide that the persons (usually the directors) who were knowingly parties to the fraud shall be **personally responsible** for debts and other liabilities of the company: s 213 Insolvency Act 1986. Fraudulent and wrongful trading are discussed later in this text.

5.2.4 Disqualified directors

Directors who participate in the management of a company in contravention of an order under the Company Directors Disqualification Act 1986 will be **jointly** or **severally liable** along with the company for the company's debts.

5.2.5 Abuse of company names

There have been a large number of instances where directors of a company which went into insolvent liquidation formed another company with an identical or similar name, which bought the original company's business and assets from its liquidator.

S 216 Insolvency Act 1986 now prevents a director or shadow director of a company that goes into insolvent liquidation being involved for the next five years with the directing, managing or promoting of a business which has an **identical name** to the original company, or a **name similar** enough to suggest a connection. Breach of these rules is an offence of strict liability and proof of intent is not required: *R v Cole & Others 1997*. The directors concerned will be **jointly** or **severally liable** along with the company for its debts if they contravene this section.

5.2.6 Liability for use of company name in incorrect form

A company is identified by its name which distinguishes it from other companies. Every company is required to exhibit its name in its correct form outside every place of business, on its seal (if it has one) and on its business letters and other documents such as bills of exchange.

If the rule is broken an **officer** of the company responsible for the default may be fined. As regards business documents, he is **personally liable** to the creditor if the company fails to pay the debt: s 349.

Penrose v Martyr 1858
The facts: A company secretary accepted a bill of exchange drawn on the company on which its name was incorrectly written by omitting the word 'limited' from the name. The company defaulted.

Decision: The secretary was personally liable on the bill.

Durham Fancy Goods Ltd v Michael Jackson (Fancy Goods) Ltd 1968
The facts: A creditor drew a bill on the company and wrote on it a form of acceptance which did not state the correct name of the company (it used 'M Jackson' instead of 'Michael Jackson' in full). The defendant signed the acceptance for the company.

Decision: The defendant was not liable since the error had been introduced by the claimant. But for that fact he would have been liable.

Exam focus point

The distinction between these two cases may not be immediately obvious. However, they raise two points which you should **consider and apply** if such an issue came up in the exam.

(1) In the first case, the element of the company's name which indicated its **status** was omitted. This could have misled creditors into thinking that they were dealing with a company whose members had unlimited liability for company debts. This makes the omission particularly serious.

(2) The three cases (two above and the Jenice Ltd case) also show the attitude of the courts, aiming to keep the **spirit of the law** (not misleading people as to the nature of the company) and not punishing people unnecessarily for small mistakes or typos.

The fact that a company name is incorrect does not make the document ineffective, provided that it is clear that it was intended to name that company: *Bird (London) Ltd v Thomas Cook & Son (Bakers) Ltd 1937*.

S349 provides that when a company's name was given wrongly on a cheque or other financial instrument, this was a mistake and it was unfortunate for the officer responsible that the creditor could proceed against him personally. This applied even to trifling errors in the company's name: *Hendon v Adelman 1973*.

However, more recently the High Court gave an interpretation of s 349 which is more generous to company directors and other officers.

Jenice Ltd and Others v Dan 1993
The facts: Mr Dan was a director of a company called Primekeen Ltd. The bank incorrectly printed the company's cheques in the name of 'Primkeen Ltd'. Mr Dan signed several of these. They were dishonoured and returned by the various claimants including Jenice. Primekeen Ltd then went into creditors' voluntary winding up and the various claimants sued Mr Dan as personally liable on the cheques because of s 349(4).

Decision: Mr Dan was not liable. The purpose of s 349(4) was to ensure that outsiders knew they were dealing with a company and that the liability of its members was limited. There was no doubt that in this case outsiders would have known that they were dealing with a limited company, so no mischief had been done. The correctness of this decision is in doubt.

Exam focus point

It is very important to know the statutory ways of lifting the veil as their omission can be a serious weakness in many answers.

5.3 Lifting the veil to prevent evasion of obligations

A company may be identified with those who control it, for instance to determine its residence for tax purposes. The courts may also ignore the distinction between a company and its members and managers if the latter use that distinction to **evade** their **existing legal obligations**.

Gilford Motor Co Ltd v Horne 1933
The facts: The defendant had been employed by the claimant company under a contract which forbade him to solicit its customers after leaving its service. After the termination of his employment he formed a company of which his wife and an employee were the sole directors and shareholders. However he managed the company and through it evaded the covenant by which he himself was prevented from soliciting customers of his former employer.

Decision: An injunction requiring observance of the covenant would be made both against the defendant and the company which he had formed as a 'a mere cloak or sham'.

5.3.1 Public interest

In time of war it is not permitted to trade with 'enemy aliens'. The courts may draw aside the veil if, despite a company being registered in the UK, it is suspected that it is controlled by aliens: *Daimler Co Ltd v Continental Tyre and Rubber Co Ltd 1916.*

The question of nationality may also arise in peacetime, where it is convenient for a foreign entity to have a British facade on its operations.

Re F G Films Ltd 1953
The facts: An English company was formed by an American company to 'make' a film which would obtain certain marketing and other advantages from being called a British film. Staff and finance were American and there were neither premises nor employees in England; the film itself was produced in India.

Decision: The British company was the American company's agent and so the film did not qualify as British. Effectively, the corporate entity of the British company was swept away and it was exposed as a 'sham' company.

5.3.2 Evasion of liabilities

The veil of incorporation may also be lifted where directors themselves ignore the separate legal personality of two companies and transfer assets from one to the other in disregard of their duties in order to avoid an existing liability: *Creasey v Breachwood Motors Ltd 1992.*

Re H and Others 1996
The facts: The court was asked to rule that various companies within a group, together with the minority shareholders, should be treated as one entity in order to restrain assets prior to trial.

Decision: The order was granted. The court thought there was evidence that the companies had been used for the fraudulent evasion of excise duty.

Re H can be contrasted with *Yukong Line Ltd v Rendsburg 1998* in which a company broke a contract, thereby leaving itself open to being sued for damages. A director-shareholder transferred all the company's money to a third party so that when the claimant sued there was no money to pay damages. The court refused to lift the veil; when the money was transferred the company did not have an existing liability to pay the claimant.

5.3.3 Evasion of taxation

The court may lift the veil of incorporation where it is being used to conceal the nationality of the company.

Unit Construction Co Ltd v Bullock 1960
The facts: Three companies, wholly owned by a UK company, were registered in Kenya. Although the companies' constitutions required board meetings to be held in Kenya, all three were in fact managed entirely by the holding company.

Decision: The companies were resident in the UK and liable to UK tax. The Kenyan connection was a sham, the question being not where they ought to have been managed, but where they were managed.

5.3.4 Quasi-partnership

An application to wind up a company on the 'just and equitable' ground under s 122(1)(g) Insolvency Act 1986 may involve the court piercing the veil to reveal the company as a **quasi-partnership.** This may happen where the company only has a few members, all of whom are actively involved in its affairs. The individuals who have operated contentedly as a company for years fall out, and one or more of them seeks to remove the others.

The courts are willing in such cases to treat the central relationship between the directors as being that of partners, and rule that it would be unfair therefore to allow the company to continue with only some of its original members. This was illustrated by the case of *Ebrahimi v Westbourne Galleries Ltd 1973* which is discussed further in Chapter 18.

5.3.5 Misleading advice

Following *Williams v Natural Life Health Foods Ltd 1998*, it seems that a director (as opposed to the company he is acting for) will only be held personally liable for the consequences of negligent advice if he explicitly assumes liability for that advice and the claimant relies on the assumption of liability.

Question

Quasi-partnership

Sandy and Pat have carried on business together for twenty years, most recently through a limited company in which each holds 500 shares. They share the profits equally in the form of directors' remuneration. Pat's son Craig joins the business, buying 100 shares from each of Sandy and Pat. Disputes arise and Pat and Craig use their voting majority to remove Sandy from the board. Advise Sandy.

Answer

Sandy cannot prevent her removal from her directorship. However, a court may find that, on the basis of the past relationship, it is unjust and inequitable to determine the case solely on legal rights and could, on equitable principles, order liquidation of the company.

The veil of the company may be lifted to reveal a quasi-partnership.

5.4 Group situations

The principle of the veil of incorporation extends to the holding company/subsidiary relationship. Although holding companies and subsidiaries are part of a group under company law, they retain their **separate legal personalities**.

In, *Adams v Cape Industries 1990*, three reasons were put forward for identifying the companies as one, and lifting the veil of incorporation. They are:

- The subsidiary is acting as **agent** for the holding company.
- The group is to be treated as a **single economic entity** because of some statutory provision.
- The **corporate structure** is being used as a **facade** (or sham) to conceal the truth.

Exam focus point

> Reference to lifting the veil in group situations should be the final point you make a in a general lifting the veil question. You should refer to the *Cape Industries* case and state the three reasons for lifting the veil in groups which it sets out.

5.5 Summary of situations in which veil can be lifted

The veil is lifted to identify the owners with the company concerned. The instances in which it will be lifted are as follows.

Lifting the veil by statute to enforce the law

- Liability of sole member for a company's debts
- Liability for trading without a trading certificate
- Fraudulent and wrongful trading
- Disqualified directors
- Abuse of company names
- Liability for use of company name in the wrong form

Evasion of obligations

- Legal obligations
- Public interest
- Evasion of liabilities
- Evasion of taxation
- Quasi partnership
- Misleading advice

Group situations

- Subsidiary acting as agent for the holding company
- The group is to be treated as a single economic entity
- The corporate structure is being used as a sham

5.6 Lifting the veil and limited liability

The above examples of lifting the veil include examples of where, if they have broken the law, **directors** can be made **personally liable** for a company's debts. This is very rare.

If those directors are also members, limited liability **does not apply** in these instances. This is the only time that limited liability is overridden and that the **member** becomes **personally liable** for the company's debts **due to his actions as a director.**

6 Distinction between partnerships and companies 12/01, 12/04

Exam questions regularly ask you to describe the distinction between partnerships and companies. It is therefore important to know what the key differences are.

The most important difference between a company and a partnership has been mentioned at some length in this chapter. It is that a company has a **separate legal personality** from its members, while a traditional partnership does not.

This basic quality of a company gives rise to a number of characteristics which mark it out from a partnership. These are outlined below. The other key differences relate to the **formality** of a company as opposed to a partnership and the **regulations** it has to adhere to.

Factor	Company	Partnership
Entity	Is a legal entity separate to its members?	Has no existence outside of its members.
Liability	Members' liability can be limited	Partner's liability is usually unlimited
Size	May have any number of members (at least 2 for a public company)	Some partnerships are limited to twenty members (professional partnerships excluded)
Succession	Perpetual succession – change in ownership does not affect existence	Traditional partnerships are dissolved when any of the partners leaves
Owners' interests	Members own transferable shares	Partners cannot assign their interests in a partnership
Assets	Company owns the assets	Partners own assets jointly
Management	Company must have at least one director	All partners can participate in management
Constitution	Company must have a written constitution (memorandum)	A partnership may have a written partnership agreement
Accounts	A company must usually deliver accounts to the registrar	Partners do not have to send their accounts to a registrar
Security	A company may offer a floating charge over its assets	A partnership may not usually give a floating charge on assets
Withdrawal of capital	Strict rules concerning repay-ment of subscribed capital	More straightforward for a partner to withdraw capital

Revise this table above when you have studied the rest of the book and know more of the details concerning the distinctive factors above.

Chapter roundup

- Partnership is 'the relation which subsists between persons carrying on a business in common with a view of profit'.
- A traditional partnership is **not** a separate legal person distinct from its members, it is **merely** a 'relationship' between persons.
- While the provision of a partnership is informal in theory, there may be considerable formalities to agree between the partners in practice.
- The internal regulation of partnerships is governed by the Partnership Act 1890. This sets out the basic rights and duties of a partner.
- The rights and duties may be expressly denied in a Partnership agreement. There is no compulsion to have a partnership agreement.
- One important issue for partnerships is the distinction between partnership property and the property of the partners.
- The two key issues in the external relationships of partners are:
  - The authority of the partners to transact with third parties
  - The resulting liability to partners
- The Partnership Act states when partnership is terminated. The following reasons can be expressly excluded in a partnership agreement:
  - Death of a partner
  - Bankruptcy of a partner
- There is no formal supervision of partnerships.
- Limited Liability Partnerships are a hybrid of partnerships and companies. They require incorporation, and have several of the publicity requirements of companies.
- A company has a separate legal identity from its members.
- Separate legal identity produces the following features.
  - Limited liability of members
  - Transferable shares in ownership
  - Perpetual succession
  - Company owns it own assets
  - Capital provided by members
  - Detailed supervision arises
  - Management is effected by directors
  - A written constitution is necessary
- A 'veil of incorporation' is drawn between the members and the company. It may be lifted:
  - To enforce the law
  - When people are seeking to evade their obligations
  - In certain group situations

Quick quiz

1 What is the statutory definition of Partnership?

2 A partnership is formed when parties agree to run a business in common.

True ☐

False ☐

3 What are the five key rights of partners?

(1) ....

(2) ....

(3) ....

(4) ....

(5) ....

4 Complete the following definition.

Partnership .... is assets beneficially .... by the partner (the firm). It does not have to be in ....shares.

5 Complete the diagram showing partner's liability.

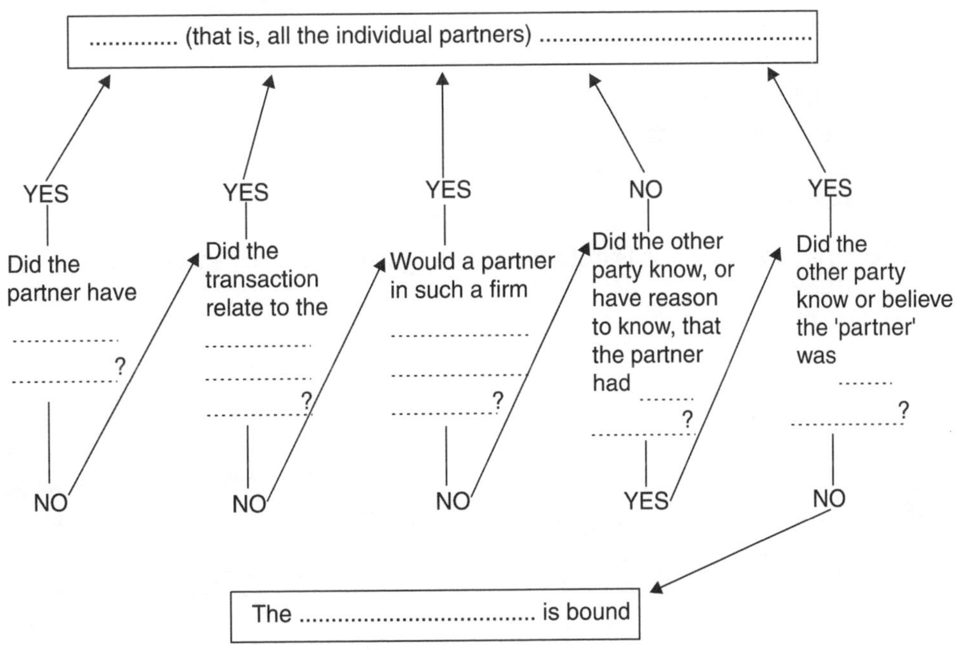

6 Complete the definition using the words in the box below.

..................................liability is a............................ offered to .... of certain types of company. In the event of .... , the members will only be asked to .... identifiable amounts to the assets of the business.

(1)	business	(3)	members	(5)	protection
(2)	Limited	(4)	failure	(6)	contribute

7 Name two circumstances in which members of a limited company will be to contribute at liquidation.

(1) ....

(2) ....

8 Put the examples given below in the correct category box.

WHEN THE VEIL OF INCORPORATION IS LIFTED		
To enforce law	**To enforce obligations**	**To expose groups**

- Liability of sole member for a company's debts
- Liability for use of company name in the wrong form
- Legal obligations
- Quasi partnership
- Disqualified directors
- Fraudulent and wrongful trading
- Need to treat as single economic entity
- Corporate structure a sham
- Public interest

9 Name six factors which help to distinguish between companies and partnerships.

(1) ....

(2) ....

(3) ....

(4) ....

(5) ....

(6) ....

Answers to quick quiz

1 Partnership is the relation which subsists between persons carrying on a business in common with a view of profit.

2 True

3 (1) Involved in decision-making
(2) Share in profits
(3) Exam accounts
(4) Insist on openness and honesty
(5) Veto new partners

4 Property, owned, equal

5

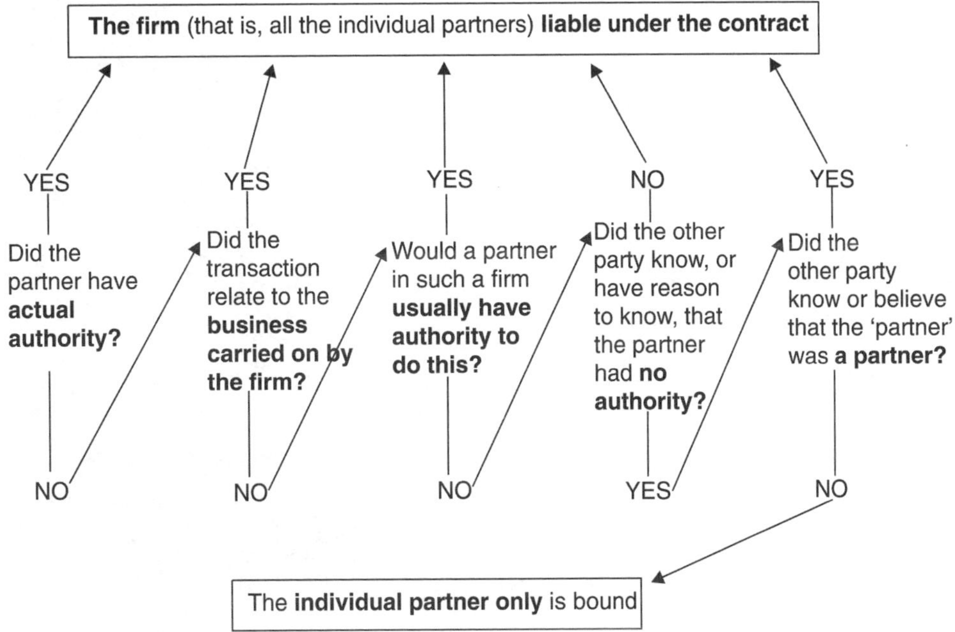

6 (2), (5), (3), (1), (4), (6)

7 (1) It is limited by guarantee, and they have pledged a guarantee
(2) It is limited by shares, and their shares are not fully paid up

8

WHEN THE VEIL OF INCORPORATION IS LIFTED

To enforce law	To enforce obligations	To expose groups
Liability of a sole member for debts	Legal obligation	Single economic ability
Wrong use of company name	Quasi partnership	Corporate structure a sham
Disqualified directors	Public interest	
Fraudulent / Wrongful } trading		

9 Any of:

(1) Entity (separate or not)
(2) Liability (of members/partners)
(3) Size (restrictions)
(4) Succession
(5) Owners' interests
(6) Ownership of assets
(7) Management
(8) Constitution
(9) Account
(10) Security
(11) Capital withdrawal

Now try the question below from the Exam Question Bank

Number	Level	Marks	Time
Q12	Examination	20	36 mins

Part D
Company formation and constitution

11

Formation and publicity

Topic list	Syllabus reference
1 Types of company	4(b)
2 Registration procedures	5(a)
3 Commencement of business	5(a)
4 Promoters and pre-incorporation contracts	5(a)
5 Public accountability	5(d)
6 Statutory books and returns	5(d)
7 Annual accounts	5(d)
8 Accounting records	5(d)
9 The annual return	5(d)

Introduction

In Chapter 10 of this Study Text you were introduced to the idea of the separate legal personality of a company. In section 1 of this chapter, we consider the types of company which can be registered.

Sections 2 to 4 of this chapter concentrate on the **procedural aspects** of **company formation**. Important topics in these sections include the formalities that a company must observe in order to be formed, and the liability of promoters for pre-incorporation contracts.

Sections 5 to 9 of this chapter consider the concept of the **public accountability** of **limited companies**. Later on in your coverage of the syllabus you will meet references to a company's obligation to publicise certain decisions, so it is important to understand at this stage how and why this should be done.

These topics can easily be examined in factual Section A question, as was the case on the Pilot paper. However, this does not preclude them from forming some of a Section B question.

1 Types of company

6/02

FAST FORWARD

A limited company is one where the members' liability for the debts of the company is limited to the amount unpaid on their shares.

Limited companies may be registered as public or private companies. Unlimited companies are always private.

1.1 Limited and unlimited companies

The meaning of limited liability has already been explained. It is the **member**, not the company, whose liability for the company's debts may be limited.

1.2 Liability limited by shares

Liability is usually **limited by shares.** This is the position when a company which has share capital states in its memorandum of association that 'the liability of members is limited'.

1.3 Liability limited by guarantee

Alternatively a company may be **limited by guarantee.** Its memorandum of association states the amount which each member **undertakes** to **contribute** in a liquidation. A creditor has no direct claim against a member under his guarantee, nor in this case can the company require a member to pay up under his guarantee until the company goes into liquidation.

Companies limited by guarantee are appropriate to **non-commercial activities**, such as a charity or a trade association which aim to keep income and expenditure in balance but also have the members' guarantee as a form of reserve capital if it becomes insolvent.

1.4 Unlimited liability companies

Key term

An **unlimited company** is a company in which members do not have limited liability. Its memorandum makes no reference to members' liability.

In the event of business failure, the liquidator can then require members to contribute as much as may be required to pay the company's debts in full.

A unlimited company **can only be a private company**, as by definition, a **public company is always limited.**

An unlimited company has two main advantages.

(a) It need not **file** a copy of its **annual accounts** and reports with the registry, unless during the relevant accounting reference period (s 254(1-3)):

   (i) It is (to its knowledge) a **subsidiary** of a limited company.

   (ii) **Two** or more **limited companies** have **exercised rights** over the **company**, which (had they been exercised by only one of them) would have **made** the **company** a **subsidiary** of that one company.

   (iii) It is the **parent company** of a limited liability company.

   (iv) It is a **promoter** of a **trading stamp scheme**.

(b) An unlimited company **may without formality purchase its shares** from its own members.

The unlimited company certainly has its uses. It provides a corporate body (a separate legal entity) which can conveniently hold assets to which liabilities do not attach.

1.5 Public and private companies

Key terms

A **public company** is a company whose memorandum states that it is public and that it has complied with the registration procedures for such a company.

A **private company** is a company which has not been registered as a public company under the Companies Act. The major practical distinction between a private and public company is that the former may not offer its securities to the public.

Since 1980 a **public** company is a company registered as such under the Companies Acts with the Registrar of Companies. Any company not registered as public is a private company: s 1(3). In practice, less than 1% of registered companies are public companies.

A public company may be one which was originally incorporated as a public company or one which re-registered as a public company having been previously a private company.

1.6 Conditions for being a public company

1.6.1 Registrar's certificate

A public company is such because the Registrar of Companies (referred to as 'the registrar' in the remainder of this text) has issued a certificate that the company has been registered as a public company. The conditions for this are:

(a) The **name** of the company identifies it as a public company by ending with the words 'public limited company' or 'plc' or their Welsh equivalents, 'ccc', for a Welsh company: s 33.

(b) The **memorandum of association** of the company states that 'the company is to be a public company' or words to that effect: s 1(3)(a).

(c) The **authorised capital** of the company is not less than the authorised minimum (s 11) which is currently £50,000: s 118.

(d) It is a **limited company**.

With regard to the minimum authorised capital of £50,000 contained in s 118:

(a) A company originally incorporated as a public company will not be permitted to trade until its **allotted** share capital is at least £50,000: s 117.

(b) A private company which re-registers as a public company will not be permitted to trade until it has **allotted** share capital of at least £50,000; under s 101, this need only be paid up to one quarter of its nominal value (plus the whole of any premium).

(c) A private company which has an authorised and allotted share capital of £50,000 or more may of course continue as a private company; it is always optional to become a public company.

(d) A company limited by guarantee which has no share capital, and an unlimited company, cannot be public companies.

1.6.2 Minimum membership

A public company must have a minimum of **two members**: s 1.

1.7 Private companies

A private company is the residual category and so need not satisfy any special conditions.

Private companies are generally small to medium enterprises in which some if not all shareholders are also directors and **vice versa**. Ownership and management are thus often combined in the same individuals. In that situation, it is unnecessary to impose on the directors complicated restrictions to safeguard the interests of members and thus a number of rules that apply to public companies are reduced for private companies.

1.8 Differences between private and public companies

The more important differences between public and private companies imposed by law relate to the following factors.

1.8.1 Directors

The main differences are:

(a) A **public** company must have at least **two directors:** a **private** company need only have **one director**: s 282.

(b) The rules on **loans to directors** are much **more stringent** in their application to **public companies** and their subsidiaries than to private companies: s 330.

(c) A **public company**, except by ordinary resolution with special notice, may **not appoint a director aged over 70**: s 293.

1.8.2 Capital

The main differences are:

(a) There is a minimum amount of **£50,000** for a **public** company, **no minimum** for a **private** company.

(b) A public company may **raise capital** by **offering** its **shares** or debentures to the public; a **private** company is **prohibited** from doing so.

(c) Both **public** and **private companies** must as a general rule **offer** to **existing members first** any ordinary shares to be allotted for cash: ss 89 – 94. However a **private** company **may permanently disapply** this rule by its articles. A **public company** can only do so for a limited period **not exceeding five years**: s 95.

1.8.3 Dealings in shares

Only a **public company** can obtain a **Stock Exchange** or other investment exchange **listing** for its shares. To obtain the advantages of listing the company must agree to elaborate conditions contained in a **listing agreement** with The International Stock Exchange. However, not all public companies are listed.

1.8.4 Accounts

(a) A **public** company has **seven** months from the end of its accounting reference period in which to produce its statutory audited accounts. The period for a **private** company is **ten** months: s 244(1).

(b) A **private** company, if qualified by its size, may have **partial exemption** from various **accounting provisions** (discussed later in this text). These remissions are not available to a public company or to its subsidiaries (even if they are private companies): ss 246, 248 and 250.

(c) A **listed public company** may prepare a **summary financial statement** to be sent to members instead of full accounts in certain circumstances: s 251(1).

(d) The **members** of a **private** company may elect to **dispense with** the laying of **accounts** and reports before a general meeting: s 252.

1.8.5 Commencement of business

A **private** company can commence business **as soon** as it is **incorporated**. A **public** company if incorporated as such must first **obtain a certificate from the registrar**.

1.8.6 General meetings

A member of a **public** company may appoint **more than one proxy** but the proxy has **no statutory right to speak**. A member of a **private** company may only **appoint one proxy** but he **may speak**: s 372.

1.8.7 Identification

The rules on identification as public or private are as follows.

(a) The word **'limited'** or **'Ltd'** in the name denotes a private company; **'public limited company'** or **'plc'** must appear at the end of the name of a public company: s 25.

(b) The **memorandum of association** of a **public** company must include a clause describing it as a public company. Nothing of this kind is prescribed for a private company.

1.8.8 Interests in securities

There are **special disclosure requirements** for persons who have beneficial interests in the voting shares of a public company: ss 198 – 220.

The main advantage of carrying on business through a public rather than a private company is that a public company, by the issue of listing particulars, may obtain a **listing** on The Stock Exchange and so mobilise capital from the investing public generally.

Private companies may be broadly classified into two groups, independent (also called **free-standing)** private companies and **subsidiaries** of other companies.

Question

Types of company

Alex, Barry and Carol have operated as a partnership for five years trading in domestic carpets. The business has been successful and they are now considering expanding the business operations by opening three new shops and an additional wholesale unit. The partners are aware that the expansion will require new business capital. They are considering the formation of a company rather than continuing as a partnership.

What types of company may be formed under the Companies Act 1985? Which type of company is suitable for this business.

Answer

The main categories of companies which may be formed under the Companies Act 1985 are a public company, limited by shares, and a private company, which may be limited by shares or by guarantee or be an unlimited company.

A private company limited by shares is the most suitable type for a small business venture of this kind. It offers the advantages of being a corporate entity separate from its members, giving them the protection of limited liability.

The main restriction on a private company is that it may not offer its shares or debentures to the public. But it is subject to fewer restrictions than a public company in respect of dividends and loans to directors. It may use capital to finance the purchase of its own shares and it may give financial assistance for the purchase of its shares. If the company ranks as a small or a medium-sized company for purposes of its annual accounts, the accounts delivered to the registrar need not contain all the material required in the accounts of a public company. The 'elective regime' of the Companies Act 1989 allows further elements of new flexibility to a private company in respect of the AGM, share allotment, auditors, accounts and required majorities for authorisation of meetings at short notice. Public and private companies

2 Registration procedures

Pilot paper, 6/02

FAST FORWARD

To obtain a certificate of incorporation, various documents must be sent to the registrar.

- **Memorandum** of association
- **Articles** of association
- Form 10 giving **particulars** of **first director(s)** and **secretary** and **address** of registered office
- **Registration fee**

Most companies are formed by registration under the Companies Act 1985.

A company is formed by the issue of a **certificate of incorporation** by the Registrar of Companies. The certificate:

- Identifies the company by its **name** and **serial number** at the registry
- States (if it be so) that it is **limited** and (if necessary) that it is a public company

2.1 Documents to be delivered to the registrar

The documents to be delivered to the registrar (delivery can be electronic – over 50% of incorporation are on-line) to obtain registration are as follows.

Documents	Description
Memorandum of association	The memorandum is signed by at least two **subscribers** or one in the case of single member private companies, dated and witnessed. Each subscriber agrees to subscribe for at least one share: s 1(1).
Articles of association	Articles are signed by the same subscriber(s), dated and witnessed. Alternatively the memorandum of a company limited by shares may be endorsed 'registered without articles of association'. The statutory **Table A articles** then become the company's articles in their entirety.
Statement in the prescribed form (known as Form 10)	The statement gives the particulars of the first **director**(s) and **secretary** and of the **first address** of the registered office. The persons named as directors and secretary must sign the form to record their consent to act in this capacity. When the company is incorporated they are deemed to be appointed.

Documents	Description
Statutory declaration (Form 12)	The declaration is made by a solicitor engaged in the formation of the company or by one of the persons named as director or secretary that the **requirements** of the **Companies Act** in respect of registration have been **complied** with: s 12(3).
Registration fee	A registration fee of £20 is also payable on registration.

Exam focus point

In law exams students' answers often just state that the company needs to file its memorandum and articles with the registrar, and do not mention the other documents. Without them the company would not be registered, so remember to mention them if you are doing a question on incorporation.

Another common weakness is failing to provide a brief explanation of each of the relevant documents. Note that a public company needs to send in a form 117, as well.

2.2 Certificate of incorporation

FAST FORWARD

A private company may carry on business as soon as it is incorporated. A public company requires a **s 117 certificate.**

The registrar considers whether the documents are formally in order and whether the objects specified in the memorandum appear to be **lawful.** If he is satisfied, he gives the company a '**registered number**' (s 705), issues a **certificate of incorporation** and publishes a **notice in the London Gazette** that it has been issued: ss 13 and 711.

Key term

The **certificate of incorporation** is a certificate issued by the Registrar of Companies which denotes that a company has been formed and has legal incorporated status.

The certificate of incorporation is conclusive evidence that:

- All the **requirements** of the **Companies Act** have been **followed.**
- The company is a **company authorised** to be **registered** and has been **duly registered.**
- If the certificate states that the company is a **public company** it is conclusive.

If irregularities in formation procedure or an error in the certificate itself are later discovered, the certificate is nonetheless **valid** and **conclusive**: *Jubilee Cotton Mills Ltd v Lewis 1924.*

The certificate of incorporation is not conclusive on the **legality** of the **objects** for which the company is formed (as stated in the memorandum of association). If they are subsequently found to be unlawful a petition may be presented for the compulsory winding up of the company, or the Attorney General may apply for cancellation of the registration.

R v Registrar of Companies (ex p Attorney-General) 1991
The facts: A woman named Lindi St Claire succeeded in having her company, Lindi St Claire (Personal Services) Ltd, registered despite the fact that its object was to promote her services as a prostitute. The Attorney-General applied for a reversal of the decision on the grounds that it was not a lawful purpose.

Decision: 'It is well-established law that a contract made for sexually immoral purposes is against public policy and therefore illegal'. The registration was reversed. 'Had she been less frank, for example by stating that the primary object was 'to carry on the business of masseuses and to provide related services', she would probably have got away with it' *Gower's Principles of Modern Company Law.*

2.3 Companies 'off the shelf'

Because the registration of a new company can be a lengthy business, it is often easiest for people wishing to operate as a company to purchase an **'off the shelf' company**.

This is possible by contacting enterprises specialising in registering a stock of companies, ready for sale when a person comes along who needs the advantages of incorporation.

Normally the persons associated with the company formation enterprise are registered as the company's subscribers, and its first secretary and director. When the company is purchased, the **shares** are **transferred** to the **buyer**, and the registrar is notified of the director's and the secretary's resignation.

The principal **advantages** of purchasing an off the shelf company are as follows.

(a) The **following documents** will **not need** to be **filed** with the Registrar of Companies:

- Memorandum and articles
- Statement in the prescribed form
- Statutory declaration
- Fee

This is because the specialist has already registered the company. It will therefore be a quicker, and very possibly cheaper, way of incorporating a business.

(b) There will be **no risk** of **potential liability** arising from pre-incorporation contracts (discussed below). The company can trade without needing to worry about waiting for the registrar's certificate of incorporation.

The **disadvantages** relate to the changes that will be required to the off-the-shelf company to make it compatible with the members' needs.

(a) The **objects** set out in the company's memorandum may **not be appropriate**.

(b) The off-the-shelf company is likely to have **Table A articles**. The directors may wish to amend these.

(c) The directors may want to **change** the **name** of the company.

(d) The **subscriber shares** will need to be **transferred**, and the transfer recorded in the register of members. Stamp duty will be payable.

(e) The directors may wish to have the **authorised share capital increased**.

Question

Documents required on formation of a company

What are the documents which must be delivered to the registrar on formation of a company?

Answer

- The Memorandum of association
- The Articles of association
- Form 10 (on directors and secretary)
- Form 12 (declaration of compliance)
- Fee of £20

2.4 Re-registration procedures

FAST FORWARD

Companies can re-register from private to public and vice versa, or can change status from limited to unlimited.

	Re-registering as a public company	Re-registering as a private company
Resolution	The **shareholders must agree** to the company going public • Convene a general meeting • Pass a **special resolution** (75% majority – Alters the memorandum and if necessary, the articles	The **shareholders must agree** to the company going private • Convene a general meeting • Pass a **special resolution** (75% majority of those present and voting) – Alters the memorandum and if necessary, the articles
Application	The **company must** then **apply** to the registrar to go public • Send application to the registrar • Send additional information to the registrar, comprising – Copy of altered memorandum and articles – Balance sheet and related auditors' statement – Statutory declaration – Valuation report on assets bought since balance sheet date	The **company must** then **apply** to the registrar to go private • Send the application to the registrar
Approval	The registrar must be convinced the **application is in order.** If he is, he issues a certificate of re-registration.	The registrar issues a certificate of re-registration.
Compulsory re-registration	If the **share capital** if a public company **falls below £50,000**, it must re-register as a private company.	There is **no such compulsion** for a private company.

2.5 Re-registering a limited company as unlimited

A private company originally formed with limited liability may re-register as unlimited under the procedure of ss 49 – 50.

(a) **Application** in the prescribed form signed by a director or by the secretary is made to the **registrar**; the application sets out the necessary changes to the memorandum.

(b) The application must be accompanied by the **written consent** of **every member** of the company to the unlimited liability now imposed on him, by a **statutory declaration** and a **copy** of the **altered memorandum** and articles.

(c) The registrar issues his **certificate of re-registration** as an unlimited company and the changes then take effect.

A company can only change from limited liability to unlimited once; it cannot change back again.

By special resolution (75% majority of those present and voting) a limited company may, if its articles so authorise, alter its memorandum so as to render its managing director, directors or managers liable without limit for the company's debts: s 307.

2.6 Re-registering an unlimited company as limited

An unlimited company may re-register as limited under a similar procedure except that:

(a) The decision is taken by passing a **special resolution** (it is not necessary to obtain the consent of every member).

(b) If the company goes into **liquidation** within **three years** of **re-registration** every person who was a member at the date of re-registration is **liable without limit** in respect of any outstanding debts and liabilities which were incurred before the date of re-registration. Anyone who had ceased to be a member before re-registration may in some circumstances be similarly liable if liquidation begins within a year of ceasing to be a member: ss 51 – 52.

The purpose of these rules is to prevent members of an unlimited company which is on the verge of insolvency from escaping liability for its debts by re-registering it with limited liability before the crash comes.

In this case also only one change, from unlimited to limited liability, is permitted. The company may not reverse the change.

A company limited by shares **cannot** re-register as a company limited by guarantee or **vice versa**.

3 Commencement of business

3.1 Private company

A **private company** may do business and exercise its borrowing powers from the date of its incorporation. After registration the following procedures are important.

(a) A **first meeting** of the directors should be held at which the chairman, secretary and sometimes the auditors are appointed, shares are allotted to raise capital, authority is given to open a bank account and other commercial arrangements are made.

(b) A **return of allotments** should be made to the registrar: s 88.

(c) Within the first nine months of its existence the company should give notice to the registrar of the **accounting reference date** on which its annual accounts will be made up: s 224. If no such notice is given within the prescribed period, companies are deemed to have an accounting reference date of the **last day of the month** in which the **anniversary of incorporation** falls.

3.2 Public company

A **public company** incorporated as such may not do business or exercise any borrowing powers unless it has obtained a **trading certificate** from the registrar: s 117. A private company which is re-registered as a public company is not subject to this rule.

To obtain the registrar's certificate under s 117 a public company makes application on **Form 117** signed by a director or by the secretary with a statutory declaration made by the director or secretary which states:

Form 117

- The nominal value of the allotted share capital is not less than £50,000
- The amount paid up on the allotted share capital, which must be at least one quarter of the nominal value and the entire premium if any; effectively this imposes a minimum of paid up capital of £12,500: s 101
- Particulars of preliminary expenses and payments or benefits to promoters

If a public company does business or borrows before obtaining a certificate the other party is protected since the **transaction is valid**. However the company and any officer in default is **punishable** by a **fine**. Moreover the other party may call on the directors to obtain a s 117 certificate. If they fail to do so within 21 days they must **indemnify him** against any loss: s 117(7) and (8).

If a public company fails to obtain a s 117 certificate within a year of incorporation a petition may be presented for its **compulsory winding up:** s 122(1)(b) Insolvency Act 1986.

Exam focus point

Remember these rules only apply to **public companies** so you would only mention them if you were asked about the formation and commencement of business of public companies.

4 Promoters and pre-incorporation contracts 12/02

FAST FORWARD

A promoter is a person who undertakes to form a company.

A promoter is in a **fiduciary position** to the company and must disclose any personal advantage he obtains from acting as promoter.

If a contract purports to be made by a company before the company has been formed, the person making the contract is held **personally** liable.

A company cannot form itself. The person who does so is called a 'promoter'. These were introduced as an example of an agent in Chapter 9.

Key term

A **promoter** is ' one who undertakes to form a company with reference to a given project and to set it going and who takes the necessary steps to accomplish that purpose': *Twycross v Grant 1877.*

In addition to the person who takes the procedural steps to get a company incorporated, the term 'promoter' includes anyone who makes **business preparations** for the company. However a person who acts merely in a professional capacity in company formation, such as a solicitor or an accountant, is not on that account a promoter.

4.1 Skill and care

Promoters have the general duty to exercise **reasonable skill and care.**

4.2 Fiduciary duty of promoters

If the promoter is to be the owner of the company (as in *Salomon's* case) there is no conflict of interest and it does not matter if the promoter obtains some advantage from the incorporation, for example by selling his existing business to the company in return for 100% of the shares.

If, however, some or all the shares of the company when formed are to be allotted to persons other than the promoter, this raises the issue of how the promoter should act as **agent** of the company. As an agent of the future company the promoter has the customary fiduciary duties of an agent (See Chapter 9).

4.2.1 Disclosure of interest

(a) A promoter must account for any **benefits obtained** through acting as a promoter.

(b) A promoter must not put himself in a position where his own **interests conflict** with those of the company.

(c) A promoter must provide **full information** on his transactions and account for all monies etc arising from them. The promoter must therefore make **proper disclosure** of any personal advantage to **existing** and **prospective** company **members** or to an **independent board of directors**. It will not be enough to disclose the transaction to the board, if the board has been appointed by, or is connected to, the promoter: *Erlanger v New Sombrero Phosphates Co 1878.*

4.2.2 Wrongful profits

There are two types of profit which a promoter may make, one legitimate and the other wrongful.

(a) A **legitimate** profit is made by a promoter who acquires interest in property **before promoting** a company and then makes a profit when he sells the property to the promoted company provided he discloses it: *Re Lady Forrest (Murchison) Gold Mine Ltd 1901.*

(b) A **wrongful** profit is made by a promoter who enters into and makes a profit personally in a contract as a promoter. He is in breach of fiduciary duty.

Nowadays a promoter of a public company makes his disclosure of legitimate profit through the listing particulars or the prospectus. If he makes proper disclosure of a legitimate profit, he may retain it.

4.2.3 Remedy for breach of fiduciary duty

If the promoter does not make a proper disclosure of legitimate profits or if he makes wrongful profits the primary remedy of the company (as in *Erlanger's* case above) is to **rescind** the **contract** and **recover its money**.

However sometimes it is too late to rescind because the property can no longer be returned or the company prefers to keep it. In such a case the company can **only recover** from the promoter his **wrongful profit**, unless some special circumstances dictate otherwise.

The promoter can also be made to account for legitimate profits arising from the sale of property to the company if they arose from a **collateral transaction** (pledging on the sale of property): *Gluckstein v Barnes 1900.*

A promoter may also be sued for damages for breach of his fiduciary duties: *Re Leeds and Hanley Theatres of Varieties Ltd 1902.*

If there is a **prospectus offer**, the promoter has a statutory liability to compensate any person who has acquired securities to which the prospectus relates and suffered loss in respect of them as a result of any untrue or misleading statement, or omission: s 166 Financial Services Act 1986.

Statutory and listing regulations together with rigorous investigation by merchant banks have greatly lessened the problem of the dishonest promoter.

4.3 Pre-incorporation expenses

A promoter usually incurs expenses in preparations, such as drafting legal documents, made before the company is formed. He has no automatic right to recover his expenses from the company. However he can generally arrange that the first directors, of whom he may be one, agree that the company shall pay the bills or refund to him his expenditure.

4.4 Pre-incorporation contracts

Key term

A **pre-incorporation contract** is a contract purported to be made by a company or its agent at a time before the company has received its certificate of incorporation.

As an abstract person a company cannot make contracts for itself. It does so through agents. Therefore, as a principal it may ratify a contract afterwards. Ratification has retrospective effect to the time when the agent made the contract. A company can **never ratify** a contract made on its behalf **before it was incorporated**. It did not exist when the pre-incorporation contract was made; it cannot be made a party to it.

4.4.1 Novation

A company may enter into a **new contract** (novation) on **similar terms** after it has been incorporated. However there must be **sufficient evidence** that the company has made a new contract. Mere recognition of the pre-incorporation contract by performing it or accepting benefits under it is not the same as making a new contract.

4.5 Liability of promoters for pre-incorporation contracts

As the company is not bound by a pre-incorporation contract the person who made the contract on its behalf was **warranting to the other party** that his **principal** (the company) **existed** when in fact **it did not**. As agent, the **promotor** is therefore liable for damages for breach of warranty of authority: *Kelner v Baxter 1866.*

Liability is now determined by s 36C(1).

> 'A contract which purports to be made by or on behalf of a company at a time when the company has not been formed has effect, subject to any agreement to the contrary, as one made with the person purporting to act for the company or as agent for it, and he is personally liable on the contract accordingly.'

This statutory rule leaves the company's agent liable on a contract to which he is deemed to be a party. The agent may also be entitled to enforce the contract against the other party and so he could transfer the right to enforce the contract to the company.

The effect of s 36C(1) was considered by the Court of Appeal in 1981 in the case below.

Phonogram Ltd v Lane 1981
The facts: At the time when the contract was made no action at all had been taken to form a company and both parties were aware of this. The defendant (who was the promoter of the new company) relied on that fact (as indicated in the court's finding below) and also argued that there was an implied 'agreement to the contrary' that he should not be liable on the contract.

Decision:

(a) Although the EU directive (on which the law was based) refers to contracts made for a company 'in formation', s 36C(1) is more widely expressed; it refers to 'a time when the company has not been formed', that is, any time before there is an existing company.

(b) S 36C (1) refers to a contract which 'purports to be made by the company'. It makes no difference that the other party knows there is no company nor is it material whether the contract is made in the name of itself or by a person as agent for it.

(c) An 'agreement to the contrary' must be an express agreement; it cannot be merely implied.

Lane was therefore liable to repay moneys paid over when the contract was made, as its terms had not been fulfilled.

4.6 Other ways of avoiding promoter liability

There are various other ways for promoters to avoid liability for a pre-incorporation contract.

(a) The contract remains as a **draft** (ie not binding) until the company is formed. The promoters are the directors, and the company has the power to enter the contract. Once the company is formed, the directors take office and the company enters into the contract.

(b) If the contract has to be finalised before incorporation it should contain a clause that the personal liability of promoters is to cease if the company, when formed, enters a **new contract** on identical terms.

(c) The promoters in the contract declare themselves to be **trustees** for the company. (You can have an unborn beneficiary of a trust.)

A common way to avoid the problem concerning pre-incorporation contracts is to buy a company **'off the shelf'** (see Section 2 of this chapter). Even if a person contracts on behalf of the new company before it is bought the company should be able to ratify the contract since it existed 'on the shelf' at the time the contract was made. It does not matter that the name of the shelf company is changed once it is bought and the company ratifies in its new name: *Oshkosh B'Gosh Inc v Dan Marbel Inc Ltd 1989.*

Exam focus point

You studied the laws of agency at Chapter 9, and have now learnt about two examples of the law of agency working in business: partnership and promoters. The examine could examine various parts of the syllabus by bringing such examples together.

5 Public accountability

FAST FORWARD

The statutory publicity requirements are designed to ensure that corporate bodies (especially limited liability companies) are open to public enquiry where this is in the public interest. This is achieved primarily by the requirements to:

– **Maintain registers** which can be inspected by the public
– **Notify the registrar** of certain important transactions
– **File with** the **registrar annual audited accounts** and the **annual return**

Under company law the privileges of trading through a separate corporate body is matched by the duty to provide information which is available to the public about the company.

5.1 Availability of information

Basic sources of information on UK companies

- Its **file at the Companies Registry** in which the registrar holds all documents delivered to him by the company for filing. Any member of the public, for example someone who intends to do business with the company, may inspect the file, inspection can be physical or electronic
- The **registers and other documents** which the company is required to hold at its registered office (or in some cases at a different address).
- **The London Gazette** in which the company itself or the registrar is required to publish certain notices or publicise the receipt of certain documents.
- The **company's letterheads** and other forms which must give particulars of the company's place of registration, its identifying number and the address of its office: s 351.

5.2 The role of the registrar

The registrar's full title is the Registrar of Companies (the registrar) and his department within the Department of Trade and Industry is usually called the Companies Registry (the registry) (in full it is 'the Companies Registration Office').

In its memorandum of association a company must state whether its registered office is to be situated in **England** (which includes Wales) **or** in **Scotland**: s 2. If in England its file is held at the Companies Registry at Cardiff. If the registered office is in Scotland the company's file is at the registry at Edinburgh.

Throughout its existence the company deals only with the registry which holds its file. For example, an English company which creates a charge over its property in Scotland gives notice to the registry at Cardiff not Edinburgh.

The company is identified by its **name** and **serial number** which must be stated on every document sent to the registry for filing.

5.3 Contents of the registry file

On first incorporation the company's file includes a copy of its certificate of incorporation and the original documents presented to secure its incorporation.

If a company has been in existence for some time the file is likely to include the following.

- Certificate of incorporation
- S 117 public company trading certificate
- Each year's annual accounts and return
- Copies of special, extraordinary and some ordinary resolutions
- A copy of the **altered** memorandum or articles of association if relevant
- Notices of various events such as a change of directors or secretary
- If a company issues a prospectus, a signed copy with all annexed documents

6 Statutory books and returns 6/02

A company must keep **registers** of certain aspects of its constitution. To make inspection of the registers reasonably easy for persons who are entitled to have access to them, the company must keep them at specified places.

STATUTORY REGISTERS		
Register	*Must be kept at registered office?*	*Relevant CA85 section*
Register of **members**	NO	s 352
Register of **directors and secretaries**	YES	s 288
Register of **directors' interests** in shares and debentures of the company	NO	s 325
Register of **charges**	YES	s 411
Minutes of general meetings of the company	YES	s 382
Minutes of directors' and **managers' meetings**	YES	s 382
Register of **written resolutions**	YES	s 382A
Register of **substantial interests** in shares (Public company ONLY) (a substantial interest is 3% or more of the nominal value of any class of share)	NO	s 211

Exam focus point

This is a stage two exam and the examiner will expect you to have a good knowledge of the Companies Act (say, key section numbers). However, the first two columns of this table (ie the law itself) are the most important ones; you **must** learn these.

6.1 Register of members

Every company must, under s 352, keep a register of members and enter in it:

(a) The **name** and **address** of **each member**

(b) **The class** (if more than one) to which he belongs unless this is indicated in the particulars of his shareholding

(c) If the company has a share capital, the **number of shares** held by each member. In addition:

   (i) If the shares have **distinguishing numbers**, the member's shares must be identified in the register by those numbers

   (ii) If the company has more than one class of shares the member's shares must be **distinguished** by their **class**, such as preference, ordinary, non-voting shares (and such like)

(d) The date on which each member **became** and eventually the date on which he **ceased** to be a member

6.1.1 Location of register of members

The register of members **may** be kept:

- At the registered office
- At another office of the company
- At the office of a professional registrar

but if it is kept at one of the last two, the other place **must**

- Be in England and Wales.
- Have its address notified to the registrar: s 353.

Any member of the company can inspect the register of members of a company without charge; a member of the public must pay but has the right of inspection.

6.2 Register of charges

The register must contain:

- **Details of charges** affecting the company property or undertaking
- **Brief descriptions** of property charged
- The **amount** of the charge
- The **name** of the person entitled to the charge

A company must also keep copies of every instrument creating a charge at its registered office: s 421. Any person may inspect the charges register; members and creditors may inspect free of charge.

6.3 Register of directors and secretaries

The register of directors and secretaries must contain the following details in respect of a director who is an individual: s 288.

- **Present and former forenames and surnames***
- **Residential address***
- **Nationality**
- Business **occupation**
- Particulars of other **current and former directorships** held in the last five years
- **Date of birth**

Only the * items are required for company secretaries.

The register must include shadow directors (discussed in a later chapter) as well as normal directors.

The register must be open to inspection by a member (free of charge), or by any other person (for a fee).

6.4 Register of directors' interest in shares and debentures

The register of **directors' interests in shares** and debentures must be maintained by the company (s 324), showing details of holdings and rights under s 325 and Schedule 13 para 14. Interests include those of a **director's spouse** and **minor children** (under 18). The directors must notify the interest (which may be unspecified) within **five days** of his becoming aware of it. The company must then amend the register within **three days**.

6.4.1 Location of register of directors' interests

The register of directors' interests and any register of substantial interests in the voting shares of a public company must be kept in the same place, **either** at the company's **registered office** or where the **register of members is kept**.

6.5 Register of debentureholders

Companies with debentures issued nearly always keep a **register of debentureholders**, but there is no statutory compulsion to do so. If a register of debentureholders is maintained, it should not be held outside England and Wales, and should generally be kept at the **registered office**.

6.6 Directors' service agreements

Copies of directors' service agreements should be kept with the register of members, at the company's principal place of business, or at the registered office.

7 Annual accounts

The directors must, in respect of each accounting reference period of the company:

- **Prepare** a **balance sheet** and **profit and loss account** which give a **true and fair view:** s 226
- **Lay** before the company in general meeting **accounts** for the period: s 241 (with exceptions as described below)
- **Deliver** to the **registrar** a copy of those accounts: s 242 . Currently most private companies are permitted to file abbreviated accounts.

7.1 Approval and signing of accounts

The company's board of directors must **approve** the **annual accounts**. When directors approve annual accounts knowing that they do not comply with the Act, or regardless as to whether they do or not, they are **guilty** of an **offence**: s 233(5).

7.2 Laying and filing of accounts

The following requirements relate to the laying and filing of accounts.

(a) A company is required to **lay its accounts** and the directors' and auditors' reports before **members** in **general meeting** (unless it is a private company which has dispensed with this requirement by an elective resolution): s 241.

(b) It must **deliver** a **copy** to the **registrar** within a maximum period reckoned from the date to which the accounts are made up: s 242. The standard permitted interval between the end of the accounting period and the issue of accounts is **seven months** for a **public** and **ten months** for a **private company.**

7.3 Dispensing with laying accounts

The members of a **private** company, by **elective resolution** under s 379A (unanimous approval), may decide to **dispense** with the **laying of accounts** and reports before a general meeting: s 252.

7.4 Auditors' and directors' reports

The accounts must be audited and the auditors' report must be attached to the copies issued to members, delivered to the registrar or published. However a company which is **'dormant'** may exclude this requirement: ss 235, 233 and 250. Exemptions also apply to **small companies**.

The accounts must also be accompanied by a **directors' report** giving information on a number of prescribed matters: s 234. Directors of companies quoted on the Stock Exchange must also prepare a directors' remuneration report: S 234B.

7.5 Operating and financial review

The Companies Act 1985 (Operating and Financial Review) Regulations 2005 require **quoted** companies to produce an Operating and Financial Review (OFR) annually. The OFR is designed to give a balanced and full analysis of the performance of the company (and any subsidiaries) trends and factors underlying its development, performance and position and which are likely to affect future developments.
The OFR must include:

- statement of the business objectives and strategies of the company
- a statement of resources
- a description of risks and uncertainties facing the company
- a description of the company's capital structure, objectives and liquidity

7.6 Circulation of accounts

Each **member** and **debentureholder** is entitled to be sent a copy of the **annual accounts**, together with the directors' and auditor's reports, at least 21 days before the meeting before which they shall be laid: s 238(1).

Anyone else entitled to **receive** notice of a general meeting, including the company's auditor, should **also be sent** a copy. At any other time any member or debenture holder is entitled to a copy free of charge within seven days of requesting it: s 239(1).

7.7 Summary financial statements

A **listed public** company may prepare a summary financial statements to be circulated to members instead of the full accounts: s 251(1).

8 Accounting records

A company is required by s 221 to keep accounting records sufficient to **show and explain** the company's transactions. At any time, it should be possible:

- To **determine** with reasonable accuracy the **company's financial position**
- To ascertain that any **balance sheet or profit and loss account** prepared is **done so** in **accordance with the Act**

Certain records are required by the Act.

- Daily entries of **sums paid** and **received**, with details of the source and nature of the transactions
- A **record** of **assets** and **liabilities**
- **Statements of stock** held by the company at the end of each financial year
- **Statements of stocktaking** to back up the records in (c)
- **Statements of goods bought and sold** (except retail sales), together with details of buyers and sellers sufficient to identify them

The requirements (c) to (e) above apply only to businesses involved in dealing in goods.

Accounting records must be kept for **three** years (in the case of a **private** company), and **six** years in that of a **public** one: s 222(5).

Accounting records should be kept at the company's **registered office** or at some other place thought fit by the directors. Accounting records should be open to **inspection** by the **company's officers**. Shareholders have **no statutory rights** to inspect the records, although they may be granted the right by the articles.

9 The annual return

Every company must make an annual return to the registrar under ss 363 – 364A.

The annual return is made up to a 'return date', which is either the **anniversary of incorporation** or the **anniversary of the date** of the previous return (if this differs). The return must be delivered to the registrar within **28 days** of the return date: s 363.

The **return** must be **signed** by a director or a secretary, and **accompanied** by a fee of £15.

The form of the annual return prescribed for a company which has share capital is:

- The address of the registered office of the company
- The address (if different) at which the register of members or debentureholders is kept
- The type of company and its principal business activities
- The total number of issued shares and their aggregate nominal value
- For each class of shares, the total number of shares in that class and their total nominal value
- The names and addresses of members of the company
- The names and addresses of those who have ceased to be members since the last return
- The number of shares of each class held by members at the return date
- Whether the company has chosen to dispense with the laying of accounts and holding an AGM
- The names and addresses of directors and secretary
- For each director: date of birth, nationality, business occupation, other directorships

Question

Statutory records

In the absence of a company taking advantage of alternative provisions under the Companies Act 1985, what statutory records must be kept at a company's registered office?

Answer

The Companies Act 1985 requires the following documents to be kept at a company's registered office

(a) Register of members (s 352) and an index of members if there are more than 50

(b) Register of directors and secretaries (s 288) containing the details specified

(c) Register of directors' interest in shares and debentures of the company and its associates: s 325

(d) Register of fixed and floating charges over the company's property and undertakings, together with copies of the charges: s 411

(e) Minutes of general meetings of the company's members: s 382

(f) Register of notifiable interests in shares

(g) Register of debenture-holders if there is one

Chapter roundup

- This chapter began by explaining the process companies need to go through to become incorporated and commence business. We then discussed the role of promoters in forming a company, and the dangers of entering into contracts before the company is formed, and looked at the publicity requirements that a company is obliged to fulfil.
- A limited company is one where the members' liability for the debts of the company is limited to the amount unpaid on their shares.
- Limited companies may be registered as public or private companies. Unlimited companies are always private.
- A company is formed by the issue of a **certificate of incorporation**.
- To obtain a certificate of incorporation, various documents must be sent to the registrar.
  - **Memorandum** of association
  - **Articles** of association
  - Form 10 giving **particulars** of **first director(s)** and **secretary** and **address** of registered office
  - **Registration fee**
- A private company may carry on business as soon as it is incorporated. A public company requires a **s 117 certificate.**
- A **promoter** is a person who **undertakes** to **form** a company.
- A promoter is in a **fiduciary position** to the company and must disclose any personal advantage he obtains from acting as promoter.
- If a contract purports to be made by a company before the company has been formed, the person making the contract is held **personally** liable.
- The statutory publicity requirements are designed to ensure that corporate bodies (especially limited liability companies) are open to public enquiry where this is in the public interest. This is achieved primarily by the requirements to:
  - **Maintain registers** which can be inspected by the public
  - **Notify the registrar** of certain important transactions
  - **File with** the **registrar annual audited accounts** and the **annual return**
- The statutory registers which must be kept are:
  - Register of **members**
  - Register of **directors and secretaries**
  - Register of **directors' interests**
  - Register of **charges**
  - **Minutes** of **meetings**
  - Register of **written resolutions**
  - Register of **substantial interests** (3% or more) for public companies only
- The directors must prepare a balance sheet and profit and loss account in respect of each accounting period. The accounts must be:
  - **Brought before the company in general meeting**
  - **Delivered** to the **registrar**
- Every company must make an **annual return** to the registrar. You should learn the principal contents of the annual return.

Quick quiz

1 A company must keep at its registered office a register of directors and secretary. What details must be revealed concerning the secretary?

A Full name
B Address
C Nationality
D Date of birth
E Directorships in other companies currently held
F Directorships in other companies held in the last five years

2 If no notice of the accounting reference date is given within nine months, what is a company's accounting reference date deemed to be?

3 If a public company does business or borrows before obtaining a certificate from the registrar under s 117 Companies Act 1985, the transaction is:

A Invalid, and the third party cannot recover any loss
B Invalid, but the third party may recover any loss from the directors
C Valid, and the directors are punishable by a fine
D Valid, but the third party can sue the directors for further damages

4 A company can confirm a pre-incorporation contract by performing it or obtaining benefits from it.

True ☐

False ☐

5 What is an off-the-shelf company, and what is its significance in company formation?

6 The register of members must be kept at a company's registered office.

True ☐

False ☐

7 Which of the following details is the register of members required to include?

A Names, addresses and date of birth of members
B The amount paid to the company for the shares
C Date of presentation of the share certificate
D Date on which a person ceases to be a member
E Nominal value of the shares

8 If a certificate of incorporation is dated 6 March, but is not signed and issued until 8 March, when is the company deemed to have come into existence?

Answers to quick quiz

1 A and B. C to F are required of directors, but not of the secretary.

2 The last day of the month in which the anniversary of incorporation falls.

3 C

4 False, as demonstrated in *Re Northumberland Avenue Hotel Company Ltd 1886.* The company must make a *new* contract on similar terms

5 An off the shelf company is a dormant company available for purchase by those wishing to set up a company. Purchase of an off-the-shelf company means that formation formalities are avoided, and there is no risk of liability for pre-incorporation contracts.

6 False. It can be kept where it is made up, at another office of the company or at the office of a professional registrar, provided that other place is in the same domicile.

7 B, D and E are correct. The date of presentation is not required, so C is incorrect. The register should include the members' names and addresses, but not their dates of birth, so A is incorrect.

8 6 March. The date on the certificate is conclusive; the facts are similar to *Jubilee Cotton Mills v Lewis 1920.*

Now try the question below from the Exam Question Bank

Number	Level	Marks	Time
Q13	Examination	10	18 mins

12

Memorandum of association

Topic list	Syllabus reference
1 Purpose and contents of the memorandum	5(b)
2 Company name	5(b)
3 The objects clause	5(c)
4 Other clauses in the memorandum	5(b)
5 Alteration of the memorandum	5(b)

Introduction

In the previous chapter the memorandum of association was mentioned briefly as one of the documents required to be submitted to the registrar of companies.

However students often seem to confuse the memorandum with other documents, in particular the articles. The key point to remember is that the **memorandum** primarily governs the relationship of a company to the **outside world**; the **articles** (dealt with in Chapter 13) govern the company's **internal** affairs.

In this chapter and the next we cover the purposes of, and clauses in, the memorandum.

Certain areas may well come up in the exam. **Restrictions** on the **name** a company can choose are very examinable; you must appreciate the statutory rules a company must follow when choosing its name, and the possibility it may be subject to a **passing-off action** if its name is similar to another business.

The memorandum also contains the objects clause. This is an important aspect of legal personality, the capacity to contract. Also significant is the concept of **ultra vires**, a term used to describe transactions that are outside the scope of the objects clause.

Another significant clause in the memorandum is the **registered office clause**. You need to appreciate the reasons why a company is required to have a registered office.

The memorandum of association and the regulation associated with the name clause could easily be examined in Section A or as a section of a Section B scenario question.

1 Purpose and contents of the memorandum 6/03

FAST FORWARD

The memorandum is extremely important to a company because it governs the relation of a company to the outside world.

Key term

The **memorandum of association** is the document which, with the articles of association, provides the legal constitution of a company.

The purpose of the memorandum and articles of association (for short 'the memorandum' and 'the articles' in the remainder of this text) is to define what the company is and how its business and affairs are to be conducted.

Together the memorandum and articles bind the company and its members in a contractual relationship: s 14. For historical reasons these are two separate documents.

If there is any **inconsistency** between the articles and the memorandum, the **memorandum** prevails.

The original memorandum must be presented to the registrar to obtain registration of the new company. Whenever the memorandum is altered a copy of the complete altered text must be delivered to the registrar for filing: s 18.

1.1 Contents of the memorandum 12/03

S 1(3) and s 2 prescribe the form of the memorandum for the various types of company as below:

MEMORANDUM OF ASSOCIATION

	Private company limited by shares	Private company limited by guarantee	Public company	Unlimited company
Name	✓	✓	✓	✓
Statement company is a **public company**			✓	
Location of **registered office**	✓	✓	✓	✓
Objects clause	✓	✓	✓	✓
Limited liability	✓	✓	✓	
Authorised share capital	✓		✓	
Statement of amount each member will **contribute in winding up**		✓		
Declaration of association	✓	✓	✓	✓

In addition to the above clauses, which are obligatory, the memorandum may include optional clauses if so desired.

Exam focus point

You should ensure, as a minimum, that you know the contents of the memorandum of private company limited by shares (s 2). The variations for public companies and companies limited by guarantee are logical and therefore should be easy to remember. Private companies limited by shares have no flexibility with their memorandum: the clauses above are mandatory.

1.1.1 Declaration of association

Every memorandum must also end with a **declaration of association** by which the subscribers state their wish to form the company. For a private company limited by shares the declaration is as follows.

'We, the subscribers to this memorandum of association, wish to be formed into a company, pursuant to this memorandum, and we agree to take the number of shares shown opposite our respective names.'

Names and addresses of subscribers	*Number of shares taken by each subscriber*
Henrietta Carrot (Address)	One
Henry Jones (Address)	One
Total number of shares taken	Two

Dated the first day of February 19XX
Witness to the above signatures

George Brown
(Address)

2 Company name 6/03, 12/03

FAST FORWARD

Except in certain circumstances the name must end with the words limited (Ltd), public limited company (plc) or the Welsh equivalents.

No company may use a name which is:
- The **same** as that of an existing company
- A **criminal offence** or offensive
- Suggest a connection with the government or local authority (unless approved)

2.1 Statutory rules on the choice of company name

The choice of name (whether the first name or a name adopted by change of name later) of a limited company must conform to ss 25 to 31, as follows.

(a) The name must **end** with the word(s):

- **Public limited company** (abbreviated **plc**) if it is a public company
- **Limited** (or Ltd) if it is a private limited company, unless permitted to omit 'limited' from its name (see below)
- The Welsh equivalents of either (i) or (ii) may be used by a Welsh company (s 25)

(b) No company may have a name which is the **same** as that of any existing company appearing in the statutory index at the registry. For this purpose two names are treated as 'the same' in spite of minor or non-essential differences; for instance the word 'the' as the first word in the name is ignored. 'John Smith Limited' is treated the same as 'John Smith' (an unlimited company) or 'John Smith & Company Ltd': s 26(3).

(c) No company may have a name the use of which would in the registrar's opinion be a **criminal** offence or which he considers **offensive:** s 26(1).

(d) Official approval is required for a name which in the registrar's opinion suggests a **connection** with the **government** or a **local authority** or which is subject to **control**: s 26(2). Words such as 'International' or 'British' are only sanctioned if the size of the company matches its pretensions.

A name which suggests some professional expertise such as 'optician' will only be permitted if the appropriate representative association has been consulted and raises no objection.

The general purpose of the rule is to **prevent** a company **misleading** the public as to its real circumstances or activities. Certain names may be approved by the Secretary of State on written application.

2.2 Omission of the word 'limited'

A private company limited by guarantee and a company licensed to do so before 25 February 1982 may omit the word 'limited' from its name if the following conditions of s 30 are satisfied.

(a) The objects of the company must be the **promotion** of either commerce, art, science, education, religion, charity or any profession (or anything incidental or conducive to such objects).

(b) The memorandum or articles must require that the **profits** or other income of the company are to be **applied to promoting** its objects and no dividends may be paid to its members. Also on liquidation the **assets** (otherwise distributable to members) are to be **transferred** either to **another body** with similar objects or to a **charity**.

(c) A **statutory declaration** in the prescribed form must be delivered to the registrar stating that the company satisfies conditions (a) and (b) above.

2.3 Change of name

A company may change its name by:

- Passing a **special resolution** (75% majority of those present and voting)
- Obtaining the **registrar's certificate of incorporation** that he has registered the company under a new name: s 28

The change is **effective from when the certificate is issued**, although the company is still treated as the same legal entity as before.

The same limitations as above apply to adoption of a name by change of name as by incorporation of a new company.

2.3.1 Registrar intervention

The registrar can **compel** a company to **change its name** (within such time as he may allow) if:

(a) The name is the **same** as or in the registrar's opinion too like the name of another company which was or should have been on the register when the name was adopted, or if **misleading information** or assurances were given to secure registration: s 28.

(b) The company's **name** gives so **misleading** an indication of its activities as to be likely to cause harm to the public: s 32.

The Registrar successfully applied to require the 'Association of Certified Public Accountants' to change its name. The association did not require its members to have any particular qualifications yet the name might have led people to suppose its members had recognised accounting qualifications (*Association of Certified Public Accountants v Secretary of State for Trade and Industry 1997*).

Except where the public is likely to be misled and prejudiced by a company name, there is a time limit on the registrar's power to order a change of name.

(a) If the name is 'too like' another company name on the index of companies, the period is **12 months** from the date when the name was registered (on formation of the company or on voluntary change of name).

(b) If the company supplied misleading information to obtain registration of the name or fails to observe undertakings given to obtain it the period is extended to **5 years**.

2.4 Passing-off action

A person who considers that his rights have been infringed can apply for an injunction to restrain a company from using a name (**even if** the name has been duly registered) which suggests that the latter company is carrying on the business of the complainant or is otherwise connected with it.

A company can be **prevented** by an **injunction** issued by the court in a **passing-off action** from **using** its **registered name** if in doing so it causes its goods to be confused with those of the claimant, who need not be another company.

> *Ewing v Buttercup Margarine Co Ltd 1917*
> *The facts:* The claimant, a sole trader, had since 1904 run a chain of 150 shops in Scotland and the north of England through which he sold margarine and tea. He traded as 'The Buttercup Dairy Co'. The defendant was a registered company formed in 1916 with the name above. It sold margarine as a wholesaler in the London area. The defendant contended that there was unlikely to be confusion between the goods sold by the two concerns.
>
> *Decision:* An injunction would be granted to restrain the defendants from the use of its name since the claimant had the established connection under the Buttercup name; he planned to open shops in the south of England and if the defendants sold margarine retail, for which their objects clause provided, there could be confusion between the two businesses.

If, however, the two companies' businesses are different, confusion is unlikely to occur, and hence the courts will refuse to grant an injunction: *Dunlop Pneumatic Tyre Co Ltd v Dunlop Motor Co Ltd 1907.*

The complaint will not succeed if the complainant lays claim to the exclusive use of a word which has a general use: *Aerators Ltd v Tollit 1902.*

xam focus oint

When approaching questions concerned with companies' names remember both the statutory restrictions and passing off.

Question — **Passing-off action**

National Shaving Products Ltd was incorporated on 1 June 20X0. On 1 November 20X0 the directors received a letter from Nottinghamshire Shaving Products Ltd stating that it was incorporated in 19X4, that its business was being adversely affected by the use of the new company's name, and demanding that National Shaving Products Ltd change its name.

Advise National Shaving Products Ltd.

Answer

Nottinghamshire Shaving Products Ltd may seek to bring a 'passing-off action', a common law action which applies when one company believes that another's conduct (which may be the use of a company name) is causing confusion in the minds of the public over the goods which each company sells. Nottinghamshire Shaving Products Ltd would apply to the court for an injunction to prevent National Shaving Products Ltd from using its name.

However, in order to be successful, Nottinghamshire Shaving Products Ltd will need to satisfy the court, first, that confusion has arisen because of National Shaving Products Ltd's use of its registered name and, secondly, that it lays claim to something exclusive and distinctive and not something in general use: *Aerators Ltd v Tollit 1902.*

Appeal to Registrar

Alternatively Nottinghamshire Shaving Products Ltd might object to the Registrar of Companies that the name National Shaving Products Ltd is too like its own name and is causing confusion, thus appealing to the Registrar of Companies to exercise its power under s 28 CA 1985 to compel a change of name. In these circumstances, the Registrar would invite written submissions from each company, on which he would base his decision (against which there is no appeal).

2.5 Publication of the company's name

The company's name must appear legibly and conspicuously:

- **Outside** the **registered office** and **all places of business**: s 348
- On the **common seal** (if the company has one): s 350
- On all **business letters**, **notices** and **official publications**
- On all **cheques**, **orders**, **receipts** and **invoices** issued on the company's behalf: s 349

2.6 Business names other than the corporate name

Key term

A **business name** is a name used by a company which is different from the company's corporate name or by a firm which is different from the name(s) of the proprietor or the partners.

Most companies trade under their own registered names. However a company may prefer to use some other name. If it does so it becomes subject to the Business Names Act. The rules require any person (company, partnership or sole trader) who carries on business under a different name from his own:

(a) To **state** its **name** (the registered name of the company if it is a company) and **address** on all **business letters**, invoices, receipts, written orders for goods or services and written demands for payment of debts: s 4(1)(a) BNA

(b) To **display** its **name** and **address** in a **prominent position** in any **business premises** to which its customers and suppliers have access: s 4(1)(b) BNA

(c) On **request** from any **person** with whom it does business to give **notice** of its name and address: s 4(2)

The address (in Great Britain) must be one at which service of a document relating to the business will be legally effective: s 4 BNA.

Question

Company name

John Henry Smith trades as 'Fulham Drapers' through a company registered with the name John Henry Smith (Fulham Drapers) Ltd. Smith and his wife are the only shareholders and directors. No competitor objects to his trading as 'Fulham Drapers' but it brings his company under the 'business name' as well as the 'company name' rules summarised above. He has a retail shop and a warehouse in the mews behind it to which his suppliers make deliveries. He keeps his books of account at his house elsewhere in order to write them up when he has time for it.

What must he display and where in relation to his **company** name?

Answer

To comply with the law he must ensure that the following is the case.

(a) The registered name of the company (in its correct form) is printed on all his business stationery, including letterheads, invoices, receipts, orders, demands for payment, business cards, and so on. The bank supplies cheques on which the company name is printed. When the company issues a document under seal it bears the imprint of the seal on which the company name appears. The name of the company is shown at the entrance to the shop and to the warehouse.

(b) The address of the registered office is on the letterheads and order forms, and outside the shop and the warehouse.

(c) The fact that the company is registered in England and its registry number are given on letterheads and order forms.

(d) When Smith calls on customers he carries business cards bearing the name of the company and the address of the registered office – ready to hand over if demanded.

He need not display any particulars outside his house since this is not a place of business nor do customers or suppliers have access to it. He should have 'Fulham Drapers' at his shop and on his stationery.

2.7 Section summary

- A company is subject to **statutory** rules on its choice of name.
  - The name must end in Ltd/plc (apart from some exceptions).
  - The name cannot be the same as another name on the registry.
  - The name cannot be a criminal offence or offensive.
  - Certain names require permission before they can be used.
- A company may also be subject to a **passing-off action** if its name is similar to another business's.
- A company may **change** its **name voluntarily** or be **required by the registrar** to change its name.
- The company's **name** must be **displayed** on **documents** and at its **place of business**.
- Further rules govern a company which has a different **business name** to its company name.

3 The objects clause 6/05

FAST FORWARD

If a company enters into a contract which is outside its objects, that contract is said to be **ultra vires**, ie beyond the powers of the company, and therefore void. However the rights of third parties to the contract are protected by S35.

Members have the right to restrain a company from an ultra vires act, but that right is only effective if exercised prior to the act being done.

Key term

The **objects clause** is a clause in the memorandum of association of a company which states the activities which a company intends to follow. If a company pursues an activity outside the scope of that clause, any such actions are **ultra vires.**

The objects clause sets out the 'aims' and 'purposes' of the company. There are two main reasons for including it in the memorandum.

(a) Firstly, the investor wants to know for what **purpose** his capital is going to be used.

(b) The objects clause also allows a third party to know whether his proposed contract is within the company's capacity, and therefore whether it will be **enforceable**. A transaction outside the terms of the objects clause is **ultra vires** ('beyond the power') and, in principle at least, unenforceable.

In practice the use of long and varied objects clauses allowing companies to do almost anything negates these reasons.

3.1 Content of the objects clause

Prior to the Companies Act 1989, the objects clauses of companies could potentially be very important. The new act introduced the 'general commercial company' clause which is very important in modern objects clauses.

Exam focus point

The next few paragraphs will summarise the historical position. However, it is important that you do not worry too much about the history of objects clauses. It is far more important that you understand the issue of the general commercial clause, discussed below.

Objects clauses drafted before the 1989 Act could be **long and complex**, because the people drafting them wanted to ensure that the clause was as long as possible**, to avoid falling foul of the ultra vires rule**.

Such objects clauses often also contained a **general clause** (sometimes known as a *Cotman v Brougham* clause) which stated that each 'object' stated should be **construed as an object in its own right**, and not as a sub-objects of the ones preceding it.

Another feature that objects clauses could contain was a **subjective sub-clause**, stating that the directors could carry on any business whatsoever that they considered profitable. This is sometimes known as a *Bell Houses clause*, after the case where such a clause was disputed. Under the rule given in 3.4, such a clause would not be restricted to the scope of any other clauses.

Lastly on this issue, it is important to remember that while new companies will fall under the provisions of the Companies Act 1989, discussed below, there are many existing companies whose memorandums were drafted prior to 1989, that will still contain complicated clauses such as those discussed here.

3.2 Object as a 'general commercial company'

The Companies Act 1989 reformed the rules relating to the objects clause so that there would be no necessity for the objects clause to be long and complex to cover every eventuality. However, in practice new companies still use long objects clauses and simply add on the S3A clause. A company's objects

clause can merely state that the company's object is to **'carry on business as a general commercial company'**: s 3A. The legislation specifically states this to mean that:

- The object of the company is to carry on any **trade** or **business** whatsoever.
- The company has power to do all such things as are **incidental** or **conducive** to the carrying on of any trade or business by it.

3.3 Alteration of the objects

A company may under s 4(1) alter its objects by **special resolution** for any reason.

S 5 provides a procedure for a dissenting minority to apply to the court to modify an otherwise valid alteration of the objects clause. The conditions are as follows.

(a) Application to the court must be made **within 21 days** from the passing of the special resolution to alter the objects.

(b) The applicants must hold in aggregate at least **15 per cent** of the issued share capital or 15 per cent of any class of shares. They must not originally have voted in favour of the alteration nor consented to it. They may appoint one or more of their membership to apply to the court on their behalf: s 5(3).

Once such an objection is made the alternative which was approved can only come into effect insofar as the court allows: s 4(2).

3.4 Contractual capacity and ultra vires 12/04

Key term

Ultra vires is where a company exceeds the objects specified in the memorandum of association; it acts outside its capacity and the resulting transactions are void.

Since a company's capacity to contract is defined in its objects clause it has always followed that, however widely this is drawn, some acts went beyond its capacity or 'power'. The Latin term for this is **ultra vires**; in principle, the law would not allow such an act to be legally enforceable because of lack of capacity.

Ashbury Railway Carriage & Iron Co Ltd v Riche 1875
The facts: The company had an objects clause which stated that its objects were to make and sell, or lend on hire, railway carriages and wagons and all kinds of railway plant, fittings, machinery and rolling stock; and to carry on business as mechanical engineers. The company bought a concession to build a railway in Belgium, subcontracting the work to the defendant. Later the company repudiated the contract.

Decision: Constructing a railway was not within the company's objects so the company did not have capacity to enter into either the concession contract or the sub-contract. The contract was void for ultra vires and so the defendant had no right to damages for breach. The members could not ratify it and the company could neither enforce the contract nor be forced into performing its obligations.

The approach taken by the Companies Act 1989 introducing a new S3A into the 1985 Act is to **give security to commercial transactions for third parties**, whilst preserving the rights of shareholders to restrain an action on the grounds that it is ultra vires. Consequently the *ultra vires* rule is now of limited importance.

S 35(1) provides as follows:

> 'the validity of an act done by a company **shall not be called into question** on the ground of lack of capacity **by reason of anything in the company's memorandum**.'

The effect of the ultra vires rule continues to operate **internally** between the company and its members. S 35(2) provides that a member can gain an injunction to restrain the doing of an ultra vires act **before it is done**. However, **after the event, there will be no right to challenge the action** (by virtue of its validation under s 35(1)). The members are, in practice, unlikely to learn of the action until after it has been done.

The directors have a duty (to the company) to ensure that the assets of the company are not used for ultra vires purposes. If they have breached this duty, the action can only be **ratified** by **special resolution**: s 35(3). **Relief** from **liability** from the directors or any other person will require a **separate special resolution**. Thus, a transaction may be binding (by virtue of S35) but the directors could be liable for entering into a contract which is *ultra vires*.

Where a company enters into a transaction which is authorised by the objects clause or enforceable by virtue of S35 a company can seek to avoid the contract if the directors (or other agent) who acted on behalf of the company in entering into the contract were not authorised to do so. The ability of a company to evade a contract by pleading lack of authority is now modified by Section 35A. Section 35A states.

> '**in favour of a person dealing with a company in good faith**, the **power of the board of directors to bind the company**, or authorise others to do so, shall be deemed to be free of any limitation under the company's constitution.'

There are a number of points to note about s 35A(1).

(a) The section applies in favour of the **person dealing with the company** (the company is protected under s 35(3)).

(b) In contrast with s 35(1), **good faith** is required. The company has, however, to prove lack of good faith in the third party and this may turn out to be quite difficult: s 35A(2).

(c) The section covers not only acts beyond the capacity of the company, but acts beyond **'any limitation under the company's constitution'**.

3.5 Protection of the company in contracts with directors

The wide scope of ss 35 and 35A could be used to validate questionable transactions between the directors and the company. S 322A deals with this situation, allowing any **ultra vires** transactions with a director or connection of a director to be **voidable** at the instance of the company. The transaction will not however be voidable if ratified, where third party rights intervene, or where restitution can no longer be made.

The section also provides that, whether or not the transaction is avoided, the persons covered by the section (and any director who authorised the transaction) is liable to account to the company for profit made or loss and damage caused.

3.6 Powers of the company

The objects clause may contain a list of permissible transactions, **express powers.** These include the ability to borrow funds, to give security by creating charges over property, to give guarantees, and possibly to make gifts. Other powers may be implied by what the company does.

Certain powers are held to be **subordinate** to **the main objects**, and cannot be converted into independent objects. The most important example is **borrowing.** In *Re Introductions Ltd 1970,* the court held that the power to borrow 'cannot mean something in the air.' Borrowing is not an end in itself and must be used for the purposes of the company.

The principle formulated in *Re Introductions* (that a power can be exercised only in pursuance of an object of the company) was itself modified in the important case of *Rolled Steel Products (Holdings) Ltd v British Steel Corpn 1986.* In this case it was stated that where a transaction was entered into by the company, eg borrowing, in accordance with a power then the company could not plead *ultra vires* if the third party had no reason to suppose that the exercise of the power was not in pursuance of an object. Hence if the directors were, unknown to the third party, using the power to pursue a purpose not authorised by the objects then the directors were in breach of duty (the company might claim that the directors could not bind the company) but the transaction was **not** *ultra vires.*

If transactions are entered into to **further** the **objects** of the company or to exercise its powers, it does not matter that in the absence of fraud, the transaction does not benefit the company. So for example in *Re Horsley and Weight Ltd 1982* there was an express power to grant pensions to former directors. The objection was raised that, in the absence of benefit to the company, that it had no power to reduce its assets by a transaction of this kind. The court held that there was no limit on an express power.

If the company's powers have been misused by the directors, normally the members may **ratify** the **contract**. However this cannot be done when the company property is **misappropriated,** since to ratify a misappropriation would be a fraud on the minority.

If powers are used **illegally,** the transaction will always be void.

3.7 Section summary

- The objects clause sets out the **purpose** and **capacity** of the company.
- If the company acts **beyond its capacity**, it acts ultra vires.
- **Third parties** can enforce ultra vires transactions, and in addition can enforce transactions that the company's directors have no authority to enter.
- Nowadays a company can avoid the threat of ultra vires by adopting the **'general commercial company'** objects clause.
- Certain **powers** of the company, particularly the power to borrow, are **not independent**, and must be used for the purposes of the company. But when a power could be used legitimately and is used for a purpose which does not support the object, the company cannot rely on *ultra vires* to avoid the transaction.
- A company's objects clause may be **altered** by **special resolution.**

Question — **Ultra vires**

Peter is acting as a proprietor of a private limited company. He has heard of the doctrine of *ultra vires* and that its legal difficulties can be minimised by sensible drafting of the objects clause. How should the objects clause be drafted to avoid unnecessary problems?

Answer

The doctrine of *ultra vires* means that a transaction which has been entered into outside the objects and powers contained in the company's Memorandum of Association is, in principle, void. As a result of the sweeping validation provisions of the Companies Act 1989, such transactions are almost always enforceable in relation to third parties. However, the rule remains in operation internally to define part of the officer/member relationship. Acting *ultra vires* may well be disadvantageous to the company, and the drafting of the objects clause remains important.

The simplest option is merely to adopt the option available under s 3A. This provides that it is possible to register a company with objects which merely state that the company's object is to 'carry on business as a general commercial company'. S 3A specifically states this to mean that:

'(a) The object of the company is to carry on any trade or business whatsoever, and

(b) The company has power to do all such things as are incidental or conducive to the carrying on of any trade or business by it.'

Exam focus point

Make sure you understand how s 35 protects third parties.

4 Other clauses in the memorandum

FAST FORWARD

The clauses other then the name and the objects clause are the registered office clause, the limited liability clause, the capital clause and the association clause, listing the first subscribers.

4.1 Registered office clause

Key term

The **registered office** is a business address to which all communications with a company may be sent.

The memorandum does **not** state the address of the registered office but only that it will be situate in England and Wales (or Wales alone if it is to be a Welsh company – s 2(2)). This fixes the **domicile** of the company which, unlike other matters comprised in the memorandum, is **unalterable**.

The registered office need not have any close connection with the company. Some companies arrange with their accountants or solicitors to make the latter's office premises the registered office of the company.

The first address of the registered office is given in the **documents presented** to secure **incorporation**. The address of the registered office is also shown on **letterheads** and the company's **annual return**.

4.1.1 Changing the address of the registered office

The directors can alter the address of the registered office. However the new address, like the old, must be within the **country specified** in the **memorandum**.

If the address of the registered office is changed:

- Notice of the new address must be **given** to the **registrar** who gives notice in the *London Gazette*.
- The **change takes effect after** the **registration**: s 287(3).
- Documents may still be served on the company at the **former address** for a further 14 days.

The importance of the registered office is that:

(a) If a **legal document**, such as a writ, has to be **served** on a company this may be done by delivering it at the registered office or by sending it by post (preferably recorded delivery) to that office: s 725. The company cannot then deny that it has received the document.

(b) Various **registers** and other documents are held either at the registered office (or in some cases at another address).

(c) All registers and other documents must be kept **open for inspection** for at least two hours on every business day.

4.2 Limited liability

The memorandum states, if it is so, that the liability of the members is limited. If the company is a guarantee company, the memorandum also states the amount which the members are liable to contribute in a winding up.

The memorandum of association of a limited liability company may provide that the liability of its managing director, directors and managers for the company's debts shall be unlimited: s 306 (1).

4.3 The capital clause

Key term

> The **capital clause** is a clause that appears in the memorandum of association of a company which specifies the amount of share capital and its division into shares of a fixed amount.

A limited company which has a share capital must in its memorandum state:

- The **amount** of share capital with which it proposes to be registered
- The **division** of that capital into shares of a fixed amount: s 2(5)(a)
- The **nominal value** of each share

As a simple example: 'the capital of the company is £100 divided into 100 shares of £1 each'. It represents the company's **authorised share capital**.

4.4 Subscribers to the memorandum

The persons who sign as subscribers to the memorandum automatically become the **first members** of the company when it is incorporated: s 22(1). They also then become **liable to pay** the agreed amount for their subscriber shares; this must be in cash: s 106.

The subscribers also **sign** the **articles** and the **form appointing the first directors** (who may be themselves) and secretary.

4.5 Additional clauses

The contents of the memorandum are normally restricted to the compulsory clauses as described above. All additional material goes into the articles. However there is no rule which requires that this should be so. It sometimes happens that particular clauses are included in the memorandum rather than the articles because it is then **more difficult** to **alter them**.

5 Alteration of the memorandum

The compulsory clauses of the memorandum may be altered as follows.

Clause	Means of alteration
Name clause	Special resolution (75% majority of those present and voting) and registrar's certificate
Country of registered office	Unalterable
Objects clause	Special resolution (75% majority of those present and voting) with right of minority objection (see next chapter)
Limited liability – unlimited to limited	Special resolution (75% majority of those present and voting) and registrar's certificate.
Limited liability – limited to unlimited	Consent of all members and registrar's certificate

Clause	Means of alteration
Removal of clause stating public company is such	Special resolution and re-registration as a private company
Authorised capital	Whatever resolution articles prescribe (generally ordinary resolution – simple majority)

5.1 Alteration of optional additional clauses

As regards optional additional clauses included in the memorandum instead of the articles, there is a general power of **alteration by special resolution**. Members who hold at least 15% in nominal value of the company's shares or any class can apply to the court to prevent the alteration. Moreover this general power of alteration is subject to the following exceptions and restrictions of s 17.

(a) The clause can be **'entrenched'** by expressly providing that it shall not be altered. The general power of alteration is then excluded: s 17(2)(b).

(b) If the memorandum specifies a **special alteration procedure** it must be followed.

(c) If the clause defines the **rights** attached to a class of shares, those rights may only be varied by **variation of rights procedure**.

(d) If the **court has ordered** that an alteration shall be made to a clause of the memorandum or that an existing clause shall not be altered then it cannot be altered except with the **consent of the court**.

(e) **No alteration** of the memorandum or articles can compel a member to **subscribe** for additional shares or to pay more than he previously agreed in respect of shares already held unless the member agrees in writing: s 16.

When the memorandum is altered in any way the company must deliver to the registrar within 15 days of making the alteration:

- A **signed copy** of the resolution by which the alteration is made: s 380
- A **copy** of the **altered memorandum** itself

Until this has been done the company cannot rely on the amended memorandum against 'other persons': S42.

Exam focus point

Do not confuse alteration of the memorandum with alteration of the articles (which requires a special resolution).

Chapter roundup

- In this chapter we have seen that the memorandum is extremely important to a company because it governs the relation of a company to the outside world. Its contents (and the individual rules relating to its content) should be thoroughly learnt.
- The contents are summarised as follows.
  - The **name** of the company
  - Whether the **registered office** is to be situated in England and Wales, or Scotland
  - The **objects** of the company
  - The **limited liability** of members
  - The **authorised share capital**
  - **Declaration of association**
- Except in certain circumstances the name must end with the words limited (Ltd), public limited company (plc) or the Welsh equivalents.
- No company may use a name which is:
  - The **same** as that of an existing company
  - A **criminal offence** or offensive
  - Suggest a **connection** with the **government or local authority** (unless approved)
- If a company enters into a contract which is outside its objects, that contract is said to be **ultra vires.** However the rights of third parties to the contract are protected by S35.
- Members have the right to restrain a company from an ultra vires act, but that right is only effective if exercised prior to the act being done.
- Under the provisions of the Companies Act 1985, a company may outflank the ultra vires rule by stating that the object of the company is to carry on business as a **general commercial company**.
- A company's **objects** can be **altered** by passing a **special resolution**.

Quick quiz

1 What are the compulsory clauses of a public company memorandum (in the correct order)?

2 A resolution has been passed to alter the objects clause. A dissenting minority may apply to the court to cancel the alteration. The application must be made within 14/21 days by the holders of 10%/15% of the issued share capital.

3 If a company adapts the recommended wording in s 3A, what will its objects clause say?

4 On what grounds may the Registrar refuse to register a company's name?

5 A company has been formed within the last six months. Another long-established company considers that because of similarity there may be confusion between it and the new company. The long-established company must bring a passing-off action if it is to prevent the new company using its name.

True ☐

False ☐

6 When a company changes its registered office, for what period after the registration of the change can documents still be served at the old office?

7 The memorandum can contain additional optional clauses in addition to the compulsory clauses, and these can be 'entrenched' by providing that they cannot be altered.

True ☐

False ☐

Answers to quick quiz

1 Statement company is a public limited company
Location of registered office
Objects clause
Limited liability
Authorised share capital
Declaration of association

2 21 days and 15% under s 5.

3 The company's object is to carry on business as a general commercial company.

4 It does not end with the words limited or public limited company.
It is the same as that of an existing company.
It constitutes a criminal offence or is offensive.
Official approval has not been obtained or the name is misleading in other ways.

5 False. The long-established company can also complain to the Registrar within 12 months of the date that the new company was registered.

6 14 days

7 True: s 17 (2) (b) provides.

Now try the question below from the Exam Question Bank

Number	Level	Marks	Time
Q14	Examination	10	18 mins

13

Articles of association

Topic list	Syllabus reference
1 The purpose and scope of the articles	5(b)
2 The memorandum and articles as contracts	5(b)
3 Alteration of the articles	5(b)
4 Shareholders' agreements	5(b)

Introduction

Having considered in detail the memorandum of association we now turn to the articles of association which are the **internal rules** of the company.

The memorandum, as we have seen, needs only to state the company's name, objects, domicile, shares (if any) and, if such be the case, that the liability of the members is limited and that it is a public company. Everything else is regarded as a matter of administration to be dealt with in the articles of association.

You must appreciate how the articles are **binding** on the **company** and its **members**, and the consequences of this. The other significant area in this chapter is the **legal restrictions** on **altering articles**.

The articles could be examined in conjunction with the memorandum in either of Sections A or B. There may be other connections in the exam in a Section B question, for example, protection members might have by the articles which could link with a question on minority protection or directors' acts.

On the pilot paper, the articles were linked with directors in a Section B question.

1 The purpose and scope of the articles 6/03

FAST FORWARD

Articles of association is the document which, along with the memorandum of association, provides the legal constitution of a company. The articles of association define the rules and regulations governing the management of the affairs of the company, the rights of the members (shareholders), and the duties and the powers of the directors.

1.1 Difference between memorandum and articles

The articles of association deal mainly with matters affecting the **internal conduct** of the company's affairs. The memorandum differs from the articles in that it deals with the constitution of the company mainly as it affects **outsiders**. In case of conflict the memorandum prevails over the articles.

CONTENTS OF ARTICLES	
Appointment of directors Powers of directors Board meetings Calling general meetings Conduct of general meetings Dividends	Accounts Class rights Issue of shares Transfer of shares Alterations of capital structure Company secretary

1.2 Table A articles 6/04

FAST FORWARD

Table A contains the specimen format for the articles. It applies unless excluded expressly or by implication.

A company limited by shares may adopt all or any part of the statutory standard Table A model articles made under s 8. If no other articles are submitted, Table A is deemed to apply.

A company limited by shares may have its own full-length special articles. Listed companies must, since Stock Exchange rules require that the articles shall include a number of special provisions differing from the standard model.

The articles of a company limited by shares usually make clear how far Table A applies by starting with:

- Either a **statement** that **Table A shall not apply** (because full length special articles follow), or
- That **Table A shall apply** with **only the modifications** and exclusions which follow

If no such statement is made the special articles override Table A where they cover the same subjects, but Table A applies to any matter on which there is nothing in the special articles.

A company **limited by guarantee**, an **unlimited company** and a **'partnership company'** must adopt **special articles**. However there are statutory models to which these special articles must conform so far as the circumstances permit: s 8.

Exam focus point

> You should be aware of the contents of Table A as companies asked about in the exam will often have Table A articles in force. Specific Table A articles are also covered where relevant elsewhere in this Text.

THE STATUTORY MODEL ARTICLES OF ASSOCIATION (TABLE A)

A summary of the 1985 Table A

1 The Companies Act 1985 contained a new model Articles of Association (Table A). This is summarised below, but note that many companies incorporated before 1st July 1985 may not have adopted this yet. At any rate, most companies have their own individual Articles, or tailor Table A to suit their needs. Every company is required to have articles. It may either adopt special articles in substitution for Table A or it may adopt Table A in its entirety or with modifications. Most public and some private companies adopt full length special articles. The majority of private companies are subject to Table A with a few modifications expressed in short articles which begin:

'The articles of association of the company are Table A of the Companies Act (date) except as expressly provided by these articles.'

Then follow a few clauses which modify the Table A wording or exclude a complete passage.

2 Unlike the previous versions the 1985 Table A is not printed as part of a schedule of the Act. It is promulgated by statutory regulations (The Companies (Alteration of Table A etc) Regulation 1984 – s 1 1984/1717) and it came into effect on 1 July 1985.

3 Although the 1985 version of Table A was made by statutory powers given to the Secretary of State for Trade and Industry its content is in most respects in accordance with the advice of the Law Society, which undertook a comprehensive review of the earlier (1984) Table A and put forward a draft for consideration by the DTI. Apart from updating Table A the aim was to make it no longer duplicate some (but not all) provisions of the Companies Act. Where the Act gives a power which the company may exercise without any corresponding provision in its own articles, Table A omits all reference to it.

4 One such case is the procedure for variation of rights attached to a class of shares. Section 125(2) confers a general power to vary class rights, *unless* the articles vary or exclude it. The 1985 Table A, unlike the previous versions, is therefore silent on this subject. Where the articles are in Table A form the company simply resorts to the unfettered power of variations given by the Act.

5 The remaining paragraphs of this note are a summary of the provisions of the current (1985) Table A. In answering examination questions it should be assumed, unless the question itself gives information to the contrary, that the company's articles are in this form. It is not necessary – or possible – to memorise *all* the provisions of Table A but a general knowledge of the more important articles of Table A is certainly required. Table A itself is sometimes referred to as 'regulations' but in this note (and elsewhere in the text) we refer to 'articles' of Table A since that is essentially what they are.

Share capital and shares (Articles 2 – 35)

6 The company may issue shares with whatever rights or restrictions as the company by ordinary resolution may determine. This includes the issue of redeemable shares of any type (Article s2 and 3). The company may pay commission as authorised by the Companies Act. This may be made partly or wholly by shares (Art 4)

7 The company is prohibited from recognising the interest of a third party in shares registered in the name of a member; the company deals only with members in connection with rights to shares (Art 5). The register of members will not, therefore, make note of the fact that share are held in trust.

8 A member is entitled to one or more share certificates for his shares and may obtain replacement for a lost certificate (Arts 6 and 7).

9 The company has a lien on partly paid shares for sums still outstanding on those shares (Article 8). There is power to sell shares if the holder defaults in payment of calls (Arts 9 – 11). There is a procedure for making calls and forfeiture in case of non-payment. (Arts 12 –22)

10 The procedure for transfer and transmission of shares (Arts 23-31) is described in the chapter on shares. There is no discretionary power to refuse to register a transfer for a fully paid share. If the company needs such a power it must adopt a special article to that effect.

11 The power to alter share capital follows ss 121 (alteration) and 135 (reduction) of the Act since those powers are only available if the articles authorise them (Arts 32 – 34). There is no longer a power to convert shares into stock but a company may adopt a special article covering it (s 121(2)(c) permits it).

12 The company may purchase its own shares in accordance with the statutory provisions (Art 35 and ss 159 – 181).

Meetings (Articles 36 – 63)

13 The procedure for convening and conducting general meetings is set out in detail later in this text.

14 Article 37 requires that, when members requisition an Extraordinary General Meeting, the directors shall set a date for it within 8 weeks. S 368(8) now overrides this article and provides that a requisitions EGM must be held within 28 days of issuing the notice of the meeting.

15 The notice convening a meeting no longer distinguishes between ordinary had special business. In all cases the requirement is that the notice shall specify 'the general nature of the business to be transacted'. here the overriding requirement of the Act (s 378) is, as before, that the full text must be given of any special or extraordinary resolution (this is not mentioned in Table A). If a meeting is an annual general meeting the notice must state it to be such.

16 A meeting may only transact business if 'a quorum is present' (Article 40). The quorum requirement is no longer limited to the number present at the outset; under Article 41 if a quorum ceases to be present the meeting is adjourned.

17 If a meeting is adjourned for 14 days or more, seven clear days notice of the adjourned meeting must be given.

18 In arranging a poll the chairman has power to appoint scrutineers, who need not be members (in practice it is usual to appoint the auditors) (Article 49).

Directors (Articles 64 – 98)

19 The minimum number of directors is two. There is no maximum (Article 64). Many companies find it convenient to fix a maximum by a special article to that effect.

20 A director may appoint as his alternate (to vote for him in his absence) another director or any other person of his choice whom the other directors may approve. An alternate director is declared to be a 'director' for all purposes including the many provisions of the act (Articles 65 – 69).

21 The directors have delegated authority to exercise all the powers of the company except where restricted by (a) the Act (b) the memorandum or articles of (c) a special resolution. These restrictive provisions cannot be exercised retrospectively to invalidate what the directors have already done under their existing powers (Article 70). A meeting of directors at which a quorum is present may exercise all the powers exercisable by directors.

22 The above general power of management includes (though it is not expressly stated) the company's power to borrow money. If, as will often be the case, the company decides to impose a limit on the amount which the directors may borrow without obtaining sanction in general meeting the company must adopt a special article.

23 Article 71 specifically allows directors to appoint agents, who may, if authorised, delegate.

24 There are articles on appointment and retirement of directors, disqualification, interest in transactions of the company, and board meetings. The substance of these provisions is described in the sequence of chapters on directors in the text.

Dividends, accounts, bonus issues (Articles 102 – 110)

25 These are straightforward provisions, mainly on procedure, which are somewhat simpler than in the previous Table A because the Table A articles no longer reproduce the requirements of the Act, for instance on maintaining accounting records (Article 109, which is now concerned with the right of members to inspect records). The company must of course comply with the Act: since the Act is very detailed in its requirements on accounting records it is unnecessary to reproduce it in all the articles.

26 Article 110, on capitalisation of profits, allows directors:

(a) to capitalise undistributed profits, share premium account or capital redemption reserve;

(b) to apply profits to paying up amounts unpaid on shares, or to paying up and allotting shares as fully paid;

(c) to authorise any person to enter the company into an agreement that shares or debentures should be treated as fully paid. Such agreement would be binding on all members

Notices (Articles 111 – 116)

27 These articles set out how the company may validly deliver notices to its members, for example to convene general meetings.

Winding-up and indemnity (Articles 117 – 118)

28 The liquidator is authorised, with the sanction of an extraordinary resolution passed in general meeting, to distribute assets in specie to members – he need not sell them in order to distribute their value in cash (Article 117). Officers are indemnified by the company against the expenses of a successful defence against legal proceedings in which negligence is alleged against them (Article 118).

1.3 Interaction of statute and articles

There are two aspects to consider.

(a) The Companies Act may permit companies to do something **if** their **articles** also authorise it. For example a company may reduce its capital if its articles give power to do this: s 135. If, however, they do not, then the company must alter the articles to include the necessary power before it may exercise the statutory power.

(b) The Companies Act will **override** the articles:

- If the Companies Act **prohibits something**
- If something is permitted by the Companies Act **only** by a **special procedure** (such as passing a special resolution in general meeting)

1.4 Form of articles

The articles must be printed and divided into numbered paragraphs: s 7(3). The first articles presented to obtain registration of a new company are signed by the subscribers to the memorandum, dated and witnessed.

1.5 Section summary

- Articles deal with the **internal conduct** of a company's business.
- Most companies limited by shares have their articles in **Table A form.**
- The Companies Act allows companies to do certain things if their **articles permit.**
- However, articles cannot override **statutory prohibitions** or **procedures.**

2 The memorandum and articles as contracts **6/04**

A company's memorandum and articles bind, under s 14:

- **Members** to **company**
- **Company** to **members** (but see below)
- **Members** to **members**

The company's articles do **not** bind the company to third parties.

This principle applies only to rights and obligations which affect members **in their capacity as members**.

> *Hickman v Kent or Romney Marsh Sheepbreeders Association 1915*
> *The facts*: The claimant (H) was in dispute with the company which had threatened to expel him from membership. The articles provided that disputes between the company and its members should be submitted to arbitration. H, in breach of that article, began an action in court against the company.
>
> *Decision:* The proceedings would be stayed since the dispute (which related to matters affecting H as a member) must, in conformity with the articles, be submitted to arbitration.
>
> *Beattie v E C F Beattie Ltd 1938*
> *The facts:* In this case the articles also provided for arbitration on disputes. The company sued its managing director to recover money improperly paid to him. The managing director applied to have the action stayed as he contended that the dispute should be submitted to arbitration.
>
> *Decision:* The claim was against the defendant as a director and the arbitration clause was limited to disputes with members as such. He could not rely on the arbitration clause. (See also *Eley's* case below.)

The principle that only rights and obligations of members are covered by s 14 applies when an outsider who is also a member seeks to rely on the articles in support of a claim made **as an outsider**.

> *Eley v Positive Government Security Life Assurance Co 1876*
> *The facts:* E, a solicitor, drafted the original articles and included a provision that the company must always employ him as its solicitor. E became a member of the company some months after its incorporation. He later sued the company for breach of contract in not employing him as a solicitor.
>
> *Decision:* E could not rely on the article since it was a contract between the company and its members and he was not asserting any claim **as a member**.

Rights that are **rights linked to shares** and which are stated in the articles will be effective, even if those rights cover issues other than the position of members, for example the appointment of directors: *Cumbrian Newspapers Group Ltd v Cumberland and Westmoreland Herald Newspaper and Printing Co Ltd 1986*.

Exam focus point

Questions with facts similar to the *Eley* case often occur in exams. Note, however, that the company may be liable for damages to the aggrieved party if there is a separate contract **as well as** the provisions in the articles. (See *Southern Foundries (1926) Ltd v Shirlaw 1940* below).

2.1 Articles as contract between members

S 14 gives to the memorandum and articles the effect of a contract made between (a) the company and (b) its members individually. It can also impose a contract on the members **in their dealings with each other**.

> *Rayfield v Hands 1958*
> *The facts:* The articles required that (a) every director should be a shareholder and (b) the directors must purchase the shares of any member who gave them notice of his wish to dispose of them. The directors, however, denied that a member could enforce the obligation on them to acquire his shares.
>
> *Decision:* There was 'a contract ... between a member and member-directors in relation to their holdings of the company's shares in its article' and the directors were bound by it.

Articles are usually drafted so that each stage is a **dealing between** the **company** and the **members**, to which s 14 clearly applies, so that:

- A member who intends to transfer his shares must, if the articles so require, give notice of his intention to the company.
- The company must then give notice to other members that they have an option to take up his shares.

2.2 Articles as supplement to contracts

FAST FORWARD

The articles can be used to establish the terms of a contract existing elsewhere.

If an outsider makes a separate contract with the company and that contract contains no specific term on a particular point but the articles do, then the contract is deemed to incorporate the articles to that extent. One example is when services, say as a director, are provided under contract without agreement as to remuneration: *Re New British Iron Co, ex parte Beckwith 1898.*

If a contract incorporates terms of the articles it is subject to the company's **right** to **alter** its articles: *Shuttleworth v Cox Bros & Co (Maidenhead) Ltd 1927.* However a company's articles cannot be altered to deprive another person of a right already earned, say for services rendered **prior** to the alteration: *Swabey v Port Darwin Gold Mining Co 1889.*

2.3 Section summary

- Articles bind the **members** to the **company**, the **company** to **members** and **members** to other **members**.
- They do **not** bind the **company** to **third parties.**
- The articles only **apply** to **rights of membership**; they **do not apply** to **rights other than membership rights** that members possess.
- Articles can be used to **supplement contracts**, to supply missing contract terms.

Exam focus point

Remember the articles only create contractual rights/obligations in relation to rights **as a member**.

Question **s 14 Companies Act 1985**

S 14(1) Companies Act 1985 provides as follows.

'Subject to the provisions of the Act, the memorandum and the articles when registered, bind the company and its members to the same extent as if they respectively had been signed and sealed by each member, and contained covenants on the part of each member to observe all the provisions of the memorandum and of the articles.'

In your own words explain what this provision means.

Answer

The effect of s 14 Companies Act 1985 is that, without obtaining from a new member any express agreement to that effect, the memorandum and articles of the company are a **binding agreement** between the member and the company.

A member must comply with the obligations imposed on him in relation to his shares. The company on its side must permit him to exercise his member's rights to vote or to receive a dividend.

The articles, if so expressed, may also constitute a contract between members: *Rayfield v Hands 1958.*

3 Alteration of the articles **Pilot paper, 6/02, 6/04**

FAST FORWARD

The articles may be altered by a **special resolution**. The basic test is whether the alteration is for the **benefit of the company as a whole.**

A company has a statutory power to alter its articles by **special resolution:** s 9(1). The alteration will be valid and binding on **all** members of the company.

An article **cannot** be made unalterable by:

(a) **Declaring** it to be **unalterable** in the articles

(b) **Making** a **separate contract** by which the company undertakes not to alter it

(c) Providing that a **larger majority** shall be required than three quarters of the votes cast on a special resolution to make an alteration: *Malleson v National Insurance & Guarantee Corporation 1894*

If all the members of the company agree to an alteration of the articles but do not hold a general meeting and pass a special resolution, this is still an effective alteration under the **'assent principle':** *Cane v Jones 1980*, but the amendment only binds those who were shareholders at the time of the alleged alteration and those who became shareholders knowing of the alleged alteration.

3.1 Making the company's constitution unalterable

FAST FORWARD

A company can, by various measures (for example **weighted voting rights**), ensure that articles are unalterable.

There are devices by which some provisions of the company's constitution can be made unalterable (without the consent of the member who wishes to prevent any alteration).

(a) The clause can be **inserted in the memorandum** instead of the articles and be described as unalterable (an 'entrenched' article). The right to alter an item in the memorandum which would have been in the articles does not apply in this case: s 17.

(b) The articles may give to a member **additional votes** so that he can block a resolution to alter articles on particular points (including the removal of his weighted voting rights from

the articles): *Bushell v Faith 1970*. However, to be effective, the articles must also limit the powers of members to alter the articles that give extra votes.

(c) The articles may provide that when a meeting is held to vote on a proposed alteration of the articles the **quorum present must include** the **member concerned**. He can then deny the meeting a quorum by absenting himself.

(d) Where a clause that could have been in the articles is in the memorandum it may be altered by a special resolution; however, **application may be made to the court** to have the alteration cancelled: s 17(1).

3.2 Restrictions on alteration

Even when it is possible to hold a meeting and pass a special resolution, alteration of the articles is restricted by the following principles.

(a) The alteration is **void** (under s 9 itself) if it **conflicts with the Companies Act** or with the **memorandum:** *Welton v Saffery 1897*.

(b) In various circumstances, such as to protect a minority (s 459) or in approving an alteration of the objects clause (s 5(5)), the **court may order** that an alteration be made or, alternatively, that an existing article shall not be altered.

(c) A **member may not be compelled** by alteration of the articles to **subscribe for additional shares** or to accept increased liability for the shares which he holds unless he has given his consent: s 16.

(d) An alteration of the articles which varies the rights attached to a class of shares may only be made if the **correct rights variation procedure** has been followed to obtain the consent of the class: s 125. A 15 per cent minority may apply to the court to cancel the variation under s 127.

(e) A person whose **contract** is contained in the **articles cannot obtain** an **injunction** to prevent the articles being altered, **but** he may be entitled to **damages** for breach of contract (see *Southern Foundries (1926) Ltd v Shirlaw 1940* below).

(f) An **alteration may not be made** with **retrospective effect** so as to take away from a member rights which he has acquired by performing a contract (as in *Swabey's* case). However there is no objection to an alteration which applies new conditions in an existing situation: *Allen v Gold Reefs of West Africa Ltd 1900* (for the facts see below).

(g) An alteration may be **void** if the **majority** who approve it are **not acting bona fide in what they deem to be the interests of the company as a whole** (see below).

3.3 The bona fide test

The case law on this subject is an effort to hold the balance between two principles:

(a) The **majority** is **entitled** to **alter articles** even though a minority considers that the alteration is prejudicial to its interests.

(b) A minority is entitled to protection against an alteration which is intended to **benefit** the **majority** rather than the company and which is **unjustified discrimination** against the minority.

Principle (b) tends to be restricted to **some cases** where the majority seeks to **expel** the minority from the company.

The most elaborate analysis of this subject was made by the Court of Appeal in the case of *Greenhalgh v Arderne Cinemas Ltd 1946*. Two main propositions were laid down by Evershed MR.

- **'Bona fide for the benefit of the company as a whole'** is a **single test** and also a **subjective test** (what did the majority believe?). The court will not substitute its own view.
- 'The company as a whole' means, in this context, **the general body of shareholders.** The test is whether every 'individual hypothetical member' would in the honest opinion of the majority benefit from the alteration.

3.3.1 Benefit of the company as a whole

If the company as a body of shareholders benefits, this may be as a result of the alteration improving or maintaining existing management: *Rights and Issues Investment Trust Ltd v Stylo Shoes Ltd 1965*, where alterations in voting rights were designed to preserve continuity of management.

If the purpose is to benefit the company as a whole the alteration is valid even though it can be shown that the minority does in fact suffer special detriment and that other members escape loss. In *Allen v Gold Reefs of West Africa Ltd 1900* the articles were altered to extend the company's lien from just partly paid shares to all shares. In fact only one member held fully paid shares. The court overruled his objections on the grounds that:

- The alteration was for the benefit of the company as a whole and applied to any member who held fully paid shares.
- The members held their shares subject to the memorandum and articles, and hence were subject to any changes to those documents.

3.3.2 Expulsion of minorities

Expulsion cases are concerned with:

- Alteration of the articles for the purpose of **removing** a **director from office**
- Alteration of the articles to permit a majority of members to **enforce** a **transfer** to themselves of the shareholding of a minority

The action of the majority in altering the articles to achieve 'expulsion' will generally be treated as **valid** even though it is discriminatory, if the majority were concerned to **benefit the company** or to remove some detriment to its interests.

If on the other hand the majority was **blatantly seeking** to secure an **advantage** to themselves by their discrimination, the alteration made to the articles by their voting control of the company will be invalid. The cases below illustrate how the distinctions are applied in practice.

Shuttleworth v Cox Bros & Co (Maidenhead) Ltd 1927
The facts: Expulsion of director appointed by the articles who had failed to account for funds was held to be valid.

Sidebottom v Kershaw, Leese & Co Ltd 1920
The facts: The articles were altered to enable the directors to purchase at a fair price the shareholding of any member who competed with the company in its business. The minority against whom the new article was aimed did carry on a competing business. They challenged the validity of the alteration on the ground that it was an abuse of majority power to 'expel' a member.

Decision: There was no objection to a power of 'expulsion' by this means. It was a justifiable alteration if made *bona fide* in the interests of the company as a whole. On the facts this was justifiable.

Brown v British Abrasive Wheel Co 1919
The facts: The company needed further capital. The majority who held 98 per cent of the existing shares were willing to provide more capital but only if they could buy up the 2 per cent minority. As the minority refused to sell the majority proposed to alter the articles to provide for compulsory acquisition on a fair value basis. The minority objected to the alteration.

Decision: The alteration was invalid since it was merely for the benefit of the majority. It was not an alteration 'directly concerned with the provision of further capital' and therefore not for the benefit of the company.

Dafen Tinplate Co Ltd v Llanelly Steel Co (1907) Ltd 1920
The facts: The claimant was a minority shareholder which had transferred its custom from the defendant company to another supplier. The majority shareholders of the defendant company therefore sought to protect its interests by altering the articles to provide for compulsory acquisition of the claimant's shares. But the new article was not restricted (as it was in Sidebottom's case above) to acquisition of shares on specific grounds where benefit to the company would result. It was simply expressed as a power to acquire the shares of a member. The claimant objected that the alteration was invalid since it was not for the benefit of the company.

Decision: The alteration was invalid because it 'enables the majority of the shareholders to compel any shareholder to transfer his shares' and that wide power could not 'properly be said to be for the benefit of the company'. The mere unexpressed intention to use the power in a particular way was not enough.

If therefore the majority intend that the power to acquire the shares of a minority is to be restricted to specific circumstances for the benefit of the company, they should ensure that this restriction is included in the new article.

3.4 Separate contracts

As explained above, the court will not grant an injunction to restrain an alteration of the articles merely because that alteration is a breach of a separate contract.

A group of cases relates to the **dismissal of a managing director**. The articles invariably authorise the board of directors to appoint one or more directors to the office of managing director or 'other executive office': Table A Article 84.

The board of directors may terminate the appointment before it has expired and the members in general meeting may terminate it by removing the director from the office of director. If he is no longer a director he is not qualified under the terms of the articles to be a managing director.

The cases turn on whether there is a **separate contract of service**. If there is such a contract, dismissal, whether under the original articles or by means of alteration of the articles, may be a breach of contract for which damages may be claimed.

(a) If the appointment is for an **unspecified period**, the power to dismiss is then unfettered by any contract and no liability for damages falls on the company: *Read v Astoria Garage (Streatham) Ltd 1952.*

(b) The appointment may be made for an **agreed period** even if it be of indefinite duration. Termination before the period has expired is a breach of contract since the power to terminate is then 'subject to the terms of an agreement'.

Nelson v James Nelson & Sons Ltd 1914
The facts: N was appointed joint Managing Director 'for so long as he shall remain a director'. The board revoked the appointment and N claimed for damages.

Decision: The articles gave the board power to appoint for 'such period as they deem fit' and they had fixed a period (so long as he shall remain a director). The power to revoke was subject to that agreement and so there had been a breach of contract.

(c) The appointment may be made **under the articles** and supported by a **separate service agreement of fixed duration**. Termination before the service agreement has expired is a breach of that agreement.

Southern Foundries (1926) Ltd v Shirlaw 1940
The facts: In 1933 S entered into a written agreement to serve the company as Managing Director for ten years. In 1936 F Co gained control of the company and used their votes to alter its articles to confer on F Co power to remove any director from office. In 1937 F Co exercised the power by removing S from his directorship and thereby terminated his appointment as Managing Director (which he could only hold so long as he was a director).

Decision: The alteration of the articles was not a breach of the service agreement but the exercise of the power was a breach of the service agreement for which the company was liable.

By its decision in *Shirlaw's* case the House of Lords made clear that the company cannot be prevented from altering its articles by a service agreement but it may be liable for damages if it thereby commits a breach of the agreement.

Exam focus point

The *Shirlaw* case is also important in the area of removal of directors.

Question

Alteration of articles

Norman has been appointed as managing director of George Ltd under a service agreement which will expire in four year's time. The company proposes to alter its articles to allow its holding company to remove any director from office. It proposes to exercise this power to remove Norman from the board, thus automatically removing him from his position as managing director. Norman does not want to be removed; what can he do to protect his position?

A Norman has no remedy; the alteration of the articles and the exercise of the new power are unfettered by his service contract as managing director, so no claim for an injunction or damages can arise.

B Norman can apply to the court under s 459 for an injunction restraining the company from making the alteration.

C Norman cannot restrain the company either from making the alteration or from removing him from the board, but he can claim damages for breach of contract.

D Norman cannot restrain the company from making the alteration, but may obtain an order for specific performance of his service contract as managing director.

Answer

C. A company cannot be prevented from altering its articles, (and the right to remove a director is also given in s 303). Because however Norman's contract does specify a fixed term he can claim damages for breach of contract; the authority is *Southern Foundries v Shirlaw 1940*.

3.5 Filing of alteration

Whenever any alteration is made to the articles a **copy** of the **altered articles** must be delivered to the registrar **within 15 days**, together with a signed copy of the special resolution by which the alteration is made: ss 18 and 380. The registrar gives notice in the *Gazette*: s 711. Until this has been done the company cannot rely on the amended article against 'other persons': S42.

3.6 Section summary

- Articles can be **altered** by **special resolution**.
- Alteration of articles must be **bona fide** for the **benefit of the company** as a whole, that is the general body of shareholders.
- There are **other restrictions** on altering articles in certain circumstances (subscription for additional shares, variation of class rights).
- **Alteration of articles** may **breach separate contracts of service** and the company may be liable for damages.
- There are **various methods** for **making articles unalterable**.

Question **Binding nature of articles**

Would a company secretary be able to enforce a clause on the articles of association which stated that he should hold office for ten years if he were removed before the expiration of ten years?

Answer

The memorandum and articles are a binding contract under s 14 only in respect of the rights and obligations of members in that capacity. The issue raised by this part of the question is based on the facts of *Eley v Positive Life Assurance Co 1875,* where the articles provided that the company should always employ Eley as its solicitor and he was also a member of the company. He was unable to enforce the article against the company since it did not relate to his position as a member but to his professional services.

If, however, the secretary was claiming remuneration at a rate stated in the articles for services already given to the company he could probably rely on this statement as evidence of the terms agreed between him and the company apart from the articles. This was the position when a director claimed fees for services already given: he was entitled to the rate stated in the articles: *Re New British Iron Co ex p Beckwith 1898.*

4 Shareholders' agreements

FAST FORWARD

A company's memorandum and articles may be supplemented by a **shareholders' agreemen**t which offers shareholders more protection.

Shareholders' agreements sometimes supplement a company's memorandum and articles of association. They are concerned with the running of the company; in particular they often contain terms by which all or some of the shareholders agree among themselves how they will vote on various issues.

Shareholders' agreements often offer more protection to the interests of shareholders than do the articles of association. Individuals have a **power of veto** over any proposal which is contrary to the terms of the agreement. This enables a minority shareholder to protect his interests against unfavourable decisions of the majority.

Chapter roundup

- In this chapter we have discussed the format and legal effect of the articles and how the articles can be altered.
- **Table A** contains the specimen format for the articles. It applies unless excluded expressly or by implication.
- The articles constitute a contract between:
  - Company and members
  - Members and the company
  - Members and members
- The articles **do not constitute** a contract between the **company** and **third parties**, or members in a **capacity** other than as **members** (the *Eley* case).
- The articles can be used to establish the terms of a contract existing elsewhere.
- The articles may be altered by a **special resolution**. The basic test is whether the alteration is for the **benefit of the company as a whole.**
- A company can, by various measures (for example **weighted voting rights**), ensure that articles are unalterable.
- A company's memorandum and articles may be supplemented by a **shareholders' agreement** which offers shareholders more protection.

Quick quiz

1 How do the articles of a company limited by shares make clear how far Table A applies?

2 A company can alter its articles by ordinary resolution.

True ☐

False ☐

3 In which of the following situations will an alteration of the articles be effective?

A Where an alteration is made that conflicts with the provisions of the memorandum

B Where an alteration is made which is intended to benefit the majority of shareholders rather than the company as a whole, and which causes special detriment to the minority

C Where an alteration is made which the majority honestly believe will benefit the company as a whole, but which has the effect of causing special detriment to the minority

D Where an alteration is made which compels non-consenting members to subscribe for additional shares

4 If a contract contains terms included in the articles, someone who is a party to the contract can take out an injunction to prevent the company from altering its articles.

True ☐

False ☐

5 Where the Companies Act permits a company to do something if its articles authorise it, but there is no provision actually made in the articles of the company on the matter, what is the position?

A Since the Act overrides any conflict with a company's articles, the company can exercise the statutory power.

B The company can exercise the statutory power, but must alter its articles to include the necessary power before exercising the statutory power.

C The company can exercise the statutory power, but must alter its articles to include the necessary power within six months.

D The company can exercise the statutory power, but must alter its articles to include the necessary power within twelve months.

6 What is the difference, as far as termination of the contract is concerned, between a service contract with a managing director for an unspecified period, and one for an agreed period of indefinite duration?

7 If the articles provide that certain articles can only be altered by a vote in favour of 90%, the members are bound by that provision.

True ☐

False ☐

8 What is the main advantage of a shareholder agreement?

Answers to quick quiz

1 The articles start with either a statement that Table A should not apply, or a statement that Table A should apply only with the modifications and exclusions that follow.

2 False. Special resolution is required.

3 C is correct. The articles can never override the memorandum (s 9), so A is incorrect. The courts will apply the test of what benefits the company as a whole, as illustrated by *Brown v British Abrasive Wheel Co 1919* so B is incorrect. D is incorrect under s 16.

4 False. Another contract cannot prevent the company altering its articles. Damages may be payable however for breach of contract.

5 B is correct. A is true, but not relevant, as there is no conflict with the articles. C and D are not true.

6 Under a contract for an unspecified period, no damages will be payable if the contract is terminated: *Read v Astoria Garage (Streatham Ltd) 1962*. Under a contract for an agreed period of indefinite duration, damages will be payable: *Nelson v James Nelson & Sons Ltd 1914*.

7 False. The right to alter articles by a special resolution overrides any such provision

8 Individuals can be given a power of veto.

Now try the question below from the Exam Question Bank

Number	Level	Marks	Time
Q15	Examination	10	18 mins

Part E
Company administration and management

14 Meetings

Topic list	Syllabus reference
1 The importance of meetings	8(a)
2 General meetings	8(a)
3 Convening a meeting	8(a)
4 Quorum	8(a)
5 Proxies	8(a)
6 Types of resolution	8(b)
7 Proceedings at meetings	8(a)
8 Class meetings	8(a)
9 Single member private companies	8(a)(b)

Introduction

In this chapter we consider the **procedures** by which companies are controlled by the shareholders, namely general meetings. **General meetings** afford members a measure of protection of their investment in the company. There are many transactions which, under the Act, cannot be entered into without a **resolution** of the company in general meeting.

Moreover, a general meeting at which the annual accounts and the auditors' and directors' reports will be laid must normally be held annually, thus affording the members an opportunity of questioning the directors on their **stewardship**.

For the exam you must be quite clear about the different types of resolution, when each type is used, and the percentage vote needed for each type to be passed.

This topic lends itself to factual Section A questions. However, resolutions in particular are important in many areas of the corporate part of the syllabus and meetings of members are an important controls on the acts of the directors, so this topic could easily be incorporated into Section B questions.

1 The importance of meetings

1.1 Decisions reserved for members

Although the management of a company, including important decisions on, for instance, making business contracts, is in the hands of the directors in board meetings, the **decisions which affect the existence of the company, its structure and scope, are reserved to the members** in general meeting.

1.2 Control over directors

The members in general meeting can exercise control over the directors, though only to a limited extent.

(a) Under normal procedure (Table A Article 73) one third of the directors retire at each annual general meeting though they may offer themselves for re-election. The company may remove directors from office by **ordinary resolution**: s 303, or in accordance with the company's memorandum or articles.

(b) Member approval in general meeting is required if the directors wish to:

- **Exceed their delegated power** or to use it for other than its given purpose
- **Allot shares**
- **Make a substantial contract** of sale or purchase with a director
- Grant a director a **long-service agreement**: ss 80, 320 and 319

(c) The **appointment and removal of auditors** is normally done in general meeting: s 385.

1.3 Resolution of differences

Finally, general meetings are the means by which members resolve differences between themselves by voting on resolutions.

The decision of a general meeting is only valid and binding if the meeting is **properly convened** by notice and if the **business** of the meeting is **fairly** and **properly conducted**. Most of the rules on company meetings are concerned with the issue of notices and the casting of votes at meetings to carry resolutions of specified types.

2 General meetings 12/01

Notice of general (sometimes called ordinary) meetings must be given **14 or 21 days** in advance of the meeting.
The notice should contain **adequate information** about the meeting.

There are two kinds of general meeting of members of a company:

- **Annual general meeting** (AGM)
- **Extraordinary general meeting** (EGM)

Exam focus point

You should appreciate the difference between AGMs and EGMs.

2.1 Annual general meetings

The AGM plays a major role in the life of a company although often the business carried out seems fairly routine. It is a statutorily protected way for members to have a regular assessment and discussion of their company and its management.

	Rules for directors calling an AGM
Timing s 366	• Every company **must** hold an AGM in **each** (calendar) **year** • Not more than **fifteen months** may elapse between meetings • First AGM must be held within **eighteen months** of incorporation • That is first AGM doesn't have to be in the first or following calendar year
Notice s 369	• Must be **in writing** and **in accordance with the articles** • At least **21 days** notice should be given • **Shorter** notice is only valid if **all** members agree to attend • The notice **must specify** the meeting of an AGM
Dispensation s 366A	• **Private** companies may **dispense** with holding an AGM • They must pass an **elective resolution** (see later)
Default s 357	• If the **directors fail to call an AGM**, the members may apply to the DTI • If they do, the **DTI may call the AGM** • They may give any direction necessary: modify the articles or file a quorum of one

2.2 Extraordinary general meetings

2.2.1 Directors

The **directors** have power under the articles to convene an EGM whenever they see fit: Table A Article 37.

2.2.2 Members

The directors may be required to convene an EGM by **requisition of the members**.

	Rules for members requisitioning an EGM (s 368)
Shareholding	• The requisitioning members (there must be at least two) **must hold** at least **1/10** of the **paid up** share capital **holding voting rights** • If there is no share capital, they **must** represent **1/10** of the **voting rights**
Requisition	• They must deposit a **signed requisition** at the **registered office** (a requisition by fax has been upheld) • This must state the 'objects of the meeting': the **resolutions proposed**
Date	• The meeting must be called within **28 days** of the notice • If the directors have not called the meting within 21 days of the members issuing the notice, **the members** may convene the meeting for a date within 3 months of the deposit of the requisition
Quorum	• Under Table A (Article 41) if no quorum is present, the meeting is adjourned

2.2.3 Court order

The court, on the application of a director or a member, may order that an EGM shall be held and may give instructions for that purpose including fixing a quorum of one.

This is a method of last resort to resolve a deadlock such as the refusal of one member out of two to attend (and provide a quorum) at an EGM: s 371.

2.2.4 Auditor requisition

An auditor who gives a statement of circumstances for his resignation or other loss of office (s 394) in his written notice may also requisition a meeting to receive and consider his explanation: s 392A.

2.2.5 Loss of capital by public company

The directors of a public company **must** convene an extraordinary general meeting if the **net assets fall to half or less of the amount of its called-up share capital: s 142.**

3 Convening a meeting

A meeting cannot make valid and binding decisions until it has been properly convened. Regulations relating to the calling of meetings are usually laid down in the articles but there are certain statutory rules.

(a) The meeting must generally be **called by** the **board of directors** or other competent person or authority.

(b) The notice must be issued to members in advance of the meeting so as to give them **14 to 21 days** 'clear notice' of the meeting. The members may agree to waive this requirement (see below).

(c) The **notice** must be sent to every member (or other person) entitled to receive the notice.

(d) The notice need **not** be sent to:

- A member whose only shares do not give him a right to attend and vote (as is often the position of **preference shareholders**)
- A **joint holder** of voting shares who is **not the first named holder** on the register

(e) If, however, the business to be done must by law be **'disclosed'** to all members, then notice of it must be sent **even** to members who are not entitled to vote on it (see *Re Duomatic 1969* below).

(f) The notice must include any information **reasonably necessary** to enable shareholders to know in advance what is to be done.

3.1 Timing of notices

For an AGM or an EGM at which a **special resolution** is proposed, the required period of notice is **21 days**. In any other case the **standard period** is **14 days:** s 369.

Members may – and in small private companies often do – waive the required 21 or 14 days notice. For a waiver:

(a) All **members** must consent in respect of an **AGM**.

(b) In **any other case** a **majority of members** who hold at least **95 per cent** of the **issued shares** carrying voting rights (or if the company has no share capital, who represent 95 per cent of the voting rights) is required. This may be reduced (under s 369(4)) for a private company which passes an elective resolution to this effect, but not to less than **90 per cent**.

The following specific rules by way of exception should be remembered.

(a) When **special notice** of a resolution is given to the company in three circumstances mentioned below, it must be given **28 days or 6 weeks** in advance as prescribed.

(b) In a **creditors' voluntary winding up** there must be at least **7 days notice** of the **creditors' meeting** (to protect the interests of creditors). The members may shorten the period of notice down to 7 days but that is all: s 98 IA.

3.1.1 Further requirements of Table A

The articles may follow Table A (Articles 38-39 and 111-116) and provide as follows.

(a) Notice must be given to all members who have a **registered address** in the United Kingdom, to **personal representatives** of a deceased member and the trustee of a bankrupt member, to the **first-named** only of **joint holders** and to the **directors** and to the **auditors**. However, failure to give notice to any person does not invalidate the proceedings of the meeting if the omission was **accidental**.

(b) **Notices** may be given to members **personally** or sent to them by **post** or other delivery to their registered address. If the notice is properly addressed and stamped the addressee is deemed to receive it **48 hours** after posting.

(c) **21 or 14 days** notice must be **clear days** notice, the day of receipt and the day of the meeting being excluded in reckoning what notice is to be given. For an AGM on Thursday 25th, for example the notices must be posted 24 days before on Monday 1st; Wednesday 3rd is the deemed day for the receipt; 21 days notice begins on Thursday 4th and expires on Wednesday 24th – the day before the meeting.

3.2 Special notice of a resolution

Key term

Special notice is notice of 28 days which must be given to a company of the intention to put certain types of resolution at a company meeting.

Special notice must be given **to the company** of the intention to propose a resolution for any of the following purposes.

- To **remove** an **auditor** or to **appoint** an **auditor other** than the **auditor** who was **appointed** at the **previous year's meeting**: s 391A
- To **reappoint** a **director aged more than 70** where the age limit applies: s 293
- To **remove a director from office** or to appoint a substitute in his place after removal: s 303

When special notice is given under s 379 the sequence is as follows.

3.2.1 Member gives notice

The member gives special notice of his intention to the company at **least 28 days** before the date of the meeting at which he intends to move his resolution.

If, however, the company calls the meeting for a date less than 28 days after receiving the special notice that notice is deemed to have been **properly given**.

3.2.2 Company decides whether to include resolution

On receiving special notice the company may be obliged under s 376 to include the resolution in the AGM notice which it issues.

3.2.3 21 days notice to members

If the company gives notice to members of the resolution it does so by a **21 day notice** to them that special notice has been received and what it contains.

If it is not practicable to include the matter in the notice of meeting, the company may give notice to members by newspaper advertisement or any other means permitted by the articles.

3.2.4 Copy sent to directors or auditors

If special notice is received of intention to propose a resolution for the removal from office of a director or to change the auditor, the company must send a copy to the **director** or **auditor**, so that he may exercise his statutory right to defend himself by issuing a memorandum and/or addressing the meeting in person.

The essential point is that a special notice is given **to the company**; it is not a notice from the company to members although it will be followed (usually) by such notice.

3.3 Requisitioning a resolution

The **directors** normally have the right to decide what resolutions shall be included in the notice of a meeting. However, apart from the requisition of an EGM, members can also take the initiative to requisition certain resolutions.

	Rules for members requisitioning a resolution
Qualifying holding s 376	• The members must represent **1/20** of the voting rights, or • Be at least 100 members holding shares with an average paid up of £100, per member
Resolution s 377	• May given notice to members of proposed resolution by delivering a **requisition** at least 6 weeks in advance of an AGM or EGM
Statement s 377	• May circulate to members a statement (<1,000 words) by delivering a **requisition** at least 1 week in advance of an AGM or EGM

In either instance, the **requisitionists** must bear the incidental costs unless the company otherwise resolves.

> *Pedley v Inland Waterways Association Ltd 1977*
> *The facts:* P wanted to propose an ordinary resolution at the AGM of Inland Waterways for the removal of all the directors. He gave the company secretary 28 days special notice but was told that the resolution could not be accepted because P did not fall into either category of member entitled under s 376 to require the company to include his resolution in the notice of AGM.
>
> *Decision:* Unless a member was able to satisfy the statutory requirements (s 376) or rely on a specific provision in the articles, the member had no right to compel the inclusion of the item in the agenda of the AGM. The rights of members to move resolutions for removal of directors (or auditors) are therefore much restricted by that procedural rule.

Exam focus point

The right of members to have resolutions included on the agenda of meetings is asked frequently in law exams, since it is an important issue if some of the members disagree with the directors.

3.4 Content of notices

The notice of a general meeting must contain adequate information on the following points.

(a) The **date, time** and **place** of the meeting must be given.

(b) An **AGM** or a **special** or **extraordinary resolution** must be described as such.

(c) Information must be given of the business of the meeting **sufficient** to enable members (in deciding whether to attend or to appoint proxies) to **understand what will be done** at the meeting.

   (i) The articles usually provide that the notice shall 'specify the general nature of the business to be transacted' Table A Article 38.

(ii) A distinction is normally made between routine business of an AGM, and non-routine business of any type of meeting. The contrast generally made is between **'ordinary'** and **'special'** business.

3.4.1 Routine business

In issuing the notice of an AGM it is standard practice merely to list the items of ordinary or routine business to be transacted, such as the following.

- Declaration of dividends (if any)
- Election of directors
- Appointment of auditors and fixing of their remuneration

The articles usually include (Table A Article 77) a requirement that members shall be informed of any intention to **propose** the **election** of a director, other than an existing director who retires by rotation and merely stands for re-election.

3.4.2 Special business

The nature of non-routine business makes it necessary to set out in the notice convening the meeting the full **verbatim** text of the relevant resolution.

The particular reasons for giving its text in full are:

(a) A special or extraordinary resolution is defined by s 378 as a resolution 'of which **notice specifying** the **intention** to **propose** the **resolution** .... has been **duly given**'. Accordingly the notice must set out 'the resolution' in full (see *Re Moorgate Mercantile Holdings Ltd 1980* described later in this chapter).

(b) When an ordinary resolution is not routine the notice of the meeting must **'specify the general nature of that business'** (Table A Article 38). Generally the full text of the resolution is given, together with any other material and relevant information which is not given in the text of the resolution itself.

Kaye v Croydon Tramways Co 1898
The facts: The notice set out a resolution to approve the sale of the company's business. It did not, however, disclose that under the sale agreement the directors were to be paid large amounts as compensation.

Decision: The notice did not properly disclose the nature of the business to be done at the meeting. The resolution was therefore invalid (as passed at a meeting not properly convened by notice).

Baillie v Oriental Telephone & Electric Co Ltd 1915
The facts: A special resolution was passed to give retrospective approval to the payment (by a subsidiary company) of increased directors' remuneration. The notice and the accompanying circular set out the text of the special resolution in full and the reasons for it but did not disclose the very large sums, £45,000 in all, which had in fact been paid to the directors under a percentage formula. A shareholder later applied to the court for a declaration that the resolution was invalid since insufficient information had been given.

Decision: The resolution was invalid since insufficient information had been given in the notice convening the meeting.

3.5 Section summary

- Meetings must be called by a **competent person** or authority.
- **Clear notice** (21 days AGM/EGM with special resolutions, 14 days otherwise) must be given to members.
- **Notice** must be **sent to all members** entitled to receive it.

- **Special notice of 28 days** of intention to propose certain resolutions (removal of directors/auditors) must be given.
- The notice convening the meeting must give certain details.
  - Date, time and place of the meeting
  - Identification of AGM, special and extraordinary resolutions
  - Sufficient information about business to be discussed at the meeting to enable shareholders to know what is to be done

Question — Removal of director

How can members remove a director from office? What is the significance of special notice in this context?

Answer

Where the articles provide a method for removing a director, that method can be adopted. In addition, there is a procedure under ss 303-304 Companies Act 1985 by which a company may by ordinary resolution remove any director from office, notwithstanding any provision to the contrary in the articles or in a contract such as a director's service agreement. So the provision in the articles maybe ineffective.

However, this procedure requires that special notice shall be given to the company at least 28 days before the meeting of the intention to propose such a resolution. Moreover, the directors are not required to include the resolution in the notice of the meeting (and it cannot then be put to the vote) unless the person who intends to propose it has (with any support from other members) a sufficient shareholding as required by s 376: *Pedley v Inland Waterways Association Ltd 1977.*

If a company receives special notice it must forthwith send a copy to the director concerned who has the right to have written representations of reasonable length circulated to members and to speak before the resolution is put to the vote at the meeting.

Question — EGM

When is a company compelled to call an extraordinary general meeting?

Answer

Members of a company who hold not less than one tenth of the company's paid up share capital carrying voting rights, may requisition the holding of a extraordinary general meeting. As this is a public company it must have a share capital and the alternative qualification does not arise. The directors are then required within 21 days of the deposit of the requisition to issue a notice convening the meeting to transact the business specified in the requisition, for a date not more than 28 days hence: s 368.

An auditor who resigns giving reasons for his resignation may requisition an extraordinary general meeting so that he may explain to members the circumstances of his resignation: s 392A.

If the net assets of a public company are reduced to less than half in value of its called-up share capital, it is the duty of the directors to convene (within 28 days of becoming aware of this situation) an extraordinary general meeting to consider what, if any, steps should be taken: s 142.

The Department of Trade (s 367) and the court (s 371) have statutory power in certain circumstances to direct that a meeting shall be held.

4 Quorum

FAST FORWARD

The **quorum** for meetings may be two or more (except for single member private companies).

Key term

A **quorum** is the minimum number of persons required to be present at a particular type of (company) meeting. In the case of shareholders' meetings, again the Table A figure is two, in person or by proxy, but the articles may make other provisions.

There is a legal principle that a 'meeting means a coming together of more than one person' (*Sharp v Dawes* below). Hence it follows that as a matter of law **one person generally cannot be a meeting.**

Sharp v Dawes 1876
The facts: At the meeting only one shareholder was present together with the secretary who was not a member (and did not count among those 'present'). The shareholder took the chair, proposed and voted for a resolution to make a call on shares. Dawes (another shareholder) refused to pay the call on his shares.

Decision: The call was invalid since no meeting had been held.

The rule that at least two persons must be present to constitute a 'meeting' does not require that both persons must be members. Every member has a **statutory right to appoint a proxy** to attend as his representative.

Hence one member and another member's proxy may together provide the quorum (if it is fixed, as is usual, at 'two members present in person or by proxy'). However one member who is also the proxy appointed by another member cannot by himself be a meeting, since a minimum of two individuals present is required: *Re Sanitary Carbon Co 1877.*

There may, however, be a meeting attended by one person only, if:

(a) It is a **class meeting** and all the **shares** of that class are **held** by **one member.**

(b) The **DTI** or the **court**, in exercising a power to order a general meeting to be held, **fixes** the **quorum** at one: ss 367 and 371; this means that in a two-member company, a meeting can be held with one person if the other deliberately absents himself to frustrate business.

(c) The company is a **single member private company**: s 370A (see later).

The articles usually fix a **quorum** for general meetings which may be as low as two (the minimum for a meeting) but may be more – though this is unusual.

The Table A **quorum** is two persons **entitled to vote** who may be members, proxies or authorised representatives of corporate members: Article 40.

4.1 Inquorate meetings

If the articles do fix a quorum of two or more persons present, the meeting lacks a quorum (it is said to be an 'inquorate' meeting) if either:

- The **required number** is **not present** within a **stipulated time** (usually half an hour) of the appointed time for commencing a meeting.
- The **meeting begins** with a **quorum** but the **number present dwindles** to less than the quorum – unless the articles provide for this possibility.

The articles usually (Table A Article 40) provide for automatic and compulsory adjournment of an inquorate meeting. However, decisions made at an inquorate meeting may be enforceable by a third party by virtue of S35A.

The articles can provide that a meeting which begins with a quorum may continue despite a reduction in numbers present to less than the quorum level. (Table A does not allow this.) However, there must still be two or more persons present: *Re London Flats Ltd 1969.*

5 Proxies

FAST FORWARD

Proxies can attend and vote on behalf of members. Only private company proxies have the right to speak.

A **proxy** is a person appointed by a shareholder to vote on behalf of that shareholder at company meetings.

Any member of a company which has a share capital, if he is entitled to attend and vote at a general or class meeting of the company, has a statutory right (s 372) to appoint an agent, called a 'proxy', to attend and vote for him.

Rules for appointing proxies		
Basic rule	• Any member may appoint a proxy • The proxy does not have to be a member	
Private company	• Member may appoint **one** proxy • Proxy may **speak** at meeting	ARTICLES MAY VARY THIS RIGHT
Public company	• Member may appoint **more than one** proxy • Proxy may **not speak** at meeting	
Voting	• Proxy **may vote** on **poll** but **not** on **show of hands**	ARTICLES MAY VARY THIS RIGHT
Notice	• Every notice of a meeting must **state** the member's right to a proxy	
Cards	• Directors may issue proxy appointment cards to all members • Articles may require that cards are **only valid** if received up to 48 hours before meeting	ARTICLES MAY **NOT** LENGTHEN THIS PERIOD

A member who has sent in a proxy card **may revoke it** and is deemed to do so if he attends the meeting in person and votes.

A company which is a member of another company may appoint a proxy. Alternatively it may by resolution of its directors appoint a **representative** to attend the meeting. Such a company representative at meetings has the right to speak and to vote on a show of hands as an individual member: s 375.

Although a proxy may not vote on a show of hands he has the same right to demand or join with other members in demanding a poll as the member whom he represents: s 373.

6 Types of resolution 12/02

FAST FORWARD

A meeting can pass three types of resolution.

- An **ordinary resolution**.
- An **extraordinary resolution**.
- A **special resolution**.

An **elective resolution** may be passed by a private company in certain situations, for example to dispense with the annual appointment of auditors.

Anything that a private company can do by a resolution of a general meeting or a class meeting may also be done by a **written resolution**.

A meeting reaches a decision by passing a resolution. There are **three major kinds** of resolution, and an additional two, for **private** companies, introduced by the Companies Act 1989.

	Type of resolution
Ordinary	Requires simple (50%+) majority of the votes cast 14 days notice
Extraordinary	Requires 75% majority of the votes cast 14 days notice
Special	Requires 75% majority of the votes cast 21 days notice
Elective	Five situations (see below) All members must vote in favour 21 days notice
Written	Can be used for all GM resolutions except those needing special notice All members must vote in favour

6.1 Differences between ordinary, special and extraordinary resolutions

Apart from the required size of the majority and period of notice, the main differences between the types of resolution are as follows.

(a) The **text** of **special** and **extraordinary** resolutions must be **set out** in **full** in the notice convening the meeting (and they must be described as special or extraordinary resolutions): s 378. This is not necessary for an ordinary resolution if it is routine business.

(b) A **signed copy** of every **special** and **extraordinary resolution** (and equivalent decisions by unanimous consent of members) must be **delivered** to the **registrar** for filing. **Some ordinary resolutions**, particularly those relating to share capital, have to be **delivered** for filing but many do not.

6.2 Special resolutions

A special resolution is required for **major changes** in the company such as the following.

- A change of name
- Alteration of the objects or of the articles
- Reduction of share capital
- Winding up the company
- Presenting a petition by the company for an order for a compulsory winding up

6.3 Extraordinary resolutions

An extraordinary resolution suffices to put the company into creditors' voluntary liquidation (where the shorter period of notice may be an advantage).

6.4 Elective resolutions

The elective resolution required is part of a wider scheme of de-regulation for **private** companies introduced by the 1989 Companies Act. An elective resolution may be passed by a **private** company (**ONLY**) in any one of five situations.

- To confer **authority to issue shares indefinitely** or for a **fixed period** which may **exceed five years**: s 80A
- To **dispense with the laying of accounts** before a general meeting, unless a member or the auditors require it: s 252
- To **dispense with holding an AGM** unless a member requires it: s 366A
- To **reduce the 95% majority** needed to consent to short notice under ss 369(4) or 378(3), to a figure of not less than **90%**
- To **dispense with the annual appointment of auditors** (so that the incumbent auditors are automatically reappointed): s 386

To pass such a resolution, **all** the members entitled to attend and vote must agree: s 379A. **21 days notice** is required. This can be waived provided all members entitled to attend and vote at the meeting agree. The resolution must be **registered** within 15 days.

An elective resolution may be **revoked** by **ordinary resolution** (s 379A(3)) but this must also be **registered**: s 380(4).

6.5 Written resolutions

Anything that a **private** company could do by a resolution of a general meeting or a class meeting may be done by a written resolution.

All **members entitled** to **attend** and **vote** must **sign** the **resolution**: s 381A(1). This may be achieved by sending each member a separate document, as long as they all set out the resolution. The date of the resolution is the date of the last member's signature. The company must keep a record of written resolutions.

The procedure can be used to bypass **any** of the other four types of resolution: s 381(A)(b). A written resolution suffices, because such a resolution is provided to be **equivalent** to a resolution passed in general meeting.

Three further points should be noted concerning written resolutions.

(a) Written resolutions can be used **notwithstanding any provisions** in the company's **articles**.

(b) A written resolution **cannot** be **used to remove a director or auditor** from office, since such persons have a right to **speak** at a **meeting**.

(c) **Copies of written resolutions** should be **sent to auditors** at or before the time they are sent to shareholders. Under s 381B auditors do not have the right to object to written resolutions. If the auditors are not sent a copy, the resolution remains valid; however the directors and secretary will be liable to a fine. The purpose of this provision is to ensure auditors are kept informed about what is happening in the company.

Exam focus point

You need to be able to:

(a) Define each type of resolution and give examples of when each is used

(b) State for a specific situation what resolution should be used

(c) Understand the aims of the written and elective resolution procedures

(i) Written resolutions – enable the company to carry on business without calling meetings
(ii) Elective resolutions – enable the company to dispense with certain statutory requirements

Question

Types of resolution

Briefly explain the main features of the following types of resolution which may be passed at a general meeting of a company:

(a) An ordinary resolution
(b) An extraordinary resolution
(c) A special resolution

Answer

(a) **Ordinary resolutions** require a **simple majority** of votes cast (ie over 50%). Usually **14 days notice** is sufficient. Ordinary resolutions of a routine nature need not be set out in full in the notice of an annual general meeting, and most ordinary resolutions need not be filed with the Registrar of Companies.

In certain circumstances, however, **special notice** of 28 days is required, namely for removal of an auditor or appointment of an auditor who was not appointed at the previous year's meeting (s 391A), for reappointment of a director aged over 70 where the age limit applies (s 293) and for removal of a director or appointment of a substitute director following such removal (s 303).

In these cases, 28 days special notice must be given to the company and to all company members at the same time and in the same form as notice of the meeting. If it is impracticable, however, to include notice of the resolution in the notice of the meeting, the company may give notice to members by newspaper advertisement or other means permitted by the articles, not less than 21 days before the meeting.

(b) **Extraordinary resolutions** require a **majority of 75%** of the votes cast at the meeting (in person or by proxy) and **14 days' notice** of the intention to propose such a resolution. The **text** of the resolution should be **set out** in the notice of the meeting and the **resolution** should be **filed** with the **Registrar** within 15 days of being passed: s 380.

Matters for which an extraordinary resolution will be required may be specified in the company's articles. An extraordinary resolution is required under the Companies Act to **vary class rights** in certain circumstances The Insolvency Act 1986 also provides that an extraordinary resolution is required to begin a **voluntary winding up** where the company is unable to meet its debts and to give certain powers to the liquidator in a member's voluntary winding-up.

(c) **Special resolutions** also require a **75% majority** of votes cast (in person or by proxy) but require **21 days notice** of the intention to propose such a resolution (members holding shares constituting 95% or more of share capital can waive the notice requirement: s 378(3)). Various provisions in the Companies Acts specify that a special resolution will be required, including a **change of name**, **alteration of the articles** (s 9) **or objects** clause (s 4) of the company, **reduction of the share capital** (s 135), **re-registration** as a public (s 43) or private (s 53) company, authorisation of the redemption or **purchase of the shares** of a private company out of capital (s 173) and presentation of a petition for a **compulsory winding-up order**.

As with extraordinary resolutions, the **text** of the notice should be **set out in the notice** of the meeting, and the resolution should be **filed** with the **Registrar** within 15 days of being passed: s 380.

7 Proceedings at meetings

FAST FORWARD

Voting at general meetings may be on a **show of hands** or a **poll**.

A meeting can only reach binding decisions if:

- It has been properly **convened** by notice.
- A **quorum is present.**
- A **chairman presides**.
- The **business** is **properly transacted** and **resolutions** are **put to the vote.**

There is no obligation to allow a member to be present if his shares do not carry the right to attend and vote. However full general meetings and class meetings can be held when shareholders not entitled to vote are present: *Carruth v ICI 1937.*

7.1 The chairman

The articles usually provide that the **chairman** of the board of directors **is to preside** at general meetings; in his absence another director chosen by the directors shall. In the last resort a member chosen by the members present can preside.

The chairman derives his authority from the articles and he has **no casting vote unless** the **articles give him one**. His duties are to **maintain order** and to **deal** with the **agenda** in a methodical way so that the business of the meeting may be properly transacted.

7.2 Adjournment

The chairman

- **May dissolve** or **adjourn** the **meeting** if it has become disorderly or if the members present agree.
- **Must** adjourn **if** the **meeting instructs him** to do so.

If he tries to end the meeting before it is proper to do so the members may elect a new chairman and continue the meeting: *Stoughton v Reynolds 1736.*

Moreover, the articles may provide that the chairman of a meeting can adjourn a general meeting **only with its consent**. The chairman, however has a residual **common-law power** to hold a meeting over if this is essential for the business to be conducted in a proper way and where the machinery of the articles has effectively broken down.

Byng v London Life Assurance 1989

The facts: The annual general meeting of the company was duly convened at the Barbican Cinema in London. Due to the number of people attending, several rooms were used and the proceedings were linked by audio-visual technology. This failed halfway through, leaving approximately 1,000 angry members outside the meeting. Matters became difficult and the Chairman walked out, declaring that the meeting would reconvene at the Café Royal that afternoon. At the Café Royal, the

'meeting' passed one resolution on the agenda. A shareholder contended that the chairman needed the consent of the meeting for an adjournment, so the subsequent meeting and resolutions were invalid.

Decision: On the particular facts the chairman's actions were unreasonable (he knew that a substantial number of the members who attended the original meeting would not only not be able to attend the adjourned meeting, but moreover would be unable to register a proxy vote). However, the mere fact that a meeting is incapable of conducting any business (since members have been wrongly excluded) does not mean that it is a nullity incapable of being treated as a meeting for any legal purpose whatsoever. In principle, the chairman does have the residual common-law power to adjourn in circumstances where the machinery of the articles has broken down.

Each item of business comprised in the notice should be taken separately, discussed and put to the vote.

7.3 Amendments to resolutions

Members may propose amendments to the resolution. The chairman should reject any amendment which is outside the limits set by the notice convening the meeting.

If the relevant business is an ordinary resolution it may be possible to amend it so as to **reduce its effect** to something less (provided that the change does not entirely alter its character). An ordinary resolution authorising the directors to borrow £100,000 might be amended to substitute a limit of £50,000 (but not to increase it to £150,000 as £100,000 would have been stated in the notice).

It is **not possible** to pass a special or extraordinary resolution which differs in substance from the text set out in the notice.

Re Moorgate Mercantile Holdings Ltd 1980
The facts: A special resolution set out in the notice provided for total cancellation of a share premium account balance of £1,356,900.48 since the assets which it represented had been lost (a form of reduction of share capital). At the meeting the resolution was amended, for technical reasons, to reduce the balance to £321.17 and it was passed in that form.

Decision: The resolution as passed was invalid since it was not the **special resolution** of which notice had been given. Even the retention of £321 out of £1.4m is a change of substance.

If the chairman wrongly rejects an amendment and the resolution is carried in its original form it is invalid. If he allows the amendment to be discussed it should be put to the vote before the original resolution. If the amendment is carried the resolution as amended is then put to the vote.

7.4 Voting and polls 12/01

The **rights of members** to **vote** and the **number of votes** to which they are entitled in respect of their shares are fixed by the **articles**.

One vote per share is normal but some shares, for instance preference shares, may carry no voting rights in normal circumstances. To shorten the proceedings at meetings the procedure is as follows.

7.4.1 Voting on a show of hands

Key term

A **show of hands** is a method of voting for or against a resolution by raising hands. Under this method each member has one vote irrespective of the number of shares held, in contrast to a poll vote.

On putting a resolution to the vote the chairman calls for a show of hands. One vote may be given by each member present in person; proxies do not vote.

Unless a poll is then demanded, the chairman's declaration of the result is conclusive. However it is still possible to challenge the chairman's declaration on the grounds that it was fraudulent or manifestly wrong.

> *Re Caratal (New) Mines Ltd 1902*
> *The facts:* A special resolution was put to the vote on a show of hands. The chairman counted the hands raised 'for' and 'against' and said '6 for and 23 against but there are 200 voting by proxy and I declare the resolution carried'. This declaration was later challenged in court.
>
> *Decision:* The declaration was invalid since on the chairman's own figures there was no majority on a show of hands. Proxies may vote on a poll (which had not been held) but not on a show of hands and should have been disregarded.

7.4.2 Polls

Key term

A **poll** is a method of voting at company meetings which allows a member to use as many votes as his shareholding grants him.

If a real test of voting strength is required a poll may be demanded. The result of the previous show of hands is then disregarded.

On a poll every member and also proxies representing absent members may cast the full number of votes to which they are entitled. A poll need not be held at the time but may be postponed so that arrangements to hold it can be made.

A poll may be demanded by:

- Not **less than five members** (unless the articles permit a lesser figure)
- Member(s) representing **not less than one tenth of the total voting rights**
- Member(s) holding shares which represent **not less than one tenth of the paid-up capital**

As an example the articles may well provide that three people may demand a poll but cannot validly say that at least six people are required. Such a rule would be void and five people could demand a poll.

Any provision in the articles is void under s 373 if it seeks to prevent such members demanding a poll or to exclude the right to demand a poll on any question other than the election of a chairman by the meeting or an adjournment.

When a poll is held it is usual to appoint 'scrutineers' and to ask members and proxies to sign voting cards or lists. The votes cast are checked against the register of members and the chairman declares the result.

7.5 Result of a vote

In voting either by show of hands or on a poll, the number of votes cast determines the result. Votes which are not cast, whether the member who does not use them is present or absent, are simply disregarded. Hence the majority vote may be much less than half (or three quarters) of the total votes which could be cast.

7.6 Minutes

Key term

Minutes are a record of the proceedings of meetings. Company law requires minutes to be kept of all company meetings including general, directors' and managers' meetings.

Every company is **required to keep minutes** which are a formal written record of the proceedings of its general meetings: s 382.

These minutes are usually kept in **book form**. If a loose-leaf book is used to facilitate typing there should be safeguards against falsification, such as sequential prenumbering.

The chairman **normally signs** the minutes. If he does so, the signed minutes are admissible evidence of the proceedings, though evidence may be given to contradict or supplement the minutes or to show that no meeting at all took place.

Members of the company have the **right to inspect** minutes of general meetings: s 383. The minutes of general meetings must be held at the registered office available for inspection by members who are also entitled to demand copies.

7.7 The assent principle

A unanimous decision of the members is sometimes treated as a substitute for a formal decision in general meeting properly convened and held, and is equally binding.

> *Parker & Cooper Ltd v Reading 1926*
> *The facts:* The directors had issued a debenture which, for technical reasons, was invalid. All four shareholders had from time to time discussed the transaction and had indicated their individual assent to it. The liquidator sought later to repudiate the debenture.
>
> *Decision:* The 'assent principle' applied to validate the transaction although no meeting of any kind had been held.

Unfortunately, it is not at all clear when formal procedures can be ignored and decisions 'passed' by assent of the members.

Finally the assent principle of unanimity of the members has been extended to cover cases where every member had the opportunity to object but either voted in favour or merely abstained: *Re Bailey Hay & Co Ltd 1971.*

8 Class meetings

Class meetings are of two kinds.

(a) If the company has more than one class of share, for example if it has 'preference' and 'ordinary' shares, it may be necessary to call a meeting of the holders of one class of shares, to approve a proposed **variation** of the **rights** attached to their shares.

(b) Under the procedure for a **'scheme of arrangement'** (s 425), the holders of shares of the same class may nonetheless be divided into **separate** classes (for whom separate meetings are required) if the scheme proposed will affect each group differently.

When separate meetings of a class of members are held, the same procedural rules as for general meetings apply (but there is a different rule on quorum).

8.1 Quorum

Under s 125 the standard general meeting rules, on issuing notices and on voting, apply to a class meeting.

However the **quorum** for a class meeting is fixed at two persons who hold, or represent by proxy, at least one third in nominal value of the issued shares of the class (unless the class only consists of a single member).

If no quorum is present, the meeting is **adjourned** (under the standard adjournment procedure for general meetings). When the meeting resumes, the quorum is **one** person (who must still hold at least one third of the shares).

9 Single member private companies

Following s 382B, if the sole member takes any decision that could have been taken in general meeting, that member shall (unless it is a written resolution) provide the company with a written record of it. This allows the sole member to conduct members' business informally without notice or minutes.

Filing requirements still apply, for example, in the case of alteration of articles.

The single member company must hold an annual general meeting unless it has opted out by elective resolution.

If the single member company has passed an elective resolution dispensing with holding an AGM and has also dispensed with the laying of accounts before a general meeting, the effect will be that no meeting of members will be required. The written resolution procedure may be used.

Written resolutions cannot be used to remove a director or auditor from office as these resolutions require special notice.

Chapter roundup

- In this chapter we have discussed the various types of meeting that a company holds.
- In particular we have concentrated on the formalities and proceedings of general meetings.
- There are two types of general meeting of a company.
  - **Annual general meeting**
  - **Extraordinary general meeting**
- Notice of general meetings must be given **14 or 21 days** in advance of the meeting.
- The notice should contain **adequate information** about the meeting.
- The **quorum** for meetings may be two or more (except for single member private companies).
- **Proxies** can attend and vote on behalf of members. Only private company proxies have the right to speak.
- A meeting can pass three types of resolution.
  - An **ordinary resolution**, carried by a simple majority of votes cast and requiring 14 days notice
  - An **extraordinary resolution**, carried by a 75 per cent majority of votes cast and requiring 14 days notice
  - A **special resolution**, requiring a 75 per cent majority of votes cast and 21 days notice
- An **elective resolution** may be passed by a private company in certain situations, for example to dispense with the annual appointment of auditors.
- Anything that a private company can do by a resolution of a general meeting or a class meeting may also be done by a **written resolution**.
- Voting at general meetings may be on a **show of hands** or a **poll**.
- A unanimous decision of the members is often treated as a substitute for a formal decision for general meetings and is equally binding (the **assent principle**).

Quick quiz

1 Which of the following decisions can only be taken by the members in general meeting?

A Alteration of objectives
B Alteration of articles
C Change of name
D Reduction of capital
E Appointment of a managing director

2 **Fill in the blanks** in the statements below.

A poll may be demanded:

A By not less than .... members

B By members representing not less than .... of the total voting rights

C By members holding shares representing not less than .... of the paid-up capital

3 Before a private company can hold an extraordinary general meeting on short notice, members holding a certain percentage of the company's shares must agree. Which one of the following percentages is correct?

51%	60%
75%	90%

4 A company holds an AGM on 1 November 20X0 and holds its next AGM on 2 January 20X2. Is this legal?

5 Give three examples of routine items of business of the AGM for which it is unnecessary to include in the notice the text of the relevant resolutions.

6 Under s 372, a member of a public company may only appoint one proxy, but the proxy has a statutory right to speak at the meeting.

True ☐

False ☐

7 Match the following with the relevant notice period.

A Special resolution	(i) 14 days
B Extraordinary resolution	(ii) 21 days
C Special notice given to a company of an ordinary resolution	(iii) 28 days

8 List the purposes for which a private company may use an elective resolution.

Answers to quick quiz

1 A, B, C and D. The board can appoint someone to be managing director, so E is incorrect.

2 A poll may be demanded:

A By not less than five members
B By members representing not less than one tenth of the total voting rights
C By members holding shares representing not less than one tenth of the paid-up capital

3 90%

4 No. Although the company has held the second AGM within 15 months of the first AGM, it should also have held the second AGM in the following calendar year, 20X1.

5 Declaration of dividends
Election of directors
Appointment of auditors and fixing of their remuneration

6 False. A *private* company member has the right only to appoint one proxy who can speak. Public company members can appoint more than one proxy, but they have no statutory right to speak.

7 Special resolution *21 days*
Extraordinary resolution *14 days*
Special notice given to a company of an ordinary resolution *28 days*

8 To confer authority to issue shares indefinitely or for a fixed period which may exceed five years
To dispense with the laying of accounts before a general meeting, unless a member or the auditors require it
To dispense with holding an AGM unless a member requires it
To reduce the 95% majority needed to consent to short notice to a figure of not less than 90%
To dispense with the annual appointment of auditors

Now try the question below from the Exam Question Bank

Number	Level	Marks	Time
Q16	Examination	20	36 mins

15

Officers and auditors

Topic list	Syllabus reference
1 Who and what is a director?	7(a)
2 The board of directors	7(a)
3 Company secretary	7(b)
4 Auditors	7(c)

Introduction

A company, being an abstract person, cannot manage itself. Company law therefore requires that every company shall have one or more directors and a secretary. Since directors are in control of the assets (which are often very valuable), they are subject to an elaborate code of rules which broadly cover three main topics (given in bold):

(a) **Who is a director** (and therefore subject to the rules)

(b) How a director is appointed to his office and when does he cease to be a director?

(c) **What standard of honest and disinterested service is required of directors** and also what standard of competence; this principle is developed by a number of statutory rules on particular transactions

(d) **What are the powers of directors** and how they exercise those powers, whether the members of the company control them in their management function and whether the company whom they represent is liable if the directors exceed their delegated powers

This chapter covers the topics mentioned in (a) above and the next two chapters deal with (b), (c) and (d).

Introduction (cont)

Company secretaries have less power than directors, but recently the law has begun to recognise the '**apparent authority**' of company secretaries in **administrative matters**. This chapter explores the appointment, powers and duties of company secretaries.

Company officers, particularly directors, act as 'stewards' of the company for the shareholders. Company law requires that many companies have an audit. The purpose of an audit is that an independent person (the auditor) gives the shareholders an opinion on the financial statements.

This chapter looks at the rules surrounding appointment of auditors and their duties and powers.

Directors are an important part of companies and their duties and powers are heavily regulated. They are likely to be regularly examined in Section B. This chapter provides the basis on which Chapters 16 and 17 build.

Company secretaries and auditors are also important. They seem more likely to be examined in Section A, as company secretaries were in the pilot paper.

1 Who and what is a director?

FAST FORWARD

Any person who occupies the position of director is treated as such, the test being one of function, ie what they actually do.

Key term

A **director** is a person who is responsible for the overall direction of the company's affairs.

Any person who occupies the position of director is treated as such: s 741. The test is one of **function** ie what the person actually does.

The directors' function is to take part in **making decisions** by **attending meetings** of the board of directors. Anyone who does that is a director whatever he may be called.

A person who is given the title of director, such as 'sales director' or 'director of research', to give him status in the company structure is not a director in company law unless by virtue of his appointment he is a **member** of the **board** of **directors**, or he carries out functions that would be properly discharged only by a director. Anyone who is held out by a company as a director, and who acts as a director although not validly appointed as one, is known as a **de facto** director.

Undischarged bankrupts and disqualified persons may not be directors.

1.1 Shadow directors

Key term

A **shadow director** is a person in accordance with whose instructions other directors are accustomed to act.

A person might seek to avoid the legal responsibilities of being a director by not accepting formal appointment as a director but using his power, say as a major shareholder, to manipulate the acknowledged board of directors.

Company law seeks to prevent this abuse by extending several statutory rules to **shadow directors**: s 741(2). Shadow directors are directors for legal purposes if the board of directors are accustomed to act in **accordance with their directions** and **instructions**. (This rule does not apply to professional advisers merely acting in that capacity.)

Thus, for example, the rules on loans to, and transactions with, directors also apply to shadow directors.

1.2 Alternate directors

Key term

An **alternate director** is a person who acts as a director in place of another.

A director may if the articles permit him to do so (Table A Arts 65 – 69) appoint an **alternate director** to attend and vote for him at board meetings which he himself is unable to attend. Such an alternate may be another director, in which case he has the vote of the absentee as well as his own. More usually he is an outsider.

Some company articles stipulate that the appointment of an alternate (unless he is another director) must be approved by the board.

An alternate director is a 'director' to whom the relevant rules of company law apply: Table A Art 69.

1.3 Executive directors **6/03**

Key term

An **executive director** is a director who performs a specific role in a company under a service contract which requires a regular, possibly daily involvement in management.

A director may also be an employee (usually a member of the management) of his company. Since the company (represented by the board of which he is a member) is also his employer there is a potential conflict of interest which in principle a director is required to avoid.

To make it possible for an individual to be both a director and employee the articles (Table A Art 84) usually make express provision for it but prohibit the director from voting at a board meeting on the terms of his own employment.

If the articles permit, a director may also have some connection, say as a consultant or professional adviser, with the company and earn remuneration paid by the company in that capacity.

Directors who have additional management duties as employees may be distinguished by special titles, such as 'Finance Director'. However (except in the case of a Managing Director) any such title does not affect their personal legal position. They have two distinct positions as (a) a member of the board of directors and (b) a manager (usually working full time) with management responsibilities as an **employee**. On the other hand a director who is 'non-executive' (as many directors of public companies are) only acts as a member of the board of directors.

1.4 Non-executive directors **6/03**

Key term

A **non-executive director** does not generally have a function to perform in a company's management. His usual involvement is to attend board meetings only.

In listed companies, boards of directors are felt more likely to be fully effective if they comprise both able executive directors and strong, independent non-executive directors.

The main tasks of the NEDs are as follows:

- **Contribute** an **independent view** to the board's deliberations
- **Help the board provide** the company with **effective leadership**
- **Ensure** the **continuing effectiveness** of the **executive directors** and management
- **Ensure high standards** of **financial probity** on the part of the company

Non-executive and shadow directors are subject to the same statutory and fiduciary duties as executive directors: *Re Wimbledon Village Restaurant Ltd 1994.* A non-executive director has been disqualified for failing to read the accounts of a company which subsequently went into insolvent liquidation: *Re Continental Assurance Co of London plc 1996.*

1.5 Managing directors

Key term

A **managing director** is one of the directors of the company appointed to carry out overall day-to-day management functions.

If the articles provide for it (Table A Article 84) the board may appoint one or more directors to be **Managing Directors**. A Managing Director ('MD') does have a special position and has wider apparent powers than any director who is not appointed an MD.

One company may be a director of another. In that case the director company sends an individual to attend board meetings as its representative.

1.6 Number of directors

Every company must have at least **one** director and for a **public** company the minimum is **two**: s 282. There is no statutory maximum but the articles usually impose a limit.

The same person may be a director (if there is more than one) and also company secretary. A sole director may not also be secretary. Another company may be either director or secretary.

To prevent avoidance of the rule that a single individual may not double the roles of sole director and secretary, s 283(4) provides that if Company A, which has a sole individual director (X), is sole director or secretary of Company B then X may not be secretary or sole director respectively of Company B.

1.7 Powers and duties

The powers and duties of directors are looked at in detail in Chapters 16 and 17.

2 The board of directors

Key term

The **board of directors** is the elected representative of the shareholders acting collectively in the management of a company's affairs.

One of the basic principles of company law is that the **powers** which are delegated to the directors under the articles (Table A Article 70) are given to them as a **collective body.** We shall look at the powers which directors have in more detail in Chapter 16.

The **board meeting** is the **proper place for the exercise of the powers** (unless they have been validly passed on, or 'sub-delegated', to committees or individual directors).

> *Re Portuguese Consolidated Copper Mines Ltd 1889*
> *The facts:* The power to allot shares was vested in the directors, of whom there were four. Two directors met, without proper notice of a meeting given to the other two. The two directors present decided that a quorum should be two and allotted shares in response to an application. On a later occasion these two directors and one of the others met, approved the allotment and also the quorum of two. The fourth director sent in a letter, which arrived later still, giving his agreement.
>
> *Decision:* As there had been no board meeting, properly convened and held, the allotment was invalid.

2.1 Face-to-face board meetings

One of the debatable points about the nature of a board meeting is how far the presence of all the directors in one place is required to constitute the meeting.

(a) It is considered that if all the directors are **in communication**, usually by telephone, though not assembled together, this suffices to constitute a board meeting. Some companies have begun to include in their articles a provision for a 'board meeting' of this kind.

(b) It is also clear that even if all the directors are present in one place, there can be no board meeting if **proper notice** has **not** been **given**, and if any of the **directors object** to holding the meeting in those circumstances.

Baron v Potter 1914
The facts: B and P were the only directors and P, as chairman, had a casting vote. He could not use it since B refused to attend board meetings for which a quorum was two. P met B as he arrived at Paddington Station, called a board meeting forthwith despite B's protests and used his casting vote to carry a resolution to appoint additional directors who would support P. On the following day there was an EGM at which B was able to carry a resolution to appoint additional directors who would support B. P objected that only the board had power to appoint additional directors. B denied that the board had met and, in meeting, had co-opted P's nominees.

Decision: A board meeting must be called at a reasonable time and place; the meeting at Paddington Station was therefore not a board meeting properly convened. As the directors were unable to exercise their powers of co-opting directors the general meeting could do so.

2.2 Signed resolution as a substitute for a board meeting

As with general meetings, there is a 'signed resolution' procedure (Table A Article 93). Any resolution signed by **all** the directors who are entitled to notice of a board meeting (including alternate directors, on behalf of their 'appointor' directors) will be 'as valid and effectual as if it had been passed at a meeting of directors... duly convened and held.'

2.3 Content of the notice

There is **no legal requirement** for a **notice** issued to convene a board meeting **to specify the business** which it is to transact.

There are however, **practical reasons** why notice of the business, in the form of an agenda, is usually given. Some items of business are discussion of lengthy papers, such as management reports or proposals for new projects. Directors cannot usually discuss such matters adequately without having read the papers before the meeting.

The agenda will vary according to the type and formality of the meeting and the particular business to be discussed. A typical agenda might include the following.

- Membership
- Apologies for absence
- Minutes of the last meeting
- Matters arising from the minutes
- Business of the present meeting, presentation of reports, resolutions etc.
- Any other business
- Date of the next meeting

2.4 Period of notice

The period of notice given to convene a board meeting need be **no longer** than is **reasonable** to enable directors to attend. Even five minutes' notice has been held reasonable, where the director in question was free to attend and close at hand: *Browne v La Trinidad 1887*.

If no prior notice is given, the mere presence of all the directors does not permit a meeting to be held, should any of them object: *Baron v Potter 1914*.

2.5 Quorum for a board meeting

In order to constitute a board meeting, as any other meeting, a properly appointed **chairman** must preside, and a **quorum** must be present.

Most companies have articles (Table A Article 89) which provide that:

'The quorum for the transaction of the business of the directors may be fixed by the directors and unless so fixed at any other number shall be two.'

Table A Article 90 provides for a fall in number of directors to less than quorum level.

> 'The continuing directors or a sole continuing director may act notwithstanding any vacancies in their number but, if the number of directors is less than the number fixed as the quorum, the continuing directors or director may act only for the purpose of *filling vacancies* or of *calling a general meeting*.'

Note also that on each item of business, any director who is disqualified from voting by having a personal interest may have to be excluded in reckoning the quorum for that item.

2.6 The chairman

The directors of a company may appoint one of their number to be **chairman** of the board of directors.

If there is no chairman of the board, or if the appointed chairman is unwilling to preside at a meeting, or fails to attend within **five minutes** of the intended start of the meeting, the directors present may appoint another director to be chairman of that meeting.

The same procedure applies to general meetings, at which the chairman of the board of directors will normally preside. If no director is present and willing to act as chairman **within fifteen minutes** of the intended start of the meeting, the members present can choose one of themselves to act as chairman.

The directors may at any time remove the chairman of the board from his office.

The chairman presides at meetings of the board, and is responsible for:

- Ensuring that the functions of the board are carried out
- Ensuring that the meeting proceeds in an efficient manner, without unnecessary or irrelevant discussion, and with a reasonable cross-section of views being heard
- Providing an agenda for the board meetings (and any necessary documentation, although the secretary would handle the paperwork)

2.7 Conduct of board meetings

There are some aspects of procedure which should be strictly observed.

(a) The discussion should **follow** the **sequence** of the **agenda**, and be confined at each stage to the item currently under discussion.

(b) Although it is not usually necessary to take a vote, the chairman should sum up **'the sense of the meeting'**, so that a suitably worded decision or conclusion may be formulated for inclusion in the minutes.

(c) If a vote does appear to be necessary, it will be along the lines of a show of hands or voice vote. The usual procedure is to **'go round the table'** inviting each member of the board to declare his vote for or against. If any member abstains, perhaps because a personal interest does not allow him to vote, this should be noted and recorded.

(d) Each member of the board, including the chairman, has **one vote**. The **articles** may provide otherwise, say by weighted voting or a veto given to a particular member. The chairman may also be given a casting vote, with which to resolve a tied issue.

2.8 Sole director and board meetings

The questions was raised in *Re Neptune Vehicle Washing Equipment Ltd 1995* whether a sole director had to comply with s 317 and if so how. It was held that a sole director could hold a meeting with a company secretary or by himself. Even if holding a meeting alone a director had to make and minute a declaration of interests in contracts, pausing for thought over potential conflicts of interest.

3 Company secretary — Pilot paper, 6/05

FAST FORWARD

Every company must have a secretary. The secretary may not also be the sole director.

Key term

The **secretary** is an officer of a company appointed to carry out general administrative duties.

3.1 Appointment

The rules governing appointment of a company secretary to **all companies** are as follows.

(a) Every **company must have** a **secretary**.

(b) A **sole director cannot also** be the **secretary**. A corporation may be a secretary to a company but Company A cannot have Company B as its secretary if Company B has a sole director who is also the sole director of Company A: s 283.

(c) Single member private companies must also have a secretary who is not the sole director/member.

The directors of a **public company** must **also** take all reasonable steps to ensure that the secretary is suitably qualified for the post by **knowledge and experience**. Under s 286, **a public company secretary may be anyone who fulfils one of the following criteria**:

- Was the **secretary** or **secretary's assistant** on **22 December 1980**
- Has been a **public company secretary** for at least **three** out of the **five years** previous to appointment
- Is a **member** of ACCA, ICAEW, ICAS, ICAI, ICSA, CIMA or CIPFA
- Is a **barrister**, **advocate** or **solicitor** in the UK
- Is a **person** who, by virtue of holding or **having** held **any other position** or being a member of any other body, **appears** to the directors to be **capable**

Two or more persons may be appointed **joint secretaries**. A company may appoint a deputy secretary who assists or acts in place of the secretary: s 283.

The term 'officer' includes the secretary.

Exam focus point

Do not forget the distinction between the rules affecting the appointment of a secretary of a private company with that of a public company.

Whenever there is a change of secretary notice must be given to the registrar within 14 days: s 288(2).

3.2 Duties

The Act does not define the general duties of a company secretary since these will vary according to the size of the company and of its headquarters. The standard minimum duties of the secretary are as follows.

3.2.1 To make the arrangements incidental to board meetings

The secretary usually:

- Convenes the meetings (Table A Article 88)
- Issues the agenda
- Collects or prepares the papers for submission to each meeting
- Attends the meeting
- Drafts the minutes
- Communicates decisions taken to employees or to outsiders

3.2.2 To maintain the register of members

The secretary has this responsibility unless the work is contracted out to professional registrars.

The secretary also keeps the other statutory registers and prepares the notices, returns and other documents which must be delivered to the registrar.

3.2.3 Acting as general administrator and head office manager

Duties include:

(a) Dealing with staff matters, office equipment and pensions, and conducting the company's correspondence with its legal advisers, members, government departments, trade associations and so on

(b) Being responsible for the accounts and taxation aspects of the company's business, unless the company has an accountant or finance department

3.2.4 Corporate governance

The report of the Committee on the Financial Aspects of Corporate Governance ('Cadbury Committee'), published in December 1992, gave a new dimension to the company secretary's function.

The report states that the secretary has a key role in ensuring that board procedures are observed and regularly reviewed. The report also stated that the company secretary may be seen as a source of guidance on the responsibilities of the board and its chairman.

Thus the directors have a duty to appoint to the position of secretary a person capable of carrying out this role, and to ensure that he remains so. Any question of the secretary's removal should be a matter for the board as a whole.

The secretary will have a primary responsibility for a number of matters raised in the report. These include:

(a) The **statement of compliance** with the Combined Code of Best Practice in the report and accounts and reasons for any areas of non-compliance

(b) **Providing information** to **non-executive directors** to enable them to carry out their function effectively

(c) Preparation of a **formal schedule of matters** reserved for the board's decision

3.3 The secretary as agent

FAST FORWARD

Secretaries can bind the company to the extent of their **'apparent authority'**. This usually means contracts of an administrative nature only, (*Panorama Developments* case).

Many of the functions of the company secretary have developed in recent years as the size of companies has increased and their administration has come to require a specialist competent to deal with a variety of complicated matters.

At one time the functions of the secretary were very limited and he dealt with them strictly in accordance with instructions given to him. The law therefore treated him as a **mere subordinate** lacking authority to enter into contracts or to speak for the company.

In 1971 however the Court of Appeal applied the **principle of apparent authority** and recognised that it is a normal function of a company secretary to enter into contracts connected with the **administration** of the company, and hence the secretary has **apparent authority** to enter such contracts as far as a third party is concerned.

> *Panorama Developments (Guildford) Ltd v Fidelis Furnishing Fabrics Ltd 1971*
> *The facts:* B, the secretary of a company, ordered cars from a car hire firm, representing that they were required to meet the company's customers at London Airport. Instead he used the cars for his own purposes. The bill was not paid, so the car hire firm claimed payment from B's company.
>
> *Decision:* B's company was liable, for he had apparent authority to make contracts such as the present one, which were concerned with the administrative side of its business. The decision recognises the general nature of a company secretary's duties.

The court also said that, if the issue had arisen, it might not have treated the secretary as having apparent authority to make commercial contracts such as buying or selling trade goods, since that is not a **normal duty** of the company secretary.

The company might by its actions give the secretary apparent authority to make commercial contracts but **positive actions** would be required; merely appointing someone company secretary would not be enough.

Exam focus point

The *Panorama* case was an important development in the law on the authority of the secretary. Note here the connection with the law of **agency** again.

Question

Authority of company secretary

Faith is the company secretary of Recycle Ltd. In March 20X5 she hired a car from Kingfisher Ltd. She told Kingfisher Ltd that the car was for company business, but she asked for it to be delivered to her home address. Faith then used the car for private purposes and has now disappeared without paying the hire charge.

Advise the directors of Recycle Ltd whether they are bound by the agreement with Kingfisher Ltd.

Answer

The general duties and authority of a company secretary are not defined in the Companies Act. It is now accepted that a company secretary's general function is to enter into contracts connected with the administration of the company. In *Panorama Developments (Guildford) Ltd v Fidelis Furnishing Fabrics Ltd 1971* it was accepted that a company secretary was usually held out as having authority to enter into contracts of an administrative nature (as opposed to commercial contracts such as buying or selling trade goods) and so such activity would be regarded as being within his or her ostensible authority.

The contract entered into by Faith in the name of the company is one of an administrative nature within her apparent authority as company secretary. As a result Recycle Ltd is bound by the contract with Kingfisher Ltd.

4 Auditors 6/03

FAST FORWARD

Every company (apart from certain small companies) must appoint appropriately qualified **auditors**.

Every company (except a dormant private company and certain small companies) must **appoint auditors** (s 384).

4.1 Appointment

4.1.1 Eligibility as auditor

Membership of a Recognised Supervisory Body is the main prerequisite for eligibility as an auditor. An audit firm may be either a body corporate, a partnership or a sole practitioner.

The Companies Act 1985 also requires an auditor to hold an **'appropriate qualification'**. A person holds an 'appropriate qualification' if he or she:

- Has satisfied **existing criteria** for appointment as an auditor under CA 1985
- Holds a **recognised qualification** obtained in the UK
- Holds an **approved overseas qualification**

4.2 Ineligibility as auditor

Under the Companies Act 1985, a person is **ineligible** for appointment as a company auditor if he or she is:

- An **officer** or **employee** of the company
- A **partner** or **employee** of such a person
- A **partnership** in which such a person is a partner
- **Ineligible** by virtue of the above for appointment as auditor of any parent or subsidiary undertaking or a subsidiary undertaking of any parent undertaking of the company, and

There exists between him or her or any associate (of his or hers) and the company (or company as referred to above) a **connection** of any description as may be specified in regulations laid down by Secretary of State

The legislation does **not** disqualify the following from being an auditor of a limited company:

- A shareholder of the company
- A debtor or creditor of the company
- A close relative of an officer or employee of the company

However, the **regulations** of the **accountancy bodies** applying to their own members are **stricter than statute in this respect**.

Under the Companies Act 1985, a person may also be ineligible on the grounds of **'lack of independence'**; the definition of lack of independence is to be determined by statutory instrument following consultation with the professional bodies

4.2.1 Procedures to appoint

FAST FORWARD

The first auditors may be appointed by the directors, to hold office until the first general meeting at which their appointment is considered; in the normal course of events, the meeting then appoints auditors to hold office until the next such meeting.

	Appointment of auditors
Members	• Usually appoint auditor in general meeting. Auditors hold office until end of next meeting at which the accounts are considered. • May appoint in general meeting to fill a casual vacancy.
Directors	• Appoint first auditors (s 385). They hold office until the end of the first meeting at which the accounts are considered. • May appoint to fill a casual vacancy (s 388)
Secretary of State	• May appoint auditors if members fail to (s 387) • Company must notify Secretary of State within 7 days of the general meeting where auditors were not appointed.

4.2.2 Dispensing with laying of accounts

Where a private company has elected, under s 252, to dispense with the laying of accounts before the company in general meeting, the auditors must be appointed by a general meeting either:

(a) **Within a period of 28 days** (the 'time for appointing auditors') after the date on which the annual accounts are sent to members

(b) If notice has been given under s 253(2) requiring the laying of accounts before the general meeting, from the **conclusion** of the **meeting**: s 385A

The auditors so appointed hold office from the end of the 28 day period (or the conclusion of the meeting) until the end of the time for appointing auditors for the next financial year.

The auditors who are in office when the election is made remain so until the end of the time for appointing auditors for the next financial year (unless the general meeting decides otherwise). The auditors in office when the election ceases to have effect remain in office until the conclusion of the next general meeting at which accounts are laid.

4.2.3 Dispensing with annual appointment of auditors

A **private** company may dispense with the obligation to appoint auditors annually, by **elective resolution** in accordance with s 379A. In this case the auditors shall be **deemed** to **be re-appointed** for each succeeding financial year whilst the election is in force:
s 386. This will be so unless:

(a) The company is **'dormant'** and therefore can resolve under s 250 to exempt itself from the obligation to submit audited accounts.

(b) A resolution has been passed under s 393 to **terminate the auditors' appointment** (see below).

When the election ceases, the auditors remain in office until the conclusion of the next general meeting at which accounts are laid, or until the end of the 'time for appointing auditors' for the next financial year.

4.2.4 Auditor remuneration

Whoever appoints the auditors has power to fix their remuneration for the period of their appointment. It is usual when the auditors are appointed by the general meeting to leave it to the directors to fix their remuneration (by agreement at a later stage). The auditors' remuneration must be disclosed in a note to the accounts: s 390A.

4.2.5 Exemption from audit

Certain **small companies** are exempt from audit provided the following conditions are fulfilled.

(a) A company is totally exempt from the annual audit requirement in a financial year if its turnover for that year is **not more** than **£5.6 million** and its **balance sheet total** is **not more than £2.8 million**.

(b) The exemptions do not apply to **public companies**, **charitable, banking** or **insurance companies** or those subject to a **statute based regulatory regime**.

(c) A company that is part of a **group** can claim exemption provided the group of which it is a member is a **small group** which satisfies the conditions of s 249B(1C).

(d) **Shareholders** holding **10%** or more of the capital of any company can veto the exemption.

(e) A **dormant company** which fulfils the criteria of s 249 (that is, qualifies for exemption from an audit as a dormant company and a small company) **does not need** a **special resolution** to achieve audit exemption.

4.3 Termination of auditors' appointment

FAST FORWARD

Auditors may leave office in the following ways.

- **Resignation**
- **Removal from office** by an ordinary resolution with special notice passed before the end of their term
- **Failing to offer themselves** for **re-election**
- **Not being re-elected** at the general meeting at which their term expires

Departure of auditors from office can occur in the following ways.

(a) Auditors may **resign** their appointment by giving notice in writing to the company delivered to the registered office.

(b) Auditors may **decline re-appointment.**

(c) Auditors may be **removed** from office before the expiry of their appointment by the passing of an ordinary resolution in general meeting: s 391. Special notice is required and members and auditors must be notified: s 391A.

(d) Auditors may **not be re-elected** when their term of office expires. Special notice must be given of any resolution to appoint auditors who were not the auditors appointed on the last occasion of the resolution and members and auditor notified.

Where a private company has **dispensed with the annual appointment** of auditors under s 386:

(a) Any **member** of the **company** may **deposit notice** in writing at the registered office proposing that the appointment of the company's auditors be brought to an end: s 393. No member may deposit more than one such notice in any financial year of the company.

(b) The directors must then **convene a general meeting** for not more than 28 days after the date of the giving of the notice, and propose a suitable resolution for termination of the auditors' appointment: s 393(2).

If the motion is passed, the auditors are not deemed to be re-appointed when otherwise they next would be; if the notice was deposited within 14 days of sending the annual accounts to the members, any deemed re-appointment for the following financial year ceases to have effect: s 393(3).

Failure by the directors to convene the meeting within 14 days of deposit of the notice results in the member(s) who deposited the notice being empowered to convene the meeting within three months: s 393(4). Reasonable expenses are recoverable by the member(s) from the company, and by the company from the directors: s 393(6).

4.4 Resignation of auditors

FAST FORWARD

However, auditors leave office, they must either:

- State there are **no circumstances** which should be brought to **members and creditors' attention**, or
- List **those circumstances**

	Procedures for resignation of auditors
Statement of circumstances	• Auditors must deposit a statement at the registered office with their resignation stating: – There are no relating circumstances which the members and creditors should know – There are relating circumstances, and what those circumstances are
Company action	• The company must send a copy of the resignation to the Registrar • If there is a statement of circumstances, the company must send a copy to every member entitled to receive the accounts • They do not have to send the statement if a court holds it to be defamatory
Auditor rights	• If the auditors have deposited a statement of circumstances, they may: – Circulate a statement of reasonable length to the members – Requisition on EGM to explain their reasons – Attend and speak at any meeting where appointment of successors is to be discussed

4.4.1 Declining to seek nomination

If the auditors decline to seek re-appointment at an Annual General Meeting, they must nevertheless deposit a **statement** that there are **no circumstances, or a list of the circumstances**, that need to be brought to members' or creditors' attention.

The reason for this provision is to prevent auditors who are unhappy with the company's affairs keeping their suspicions secret. The statement must be deposited not less than **14 days** before the time allowed for next appointing auditors.

As the case of resignation, the company must **send** a copy of the statement of circumstances to **every person entitled to receive a copy of the accounts**.

4.5 Removal from office

	Procedures for removal from office
Auditor representations	If a resolution is proposed either to • Remove the auditors before their term of office expires • Change the auditors when their term of office is complete the auditors have the right to make representations of reasonable length to the company
Company action	The company must • Notify members in the notice of the meeting of the representations • Send a copy of the representations in the notice • If it is not sent out, the auditors can require it is read at the meeting
Attendance at meeting	Auditors removed before expiry of their office may • Attend the meeting at which their office would have expired • Attend any meeting at which the appointment of their successors is discussed
Statement of circumstances	If auditors are removed at a general meeting they must • Make a statement of no circumstances • Make a statement of circumstances for members and creditors The statement must be deposited at the registered office within 24 days of date auditors cease to hold office.

Exam focus point

Remember that:

(a) A statement of circumstances/no circumstances must be deposited **however** the auditors leave office.

(b) The auditors have additional rights depending on how they leave office.

In the exam you **must** read any question on this area very carefully and not write about auditors **resigning** when the question asks about auditors **being removed** from office, for example.

4.6 Duties of auditors

The statutory duty of auditors is to report to the members whether the accounts give a **true and fair view** and have been properly prepared in accordance with the Companies Act: s 235.

To fulfil this duty, the auditors **must carry out such investigations as are necessary** to form an opinion as to whether:

(a) **Proper accounting records** have been kept and proper returns adequate for the audit have been received from branches.

(b) The **accounts** are in **agreement** with the **accounting records**: s 237.

(c) The **information** given in the **directors' report** is **consistent** with the **accounts**: s 235(3).

If the auditors are satisfied on these matters they need not be mentioned in the report.

Auditors must also consider whether **Schedule 6** of the **Companies Act**, relating to disclosure of directors' emoluments and other benefits, has been obeyed. If there is not complete disclosure in the accounts, auditors should state this fact, and supply the missing disclosures.

The auditors' report must be read before any general meeting at which the accounts are considered and must be open to inspection by members.

4.7 Powers of auditors

The Companies Act provides **statutory rights** for auditors to enable them to carry out their duties.

The **principal rights**, excepting those dealing with resignation or removal, are set out in the table below, and the following are notes on more detailed points.

s 389A(1)	*Access to records*	A right of access at all times to the books, accounts and vouchers of the company
s 389A(1)	*Information and explanations*	A right to require from the company's officers such information and explanations as they think necessary for the performance of their duties as auditors
s 390(1)(a) and (b)	*Attendance at/notices of general meetings*	A right to attend any general meetings of the company and to receive all notices of and communications relating to such meetings which any member of the company is entitled to receive
s 390(1)(c)	*Right to speak at general meetings*	A right to be heard at general meetings which they attend on any part of the business that concerns them as auditors
s 381B(2)-(4)	*Rights in relation to written resolutions*	A right to receive a copy of any written resolution proposed
s 253	*Right to require laying of accounts*	A right to give notice in writing requiring that a general meeting be held for the purpose of laying the accounts and reports before the company (if elective resolution dispensing with laying of accounts in force)

4.7.1 Rights to information

If auditors have not received all the information and explanations they consider necessary, they should state this fact in their audit report.

The Act makes it an offence for a company's officer knowingly or recklessly to make a statement in any form to an auditor which:

- Purports to convey any information or explanation required by the auditor
- Is materially misleading, false or deceptive

The penalty is a maximum of two years' imprisonment, a fine or both (s 389A(2))

Chapter roundup

- Any person who occupies the position of director is treated as such, the test being one of function.
- **Every** company must have a secretary. The secretary may not also be the sole director.
- S 286 imposes a duty on **public company directors** to satisfy themselves that the person appointed as secretary can adequately fill the position.
- Secretaries can bind the company to the extent of their **'apparent authority'**. This usually means contracts of an administrative nature only, (*Panorama Developments* case).
- Every company (apart from certain small companies) must appoint appropriately qualified **auditors**.
- The first auditors may be appointed by the directors, to hold office until the first general meeting at which their appointment is considered; in the normal course of events, the meeting then appoints auditors to hold office until the next such meeting.
- Auditors may leave office in the following ways.
  - **Resignation**
  - **Removal from office** by an ordinary resolution with special notice passed before the end of their term
  - **Failing** to **offer themselves** for **re-election**
  - **Not being re-elected** at the general meeting at which their term expires
- However auditors leave office, they must either:
  - State there are **no circumstances** which should be brought to **members and creditors' attention,** or
  - List **those circumstances**
- Auditors who are resigning can also:
  - **Circulate members** about their resignation
  - **Requisition a general meeting**, **or speak** at a general meeting

Quick quiz

1 Fill in the gaps in the following definitions, using the words in the box below.

(a) A............................ is a person responsible for the overall direction of the company.

(b) An .... is a person who acts as a director in place of another.

(c) An .... is a director who performs a specific role in a company under a service contract, which requires a regular, possibly daily involvement in management.

(d) A .... is a person in accordance with whose instructions other directors are accustomed to act.

(e) A .... is one of the directors of the company appointed to carry out overall day-to-day management functions.

managing director		alternate director
	director	
executive director		shadow director

2 Every company must have a secretary, who can be the sole director.

True ☐

False ☐

3 (a) Name three duties of a company secretary

(1) ....

(2) ....

(3) ....

(b) As agent, what does the secretary have authority to do?

4 Name two reasons a person would be ineligible to be an auditor under Companies Act 1985.

(1) ....

(2) ....

5 Name five rights of auditors

(1) ....

(2) ....

(3) ....

(4) ....

(5) ....

Answers to quick quiz

1 (a) Director
(b) Alternate director
(c) Executive director
(d) Shadow director
(e) Managing director

2 False. A secretary **can** also be a director, **but not** a **sole** director.

3 (a) (1) Arrangements re board meetings
(2) Maintain register of members
(3) General administrator/head office manager

(b) To bind the company to a contract for an **administrative** matter.

4 Any of:

(1) Is an officer/employee of the company
(2) A partner or employee of a person in (1)
(3) A partnership in which (1) is a partner
(4) Ineligible by (1), (2) and (3) to be auditor of any of the entity's subsidiaries

5 (1) Access to records
(2) Information and explanations
(3) Attendance oat/notice of general meetings
(4) Right to speak at general meetings
(5) Rights in relation to written resolutions
(6) Right to require laying of accounts

Now try the question below from the Exam Question Bank

Number	Level	Marks	Time
Q17	Examination	10	18 mins

Directors: holding office and powers

Topic list	Syllabus reference
1 Appointment of directors	7(a)
2 Vacation of office	7(a)
3 The extent of directors' powers	7(a)
4 Managing and other working directors	7(a)
5 Directors as agents	7(a)

Introduction

In this chapter we turn our attention to the appointment and the powers of the directors and also their vacation of office.

The important principle to grasp is that the **extent of directors' powers is defined by the articles**. Table A Article 70 provides that 'the business of the company shall be managed by the directors who may ... exercise all the powers of the company'. Also 'No alteration of the memorandum or articles and no such direction shall invalidate any prior act of the directors'.

Thus, if **shareholders** do not approve of the directors' acts they must either **remove them** under s 303 or **alter the articles** to regulate their future conduct. They **cannot** simply **take over** the functions of the directors. These issues are explored in the first half of the chapter.

The second half of the chapter deals, in essence, with the directors as **agents of the company**. This ties in with the **agency** part of your business law studies also discussed in connection with partnerships. The different types of authority a director can have (implied and actual) are important in this area.

The relationship of directors to the company and members is very important. It could be examined in Sections A or B, perhaps more likely in Section B, in conjunction with directors' duties, or the articles or minority protection.

1 Appointment of directors 12/03

FAST FORWARD

The method of appointing directors, along with their rotation and co-option is **controlled** by the **articles.**

A director may be appointed expressly (that is, by **appointment**), sometimes called a *de jure* director.

However, where a person acts as a director without being appointed as such (a *de facto* director) he incurs the obligations and has some of the powers of a proper director. In addition, a shadow director (see Chapter 15) is subject to many of the duties imposed on directors.

1.1 Appointment of first directors

The documents delivered to the registrar to form a company include **Form 10** giving particulars of the first directors and signed by them to signify their consent: s 13(5). On the formation of the company those persons become the first directors.

1.2 Appointment of subsequent directors

Once a company has been formed further directors can be appointed, either to **replace** existing directors or as **additional** directors.

Appointment of further directors is carried out **as the articles provide**. Most companies follow Table A which provides for

- **Co-option** of new members by existing directors, and
- **Election** of directors in general meeting.

However the articles do not have to follow these provisions and may impose different methods on the company.

When the appointment of directors is proposed at a general meeting of a public company a **separate** resolution should be proposed for the election of each director: s 292. However the rule may be waived if a resolution to that effect is first carried without any vote being given against it.

A company may by its articles or by a separate agreement permit a director to assign, or transfer his office to another person. However any such transfer is valid only if approved by **special resolution** passed in general meeting: s 308.

1.3 Publicity

In addition to giving notice (with their consent to act) of the first directors, every company must within **14 days** give **notice** to the **registrar** of any change among its directors (together with the signed consent of any new director to act).

A company is not required to show the names of its directors on its business letters and some other commercial documents. If, however, it decides to do so (as is still common practice) it must print a **complete list** of **all** its directors: s 305.

2 Vacation of office

FAST FORWARD

The articles may provide regulations for the removal of a director from office, but any such provisions are overridden by statute which allows removal by **ordinary resolution** with **special notice.**

A director may leave office in the following ways.

- **Resignation** (Table A Article 81 specifies written notice)
- Not **offering himself for re-election** when his term of office ends
- **Death**
- **Dissolution of the company**
- Being **removed** from office
- Being **disqualified**

However the director leaves office, Form 288b should be filed with the Registrar.

2.1 Rotation of directors

Table A Articles 73-80 on retirement and re-election of directors ('rotation') contains the following provisions.

(a) Every year **one-third** (or the number nearest to one-third) shall **retire**; at the first AGM of the company they all retire (Article 73).

(b) **Retiring directors** are **eligible** for **re-election** (Article 80).

(c) Those retiring shall be those **in office longest** since their last election (Article 74).

(d) If directors fail to agree who should retire and be offered for re-election, the question should be decided by lot (Article 74).

(e) A director shall be **deemed** to be **re-elected unless** the **meeting decides otherwise** (Article 75).

(f) The **directors** themselves **may fill** a **casual vacancy** by **co-option**. Such an appointee must stand for re-election at the next AGM after his appointment and does not count in determining the one-third to retire by rotation (Article 79).

(g) The company in general meeting may also elect new directors (Article 79).

(h) A managing director or any other director holding **executive** office is **not subject** to **retirement by rotation** and is excluded in reckoning the one-third in (a) above (Article 84).

Question — Rotation of directors

The board of Teddy plc has the following directors at the start of its AGM on 31 December 20X7.

	Age	*When last re-elected*
Mr Timothy	42	31 December 20X4
Mr Paul	64	31 December 20X5
Mr Henry	70	31 December 20X6
Mr Maurice	38	31 December 20X6
Mr Steven	34	31 December 20X6
Mr Gordon	43	2 May 20X7
Mr Edward	41	2 May 20X7

At the board meeting on 2 May 20X7 Mr Gordon and Mr Edward were appointed to fill casual vacancies and Mr Timothy was appointed managing director. The company's articles follow Table A as regards rotation of directors; the articles do not contain any provision about re-appointing directors who are over the statutory age limit. Which directors would be due for re-election at the AGM on 31 December 20X7?

Answer

Mr Gordon and Mr Edward must stand for re-election since they have been appointed during the year. Mr Henry must stand for re-election as he has reached the age of 70 and Teddy plc is a public company with no provision in its articles for automatic appointment of directors who are 70.

Calculation of who is to retire by rotation excludes Mr Gordon, Mr Edward, Mr Henry and Mr Timothy (as Managing Director), thus leaving three directors. One of those must therefore retire, and as Mr Paul has been in office the longest, it must be him.

2.2 Removal 12/03, 6/04

In addition to any such provisions of the articles for removal of directors, a director may be removed from office by **ordinary** resolution of which **special notice** to the company has been given by the person proposing it: s 303.

On receipt of the special notice the company must send a copy to the director who may require that a memorandum of reasonable length shall be issued to members; he also has a right to address the meeting at which the resolution is considered: s 304.

The articles cannot override the statutory power, nor can any service agreement. However, the articles can permit dismissal without the statutory formalities being observed, for example, dismissal by a resolution of the board of directors.

The **power to remove a director** is, however, **limited** in its effect in **three ways**.

Restrictions on power to remove directors	
Shareholding qualification to include the resolution	In order to propose a resolution to remove a director, the shareholder(s) involved must hold: • Either, 1/20th voting rights, • Or, represent 100 members with an average of £100 paid up on shares
Weighted voting rights	A director who is also a member may have weighted voting rights given to him under the constitution for such a eventuality, so that he can automatically defeat any motion to remove him as a director: *Bushell v Faith 1970.*
Class right agreement	It is possible to draft a shareholder agreement stating that a member holding each class of share must be present at a general meeting to constitute quorum. If so, a member holding shares of a certain class could prevent a director being removed by not attending the meeting.

Exam focus point

The courts have stressed that the s 303 power of members to remove directors is an important right, but you should remember the ways in which members' intentions might be frustrated.

2.3 Compensation to directors

The dismissal of a director may also entail payment of a **substantial sum** to settle his claim for breach of contract if he has a service agreement.

However the shareholders can prevent the company becoming committed to a long-term service agreement with a director, since a contract of service extending for a period of more than five years must be approved by the company in general meeting: s 319.

2.4 Directors' retirement

A director of a public company is deemed to retire at the end of the AGM following his 70th birthday: s 293(3). This rule is disapplied if the **articles** permit him to continue or if his continued **appointment** is **approved** by the **general meeting**.

A director may, if the articles permit, assign his office to another person, because for example he is to be abroad. Assignment must be approved by a special resolution: s 308.

2.5 Disqualification of directors

FAST FORWARD

Directors **may** be disqualified from a very wider range of company involvements under the Company Directors Disqualification Act 1986 (CDDA).

A person cannot be appointed a director or continue in office if he is or becomes disqualified under the articles or statutory rules as explained below.

2.5.1 Disqualification under articles

The articles often embody the statutory grounds of disqualification and add some optional extra grounds. Table A Art 81 provides that a director must vacate office if:

(a) He is **disqualified** by the **Act** or any rule of law (for example if he ceases to be the registered holder of qualification shares).

(b) He becomes **bankrupt** or enters into an arrangement with his creditors.

(c) He becomes of **unsound mind**.

(d) He **resigns** by notice in writing.

(e) He is **absent** for a period of **six consecutive months** from board meetings held during that period, without obtaining leave of absence **and** the other directors resolve that he shall on that account vacate office.

2.5.2 Disqualification of bankrupts

Except with leave of the court an undischarged bankrupt cannot act as a director nor be concerned directly or indirectly in the management of a company: s 11 CDDA. If he does continue to act, he becomes personally liable for the company's relevant debts.

2.5.3 Statutory disqualification of directors

The Company Directors Disqualification Act 1986 (CDDA 1986) provides that a court may formally disqualify a person from being (without leave of the court) a director (including a shadow director), liquidator, administrator, receiver or manager of a company's property or in any way directly or indirectly being concerned or taking part in the promotion, formation or management of a company: s 1.

The terms of the disqualification order are thus very wide, and include acting as a consultant to a company. The Act, despite its title, is not limited to the disqualification of people who have been directors. **Any person** may be disqualified if they fall within the appropriate grounds. These are discussed in the next chapter, in the context of directors' duties.

2.5.4 Automatic vacation of office

In addition to the grounds of disqualification described above, the articles may follow Table A in providing that a director shall automatically vacate office if he is **absent** from **board meetings** (without obtaining the leave of the board) for a **specified period** (three or six months is usual). The effect of this disqualification depends on the words used.

- If the articles refer merely to 'absence' this includes involuntary absence due to illness.
- The words 'if he shall absent himself' restrict the disqualification to periods of voluntary absence.

The period of six months is reckoned to begin from the **last meeting** which the absent director did attend. The normal procedure is that a director who foresees a period of absence, say because he is going abroad, applies for leave of absence (for a specified period) at the last board meeting which he attends; the leave granted is duly minuted. He is not then absent 'without leave' during the period.

If he fails to obtain leave but later offers a reasonable explanation the other directors may let the matter drop by simply not resolving (under the provision introduced into the current Table A Art 81) that he shall vacate office. The general intention of the rule is to impose a sanction against slackness; a director has a duty to attend board meetings when he is able to do so.

Question

Disqualification of directors

Which of the following are grounds provided under Table A Article 81 for a director being compelled to leave office?

A Becoming bankrupt
B Entering into an arrangement with personal creditors
C Becoming of unsound mind
D Resigning by notice in writing
E Being absent from board meetings for six consecutive months without obtaining leave of absence

Answer

All of them.

Question

Resolution for removal of director

A company has three members who are also directors. Each holds 100 shares. Normally the shares carry one vote each, but the articles state that on a resolution for a director's removal, the director to be removed should have 3 votes per share. On a resolution for the removal of Jeremy, a director, Jeremy casts 300 votes against the resolution and the other members cast 200 votes for the resolution. Has Jeremy validly defeated the resolution?

A No, the articles are invalid insofar as they purport to confer extra votes.

B Yes, the proceedings and articles are valid.

C Yes. Whilst the articles are invalid and the voting is therefore 200 to 100 in favour, a special resolution is required and the necessary 75% majority has not been obtained.

D No. A director is not entitled to vote on a resolution for his own removal.

Answer

B. This was confirmed in *Bushell v Faith 1970.* A is therefore wrong. C is wrong in stating the articles are invalid *and* that a special resolution is needed; an ordinary resolution will suffice to remove a director. A director can vote on his removal if he is a member; therefore D is incorrect.

Question

Vacation of office

The articles of Robert Ltd provide that if a director should 'absent himself' for a period exceeding six months from board meetings, the director shall automatically vacate office. Miles, a director, obtains a twelve month leave of absence to go abroad. Whilst abroad, he contracts a rare illness; on his return he is rushed to hospital and remains there for nine months. On the day of his release, there is a board meeting which he does not attend, and he resolves not to attend board meetings again. After a further five months he has a relapse and dies a fortnight later. At what point does he cease to be a director?

A After six months of his holiday
B After six months of hospitalisation
C At the point where he decides not to attend board meetings again
D When he dies

Answer

D. The board can grant leave of absence, and 'absenting himself' does not include forced hospitalisation. The period of six months **begins** on his release from hospital, and has not been completed when he dies.

3 The extent of directors' powers 6/03

FAST FORWARD

The **powers** of the directors are **defined** by the **articles**.
The directors have a duty to exercise their powers in what they honestly believe to be the **best interests** of the company and for the **purposes** for which the powers are given.

The powers of the directors are **defined by the articles**. The directors are usually authorised 'to manage the business of the company' and 'to exercise all the powers of the company' (Table A Article 70).

Therefore they may then take **any decision which is within the capacity** (as defined by the objects clause) of the company **unless** either **the Act** or **the articles** themselves **require** that the **decision shall be taken by the members in general meeting**.

3.1 Restrictions on directors' powers

3.1.1 Statutory restrictions

Many transactions, such as an alteration of the articles or a reduction of capital, must by law be effected by passing a **special resolution**. If the directors propose such changes they must secure the passing of the appropriate resolution by shareholders in a general meeting.

3.1.2 Restrictions imposed by articles

As an example, the articles often set a maximum amount which the directors may borrow. If the directors wish to exceed that limit, they should **seek authority** from a **general meeting**.

When the directors clearly have the necessary power, their decision may be challenged if they exercise the power in the wrong way. They must exercise their powers:

- In what they **honestly believe to be the interests of the company** (see *Re Lee Behrens & Co* for an example of a decision held void for failure to observe this principle)
- For a **proper purpose**, being the purpose for which the power is given. See *Bamford v Bamford* for an example of this principle in operation

3.1.3 Members' control of directors

As explained above there is a division of powers between the board of directors who manage the business and the members who as owners take the major policy decisions at general meetings. How, then, do the owners seek to 'control' the people in charge of their property?

- The members **appoint** the directors and may **remove** them from office under s 303 (see above).
- The members can, by **altering the articles** with a special resolution, re-allocate powers between the board and the general meeting.

However the **directors are not agents of the members** who can be instructed by the members in general meeting as to how they should exercise their powers. **The directors' powers are derived from the company as a whole** and are to be exercised by the directors as they think best in the **interests of the company**.

3.1.4 Control by the law

Certain powers (it is not entirely clear which) must be exercised for a 'proper purpose' (see Chapter 17) and all powers must be exercised *bone fide* for the benefit of the company (see Chapter 17). Failure to comply will result in the exercise of the power being set aside by the courts unless the shareholders ratify the actions of the directors.

4 Managing and other working directors

FAST FORWARD

The managing director's **actual authority** is whatever the board gives him or her. Their **apparent authority** is to make business contracts on behalf of the company.

If the articles provide for it (for example Table A Article 84) the board may appoint one or more directors to be **managing directors**.

In his dealings with outsiders the managing director has **apparent authority** as agent of the company to **make business contracts**. No other director, even if he works full time, has that **apparent** authority as a director, though if he is employed as a manager he may have apparent authority at a slightly lower level (see *Kreditbank Cassel* case).

The managing director's **actual authority** is whatever the board gives him.

Holdsworth & Co v Caddies 1955
The facts: The MD's service agreement stated that he should perform duties for the holding and subsidiary companies assigned by the holding company's board. Following disagreements, these duties were restricted by the board to the business of one subsidiary.

Decision: The MD was duly confined by a resolution of the board, although his service agreement had thereby been breached.

Although a managing director (MD) has this special status his appointment may be terminated like that of any other director (or employee); he then reverts to the position of an ordinary director.

Alternatively the company in general meeting may remove him from his office of director and he immediately ceases to be MD since being a director is a necessary qualification for holding the post of MD.

The position of any other working director (not an MD) who is also an employee is that:

(a) He does not have the apparent authority to make general contracts which attaches to the position of MD but he has **whatever apparent authority attaches** to his **management position**.

(b) His **removal** from the office of director may be a **breach** of his **service contract** if that agreement stipulates that he is to have the status of director as part of the conditions of his employment.

5 Directors as agents 12/02, 6/04

FAST FORWARD

The directors are agents of the company and when they have actual or usual authority they can bind the company. In addition a director may have ostensible authority by virtue of holding out.

Holding out is a basic rule of the law of agency. It was outlined in Chapter 9. To recap, if the principal (the company) holds out a person as its authorised agent it cannot (against a person who has relied on the representation) deny that he is its **authorised agent** and so is bound by a contract entered into by him on the company's behalf.

Key term

Ostensible authority which is sometimes called apparent authority, is the authority which an agent appears to have to a third party. A contract made within the scope of such authority will bind the principal even though the agent was not following his instructions.

Therefore if the board of directors **permits a director** to behave as if he were a **managing director** duly appointed when in fact he is not, the company may be bound by his actions.

A managing director has, by virtue of his position, **ostensible authority** to make commercial contracts for the company. Moreover if the board allows a director to enter into contracts, being aware of his dealings and taking no steps to disown him, the company will usually be bound.

It is appropriate to revisit a case mentioned in Chapter 9 to illustrate this point.

Freeman & Lockyer v Buckhurst Park Properties (Mangal) Ltd 1964
The facts: A company carried on a business as property developers. The articles contained a power to appoint a managing director but this was never done. One of the directors of the company, to the knowledge but without the express authority of the remainder of the board, acted as if he were managing director. He found a purchaser for an estate and also engaged a firm of architects to make a planning application. The company later refused to pay the architect's fees on the grounds that the director had no actual or apparent authority.

Decision: The company was liable since by its acquiescence it had represented that the director was a managing director with the authority therefore to enter into contracts that were normal commercial arrangements in that sector, and which the board itself would have been able to enter.

Exam focus point

Situations where the facts are similar to the *Freeman & Lockyer* case often occur in law exams.

In the *Freeman & Lockyer* case, Diplock L J laid down four conditions which must be satisfied in claiming under the principle of holding out. The claimant must show that:

(a) A **representation** was made to him that the **agent had** the **authority** to enter on behalf of the company into the contract of the kind sought to be enforced.

(b) Such **representation** was **made by a person** who had **'actual' authority** to **manage** the **business** of the company.

The board of directors would certainly have actual authority to manage the company. Some commentators have also argued that the managing director has actual or apparent authority to make representations about the extent of the actual authority of other company agents. (However a third party cannot rely on the representations a managing director makes about his own actual authority).

(c) He was **induced** by the **representation** to enter into the contract; he had in fact relied on it.

(d) There must be **nothing** in either the **memorandum** (the objects clause) **nor** in the **articles** (a restriction on the board's power to delegate authority) which would prevent the company from giving valid authority to its agent to enter into the contract.

It is important to note that the fourth condition has been affected by S35A (see Chapter 12) and that many restrictions can now be disregarded.

Question

Directors' powers

Under the articles of association of Recycle Ltd the directors of the company need the consent of the general meeting by ordinary resolution to borrow sums of money in excess of £50,000. The other articles are in the form of Table A.

Mary has been appointed managing director of the company and she holds 1% of the issued shares of the company. Early in May 19X5 Mary entered into two transactions for the benefit of Recycle Ltd. First, she arranged to borrow £100,000 from Conifer Bank Ltd, secured by a floating charge on the company's assets. She had not sought the approval of the members as required by the articles. Second, she placed a contract worth £10,000 with Saw Ltd to buy some agricultural machinery.

Advise the directors of Recycle Ltd whether they are bound by the agreements with Conifer Bank Ltd and Saw Ltd.

Answer

The enforceability of the loan agreement and floating charge by Conifer Bank Ltd against Recycle Ltd is determined by reference to sections 35A CA1985. The transaction is intra vires the company but beyond the authority of the managing director, Mary, in that she failed to obtain an ordinary resolution of the company as required by its articles of association.

S35A provides that, in favour of a person dealing in good faith with a company, the power of the board of directors to bind the company or (importantly in this case) to authorise others to do so, shall be deemed to be free of any limitation under the company's constitution.

There is no suggestion that Conifer Bank Ltd has not acted in good faith and it will be presumed that it has in fact acted in good faith unless the contrary is proved by the company.

The articles are in the form of Table A and thus (Art 84) allow the board to appoint a managing director. In that position, Mary has apparent authority as agent of the company to make business contracts including the type of transaction entered into here.

Under s 35A, the restriction placed on her actual authority (by the article requiring an ordinary resolution) shall be deemed not to exist in favour of the third party, Conifer Bank Ltd. The power of the board to authorise Mary to bind the company is deemed to be free of any constitutional limitation.

Chapter roundup

- The method of appointing directors, along with their rotation and co-option is **controlled** by the **articles.**
- The articles may provide regulations for the removal of a director from office, but any such provisions are overridden by statute which allows removal by **ordinary resolution** with **special notice.**
- Directors may also be required to vacate office because they have been disqualified on grounds dictated by the articles.
- Directors **may** be disqualified from a very wider range of company involvements under the Company Directors Disqualification Act 1986 (CDDA).
- In this chapter we have also shown the extent of directors' powers, and how third parties may be protected if irregularities occur.
- The **powers** of the directors are **defined** by the **articles**.
- The directors have a duty to exercise their powers in what they honestly believe to be the **best interests** of the company and for the **purposes** for which the powers are given.
- If the articles provide for it, one or more directors may be appointed by the board as **managing director**.
- The managing director has **apparent** authority to make business contracts on behalf of the company. The managing director's **actual** authority is whatever the board gives him.
- The directors may appoint one of their number to be **chairman** of the board.
- If members do not like the acts of the directors, they can **remove them** under **s 303** or change the articles.
- Where the contract is **ultra vires**, s 35 applies.
- If the principal (the company acting through the board) **holds out** a person as its authorised agent, then it is estopped from denying that he is its authorised agent.

Quick quiz

1 Table A Articles 73-80 provide a number of rules on retirement and re-election of directors. These include which of the following?

A Every year one-third (or the nearest number thereto) shall retire.

B The managing director and any other director holding executive office are not subject to retirement by rotation and are excluded from the reckoning of the one third figure.

C A director shall be deemed to be re-elected unless the meeting decides otherwise.

D If the directors fail to agree on who should retire, the question is decided by lot.

E A co-opted director must stand for re-election at each AGM after his appointment.

2 **Fill in the blanks** in the statements below.

Under Table A Article 70 directors are authorised to ……………….. the ……………….. of the company, and ……………….. the ………………..of the company.

3 What is the extent of a managing director's actual authority?

4 What are the two principal ways by which members can control the activities of directors?

A director who has been appointed managing director ceases to be managing director if he is removed from office as a director.

True ☐

False ☐

6 Summarise the rule of holding out.

Answers to quick quiz

1 A, B, C and D are correct. Article 79 provides that a co-opted director should stand for re-election at the *next* AGM after his appointment.

2 Under Table A Article 70 directors are authorised to *manage* the *business* of the company, and *exercise* all the *powers* of the company.

3 The actual authority is whatever the board gives him.

4 Appointing and removing directors in general meeting

Reallocating powers by altering the articles

5 True

6 If a company holds out a person to be its authorised agent it cannot, against someone who has relied on the representation, deny that he is its authorised agent, and is therefore bound by any contract made by him on the company's behalf.

Now try the question below from the Exam Question Bank

Number	Level	Marks	Time
Q18	Examination	20	36 mins

Directors: duties

Topic list	Syllabus reference
1 Directors' duty of care	7(a)
2 Fiduciary duties of directors	7(a)
3 Remedies against directors for breach of fiduciary duties	7(a)
4 Statutory rules on directors' duties	7(a)
5 Insider dealing	7(d)
6 Money laundering	7(a)
7 Fraudulent and wrongful trading	7(a)
8 Disqualification of directors	7(a)

Introduction

The previous chapter considered the question of how directors are appointed and when they cease to be directors and the powers that they have. In this chapter we move away from procedural matters and consider the duties of directors and the common law and statutory remedies for the breach of such duties.

The duties of directors can conveniently be discussed under two headings.

- **Duties of care and skill**
- **Fiduciary duties** of loyalty and good faith

Statute also imposes some duties on directors, specifically concerning openness when transacting with the company.

We then consider the specific statutory offences of **insider dealing**, **money laundering** and **fraudulent and wrongful trading**. Fraudulent and wrongful trading relate to insolvency situations, where directors have been guilty of fraud or failed to take appropriate steps to minimise the losses of creditors.

Both fraudulent and wrongful trading are grounds for disqualifying directors; we mentioned disqualification briefly in the last chapter, but now go into more detail as to why directors might be disqualified.

The duties of directors are extremely important. This can be seen by the wealth of criminal sanctions which have built up for when directors' duties are broken. This subject is likely to be examined regularly in Section B, as it was in the Pilot paper.

1 Directors' duty of care 6/04

FAST FORWARD

Directors have a duty of care to show **reasonable competence**.

Directors have a **common law duty of care** to show **reasonable competence**. In the case of *Re City Equitable Fire and Insurance Co Ltd 1925* below, this duty was analysed into three propositions.

(a) A director is expected to show the **degree of skill** which may **reasonably be expected** from a person of his knowledge and experience. The standard set is personal to the person in each case. An accountant who is a director of a mining company is not required to have the expertise of a mining engineer, but he should show that of an accountant.

(b) A director is **required to attend board meetings** when he is able but he has no duty to concern himself with the affairs of the company at other times (unless he has undertaken to do so). His duties are of an **intermittent** nature. If he is also a working executive of the company his extra duties are performed as an employee and not as a director.

(c) In the absence of ground for suspicion and subject to normal business practice, he is **entitled to leave** the **routine conduct** of the business **in the hands of its management** and may trust them, accepting the information and explanation which they provide, if they appear to be honest and competent.

The duty to be competent extends to **non-executive directors**, who may be liable if they fail in their duty. Again the test is personal.

> *Dorchester Finance Co Ltd v Stebbing 1977*
> *The facts:* Of all the company's three directors, S, P and H, only S worked full-time. P and H signed blank cheques at S's request; he used them to make loans which became irrecoverable. The company sued all three; P and H, who were experienced accountants, claimed that as non-executive directors they had no liability.
>
> *Decision:* All three were liable, P's and H's acts in signing blank cheques being negligent and not showing the necessary skill and care.

S214 Insolvency Act 1986 (which imposes liability for wrongful trading on directors) imposes an objective duty on directors to display such care when carrying out their functions as a director as could reasonably be expected from a competent person carrying out those functions. In other words, a director is judged by the standard of the 'reasonable' director and it is no excuse for a director to say that he or she lacked expertise if a reasonable director would possess that expertise.

This section is influencing the scope of the general duty of competence, and the courts are now beginning to judge directors by this standard rather then the personal standard set out in *Re City Equitable Fire Insurance*, unless that personal standard would impose a **higher** standard on the director.

1.1 Company's action against negligent directors

The company may recover damages from its directors for loss caused by their negligence. Something more than imprudence or want of care must be shown. It must be shown to be a case of **gross negligence**, defined in *Overend Gurney & Co v Gibb 1872* as conduct which 'no men with any degree of prudence acting on their own behalf, would have entered into such a transaction as they entered into'. However, the impact of S214 Insolvency Act 1986 has led to courts being more likely to impose liability on directors.

In the absence of fraud it was difficult to control careless directors effectively. The new statutory provisions on disqualification of directors of insolvent companies and on liability for wrongful trading (discussed below) (CDDA and IA 1986) both set out how to judge a director's competence, and provide more effective enforcement.

1.1.1 Relief of liability

The company by decision of its members in general meeting decides whether to sue the directors for their negligence. As we have seen, even if it is a case in which they could be liable the court has discretion under s 727 to relieve them of liability if it appears to the court that:

- The directors acted **honestly** and **reasonably**.
- They **ought**, having regard to the circumstances of the case, **fairly to be excused**.

Re D'Jan of London Ltd 1993
The facts: D, a director of the company, signed an insurance proposal form without reading it. The form was filled in by D's broker. An answer given to one of the questions on the form was incorrect and the insurance company rightly repudiated liability for a fire at the company's premises in which stock worth some £174,000 was lost. The company became insolvent and the liquidator brought this action under s 212 of the Insolvency Act 1986 alleging D was negligent.

Decision: In failing to read the form D was negligent. However, he had acted honestly and ought therefore to be partly relieved from liability by the Court under s 727 of the Companies Act 1985.

1.1.2 Forgiveness by members

In the absence of **fraud or bad faith** the members may vote unanimously to forgive the director's negligence, even if it is those negligent directors who control the voting and exercise such forgiveness: *Multinational Gas & Petrochemical Co v Multinational Gas and Petrochemical Services Ltd 1983*. Where there is no fraud on the minority, a majority decision is sufficient: *Pavlides v Jensen 1956*.

Where the directors' negligence causes a company to enter into an *ultra vires* transaction the shareholders can absolve them from liability by special resolution (S35 CA85)

1.2 Directors' personal liability

As a general rule a director has no personal liability for the debts of the company. But there are certain exceptions.

- Personal liability **may arise** by **lifting the veil** of incorporation. (This was discussed in Chapter 10)
- A **limited company** may by its memorandum or by **special resolution** provide that its directors shall have unlimited liability for its debts: ss 306 – 307.
- A director may be **liable** to the **company's creditors** in certain circumstances. (See section 7)

Can a director be held personally liable for negligent advice given by his company?

He can, but only when he clearly assumes personal responsibility for advice given rather than simply giving advice in his capacity as a director.

Williams and Another v Natural Life Health Foods Ltd 1998
The facts: The director was sued personally by plaintiffs who claimed they were misled by the company's brochure. The director helped prepare the brochure, and the brochure described him as the source of the company's expertise. The plaintiffs did not however deal with the director but with other employees.

Decision: The House of Lords overruled the Court of Appeal, and ruled that the director was not personally liable. In order to have been liable, there would have had to have been evidence that the director had assumed personal responsibility. Merely acting as a director and advertising his earlier experience did not amount to assumption of personal liability.

2 Fiduciary duties of directors

Pilot paper, 6/02, 12/03, 6/04, 6/05

FAST FORWARD

Directors are said to be in a **fiduciary position** in relation to the company. Because of their special position, directors owe a number of strictly applied fiduciary duties to the company.

They must exercise their powers **bona fide** what they consider to be the best interest of the company. Breach of this rule leads to the act being ultra vires, and the directors become liable to indemnify the company against any loss.

Key term

Fiduciary duty is a duty imposed upon certain persons because of the position of trust and confidence in which they stand in relation to another. The duty is more onerous than generally arises under a contractual or tort relationship. It requires full disclosure of information held by the fiduciary, a strict duty to account for any profits received as a result of the relationship, and a duty to avoid conflict of interest.

Broadly speaking directors must be **honest** and **not** allow their personal interests to conflict with their duties as directors. The directors are said to hold a **fiduciary position** since they make contracts as **agents** of the company and have control of its property.

The directors owe a fiduciary duty to the company to exercise their powers bona fide in what they honestly consider to be the interests of the company: (not necessarily what the court may consider). *Re Smith and, Fawcett Ltd 1942*

In *Regentcrest plc v Cohen 2001* the judge said, 'The question is not whether, viewed objectively by the court, the particular act .... was in fact in the interest of the company ..... rather, the question is whether the director honestly believed that his act was in the interests of the company. The issue is as to the director's state of mind.'

This duty is owed **to the company** and **not generally to individual shareholders**. The directors will not generally be liable to the members if they purchase shares without disclosing information affecting the share price: *Percival v Wright 1902.*

FAST FORWARD

The **powers of directors** must only be used for a **proper purpose**. Unlike the requirement for bona fides, breach of this rule does not lead to the act being ultra vires, but the transaction will still be invalid unless the company in general meeting ratifies it.

In exercising the powers given to them by the articles the directors have a fiduciary duty not only to act bona fide **but also only to use their powers for a proper purpose.**

The powers are restricted to the **purposes** for **which they were given**. If the directors infringe this rule by exercising their powers for a collateral purpose the transaction will be invalid **unless** the **company** in **general meeting gives approval**, which may be retrospective.

If the irregular use of directors' powers is the allotment of shares the votes attached to the new shares may not be used in reaching a decision in general meeting to sanction it.

> *Howard Smith Ltd v Ampol Petroleum Ltd 1974*
> *The facts:* Shareholders who held 55% of the issued shares intended to reject a take-over bid for the company. The directors honestly believed that it was in the company's interest that the bid should succeed. The directors therefore allotted new shares to the prospective bidder so that the shareholders opposed to the bid would then have less than 50% of the enlarged capital and the bid would succeed.
>
> *Decision:* The allotment was invalid. 'It must be unconstitutional for directors to use their fiduciary powers over the shares in the company purely for the purpose of destroying an existing majority or creating a new majority which did not previously exist'.

Any **shareholder** may **apply to the court** to declare the transaction should be set aside. However the practice of the courts is generally to **remit the issue** to the **members in general meeting** to see if the members wish to affirm the transaction.

If the majority approve what has been done (or have authorised it in advance) that decision is treated as a proper case of majority control to which the minority must normally submit.

Hogg v Cramphorn 1966
The facts: The directors of a company issued shares to trustees of a pension fund for employees to prevent a take-over bid which they honestly thought would be bad for the company. The shares were paid for with money belonging to the company provided from an employees' benevolent and pension fund account. The shares carried 10 votes each and as a result the trustees and directors together had control of the company. The directors had power to issue shares but not to attach more than one vote to each. A minority shareholder brought the action on behalf of all the other shareholders.

Decision: If the directors have acted honestly in the best interest of the company, the company in general meeting can ratify the use of their powers for an improper purpose, so the allotment of the shares would be valid. But only one vote could be attached to each of the shares because that is what the articles provided.

Bamford v Bamford 1969
The facts: The directors of Bamford Ltd allotted 500,000 unissued shares to a third party to thwart a take-over bid. A month after the allotment an EGM was called and an ordinary resolution was passed ratifying the allotment, the holders of the newly-issued shares not voting. The claimants (minority shareholders) alleged that the allotment was not made for a proper purpose.

Decision: The ratification was valid and the allotment was good. There had been a breach of fiduciary duty but the act had been validated by an ordinary resolution passed in general meeting.

These cases can be distinguished from the *Howard Smith* case (where the allotment was invalid) in that in the *Howard Smith* case the original majority would not have sanctioned the use of directors' powers. In the *Bamford* case the decision could have been sanctioned by a vote which excluded the new shareholders.

Ratification is not effective where it attempts to validate a transaction when

- It constitutes fraud on a minority.
- It involves **misappropriation of assets**.
- The transaction **prejudices creditors' interests** at a time when the company is insolvent: *West Mercia Safetywear Ltd v Dodd 1988*.

Most of the cases discussed above concern the **duty of directors** to exercise their power to allot shares. This is only one of the many powers given to directors which are subject to this **fiduciary duty**, including the powers to:

- Borrow
- Give security
- Refuse to register a transfer of shares
- Call general meetings
- Circulate information to shareholders.

2.1 Conflicts of interests

FAST FORWARD

The directors must **avoid conflicts** of duty and **personal interest**. This rule is very strictly applied.

As **agents,** directors have a **duty to avoid a conflict of interest**. In particular:

(a) The directors must **retain their freedom of action** and **not fetter their discretion** by agreeing to vote as some other person may direct.

(b) The directors owe a fiduciary duty to **avoid a conflict of duty and personal interest.**

(c) The directors **must not obtain any personal advantage** from their position as directors **without the consent of the company** for whatever gain or profit they have obtained.

2.2 Freedom of action

A director may be appointed to represent the interest of, for instance, a shareholder or debentureholder. If he finds himself in an acute conflict of interest he should **resign**: *SCWS v Meyer 1959.*

2.3 Duty and personal interest

Directors must show undivided concern for the company's interests. It is unnecessary to show that the company has been prejudiced in any way by the conflict of interest.

Aberdeen Railway Co v Blaikie Bros 1854
The facts: A railway company made a contract for the supply of goods from a firm in which the chairman of the company was a partner. The company refused to accept the goods arguing that the contract was voidable owing to the chairman's interest in the supplier firm.

Decision: A director like a trustee may not have 'a personal interest conflicting, or which possibly may conflict, with the interests of those whom he is bound to protect ... it may sometimes happen that the terms ... have been as good as could have been obtained from any other person – they may even at the time have been better. But still so inflexible is the rule that no inquiry on that subject is permitted'. Accordingly, following trust law principles the company could treat the contract as voidable at its option.

There must always be a conflict of interest where a director has an interest, even indirect, in a contract with his company. Yet such contracts have to be made, such as when a company employs one of its directors in the management of the business.

To regulate these situations, statutory and other rules do permit directors to enter into or be **interested** in **contracts** with their company subject to various conditions, principally **disclosure** under s 317. These are discussed below, in section 3.

2.4 Personal advantage 12/04

Directors may not obtain personal advantages through their being directors unless the company is aware of and approves the benefit to the director.

Regal (Hastings) Ltd v Gulliver 1942
The facts: The company owned a cinema. It had the opportunity of acquiring two more cinemas through a subsidiary to be formed with an issued capital of £5,000. However the company could not proceed with this scheme since it only had £2,000 available for investment in the subsidiary. The directors and their friends therefore subscribed £3,000 for shares of the new company to make up the required £5,000. The chairman acquired his shares not for himself but as nominee of other persons. The company's solicitor also subscribed for shares. The share capital of the two

companies (which then owned three cinemas) was sold at a price which yielded a profit of £2.80 per share of the new company in which the directors had invested. The new controlling shareholder of the company caused it to sue the directors to recover the profit which they had made.

Decision:

(a) The directors were **accountable** to the company for their profit since they had obtained it from an opportunity which came to them as directors.

(b) It was **immaterial** that the **company** had **lost nothing** since it had been unable to make the investment itself.

(c) The directors might have kept their profit if the company had **agreed** by resolution passed in general meeting that they should do so; the directors might have used their votes to approve their action since it was not fraudulent (there was no misappropriation of the company's property.)

(d) The chairman was not accountable for the profit on his shares since he did not obtain it for himself. The solicitor was not accountable for his profit since he was **not a director** and so was not subject to the rule of accountability as a director for personal profits obtained in that capacity.

Exam focus point

Questions with facts similar to the *Regal Hastings* case often occur in law exams.

Industrial Development Consultants Ltd v Cooley 1972
The facts: C was managing director of the company which provided consultancy services to Gas Boards. A Gas board was unlikely to award a particular contract to the company but C realised that, acting personally, he might be able to obtain it. He told the board of his company that he was ill and persuaded them to release him from his service agreement. On ceasing to be a director of the company C obtained the contract on his own behalf. The company sued him to recover the profits of the contract.

Decision: C was accountable to his old company for his profit.

The Canadian courts (*Peso Silver Mines Ltd v Cropper 1966*) have made a distinction between a profit gained from a transaction which the company is **unable to undertake** and one which it **could undertake but declines**. The effect of the distinction is that if the contract is offered to the company and declined on commercial grounds the directors may enter into the contract and retain their profit. However there is no English decision to this effect and it is doubtful whether the English courts would make this distinction, although this decision has been followed in Australia.

2.5 Section summary

- Directors must exercise their powers **bona fide** in the company's best interests.
- Directors must use their powers for a **proper purpose**.
- Directors must avoid **conflicts of interest**.
  - Directions of other party
  - Personal interest
  - Personal advantage

3 Remedies against directors for breach of fiduciary duties

FAST FORWARD

Remedies against directors for breach of duties include accounting to the company for a **personal gain**, **indemnifying the company**, and **rescission of contracts** made with the company.

Any **action** will normally be **taken by the company** unless it is a situation in which a member may sue under the rules of minority protection (discussed in Chapter 18).

The type of remedy varies with the breach of duty.

(a) The director may have to **account for a personal gain:** *Regal (Hastings) Ltd v Gulliver.*

(b) He may have to **indemnify the company** against loss caused by his negligence by an unlawful transaction which he has approved.

(c) If he contracts with the company in a conflict of interest the **contract may be rescinded by the company**. However under common law rules the company cannot both affirm the contract and recover the director's profit: *Burland v Earle 1902.*

(d) The court may declare that a transaction is ultra vires or unlawful*: Re Lee Behrens & Co 1932.*

3.1 Relief by company

A company may, either by its **articles** or by **passing a resolution** in general meeting, **authorise or ratify** the conduct of directors in breach of duty. There must be **full disclosure** to members of the relevant facts. At the meeting a director who is a shareholder **may** use his votes as he wishes to approve his own conduct.

There are some limits on the power of members in general meeting to sanction a breach of duty by directors or to release them from their strict obligations.

(a) If the directors **defraud** the company and vote in general meeting to approve their own fraud, their votes are invalid (*Cook v Deeks*; contrast the *North West Transportation* case where there was a personal gain by a director but no fraud).

(b) If the directors **allot shares** to alter the balance of votes in a general meeting the votes attached to those shares may not be cast to support a resolution approving the issue (see *Bamford's* case above).

3.2 Liability for acts of other directors

A director is not liable for acts of fellow directors. However if he becomes aware of serious breaches of duty by other directors, he himself may have a duty to inform members of them or to take control of assets of the company without having proper delegated authority to do so.

In such cases the director is liable for his own negligence in what he allows to happen and not directly for the misconduct of the other director.

Question

Fiduciary duties

Briefly describe the fiduciary duties owed to a company by a director.

Answer

The fiduciary duties of directors can be summarised under two headings.

(a) To exercise their powers properly
(b) To avoid a conflict of interest

Proper exercise of powers

Directors in exercising their power must act bona fide (judged subjectively) and also exercise their powers for a proper purpose (judged objectively).

Exercise of powers *bona fide* restricts directors in, for example, making gifts to persons not employed by the company: *Re W & M Roith Ltd 1967.*

Use of powers for a proper purpose means directors must use powers for the purposes for which they were given. Directors should not use powers for a collateral purpose, for example, allotting shares to prevent a takeover bid: *Howard Smith Ltd v Ampol Petroleum Ltd 1974.*

If, however, the directors use their powers for a proper purpose but act honestly in the best interests of the company, the breach of duties may be ratified retrospectively by the company: *Bamford v Bamford 1969.*

Conflict of interest

Case law provide a number of examples of conflicts of interest directors must avoid.

(a) Directors must retain their freedom of action. In certain circumstances a director may be appointed to represent the interests of a shareholder or debentureholder. If then his duty to the company conflicts with the interests of whoever appointed him, he should resign: *SCWS v Meyer 1959.*

(b) Directors should not, except with the company's consent make any arrangement where their personal interests conflict with the company's interests. In *Aberdeen Railway Co v Blaikie Bros 1854*, a contract for the supply of goods by a firm in which the company's chairman was partner was held to be voidable by the company.

(c) A director should not make personal profits from his position except with the company's consent. If no consent is given the director will be liable to account to the company for the profit. This rule extends to profits obtained from transactions with a director in that capacity with third parties. Although he does not profit at the company's expense he is nonetheless accountable to it.

In *Regal (Hastings) Ltd v Gulliver 1942* which concerned investments in shares, it was held that it was immaterial that the company would not have been able to obtain the profit from share dealings the directors obtained, since it did not have sufficient capital to make the required investment. The directors were accountable since the opportunity to make a profit had come from their being directors.

The same principle applies even if the director has ceased to be a director, if the opportunity came because the person had been a director: *Industrial Development Consultants Ltd v Cooley 1972.*

A Canadian case, *Peso Silver Mines Ltd v Cropper 1966,* drew a distinction between a situation where a director obtained a profit under a contract which the company was unable to perform (in which case the director could retain the profit), and the situation where the company was offered the opportunity to obtain the profit but declined (where the director could not retain the profit). No English case has followed this judgement. Therefore the director can only obtain personal profits if the company consents.

4 Statutory rules on directors' duties

The statutory rules operate in three different ways.

(a) Some transactions, such as loans to directors, are normally **prohibited**.

(b) Some transactions **require approval** by shareholders in general meeting and are voidable by the company unless properly disclosed and approved.

(c) Some transactions, such as directors having interests in shares, are not restricted but particulars must be **disclosed** in the annual accounts or directors' report sent to members.

(d) Some transactions must be available for member inspection (eg the register of directors' interests).

4.1 Directors' interests in company contracts

There are three possible objections to a director making or being interested in a contract with his own company.

(a) He may be obtaining a **personal advantage** from his position as director.

(b) There may be a **conflict of interest** which may affect his judgement.

(c) By **concealment** of his interest he may induce the other directors or the shareholders to approve transactions which they might have rejected if they had known of his interest.

4.1.1 Declaration of directors' interests (s 317)

The main statutory safeguard is the requirement (s 317) that a director shall always **'declare the nature of his interest'**, direct or indirect, in a contract or proposed contract with the company.

The disclosure must be made to the **first meeting** of the **directors** at which the contract is considered or (if later) the **first meeting held after** the **director becomes interested** in the contract.

If a director fails to give notice when required to do so by s 317:

(a) He commits an offence and may be **fined**.

(b) He loses the benefit of any **relieving provisions** of the articles (for example, Table A, Art 85) and the contract is probably voidable at the option of the company if the articles contain such provisions.

(c) He may be **accountable to the company** for any secret profit obtained from the contract.

A director who does give notice is not thereby relieved of his duty to avoid a conflict of interest. However the standard articles (Table A Article 94) grant wide exemptions and generally permits a director to be interested in a contract provided that:

(a) He **discloses** the nature of his interest as required by s 317.

(b) He **does not vote** and is not reckoned as one of the quorum of directors at the board meeting which approves the contract.

4.1.2 Single member companies

The requirement to declare his interest at a meeting of the company directors also applies in the case of a sole director: *Neptune (Vehicle Washing Equipment) Ltd v Fitzgerald 1995.* (It was held that a meeting could consist of one person).

Furthermore, s 322B of the Companies Act 1985 regulates the situation where a single member private company enters into a contract (other than a contract entered into in the ordinary course of the company's business) with the **sole member** of the company and the sole member is also a director of the company. The company must, unless the contract is in writing, ensure that the **terms** of the contract are:

(a) **Set out** in a **written memorandum**

(b) **Recorded** in the **minutes** of the first meeting of the directors of the company following the making of the contract

4.2 Substantial property transactions (s 320)

Shareholder approval is required for any contract (or arrangement) by which the company buys from or sells to a director of the company or of its holding company or a person connected with any such director property which exceeds **£100,000 in value** or (if less) **exceeds 10 per cent of the company's net assets** (subject to a minimum of £2,000 value): s 320.

If this approval is not obtained the contract is **voidable** by the company. The director (or person connected with him) is accountable to the company for any gain and liable to indemnify the company for any loss: s 322.

This includes a subsequent loss in value occurring after the transaction: *Re Duckwari plc 1998,* where the loss in value was caused by the collapse in the property market and the price paid for the asset was a perfectly fair one.

4.3 Material interest transactions (s 232)

A company must disclose in the annual accounts any contract or arrangement with the company (or a subsidiary) in which a director, directly or through a connected person, has an interest which was **'material'**. The other directors may decide that a director's interest in a contract is not material for disclosure.

Contracts of a value **not exceeding £1,000** or (if greater) not exceeding **one per cent of the company's assets (subject to a maximum of £5,000)** are **exempt** from this disclosure requirement: s 232 and Sch 6.

4.4 Service contracts (ss 318 and 319)

Where reference is made to a director's 'service contract' there are in fact two separate circumstances at issue.

(a) The contract may be one where the director acts solely in that capacity: that is, he attends board meetings and is publicly associated with the company. This is a contract **for services**.

(b) The contract may essentially be one of employment, where the director carries out management and executive functions. This is a contract **of service**.

A contract of service or for services is valid even if it both extends for longer than five years and the company:

- **Cannot terminate** by notice, or
- Can only terminate it in **specified circumstances** (s 319(6)),

provided it is **first** approved by an ordinary resolution. It cannot later be ratified. If the term of employment is in excess of five years etc and has not been approved by the members, the company will be able to terminate the contract at any time by giving reasonable notice.

4.5 Directors' emoluments

A director is only entitled to **fees** for his services as a director as the **articles provide**. The articles usually fix a specific amount, say £1,000 pa or provide (Table A Article 82) that it shall be such as the company in general meeting may decide.

Directors are entitled to **reimbursement** of their **expenses** by Article 83.

In practice directors prefer to have **written service contracts** setting out their entitlement to emoluments and expenses, since the articles may be changed by the members and do not give rise to legally enforceable rights.

The annual accounts must include information of directors' emoluments distinguishing directors' fees and management salaries (if any) and certain directors' pensions: s 231 and Sch 5.

4.6 Damages and compensation for loss of office

Any director may receive **non-contractual** compensation for loss of office paid to him voluntarily under ss 312 – 315. Any such compensation is lawful **only if** approved by members of the company in general meeting after proper disclosure has been made to all members, whether voting or not.

Ss 312-315 only apply to uncovenanted payments; approval is not required where the company is contractually bound to make the payment: *Lander v Premier Pict Petroleum Limited 1998.*

Compensation paid to directors for loss of office is distinguished from any payments made to directors **as employees**, for example to settle claims arising from the premature termination of the service agreements. These are contractual payments which do not require approval in general meeting: *Taupo Totara Timber Co v Rowe 1977.*

4.7 Loans to directors

Every company is prohibited by s 330 from:

- **Making a loan** to a director of the company or of its holding company
- **Guaranteeing or giving security** for a loan to any such director
- **Taking an assignment of a loan** which, if made originally by the company, would have been contrary to (a) and (b)
- **Providing a benefit to another person** as part of an arrangement by which that person enters into a transaction forbidden to the company itself by rules (a) to (c)

General exceptions to the above rule include the following.

- A company may make a loan or give a guarantee or security in respect of a loan to a director which is also its **holding company**: s 336.
- A company may **fund** a director to enable him to **perform his duties** provided that the money is **approved** in **general meeting before or afterwards**. If it is made available before approval is obtained, it must be approved at or before the next AGM and must be repaid within six months of that AGM if not so approved: s 337. In order to approve the funding, the members must be told the following.
  - The **purpose** of the expenditure
  - The **amount of funds** to be supplied
  - The **extent** to which the **company** is **liable** in relation to the transaction entered into by the director

- A **money lending company** may advance money to a director, provided it is done in the normal course of business and the terms are not more favourable than the company would normally allow: s 338.
- Any company may make a **loan** to directors provided the total of all loans does not exceed **£5,000**: s 334.
- **Group members**, even where there is relevant company status, may lend to each other: s 333.
- A **holding company** may make loans to **directors of its subsidiaries**, provided they are not directors of, or connected to directors of, the holding company.

4.7.1 Relevant companies

There are **more stringent rules for 'relevant companies**' which include **any public company** and any private company which is a member of a group which includes a public company.

The same basic rules apply to relevant as to other companies. In addition, in the case of a relevant company:

- The second and third **exceptions** described above are **limited** to a **maximum** of **£20,000** and **£100,000** respectively, although a bank is only restricted to the £100,000 limit if it is for a residence: s 338.
- There are restrictions on indirect means of enabling a director to obtain goods or services on credit by transactions called **'quasi-loans' and 'credit transactions'.**
- A company transaction with a third party who is **'connected'** with one of its directors is subject to the same rules as apply to its transactions with a director himself.

A **'quasi-loan'** is a payment to a third party on the director's behalf, with the company being indemnified later by the director: s 331.

A **'credit transaction'** is a hire purchase or conditional sale agreement, a lease or a deferred payment agreement for land or goods (and services in the case of deferred payment): s 331. A relevant company may enter into a credit transaction regarding a director if:

- It **does not exceed £10,000**, or
- It enters into it in the **ordinary course of its business** and the **terms** are **no different** than would have been offered to any third party.

A person is connected with a director of a company under s 346 if the person:

- Is the **spouse** or **child** under 18 of the director
- Is a **company** in which the **director** and any other **persons connected** with him together own at least 1/5 of the equity share capital (or control at least 1/5 of the votes)
- Is a **trustee** of a trust of which the **director or persons connected** with him are **beneficiaries**
- Is a **partner** in a firm in which the **director or a person connected** with him is also a **partner**

The same definition is applied to substantial property transactions of directors.

4.7.2 Breach of S330

S341 provides that breach of S330 results in the transaction being voidable by the company. The director who benefited from the transaction (and any connected person) is liable to account to the company for any gain made.

Where a director has purchased shares with a loan granted in breach of S330 and the shares have increased in value the company can claim that increase.

In addition, the director can be required to indemnify the company for any losses arising from a transaction in breach of S330.

A director of a **relevant** company who authorises or permits a company to enter into a transaction in breach of S330 may incur criminal liability.

4.8 Disclosures concerning directors

In order to help in the enforcement of the above rules on directors' interests, shareholdings and other transactions the law makes stringent rules on disclosure of such events. This enhances accountability to members.

4.8.1 Loans to directors

If any loan to directors, whether **prohibited or permitted**, existed during the year prescribed particulars must be **included** in the **annual accounts** for the year: s 232.

If the information is not given in the accounts the auditors must, so far as they are reasonably able to do so, include the missing particulars in their audit report: s 237(4).

4.8.2 Directors' interests in contracts

There are similar requirements for disclosure in the annual accounts of transactions in which a director had **directly** or **indirectly** a **material interest**: Sch 6 para 1. The other directors may decide whether a director's interest is 'material' (and requires disclosure).

4.8.3 Inspection of directors' service agreements

A company must make available for inspection by members a copy or particulars (if there is no written service agreement) of **contracts of employment** between the company or a subsidiary with a director of the company: s 318.

There are two exceptions to the s 318 disclosure requirements (s 319):

(a) If the contract requires the director to work **wholly** or **mainly outside the UK,** only brief particulars (the director's name and the duration of the contract) need be given.

(b) If the contract will **expire** or if the company can **terminate it without compensation within a year**, no copy or particulars need be kept available for members' inspection.

The copy or particulars must be available either at the **registered office**, or at the **principal place of business** in England: s 318(4).

Prescribed particulars of **directors' emoluments** must be given in the accounts and also particulars of any **compensation for loss of office** and directors' **pensions**: Sch 5.

The annual report must contain details of the **unexpired contract term** of any director who is standing for re-election at the next annual general meeting. It must also contain details of any **service contract** with a **notice period in excess of one year**, or where compensation for loss of office exceeded one year's salary plus benefits in kind.

5 Insider dealing 12/01, 12/03

FAST FORWARD

Insider dealing legislation prohibits people possessing inside information from:

- Dealing
- Encouraging others to deal
- Disclosure of information

Insider dealing applies to many individuals other than directors.

The facts of the following case are an example of what is now called insider dealing. Note that the directors purchased the shares when they (as directors) knew and the vendor shareholders did not know that there was the possibility of a takeover bid at a higher price.

Percival v Wright 1902

The facts: The claimants asked the company whether it could find buyers for their shares which they valued at £12.50 each. The directors purchased the shares at that price. At the time the directors knew that a third party was interested in buying the entire issued share capital at a higher price than £12.50. In fact nothing came of these negotiations. But the claimants demanded that their sale to the directors should be rescinded for non-disclosure of the possibility of re-sale by the directors at a higher price.

Decision: The directors owed no duty to members individually which obliged the directors to disclose what they knew. (Note that the decision would, today, not fall foul of the Criminal Justice Act unless the shares were listed securities.)

Part V of the **Criminal Justice Act 1993** contains the rules on insider dealing.

The offence

S 52 describes the offence as dealing in listed securities while in possession of inside information as an insider, the securities being **price-affected** by the information.

The prosecution must prove that the possessor of inside information:

- **Dealt in price affected securities**
- **Encouraged another to deal** in them
- **Disclosed** the **information**

Dealing

S 55 defines dealing as **acquiring** or **disposing** of or **agreeing to acquire or dispose** of relevant securities whether **directly** or **through an agent** or nominee or a person acting according to direction.

Encouraging another to deal

An offence is also committed if an individual, having information as an insider, **encourages another person** to deal in price-affected securities in relation to that information, **knowing** or having **reasonable cause to believe that dealing would take place.**

It is irrelevant whether:

- The **person encouraged realises** that the **securities** are **price-affected** securities.
- The **inside information is given** to that person; for example, a simple recommendation to the effect that 'I cannot tell you why but now would be a good time to buy shares in Bloggs plc' would infringe the law.
- **Any dealing takes place**, the offence being committed at the time of encouragement.

Disclosing information It is also an offence for an individual who is considered an insider to disclose the information to another person otherwise than in the proper performance of the functions of his employment, office or profession.
Securities covered by the Act S 54 states that the securities include shares, debt securities and warranties.
Inside information S 56 defines inside information as **'price sensitive information'** relating to a **particular issuer** of **securities** that are price-affected and not to securities generally. It must, if made public, be likely to have a **significant effect on price** and it must be **specific or precise**. Specific would, for example, mean information that a takeover bid would be made for a specific company; precise information would be details of how much would be offered for shares.
Insiders S 57 states that a person has information as an insider if it is (*and* he **knows** it is) inside information; and if he has it (*and* **knows** he has) from an inside source: • Through being a **director, employee or shareholder** of an issuer of securities • Through **access** because of **employment, office or profession** • If the **direct** or **indirect source** is a **person within these two** previous categories
General defences S 53 gives a general defence where the individual concerned can show that: • He did **not expect** there to be a **profit** or avoidance of loss. • He had **reasonable grounds** to **believe** that the **information** had been **disclosed widely**. • He would have done what he did even **if he had not had the information**, for example, where securities are sold to pay a pressing debt. Defences to disclosure of information by an individual are that: • He did **not expect** any person to **deal**. • Although dealing was expected, **profit or avoidance of loss was not expected**.
'Made public' S 58 defines this term, but not exhaustively, leaving final determination to the Court. Information is made public if: • It is **published** under the rules of the regulated market, such as the Stock Exchange. • It is in **public records**, for example, notices in the *London Gazette.* • It can **readily be acquired** by those likely to deal. • It is **derived** from **public information**. Information may be treated as made public even though: • It can **only** be **acquired** by **exercising diligence** or expertise (thus helping analysts to avoid liability). • It is **communicated only** to a **section** of the **public** (thus protecting the 'brokers' lunch' where a company informs only selected City sources of important information). • It can be **acquired** only by **observation**. • It is **communicated only** on a **payment of a fee** or is **published only outside the UK**.

Penalties
Maximum penalties given by s 61 are seven years' imprisonment and/or an unlimited fine. Contracts remain valid and enforceable at civil law.
Territorial scope
S 62 states that the offender or any professional intermediary must be in the UK at the time of the offence or the market must be a UK regulated market.

5.1 Problems with the laws on insider dealing

The courts may have problems deciding whether information is specific or precise. S 60(4) states that information shall be treated as relating to an issuer of securities which is a company not only when it is about the company but also where it may affect the business prospects of the company.

The requirement that price-sensitive information has a significant effect on price limits the application of the legislation to fundamental matters such as an impending takeover, or profit or dividend levels which would be out of line with market expectations.

5.2 Market abuse

The Finance and Markets Act 2000 introduced a new civil offence of 'market abuse'. This was partly in response to the perceived ineffectiveness of the insider dealing provisions in the Criminal Justice Act 1993.

Market abuse is behaviour by one person or in concert which occurs in the UK in relation to qualifying investments traded on a designated market, which satisfies one of more of the prescribed conditions and which is likely to be regarded by a regular user of the market, who is aware of the behaviour as a failure on the part of the person or persons concerned to observe the standard of behaviour reasonably expected of a person in his position in relation to the market.

The conditions (mentioned in the key term above) are:

(a) The behaviour is based on information not generally available to those using the market. If available to a regular user of the market would be regarded as relevant for decision-making.

(b) The behaviour is likely to give a regular user a false/misleading impression as to the supply/demand for or price/value of investments in question.

(c) The regular user would be likely to regard the behaviour as such that would distort the market.

The published code relating to 'market abuse' suggests that it covers not only what has been known as insider dealing, but also artificial transactions, price manipulation and the dissemination of misleading information.

The FSA can impose a penalty of whatever amount it considers appropriate on people found to have engaged in market abuse.

6 Money laundering

6.1 What is money laundering?

Key term

> **Money laundering** is the term given to attempts to make the proceeds of crime appear respectable.
>
> It covers any activity by which the apparent source and ownership of money representing the proceeds of income are changed so that the money appears to have been obtained legitimately.

Money laundering legislation in the UK is relevant to a number of different pieces of legislation, including the following:

- Drug Trafficking Offences Act 1986
- Criminal Justice Act 1993
- Proceeds of Crime Act 2002
- Terrorism Act 2000
- Anti-terrorism Crime and Security Act 2001

The offences

There are **three categories of criminal offences** in the Proceeds of Crime Act 2002.

- **Laundering**: acquisition, possession or use of the proceeds of criminal conduct or assisting another to retain the proceeds of criminal conduct and concealing the proceeds of criminal activity
- **Failure to report**: failure to disclose knowledge or suspicion of money laundering
- **Tipping off**: disclosing information to any person if disclosure may prejudice an investigation into:
  - Drug trafficking
  - Drug money laundering
  - Terrorist related activities
  - Laundering the proceeds of criminal conduct

Penalties

The law sets out the following penalties in relation to money laundering:

- 14 years' imprisonment, for knowingly assisting in the laundering of criminal funds
- 5 years' imprisonment, for failure to report knowledge or the suspicion of money laundering
- 5 years' imprisonment for 'tipping off' a suspected launderer. Suspicions must be reported to the **National Criminal Intelligence Service**. The suspected launderer must not be alerted
- 2 years' imprisonment for contravention of the systems requirements of the Money Laundering Regulations 2003 (see below)

Money laundering

Why should a professional adviser not give a warning to a client whom he suspects of money laundering?

Answer

Tipping off a suspected money launderer is an offence. Alerting the suspect would be likely to hamper any subsequent investigation by the authorities.

The money laundering process usually involves three phases:

- **Placement** – this is the actual disposal of the proceeds of the initial illegal activity
- **Layering** – this involves the transfer of monies to conceal the original source
- **Integration** – having been layered, the money has the appearance of legitimate funds

6.2 Money Laundering Regulations 2003

In the UK, the Money Laundering Regulations 2003 came into force on 1 March 2004. The new regulations impose obligations upon professionals from a wide range of sectors. These include accountants, auditors, insolvency practitioners, tax advisers and legal advisers.

There is a **legal requirement** for organisations to take the following actions.

(a) To set up procedures and establish accountabilities for senior individuals to take action to prevent money laundering

(b) To educate staff and employees about the potential problems of money laundering

(c) To obtain satisfactory evidence of identity where a transaction is for more than €15,000 or £10,000

(d) To report suspicious circumstances (according to the established procedures)

(e) Not to alert persons who are or might be investigated for money laundering

(f) To keep records of all transactions for five years

If one of the specified types of organisation identifies suspicious circumstances, a report must be made to the National Criminal Intelligence Service ('NCIS') on a Suspicious Activity Report ('SAR') form.

Individual professional bodies, including the accountancy and taxation bodies and the Law Society, have issued guidance to their members. The Second Interim Guidance for Accountants was published by the CCAB in February 2004. Accountants working in practice or in another **relevant business** must report knowledge or suspicion of money laundering to the NCIS. In order to facilitate this, a relevant business must:

(a) Appoint a nominated officer as the Money Laundering Reporting Officer (MLRO);

(b) Train employees on the requirements of the legislation, including how to recognise and deal with potential money laundering;

(c) Verify the identify of new clients and keep a record of the evidence obtained; and

(d) Establish appropriate internal procedures to forestall and prevent money laundering.

The making of a report based on knowledge, suspicion or reasonable grounds for such takes precedence over any considerations regarding client confidentiality. The Proceeds of Crime Act 2002 gives protection for any breach of duty of confidentiality in such circumstances.

Legal privilege can provide a defence for a professional legal adviser to a charge of failing to report suspicions of money laundering. The information must not have been provided to the legal adviser with the intention of furthering a criminal purpose. There is no equivalent protection available to accountants.

The legislation applies to a business operating in the UK, including those working out of a UK office for overseas clients.

7 Fraudulent and wrongful trading **12/03**

FAST FORWARD

Breach of the rules on fraudulent trading (trading with intent to defraud) or wrongful trading (trading while knowingly insolvent) can lead to directors incurring personal liability.

7.1 Fraudulent trading: s 213 IA 1986

If the court finds that the business of a company in liquidation has been carried on with **intent to defraud creditors** or for any fraudulent purpose it may declare that **any** persons who were knowingly parties to carrying on the business in this fashion shall be liable for the debts of the company as the court may decide: ss 213 and 217.

Various rules have been established to determine what is fraudulent trading:

(a) Only persons who **take the decision** to carry on the company's business in this way or play some active part are liable.

(b) **'Carrying on business'** can include a single transaction and also the mere payment of debts as distinct from making trading contracts: *Re Sarflax Ltd 1979*.

If the liquidator considers that there has been fraudulent trading he should apply to the court for an order that those responsible (usually the directors) are liable to make good to the company all or some specified part of the **company's debts**.

The liquidator should also report the facts to the Director of Public Prosecutions so that the DPP may **institute criminal proceedings**.

7.2 Wrongful trading: s 214 IA 1986

The problem which faced the creditors of an insolvent company before the introduction of 'wrongful trading' was that it was exceptionally difficult to prove the necessary fraud (in order to render directors liable for the company's debts). However, the Insolvency Act 1986 introduced a further civil liability for 'wrongful trading'. Where a director is liable under S214 the court can order him to 'make such contribution to the assets of the company as the court thinks proper.'

Directors will be liable under s 214 if the liquidator proves the following.

(a) The director(s) of the insolvent company **knew**, or **should have known**, that there was **no reasonable prospect** that the **company** could **have avoided going into insolvent liquidation**. This means that directors cannot claim they lacked knowledge if their lack of knowledge was a result of failing to comply with Companies Act requirements, for example preparation of accounts: Re Produce Marketing Consortium 1989 (see below).

(b) The director(s) did **not take sufficient steps to minimise the potential loss** to the creditors.

The section goes on to provide that the director(s) will be deemed to know that the company could not avoid insolvent liquidation if that would have been the conclusion of a **reasonably diligent person** with the **general knowledge, skill and experience** that might reasonably be expected of a person carrying out that particular director's duties (ie a reasonable occupant of a similar post).

In addition, where a director has greater skill and experience than in 'normal' director he is judged by reference to his own capacity.

7.3 Standard expected

The standard expected of a listed company director would be higher than for the director of a small owner-managed private company.

Halls v David and Another 1989
The facts: The directors sought to obtain relief from liability for wrongful trading by the application of s 727 Companies Act 1985, which states that in proceedings for negligence, default, breach of duty or breach of trust against a director, if it appears that he has acted honestly and reasonably (so that in all the circumstances he ought fairly to be excused) the court may relieve him wholly or partly from liability on such terms as it sees fit.

Decision: S 727 is not available to excuse a director from liability under s 214.

Re Produce Marketing Consortium Ltd 1989
The facts: Two months after the case above, the same liquidator sought an order against the same directors, that they should contribute to the company assets (which were in the hands of the liquidator) since they had been found liable for wrongful trading.

Decision: The directors were jointly and severally liable for the sum of £75,000 plus interest, along with the costs of the case. The judge stated that the fact that wrongful trading was not based on fraud was not a reason for giving a nominal or low figure of contribution; the figure should, however, be assessed in the light of all the circumstances of the case.

This case was significant for creditors, since the assets available for distribution in a winding-up will (potentially) be much increased by a large directors' contribution. It serves as a warning to directors to take professional advice sooner rather than later, as the prospect of making a personal contribution may prove much more expensive than winding-up at the appropriate stage.

8 Disqualification of directors 6/05

We saw in the last chapter that directors could be disqualified from acting as directors or being involved in the management of companies.

The law here is set out in the Company Directors Disqualification Act 1986 (CDDA). This was introduced in response to public disquiet with the fact that often directors of failed companies were able to walk away from the wreckage of the company with no personal liability, regardless of the reasons for which the company failed. In many cases they would then go on to start new, very similar companies (so called 'phoenix' companies) which had no liability to the previous creditors, who usually ended up with nothing.

8.1 The CDDA

The court **may** make an order on any of the following grounds.

(a) **Where a person is convicted of an indictable offence in connection with the promotion, formation, management or liquidation of a company or with the receivership or management of a company's property (s 2).**

An indictable offence is an offence which may be tried at a crown court; it is therefore a serious offence. It need not actually have been tried on indictment (at the crown court) but if it was, the maximum period for which the court can disqualify is 15 years, compared with only 5 years if the offence was dealt with summarily (at the magistrates court: s 5).

(b) **Where it appears that a person has been persistently in default in relation to provisions of company legislation.**

This legislation requires any return, account or other document to be filed with, delivered or sent or notice of any matter to be given to the registrar of companies (s 3). Three defaults in five years are conclusive evidence of persistent default.

The maximum period of disqualification under this section is five years.

(c) **Where it appears in the course of the winding up of a company that a person has been guilty of fraudulent trading**, carrying on business with intent to defraud creditors or for any fraudulent purpose.

The person does not actually have to have been convicted of fraudulent trading. The legislation also applies to anyone who has otherwise been guilty, while an officer or liquidator of the company or receiver or manager of its property, of any fraud in relation to the company or of any breach of his duty as such officer etc (s 4).

The maximum period of disqualification under this section is 15 years.

(d) **Where the Secretary of State acting on a report made by the inspectors or from information or documents obtained under the Companies Act, applies to the court for an order believing it to be expedient in the public interest.**

If the court is satisfied that the person's conduct in relation to the company makes that person unfit to be concerned in the management of a company, then it may make a disqualification order (s 8). Again the maximum is 15 years.

(e) Where a director has engaged in certain **competitor violations** (S9A, inserted by the Enterprise Act 2002). Maximum – 15 years.

(f) **Where a director has participated in wrongful trading (s 10).** Maximum – 15 years.

The court **must** make an order where it is satisfied that the following apply:

(a) A person has been a director of a company which has at any time become **insolvent** (whether while he was a director or subsequently).

(b) His conduct as a director of that company makes him **unfit** to be **concerned** in the **management** of a company (s 6). The courts may also take into account his conduct as a director of other companies, whether or not these other companies are insolvent: *Secretary of State for Trade and Industry v Ivens and Another 1997.* Directors can be disqualified under this section even if they take no active part in the running of the business: *Re Park House Properties 1998.* In such cases, the **minimum** period of disqualification is two years.

8.2 Examples of conduct leading to disqualification

Offences for which directors have been disqualified include the following.

(a) **Insider dealing**

(b) **Failure to keep proper accounting records**

(c) **Failure to read the company's accounts**

(d) **Loans** to another company for the purposes of purchasing its own shares with **no grounds for believing the money would be repaid**

(e) **Loans** to associated companies on **uncommercial terms** to the detriment of creditors

The courts have been establishing what constitutes conduct worthy of disqualification since the Act was introduced. For example in *Re Lo-Line Electric Motors Ltd 1988* the judge said that 'ordinary commercial

misjudgement is not in itself sufficient to justify disqualification. In the normal case, the conduct complained of must display a **lack of commercial probity**, although... in an extreme case of gross negligence or total incompetence, disqualification could be appropriate.'

In *Re Stanford Services* 1987 the judge said that the public is entitled to be protected from the activities of anyone who 'has shown in his conduct of a company a failure to appreciate or observe the duties attendant on the privilege of conducting business with the protection of limited liability.'

Re Uno, Secretary of State for Trade and Industry v Gill 2004

Facts: A group consisting of two furniture companies carried on trading while in serious financial difficulties, while the directors tried to find a way out of the situation. Uno continued to take deposits from customers for furniture to fund its working capital requirements.

Decision: The directors were not disqualified for acting in this way as their behaviour was not dishonest or lacking in commercial probity, and did not make them unfit to manage a company. They had been trying to explore realistic opportunities to save the businesses, and were not to blame for the eventual collapse of the businesses and the subsequent losses of customers.

8.3 Disqualification periods

In *Re Sevenoaks Stationers (Retail) Ltd 1991* the Court of Appeal laid down certain 'disqualification brackets'. The appropriate period of disqualification which should be imposed under s 6 was a minimum of two to five years if the conduct was not very serious, six to ten years if the conduct was serious but did not merit the maximum penalty, and over ten years only in particularly serious cases.

Disqualification as a director need not mean disqualification from all involvement in management: *Re Griffiths 1997,* and it may mean that the director can continue to act as an unpaid director: *Re Barings plc 1998*, but only if the court gives leave to act.

If a person breaches a disqualification order they may be liable to penalties including a fine and/or imprisonment.

8.4 Mitigation of disqualification

Examples of circumstances which have led the court to imposing a lower period of disqualification include the following.

- **Lack of dishonesty**: *Re Burnham Marketing Services Ltd 1993*
- **Loss of director's own money** in the company: *Re GSAR Realisations Ltd 1993*
- Absence of personal gain, for example excessive remuneration: Re *GSAR Realisations Ltd 1993*
- **Efforts to mitigate** the situation: *Re Burnham Marketing Services Ltd 1993*
- **Likelihood of re-offending**: *Re Grayan Building Services Ltd 1995*
- **Proceedings hanging over director** for a long time: *Re Aldermanbury Trust 1993*

8.5 Procedures for disqualification

Administrators, receivers and liquidators all have a statutory duty to report to the DTI on directors of companies in whose affairs they have become involved, where they believe the conditions in s 6 for a disqualification order have been satisfied: s 7.

The Secretary of State then decides whether to apply to the court for an order, but if he does decide to apply he must do so within two years of the date on which the company became insolvent.

Disqualification

In what circumstances can a court make a disqualification order against a director of a company?

Answer

The provisions for disqualification of directors are now contained in the Company Directors Disqualification Act 1986. A court may, by order, disqualify a person from being a director, liquidator, administrator, receiver or manager of a company, and from being concerned in the promotion or management of any company: CDDA s 1.

The order may be made in any one of the following circumstances.

(a) The director concerned is convicted of an indictable offence in connection with a company: s 2.

(b) The director concerned has been persistently in default in relation to company law requirements requiring the delivery to the Companies Registry of annual accounts, the annual return and other documents. A previous decision of a court on three previous occasions in five years that the person concerned has been in default in compliance with these requirements is conclusive evidence of 'persistent' default: s 3.

(c) The director concerned has been guilty of fraud in connection with a company then in liquidation: s 4.

(d) The court is satisfied that a director's conduct is such as to make him unfit to be concerned in the management of a company. There is a procedure and subsidiary rules for this ground of disqualification including the criteria that the company must have become insolvent either during the period the person was a director or subsequently. In this case the court must make an order if it finds that the grounds exist and a minimum of 2 years disqualification is prescribed: ss 6 and 7.

(e) Where the Secretary of State applies for disqualification in the public interest. This would arise from an investigation by DTI inspectors or documents obtained under the Companies Act: s 8.

(f) Where a director has been found guilty of certain breaches of competition law: S9A.

(g) The director has participated in wrongful trading in insolvency: s 10.

In general disqualification may be ordered for up to 15 years. But the maximum is 5 years in case (b) above or when the order is made by a magistrates' court: s 2. A person subject to disqualification may apply to the court for remission of the order.

Bankruptcy

An undischarged bankrupt may not, without leave of the court, act as a director of a company or be concerned in the management or promotion of a company: s 11.

Here the disqualification is the automatic result of the bankruptcy order made against him by the court.

Exam focus point

The examiner, David Kelly, published an article on the CDDA 1986 in the February 2005 edition of *Student Accountant*. This may indicate that it is an area of interest to him, so you should make sure that you read it.

Chapter roundup

- Directors have a duty of care to show **reasonable competence**.
- Directors are said to be in a **fiduciary position** in relation to the company. Because of their special position, directors owe a number of strictly applied fiduciary duties to the company.
- They must exercise their powers **bona fide** what they consider to be the best interest of the company. Breach of this rule leads to the act being ultra vires, and the directors become liable to indemnify the company against any loss.
- The **powers of directors** must only be used for a **proper purpose**. Unlike the requirement for bona fides, breach of this rule does not lead to the act being ultra vires, but the transaction will still be invalid unless the company in general meeting ratifies it.
- The directors must **retain their freedom of action** and not fetter their discretion by agreeing to vote as some other person may direct.
- The directors must **avoid conflicts** of duty and **personal interest**. This rule is very strictly applied.
- Remedies against directors for breach of duties include accounting to the company for a **personal gain**, **indemnifying the company**, and **rescission of contracts** made with the company.
- A compromise is reached in some situations by allowing directors to have certain interests so long as they have been disclosed (in accordance with a very rigid procedure).
- The statutory rules operate in four ways.
  - Some transactions are **prohibited**, for example, loans.
  - Some transactions **require approval** by shareholders for example, substantial and material property transactions.
  - Some transactions require **disclosure** in the annual report and accounts or in the directors' report: for example loans, emoluments.
  - Details of some transactions must be available for **member inspection** (register of directors' interests, directors' service agreements).
- **Insider dealing** legislation prohibits by people possessing inside information from:
  - Dealing
  - Encouraging others to deal
  - Disclosure of information
- **Money laundering** is the term given to attempts to make the proceeds of crime appear legitimate. Key legislation includes the Proceeds of Crime Act 2002 and the Money Laundering Regulations 2003.
- Breach of the rules on fraudulent trading (trading with intent to defraud) or wrongful trading (trading while knowingly insolvent) can lead to directors incurring personal liability.

Quick quiz

1 The directors of a company are in breach of the rule requiring them to act for a proper purpose. A general meeting can

A Do nothing that will authorise the transaction
B Authorise the transaction by ordinary resolution
C Authorise the transaction by special resolution only
D Relieve the directors of any liability under the transaction by special resolution only

2 What were the three principles laid down in the case of *Re City Equitable Fire Insurance Co Ltd 1925* in relation to a director's duty of skill and competence?

3 **Fill in the blanks** in the statement below.

Shareholder approval is required under s 320 for any contract or arrangement under which the company buys from or sells to a director property which exceeds ……………….. in value or (if less) ………………..% of the company's net assets, subject to a minimum of ……………….. .

4 Which of the following are lawful loans by public companies to directors?

A A loan of £1,000 made by a private company that makes vending machines

B A loan of £25,000 to meet legitimate expenses by a public company which manufactures cars

C A loan of £40,000 made on standard terms by a money-lending public company

D A hire purchase agreement made on standard terms during the ordinary course of business for £4,000 by a hire purchase public company

5 What does a liquidator have to prove for a director to be guilty of wrongful trading?

6 Loans to directors of a private company under £5,000 are not illegal and need not be disclosed in the company's accounts.

True ☐

False ☐

7 Under which of the following grounds *may* a director be disqualified if he is guilty, and under which *must* a director be disqualified?

A Conviction of an indictable offence in connection with a company

B Persistent default with the provisions of company legislation

C Fraudulent trading

D Public interest, as a result of an inspectors' report

E Wrongful trading

F Director of an insolvent company whose conduct makes him unfit to be concerned in the management of the company

Answers to quick quiz

1 B

2 A director is expected to show the degree of skill which may reasonably be expected from a person of his knowledge or experience.

A director is required to attend board meetings when he is able, but has no duty to concern himself with the affairs of the company at other times.

In the absence of grounds for suspicion and subject to normal business practice, a director is entitled to leave the routine conduct of the business in the hands of its management.

3 Shareholder approval is required under s 320 for any contract or arrangement under which the company buys from or sells to a director property which exceeds *£100,000* in value or (if less) *10%* of the company's net assets, subject to a minimum of *£2,000*.

4 A, C and D are lawful, as they are not over the prescribed financial limits. However the upper limit for the type of transaction mentioned in B is £20,000: s 338.

5 The director knew, or should have known, that there was no reasonable prospect that the company could have avoided going into insolvent liquidation and the director did not take sufficient steps to minimise the loss to creditors.

6 False. Loans to directors under £5,000 are legal, but loans of any size should be disclosed in the company's accounts.

7 A to E are grounds under which a director may be disqualified; F is grounds under which a director must be disqualified.

Now try the question below from the Exam Question Bank

Number	Level	Marks	Time
Q19	Examination	10	18 mins

18 Majority control and minority protection

Topic list	Syllabus reference
1 Majority control: the rule in *Foss v Harbottle*	9(a)
2 Minority protection: s 459	9(a)
3 Minority protection: common law rules	9(a)
4 'Just and equitable' winding up	9(b)
5 DTI investigations	9(c)
6 Other statutory rights of minorities	9(a)

Introduction

Every member of a company is bound by the articles to the company and to his fellow members as we saw in an earlier chapter. By implication, a member agrees to be bound by the decisions of the **majority** as expressed at a general meeting. This principle of majority rule was established in *Foss v Harbottle*.

However, while **directors** must exercise their power **bona fide** for the benefit of the company and for a proper purpose, shareholders are under no such obligation. Clearly shareholders may exercise their votes in their own interests and not those of the company. There must, therefore, be some restraint on the power of those able to command a majority vote. Minorities are therefore protected by **common law** and **statute**, and the various rules are all covered in this chapter.

You should concentrate more on the statutory rules for minority protection under s 459 than on the common law rules.

This topic may be examined along with the duties of directors and other actions a shareholder may take, including a shareholder's right to remove directors under s 303.

Minority interests could come up in almost any company scenario given in Section B. it could also be examined in Section A.

1 Majority control: The rule in Foss v Harbottle

FAST FORWARD

If the directors hold a majority of the voting shares or represent a majority shareholding, the minority has no remedy unless the rules of **minority protection apply.**

Members voting in general meeting have ultimate control of a company, and therefore its directors. However if the directors hold a majority of the voting shares or represent a majority shareholder the minority of members has no remedy if the minority feel they have been treated unfairly or the company has been treated improperly by the directors, unless the rules of minority protection apply.

Foss v Harbottle 1843

The facts: A shareholder (Foss) sued the directors of the company alleging that the directors had defrauded the company by selling land to it at an inflated price. The company was by this time in a state of disorganisation and efforts to call the directors to account at a general meeting had failed.

Decision: The action must be dismissed.

- The **company** as a person separate from its members is the **only proper plaintiff** in an action to protect its rights or property.
- The **company** in **general meeting** must decide whether to bring such legal proceedings.

Exam focus point

Remember *Foss v Harbottle* established the **need** for minority protection, not the **right** of minority protection.

In laying down the general principles of procedure the court did nonetheless recognise that 'the claims of justice' must prevail over 'technical rules'. The protection of a minority in various situations is provided by making exceptions to *Foss v Harbottle.* The common law exceptions are discussed in Section 3, but the most effective remedy is S459.

2 Minority protection: s 459 12/01, 6/03

FAST FORWARD

The principal **statutory** remedy for minorities is a s 459 action alleging the company's affairs have been conducted in an **unfairly prejudicial manner.**

The court may make **whatever order** it sees fit to settle a s 459 action (generally purchase of the petitioner's shares).

Any member may apply to the court for relief under s 459 on the grounds that the company's affairs are being or have been conducted in a manner which is **unfairly prejudicial** to the interests of the members **generally or of some part** of the members. Application may also be made in respect of a single prejudicial act or omission.

There is **no** statutory definition of what constitutes unfairly prejudicial conduct. Applications against unfairly prejudicial conduct often arise from:

(a) **Exclusion of a director** from participation in the management of a quasi-partnership company where he could legitimately have expected to be involved in management. (A 'quasi-partnership' company is a small, generally private and often family-owned company where essentially the relationship between the directors and members is equivalent to partners in a partnership.)

(b) **Discrimination against a minority**

Whatever the reason for the application, the complaint must be based on prejudice to the member as a **member** and not as an employee, nor as an unpaid creditor.

The complaint must relate to breach of the terms by which it has agreed the company should be run, and not to private acts of shareholders.

Courts will have regard to the **expectations** of members when considering whether conduct is unfairly prejudicial, particularly in quasi-partnership cases where the 'partner' expects to be involved in management. It is therefore unfairly prejudicial for the members to ignore that expectation and expel him.

> *Re Bird Precision Bellows Ltd 1986*
> *The facts:* A minority with 26% of the shares suspected the MD of this 'quasi-partnership' company of concealing bribes paid to secure contracts. When the DTI refused to investigate the minority was removed from the board. They claimed unfair prejudice under s 459.
>
> *Decision:* The claim was allowed as it was a 'quasi-partnership'.

There are however limits to claims under s 459.

(a) There has to have been an **actual act** by the company, for example a breach in the terms on which it was agreed the company could be run. A minority shareholder will not be able to obtain relief just because he has lost trust or confidence in the way the company is being run: *O'Neill v Phillips and Others 1999.*

(b) The court will take into account the **contents** of the **memorandum** and articles in deciding whether the minority had legitimate expectations: *Re Tottenham Hotspur plc 1994.* It is unlikely that 'expectations' can override the terms of the memorandum and articles when the company is a plc.

(c) In public companies, shareholders are unlikely to have a reasonable expectation of being involved in management: *Re Blue Arrow plc 1987.*

The courts may also take the petitioner's conduct into account when deciding whether certain actions are unfairly prejudicial.

> *Re R A Noble & Sons (Clothing) Ltd 1983*
> *The facts:* B had provided the capital but left the management in the hands of N, the other director, on the understanding that N would consult B on major company matters. N did not do so and B confined himself to enquiries to N on social occasions; he accepted N's vague assurances that all was well. The petition followed from a breakdown of the relationship.
>
> *Decision:* B's exclusion from discussion of company management questions was largely the result of his own lack of interest. His petition was dismissed.
>
> *Re London School of Electronics Ltd 1985*
> *The facts:* The other shareholders had removed the petitioner from his directorship after he had alleged that they were diverting business from the company to themselves. He then set up a rival business and took part of the company's connection with him.
>
> *Decision:* He had a right to relief even though he did not have 'clean hands'. The majority had to buy out the minority without any discount for the fact that his were minority shares and therefore of less value.

The courts will not sanction a s 459 action made for a purpose other than relieving a minority, for example encouraging a takeover bid: *Re Astec (BSR) plc 1998.*

2.1 Examples of conduct that has been held to be unfairly prejudicial

Unfairly prejudicial conduct need not be illegal, nor need it be intentional nor discriminatory: *Re Bovey Hotel Ventures Ltd 1983.* It is the **effect** of the conduct which is considered.

Examples of conduct that has been held to be unfairly prejudicial include the following.

(a) **Exclusion** and **removal** from the **board** where the company was one in which the director had a legitimate expectation of being involved in management: *Re Bird Precision Bellows Ltd 1986*

(b) **Improper allotment** of shares

Re D R Chemicals Ltd 1989
The facts: The majority shareholder allotted further shares to himself to increase his holding.

Decision: The allotment was a blatant case of unfairly prejudicial conduct (and also, incidentally, a breach of the Companies Act pre-emption rules).

(c) **Failure** to **call a meeting:** *Re McGuinness and Another 1988*

(d) **Making** an **inaccurate statement** to **shareholders**

Re A Company 1986
The facts: The petitioners complained that the directors had misled them in recommending acceptance of a bid by another company which the directors owned.

Decision: The directors' conduct was unfairly prejudicial since it affected members' rights to sell their shares at the best price.

(e) A managing director using **assets** for his own **personal benefit** and the personal benefit of his family and friends: *Re Elgindata Ltd 1991*

(f) **Diversion of company's business** to a director-controlled company: *Re Cumana 1986*

(g) Making a **rights issue** which minority shareholders could not take up: *Re Cumana 1986*

(h) Payment of **excessive directors' bonuses** and **pension contributions**: Re Cumana 1986

However the courts will not generally intervene in cases of dispute about **management** (even bad management).

Re A Company 1983
The facts: The petitioners' grievance was the directors' refusal to put forward a scheme of reconstruction or a proposal to purchase their shares (by the company). The directors were preoccupied with plans for diversification of the business.

Decision: The directors' duty was to manage the company to its advantage as they saw it. It was not a case of 'unfair prejudice'. In *Re Five Minute Car Wash Service Ltd 1966*, the complaint was of incompetent management causing loss but tolerated by the controlling shareholder. The petition failed.

Nevertheless on occasions the courts have intervened where continued mismanagement caused serious financial damage to the company and the minority's interests: *Re Macro (Ipswich) Ltd 1994.*

There are other instances where the courts have held that conduct was **not unfairly prejudicial**.

- **Late presentation** of **accounts**: *Re Ringtower Holdings plc 1989*
- **Failure** by a parent company **to pay** the **debts** of a **subsidiary**: *Nicholas v Soundcraft Electronics Ltd 1993*
- **Non-compliance** with the **Stock Exchange rules**, the City Code and the Cadbury Code: *Re Astec (BSR) plc 1998*

The limits on the application of s 459 remain under debate. It has been argued for example that a s 459 action could be used as a check on excessive board remuneration packages. *Re Cumana 1986* laid down the principle that excessive directors' remuneration can be conduct that is unfairly prejudicial to members' interests.

The House of Lords in *O'Neill v Phillips (1999)* stressed that the relationship of the shareholders is primarily governed by the **memorandum and articles**. Hence, where these documents have been complied with (or there has been only a minor breach) the court will not rush to find unfair prejudice. The House held that only where the memorandum and articles do not represent the understandings on which the shareholders are associated will an act which complies with these documents be, potentially, unfairly prejudiced.

> *O'Neill v Phillips (1999)*
>
> *Facts:* P originally owned all the shares (100) in a construction company but in 1985 he gave 25 shares to O, an employee: P also retired from the board effectively leaving O as managing director. The profits of the company were legally divided between P (75%) and O (25%) but P voluntarily gave up 25% of the profits so that P and O received equal profit shares and there were discussions about O's shareholding being increased to 50% of the share.
>
> In 1991 there was a downturn in the construction industry and P returned to oversee management, giving O the choice of managing, under P's direction, either the English or the German branch of the business while remaining a director of the company; O went to Germany. Later that year, P claimed to be entitled to retain 75% of the company's profits and O left the company claiming unfair prejudice.
>
> *Decision:* The House rejected O's claim. Lord Hoffman approved *Re Saul Harrison* (in which he had given the leading judgement) and stressed that 'a member of a company will not ordinarily be entitled to complain of unfairness unless there has been some breach of the terms on which he agreed that the affairs of the company would be conducted. But ...there will be cases in which equitable considerations make it unfair for those conducting the affairs of the company to rely upon their strict legal powers. Thus unfairness may consist of a breach of the rules or in using the rules in a manner which equity would regard as contrary to good faith.'
>
> On the facts of this case, O had not been excluded from management, nor had P promised or agreed to transfer any shares to O (even if O had hopes of such a transfer), nor had O been promised he would always receive 50% of the profits. Rather O had been promised, at best, 50% while he was acting as managing director. P had done nothing in breach of the memorandum and articles and there were no promises by P which could give rise to equitable considerations which might have led the court to treat O as entitled to something other then that given in the company's constitution.

The House of Lords also suggested that where one party has been excluded from management and alleges that this is unfairly prejudicial but the excluding party has made a **reasonable offer to buy out the shares of the excluded shareholder** the exclusion will not be unfairly prejudicial. An offer to buy will be reasonable only if three conditions are satisfied:

(a) A valuation is done by a competent expert;

(b) Both parties have access to information about the company which might affect the value of the shares; and

(c) The valuation values the shares without applying a discount to reflect the fact that it is a minority shareholding.

2.2 Court orders

When a petition is successful the court may make whatever order it deems fit. Courts may give, under s 461:

- An order regulating the **future conduct** of the company's affairs, for example that a controlling shareholder shall conform to the decisions taken at board meetings.
- An authorisation to any person to bring **legal proceedings** on behalf of the company; the company is then responsible for the legal costs

- An order requiring the company to **refrain** from doing or continuing an act complained of
- Provision for the **purchase of shares** of the **minority**
- **Inclusion in the memorandum or articles** of provisions which may only be altered or removed thereafter by leave of the court

Perhaps the most common type of relief is an order that either the controlling shareholder or the company shall purchase the petitioner's shares at a fair price. This ends a relationship which has probably broken down beyond repair.

(a) The shares should be valued on the basis of their **worth before** the controlling shareholders' conduct had diminished it: *SCWS v Meyer 1959*

(b) The **court** may determine what is **fair**; in particular no allowance need be made because the shares to be bought are only a minority holding and do not give control: *Re Bird Precision Bellows Ltd 1986*.

(c) Where the articles provide a method for valuing shares it should be used unless it would be unfair to the petitioner.

Question

s 459

James is the majority shareholder in Elan Ltd, holding 52% of the issued shares. The other shareholders are Chris, Martin, Jennifer and Henry, each of whom holds 12% of the shares. The minority shareholders feel that James has been abusing his position as majority shareholder and have lost confidence in him. They approach you for general advice.

Advise them on the nature of the action available under s 459 of the Companies Act 1985 on the basis of unfair prejudice to the minority.

Answer

Under s 459, any member may now apply to the court for relief on the grounds that the company's affairs are being or have been conducted in a manner which is unfairly prejudicial to the interests of the members generally or some part of the members or in respect of a particular act or omission which has been or will be prejudicial. Applications are commonly made in cases of discrimination against a minority or exclusion of a director in a quasi-partnership company.

The prejudice complained of must affect the claimant-member in his capacity as member and not as an employee or unpaid creditor. The member need not prove bad faith or even an intention to discriminate.

The court will take into account the surrounding circumstances including the parties' conduct and may make such orders as it deems fit. It might regulate the company's future affairs in some way, order the purchase of the minority's shares by the majority or by the company itself (*SCWS v Meyer 1958*), authorise some person to bring proceedings on the company's behalf, order the company to refrain from doing the act complained of or include in the company's constitution provisions which could then only be altered by the court. However, loss of confidence in itself will rarely be unfair prejudice.

Examples of types of conduct that have been held to be unfairly prejudicial include.

(a) Exclusion and removal from the board where there was a legitimate expectation of participation: *Re Bird Precision Bellows Ltd 1985*

(b) Where a managing director uses assets for his own personal benefit and the personal benefit of his family and friends: *Re Elgindata Ltd 1991*

(c) Where a majority shareholder transfers sources of profit into another company owned by the majority shareholder: *Re London School of Electronics Ltd 1986*

(d) The diversion of a company's business to a director-controlled company or the making of a rights issue which minority shareholders were not permitted to take up or the payment of excessive directors' bonuses and pension contributions: *Re Cumana 1986*

(e) The improper allotment of shares: *Re D R Chemicals Ltd 1989*

(f) The failure to call a meeting as requisitioned by the petitioner-minority: *Re McGuinness and Another 1988*

(g) The late presentation of accounts *(Re Ringtower Holdings plc 1989)* and failure by a parent company to pay the debts of a subsidiary: *Nicholas v Spendcroft Electronics Ltd 1993*

(h) Failure to increase dividends at a time when directors' remuneration was sharply increased: *Re Sam Weller 1989*

2.3 Section summary

- S 459 offers a statutory remedy to a minority if **unfairly prejudicial conduct** has occurred.
- Unfairly prejudicial conduct generally involves **discrimination against** a **minority** or **exclusion of a director** from a **quasi-partnership company.**
- There are various case law examples of unfairly prejudicial conduct.
- Bad management will not generally be treated as unfairly prejudicial conduct.
- Courts may make whatever orders they deem fit, most often **purchase of a dissenting minority's shares**.

Exam focus point

A shareholder who is unhappy about the conduct of the company's affairs will often try to obtain a remedy under s 459.

3 Minority protection: Common law rules 6/03

FAST FORWARD

A number of common law exceptions for the protection of the minority have been accepted since *Foss v Harbottle*. A minority has been allowed to bring proceedings in the following situations.

- To restrain an illegal or ultra vires decision
- To remedy certain errors in procedure
- To enforce individual rights of membership
- To prevent a **fraud** on the minority

In addition case law recognises a number of limitations to the principle of majority control (the rule in *Foss v Harbottle*). In those cases a minority can bring legal proceedings. The decisions are not entirely consistent but the principles are generally summarised as follows.

	Minority protection: common law principles
Illegal acts	No majority vote can be effective to sanction an illegal company act
Special procedure	If the law or the articles specify a 'special procedure' for an action, if the directors do not follow that procedure their act is invalid.
Individual rights of membership	If the company deprives a member of his individual rights he may sue the company to enforce his rights
Fraud/oppression	If those who control the company use their control to defraud the company the minority may bring legal proceedings against the minority

3.1 Illegal decisions

Illegal decisions taken in general meeting are not binding because a majority of members cannot decide that the company shall break the law. If they attempt to do so any member may apply to the court for a declaration that the decision is void and (if necessary) for an **injunction** to restrain the company from acting on the decision.

3.2 Failure to observe procedure

Where a majority merely disregards procedure or restrictions imposed by the articles of the company it is less certain that a minority can enforce due compliance by action in the courts. The courts have sometimes been inclined to treat these situations as mere internal matters which a majority of members should be free to regulate as they see fit.

> *Edwards v Halliwell 1950*
> *The facts:* A trade union (subject to rules of company law on this point) had rules (equivalent to articles) by which members' contributions were fixed at a specific rate which could only be increased if so decided by a two-thirds majority of votes cast in a members' ballot. A meeting decided, without holding a ballot of members, to increase the rate of subscriptions.
>
> *Decision:* The decision was invalid since it conflicted with the rules and the members who brought the action were entitled to a declaration that it was void.
>
> *Macdougall v Gardiner 1875*
> *The facts:* The articles provided that a poll must be held if demanded at the meeting by at least five members. However when five members demanded a poll the chairman refused to comply. One of the members sued for a declaration that the resolutions passed on a show of hands were invalid.
>
> *Decision:* The court would not intervene in a mere 'irregularity' of internal procedure which could be regularised by a majority approving it. (On the particular point in the case there is now a statutory right given to five members to demand a poll.)

3.2.1 Convening of meetings

A minority may also apply to the court for a remedy if a meeting is convened by a notice which does not, as the articles usually require (Table A Article 38), disclose in sufficient detail 'the general nature of the business' to be done: *Kaye v Croydon Tramways 1898* and *Baillie v Oriental Telephone Co 1915*.

However a mere technical irregularity of procedure in convening a meeting may not suffice to invalidate its decisions: *Bentley-Stevens v Jones 1974*.

The above cases may be distinguished as follows.

(a) If the articles require that some power is to be **exercised in a particular way** (as in the *Edwards* case mentioned above), an attempt by simple majority vote to override the article will be invalid. If the articles are to be altered a special resolution should be passed since that is the proper way.

(b) On the other hand, if the minority complaint is really that in exercising its voting rights the majority has, by approval of the substantive proposal, waived some **technical irregularity of procedure** (as in the *Macdougall* case) the court may well refuse to intervene.

3.3 Fraud on the company

The exception to the rule (in *Foss v Harbottle*) over fraud by a controlling majority is to protect the company (by a member's action) since the company cannot protect itself. It must be shown that:

- What was taken **belonged to the company**
- It **passed to those against** whom the claim is made
- Those who **appropriated the company's property are in control** of the company

In such cases a member may bring an action to enforce the company's rights (a derivative action). Any remedy awarded goes to the company.

3.3.1 Diversion of contracts

To divert away from the company profitable contracts which it was about to make is to deprive it of its 'property' (for the purposes of this rule).

Cook v Deeks 1916
The facts: The directors who were also controlling shareholders negotiated a contract in the name of the company. They took the contract for themselves and passed a resolution in general meeting declaring that the company had no interest in the contract. A minority shareholder sued them as trustees for the company of the benefit of the contract.

Decision: The contract 'belonged in equity to the company' and the directors could not, by passing a resolution in general meeting, bind the company to approving this action of defrauding it.

3.3.2 Passing of property to controlling shareholders

Likewise passing property to controlling shareholders (though **not** to **other third parties**: *Pavlides v Jensen 1956*) may well be equivalent to fraud even though no dishonesty is shown.

Daniels v Daniels 1978
The facts: The company was controlled by its two directors, husband and wife. It bought land for £4,250 (probate value) from the estate of a deceased person and later resold it at the same price to the lady director. She re-sold it for £120,000. A minority shareholder sued the directors but did not allege fraud. Objection was raised that a member could not sue the directors on the company's behalf for negligence (*Pavlides'* case above) but only for fraud.

Decision: The circumstances required investigation and a member might sue the directors and controlling shareholders for negligence if one of them secured benefit from the company by reason of it.

3.3.3 Discrimination against minority

The courts have taken fraud to mean not just misappropriation of company property but in some cases also discrimination against the minority.

Clemens v Clemens Bros Ltd 1976
The facts: A and B (who were aunt and niece) held 55% and 45% respectively of the shares with voting rights. A proposed to vote in favour of ordinary resolutions to increase the authorised share capital and to approve the allotment of new shares to or for the benefit of employees of the company. No more shares would be allotted to A or B but the effect of the scheme would be to reduce B's shareholding from 45% to 24.5% with the object of depriving B of her power to block a special resolution to alter the articles as A desired. B sought a declaration that A could not use her votes in this way.

Decision: A should be restrained from using her votes to deprive B of her 'negative control' (her ability to block an alteration of the articles to which B objected).

3.3.4 Remedies

The issue in the cases is often whether a shareholder in a company is entitled to recover damages for the diminution of the value of his shareholding, where such diminution was the result of loss inflicted on the company by the actions of the controlling majority.

If the company successfully sues the wrongdoers then the company's losses are made good and the shares should not lose value. If a shareholder suffers losses which are simply a reflection of the company's losses, eg dividends not paid because of the losses, a shareholder cannot recover that from the wrongdoers. *Johnson v Gore Wood & Co. 2002.*

3.4 Enforcement of individual rights of membership

A member may sue the company to enforce his personal rights against it. This is a different kind of minority action. In the other cases the minority is usually seeking to protect **the company** (and their interests in it) against others. In protecting his personal rights the member is **protecting himself against** the company.

> *Pender v Lushington 1877*
> *The facts:* The articles gave members one vote for each 10 shares held by them but subject to a maximum of 100 votes for each member. A company which was a large shareholder transferred shares to the plaintiff to increase its voting power. At the meeting the chairman rejected the plaintiff's votes. The plaintiff sued and the company relied on the argument that only the company itself could object to an irregularity of voting procedure.
>
> *Decision:* The plaintiff's votes were a 'right of property' which he was entitled to protect by proceedings against the company.

The principle of *Pender's* case is restricted to protection of **personal rights** of **membership** such as the right to vote or receive a due dividend. A member cannot sue merely to have the voting procedure of the articles observed (*Macdougall's* case above) since that is not sufficiently personal to him. He also cannot bring a **personal action** for loss in value of shares due to misappropriation of assets, as the company is the proper plaintiff for that type of action: *Stein v Blake 1998.*

3.5 Usefulness of common law remedies

Owing to changes in the statutory code the dissatisfied minority is now more likely to apply to the court for relief under ss 459 – 461 than to attempt to sue the majority under common law rules.

There are also procedural points in bringing a minority shareholders' action.

(a) The claimant may bring a **derivative** action on behalf of the company to enforce its rights or recover its property. Any benefit obtained will accrue to the company since the claim is derived from and made on behalf of the company. In such cases the court may order the company to indemnity the member.

(b) The claimant usually combines a derivative action with a **representative** action – he asserts that he sues on behalf of all other shareholders (except the defendants). He may however combine a representative action with a personal claim for damages.

Exam focus point

Minority protection questions may cover the **common law** remedies, the **statutory** protection for minorities under s 459, or both. Make sure you understand exactly what the question is asking for.

4 'Just and equitable' winding up

Dissatisfied shareholders also have these statutory remedies.

- To petition for winding-up of the company on the **just and equitable ground**
- To demand a **DTI investigation**
- To object to certain specific actions (for example changing the company's articles)

A member who is dissatisfied with the directors or controlling shareholders over the management of the company may petition the court for a winding up on the **just and equitable ground**.

For such a petition to be successful, the member must show that **no** other remedy is available. It is not enough for a member to be dissatisfied to make it just and equitable that the company should be wound up, since winding up what may be an otherwise healthy company is a drastic step.

Orders have been made for winding up in the following situations.

(a) **The substratum of the company has gone – the only main object(s) of the company (its underlying basis or substratum) cannot be or can no longer be achieved.**

Re German Date Coffee Co 1882
The facts: The objects clause specified very pointedly that the sole object was to manufacture coffee from dates under a German patent. The German government refused to grant a patent. The company manufactured coffee under a Swedish patent for sale in Germany. A contributory petitioned for compulsory winding up.

Decision: The company existed only to 'work a particular patent' and as it could not do so it should be wound up.

(b) **The company was formed for an illegal or fraudulent purpose or there is a complete deadlock in the management of its affairs.**

Re Yenidje Tobacco Co Ltd 1916
The facts: Two sole traders merged their businesses in a company of which they were the only directors and shareholders. They quarrelled bitterly and one sued the other for fraud. Meanwhile they refused to speak to each other and conducted board meetings by passing notes through the hands of the secretary. The defendant in the fraud action petitioned for compulsory winding up.

Decision: 'In substance these two people are really partners' and by analogy with the law of partnership (which permits dissolution if the partners are really unable to work together) it was just and equitable to order liquidation.

(c) **The understandings between members or directors which were the basis of the association have been unfairly breached by lawful action.**

Ebrahimi v Westbourne Galleries Ltd 1973
The facts: E and N carried on business together for 25 years, originally as partners and for the last 10 years through a company in which each originally had 500 shares. E and N were the first directors and shared the profits as directors' remuneration; no dividends were paid. When N's son joined the business he became a third director and E and N each transferred 100 shares to N's son. Eventually there were disputes; N and his son used their voting control in general meeting (600 votes against 400) to remove E from his directorship under the power of removal given by s 303 of the Companies Act 1985 (removal by ordinary resolution).

Decision: The company should be wound up. N and his son were within their legal rights in removing E from his directorship, but the past relationship made it 'unjust or inequitable' to insist on legal rights and the court could intervene on equitable principles to order liquidation.

Re A company 1983
The facts: The facts were similar in essentials to those in Ebrahimi's case but the majority offered and the petitioner agreed that they would settle the dispute by a sale of his shares to the majority. This settlement broke down however because they could not agree on the price. The petitioner then petitioned on the just and equitable ground.

Decision: An order for liquidation on this ground may only be made 'in the absence of any other remedy'. As the parties had agreed in principle that there was an alternative to liquidation (use of S459) the petition must be dismissed.

(d) **The directors deliberately withheld information so that the shareholders have no confidence in the company's management:** *Loch v John Blackwood Ltd 1924*

Question

Minority action

Austen Ltd has three directors. Darcy, Bingley and Benett. Together they own 85% of the shares in the company. They agree to sell a plot of land to Wickham for £50,000 which is what they honestly believe it to be worth. They do not, however, have the land professionally valued until later when it is shown to be worth nearer £100,000. Elizabeth and Jane are two minority shareholders who are considering bringing an action against the directors and the company.

Advise Elizabeth and Jane whether they are likely to be successful.

Answer

The type of action open to Elizabeth and Jane would be a derivative action, that is one brought by Elizabeth or Jane on behalf of the company, with the directors as defendants. However, they would be unlikely to succeed. The facts of this case resemble those of *Pavlides v Jensen 1956.* In this case it was held that mere negligence did not justify a minority action to protect the company's rights. Thus, in the absence of fraud, the sale could legitimately be approved by a majority of the shareholders.

5 DTI investigations

The DTI has statutory power to appoint an inspector (or joint inspector) to investigate:

- The **affairs** of a company: ss 431-432
- The **ownership** of a company: ss 442-443
- Suspected **infringement** by directors of **statutory** rules relating to their interests or dealings in options over shares or debentures of their company: ss 323, 324 and 446
- **Suspected insider dealing**: s 177 FSA

The DTI also has a statutory power to require a company or its officers to **produce** to the DTI **documents** and to provide an explanation of any of them (S447).

The DTI **must** appoint inspectors to investigate the affairs of a company if the **court** makes an **order** to that effect: s 432(1).

The DTI **may** in its discretion appoint inspectors to investigate the affairs of a company in any of the following situations.

(a) If the **company** itself **applies**: s 431

(b) If application is made by members:

- Who are **not less than 200** in number, or
- Who **hold at least one tenth** of the **issued shares**, or
- If the company has no share capital, by at **least one fifth** of the **members**

(c) If the DTI considers that the affairs of the company have been conducted in a **fraudulent or unlawful manner** (or that it was formed for a fraudulent or unlawful purpose) or in a manner **unfairly prejudicial** to some part of its members or that members have not been given all the information with respect to its affairs which they might reasonably expect: s 432

5.1 Powers of DTI inspectors

Inspectors have extensive statutory powers to **call for documents** and to **question informants** on oath. Refusal to comply is punishable as contempt of court: s 436. For this purpose the inspectors may question and call for documents from officers and agents of the company and any other person whom they believe has relevant information. Auditors, solicitors, bankers and sometimes receivers are 'agents'.

HUMAN RIGHTS ACT 1998

Under Article 6 of the Convention, everyone has a right to a fair trial.

Prior to the legislation in the UK, in the European Court of Human Rights, Ernest Saunders claimed under Article 6 that the use of statements made by him to DTI inspectors as evidence against him the Guinness case was a breach of his right to a fair trial.

The European Court of Human Rights ruled that the UK could not ignore this convention right by arguing that prevention of corporate frauds was in the public interest.

The incorporation of the Convention into domestic law may well have an impact on the DTI's use of information for prosecution but the DTI has stated that it will use 'compelled evidence' in disqualification proceedings.

5.2 Investigations into membership

The DTI may appoint inspectors to investigate the membership of a company (or who is interested in or in control of it through nominees): s 442.

If the inspectors' search for information encounters difficulty the DTI may by order restrict the transfer of the relevant shares, or the voting rights or payment to the holders of dividends or return of capital: s 445.

5.3 Reports of inspectors

The inspectors submit a report to the DTI. Their report is usually published and may well contain severe criticism of the shortcomings of the persons involved.

The outcome of the investigation may be civil or criminal proceedings or a petition (by the DTI) for compulsory winding up of the company or for a court order for the protection of a minority.

6 Other statutory rights of minorities

A minority of members is given a number of specific statutory rights, including the following.

Minority rights	
Subject	**Required**
Variation of class rights	Holders of 15%+ of class of shares can apply to court for cancellation
Alteration of objects	Holders of 15%+ of issued shares can apply to court for cancellation
Company meeting	Can be requisitioned by holders of 10%+ of company's voting capital
Notice of members' resolutions	Must be given by company on requisition of members holding 5%+ of voting rights/100 or more members holding shares in the company on which an average sum of £100+ per member has been paid up
Full notice of special resolution	Must be given if members with 5%+ of voting capital insist
Conversion of public company to private	50+ members or members holding 5%+ of issued share capital can apply to court for cancellation
Purchase of own shares out of capital by private company	Holders of 10%+ of shares/any class of shares can apply to court to prohibit the transaction
Financial assistance by private company	Any member can apply to court to prohibit the transaction
Poll	Can be demanded by at least 5 members/members holding 10%+ of voting rights or have 10%+ of total of all paid up shares
Off-market purchase of own shares	Poll can be demanded by individual members
Full notice of AGM	Can be demanded by individual members
Registration of limited company as unlimited	Can be prevented by individual members
DTI investigation into affairs/ownership of company	Can be requested by 200+ members/members holding 10%+ of issued shares
Public company investigation into membership of company	Can be demanded by holders of 10%+ of company's voting capital

Chapter roundup

- In this chapter we have shown that ultimate control of a company rests with its members voting in general meeting.
  - If the directors hold a majority of the voting shares or represent a majority shareholding, the minority has no remedy unless the rules of **minority protection apply.**
  - *Foss v Harbottle 1843* made it clear that the **company**, as a separate person from its members, is the **only proper plaintiff** in an action to protect the rights or property, and that the decision to bring an action must be taken by the company in general meeting.
- The principal **statutory** remedy for minorities is a s 459 action alleging the company's affairs have been conducted in an **unfairly prejudicial manner.**
- The court may make **whatever order** it sees fit to settle a s 459 action (generally purchase of the petitioner's shares).
- A number of common law exceptions for the protection of the minority have been accepted since *Foss v Harbottle.* A minority has been allowed to bring proceedings in the following situations.
  - To restrain an **illegal** or **ultra vires decision**
  - To remedy certain **errors in procedure**
  - To enforce **individual rights** of membership
  - To prevent a **fraud** on the minority
- Dissatisfied shareholders also have these statutory remedies.
  - To petition for winding-up of the company on the **just and equitable ground**
  - To demand a **DTI investigation**
  - To object to certain specific actions (for example changing the company's articles)

Quick quiz

1 *Foss v Harbottle* established the rights of minority shareholders to obtain relief from oppressive acts by the majority.

True ☐

False ☐

2 Give four examples of remedies a court may provide under s 461.

3 **Fill in the blanks** in the statements below.

S 459 gives relief on the grounds that the company's affairs are being or have been conducted in a manner that is .... to the interests of .... or ....

4 What are the four main common law exceptions to *Foss v Harbottle*?

5 Which of the following are statutory rights of individual members?

A To demand full notice of an AGM
B To prevent re-registration of a limited company as unlimited
C To apply for a cancellation of a variation of class rights
D To demand a poll on a resolution for an off-market purchase of own shares
E To require the DTI to investigate a company's membership
F To insist on full notice for a special resolution

6 **Fill in the blanks** in the statements below.

Petitions under s 459 often arise from exclusion of a director from participation in the management of a ……………….. company, or ……………….. against a minority.

7 Give four grounds under which the DTI can use its statutory power to appoint inspectors.

8 Give four examples of instances where the court has ordered a company to be wound up on the just and equitable grounds.

Answers to quick quiz

1 False. *Foss v Harbottle* emphasised the principle of *majority* rule. (It was thus evident that the minority needed protection.)

2 An order regulating the future conduct of the company's affairs
Authorising the company to bring legal proceedings
Ordering the company to refrain from actions
Providing for the purchase of shares of the minority

3 S 459 gives relief on the grounds that the company's affairs are being or have been conducted in a manner that is *unfairly prejudicial* to the interests of *members generally* or *some part of the members.*

4 The majority cannot sanction an illegal act.
Special procedures under law or the company's articles should be observed.
Individual rights of membership should be preserved.
The majority may be brought to account for defrauding the company.

5 A, B and D represent individual rights. Under s 127, C requires application by holders of at least 15% of the shares of the class. E requires 200 members or the holders of at least 10% of issued shares: s 431. F requires members holding at least 5% of voting shares: s 378.

6 Petitions under s 459 often arise from exclusion of a director from participation in the management of a *quasi-partnership* company, or *discrimination* against a minority.

7 To investigate the affairs of a company

To investigate the ownership of a company

To investigate suspected infringement by directors of statutory rules relating to interests or dealings in share or debentures

To investigate suspected insider dealing

8 The substratum of the company has gone.

The company was formed for an illegal or fraudulent purpose, or there is complete deadlock in its affairs.

The understandings between members or directors which were the basis of association have been unfairly breached.

The directors deliberately withhold information so that the shareholders have no confidence in the company's management.

Now try the question below from the Exam Question Bank

Number	Level	Marks	Time
Q28	Examination	20	36 mins

Part F
Company financing and insolvency

Share capital

Topic list	Syllabus reference
1 The nature of shares	6(a)
2 Types of capital	6(a)
3 Types of share	6(a)
4 Variation of class rights	6(a)
5 Members	6(a)
6 Allotment of shares	6(a)
7 Rights and bonus issues	6(a)
8 Consideration for shares	6(a)
9 Allotment of shares at a premium	6(a)

Introduction

In this chapter the nature of share capital is explained. You should note (and **not** confuse) the different types of capital that are important for company law purposes.

The rest of the chapter discusses procedural matters relating to the **issue** and **transfer** of shares. You will see that there are built-in safeguards to protect members' rights, **pre-emption rights** and the necessity for directors to be voted **authority** before they can **allot** shares. There are also safeguards that ensure that a company receives **sufficient consideration** for its shares. This is an aspect of **capital maintenance**, which we discuss further in the next chapter.

Capital can easily be examined in Section A. However, it could also form part of a larger scenario question in Section B.

1 The nature of shares

FAST FORWARD

A **share** is a transferable form of property, carrying rights and obligations, by which the interest of a member of a company limited by shares is measured.

Key term

A **share** is 'the interest of a shareholder in the company measured by a sum of money, for the purpose of a liability in the first place, and of interest in the second, but also consisting of a series of mutual covenants entered into by all the shareholders *inter se*': *Borland's Trustee v Steel Bros & Co Ltd 1901*.

The key points in this definition are:

- The share must be **paid for** ('liability').
- It gives a **proportionate entitlement** to dividends, votes and any return of capital ('interest').
- It is a form of **bargain** ('mutual covenants') between shareholders which underlies such principles as majority control and minority protection.

A share is a form of property, carrying rights and obligations. It is by its nature **transferable**.

A member who holds one or more shares is a **shareholder**. However some companies (such as most companies limited by guarantee) do not have a share capital. So they have members who are not also shareholders.

Information about any special rights attached to shares is obtainable from one of the following documents which are on the file at the registry:

- The **articles**, which are the normal context in which share rights are defined, or the memorandum
- A **resolution** or agreement incidental to the creation of a new class of shares; a copy must within 15 days be delivered to the registry: s 380(4)(c)
- **Particulars** of the rights of shares must be given to the registry within one month of **allotment** if the class rights are not disclosed by (a) or (b) above: s 128

2 Types of capital 12/03, 6/05

The term 'capital' is used in several senses in company legislation.

2.1 Authorised share capital

Key term

Authorised share capital (nominal share capital, registered share capital) is the type, class, number and amount of the shares which a company may issue, as empowered by its memorandum of association.

This total must be divided into shares of fixed amount (called the **'nominal'** or **'par'** value of the shares). The nominal value is just that – nominal. It is a figure chosen by the company and which has no direct correlation with the value of the shares or the assets of the company.

A company which has a share capital may, if authorised by its articles and by resolution passed in general meeting, **increase** the amount of its **authorised share capital**: s 121. The standard form of articles (Table A Article 32) requires only that an **ordinary** resolution shall be passed.

When a company has increased its authorised share capital it must within 15 days deliver to the registrar the following documents.

- **Particulars** of the **new shares** on the prescribed form: s 123
- A **printed copy** of the **resolution** authorising the increase: s 123
- A **printed copy** of the **memorandum** as altered (in its capital clause): s 18

The registrar must give notice in the *Gazette* of receipt of the resolution: s 711.

The effect of such an increase of authorised share capital is merely to add to the unissued shares which the company has 'on the shelf' available for issue. There is no increase in issued share capital unless new shares are then allotted.

2.2 Issued share capital

Key term

> **Issued share capital** (or subscribed share capital) is the type, class, number and amount of the shares held by shareholders.

A company need not issue all its share capital at once. If it retains part this is unissued share capital.

2.3 Called up share capital

Key terms

> **Called up share capital** is the amount which the company has required shareholders to pay on the shares issued.
>
> **Paid up share capital** is the amount which shareholders are deemed to have paid on the shares issued and called up.

If for example a company has issued 70 £1 (nominal) shares, has received 25p per share on application and has called on members for a second 25p, its **called up** share capital is £35 (50p per share). When the members pay the call the **'paid up'** share capital is then £35 also. Capital not yet called is **'uncalled capital'**.

2.4 Loan capital

Key term

> **Loan capital** is debentures and other long-term loans to a business.

Loan capital, in contrast with the above, is the term used to describe **borrowed money** obtained often by the issue of debentures.

3 Types of share

FAST FORWARD

> If the constitution of a company states no differences between shares, it is assumed that they are all **ordinary** shares with parallel rights and obligations. There may, however, be other types, notably **preference shares** and **redeemable shares**.

Key term

> **Equity** is the issued ordinary share capital plus reserves, statutory and otherwise, which represents the investment in a company by the ordinary shareholders. **Equity share capital** is a company's issued share capital less capital which carries preferential rights. Equity share capital normally comprises ordinary shares.

3.1 Ordinary shares

If no differences between shares are expressed then all shares are equity shares with the **same rights**, known as ordinary shares.

Key term

> **Ordinary shares** are shares which entitle the holders to the remaining divisible profits (and, in a liquidation, the assets) after prior interests, for example, creditors and prior charge capital , have been satisfied.

3.2 Class rights

Key term

> **Class rights** are those rights which by the company's constitution are attached to particular types of shares.

A company may at its option attach special rights to different shares. Examples of special rights include:

- Dividends
- Return of capital
- Voting
- The right to appoint a director

Any share which has different rights from others is grouped with the other shares carrying **identical** rights to form a class.

The most common types of share capital with different rights are **preference shares** and **ordinary shares;** there may also be ordinary shares with voting rights and ordinary shares without voting rights.

3.3 Preference shares

Key term

> **Preference shares** are shares carrying one or more preferential rights, for example a fixed rate of dividend, or a prior claim to any company profits available for distribution.

A preference share may and generally will carry a **prior right** to receive an annual dividend of fixed amount, say a six per cent dividend. Ordinary and preference shares are deemed to have identical rights, but in practice there are often **differences** between them **expressed** in the **articles** or **resolution creating them**.

Where there is a priority dividend entitlement, four points should be noted.

(a) **The right is merely to receive a dividend at the specified rate before any other dividend may be paid or declared**. It is **not** a right to compel the company to pay the dividend; the company can decline to do so, if it decides to transfer available profits to reserves instead of using the profits to pay the preference dividend.

Bond v Barrow Haematite Steel Co 1902
The facts: The company did not pay (it 'passed') its preference dividend. B and other preference shareholders contended that the company had available reserves of £240,000 from which it could have declared the dividend on their shares. The company replied that it had suffered realised losses of £200,000 on the disposal or demolition of current assets and in addition its retained fixed assets had diminished in value generally by £50,000. It therefore decided to retain the funds in question to make good losses.

Decision: The court would not overrule the directors in their decision that the 'state of the accounts did not admit of any such payment' (of preference dividend).

(b) **The right to receive a preference dividend is deemed to be cumulative unless the contrary is stated.** If, therefore, a 6% dividend is not paid in year 1, the priority entitlement is normally carried forward to Year 2, increasing the priority right for that year to 12% – and so on.

When arrears of cumulative dividend are paid, the holders of the shares at **the time when the dividend is declared**, are entitled to the whole of it even though they did not hold the shares in the year to which the arrears relate.

An intention that preference shares should not carry forward an entitlement to arrears is usually expressed by the word **'non-cumulative'**.

(c) **If a company which has arrears of unpaid cumulative preference dividends goes into liquidation, the preference shareholders cease to be entitled to the arrears unless:**

- A **dividend** has been **declared** though **not yet paid** when liquidation commences.
- The **articles** (or other terms of issue) **expressly provide** that in a liquidation arrears are to be paid in priority to return of capital to members.

(d) **Holders of preference shares have no entitlement to participate in any additional dividend over and above their specified rate.** If, for example, a 6% dividend is paid on 6% preference shares, the entire balance of available profit may then be distributed to the holders of ordinary shares.

This rule also may be expressly overridden by the terms of issue. For example, the articles may provide that the preference shares are to receive a priority 6% dividend and are also to participate equally in any dividends payable after the ordinary shares have received a 6% dividend. Preference shares with these rights are called **participating preference shares**.

In all other respects preference shares carry the **same** rights as ordinary shares **unless otherwise stated**. If they do rank equally they carry the same rights, no more and no less, to return of capital, distribution of surplus assets and voting.

In practice, it is unusual to issue preference shares on this basis. More usually, it is expressly provided that:

(a) The preference shares are to carry a **priority right** to **return of capital**.

(b) They are **not to carry a right to vote or only in specified circumstances** such as failure to pay the preference dividend, variation of their rights or a resolution to wind up.

When preference shares carry a **priority right** to **return** of **capital** the result is that:

(a) The amount paid up on the preference shares, say £1 on each £1 share, is to be repaid in liquidation or reduction of capital before anything is repaid to ordinary shareholders.

(b) Unless otherwise stated the holders of the preference shares are **not** entitled to share in surplus assets when the ordinary share capital has been repaid.

On a reduction of share capital (where the preference shares carry an entitlement to priority in repayment) it is in accordance with the rights of preference shareholders to pay them off first. They cannot object that this is a variation of their rights: it is strict observance of them (unless their rights are so expressed as to prevent it): *House of Fraser plc v ACGE Investments Ltd 1987.*

3.4 Advantages and disadvantages of preference shares

The advantages of preference shares are **greater security of income** and (if they carry priority in repayment of capital) **greater security** of capital. However in a period of persistent inflation, the entitlement to fixed income and to capital fixed in money terms is an illusion.

A number of other drawbacks and pitfalls, such as loss of arrears, winding up and enforced payment, have been indicated above. Preference shares may be said to fall between the two stools of risk and reward (as seen in ordinary shares) and security (debentures).

3.5 Redeemable shares

Redeemable shares, shares that are issued on terms that they may be bought back by a company either at a future specific date or at the shareholder's or company's option, are discussed further in Chapter 20.

Question — Types of share capital

Give brief definitions of the following types of share.

(a) Equity share
(b) Ordinary share
(c) Preference share

Answer

(a) An equity share is a share which gives the holder the right to participate in the company's surplus profit and capital. There is no limit to the size of the dividend which may be paid except the size of the profit itself. In a winding up the holder is entitled to a repayment of the normal value plus a share of surplus assets. The term equity share embraces ordinary shares, but it can also include a preference share when the terms of issue include either the right to an additional dividend or the right to surplus assets in a winding up.

(b) An ordinary share is the more common type of equity share, as discussed in (i) above. The dividend is payable only when preference dividends, including arrears have been paid.

(c) The essential characteristic of a preference share is that it carries rights not possessed by an ordinary share, for example, a prior right to receive an annual dividend of a fixed amount. There are no other implied differences between preference and ordinary shares, although there may be express differences between them, for example the preference shares may carry a priority right to return of capital. Generally preference shares do not carry voting rights in the company other than those relating to their own class. Unless otherwise stated, preference shares are assumed to be cumulative. This means that, if the company does not make sufficient profits to pay a dividend in one year, the arrears are carried forward to future years.

3.6 Section summary

- The most common right of preference shareholders is a **prior right** to receive a fixed dividend.
- This right is not a right to **compel payment** of a dividend.
- The right to receive a dividend is **cumulative** unless otherwise stated.
- Unless otherwise stated, preference shareholders:
  - **Cannot participate** in a dividend over and above their fixed dividend
  - Cease to be entitled to arrears of undeclared dividends when the company goes into liquidation
- Preference shares have **equal rights** to ordinary shares in all other respects, **unless** the **contrary** is **stated**.

4 Variation of class rights 12/02

FAST FORWARD

The holders of **issued** shares have **vested rights** which can only be altered by using a strict procedure. The standard procedure is by **extraordinary resolution** passed by at least **three quarters** of the votes cast at a **separate class meeting** or by written consent.

Key term

A **variation of class rights** is an alteration in the position of shareholders with regard to those rights or duties which they have by virtue of their shares.

The holders of issued shares have vested rights which can only be varied by the company with the consent of all the holders or with such consent of a majority as is specified (usually) in the articles.

The standard procedure for variation of class rights requires that an **extraordinary resolution** shall be passed by a **three quarters majority** cast either at a **separate meeting** of the class, or by **written consent:** s 125(2).

If any other requirements are imposed by the company's articles then these must also be followed.

4.1 Special situations

To deal with unusual special situations which in the past caused some difficulty it is provided that the following rules apply.

(a) If the class rights are set **by the memorandum or otherwise and** the **memorandum or articles provide** a **variation procedure**, that procedure must be followed for any variation: s 125 (4). But if the variation relates to the directors' power to allot shares under s 80 or s 80A, or to a reduction of share capital under s 135, consent of a **three quarters majority** of the class must be obtained if the special procedure in the articles does not include it: s 125 (3).

(b) If class **rights** are **defined otherwise than by the memorandum** and there is **no variation procedure** in the articles, consent of a **three quarters majority** of the class is both necessary and sufficient. A minority has the right to appeal to the court: s 125 (2).

(c) If **rights** are **attached by the memorandum** and there is **no variation procedure prescribed** at all, the consent of **all members** of the company is necessary to alter rights defined in the memorandum: s 125 (5).

The rules on notice, voting, polls, circulation of resolutions and quorum relating to general meetings relate also to class meetings when voting on alteration of class rights: s 125 (6). (See Chapter 14).

4.2 Minority appeals to the court

Whenever class rights are varied under a procedure contained in the memorandum or articles a minority of holders of shares of the class may apply to the court to have the variation cancelled: s 127. The objectors together must:

- Hold **not less** than **15%** of the **issued shares** of the class in question
- **Not** themselves have **consented** to or voted in favour of the variation
- **Apply** to the court within **21 days** of the consent being given by the class: s 127

The court can either approve the variation as made or cancel it as 'unfairly prejudicial': s 127 (4). It cannot, however, modify the terms of the variation.

To establish that a variation is 'unfairly prejudicial' to the class, the minority must normally show that the majority who voted in favour was seeking **some advantage** to themselves as **members** of a **different**

class instead of considering the interests of the class in which they were then voting: *Re Holders Investment Trust, 1971.*

4.3 When variation rules apply

It is only necessary to follow the variation of class rights procedure if what is proposed amounts to a **variation** of class rights. A class right is varied only if the right itself is altered. An alteration which affects **how the 'right' operates** which leaves the 'right' unchanged is not a variation.

The following situations do not constitute a variation of class rights.

(a) **To issue shares of the same class to allottees who are not already members of the class** (unless the defined class rights prohibit this).

White v Bristol Aeroplane Co Ltd 1953
The facts: The company made a bonus issue of new ordinary and preference shares to the existing ordinary shareholders who alone were entitled under the articles to participate in bonus issues. The existing preference shareholders objected that by reducing their proportion of the class of preference shares the bonus of preference shares was a variation of class rights to which they had not consented.

Decision: This was not a variation of class rights since the existing preference shareholders had the same number of shares (and votes at a class meeting) as before.

(b) **To subdivide shares of another class with the incidental effect of increasing the voting strength of that other class.**

Greenhalgh v Arderne Cinemas Ltd 1946
The facts: The company had two classes of ordinary shares, 50p shares and 10p shares. Every share carried one vote. A resolution was passed to subdivide each 50p share into five 10p shares, thus multiplying the votes of that class by five.

Decision: The rights of the original 10p shares had not been varied since they still had one vote per share as before.

(c) **To return capital to the holders of preference shares**: *House of Fraser plc v ACGE Investments Ltd 1987.*

Illustration

If a £1 share has a preference dividend of 4% so it yields 4p dividend per year it is **not** a variation to reduce the nominal value of shares to 50p, even though it reduces the dividend to 2p per year (*Re Mackenzie & Co. Ltd 1916)* because the right itself – 4% per annum – has not been changed.

(d) **To create and issue a new class of preference shares with priority over an existing class of ordinary shares**: *Re John Smith's Tadcaster Brewery Co Ltd 1953.*

The cases cited in the preceding paragraph illustrate the principle that without a '**literal variation**' of class rights (to participate in surplus assets, to have one vote per share, to be paid a dividend) there is no alteration of rights to which the safeguards of proper procedure and appeal to the court apply. The fact that the **value** of existing rights may be affected will not concern the court if the rights are unchanged.

Exam focus point

Knowledge of what does **not** constitute a variation of class rights is vital in this area.

4.4 Use of minority protection rules

If the minority in a class cannot protect itself by establishing that there has been a variation (or that what is undeniably variation is 'unfairly prejudicial') it may still obtain a remedy as a minority under the **minority protection rules** eg S459.

5 Members

FAST FORWARD

A member of a company is a person who has **agreed to become a member**, and whose name has been **entered** in the **register of members**. This may occur by

- Subscription to the memorandum
- Applying for shares
- The presentation to the company of a transfer of shares to the prospective member
- Applying (as personal representative of a deceased member or a trustee of a bankrupt).

5.1 Becoming a member

Key term

A **member** of a company is a person who has agreed to be a member and whose name has been entered in the register of members: s 22(2).

Entry in the register is **essential**. Mere delivery to the company of a transfer does not make the transferor a member – until the transfer is entered in the register.

5.2 Subscriber shares

Subscribers to the memorandum are deemed to have agreed to become members of the company. As soon as the company is formed their names should be entered in the register of members.

Other persons may acquire shares and become members:

- By **applying** and being allotted shares
- By presenting to the company for registration a **transfer** of shares to them
- By applying as **personal representative trustee** of a
  - Deceased member
  - Bankrupt member

5.3 Ceasing to be a member

A member ceases to be a member in any of the following circumstances.

- He **transfers** all his shares to another person and the transfer is registered.
- The member **dies**.
- The **shares** of a bankrupt member are **registered** in the name of his trustee.
- A **member who is a minor repudiates his shares.**
- The **trustee** of a **bankrupt member disclaims** his shares.
- The **company forfeits** or **accepts** the **surrender of shares.**
- The **company** sells them in exercise of a lien.
- The **company is dissolved** and **ceases to exist**.

5.4 The number of members

FAST FORWARD

A **public** company must have a minimum of **two** members. A **private** company needs only **one** member.

Public companies: **Minimum:** 2 members
Maximum: unlimited

Private companies: **Minimum:** 1 member
Maximum: unlimited

Single member private companies	
Secretary	The sole member/director must not also be the secretary.
Register of members	Must contain a statement that there is only one member and give his address.
Quorum	The articles are automatically amended to allow a quorum of one.
Resolutions	Must be all in writing.
Contracts	All contracts between the company and the sole member must be in writing, unless • It is in the usual course of business • It is on the company's usual commercial terms
Decisions	A written record of all decisions made by the member must be given to the company.

6 Allotment of shares 12/01

FAST FORWARD

Directors may receive the **delegated power** to allot shares, either from the articles or a resolution in general meeting.

If the directors propose to allot 'equity securities' wholly for cash, there is a general requirement to offer these shares to **holders** of **similar shares** in proportion to their holdings (pre-emption rights).

The price at which the shares are issued must be at least the nominal value.

Key term

Allotment of shares is the allocation to a person of a certain number of shares under a contract of allotment. Once the shares are allotted the holder becomes a member of the company.

The allotment of shares is a form of contract. The intending shareholder applies to the company for shares, and the company accepts the offer.

The terms 'allotment' and 'issue' have slightly different meanings.

(a) A share is **allotted** when the person to whom it is allotted acquires an unconditional right to be entered in the register of members as the holder of that share: s 738. That stage is reached when the board of directors (to whom the power to allot shares is usually given) consider the application and formally resolve to allot the shares.

However if the directors imposed a condition, for instance that the shares should be allotted on receipt of the subscription money, the allotment would take effect when payment was made.

(b) The **issue** of shares is not a defined term but is usually taken to be a later stage at which the allottee **receives** a **letter of allotment** or share certificate issued by the company as evidence of his title.

The allotment of shares of a private company is a simple and immediate matter. The name of the allottee is usually entered in the register soon after, and as a direct consequence of, the allotment of shares to him. He then becomes a member: s 22.

6.1 Public company allotment of shares

Public companies listed on the Stock Exchange usually follow a two-stage procedure.

(a) They first issue a **renounceable allotment letter** which the original allottee may for a limited period (up to six weeks) transfer to another person by signing a **form of renunciation** (included in the letter) and delivering it to the transferee. The original allottee, or the ultimate renouncee, sends in the allotment letter with a completed application for registration of the shares in his name.

(b) On receipt of **application for registration** the company enters the name of the applicant in the register of members and delivers a return of allotments to the registrar made up to show who is then on the register. The applicant becomes a member **by entry on the register** and receives a share certificate from the company.

Public companies face the further restriction that no allotment can be made unless:

(a) The shares offered are **subscribed** for in **full**, or

(b) The offer states that even if the capital is not subscribed in full, the **amount** of the **capital subscribed** for may be **allotted** in **any event**, or in the event of the conditions specified in the offer being satisfied.

If (a) applies, money must be returned forthwith to applicants at the expiry of 40 days after the first issue of the prospectus.

6.2 Directors' powers to allot shares

Directors may neither allot shares (except to subscribers to the memorandum and to employees' share schemes) nor grant options or convertible securities, without **authority from the members.**

Authority may be given either by the **articles** or by **ordinary resolution** passed in general meeting in conformity with s 80 or under the provisions of s 80A.

6.2.1 Procedure for allotment

Director's power to allot shares	
Timescale	**Public companies** • Authority to allot must be given until a **specified date** • Authority to allot must be given for a **specified period** • Authority can be received by ordinary resolution in general meeting • Extension cannot be for more than five years **Private companies** • Authority to allot can be given **indefinitely** • Authority to allot can be given for fixed periods greater than five years

Director's power to allot shares	
Maximum	**All companies** must specify a maximum number of shares which may be allotted.
Additional conditions	**All companies** may give additional conditions.
Resolution	An **ordinary** resolution is required. Signed copy must be sent to the Registrar with in 15 days.
General authority	Directors may have been given general authority to allot without further reference to general meeting. A **general meeting** must be called if • **No authority** has been given in advance • Authority is subject to certain **conditions** • Authority has **lapsed** or been used up
Breach of law	If directors have allotted without authority • The allotment is valid • Directors are punishable by fine

Exam focus point

Remember the basic distinction that (a) directors can only allot shares if they have the power to do so (given by the Articles, generally as part of their power of management) *and* (b) if they have the authority to *exercise* the power (given by the Articles or ordinary resolution under s 80).

6.3 Pre-emption rights: s 89

Key term

Pre-emption rights are the rights of existing company shareholders to be offered new equity shares issued by the company *pro rata* to their existing holding of that class of shares.

If a company proposes to allot shares described as 'equity securities' (basically ordinary shares issued for cash) wholly for cash it generally has a statutory obligation to offer those shares first to holders of similar shares in **proportion to their holdings**: s 89 (a rights issue).

The offer must be made **in writing** in the same manner as a notice of a general meeting is sent to members. It must specify a period of **not less than 21 days** during which the offer may be accepted. If not accepted within that period the offer is deemed to be declined: s 90.

Equity securities which have been offered to members in this way but are not accepted may then be allotted on the same (or less favourable) terms to non-members.

If the memorandum or articles confer special rights of pre-emption on certain members of the company only, the offer must first be made to them; shares which they do not accept must then be offered to shareholders under s 89.

If equity securities are allotted in breach of these rules the members to whom the offer should have been made may within the ensuing two years recover **compensation** for their loss, if any, from those in default: s 92. The allotment will generally be valid.

6.3.1 Exclusion of pre-emption rights: s 91

A **private** company may by its memorandum or articles permanently exclude these rules so that there is no statutory right of first refusal: s 91.

6.3.2 Disapplication of pre-emption rights: s 95

Any company may, by special resolution resolve that the statutory right of first refusal shall not apply: s 95. Such a resolution to 'disapply' the right may either:

(a) Be **combined** with the **grant to directors** of **authority to allot shares** under s 80, or

(b) May simply **permit an offer** of shares to be made for cash to a non-member (without first offering the shares to members) on a particular occasion

In case (b) the directors, in inviting members to 'disapply' the right of first refusal, must issue a circular setting out their reasons, the price at which the shares are to be offered direct to a non-member and their justification of that price.

6.4 Issues for an improper purpose

We discussed in Chapter 17 the rules that directors may issue shares for a proper purpose, and that issues to manipulate the company's shareholdings were void, unless approved by the members in general meeting. Remember that holders of shares that have been issued irregularly **cannot vote** in a general meeting to sanction the directors' actions.

6.5 Section summary

- In order to allot shares **directors**:
  - Must have the **power** given by the articles
  - Must be given **authority** to allot
- The maximum number of shares to be allotted must be specified.
- The time period during which allotment can take place must not exceed five years (private companies can disapply this rule).
- Current members have pre-emption rights unless permanently excluded (private companies) or disapplied for a specific offer or set time (all companies).

7 Rights and bonus issues

7.1 Rights issues

Key term

A **rights issue** is a right given to a shareholder to subscribe for further shares in the company, usually *pro rata* to his/her existing holding in the company's shares.

As indicated above a rights issue is an allotment (or the offer of it by renounceable allotment letter) of additional shares made to existing members. If the members do not wish to subscribe for additional shares under a rights issue they may be able to sell their rights to other persons and so obtain the value of the option.

7.2 Bonus issues

Key term

A **bonus issue** is the capitalisation of the reserves of a company by the issue of additional shares to existing shareholders, in proportion to their holdings. Such shares are normally fully paid-up with no cash called for from the shareholders.

A bonus issue is more correctly but less often called a 'capitalisation issue' (also called a 'scrip' issue). The articles of a company usually give it power to apply its reserves (including its undistributed profits and reserves which could never be distributed as dividends) to paying up unissued shares wholly or in part and then to allot these shares as a bonus issue to members.

Table A Article 110 is the standard form of articles on **bonus issues**, requiring an **ordinary** resolution. Obviously **sufficient authorised capital** must be available to make the issue; if not it must be **increased** under s 121.

8 Consideration for shares 6/04

Every share has a **nominal value** and **may not be allotted at a discount** to that.

In allotting shares every company is required to obtain in money or money's worth consideration of a value at least equal to the nominal value of the shares: s 100. To issue shares **'at par'** is to obtain equal value, say, £1 for a £1 share.

If shares are allotted at a discount on their nominal value the allottee must nonetheless pay the full nominal value with interest at the appropriate rate (5%).

Exam focus point

> The prohibition on offer of shares at a discount on **nominal** value is often confused with a company issuing shares at a price below **market** value (which is not prohibited).

8.1 Partly paid shares

The no-discount rule only requires that, in allotting its shares, a company shall not fix a price which is less than the nominal value of the shares. It may leave part of that price to be paid at some later time. Thus £1 shares may be issued partly paid – 75p on allotment and 25p when called for or by instalment. The unpaid capital passes with the shares, if they are transferred, as a debt payable by the holder at the time when payment is demanded.

8.2 Underwriting fees

A company may pay underwriting or other commission in respect of an issue of shares if so permitted by its Articles (s 97 and Table A Article 4). This means that, if shares are issued at par the net amount received will be below par value. This is not a contravention of s 100 (prohibiting allotment of shares at a discount).

8.3 Bonus issue

The allotment of shares as a 'bonus issue' is for full consideration since reserves, which are shareholders' funds, are converted into fixed capital and used to pay for the shares: s 99(4).

8.4 Money's worth

The price for the shares may be paid in **money** or **'money's worth'**, including goodwill and know-how: s 99. It need not be paid in cash and the company may agree to accept a **'non-cash' consideration** of sufficient value. For instance, a company may issue shares in payment of the price agreed in the purchase of a property.

8.5 Private companies

A private company may allot shares for inadequate consideration by acceptance of goods or services at an over value. This loophole has been allowed to exist because in some cases it is very much a matter of opinion whether an asset is or is not of a stated value.

The courts therefore have refused to overrule directors in their valuation of an asset acquired for shares if it appears reasonable and honest: *Re Wragg 1897*. However a blatant and unjustified overvaluation will be declared invalid.

8.6 Public companies

The more stringent rules which apply to public companies regarding consideration and payment are as follows.

(a) **Future services are not to be accepted as consideration:** s 99(2). A public company may, however, allot shares to discharge a debt in respect of services already rendered.

(b) The company must, at the time of allotment, receive **at least one quarter of the nominal value** of the shares and the **whole** of any premium.

(c) **Non-cash consideration** may **not** be accepted as payment for shares if an undertaking contained in such consideration is to be, or may be, **performed more than five years after the allotment: s** 102. This relates to, say, a property or business in return for shares.

(d) Any **non-cash consideration** accepted must be **independently valued:** s 103.

(e) Within **two years of receiving its certificate** under s 117, a public company **may not receive a transfer of non-cash assets from a subscriber** to the memorandum, unless its value as consideration is less then 10% of the issued nominal share capital and it has been independently valued and agreed by an ordinary resolution: s 104.

8.6.1 Future undertakings

If a public company does accept future services as consideration, on the shares being treated as paid up the holder must pay the company their **nominal value** plus any **premium** treated as paid up, and **interest** at 5% (s 107) on any such amount: s 99 (3).

8.6.2 Non-cash consideration

To enforce the five year rule the law requires that (s 102):

(a) At the time of the allotment the **allottee** must **undertake** to **perform** his side of the agreement within a specified period which must not exceed five years; if no such undertaking is given the **allottee** becomes **immediately liable** to pay cash for his shares as soon as they are allotted

(b) If the **allottee later fails** to **perform** his undertaking to transfer property at the due time he becomes liable to pay **cash** for his shares when he defaults

8.6.3 Valuation of non-cash assets

When a public company allots shares for a non-cash consideration the company must usually obtain a **report on its value** from an independent valuer: s 108. This independent valuation rule does **not** apply however to an allotment of shares made in the course of a takeover bid.

The valuation report is to be made or obtained by 'an **independent person qualified to be auditor of the company'** (by the auditor or some other qualified accountant).

However the independent person may arrange for the valuation to be made by or accept the valuation of some other person (independent of the company) if the latter appears to be competent and it seems a reasonable arrangement. For example, the auditor might arrange that a valuation of land should be made by a chartered surveyor.

The valuation report must be made to the company within the six months before the allotment: s 103(1).

On receiving the report the company must send a copy to the proposed allottee and later to the registrar (with the return of allotments): s 111.

8.6.4 Relief from liability

S.113 allows a court to relieve a person who is liable to pay the price of shares because of a breach of S99 or S103 if it is just and equitable to do so.

9 Allotment of shares at a premium 6/04

Key term

Premium is an amount paid to a company for a share in excess of the nominal value of the share.

An established company may be able to obtain consideration for new shares in excess of their nominal value. The excess, called 'share premium', must be credited to a **share premium account** (s 130).

If a company obtains non-cash consideration for its shares which exceeds the nominal value of the shares the excess should also be credited to the **share premium account**: *Henry Head & Co Ltd v Ropner Holdings 1952.*

This decision was applied in a controversial case which led to the whole situation being modified by merger relief in ss 131-133.

> *Shearer v Bercain 1980*
> *The facts:* An investment company, A Ltd, acquired the entire share capital of L Ltd and B Ltd, worth a total of £9,600, by issuing shares of nominal value £4,100. The difference was credited to share premium in accordance with s 130. The difference represented undistributed profits of L Ltd and B Ltd, and the Inspector of Taxes sought to raise an assessment to tax on these as distributable.
>
> *Decision:* The amount credited was an undistributable reserve.

Question — **Increasing a company's share capital**

Tickle plc was incorporated in December 1995 with an authorised share capital of 500,000 £1 shares which is fully issued and fully paid. The original articles of association gave the directors authority to issue the initial authorised share capital.

The directors are proposing to purchase a small workshop from Laff for £300,000 and to finance the purchase by a fresh issue of 200,000 £1 shares to Laff. In order to re-equip the workshop, they propose to raise further capital by issuing a further 200,000 shares of £1 each. The directors propose that 100,000 of these shares should be offered to existing shareholders and 100,000 to the general public. The shares to Laff, the existing shareholders and to the general public are to be offered at £1.50 for each £1 share.

(a) What preliminary checks must the directors make before proceeding with these proposals? State the steps the directors must take to give them effect?

(b) What are the rights of the existing shareholders in respect of the proposed issue of 400,000 shares?

Answer

(a) *Power to increase share capital*

Since the amount of authorised share capital, as set out in the company's memorandum of association, has been fully issued and paid, Tickle plc must increase that amount. The directors must first ensure that the company has the necessary power to increase its authorised share capital. Such power is normally contained in the articles of association and requires an ordinary resolution to be passed.

Increasing share capital

Assuming the power exists, the directors will need to convene an extraordinary general meeting and secure the passing of the resolution. They will then need to submit to the Registrar of Companies within 15 days of the resolution being passed, notice of the increase and particulars of the new shares in the prescribed form, a copy of the resolution and a copy of the memorandum of association amended accordingly: ss 18 and 123.

Power of allotment

The directors will also need to check that they have power to issue or allot the shares. Again this power is normally given in the articles of association. In order to exercise the power of allotment, the directors need to be authorised to do so, either by the articles or by ordinary resolution of the company in general meeting.

In the case of Tickle plc, if the authority is contained in the articles but is conditional or expired or in some other way insufficient to authorise the proposed issues of shares, then the directors will need to secure the passing of a second ordinary resolution at the meeting convened for the purpose of increasing the authorised share capital: s 80. A copy of any such resolution must be forwarded to the Registrar of Companies within 15 days: s 380.

Disapplication of pre-emption rights

In order to disapply pre-emption rights (see below) so that some shares can be issued to members of the public and not to existing members, a special resolution is needed to be passed by the company in general meeting. This requires a 75% majority of all votes cast, rather than a simple majority (as in the case of ordinary resolutions) and will also require 21 (not 14) clear days' notice of the meeting to be given.

Valuation of building

In order to issue shares to Laff in return for the building, the directors will need to obtain an independent valuation of the building which constitutes non-cash consideration under s 103. The report must be made or procured by someone qualified to be an auditor of the company and must be submitted to the company within the six months before allotment.

(b) S 89 provides that if a company proposes to allot shares wholly for cash, which Tickle plc intends to do in respect of 100,000 shares to the public, it must first offer those shares to existing holders of similar shares in proportion to their holdings. The shares must be offered to existing shareholders on terms the same as or more favourable than the terms proposed to be offered to non-members.

These pre-emption rights do not apply where equity securities are proposed to be offered for non-cash consideration and so will not apply in the case of the proposed issue of shares to Laff.

Existing shareholders have the right to receive a written offer of the shares. In case of contravention, they also have the right to compensation for any resulting loss, damage costs or expenses: s 92.

These rights exist unless disapplied by means of a special resolution (s 95 CA 1985).

Chapter roundup

- A **share** is a transferable form of property, carrying rights and obligations, by which the interest of a member of a company limited by shares is measured.
- If the constitution of a company states no differences between shares, it is assumed that they are all **ordinary** shares with parallel rights and obligations. There may, however, be other types, notably **preference shares** and **redeemable shares**.
- The holders of **issued** shares have **vested rights** which can only be altered by using a strict procedure. The standard procedure is by **extraordinary resolution** passed by at least **three quarters** of the votes cast at a **separate class meeting** or by written consent.
- A member of a company is a person who has **agreed to become a member**, and whose name has been **entered** in the **register of members**. This may occur by
  - Subscription to the memorandum
  - Applying for shares
  - The presentation to the company of a transfer of shares to the prospective member
  - Applying (as personal representative of a deceased member or a trustee of a bankrupt).
- **Membership** will **cease** in any of the following situations.
  - Registration of a transfer of his whole holding to another person
  - Death of the member
  - Registration of the shares of a bankrupt in the name of his trustee
  - Repudiation by a member who is a minor
  - A disclaimer of the shares by the company, or their sale in exercise of a lien
  - Dissolution of the company so that it ceases to exist
- A **public** company must have a minimum of **two** members. A **private** company may be formed and operate with only **one** member.
- Directors may receive the **delegated power** to allot shares, either from the articles or a resolution in general meeting.
- If the directors propose to allot 'equity securities' wholly for cash, there is a general requirement to offer these shares to **holders** of **similar shares** in proportion to their holdings.
- In issuing shares, a company must fix a **price** which is **equal** to or **more than** the **nominal value of the shares**. If shares are issued at a premium, the **excess** must be credited to a **share premium** account.

Quick quiz

1 What is the difference between authorised and called up share capital?

2 If a company fails to pay preference shareholders their dividend, they can bring a court action to compel the company to pay the dividend.

True ☐

False ☐

3 Which of the following are rights of preference shareholders (unless excluded by the articles)?

A The right to receive a dividend is cumulative.

B If the company goes into liquidation, preference shareholders are entitled to claim all arrears of dividend from the liquidator.

C As well as rights to their preference dividends, preference shareholders can share equally in dividends payable to ordinary shareholders.

D Preference shareholders have a priority right over ordinary shares for the return of their capital.

E Preference shareholders have equal voting rights to ordinary shareholders.

4 Give four examples of changes in share capital that do not constitute a variation of class rights.

5 If class rights are defined otherwise than by the memorandum, and there is no variation procedures in the articles, consent of a three quarters majority of the class is required to alter the class rights.

True ☐

False ☐

6 **Fill in the blanks** in the statements below.

A .... issue is an allotment of additional shares to existing members in exchange for consideration payable by the members.

A .... issue is an allotment of additional shares to existing members where the consideration is effectively paid by using the company's reserves.

7 **Fill in the blanks** in the statements below.

If there has been a variation of class rights, a minority of holders of shares of the class (who have not consented or voted in favour of the variation) may apply to the court to have the variation cancelled. The objectors must hold not less than .... of the issued shares of that class, and apply to the court within .... days of the giving of consent by that class.

Answers to quick quiz

1 Authorised share capital is the total amount of capital that a company can issue under the terms of the capital clause in its memorandum. Called up share capital is the amount payable by shareholders on the capital that has been issued

2 False. The company may decide not to pay any dividend, or may be unable to because it does not have any distributable profits. What the preference shareholders have is a right to receive their dividends before other dividends are paid or declared.

3 A and E are implied rights; the others have to be stated explicitly.

4 Issuing shares of the same class to allottees who are not already members of that class

Subdividing shares of another class, and thus increasing the voting strength of that class

Returning capital to the owners of preference shares

Creating and issuing a new class of preference shares with priority over an existing class of ordinary shares

5 True

6 A *rights* issue is an allotment of additional shares to existing members in exchange for consideration payable by the members.

A *bonus* issue is an allotment of additional shares to existing members where the consideration is effectively paid by using the company's reserves.

7 If there has been a variation of class rights, a minority of holders of shares of the class (who have not consented or voted in favour of the variation) may apply to the court to have the variation cancelled. The objectors must hold not less than *15%* of the issued shares of that class, and apply to the court within *21* days of the giving of consent by that class.

Now try the question below from the Exam Question Bank

Number	Level	Marks	Time
Q20	Examination	20	36 mins

Capital maintenance

Topic list	Syllabus reference
1 Reduction of share capital	6(c)
2 Share premium account	6(c)
3 Redemption and purchase by a company of its own shares	6(c)
4 Financial assistance for purchase of shares	6(c)
5 Dividends	6(c)
6 Loss of capital in a public company	6(c)

Introduction

The capital which a limited company obtains from its members as consideration for their shares is sometimes called **'the creditors' buffer'**. No one can prevent an unsuccessful company from losing its capital by trading at a loss. However, whatever capital the company does have must be held for the payment of the company's debts and may not be returned to members (except under procedures which safeguard the interest of creditors). That is the price which members of a limited company are required to pay for the protection of limited liability. This principle has been developed in a number of detailed applications.

- Capital may only be distributed to members under the formal procedure of a **reduction** of **share capital** or a **winding up** of the company.
- A **premium** obtained on the allotment of shares and profits used to redeem or purchase shares of the company are statutory reserves subject to the basic rules on capital.
- There are restrictions on the **purchase** by a company **of its own shares** and on giving **financial assistance** for the purchase of shares of the company or of its holding company.
- **Dividends** may only be paid out of distributable profits.

The maintenance of **capital** does not mean that the company has to retain the **cash** which it has, even if the cash was in payment for shares.

Capital maintenance can be a difficult area. The different components of this chapter could all be examined separately, in Section A, or as part of a longer Section B question, in connection with share capital, for example. Capital maintenance could also form a Section B question in its own right.

Key term

Maintenance of capital is a fundamental principle of company law that limited companies should not be allowed to make payments out of capital to the detriment of company creditors. Thus the Companies Act contains many examples of control upon capital payments. These include provisions restricting dividend payments, financial assistance to aid share purchases, the uses to which share premiums may be put, the freedom of a company to purchase its own shares, and capital reduction schemes.

Exam focus point

The rules affecting the possible threats to capital are complicated in certain areas; however, provided you know the rules, questions on capital maintenance tend to be straightforward.

1 Reduction of share capital **12/02**

FAST FORWARD

A limited company may reduce its issued share capital provided:

- It has **power** to do so in its articles.
- A **special resolution** is passed.
- The court **confirms** the reduction under s 135.

A limited company is permitted without restriction to cancel **unissued** shares and in that way to **reduce** its **authorised** share capital. That change does not alter its financial position.

If a limited company with a share capital wishes to **reduce** its **issued** share capital (and incidentally its authorised capital of which the issued capital is part) it may do so provided that:

- It has **power** to do so in its articles; if it does not have, a special resolution would be needed to alter the articles prior to the resolution in (b).
- It passes a **special resolution.**
- It obtains **confirmation** of the reduction **from the court: s 135**.

A company may wish to reduce its capital for one or more of the following reasons.

- The company has suffered a **loss** in the **value** of its **assets** and it reduces its capital to reflect that fact.
- The company wishes to **extinguish** the **interests** of some members entirely.
- The capital reduction is part of a **complicated arrangement** of capital which may involve, for instance, replacing share capital with debt capital.

There are three basic methods of reducing share capital specified in s 135(2).

Method	What happens	Effects
Extinguish or reduce liability on partly paid shares	Eg Company has nominal value £1 shares 75p paid up. Either (a) reduce nominal value to 75p; or (b) reduce nominal value to figure between 75p and £1.	Company gives up claim for amount not paid up (nothing is returned to shareholders).
Pay off part of paid up share capital out of surplus assets	Eg Company reduces nominal value of fully paid shares from £1 to 70p and repays this amount to shareholders	Assets of company are reduced by 30p in £.
Cancel paid up share capital which has been lost/ which is no longer represented by available assets.	Eg Company has £1 nominal fully paid shares but net assets only worth 50p per share. Difference debit balance on reserves. Company reduces nominal value to 50p, and applies amount to write off debit balance	Company can resume payments out of future profits without having to make good past losses.

A company could also reduce capital by cancelling statutory capital reserves such as the share premium amount, or allotting debenture stock to shareholders.

1.1 Role of court in reduction of capital

1.1.1 Protection of creditors

When the court receives an application for reduction of capital its first concern is the effect of the reduction on the company's ability to pay its debts: s 136.

If the reduction is by extinguishing liability or paying off part of paid up share capital, the court **must** generally require that **creditors** shall be **invited** by advertisement to state their objections (if any) to the reduction. Where paid up share capital is cancelled, the court **may** require an invitation to creditors.

Normally the company persuades the court to dispense with advertising for creditors' objections (which can be commercially damaging to the company). Two possible approaches are:

- To **pay off** all **creditors** before application is made to the court; or, if that is not practicable
- To produce to the court a **guarantee**, say from the company's bank, that its existing debts will be paid in full

1.1.2 Effect on different classes of shareholder

The court also considers whether, if there is more than one class of share, the reduction is fair in its effect on different classes of shareholder. If the reduction is, **in the circumstances**, a **variation of class rights** (for example removal of the right to an interest in the surplus on a winding-up) the **consent** of the class must be obtained under the variation of class rights procedure: *Re Old Silkstone Collieries Ltd 1954.*

Within each class of shares it is usual to make a uniform reduction of every share by the same amount per share, though this is **not** obligatory.

1.1.3 Other issues

The court may be concerned that the reduction should not confuse or mislead people who may deal with the company in future; for instance, it may insist that the company add 'and reduced' to its name or publish explanations of the reduction.

1.1.4 Approval by the court

If the court is satisfied that the reduction is in order, it approves the reduction by making an order to that effect.

A **copy of the court order** and of a **minute**, approved by the court, to show the altered share capital is delivered to the registrar who issues a certificate of registration.

Exam focus point

Do not confuse reduction of capital (which occurs on shares that have **already** been issued) with the issue of shares at a discount.

1.2 Section summary

- Reduction of capital can be achieved in the following ways.
  - Extinguishing/reducing liability on partly paid shares
  - Cancelling paid up share capital
  - Paying off part of paid up share capital
- Court approval is required.
- The court considers the interests of creditors and different classes of shareholder.

Question — **Reduction of share capital**

What are the main methods for a company to reduce its share capital? What procedures must it follow?

Answer

A limited company is permitted without restriction to cancel unissued shares and in that way to reduce its **authorised** share capital. That change does not alter its financial position.

If a limited company with a share capital wishes to reduce its **issued** share capital (and incidentally its authorised capital of which the issued capital is part) it may do so provided that:

(a) It has power to do so in its articles.
(b) It passes a special resolution.
(c) It obtains confirmation of the reduction from the court: s 135.

Requirement (a) is simply a matter of procedure. Articles (Table A Art 34) usually contain the necessary power. If not, the company in general meeting would first pass a special resolution to alter the articles appropriately and then proceed, as the second item on the agenda of the meeting, to pass a special resolution to reduce the capital.

There are three basic methods of reducing share capital specified in s 135(2):

(a) Extinguish or reduce liability on partly-paid shares

(b) Cancel paid up share capital which has been lost or which is no longer represented by available assets

(c) Pay off part of the paid up share capital out of surplus assets

Although these are the methods specified in s 135, they are not the only possibilities.

If method (a) or (b) is used (or is part of a more complex scheme to reduce capital) creditors must be invited to object, and their consent must be granted. An alternative is that they are paid off, which will allow the court to approve the reduction. These requirements, along with other court procedures, are contained in s 136.

It should be remembered that public companies are subject to a minimum capital requirement, currently of £50,000: s 11. This means that any public company wishing to reduce its capital below this figure will only be allowed to do so by the court if it re-registers as a private company, which is not subject to the minimum capital requirement. This situation is, of course, relatively rare.

2 Share premium account 12/01

FAST FORWARD

Any **premium** on the allotment of shares must be **put** into a **share premium** account.

Key term

Share premium is the excess received, either in cash or other consideration, over the nominal value of the shares issued.

A company which obtains for its shares a consideration in excess of their nominal value must transfer the excess to a share premium account: s 130.

2.1 Example

If a company allots its £1 (nominal) shares for £1.50 in cash, £1 per share is credited to the share capital account, and 50p to the share premium account.

Illustration

We will use the above example to illustrate the effects of the transaction on the balance sheet. The company have issued 100 shares.

	Before share issue	*After share issue*
	£	£
Cash	100	250
Share Capital	100	200
Share Premium	–	50
	100	250

The general rule is that reduction of the share premium account is subject to the **same** restrictions as reduction of share capital; **a company cannot distribute any part of its share premium account as dividend**: s 130.

2.2 Merger relief

Following the decision in *Shearer v Bercain 1980*, there is now a complicated exemption from the general rules on share premium account to regularise amalgamation of companies under the accepted 'merger accounting' procedure (first adopted in 1981).

If an acquiring company (Company X) secures at least **90 per cent** of the **equity capital** of another company (Company Y) as consideration for an allotment of shares (of Company X) any premium obtained from the excess of Company Y's assets over the nominal value of its shares need **not** be transferred to the share premium account: s 131 (merger relief).

2.3 Bonus issues

Share premium may be used to pay up fully paid shares under a bonus issue since this operation merely converts one form of fixed capital into another.

2.4 Other uses of the share premium account

The other permitted uses of share premium are to pay:

- **Capital expenses**, such as the preliminary expenses of forming the company
- A **discount on the issue of debentures** (NB shares cannot be issued at a discount)
- **A premium (if any) paid on the redemption of debentures:** s 130(2)
- **Purchase of own shares out of capital** by private companies

Exam focus point

The uses to which the share premium account can be put are generally relevant when answering a question on shares being issued at a premium.

3 Redemption and purchase by a company of its own shares

6/04

FAST FORWARD

Elaborate rules govern the ability of private and public companies to **redeem** or **purchase** their own shares. A **private** company may **purchase its own shares out of capital** subject to restrictions.

S 143 states that **a company cannot acquire its own shares** by purchase, subscription or other method.

A company can however accept shares as a gift: *Re Castiglione's Will Trusts 1958*. However the company cannot be the registered holder of the shares in its own register of members. The shares should be transferred to nominees to hold in trust for the company.

The prohibition is subject to **exceptions**. A company may:

- Purchase its own shares in compliance with a **court order**
- Issue and redeem **redeemable** shares
- **Purchase** its **own shares** under certain specified procedures
- Forfeit or **accept** the **surrender** of its shares

3.1 Redeemable shares

Key term

Redeemable shares are shares which are issued on terms which may require them to be bought back by the issuer at some future date, either at the discretion of the issuer or of the holder. Redemption must comply with the conditions of the Companies Act 1985.

Both ordinary and preference shares may be issued on terms which allow the company to redeem them. The expression redeemable shares means only shares which are redeemable from the time of issue, so shares not issued as redeemable cannot later be made so.

The conditions for the issue and redemption of redeemable shares are set out in ss 159 and 160.

	Redeemable shares
Authority s 159(1)	• The articles must give authority • The articles may be amended (special resolution) to give authority
Issued shares s 159(2)	• Some non-redeemable shares must be in issue • A company's capital must not consist entirely of redeemable shares
Paid up s 159(3)	• Redeemable shares must be fully paid at redemption
Terms s 159(3)	• The terms of redemption must provide for the payment on redemption
Redemption funds S160(1)	• The shares may be redeemed out of: – Distributable profits – Proceeds of a new issue of shares – Capital (if it is private company)
Premium s160(2)	• Any premium on redemption must be paid out of distributable profits, unless the shares are redeemed out of the proceeds of a share issue, when a premium may be paid from – Premium on share issue – Credit on share premium account
Articles	• The company may only redeem shares as allowed by – Its articles, and – Law

When shares are redeemed they are cancelled and may not be reissued.

(a) The amount of the company's **issued** share capital is **reduced** by the **nominal amount** of the shares but its authorised capital is unaltered: s 160(4).

(b) Any new shares issued to raise money to redeem shares are treated as a **replacement** for them to the extent that the nominal value of the new shares does not exceed the nominal value of the shares redeemed: s 160(5).

(c) If shares are redeemed wholly out of profits an amount equal to the nominal value of shares redeemed must be transferred to a **capital redemption reserve** which is to be treated as if it were share capital, except that it may be applied in paying up unissued shares as a bonus issue.

3.2 Purchase of own shares

A limited company may purchase its own shares by market or off-market purchase:

- **Out of profits or the proceeds of an issue of new shares** under the same rules that apply to redemption of shares
- If it is a **private company,** out of **capital;** this must by definition be an off-market purchase since no market purchase may be made of a private company's shares

A company cannot, however, purchase ordinary shares if, as a result, only redeemable shares are left.

An **unlimited** company can reduce its share capital or to purchase its own shares without complying with any statutory rules.

Two methods – 'off market purchase' and 'market purchase' – are distinguished: s 163. It is the **method of purchase**, not the type of share, which distinguishes the two procedures.

- **Market purchase** is purchase under the normal market arrangements of a recognised investment exchange.
- **Off-market purchase** is any other purchase, usually by private treaty. This will apply to shares of private companies.

	Market purchase of own shares (s 166)
Authority	The purchase must be authorised by ordinary resolution specifying • **Maximum** number of **shares** to be acquired • Maximum and minimum prices to be paid – By global sum, or – By price formula • Specify a data (< 18 months after resolution) on which authority expires
Filing	A copy of the resolution must be sent to the **Registrar** within 15 days
Charges	The authority may be **varied, revoked** or **renewed**

	Off market purchase of own shares (s 164)
Authority	A contract for the purchase of shares must be approved in advance by **special resolutions**
Inspection	A copy of the proposed contract must be available for inspection by members • At the registered office • For 15 days before the meeting for approval • At the meeting It must disclose the names of the seller
Voting	The **member** who intends to **sell** the shares should **not vote** If he does vote and the resolution would not have been carried without his vote, it is invalid He may cast votes attached to other shares which he is not selling
Public company	A public company may only be given **authority** for a **limited period** (maximum 6 months)
Filing	The company must make a **return** to the Registrar giving prescribed particulars within **28 days** of making the purchase
Changes	The authority may be **varied**, **revoked** or **renewed**

Illustration

The transaction described above may sound complicated, and it may help to see the effect of the transaction on a balance sheet. In the following illustration, the company is going to repurchase £20 of shares for cash.

	Before payment out of capital	*After payment of capital*	*Correction*
	£	£	£
Cash	250	230	230
Share Capital	100	80	80
Share Premium	50	50	50
Revaluation Reserve	50	50	50
Capital redemption reserve	–	–	20
(Capital & undistributable reserves)	200	180	200
Retained profit	50	50	30
(Distributable reserves)	250	230	230

The effect of this transaction has been circled above. In column two the capital and undistributable reserves figure has been reduced by the £20 value of the shares repurchased. As that capital and undistributable reserves is what the law considers to be 'the creditors' buffer', the transaction as it stands is unacceptable. In order to make the transaction acceptable, the transaction shown in column three must be undertaken, transfering a figure from the distributable reserves up into an undistributable reserve so that the creditors' buffer remains.

(Note. The headings given in italics are not statutory headings. They are for your reference only.)

Exam focus point

This is a law paper, not an accounting one. The above illustration and the one given later are put here in case seeing the numerical effect helps you to understand the legal principle. Do not get overly concerned about these numbers or feel that you have to learn them.

3.3 Payment for shares out of capital – private companies only

A **private limited company** which has a share capital may redeem or purchase its shares 'out of capital' by a **'permissible capital payment'** to which elaborate rules apply: s 171. These rules are designed to ensure that the company does not make itself insolvent.

The conditions are as follows.

(a) There must be general **authority** in the **articles** for redemption or purchase of shares out of capital (such as Table A Article 35).

(b) Capital may only be used to **'top up'** distributable profits and the proceeds of any issue of new shares in cases where those resources, fully used, do not suffice to make up the required amount,

$$\text{Cost of redemption or purchase} = \text{Available distributable profits} + \text{Proceeds of fresh issue} + \text{Permissable capital payment}$$

(c) A **capital redemption reserve** must be created where the amount of the permissible capital payment is less than the nominal amount of the shares redeemed or purchased: s 171(4).

If the payment is greater than the nominal amount then the capital redemption reserve, share premium account, share capital or revaluation reserve of the company may be reduced by the excess: s 171(5).

(d) A **statutory declaration of the directors** must be made and supported by a report of the auditors to the effect that after the payment is made the company will be able to pay its debts and to carry on its business for at least a year to come: s 173. These must also be delivered to the registrar: s 195.

(e) Shareholders must approve the payment by passing a **special resolution**. In this decision any vendor of shares may **not** use the votes attached to the shares which he is to sell to the company: s 173.

(f) A member who did not vote for the resolution and a creditor (for any amount) may within five weeks **apply to the court to cancel the resolution**, which may not be implemented until the five weeks have elapsed: s 176.

(g) A **notice** must be placed in the **Gazette** and in an appropriate national newspaper, **or** every creditor must be informed: s 175.

If the company goes into insolvent liquidation within a year of making a payment out of capital the persons who received the payment and the directors who authorised it may have to make it good to the company.

Illustration

The company who redeemed shares in the example above is a private limited company. It wants to redeem a further £40 of shares. However, it only has £30 of distributable profits remaining. As it is a private company (Ltd), it is allowed to make a permissible capital repayment. Once it has carried out all the legal formalities, described above, the transaction would be accounted for as follows:

	Before payment out of capital		After payment out of capital
	£		£
Cash	230	(Cr 40)	190
Share Capital	80	(Dr 40)	40
Share Premium	50		50
Revaluation Reserve	50		50
Capital redemption reserve	20	(Cr 30)	50
(Capital & undistributable reserves)	200		190
Retained profits	30	(Dr 30)	–
	230		190

In this instance, the maximum transfer has been made from distributable profits to the capital redemption reserve, but as the distributable profits were insufficient to bear the cost of the redemption, undistributable reserves have been reduced by £10, that is, a permissible capital repayment has been made.

(The accounting entries are shown in brackets.)

3.4 Default and restrictions incidental to redemption or purchase of shares

If the company issues redeemable shares but fails to redeem them at an agreed time, or if it agrees to purchase shares and then defaults under the contract, then the shareholder concerned may apply to the court for an order for specific performance. The shareholder will not succeed if the company is unable to meet the cost of redemption or purchase out of distributable profits: s 178.

A company which has made a contract for the purchase of its shares may not assign to another person the right to acquire the shares. If it wishes to cancel the agreement the cancellation must be approved by special resolution: s 167.

3.5 Subsidiary not to be a member of its holding company

The restrictions on acquisition by a company of its own shares are extended by a general prohibition against a subsidiary being a member of its holding company: s 23.

A subsidiary may, however, be a member of its holding company if it holds the shares as trustee or personal representative of a deceased person. The prohibition also does not apply where the subsidiary is concerned only as a market maker, as defined by s 23(3).

A problem can arise when Company A holds shares in Company B and later becomes a subsidiary of Company B. Company A may not vote at meetings of Company B but it still retains the shares (of Company B) as its property. In such a case Company A may end an awkward situation by arranging to sell the shares to a third party.

3.6 Section summary

- All companies can issue and redeem **redeemable shares** provided their **articles allow it**.
- A company issuing redeemable shares must have **non-redeemable shares** in issue.
- Various conditions apply to redemption, including shares being fully paid and payment being made on redemption.
- All companies can purchase their own shares out of **profits** or the **proceeds** of a **fresh issue**.
- Purchase can be by **market** or **off-market** purchase.
- A private company can purchase its shares out of capital subject to **strict conditions.**

Exam focus point

Do not confuse purchase of own shares with reduction of capital under s 135.

4 Financial assistance for purchase of shares

FAST FORWARD

A **public** company may not give **financial assistance** to a third party to purchase shares in the company. A private company can do so, however, under certain conditions.

- Two tests are applied to any suspect financial transactions.
  - What was its purpose?
  - Did the directors act *bona fide* in the interests of the company and not the third party?

Key term

Financial assistance is the provision of benefit by a company to a person to put that person in funds so that s/he may purchase shares in the company.

Giving financial assistance to a third party to enable him to buy the company's shares can take many forms. Hence it is difficult to prohibit altogether or to regulate. The relevant rules (ss 151 – 158) comprise:

- A general prohibition
- A procedure by which a private company may give such assistance
- A complex set of definitions and exceptions intended to determine which transactions are or are not prohibited

Transactions of this kind are usually very complicated.

Belmont Finance Corporation Ltd v Williams Furniture Ltd (No 2) 1980
The facts: G wished to purchase the shares of B Co at an agreed price of £489,000 but G did not have that sum available. The directors of B Co arranged to buy from G the issued shares of M Co for £500,000. G was thus able to purchase the shares of B Co with money which had come from B Co. B Co later claimed that there had been an infringement of the law. The directors and other defendants argued that the purchase of the shares of M Co had been a commercial transaction in the interests of B Co.

Decision: The purchase of the M Co shares was an artificial transaction undertaken for the purpose of financing the sale of the capital of B Co. B Co's claim was upheld; the M Co shares had not been purchased as part of a commercial transaction in B Co's interests. B Co's directors were found to be in breach of their fiduciary duties and had to account as constructive trustees to B Co for the funds advanced.

The *Belmont* case illustrated the most important problem of the law in this area. On the one hand it can be difficult to see whether a specific transaction is lawful. On the other hand any rule which is too simple or too specific tends to be evaded by unscrupulous people.

4.1 The rule against financial assistance

The general rules apply to **all public companies**, and all private companies who do not follow the procedures outlined below.

(a) A company is **prohibited** from **giving** any **financial assistance** for the **purpose** of the **acquisition** of **shares** either of the company or of its holding company or to **discharge liabilities** incurred in making the acquisition (subject to certain exceptions).

(b) The prohibition applies to assistance **given either directly or indirectly**, before or after, or at the time of the acquisition. An example of assistance given **after** acquisition is if the company repays or guarantees an earlier loan.

(c) 'Financial assistance' is elaborately defined to mean:

- A **loan**
- A **guarantee indemnity** or **security**
- **Purchase** of such **rights** from a third party
- **'Any other financial assistance** given by a company which **reduces** to a material extent, its **net assets':** s 152

Two main tests have to be applied to any **suspect transaction**.

- What was its **purpose**? It is not objectionable if its **principal purpose** was **not** to give financial assistance for the purchase of the shares nor if it was an incidental part of some **larger purpose** of the company: s 153(1)(a).
- What was the state of mind of the directors in approving the transaction? Did they act in **good faith** in what they deemed to be the interests of the company and not of a third party: s 153 (1)(b).

In the *Belmont* case the preliminary purchase of the M Co shares might have qualified as a *bona fide* commercial investment, but it would fail the purpose test, since it was undertaken for the purpose of financing the purchase of the shares of B Co.

The case below illustrates the application of these tests.

Brady v Brady 1988

The facts: Two brothers, D and E, managed a company, X Ltd. They were in such deadlock that X Ltd was heading for liquidation. It was agreed that half of X Ltd's assets would be transferred to Y Ltd, beneficially owned by D, X Ltd to be beneficially owned by E. To this end, Y Ltd was to buy all of D's shares in X Ltd, so leaving E as sole beneficial owner of X Ltd. D then refused to go ahead and E sought an order for specific performance.

Decision:

(a) The House of Lords held that the principal purpose of the scheme was to reduce indebtedness (and hence the scheme amounted to financial assistance).

(b) The House of Lords rejected the argument that the reduction of indebtedness was incidental to some larger purpose of the company. They drew a distinction between purpose and reason for a purpose. The **reason** for the assistance was the division of the group but the sole **purpose** was financial assistance.

Their lordships went on to conclude that, notwithstanding (a) and (b) above specific performance could be granted. The transaction was in good faith in the company's interests and the company was, as a private company, allowed the relaxation in ss 155-158 (discussed below).

However the main implication of the case is that the terms 'principal purpose' and 'incidental part of larger purpose' will be interpreted very restrictively.

Exam focus point

Brady v Brady is a very important case in this area.

If a company provides financial assistance for example by an unlawful loan, it cannot recover the money since the contract is illegal. But if the company thereby suffers loss it may claim damages from the directors responsible as constructive trustees: *Selangor United Rubber Estates Ltd v Cradock 1968* and *Guinness plc v Saunders and Another 1988.*

A director or other officer of a company which infringes these rules commits a criminal offence punishable by fine or imprisonment: s 151(3).

4.2 Giving financial assistance: private companies

A **private company may give financial assistance** for the acquisition of its own shares or the shares of its holding company, subject to the **following conditions** of ss 155 – 158.

- The financial assistance given **must not reduce the net assets** of the company or, if it does, the financial assistance is to be provided out of distributable profits.
- There must be a **statutory declaration of solvency** by the directors of the company (with a report by the auditors) of the same type as is prescribed when a private company purchases its own shares by a payment out of capital.
- A **special resolution** must be passed to approve the transaction. Normally this is a resolution of the company which gives the assistance.
- A right to **apply to the court** is given to members holding at least 10% of the issued shares (or of a class of shares). To permit them to exercise this right there is a four week standstill on the implementation of the resolution.

The procedure described above is not available to any group of companies which includes a public company.

4.3 Other exceptions from the financial assistance rules

S 153(3) states that certain specified transactions are **not** prohibited by s 151. These are:

- **Payment** of a **dividend** out of profits (the most important exception)
- **Distribution** of **assets** in winding up
- **Allotment** of **bonus shares**
- **Reduction** of **capital** approved by the court
- **Redemption** or **purchase of shares** under the appropriate procedures
- **Certain transactions** incidental to reconstruction, amalgamation and liquidation under the relevant provisions of the Companies Act

Three specific exceptions are also made. A company is not prohibited from entering into any of the following transactions: s 153(4).

- Making a loan if **lending is part of its ordinary business**, and the loan is made in the ordinary course of its business; this exception is restricted to money-lending companies
- Providing money in good faith and in the best interests of the company for the purpose of an **employees' share scheme** or for other share transactions by *bona fide* employees or connected persons
- **Making loans** to persons (other than directors) employed in good faith by the company with a view to those **persons acquiring fully paid shares** in the company or its holding company to be held by them as beneficial owners

Exam focus point

Do not confuse a company purchasing its own shares with a company providing financial assistance for **someone else** to purchase its shares.

4.4 Section summary

- S 151 prohibits a company giving **financial assistance** for the purchase of its own shares.
- Financial assistance is defined to include many arrangements, although certain transactions do not count as financial assistance.
- The courts have been reluctant to accept the following arguments.
  - Financial assistance was not the principal purpose of transactions.
  - Financial assistance was an incidental part of some larger purpose.
- **Private companies** are allowed to give financial assistance under certain stringent conditions.

5 Dividends 6/02, 6/05

FAST FORWARD

Dividends may only be paid out of **distributable profits**, defined as **accumulated realised profits** less **accumulated realised losses**.

Key term

A **dividend** is an amount payable to shareholders from profits or other distributable reserves.

Dividends may only be paid by a company out of profits available for the purpose: s 263.

Key term

Profits available for distribution are accumulated realised profits (which have not been distributed or capitalised) less accumulated realised losses (which have not been previously written off in a reduction or reorganisation of capital).

The power to declare a dividend is given by the articles which usually follow the model of Table A.

(a) The **company** in **general meeting** may declare dividends.

(b) No dividend may exceed the **amount recommended** by the directors who have an implied power in their discretion to set aside profits as reserves: Table A Article 102.

(c) The directors may declare such **interim dividends** as they consider justified: Article 103.

(d) Dividends are normally declared payable on the **paid up amount** of **share capital**. For example a £1 share which is fully paid will carry entitlement to twice as much dividend as a £1 share 50p paid: Article 104.

(e) A dividend may be paid **otherwise than in cash**: Article 105.

(f) Dividends may be paid by **cheque** or **warrant** sent through the post to the shareholder at his registered address: Article 106.

Listed companies generally pay two dividends a year; an interim dividend based on interim profit figures, and a final dividend based on the annual accounts and approved at the AGM.

A **dividend is a debt only** when it is **declared** and **due for payment**. A shareholder (ordinary or preference) is not entitled to a dividend unless it is declared in accordance with the procedure prescribed by the articles and the declared date for payment has arrived. The directors may decide to withhold profits and cannot be compelled to recommend a dividend.

Bond v Barrow Haematite Steel Co 1902

The facts: The company suffered a realised loss of £200,000 and the directors decided that the remaining £50,000 otherwise available for payment of dividends should be held back to make good a general depreciation in value of assets. The preference shareholders sued to compel the company to pay the preference dividend arguing (as was the position at the time) that the company was not bound to make a provision for depreciation of retained assets.

Decision: The directors must be the judge of what (if anything) the company could afford to distribute in dividends. The court would not overrule their opinion that the sum in question should not be distributed.

5.1 Payment 'in specie'

If the articles refer to 'payment' of dividends this means **payment in cash**. A power to pay dividends **in specie** (otherwise than in cash) is not implied but may be expressly created (see Table A Article 105). **Scrip dividends** are dividends paid by the issue of additional shares.

5.2 Distributable profits

Any provision of the articles for the declaration and payment of dividends is subject to the overriding rules of ss 263-281 – no dividend may be paid except out of profits distributable by law.

The profits which may be distributed as dividend are **accumulated realised profits**, so far as not previously utilised by distribution or capitalisation, **less accumulated realised losses**, so far as not previously written off in a reduction or reorganisation of capital duly made: s 263(3).

The word **'accumulated'** requires that any **losses** of **previous years** must be included in reckoning the current distributable surplus.

A profit or loss is deemed to be **realised** under s 262(3) if the profit or loss falls is treated as realised in accordance with generally accepted accounting principles. Hence, accounting standards in issue, plus generally accepted accounting principles (GAAP), should be taken into account when determining realised profits and losses.

Depreciation must be treated as a **realised loss**, and debited against profit, in determining the amount of distributable profit remaining.

However, a revalued asset will have deprecation charged on its historical cost and the increase in the value in the asset. the Companies Act allows the depreciation provision on the valuation increase to be treated also as a realised profit.

Effectively there is a cancelling out, and at the end only depreciation that relates to historical cost will affect dividends: s 275.

Illustration

Suppose that an asset purchased for £20,000 has a 10 year life. Provision is made for depreciation on a straight line basis so the annual depreciation charge of £2,000 must be deducted in reckoning the company's realised profit less realised loss.

Suppose now that after five years the asset is revalued to £50,000 and in consequence the annual depreciation charge is raised to £10,000 (over each of the five remaining years of the asset's life).

The effect of s 275 is that £8,000 of this amount may be reclassified as a realised profit. The net effect is that realised profits are reduced by only £2,000 in respect of depreciation, as before.

If, on a general revaluation of all fixed assets (or all except goodwill), it appears that there is a diminution in value of any one or more assets, then any related provision(s) need **not** be treated as a realised loss.

S 269 states that if a company shows development expenditure as an asset in its accounts it must usually be treated as a realised loss in the year it occurs: s 269. However it can be carried forward in special circumstances (generally taken to mean in accordance with SSAP 13 *Accounting for research and development*).

5.3 Dividends of public companies

FAST FORWARD

A public company may also only pay a dividend if its net assets are at the time, not less than the aggregate of its called up share capital and undistributable reserves.

The above rules on distributable profits apply to all companies, private or public. A public company is subject to an additional rule which may diminish but **cannot** increase its distributable profit as determined under the above rules.

A public company may only make a distribution if its **net assets are**, at the time, **not less than the aggregate of its called-up share capital and undistributable reserves**. The dividend which it may pay is limited to such amount as will leave its net assets at not less than that aggregate amount: s 264(1).

Undistributable reserves are defined in s 264(3) as:

(a) **Share premium account**

(b) **Capital redemption reserve**

(c) Any **surplus** of **accumulated unrealised profits** over **accumulated unrealised losses** (known as a revaluation reserve); however a deficit of accumulated unrealised profits compared with accumulated unrealised losses must be treated as a realised loss

(d) Any **reserve** which the company is **prohibited** from **distributing** by **statute** or by its memorandum or articles

Illustration

Suppose that a public company has an issued share capital (fully paid) of £800,000 and £200,000 on share premium account (which is an undistributable reserve). If its assets less liabilities are less than £1 million it may not pay a dividend. If however its net assets are say £1,250,000 it may pay a dividend but only of such amount as will leave net assets of £1 million or more, so its maximum permissible dividend is £250,000.

The dividend rules apply to every form of distribution of assets of the company to its members except the following (s 263)

- The **issue of bonus shares** whether fully or partly paid
- The redemption or purchase of the company's shares out of capital or profits
- A reduction of share capital
- A distribution of assets to members in a winding up

Exam focus point

You must appreciate how the rules relating to public companies in this area are more stringent than the rules for private companies.

Question

Distribution of profit

What are the main rules affecting a company's ability to distribute its profits as dividends?

Answer

Dividends may only be paid by a company out of profits available for the purpose: s 263. There is now a detailed code of statutory rules which determines what are distributable profits. This statutory code replaces much of the confused and uncertain case-law which previously applied. The profits which may be distributed as dividend are accumulated realised profits, so far as not previously utilised by distribution or capitalisation, less accumulated realised losses, so far as not previously written off in a reduction or reorganisation of capital duly made.

The word 'accumulated' requires that any losses of previous years must be included in reckoning the current distributable surplus.

The word 'realised' presents more difficulties. It clearly prevents the distribution of an increase in the value of a retained asset resulting from revaluation. However, it does not prevent a company from transferring to profit and loss account, for example, profit earned on an uncompleted contract, if it is in accordance with generally accepted accounting principles. Sch 4 para 36A requires that:

> 'It shall be stated whether the accounts have been prepared in accordance with applicable accounting standards and particulars of any material departure from those standards and the reasons for it shall be given.'

There is no mention here of realised profits and so it would seem that there is no statutory guidance on this point. Nevertheless, in view of the authority of accounting standards, it is unlikely that profits determined in accordance with accounting standards would be considered unrealised. A realised capital loss will reduce realised profits.

The above rules on distributable profits apply to all companies, private or public. A public company is subject to an additional rule (s 264) which may diminish but cannot increase its distributable profit as determined under the above rules.

A public company may only make a distribution if its net assets are, at the time, not less than the aggregate of its called-up share capital and undistributable reserves. The dividend which it may pay is limited to such amount as will leave its net assets at not less than that aggregate amount.

5.4 Relevant accounts

The question whether a company has profits from which to pay a dividend is determined by reference to its **'relevant accounts'** which are generally the last annual accounts to be prepared and laid in general meeting.

If the auditor has qualified his report on the accounts he must also state in writing whether, in his opinion, the subject matter of his qualification (if it relates to statutory accounting requirements) is **material** in determining whether the dividend may be paid: s 271. If this statement is not made, the dividend may be treated as **ultra vires** and repayable: *Re Precision Dippings Marketing Ltd and Others 1985.*

A company may produce **interim accounts** if the latest annual accounts do not disclose a sufficient distributable profit to cover the proposed dividend. It may also produce **initial accounts** if it proposes to pay a dividend during its first accounting reference period or before its first accounts are laid before the company in general meeting. These accounts may be unaudited, but they must suffice to permit a proper judgement to be made of amounts of any of the relevant items.

If a **public** company has to produce initial or interim accounts, which is unusual, they must be full accounts such as the company is required to produce as final accounts at the end of the year. They need not be audited. However the auditors must, in the case of initial accounts, satisfy themselves that the accounts have been 'properly prepared' to comply with the Act. A copy of any such accounts of a public company (with any auditors' statement) must be delivered to the registrar for filing: s 272.

5.5 Infringement of dividend rules

If a dividend is paid otherwise than out of distributable profits the company, the **directors and** the **shareholders** may be involved in making good the unlawful distribution.

The directors are held responsible since they either recommend to members in general meeting that a dividend should be declared or they declare interim dividends.

(a) **They are liable if they recommend or declare a dividend which they know is paid out of capital**: *Re Exchange Banking Co 1882 (called Flitcroft's case).*

(b) **The directors are liable if without preparing any accounts they declare or recommend a dividend which proves to be paid out of capital.** It is their duty to satisfy themselves that profits are available.

Re Oxford Benefit Building and Investment Society 1886

The facts: The articles provided that dividends might be paid out of 'realised profits'. The directors 'never attempted in any report or balance sheet to distinguish realised profit from estimated profits ... or to ascertain out of what fund the dividends were actually paid'.

Decision: This was perhaps only 'gross carelessness' though the good faith of the directors was 'extremely questionable'. They must make good the dividends improperly paid.

(c) **The directors are liable if they make some mistake of law or interpretation of the memorandum or articles which leads them to recommend or declare an unlawful dividend.** However in such cases the directors may well be entitled to relief under s 727 (acts performed 'honestly and reasonably').

The directors may however honestly rely on proper accounts which disclose an apparent distributable profit out of which the dividend can properly be paid. They are not liable if it later appears that the assumptions or estimates used in preparing the accounts, although reasonable at the time, were in fact unsound.

Re Mercantile Trading Co 1869 (called Stringer's case)
The facts: The company was formed in England to trade with the Confederate Southern States during the American Civil War. In 1864 accounts were prepared in which ships running the northern blockade of southern ports, cotton stock situate in the southern states and a debt due from the Confederate Government were shown as assets valued at full value. On the basis of these accounts there was a profit from which the proposed dividend could be paid. With the defeat of the southern confederacy the company lost its assets – ships had been sunk, the cotton had been appropriated by the northern states and the debt was worthless. The company went into liquidation. The liquidator sought to obtain reimbursement of the dividend from the managing director (Stringer) on the grounds that the balance sheet had been 'delusive' and had caused dividends to be paid out of capital.

Decision: In the absence of fraud (none was alleged) and in view of the known hazards (which had made it impossible to obtain insurance cover) the directors were justified in preparing their accounts as they had done. It was not then inevitable or foreseeable that the southern confederacy would be defeated. There is no requirement that a company must have 'actual cash in hand' to the full amount of the dividend declared. The claim against Stringer was dismissed.

The position of members is as follows.

- A member may obtain an **injunction** to restrain a company from paying an unlawful dividend.
- Members voting in general meeting **cannot authorise** the payment of an unlawful dividend nor release the directors from their liability to pay it back.
- The company can **recover from members** an **unlawful dividend** if the **members know** or had **reasonable grounds** to believe that it is unlawful: s 277(1).

- If the directors have to make good to the company an unlawful dividend they may claim **indemnity from members** who at the time of receipt knew of the irregularity.
- Members knowingly receiving an unlawful dividend may **not bring an action** against the directors.

If an unlawful dividend is paid by reason of error in the accounts the company may be unable to claim against either the directors or the members. The company might then have a claim against its auditors if the undiscovered mistake was due to negligence or misfeasance on their part.

Re London & General Bank (No 2) 1895
The facts: The auditor had drawn the attention of the directors to the fact that certain loans to associated companies were likely to prove irrecoverable. The directors refused to make any provision for these potential losses and they persuaded the auditor to confine his comments in his audit report to the uninformative statement that the value of assets shown in the balance sheet 'is dependent on realisation'. A dividend was paid in reliance on the apparent profits shown in the accounts. The company went into liquidation and the liquidator claimed from the auditor compensation for loss of capital due to his failure to report clearly to members what he well knew affecting the reliability of the accounts.

Decision: The auditor has a duty to report what he knows of the true financial position: otherwise his audit is 'an idle farce'. He had failed in this duty and was liable.

5.6 Section summary

- Various rules have been created to ensure that dividends are only paid out of available profits.
- Distributable profits may be defined as 'accumulated realised profits ... less accumulated realised losses'.
- **'Accumulated'** means that any losses of previous years must be included in reckoning the current distributable surplus.
- **'Realised'** profits are determined in accordance with generally accepted accounting principles.
- A public company may only make a distribution if its **net assets** are, at the time, **not less than the aggregate of its called up share capital and undistributable reserves**. It may only pay a dividend which will leave its net assets at not less than that aggregate amount.
- In certain situations the **directors** and **members** may be liable to make good to the company the amount of an **unlawful dividend**.

6 Loss of capital in a public company

If the net assets of a public company are half or less of the amount of its called up share capital there must be an extraordinary general meeting: s 142.

Where the directors' duty arises they must issue a notice to **convene a meeting** within **28 days** of becoming aware of the need to do so. The meeting must be convened for a date within 56 days of their coming to know the relevant facts.

The directors have no obligation to lay a report or proposals before the meeting though in practice they would be wise to take the initiative in doing so.

The purpose of this procedure is to enable shareholders to consider 'whether any, and if so what, measures should be taken to deal with the situation'.

If the capital falls below £50,000, the company must re-register as private.

Chapter roundup

- We have seen in this chapter that the rules which dictate how a company is to manage and maintain its capital exist to maintain the delicate balance between the members' enjoyment of limited liability and the creditors' requirements that the company shall remain able to pay its debts.
- A limited company may reduce its issued share capital provided:
  - It has **power** to do so in its articles.
  - A **special resolution** is passed.
  - The court **confirms** the reduction under s 135.
- Any **premium** on the allotment of shares must be **put** into a **share premium** account.
- Elaborate rules govern the ability of private and public companies to **redeem** or **purchase** their own shares.
- A **private** company may **purchase its own shares out of capital** subject to restrictions.
- A **public** company may not give **financial assistance** to a third party to purchase shares in the company. A private company can do so, however, under certain conditions.
- Two tests are applied to any suspect financial transactions.
  - What was its purpose?
  - Did the directors act *bona fide* in the interests of the company and not the third party?
- Dividends may only be paid out of **distributable profits**, defined as **accumulated realised profits** less **accumulated realised losses**.
- A public company may also only pay a dividend if its **net assets** are at the time, **not less than the aggregate of its called up share capital and undistributable reserves.**

Quick quiz

1 Where application is made to the court for approval of a reduction in capital, the court may require that creditors should be invited by advertisement to state their objections. In which of the following ways can the need to advertise be avoided?

A Paying off all creditors before application to the court
B Producing a document signed by the directors stating the company's ability to pay its debt
C Producing a guarantee from the company's bank that its existing debts will be paid in full
D Renouncement by existing shareholders of their limited liability in relation to existing debts
E Production of a comfort letter from a holding company

2 If a private company goes into insolvent liquidation within a certain period of making a payment for its own shares out of capital, the persons who received the payment and the directors who authorised it may have to make it good to the company. What is the period of time?

3 months	6 months
12 months	2 years

3 A share premium account can be used for bonus issues of shares or discounts on the issue of debentures.

True ☐

False ☐

4 **Fill in the blanks** in the statements below.

When a company redeems or purchases its own shares, it must create a .... when the amount of the permissible capital payment is less than the nominal amount of the shares redeemed or purchased.

5 Which of the following statements are true of redeemable shares?

A The articles must give authority for the issue of redeemable shares.
B A company's capital cannot consist entirely of redeemable shares.
C Redeemable shares may only be redeemed if they are fully paid.
D Redeemable shares may only be redeemed from distributable profits, not capital.
E The terms of redemption must provide for payment on redemption.

6 No company may give financial assistance for the purchase of its own shares unless that assistance is for certain specified purposes.

True ☐

False ☐

7 **Fill in the blanks** in the statements below.

Distributable profits may be defined as .... profits less .... losses.

8 If a company makes an illegal dividend, who may be involved in making good the unlawful distribution?

A The company
B The directors
C The shareholders

9 Give four examples of undistributable reserves.

10 What normally are a company's relevant accounts in the context of payments of dividends?

Answers to quick quiz

1 A and C. The only guarantee that the courts will accept is from the company's bank.

2 12 months

3 True

4 When a company purchases its own shares, it must create a *capital redemption reserve* when the amount of the permissible capital payment is less than the nominal amount of the shares redeemed or purchased.

5 A, B, C and E are correct. D is wrong, as shares can be redeemed out of the proceeds of a fresh issue, and a private company can redeem shares out of capital.

6 False. A private company may give financial assistance for any reason providing it follows the procedures in ss 155-158.

7 Distributable profits may be defined as *accumulated realised* profits less *accumulated realised* losses.

8 All three may be liable.

9 Share premium account

Capital redemption reserve

A surplus of accumulated unrealised profits over accumulated unrealised losses

Any reserve which the company is prohibited from distributing by statute or by its memorandum and articles

10 The relevant accounts are the last accounts to have been prepared and laid in general meeting.

Now try the question below from the Exam Question Bank

Number	Level	Marks	Time
Q21	Examination	20	36 mins

Borrowing and loan capital

Topic list	Syllabus reference
1 Borrowing	6(b)
2 Debentures	6(b)
3 Debentureholders' remedies	6(b)
4 Charges	6(b)
5 Registration of charges	6(b)
6 Administrative receivers	6(b)
7 Administration	10(c)
8 Avoidance of floating charges	6(b)
9 Transactions at an undervalue and preferences	6(b)

Introduction

The last few chapters have been concerned with share capital. In this chapter on borrowing and loan capital, you should note that the interests and position of a lender is very different from that of a shareholder.

This chapter covers how loan capital holders protect themselves, specifically through taking out **fixed or floating charges**.

You need to understand the differences between fixed and floating charges, and also how they can protect loan creditors, for example by giving chargeholders the ability to appoint a receiver or, under the Enterprise Act 2002, an administrator.

Loan capital was examined in Section A of the Pilot paper. It could easily be examined also as some of a Section B question in connection with other types of capital or in connection with liquidation, which is explored in the next chapter.

1 Borrowing

A company whose objects are to carry on a trade or business has an **implied power to borrow** for purposes **incidental to the trade or business**. A non-trading company must have an express power to borrow since it is not implied.

In delegating the company's power to borrow to the directors it is usual, and essential in the case of a company whose shares are listed on the Stock Exchange, to impose a **maximum** limit on the **borrowing** arranged by directors.

A contract to repay borrowed money may in principle be unenforceable if either:

- It is money borrowed for an **ultra vires** purpose and this is known to the lender.
- The directors **exceed their borrowing powers** or have no powers to borrow.

However:

- In both cases the lender will probably be **able** to **enforce** the contract by virtue of ss 35(1) or 35A (see Chapter 13).
- If the contract is within the capacity of the company but beyond the delegated powers of the directors the company may **ratify** the **loan contract**.

If there is a power to borrow, there is also a power to create charges over the company's assets as security for the loan: *Re Patent File Co 1870.*

2 Debentures **6/04**

FAST FORWARD

A **debenture** is a document stating the terms on which a company has borrowed money. There are three main types.

- A **single debenture**
- **Debentures issued as a series** and usually registered
- **Debenture stock** subsidised by a large number of lenders.

Key term

A **debenture** is the written acknowledgement of a debt by a company, which may be given under its seal, and normally containing provisions as to payment of interest and the terms of repayment of principal. A debenture may be secured on some or all of the assets of the company or its subsidiaries.

A debenture may create a **charge** over the company's assets as security for the loan. However a document relating to an unsecured loan is also a debenture in company law.

A debenture is usually a formal legal document, often in printed form. Broadly, there are three main types.

(a) **A single debenture**

If, for example, a company obtains a secured loan or overdraft facility from its bank, the latter is likely to insist that the company seals the bank's standard form of debenture creating the charge and giving the bank various safeguards and powers.

(b) **Debentures issued as a series and usually registered**

Different lenders may provide different amounts on different dates. Although each transaction is a separate loan, the intention is that the lenders should rank equally *(pari passu)* in their right to repayment and in any security given to them. Each lender therefore receives a debenture in identical form in respect of his loan.

The debentures are transferable securities. The normal conditions require the company to maintain a register of debentureholders (unless they are bearer debentures).

(c) **The issue of debenture stock subscribed to by a large number of lenders**

Only a public company may use this method to offer its debentures to the public and any such offer is a prospectus; if it seeks a listing on The Stock Exchange then the rules on listing particulars must be followed.

Each lender has a right to be **repaid** his **capital** at the **due time** and to receive **interest** on it until **repayment**. This form of borrowing is treated as a single global loan 'stock' in which each debenture stockholder has a specified fraction (in money terms) which he or some previous holder contributed when the stock was issued. Debenture stock is transferable in multiples of, say, £1 or £10.

A company will maintain a register of debenture stockholders.

One advantage of debenture stock over debentures issued as single and indivisible loan transactions is that the holder of debenture stock can sell part of his holding, say £1,000 (nominal) out of a larger amount.

2.1 Debenture trust deed

A **debenture trust deed** usually contains the following major elements.

(a) **The appointment usually of a trustee for prospective debenture stockholders**. The trustee is usually a bank, insurance company or other institution but may be an individual.

(b) **The nominal amount of the debenture** stock is defined, which is the maximum amount which may be raised then or later. The date or period of repayment is specified, as is the rate of interest and half-yearly interest payment dates.

(c) If the debenture stock is secured **the deed creates a charge or charges** over the assets of the company.

(d) The trustee is authorised to **enforce the security** in case of default and, in particular, to appoint a receiver with suitable powers of management.

(e) The company enters into **various covenants**, for instance to keep its assets fully insured or to limit its total borrowings; breach is a default by the company.

(f) There may be elaborate provisions for a **register** of debenture stockholders, **transfer of stock** and **meetings** of debenture stockholders.

The main advantages of the use of a debenture trust deed are as follows.

(a) The **trustee** with appropriate powers can **intervene promptly** in case of default.

(b) **Security** for the debenture stock in the form of charges over property can be **given to a single trustee**.

(c) The **company** can **contact a representative of the debentureholders** with whom it can negotiate.

(d) By calling a **meeting of debentureholders**, the trustee can consult them and obtain a decision binding on them all.

(e) The **debentureholders** will be able to **enjoy the benefit of a legal mortgage** over the company's land. This would not be possible without trustees since under the Law of Property Act 1925, a legal estate in land cannot be vested in more than four persons.

2.2 Register of debentureholders

Company law does not require a register of debentureholders be maintained. However, a company is normally required to maintain a register by the debenture or debenture trust deed when debentures are issued as a series or when debenture stock is issued.

When there is a register of debentureholders, the following regulations apply.

(a) The company is required by law to keep the **register** in the **same country** as its registered office, either at that office or, if the register is made up elsewhere, at an **address** of which notice is given to the registrar: s 190.

(b) The register of debentureholders must be open to **inspection** by **any person**. Any person may obtain a copy of the register or part of it. A holder of debentures issued under a trust deed may require the company (on payment) to supply him with a copy of the deed: s 191.

(c) The register should be **properly kept** in accordance with s 722 and s 723.

2.3 Rights of debentureholders

The position of debentureholders is best described by comparison with that of shareholders. At first sight the two appear to have a great deal in common.

- Both **own transferable company securities** which are usually long-term investments in the company.
- The **issue procedure** is much the same. An offer of either shares or debentures to the public is a prospectus as defined by s 744.
- The **procedure** for **transfer** of registered shares and debentures is the same.

There are however important and more fundamental differences.

Factor	Shareholder	Debenture holder
Role	Is a proprietor or owner of the company	Is a creditor of the company
Voting rights	May vote at general meetings	May not vote
Cost of investment	Shares may not be issued at a discount	Debentures may be offered at a discount
Return	Dividends are only paid • Out of distributable profits • When directors declared them	Interest must be paid when it is due
Redemption	Statutory restrictions on redeeming shares	No restriction on redeeming debentures
Liquidation	Shareholders are the last people to be aid in a winding up	Debentures must be paid back before shareholders are paid

From the investor's standpoint debenture stock is often preferable to preference shares since the former offers greater security and yields a fixed income.

2.4 Advantages and disadvantages of debentures (for the company)

Advantages	Disadvantages
Easily traded	May have to pay high interest to make them attractive
Terms clear and specific	Interest payments mandatory
Asset floating charged may be traded	Interest payments may upset shareholders if dividends fall
Popular due to guaranteed income	Debenture-holder's remedies of liquidators or receivers may be disastrous for the company
Interest tax-deductible	
No restrictions on issue or purchase by a company	Crystallisation of a floating charge can cause trading difficulties for a company

Question

Shareholders and debentureholders

Explain how the rights of the shareholders of a company differ from the rights of its debentureholders.

Answer

Rights of shareholders and debentureholders

Shareholders are members of the company. Debentureholders are creditors but not members of the company. Their relationships with the company differ in the following principal respects.

What governs the relationship

A company's relationship with its shareholders is governed by

(a) Its memorandum and articles which operate as a contract between them and between the shareholders and each other (s 14), and

(b) The Companies Act

The relationship between a company and its debentureholders is regulated by:

(a) The terms of the trust deed or other formal document, and
(b) (Different) provisions of the Companies Act

The major practical differences are set out below.

Voting

As members of the company, shareholders have the right to attend and vote at meetings. Debentureholders have no such automatic rights; they may however have votes if the articles and deed allow.

Income

A shareholder, even if he holds preference shares on which fixed dividends are due on specific days, can only receive dividends out of distributable profits. In addition he cannot force the company to pay dividends: *Bond v Barrow Haematite Steel Co 1902.*

By contrast interest at the agreed rate must be paid on debentures even if that interest has to be paid out of capital.

Rights on securities

The Companies Act confers pre-emption rights on shareholders, entitling them to first call on any new shares which are to be issued: s 89.

Debentureholders have no right of objection to further loans and debentures being taken out, unless the trust deed sets out restrictions. However there is no statutory restriction on debentureholders having debentures redeemed or purchased by the company. By contrast there are detailed rules regulating redemption or purchase of a company's own shares.

Rights if aggrieved

Shareholders have the right to complain to the court if directors are allowing ultra vires transactions (s 35 (2)) or acting in a manner unfairly prejudicial to their interests (s 459). Shareholders can by simple majority remove directors from the board: s 303.

Debentureholders may have rights under the trust deed if the company breaches the agreement. These include:

(a) The right to appoint a receiver, or
(b) The right if given to enforce charges and sell the property under the charge to realise their debts

Their consent may also be required before the company deals with certain of its assets, when the debentureholders have secured their loan by means of a fixed charge over those assets.

Rights on liquidation

In liquidation debentureholders must be repaid in full before anything is distributed to shareholders.

3 Debentureholders' remedies

FAST FORWARD

A **secured** debentureholder may enforce the security if the company defaults on payment of interest or repayment of capital.

- He may take possession of the asset subject to the charge and sell it.
- He may apply to the court for its transfer to his ownership by a foreclosure order.
- He may appoint a receiver of it (which is the usual first step).

3.1 Rights of unsecured debentureholders

Any debentureholder is a creditor of the company with the normal remedies of an unsecured creditor. He could:

- **Sue** the company for debt and seize its property if his judgement for debt is unsatisfied
- Present a petition to the court for the **compulsory liquidation** of the company
- Present a petition to the court for an **administration order**, that is, a temporary reprieve to try to rescue the company

3.2 Rights of secured debentureholders

A **secured** debentureholder (or the trustee of a debenture trust deed) may enforce the security. He may:

- Take **possession of the asset** subject to the charge if he has a legal charge (if he has an equitable charge he may only take possession if the contract allows)

- **Sell it** (provided the debenture is executed as a deed)

- Apply to the court for its **transfer** to his ownership by foreclosure order (rarely used and only available to a legal chargee)
- Appoint a **receiver** of it

The **appointment of a receiver** is the usual **first** step.

Exam focus point

The last part of a question on charges may well ask what debentureholders can do if a company defaults.

3.3 Receivers

The debenture (or debenture trust deed) usually gives power to the debentureholders (or their trustee) to appoint a receiver in specified circumstances of default by the company. The debenture also generally provides that the receiver, when appointed:

(a) Shall have **suitable powers** of **management** and disposal of the assets under his charge

(b) Shall be an **agent** of the **company** and not of the debentureholders by whom he is appointed; the purpose of this stipulation is to safeguard the debentureholders against liability for any wrongful act of the receiver

4 Charges 6/04

FAST FORWARD

A charge over the assets of a company gives a creditor a **prior claim** over other creditors to payment of his debt out of these assets.

Key term

A **charge** is an encumbrance upon real or personal property granting the holder certain rights over that property, usually as security for a debt owed to the charge holder. The most common form of charge is by way of legal mortgage, used to secure the indebtedness of borrowers in house purchase transactions. In the case of companies, charges over assets are most frequently granted to persons who provide loan capital to the business.

A charge **secured** over a company's assets gives to the creditor (called the 'chargee') a prior claim (over other creditors) to payment of his debt out of those assets. Charges are of two kinds, fixed and floating.

Key term

A **fixed charge** is a form of protection given to secured creditors relating to specific assets of a company. The charge grants the holder the right of enforcement against the identified asset (in the event of default in repayment) so that the creditor may realise the asset to meet the debt owed. Fixed charges rank first in order of priority in liquidation.

Fixed or specific charges attach to the relevant asset as soon as the charge is created. By its nature a fixed charge is best suited to fixed assets which the company is likely to retain for a long period. If the company does dispose of the asset it will either repay the secured debt out of the proceeds of sale so that the charge is discharged at the time of sale, or pass the asset over to the purchaser still subject to the charge.

Key term

A **floating charge** has been defined (*Re Yorkshire Woolcombers Association Ltd 1903*) as:

(a) A charge on a class of assets of a company, present and future . . .

(b) Which class is, in the ordinary course of the company's business, changing from time to time and . . .

(c) Until the holders enforce the charge the company may carry on business and deal with the assets charged.

Floating charges do not attach to the relevant assets until the charge crystallises. A floating charge is not restricted however to current assets such as book debts or stock in trade. A floating charge over 'the undertaking and assets' of a company (the most common type) applies to future as well as to current assets.

4.1 Identification of charges as fixed or floating

FAST FORWARD

Charges may be either **fixed**, which attach to the relevant asset on creation, or **floating**, which attach on 'crystallisation'. For this reason it is not possible to identify the assets to which a **floating** charge relates (until **crystallisation**).

It is not always immediately apparent whether a charge is fixed or floating. Chargees often do not wish to identify a charge as being floating when it was created since this means that, if a receiver is appointed, preferential creditors must first be paid out of the charged assets: s 40 Insolvency Act 1986 (IA).

Thus a charge contract will often declare the charge as fixed, or fixed and floating, whether it is or not. However the label attached by parties in this way is not a conclusive statement of the charge's legal nature: *Street v Mountford 1985.*

The general rule is that a charge over assets will not be registered as fixed if it envisages that the company will still be able to deal with the charged assets without reference to the chargee.

> *R in Right of British Columbia v Federal Business Development Bank 1988*
> *The facts:* In this Canadian case the Bank had a charge over the company's entire property expressed as 'a fixed and specific mortgage and charge'. Another term allowed the company to continue making sales from stock in the ordinary course of business until notified in writing by the bank to stop doing so.
>
> *Decision:* The charge was created as a floating, not a fixed, charge.

The courts have found exceptions to the general rule concerning permission to deal.

(a) In *Re GE Tunbridge Ltd 1995* it was held that as the three criteria stated in the *Yorkshire Woolcombers* case applied, the charge over certain fixed assets was a floating charge even though the company was required to obtain the chargee's permission before dealing with the assets.

(b) In *Re Cimex Ltd 1994* the court decided that the charge in dispute was a fixed charge because the assets did not in the ordinary course of business change from time to time; this was despite the company being able to deal with the assets without the chargee's permission.

Charges expressed to be fixed which cover present and future book debts are particularly tricky. Again the general rule applies: if the company is allowed to deal with money collected from debtors without notifying the chargee the charge is floating (*Re Westmaze Ltd 1998*); if the money collected must be paid to the chargee, say in reduction of an overdraft, the charge is fixed: *Siebe Gorman & Co Ltd v Barclays Bank Ltd 1979.* This decision was approved by the Court of Appeal in *Re Spectrum Plus Ltd 2004*, but this decision has been itself appealed, so things remain uncertain.

In *Re New Bullas Trading Ltd 1994* it was held that contracting parties could provide that future book debts should be subject to a fixed charge while they were uncollected and that the proceeds should be subject to a floating charge once paid into a specific bank account.

4.1.1 Problems with fixed charges

If a fixed charge is created to secure a debt within six months before a company becomes insolvent then it *may* be invalid as a preference: s 239 IA. When he comes to enforce the charge, the chargee may find that the value of the asset does not fully discharge the debt. In a liquidation, the unpaid balance then falls to be an unsecured debt.

4.2 Floating charges

FAST FORWARD

A floating charge has been defined as:

- A charge on a **class** of assets, present and future
- Which class **changes from time to time** in the **ordinary course of business**
- Until the **charge** is enforced, the company can deal with the **charged assets**

A floating charge is often created by express words. However no special form of words is essential. If a company gives to a chargee rights over its assets while retaining freedom to deal with them in the ordinary course of business until the charge crystallises, that will be a charge which 'floats'. The particular assets subject to a floating charge cannot be identified until the charge attaches by crystallisation.

The same rules on registration (dealt with later) and preference apply to a floating as to a fixed charge. Additionally a floating charge, if created **within twelve months** before liquidation, may become **void automatically** on liquidation: s 245 IA.

4.2.1 Crystallisation of a floating charge

Key term

Crystallisation of a floating charge occurs when it is converted into a fixed equitable charge: that is, a fixed charge on the assets owned by the company at the time of crystallisation: *Re Griffin Hotel Co Ltd 1941.*

Events causing crystallisation are as follows.

(a) The **liquidation** of the company

(b) **Cessation** of the company's **business**: *Re Woodroffes (Musical Instruments) Ltd 1986*

(c) **Active intervention** by the chargee, generally by way of appointing a receiver

(d) If the **charge contract so provides**, when notice is given by the chargee that the charge is converted into a fixed charge (on whatever assets of the relevant class are owned by the company at the time of the giving of notice): *Re Brightlife 1987*

(e) The **crystallisation** of **another floating charge** if it causes the company to cease business.

Floating charge contracts sometimes make provision for 'automatic crystallisation': that is, the charge is to crystallise when a **specified event** – such as a breach of some term by the company – occurs, whether or not:

- The chargee learns of the event.
- The chargee wants to enforce the charge as a result of the event.

Such clauses have been accepted by the court if they state that, on the event happening, the floating charge is converted to a fixed one: *Re Brightlife 1987.* Clauses which provide only that a company is to cease to deal with charged assets on the occurrence of a particular event have been rejected.

4.3 Comparison of fixed and floating charges

A fixed charge is normally the more satisfactory form of security since it confers immediate rights over identified assets. A floating charge has some advantage in being applicable to current assets which may be easier to realise than fixed assets subject to a fixed charge. If for example a company becomes insolvent it may be easier to sell its stock than its empty factory.

The principal **disadvantages** of **floating charges** are as follows.

(a) The **holder** of a floating charge **cannot be certain** until the charge crystallises (often through the company failing) which assets will form his security.

(b) Even when a floating charge has crystallised over an identified pool of assets the **chargeholder** may find himself **postponed** to the claim of **other creditors** as follows.

   (i) A **judgement creditor or landlord** who has seized goods and sold them may retain the proceeds if received before the appointment of the debentureholder's receiver: s 183 IA.

   (ii) **Preferential debts** may be paid out of assets subject to a floating charge unless there are other uncharged assets available for this purpose: ss 40 and 175 IA.

   (iii) The **holder** of a **fixed charge** over the same assets will usually have priority over a floating charge on those assets even if that charge was created before the fixed charge (see below).

   (iv) A creditor may have sold goods and delivered them to the company on condition that he is to retain legal ownership until he has been paid (a **Romalpa** clause).

   (v) The Enterprise Act 2002 also introduce a clause into the Insolvency Act 1986 stating that a '**prescribed part**' of the company's **net property** will be **available to unsecured creditors**, regardless of any charges over that property. This introduces an element of 'proportionality' for unsecured creditors. The amount of money that is to be so prescribed, or 'ring-fenced' to put it another way, will be set by the Secretary of State by statutory instrument.

(c) A **floating charge** may become **invalid automatically** if the company creates the charge to secure an existing debt and goes into liquidation within a year thereafter (s 245 IA); the period is only six months with a fixed charge.

4.3.1 Preferential debts

Preferential debts have been limited by the Enterprise Act 2002 and now comprise:

- Remuneration and holiday pay owed to employees
- EC levies on coal and steel production

4.4 Priority of charges

FAST FORWARD

On liquidation a **fixed charge** on assets has preference. Assets subject to a **floating charge** may be used to settle **preferential debts** and a proportion of the assets are also ring-fenced for the benefit of unsecured creditors.

If different charges over the **same** property are given to different creditors their priority must be determined.

Illustration

If charges are created over the same property to secure a debt of £5,000 to X and £7,000 to Y and the property is sold yielding only £10,000 either X or Y is paid in full and the other receives only the balance remaining out of £10,000 realised from the security.

Leaving aside the question of registration (discussed below), the main points to remember in connection with the priority of any charges are as follows.

(a) **Legal charges** rank according to the **order of creation**. If two successive legal charges over the same factory are created on 1 January and 1 February the earlier takes priority over the later one.

(b) An equitable charge created before a legal charge will only take priority over the latter if, when the latter was created, the **legal chargee** had **notice** of the equitable charge.

(c) A **legal charge created before** an **equitable one** has **priority**.

(d) **Two equitable charges** take priority according to the **time of creation**.

If a floating charge is created and a fixed charge over the same property is created later, the **fixed** charge will rank **first** since it attached to the property at the time of **creation** but the **floating** charge attaches at the time of **crystallisation**. Once a floating charge has crystallised it becomes a fixed charge and a fixed charge created subsequently ranks after it.

A creditor to whom a floating charge is given may seek to protect himself against losing his priority by including in the terms of his floating charge a prohibition against the company creating a fixed charge over the same property which would otherwise take priority (sometimes called a **'negative pledge clause'**).

If the company breaks that prohibition the creditor to whom the fixed charge is given nonetheless obtains priority, unless at the time when his charge is created he has **actual** knowledge of the prohibition: *Wilson v Kelland 1910.*

If a company sells a charged asset to a third party the following rules apply.

- A chargee with a legal charge still has recourse to the property in the hands of the third party – the **charge** is **automatically** transferred with the property.
- Property only remains charged by an equitable charge if the **third party** had **notice** of it when he acquired the property.

4.5 Section summary

- **Fixed charges** attach to assets (generally fixed assets) from **creation**.
- Floating charges have three characteristics.
  - A charge on a **class** of assets
  - The **class** is **changing from time to time**
  - The **company can deal** with the **assets** until the charge is enforced
- Floating charges **crystallise** (conversion into a fixed equitable charge) on the happening of certain relevant events.
- Floating charges rank behind a number of other creditors on liquidation.

Exam focus point

This is an important section for your exam. You should be aware of what fixed and floating charges are, and what the implications are of the differences between them.

5 Registration of charges

FAST FORWARD

In order to be valid and enforceable, a charge must be properly registered within 21days.

5.1 The registration process

Certain types of charges created by a company should be registered within **21 days** with the registrar: s 395 (1) and s 399 (1).

Charges securing a debenture issue and floating charges are specifically registrable: s 396 (1).

Other charges that are registrable include charges on:

- Uncalled share capital or calls made but not paid
- Land or any interest in land, but not rent or other periodic sums from the land
- Book debts
- Goodwill or any intellectual property
- Ships or aircraft or any share in a ship

Registration of a charge created or evidenced by an instrument which, if executed by an individual, would require registration as a **bill of sale** is also required.

The company is responsible for registering the charge but the charge may also be registered as a result of an application by another person interested in the charge.

The registrar should be sent **copies of the instrument** by which the charge is created or evidenced: s 395(1). The registrar also has to be sent **prescribed particulars of the charge**.

- The date when the charge was created
- The amount of the debt which it secures
- The property to which the charge applies
- The person entitled to it

Additional particulars may be included but this does not make them known by constructive notice to anyone unaware of them.

The registrar files the particulars in the companies charges register which he maintains (s 401) and notes the date of delivery. He also issues a certificate which is conclusive evidence that the charge had been duly registered.

Exam focus point

> Note that 15 September 2003 is now an important cut-off date in determining whether the holders of a floating charge may appoint an administrative receiver or not. This is explained in the section below on Administrative Receivers.

5.2 Delivery of inaccurate particulars

The law does not deal with this problem since the registrar's certificate carries a warranty that the registered particulars are accurate.

5.3 Delivery of further particulars

A mistake in registered particulars can only be ratified by **court order**, with the subsequent registration of a memorandum of satisfaction, if this:

- Involves a reduction in the amount secured, or
- The registration of a completely new charge, if the amount secured was increased or the property charged changed: s 404

5.4 Time period for delivery of particulars

The 21 day period for registration runs from the **creation** of the **charge**, or the acquisition of property charged, and not from the making of the loan for which the charge is security: s 395(1). Creation of a charge is usually effected by execution of a document. However, it may result from informal action.

5.5 The effect of non-delivery

We have seen that the duty to deliver particulars falls upon the company creating the charge and if no one delivers particulars within 21 days, the company is liable to a fine, as are its officers: s 399(3).

Non-delivery in the time period results in the **charge** being **void** against an administrator, liquidator or any creditor of a company.

Non-delivery of a charge means that the sum secured by it is payable forthwith on demand: s 395 (2).

5.6 Late delivery of particulars

The rules governing late delivery are the same as governing registration of further particulars, ie a **court order** is required for registration.

A charge can only be registered late if it is registered **'without prejudice to the rights of parties acquired prior to the time when the charge is actually registered'**. Therefore if a fixed charge is created but not presented for registration until nine months after it should have been, a fixed charge created and registered correctly during that nine month period will have priority over the earlier created charge: *Re Monolithic Building Co 1915*.

5.7 Register of charges

Every company is under an obligation to keep a copy of documents creating charges, and a register of other charges, at its registered office: s 406 (1) and 407 (3).

5.8 Section summary

- Floating charges and charges creating a debenture are registerable, along with many other charges.
- The registrar should be sent a **copy** of the charge together with **particulars** of it.
- The registrar issues a certificate which is conclusive evidence of registration.
- Charges should be registered within **21 days** of creation.
- **Non-delivery renders** the **charge void.**
- A **court order** is required for **late registration** to be allowed, or **further particulars** to be accepted.

Question — **Fixed and floating charges**

Discuss how fixed and floating charges differ, and the circumstances in which each type of charge might be used.

Answer

In company law a 'charge' of any type gives to the holder of the charge a priority claim to payment of what is owing to him out of the value of the property subject to the charge. As such the charge gives an advantage over the other creditors of the company who are postponed to the claim of the holder of the charge.

A **fixed charge** attaches at the moment of its creation to the relevant property. From then on the company cannot dispose of the property except subject to the charge. Few purchasers are willing to buy property if in doing so they also accept the burden of the existing charge, the liability to pay the company's debt. It normally happens that if the company wishes to sell property which is subject to a fixed charge it repays its debt out of the proceeds of sale and the creditor on receiving payment releases the property from his charge so that it passes unencumbered to the ownership of the purchaser.

This procedure is workable in connection with fixed assets which are not often sold. It would not generally be practicable to create a fixed charge over current assets which by their nature are constantly 'turned over', sold and replaced in the course of the company's business.

A company may however create a **floating charge** over any kind of asset, including current assets. A floating charge does not attach to the charged property at once and the company is free to dispose of the property unencumbered to a purchaser and also to create subsequent fixed charges over it (if the property subject to the floating charge is a fixed asset – as it may be).

The floating charge attaches to the property in various circumstances such as cessation of normal business, commencement of liquidation or default by the company in its obligations to the holder of the charge followed by intervention on his part. The floating charge is said to 'crystallise' in these cases and thereupon it attaches to whatever property of the type charged the company may then own.

A floating charge may be postponed to a subsequent fixed charge if the latter charge is created before the floating charge crystallises. A floating charge is also postponed to those unsecured debts of the company which are 'preferential' unless there are uncharged assets from which preferential debts can be paid: s 40 Insolvency Act 1986.The categories of preferential creditor are few under the Enterprise Act 2002 and comprise principally remuneration and holiday pay owed to employees.

The advantage of a floating charge is its potentially wide scope as it commonly extends to all property of the company. Its disadvantage is the uncertainty as to what property will remain when it crystallises and the risk that it will be postponed to other claims.

6 Administrative receivers

Key term

'An **administrative receiver'** is a receiver who is appointed under a floating charge extending over the whole or substantially the whole of the company's property.

He is in charge of the company's business, and he must be a qualified insolvency practitioner.

The secured creditor exercises a contractual power to appoint an administrative receiver when one of the specified 'trigger' events happen, such as failure to repay interest or profits falling below a certain level. However, he must first **demand repayment** in **writing** of the company's indebtedness and only on default can he appoint a receiver.

A receiver is appointed **in writing** and the appointment takes effect only if the person appointed accepts it not later than the next following day after the notice of appointment is delivered to him.

It is extremely important to note that the Enterprise Act 2002 amends the Insolvency Act 1986 by stating that 'the holder of a qualifying floating charge in respect of a company's property may **not** appoint an administrative receiver of the company'. **This means that the rules outlined above apply only in respect of charges registered prior to 15 September 2003.**

Exam focus point

Make sure that you read any question involving the insolvency of a company very carefully, as any dates given may be critical.

6.1 The effect of the administrative receiver's appointment

The immediate effect of any appointment of an administrative receiver is as follows.

(a) He **assumes control** of the **assets** subject to the charge and the directors' powers in respect of those assets are suspended during the receivership.

(b) Every **letter, order, invoice** etc issued by the company must state that a receiver has been appointed (for example, 'In receivership' on the letterheads): s 39 IA.

(c) If he is appointed by the court or by the debentureholders as their agent, not the company's, his appointment operates to **dismiss employees** of the company automatically (though he may re-engage them if he wishes).

(d) Any **floating charge crystallises**.

(e) Publicity. Within **28 days** of being appointed he must send a **notice** of his appointment to all known **creditors** of the company: s 46 IA. The company must send the administrative receiver a statement of affairs within 28 days: s 47 IA. This will show its assets and liabilities and its creditors.

(f) The receiver within **three months** sends a copy of a **statement** and of his comments on it (or of a summary) **to the registrar**, the company and the debentureholders (and also to the court if he was appointed by the court): s 48 IA. This must cover:

- The **events** leading up to his appointment
- Any **disposal** or proposed disposal of **assets**
- The **carrying** on of the company's **business**
- The amounts expected to be available to other creditors

He must also send a **copy** to **unsecured creditors** and convene a meeting where they can consider it.

6.2 Powers of an administrative receiver

An administrative receiver is automatically given a long list of **statutory powers**, unless the debenture provides to the contrary (Schedule 1 and s 42 IA). These include powers to carry on business, borrow money and sell property.

Unless appointed by the court, the receiver is an agent of the company unless or until it goes into liquidation: s 44 IA. As agent:

(a) He is **personally liable** on contracts made in the course of his duties as receiver.
(b) He is **entitled** to an **indemnity** for that liability out of the company's assets.
(c) He can **bind** the **company** by his acts.

6.3 Functions of the administrative receiver

The function of a receiver is to manage or to realise the assets which are the security with a view to paying out of those assets what is due to the debentureholders whom he represents (plus the expenses including his own remuneration). If he is able to discharge these debts he vacates his office of receiver and the directors resume full control.

The **directors** remain in office and can exercise such of their powers as have not passed to the receiver; for example, they may convene a general meeting for the purpose of resolving to wind up the company. They may also take action to **safeguard** the **property** and **interests** of the company, if the receiver is unable or unwilling to do so.

The general responsibility of the receiver is to the **debentureholders** rather than to the company even if he is formally an agent of the company. The company as principal cannot instruct him on the exercise of his powers.

The essential distinction between a receiver and a liquidator is that the **receiver** merely **represents** the **secured debentureholders** with control of the assets which are their security – his task is to obtain payment of what is owed to them alone. A **liquidator** is appointed to **realise all the assets**, to pay all the debts of the company and to distribute any **surplus** remaining to the shareholders.

6.4 Priority of claims in receivership

The order of application of assets in the hands of the receiver is as follows.

(a) **Payment** of **expenses** of **selling property** or other realisation

(b) The **receiver's expenses** and his claims (if any) against the company under his indemnity; creditors to whom he is personally liable are subrogated to his rights against the company (if he becomes bankrupt), and so their claims come in at this point

(c) Any **expenses** of the **debenture trust deed** including the trustee's remuneration and the costs (if any) of an application to the court to appoint the receiver

(d) **Preferential debts** (if the charge was created as a floating one: s 40 IA)

(e) The **capital** and **interest** of the secured debt

6.5 Official receiver appointed by the court

If the debenture does not give adequate power to appoint a receiver (or to vest him with powers of management) the debentureholders (or their trustee) may apply to the court to appoint the official receiver with appropriate powers: s 32 IA. The court will only make the appointment if:

- **Principal** or **interest** on the **debenture** is in **arrears**
- The **company** has **begun** to be **wound up**
- The **security** is in **jeopardy**

The official receiver appointed by the court is **not** an agent of the debentureholders nor of the company. He is an **officer** of the **court** whose remuneration is fixed by the court (to be paid by the company). As an officer of the court he has its authority for what he does and it may be contempt of court to obstruct him.

6.6 Other circumstances in which an administrative receiver may be appointed

Besides the exception regarding floating charges **registered prior to 15 September 2003**, there are a number of other instances where a qualifying floating charge holder (QFCH) may continue to appoint an administrative receiver. These are where the floating charges relate to:

- A capital market arrangement of £50 million or more involving the use of a capital market investment
- A public-private partnership
- A utility project for a regulated business
- A financed project of a 'project company'
- A 'market-charge', 'system-charge' or 'collateral security charge'
- A registered social landlord

7 Administration

Key term

An **administration order** is an order of the court which puts an **insolvency practitioner** in **control** of the company with a defined programme.

Its effect is to **insulate** the company **from its creditors.** Its principal purpose is company rescue (as a going concern).

Exam focus point

Do not confuse an administration order with an administrative receiver. They are mutually exclusive.

- An administration order is applied for by parties to freeze debt collection, sometimes called a moratorium.
- An administrative receiver is appointed by secured creditors to manage a company's assets under a charge

7.1 Advantages of an administration order

The advantages **over a liquidation** are:

- It does not result in the company being dissolved

The advantages **over appointment of an administrative receiver are:**

- Any creditor can apply for an administration order, not just secured creditors
- It prevents any creditor applying for a compulsory liquidation
- An administrator may challenge past transactions of the company

7.1.1 Administration orders and receiverships are mutually exclusive

Anyone petitioning for an administration order must give notice of the fact to anyone who is entitled to put in a receiver or to anyone who has actually put one in. The secured creditor on receiving the notice can then appoint a receiver. If he does, an administration order cannot be made.

If a **receiver is already in place** and the secured creditor does not consent to that receiver stepping down, then again **an administration order cannot be made**. On the other hand once an administration order is made it will no longer be possible for a creditor to appoint a receiver.

7.1.2 Administration orders and liquidations are mutually exclusive

Once a **winding up resolution has been passed** or the court has ordered the company to be wound up, an **administration order can no longer be made**. On the other hand once an administration order has been made it will no longer be possible to petition the court for a winding up order.

7.1.3 What is administration?

Administration is an insolvency process by which an insolvent company can apply to have an insolvency practitioner appointed to run the company while it works out a programme to rescue the company. The company is insulated from its creditors during the process.

While administration as a concept existed prior to the Enterprise Act 2002 the law relating to administration (previously set out in Part II of the Insolvency Act 1986) has been completely replaced.

7.2 Purpose of administration

The overriding purpose of administration under the Enterprise Act 2002 is **company rescue** as a going concern. There are in total three objectives which are hierarchical:

(a) Company rescue is primary purpose

(b) If that is not possible, or if the second objective would better benefit the creditors as a whole, the administrator may seek to obtain a better result than an immediate winding-up would produce. For example, he may trade on for a while and then look for a sale as a going concern.

(c) Only if these both fail may the administrator realise property in order to make a distribution.

Under the older legislation, the administrator had to state in advance which one of four specified purposes he was going to pursue. Now it is assumed that he will not seek to realise property unless he can explain why the first two objectives are not possible.

7.3 Appointment of an administrator by the court

Any of the following parties or a combination may apply to the court to obtain an administration order for the company:

- The company
- The directors of the company
- One or more creditors of the company
- The Justices' Chief Executive of the Magistrates' Court following non-payment of a fine imposed on the company.

You should note that **individual shareholders** of the company **may not apply** for an administration order. The company may apply if more than 50% of the shareholders agree (this majority can be varied by the articles of association).

The court may grant the administration order if it is satisfied that:

- The company is, or is likely to be, unable to pay its debts; and
- The administration order is reasonably likely to achieve the purposes of administration

The application for administration order will name a person whom the applicants want to be appointed administrator. Subject to any objection by interested parties (discussed below) the court will appoint this person to be administrator if they grant the order.

7.4 Appointment of administrator by floating chargeholder

Although for floating charges registered after 15 September 2003, the holders will not be allowed to appoint an administrative receiver to realise their debt, they are now allowed to **appoint an administrator without application to the court**.

The floating chargeholder must hold a floating charge which entitles him to appoint an administrator and the charge must relate to the whole or substantially the whole of the company's property. In practice, in the majority of cases, such floating charges are held by banks.

The floating chargeholder may not so appoint an administrator if:

- He has not given 2 days written notice to the holder of any prior floating charge where that person has the right to appoint an administrator unless that chargeholder has consented to the appointment
- His floating charge is not enforceable
- The company is in liquidation
- A provisional liquidator has been appointed under s135 Insolvency Act 1986
- An administrative receiver is already in office
- An administrator is already in office

After any relevant two day notice period (see above), the floating chargeholder will file the following documents at court:

- A notice of appointment identifying the administrator in the prescribed form
- A statement by the administrator that he consents to the appointment

- A statement by the administrator that, in his opinion, the purpose of the administration is likely to be achieved
- A statutory declaration by the floating chargeholder that he qualifies to make the appointment

Once these documents have been filed, the appointment is valid. The appointer must notify the administrator and other people prescribed by regulation of the appointment as soon as is reasonably practicable.

7.5 Appointment of an administrator by the company or its directors

The process by which a company may commence the procedure to appoint an administrator will depend upon its own procedures in the articles of association. Some companies may wish to amend the articles of association to set out a procedure for so doing.

A company or its directors may appoint an administrator if:

- They have not done so in the last 12 months or been subject to a moratorium as a result of a voluntary arrangement with its creditors in the last 12 months
- The company is, or is likely to be, unable to pay its debts
- No petition for winding up nor any administration petition in respect of the company has been presented to the court and is outstanding
- The company is not in liquidation or provisional liquidation
- No administrator is already in office
- No administrative receiver is already in office

The company or its directors must give five days notice to any floating chargeholders entitled to appoint an administrative receiver or an administrator.

This means that the **floating chargeholders may** appoint their own administrator within this time period, so **block the company's choice of administrator**, or, if the debt arrangement is pre-Enterprise Act 2002, **block the administration process** entirely by appointing an administrative receiver.

Once the five day notice period is over, the company or its directors must, as soon as reasonably practicable, file at court:

- The notice identifying the proposed administrator in the prescribed form
- A statutory declaration that:
  - The company is, or is unlikely to be, unable to pay its debts
  - The company is not in liquidation
  - As far as the person making the statement can ascertain there is no restriction in making the appointment

If the chargeholder consents, does not reply or does not appoint their own administrator, the appointer must make the appointment within 10 business days. They must also file a notice of appointment at court, which includes:

- A notice identifying the administrator in the prescribed form
- A statement by the administrator that he consents to the appointment and that in his opinion the purposes of administration are reasonably likely to be achieved
- A statutory declaration that the appointer is entitled to appoint and that the appointment is in accordance with the Schedule to the Insolvency Act 1986.

7.6 Effect of administrator appointment

There are various effects of the appointment of an administrator:

Effects of appointment	
By any method	A **moratorium** over the company's debts commences (that is, no creditor can enforce the debt during the administration period without the court's permission). This is the advantageous aspect of being in administration. The court must give its permission for: • Security over company property to be enforced • Goods held under hire purchase to be repossessed • A landlord to conduct forfeiture by peaceable entry • Commencement/continuation of any legal process against the company The powers of management are subjugated to the authority of the administrator and they can only act with his consent.
By court order	All outstanding **petitions for winding-up** of the company are **dismissed**. Any **administrative receiver** in place must **vacate office**. You should note, however, that the court cannot agree to an administration order unless any such administrative receiver agrees, or the floating charge under which he has been appointed is invalid.
By floating charge holder	All outstanding **petitions for winding-up** of the company are **suspended**.

You should note that the **directors/company cannot apply** out of court for an administration order **when a winding up petition has been presented** at court. This is so that the directors/company do not try to use administration as a way of avoiding or delaying a winding up procedure being commenced.

7.7 Interim moratorium

An interim moratorium will also exist where:

- An administration application has been issued but not heard by the court
- An order has been granted but has not yet taken effect
- Notice of intention to appoint an administrator has been filed at court

Such an interim moratorium does not prevent an administrative receiver being appointed, nor does it prevent a floating chargeholder from appointing an administrator, nor a winding up petition being presented.

7.8 Duties of the administrator

The administrator is an **agent of the company**. He therefore owes fiduciary duties to the company. He also has the following legal duties:

Duties of the administrator
As soon as **reasonably practicable** after appointment he must:
• Send notice of his appointment to the company
• Publish notice of his appointment
• Obtain a list of company creditors and sent notice of appointment to each
• Within 7 days of appointment, send notice of appointment to Registrar of Companies

- Require certain relevant people to provide a **statement of affairs** of the company
- Ensure that every **business document** of the company **bears the identity** of the administrator and a statement that the affairs, business and property of the company are being managed by him.
- Consider the statements of affairs submitted to him and set out his **proposals** for achieving the aim of administration. His proposals must be **sent to the Registrar of Companies**, the company's **creditors** and made available to **every member of the company** as soon as is reasonably practicable, and **within eight weeks**.

The **statement of affairs** must be provided by the people from whom it is requested within 11 days of it being requested. It is in a prescribed form, and contains:

- Details of the company's property
- The company's debts and liabilities
- The names and addresses of the company's creditors
- Details of any security held by any creditor.

Failing to provide a statement of affairs, or providing a statement in which the writer has no reasonable belief of truth is a criminal offence punishable by fine.

7.9 Administrator's proposals and powers

The administrator must either set out his proposals for achieving the aim of the administration, or must set out why he does not consider it reasonable and practicable that the company be rescued. If the latter, and appropriate, he will also set out why the creditors as a whole would benefit from winding up.

The proposal must not affect the right of a secured creditor to enforce his security, result in preferential debt being paid otherwise than in priority to non-preferential debt or result in one preferential creditor being paid a smaller proportion of his debt than another.

The administrator must call a meeting of creditors within 10 weeks of his appointment to approve his proposals. The creditors may either accept or reject the proposals.

Creditors meeting	
Approve the proposals, or modify them with the administrator's consent	The administrator must then report the decision to the Court and the Registrar of Companies. Once the proposals have been agreed, the administrator cannot make any substantial amendment without first gaining the creditors' consent.
Reject the proposals	If the proposals are rejected, the court can order: • The administrator's appointment ceases to have effect • An adjournment • An interim order on a suspended winding-up petition • Any order it sees fit

7.9.1 Administrator's powers

The powers of the administrator are summed up in s 59 (1):

> 'The administrator of a company may do anything necessarily expedient for the management of the affairs, business and property of the company.'

The administrator takes on the powers previously enjoyed by the directors and the following specific powers to:

- Remove or appoint a director
- Call a meeting of members or creditors
- Apply to court for directions regarding the carrying out of his functions
- Make payments to secured or preferential creditor
- With the permission of the court, payments to unsecured creditors

Although the administrator with usually require the permission of the court to make payments to unsecured creditors, it is possible not to if the administrator feels that to pay the unsecured creditor will assist the achievement of the administration (for example, if the company has been denied further supplies by a major supplier unless payment is tendered).

Any creditor or member of the company may apply to the court if they feel that the administrator has acted or will act in a way that has harmed or will harm his interest. The court may take various actions against the administrator.

7.10 End of administration

The administration period ends when:

- The administration has been successful
- Twelve months have elapsed from the date of the appointment of administrator
- The administrator applies to the court to end the appointment
- A creditor applies to the court to end the appointment
- A public-interest winding up petition is granted

The administrator automatically vacates office after 12 months of his appointment. This time period can be expended by court order or by consent from the appropriate creditors.

Alternatively, the administrator may apply to the court when he thinks:

- The purpose of administration cannot be achieved
- The company should not have entered into administration
- The administration has been successful (if appointed by the court)

He must also apply to the court if required to by the creditor's meeting.

Where the administrator was appointed by a chargeholder or the company/its directors, when he feels that the purposes of administration have been achieved, he must file a notice with the court and the Registrar of Companies.

8 Avoidance of floating charges

Liquidation automatically renders void, under s 245, any floating charge created within the period of 12 months (or in the case where the charge was created in favour of a 'connected person', two years) subject to the following exceptions.

(a) The charge is **valid** if the company was **solvent** at the time when the charge was created, unless as a result of the transaction under which the charge was created the company became unable to pay its debts. This exception does not apply where the charge was created in favour of a **'connected person'**. Note that a company is not solvent unless it can pay its **debts in full** as they fall **due**.

(b) If the company was not solvent at the time the charge was created, the floating charge is still valid to the extent of **money paid** or **goods and services** received by the company at the same time or after the charge is created, or discharge or reduction of the company's liability.

Only the charge (as security), not the debt, becomes void: s 247.

9 Transactions at an undervalue and preferences

When a company goes into liquidation the court may avoid transactions at an undervalue and preferences.

A transaction **'at an undervalue'** is a gift or a transaction in the two years previous to liquidation (or administration), by which the company gives consideration of greater value than it receives, for instance a sale at less than full market price: s 238. However, such a transaction does not become void if the company enters into it:

- In **good faith**
- For the **purpose of carrying on its business**
- **Believing on reasonable grounds** that it will benefit the company

A company **'gives preference'** to a creditor or guarantor of its debts if it does anything by which his position will be benefited if the company goes into insolvent liquidation *and* the company does this with the intention of producing that result: s 239.

If at the time of the undervalue or preference the company was unable to pay its debts, or became so by reason of the transaction, and the company later goes into liquidation or administration, the liquidator or the administrator can apply to the court for an order to restore the position to what it would have been if no such transaction had taken place.

The relevant period which brings the avoidance powers into operation in relation to a transaction are as follows.

- **Undervalues two years** before the commencement of liquidation
- **Preferences**
  - With a person **unconnected** with the company **six months** before the commencement of liquidation
  - With a person **connected** with the company **two years** prior to commencement

Unless the person in whose favour the undervalue or preference operates is connected with the company, the company must be **insolvent** at the time of entering into the disputed transaction, or must have become so in consequence of it, if it is to be disputed by the court.

If the court is satisfied that a preference has been given it can (under s 241):

- **Order return** of **property** or of the proceeds of its sale
- **Discharge any security** given
- **Order payment** in respect of benefit to the liquidator
- **Renew guarantee obligations** discharged by the preference
- **Charge property**

The term 'connected persons' appears in the law both in the context of preferences and transactions at an undervalue and also in relation to floating charges. A person is **'connected'** with the company if he is:

- A **director** or **shadow director** (see chapter on directors) of the company
- An **associate** of a director, shadow director or the company itself

These provisions are summarised below.

Transaction with		Transactions at an undervalue	Preference
Unconnected person	Time period before commencement	2 years	6 months
	Company insolvent at that time?	Yes	Yes
Connected person	Time period before commencement	2 years	2 years
	Company insolvent at that time?	Yes	No

Chapter roundup

- In this chapter we have discussed the formalities governing a company's borrowing. **Debentures** are important instruments of borrowing, and the security companies give in the form of **charges** supports debentures.
- A **debenture** is a document stating the terms on which a company has borrowed money. There are three main types.
  - A **single debenture**
  - **Debentures issued as a series** and usually registered
  - **Debenture stock** subsidised by a large number of lenders. Only this form requires a **debenture trust deed**, although the others may often incorporate one
- A **secured** debentureholder may enforce the security if the company defaults on payment of interest or repayment of capital.
  - He may take possession of the asset subject to the charge and sell it.
  - He may apply to the court for its transfer to his ownership by a foreclosure order.
  - He may appoint a receiver of it (which is the usual first step).
- A charge over the assets of a company gives a creditor a **prior claim** over other creditors to payment of his debt out of these assets.
- Charges may be either **fixed**, which attach to the relevant asset on creation, or **floating**, which attach on 'crystallisation'. For this reason it is not possible to identify the assets to which a **floating** charge relates (until **crystallisation**).
- A **floating charge** has been defined as:
  - A charge on a **class** of assets, present and future
  - Which class **changes from time to time** in the **ordinary course of business**
  - Until the **charge** is enforced, the company can deal with the **charged assets**
- On liquidation a **fixed charge** on assets has preference. Assets subject to a **floating charge** may be used to settle **preferential debts** and a proportion of the assets are also ring-fenced for the benefit of unsecured creditors.
- **Administration** is a stay of execution. It is designed to have the principal objective of company rescue as a going concern. A moratorium is imposed by the court on creditors' actions against the company in order to achieve certain objectives.
- A **transaction at an undervalue** is a gift or a transaction in the two years before liquidation or administration, by which the company gives consideration of greater value than it received: s 238 IA. Such a transaction is **void** unless the company acted in good faith and for the purpose of carrying on its business, and believed on reasonable grounds that it would benefit the company.
- A company gives **preference** to a creditor or to a guarantor of its debts if it acts so as to benefit that person's position if the company goes into insolvent liquidation *and* does so with the intention of producing that result: s 239 IA. The transaction will be void if it was created within the 6 months before the commencement of liquidation.

Quick quiz

1 Which of the following are correct statements about the relationship between a company's ordinary shares and its debentures.

A Debentures do not confer voting rights, whilst ordinary shares do.
B The company's duty is to pay interest on debentures, and to pay dividends on ordinary shares.
C Interest paid on debentures is deducted from pre-tax profits, share dividends are paid from net profits.
D A debentureholder takes priority over a member in liquidation.

2 What are the elements of the definition of a floating charge?

3 Company law requires a company to maintain a register of charges, but not a register of debentureholders.

True ☐

False ☐

4 In which of the following situations will crystallisation of a floating charge occur?

A Liquidation of the company
B Disposal by the company of the charged asset
C Cessation of the company's business
D After the giving of notice by the chargee if the contract so provides
E The appointment of an administrative receiver

5 Certain types of charges need to be registered within 28 days of creation.

True ☐

False ☐

6 Certain transactions may be avoided if they occur within a certain time period of insolvency. Match the time period with the transaction.

(a)	Floating charge in favour of an unconnected person	(i)	6 months
(b)	Transaction at an undervalue	(ii)	1 year
(c)	Preference in favour of an unconnected person	(iii)	2 years

7 What particulars of a charge must the Registrar be sent when the charge is registered?

8 What steps can a secured debentureholder take to enforce his security?

Answers to quick quiz

1 A, C and D are correct. Whilst the company has a contractual duty to pay interest on debentures, there is no necessity for it to pay dividends on shares. B is therefore incorrect.

2 The charge is:

(a) A charge on a class of assets, present and future

(b) Which class is in the ordinary course of the company's business changing from time to time

(c) Until the holders enforce the charge, the company may carry on business and deal with the assets charged

3 True

4 A, C, D and E are true. As the charge does not attach to the asset until crystallisation, B is untrue.

5 False. Certain charges such as charges securing a debenture issue and floating charges need to be registered within 21 days.

6 Floating charge in favour of an unconnected person *1 year*
Transaction at an undervalue *2 years*
Preference in favour of an unconnected person *6 months*

7 A copy of the charge
The date that the charge was created
The amount of the debt which it secures
The property to which the charge applies
The person entitled to it

8 Take possession of the asset subject to the charge
Sell it
Apply to the court for a transfer to his ownership
Appoint a receiver of it

Now try the question below from the Exam Question Bank

Number	Level	Marks	Time
Q22	Examination	10	18 mins

22

Liquidation

Topic list	Syllabus reference
1 Liquidation	10
2 Compulsory liquidation	10(b)
3 Voluntary liquidation	10(a)
4 Differences between compulsory and voluntary liquidation	10(b)
5 Revision: Insolvency situations	10

Introduction

In Chapter 21 we introduced two debenture-holder remedies against a company

- Petition the court for a compulsory liquidation
- Petition the court for an administration order

A secured debenture-holder may also appoint a receiver to take charge of the secured asset. In this chapter we will continue to consider the effects of financial difficulties on a company.

A company in financial difficulties may

- Be **liquidated**, which will result in the company being dissolved
- Go into **administration**, which allows a liquidator to take measures to 'save' the company from liquidation.

There are different types of liquidation

- Voluntary liquidation by members or creditors
- Compulsory liquidation

This chapter will explore what each types of liquidation means the what the procedures for the company are.

Introduction (cont)

In the previous chapter we discussed why administration is often considered a good alternative to liquidation, and what the procedures for a company in administration are.

However, it is important to note that **a company does not have to be in financial difficulties to go into liquidation**. Sometimes the members may choose to liquidate a company for other reasons.

This chapter looks at the end of the life of a company. It would be examined in conjunction with many areas of company law, for example:

- The initial decision to incorporate
- Directors, fraudulent and wrongful trading
- Financing

It could therefore be examined in either part of the paper.

Statutory references in this chapter are to the Insolvency Act 1986 (as amended by the Insolvency Act 1994 and the Insolvency Act 2000) unless stated otherwise.

1 Liquidation 6/02, 6/04

FAST FORWARD

There are three types of liquidation:

– Compulsory winding up
– Members' voluntary winding up
– Creditors' voluntary winding up

Key term

Liquidation means that the company must be dissolved and its affairs 'wound up', or brought to an end.

The assets are realised, debts are paid out of the proceeds, and any surplus amounts are returned to members. Liquidation leads on to dissolution of the company. It is sometimes referred to as **winding up**.

Liquidation begins with a formal decision to liquidate.

If the members in general meeting resolve to wind up the company that is a voluntary winding up. This may be either a members' or a creditors' **voluntary** winding up, depending on whether the directors believe that the company will or will not be able to pay its debts in full. Voluntary winding up is considered in more detail in section 3.

Creditors must have a decisive part in the liquidation of an insolvent company since the remaining assets belong to them, and hence insolvent companies which make the decision to liquidate undergo winding up in a creditors' voluntary liquidation.

Although voluntary liquidation is simpler, quicker and less expensive, it is possible only if a majority of votes is cast in general meeting on a resolution to liquidate.

A company may, however, be obliged to wind up by a **compulsory** liquidation, ordered by the court on a petition usually presented by a creditor or a member.

Whether liquidation is voluntary or compulsory it is in the hands of the liquidator (or joint liquidators), who take over control of the company from its directors.

1.1 Liquidator

The office of liquidator must be filled by an **authorised insolvency practitioner**: s 230 IA. This authorisation is issued by either the professional body to which the practitioner belongs or by a licensing board administered by the DTI. Only persons who are:

- Fit and proper, and
- Up to the required standard in respect of education, practical training and experience

will receive such authorisation: s 390.

1.2 Liquidator's reports on directors

The liquidator now has a **statutory duty to report** on the directors of the insolvent company to the Secretary of State where he considers that any **director is unfit to be concerned in the management** of a company: s 7 CDDA.

1.3 Common features of all types of liquidation

Although liquidation may begin in different ways and there are differences of procedure the working method is much the same in every type of liquidation and the same legal problems can arise. In particular, the following occur at the onset of any liquidation.

- **No** further **share dealings** or **changes in membership** will be permitted (unless the court sanctions a rectification or other change).
- All invoices, orders, letters and other company documents must state prominently that the company is in liquidation.
- The **directors' power** to manage **ceases**.

2 Compulsory liquidation

As discussed in Chapter 18, a **creditor** may apply to the court for a compulsory winding up. There are seven statutory reasons he can give, which can all be found in s122 of the Act. We shall consider the two most important here.

	Statutory reasons for compulsory liquidation
s122(1)(f)	Company is unable to pay its debts
s122(1)(g)	It is just and equitable to wind up the company

The **DTI** may petition for the compulsory winding up of a company:

- If a public company has not obtained a s177, trading certificate within one year of incorporation
- Following a report by DTI inspectors that it is in the public interest and just and equitable for the company to be wound up.

2.1 Company unable to pay its debts

A creditor who petitions on the grounds of the company's insolvency may rely on any of three situations to show (as he is required to do) that the company is unable to pay its debts: s 123.

(a) A **creditor** (or creditors) **to whom the company owes more than £750 serves** on the company at its registered office a **written demand** for payment and the **company neglects**, within the next **21 clear days**, either to **pay the debt** or to offer reasonable security for it.

If the company denies it owes the amount demanded on apparently reasonable grounds, the court will dismiss the petition and leave the creditor to take legal proceedings for debt.

(b) A creditor obtains judgement against the company for debt, and attempts to enforce the judgement but is unable to obtain payment, because no assets of the company have been found and seized.

(c) A creditor satisfies the court that, taking into account the contingent and prospective liabilities of the company, it is unable to pay its debts. The creditor may be able to show this in one of two way, by proof that:

- The company cannot pay its debts as they fall due – the **commercial insolvency test**
- The company's assets are less than its liabilities – the **balance sheet test**.

This is a residual category. Any suitable evidence of actual or prospective insolvency may be produced.

2.2 The just and equitable ground

The just and equitable ground was discussed in Chapter 19. It is usually relied on by a member (contributory) who is dissatisfied with the directors or controlling shareholders over the management of the company.

It must be shown that **no** other remedy is available: s 125(2). Each decision is linked closely to the particular facts of the case.

The cases outlining reasons for fair and equitable winding up are outlined on page 320.

Reasons for just and equitable winding up	
Object of the company has finished	*Re German Date Coffee Co 1882*
Management deadlock	*Re Yenidje Tobacco Co Ltd 1916*
Quasi-partnership breaks down	*Ebrahimi v Westbourne Galleries 1973*

2.3 Proceedings for compulsory liquidation

When a petition is presented to the court a copy is delivered to the company in case it objects. It is advertised so that other creditors may intervene if they wish.

The petition **may** be presented by a member. If the petition is presented by **a member** he **must show** that:

(a) The company is **solvent** or alternatively refuses to supply information of its financial position. (The court will not order compulsory liquidation on a member's petition if he has nothing to gain from it. If the company is insolvent he would receive nothing since the creditors then take all the assets,) and

(b) He has been a registered shareholder for at least six of the 18 months up to the date of his petition. However this rule is not applied if the petitioner acquired his shares by allotment direct from the company or by inheritance from a deceased member or if the petition is based on the number of members having fallen below two: s 124.

2.3.1 Provisional liquidator

Once the court has been petitioned, a provisional liquidator may be appointed by the court: s 135. The **official receiver** is usually appointed, and his powers are conferred by the court. These usually extend to taking control of the company's property and applying for a special manager to be appointed: ss 144 and 177.

Key term

The **official receiver** is an officer of the court. He/she is appointed as liquidator of any company ordered to be wound up by the court, although an insolvency practitioner may replace him/her.

2.4 Effects of an order for compulsory liquidation

The effects of the **order**, which may be made some time after a provisional liquidator is appointed, are as follows.

(a) The **official receiver** (an official of the DTI whose duties relate mainly to bankruptcy of individuals) **becomes liquidator**: s 136.

(b) The liquidation is **deemed to have commenced at the time** (possibly several months earlier) **when the petition was first presented**.

(c) Any **disposition** of the **company's property** and any transfer of its shares subsequent to the commencement of liquidation is **void** unless the court orders otherwise: s 127.

(d) Any **legal proceedings** in progress against the company are halted (and none may thereafter begin) unless the court gives leave. Any seizure of the company's assets after commencement of liquidation is void: ss 130 and 128.

(e) The **employees** of the company are **automatically dismissed**. The provisional liquidator assumes the powers of management previously held by the directors.

(f) Any **floating charge crystallises**.

The assets of the company may remain the company's legal property but under the liquidator's control unless the court by order vests the assets in the liquidator.

The business of the company may continue but it is the liquidator's duty to continue it with a view only to realisation, for instance by sale as a going concern.

Within 21 days of the making of the order for winding up (or of the appointment of a provisional liquidator) a **statement of affairs** must be delivered to the liquidator (official receiver) verified by one or more directors and by the secretary (and possibly by other persons). The statement shows the assets and liabilities of the company and includes a list of creditors with particulars of any security: s 131.

The official receiver may require that any officers or employees concerned in the recent management of the company shall join in submitting the statement of affairs.

2.4.1 Investigations by the official receiver

The official receiver **must investigate** (s 132):

- The causes of the failure of the company, and
- Generally the promotion, formation, business dealings and affairs of the company.

The official receiver **may report** to the court on the results.

(a) The official receiver may require the public examination in open court of those believed to be implicated (a much feared sanction).

(b) Further, the official receiver is now empowered to apply to the court for public examination where half the creditors or three-quarters of the contributories (in value in either case) so request: s 133. Failure to attend, or reasonable suspicion that the examinees will abscond, may lead to arrest and detention in custody for contempt of court: s 134. Meetings of contributories and creditors

Key term

Contributories are members of a company.

At winding up, the member may have to make payments to the company in respect of any unpaid share capital or guarantees (see Chapter 10).

The official receiver has 12 weeks to decide whether or not to convene separate meetings of creditors and contributories. The meetings provide the creditors and contributories with the opportunity to appoint their own nominee as permanent liquidator to replace the official receiver, and a liquidation committee to work with the liquidator.

If the official receiver believes there is little interest and that the creditors will be unlikely to appoint a liquidator he can dispense with a meeting, informing the court, the creditors and the contributories of the decision. He can always be required to call a meeting if at least 25 per cent in value of the creditors require him to do so: s 136.

If no meeting is held, or one is held but no liquidator appointed, the official receiver continues to act as liquidator. If the creditors do hold a meeting and appoint their own nominee he automatically becomes liquidator subject to a right of objection to the court: s 139. Any person appointed to act as liquidator must be a qualified insolvency practitioner.

At any time after a winding up order is made, **the official receiver may ask the Secretary of State to appoint a liquidator** (who would be a qualified insolvency practitioner). Similarly, he may request an appointment if the creditors and members fail to appoint a liquidator: s 137.

If separate meetings of creditors and contributories are held and those meetings nominate different persons to act as liquidators, it is the **creditors' nominee** who **takes precedence**, subject again to a right of objection to the court: s139(4).

Notice of the order for compulsory liquidation and of the appointment of a liquidator is given to the registrar and in the **London Gazette**.

If, while the liquidation is in progress, the liquidator decides to call meetings of contributories or creditors he may arrange to do so under powers vested in the court: s 195.

2.5 Completion of compulsory liquidation

When the liquidator completes his task he reports to the DTI, which examines his accounts. He may apply to the court for an order for dissolution of the company.

An official receiver may also apply to the registrar of companies for an early dissolution of the company if its realisable assets will not cover his expenses and further investigation is not required: s 202.

Question — Compulsory liquidation order

What are the six effects of a compulsory liquidation order?

Answer

- Official receiver appointed as liquidator
- Liquidation deemed to have commenced at time when petition first presented
- Disposition of company property since commencement of liquidation deemed void
- Legal proceedings against the company are halted
- Employees are dismissed
- Any floating charge crystallises

3 Voluntary liquidation **6/04**

There are two types of voluntary liquidation

- A **members' voluntary winding up**, where the company is **solvent** and the members merely decide to 'kill it off'
- A **creditors' voluntary winding up**, where the company is **insolvent** and the members resolve to wind up in consultation with creditors.

The main differences between a members' and a creditors' voluntary winding up are set out below.

Function	Winding up	
	Members'	Creditors'
(1) Appointment of liquidator	By members	Normally by creditors though responsible to both members and creditors
(2) Approval for liquidator's actions	General meeting of members	Liquidation committee
(3) Liquidation committee	None	Up to 5 representatives of creditors and 5 representatives of members

The effect of the voluntary winding up being a creditors' one is that the creditors have a decisive influence on the conduct of the liquidation.

Meetings in a creditors' voluntary winding up are held in the same sequence as in a members' voluntary winding up but meetings of creditors are called at the same intervals as the meetings of members and for similar purposes: ss 105 – 106.

In both kinds of voluntary winding up, the court has the power to appoint a liquidator (if for some reason there is none acting) or to remove one liquidator and appoint another: s 108.

3.1 Members' voluntary liquidation

	Type of resolution to be passed
Ordinary	This is **rare**. If the articles specify liquidation at a certain point, only an ordinary resolution is required
Special	A company may resolve to be wound up by special resolution
Extraordinary	If a company cannot continue in business due to its liabilities it may resolve to be wound up by extraordinary resolution This allows the company to go into liquidation on 14 days notice.

The winding up commences on the passing of the resolution. A signed copy of the resolution must be delivered to the registrar within 15 days. A liquidator is usually appointed by the same resolution (or a second resolution passed at the same time).

3.1.1 Declaration of solvency

A voluntary winding up is a members' voluntary winding up **only** if the directors make and deliver to the registrar a **declaration of solvency**: s 89.

This is a statutory declaration that the directors have made full enquiry into the affairs of the company and are of the opinion that it will be able to pay its debts, together with interest (at the rate applicable under s 189(4)) on those debts, in full, within a specified period not exceeding 12 months.

(a) The declaration is made by all the directors or, if there are more than two directors, by a **majority** of them.

(b) The declaration includes a statement of the company's assets and liabilities as at the latest practicable date before the declaration is made.

(c) The declaration must be:

- Made not more than five weeks before the resolution to wind up is passed, and
- Delivered to the registrar within 15 days after the meeting: s 89.

If the liquidator later concludes that the company will be unable to pay its debts he must call a meeting of creditors and lay before them a statement of assets and liabilities: s 95.

It is a **criminal offence** punishable by fine or imprisonment for a director to make a declaration of solvency without having **reasonable grounds** for it – if the company proves to be insolvent he will have to justify his previous declaration or be punished.

In a members' voluntary winding up the **creditors play no part** since the assumption is that their debts will be paid in full. The liquidator calls special and annual general meetings of contributories to whom he reports:

(a) Within three months after each anniversary of the commencement of the winding up the liquidator must call a meeting and lay before it an account of his transactions during the year: s 93.

(b) When the liquidation is complete the liquidator calls a meeting to lay before it his final accounts: s 94.

After holding the final meeting the liquidator sends a copy of his accounts to the registrar who dissolves the company three months later by removing its name from the register: s 201.

3.2 Creditors' voluntary liquidation

If no declaration of solvency is made and delivered to the registrar the liquidation proceeds as a creditors' voluntary winding up even if in the end the company pays its debts in full: s 96.

To commence a creditors' voluntary winding up the directors convene a general meeting of members to pass an **extraordinary resolution**. They must also convene a meeting of creditors: (s 98), giving at least seven days notice of this meeting. The notice must be advertised in the **London Gazette** and two local newspapers. The notice must either:

- Give the name and address of a qualified insolvency practitioner to whom the creditors can apply before the meeting for information about the company, **or**

- State a place in the locality of the company's principal place of business where, on the two business days before the meeting, a list of creditors can be inspected.

The meeting of members is held first and its business is as follows:

- To resolve to wind up: s 98
- To appoint a liquidator, and
- To nominate up to five representatives to be members of the liquidation committee: s 101.

The creditors' meeting should preferably be convened on the same day at a later time than the members' meeting, or on the next day, but in any event within fourteen days of it: s 98.

One of the directors presides at the creditors' meeting and lays before it a full statement of the company's affairs and a list of creditors with the amounts owing to them. The meeting may nominate a liquidator and up to five representatives to be members of the liquidation committee.

If the creditors nominate a different person to be liquidator, their choice prevails over the nomination by the members.

Of course, the creditors may decide not to appoint a liquidator at all. They cannot be compelled to appoint a liquidator, and if they do fail to appoint one it will be the members' nominee who will take office.

However even if creditors do appoint a liquidator there is a period of up to two weeks before the creditors' meeting takes place at which they will actually make the appointment. In the interim it will be the members' nominee who takes office as liquidator.

In either case the presence of the members' nominee as liquidator has been exploited in the past for the purpose known as **'centrebinding'**.

> *Re Centrebind Ltd 1966*
> *The facts:* The directors convened a general meeting, without making a statutory declaration of solvency, but failed to call a creditors' meeting for the same or the next day. The penalty for this was merely a small default fine (at present a maximum of £200). The liquidator chosen by the members had disposed of the assets before the creditors could appoint a liquidator. The creditors' liquidator challenged the sale of the assets (at a low price) as invalid.
>
> *Decision:* The first liquidator had been in office when he made the sale and so it was a valid exercise of the normal power of sale.

In a 'centrebinding' transaction the assets are sold by an obliging liquidator to a new company formed by the members of the insolvent company – in order to defeat the claims of the creditors at minimum cost and enable the same people to continue in business until the next insolvency supervenes.

The government has sought to limit the abuses during the period between the members' and creditors' meetings. The powers of the members' nominee as liquidator are now restricted under s 166 to:

- Taking control of the company's property,
- Disposing of perishable or other goods which might diminish in value if not disposed of immediately, and
- Doing all other things necessary for the protection of the company's assets.

If the members' liquidator wishes to perform any act other than those listed above, he will have to apply to the court for leave.

Question — Voluntary liquidation

What are the key differences between a creditors' voluntary liquidation and a members' voluntary liquidation?

Answer

Creditors' voluntary liquidation	Members' voluntary liquidation
Company is insolvent	Company is solvent
Creditors (usually) appoint liquidator	Members appoint liquidator
Liquidation committee approve liquidator's action	Members appropriate liquidator's actions in general meeting

4 Differences between compulsory and voluntary liquidation

The main differences in legal consequences between a compulsory and a voluntary winding up are as follows.

	Differences
Timing	A voluntary winding up commences on the day when the resolution to wind up is passed. It is not retrospective. A compulsory winding up, once agreed to by the court, commences on the day the petition was presented: s 129(2).
Receiver	The official receiver plays no role in a voluntary winding up. The members or creditors select and appoint the liquidator and he is not an officer of the court.
Legal proceedings	There is no automatic stay of legal proceedings against the company nor are previous dispositions or seizure of its assets void in a voluntary winding up. However the liquidator has a general right to apply to the court to make any order which the court can make in a compulsory liquidation. He would do so, for instance, to prevent any creditor obtaining an unfair advantage over other creditors: s 112.
Management and staff	In any liquidation the liquidator replaces the directors in the management of the company (unless he decides to retain them). However, the employees are not automatically dismissed by commencement of voluntary liquidation. Insolvent liquidation may amount to repudiation of their employment contracts (provisions of the statutory employment protection code apply).

5 Revision: Insolvency situations

As has been discussed in this and the previous Chapter, various situations could arise when a company gets into financial difficulties.

Exam focus point

It is vital that you do not confuse the various implications for a company of getting into financial difficulties. This can be a difficult area to keep clear in your head, particularly given that many of the terms introduced in these two Chapters and the personnel sound very similar to each other.

Given the possibility of confusion arising in this area, the following scenarios are given for you to work through, to ensure that you understand the implications for the company in each situation.

5.1 Company defaults on secured debt

As discussed in Chapter 21, when the company defaults on secured debt, the creditor can usually take one of four steps under the terms of his security:

- Take possession of the relevant asset
- Sell the asset
- Apply to the court to have the asset transferred to him
- Appoint a receiver of it or for newer charges, an administrator.

The most common result is that a receiver, or an administrator, is appointed. The next two scenarios will outline this in relation to both fixed and floating charges.

Illustration

Fixed charge

X Ltd has a mortgage with ABC Bank which is secured by a fixed charge over the building to which it relates. X Ltd fails to keep up its payments to ABC Bank. Under the terms of its security, ABC Bank appoints a receiver of the building, who sells the building and realises the debt.

Once the bank had realised its debt, the receiver would leave and the business would be left to continue (as best it could without its premises). In such a situation, liquidation might follow this act of the receiver if the business could not longer operate (see illustration 3 below.)

Illustration

Floating charge

Y Ltd has a loan from EFG Bank which is secured by a fixed and floating charge registered before 15 September 2003 over the company's assets. Y Ltd defaults on the loan. EFG Bank demands in writing that the repayment be made. Y Ltd continues to default on the loan. Under the terms of its security, EFG Bank appoints an administrative receiver to take control of the company's assets. The company is put in receivership.

Similarly to a receiver being appointed under a fixed charge, the administrative receiver's purpose is to realise the debt for the creditor. He may achieve this by selling the business as a going concern or by breaking up the business and realising individual assets.

Unsecured creditors may apply for a petition for a compulsory winding up (see illustration 3) during the course of an administrative receivership. The two can run simultaneously.

5.2 Company defaults on unsecured debt

An unsecured creditor has the following rights against a company who has defaulted on a debt:

- Sue the company for the debt/seize the asset if his judgement is not satisfied
- Petition the court for the compulsory liquidation of the company
- Petition the court for an administration order

It is important to note that a secured creditor also has these remedies open to him. However, a secured creditor has more to gain from appointing a receiver as discussed above than commencing liquidation proceedings.

Illustration

Petition for compulsory liquidation

A has sold goods worth £29,567 to B on credit. B Ltd has exceeded the credit terms extended and A has presented B Ltd with a written demand to their registered office, which B Ltd has not responded to after a month. B Ltd have sold on the goods which they purchased from A and do not dispute the value of the invoice.

A can apply to the court for the compulsory winding up of the company because the company has not paid its debts.

The court appoints the official receiver to be the provisional liquidator until it gives an order for compulsory liquidation.

Illustration

Petition for administration order

A has sold goods worth £29,567 to B Ltd on credit. B Ltd has exceeded the credit terms extended. A has discovered that the management of B Ltd is experiencing difficulties, but believes that the business is sound and that the debt could be paid if the business was managed properly. A is also aware that B Ltd has a loan from the bank which is secured by a floating charge.

A suspects that if the bank exercises its right to bring in an administrative receiver, the business will be wound up and that the unsecured debts might not be paid. It therefore applies to the court for an administration order so that debt collection will be frozen while an action plan is undertaken to ensure that debts can be paid.

An unsecured creditor would benefit from an administration order over a compulsory liquidation as once an administration order has been granted, secured creditors are barred from appointing receivers to realise their debts.

Remember that 'in receivership' and in liquidation, the priority of claims is as follows:

- Expenses of selling assets
- Receiver's expenses
- Preferential debt
- Debt secured under a floating charge
- (By implication) any other unsecured debt (with rights over a 'ring-fenced' element)

The administration order can represent a good alternative to liquidation to the unsecured creditor.

5.3 Actions of members

The only way that a company can be wound up is if its members determine that this should be so. In this case, a voluntary winding up would take place.

Exam focus point

The following are issues which as a minimum you must learn and remember:

- Distinction between liquidator/receiver/official receiver/administrator
- A company can be in receivership and liquidation at the same time
- Once an administration **order** has been passed, no receiver can be appointed or liquidation proceedings started (although they can until the court grants the petition)
- A secured creditor will usually enforced his security and appoint a receiver, where possible, or an administrator
- A voluntary liquidation is always instigated by the members

You should consider the advantages of administration as opposed to liquidation from the point of view of all the parties involved.

Advantages of administration	
To the company	It does not necessarily cease to exist at the end of the process. Liquidation will always result in the company being wound up. It also provides temporary relief from creditors to allow breathing space to formulate rescue plans.
To the members	They will continue to have shares in the company which has not been wound up. If the administration is successful, regenerating the business should enhance share value and will restore any income from the business (dividends or any salary for owner-managed business).
To the creditors	Creditors should obtain a return in relation to their past debts from an administration. Unsecured creditors will benefit from the 'prescribed part' of asset realisations. Any creditor may apply to the court for an administration order, while only certain creditors may apply for other forms of relief from debt, for example, the use of receivers or an application for winding up. Floating chargeholders may appoint an administrator without reference to the court. It may also be in the interests of the creditors to have a continued business relationship with the company once the business has been turned around.

Chapter roundup

- In this chapter we have seen the importance of distinguishing between types of liquidation and also between liquidation and dissolution. The chapter contains most of the procedural information which you need to know on how a liquidation commences and proceeds.
- It is important to be able to distinguish between and discuss the procedures involved with
  - Compulsory winding up
  - Members' voluntary winding up
  - Creditors' voluntary winding up
- Winding up is a drastic and costly procedure, to be avoided if possible. An administration order is an alternative.

Quick quiz

1 Complete the following definition

.... means that a company must be .... and its affairs wound up.

2 Name three common features of liquidations.

(1) ....

(2) ....

(3) ....

3 What are the two most important reasons for **compulsory liquidation?**

(1) ....

(2) ....

4 A members' voluntary winding up is where the members decide to dissolve a healthy company.

True ☐

False ☐

5 Rearrange the list in order of proceedings in a creditors' voluntary winding up

(a) Creditors' meeting
(b) Liquidator appointed
(c) Directors' notice of meeting outlines situation
(d) Members' meeting
(e) Liquidation committee nominated

6 Complete the following definition, using the words given below.

An .... is an order of the .... which puts

an..................... .... in control of the business with a ....

....

(1) Court	(4) Programme	(6) Insolvency
(2) Defined	(5) Administration	(7) Order
(3) Practitioner		

7 Name two advantages of administration

(1) ....

(2) ....

Answers to quick quiz

1 Liquidation, dissolved

2 (1) No further changes in membership permitted
(2) All documents must state prominently that company is in liquidation
(3) Directors' power to manager ceases

3 (1) Company is unable to pay its debts
(2) It is just and equitable to wind up the company

4 True

5 (c)
(d)
(a)
(b)/(e). Both these steps occur at the creditors' meeting

6 (5), (7), (1), (6), (3), (2), (4)

7 (1) It does not result in the dissolution of the company
(2) It prevents creditors applying for compulsory liquidation

Subsidiary advantages are

(3) All creditors can apply for an administration order
(4) The administrator may challenge past transactions of the company

Now try the question below from the Exam Question Bank

Number	Level	Marks	Time
Q23	Examination	20	36 mins

Part G
Law of employment

The employment contract

23

Topic list	Syllabus reference
1 What is an employee?	11(a)
2 Why does it matter?	11(a)
3 Employment contract: basic issues	11(a)
4 Common law duties	11(a)
5 Statutory duties	11(a)
6 Varying the terms of an employment contract	11(a)
7 Continuous employment	11(a)

Introduction

The law of employment was developed under common law principles as an application of the law of contract. In recent years **statutory rules** have been enacted to give the **employee protection** both against dismissal and unfair treatment. These matters will be considered in Chapters 24 and 25.

In this Chapter we shall consider two basic issues:

(a) What is 'an employee'?
(b) What is a contract of employment?

Statutory references in this chapter are to the Employment Rights Act 1996 (ERA 1996) unless otherwise noted.

The pilot paper examined the distinction between employees and the self employed in Section A. However, you should not rule out the possibility of them being examined in Section B, as indeed was the case in the December 2003 exam.

1 What is an employee?

Pilot paper, 12/03

FAST FORWARD

It is important to distinguish between a **contract of service** (employment) and a **contract for services** (independent contractor). Each type of contract has different rules for taxation, health and safety provisions, protection of contract and vicarious liability in tort and contract.

A general rule is that an employee is someone who is employed under a **contract of service**, as distinguished from an independent contractor, who is someone who works under a **contract for services**.

However, it is important to note that some statutory provisions apply to 'workers' and this term is wider than 'employees' and includes those personally performing work or services unless truly self-employed.

Key terms

An **employee** is 'an individual who has entered into or works under a contract of employment'. (ERA 1996)

A **contract of employment** is 'a contract of service or apprenticeship, whether express or implied, and (if it is express) whether it is oral or in writing.'

In practice this distinction depends on many factors. As we will discuss in section 2 it can be very important to know whether an individual is an employee or an independent contractor. The courts will apply a series of **tests**.

Primarily, the court will look at the **reality of the situation**. This may be in spite of the form of the arrangement.

> *Ferguson v John Dawson & Partners 1976*
> *The facts*: A builder's labourer was paid his wages without deduction of income tax or National Insurance contributions and worked as a self-employed contractor providing services. His 'employer' could dismiss him, decide on which site he would work, direct him as to the work he should do and also provided the tools which he used. He was injured in an accident and sued his employers on the basis that they owed him legal duties as his employer.
>
> *Decision*: On the facts taken as a whole, he was an employee working under a contract of employment.

Where there is some **doubt** as to the nature of the relationship the courts will then look at any **agreement between the parties**.

> *Massey v Crown Life Assurance 1978*
> *The facts*: The claimant was originally employed by an insurance company as a departmental manager; he also earned commission on business which he introduced. At his own request he changed to a self-employed basis. Tax and other payments were no longer deducted by the employers but he continued to perform the same duties. The employers terminated these arrangements and the claimant claimed compensation for unfair dismissal.
>
> *Decision*: As he had opted to become self-employed and his status in the organisation was consistent with that situation, his claim to be a dismissed employee failed.

It can still be unclear whether a person is an employee or an independent contractor. Historically, the tests of **control, integration** into the employer's organisation, and **economic reality** (or the multiple test) have been applied in such cases.

The fundamental prerequisite of a contract of employment is that there must be **mutual obligations** on the employer to provide, and the employee to perform, work.

1.1 The control test

The court will consider whether the employer has **control** over the way in which the employee performs his duties.

> *Mersey Docks & Harbour Board v Coggins & Griffiths (Liverpool) 1947*
> *The facts:* Stevedores hired a crane with its driver from the harbour board under a contract which provided that the driver (appointed and paid by the harbour board) should be the employee of the stevedores. Owing to the driver's negligence a checker was injured. The case was concerned with whether the stevedores or the harbour board were vicariously liable as employers.
>
> *Decision:* In the House of Lords, that the issue must be settled on the facts and not on the terms of the contract. The stevedores could only be treated as employers of the driver if they could control in detail how he did his work. But although they could instruct him what to do, they could not control him in how he operated the crane. The harbour board (as 'general employer') was therefore still the driver's employer.

1.2 The integration test

The courts consider whether, if the employee is so skilled that he cannot be controlled in the performance of his duties, he was **integrated** into the employer's organisation.

> *Cassidy v Ministry of Health 1951*
> *The facts:* The full-time assistant medical officer at a hospital carried out a surgical operation in a negligent fashion. The patient sued the Ministry of Health as employer. The Ministry resisted the claim arguing that it had no control over the doctor in his medical work.
>
> *Decision:* In such circumstances the proper test was whether the employer appointed the employee, selected him for his task and so integrated him into the organisation. If the patient had chosen the doctor the Ministry would not have been liable as employer. But here the Ministry (the hospital management) made the choice and so it was liable.

The control and integration tests are important, but **no longer decisive** in determining whether a person is an employee.

1.3 The multiple (economic reality) test

They also consider whether the employee was **working on his own account**.

> *Ready Mixed Concrete (South East) v Ministry of Pensions & National Insurance 1968*
> *The facts:* The driver of a special vehicle worked for one company only in the delivery of liquid concrete to building sites. He provided his own vehicle (obtained on hire purchase from the company) and was responsible for its maintenance and repair. He was free to provide a substitute driver. The vehicle was painted in the company's colours and the driver wore its uniform. He was paid gross amounts (no tax etc deducted) on the basis of mileage and quantity delivered as a self-employed contractor. The Ministry of Pensions claimed that he was in fact an employee for whom the company should make the employer's insurance contributions.
>
> *Decision:* In such cases the most important test is whether the worker is working on his own account (the *entrepreneurial* test or *multiple* test). On these facts the driver was a self-employed transport contractor and not an employee.

In *Franks v Reuters Ltd 2003*, the difficult issue of whether an agency worker can at some point become an employee of the client was directly addressed. The agency worker had been providing services to the client for some six years engaged in a variety of jobs, and was effectively so thoroughly integrated with the employer's organisation as to be indistinguishable from the employer's staff. The court considered that too much emphasis had been placed in the tribunal on considering whether there is a mutuality of obligations without looking at the totality of the evidence.

Mummery LJ, said that an implied contract of employment did not arise simply by virtue of the **length of the employment**, but it could well be a factor in applying the overall tests appropriate to establish (or otherwise) an employment status. The case was remitted to the tribunal for further consideration, but the length of an assignment of an agency worker clearly has implications for the development of other indications of an employment relationship, with those utilising the services of the worker forgetting the true nature of the relationship and behaving towards the work as if he or she was an employee. It may be that at this point the relevant approach also starts to involve the 'integration' test.

1.4 Relevant factors

Significant factors are as follows.

- Does the employee use his **own tools and equipment** or does the employer provide them?
- Does the alleged employer have the power to **select or appoint** its employees, and may it dismiss them?
- **Payment of salary** is, as mentioned above, a fair indication of there being a contract of employment.
- **Working for a number of different people** is not necessarily a sign of self-employment. A number of assignments may be construed as 'a series of employments'.

In difficult cases, the court will also consider whether the employee can delegate all his obligations, whether there is restriction as to place of work, whether there is a **mutual obligation** and whether holidays and hours of work are agreed.

> *O'Kelly v Trusthouse Forte Plc 1983*
> *The facts:* The employee was a 'regular casual' working when required as a waiter. There was an understanding that he would accept work when offered and that the employer would give him preference over other casual employees. The industrial tribunal held that there was no contract of employment because the employer had no obligation to provide work and the employee had no obligation to accept work when offered.
>
> *Decision:* The Court of Appeal agreed with this finding. Whether there is a contract of employment is a question of law but it depends entirely on the facts of each case; here there was no 'mutuality of obligations' and hence no contract.

The decision whether to classify an individual as an employee or not is also influenced by policy considerations. For example, an employment tribunal might regard a person as an employee for the purpose of unfair dismissal despite the fact that the tax authorities treated him or her as self-employed *Airfix Footwear Ltd v Cope 1978*.

> *The facts:* The EAT was concerned with a classic outworking arrangement under which the applicant (having been given training and thereafter supplied with the necessary tools and materials) generally worked five days a week making heels for shoes manufactured by the respondent company. She was paid on a piece work basis without deduction of income tax or NIC.
>
> *Decision:* Working for some seven years, generally for five days a week, resulted in the arrangement being properly classified as employment under a contract of employment.

2 Why does it matter?

The first thing that it is important to note is that much of the recent legislation which gives protection to employees **extends further than employees**. Much of it is drafted to cover 'workers' which has a wide definition to cover most people providing services to others outside of the course of (their own) business.

This has reduced the importance of the distinction between employee and independent contractor in this area.

However, there are several other practical reasons why the distinction between a contract of service and a contract for services is important.

SIGNIFICANCE OF THE DISTINCTION		
	Employed	**Self-employed**
Social security	Employers must pay secondary Class 1 contributions on behalf of employees Employees make primary Class 1 contributions There are also differences in statutory sick pay and levies for industrial training purposes	Independent contractors pay Class 2 and 4 contributions
Taxation	Deductions must be made by an employer for income tax under PAYE (Schedule E) from salary paid to employee	The self-employed are taxed under Schedule D and are directly responsible to the Inland Revenue for tax due
Employment protection	There is legislation which confers protection and benefits upon employees under a contract of service, including • Minimum periods of notice • Remedies for unfair dismissal	
Tortious acts	Employer is generally vicariously liable for tortious acts of employees, committed in the course of employment	Liability of person hiring an independent contractor for contractors' acts severely limited unless there is strict liability
Implied terms	There are rights and duties implied by statute for employers and employees This will affect things such as copyrights and patents.	These implied rights and duties do not apply to such an extent to a contract for services
VAT		An independent contractor may have to register for, and charge VAT.
Bankruptcy	In liquidation, an employee has preferential rights as a creditor for payment of outstanding salary and redundancy payments, up to certain limits	
Health and safety	There is significant common lay and regulation governing employers' duties to employees with regard to health and safety	The common law provisions and much of the regulation relating to employees also related to independent contractors

Exam focus point

If you are asked about the importance of the distinction between employees and independent contractors in the exam, make sure that you highlight the fact that it is important for the practical reasons given above, but also that the recent legislative trend has been to extend protection to 'workers' beyond the traditional definition of employees.

3 Employment contract: basic issues

FAST FORWARD

There are no particular legal rules relating to the commencement of employment - it is really **just like any other contract** in requiring offer and acceptance, consideration and intention to create legal relations.

The definition of an employment contract was given in section 1. To recap, it is a contract of service which may be **express** or **implied**. If express, it can be either **oral** or **written**. In essence, then, an employment contract can be a simple, straightforward agreement. The contact must, of course, comply with the usual rules relating to the formation of a valid contract.

Question

Essential elements of a contract of employment

As with any other contract, agreements for employment require offer and acceptance, consideration and the intention to create legal relations. How are these three essential elements manifested in a contract of employment?

Answer

Generally the offer comes from the employer and acceptance from the employee, who may write a letter or simply turn up for work at an agreed time. Consideration comprises the promises each party gives to the other - a promise to work for a promise to pay. If there is no consideration, a deed must be executed for there to be a contract of employment. The intention to create legal relations is imputed from the fact that essentially employment is a commercial transaction.

At the one extreme, an employment contract may be a document drawn up by solicitors and signed by both parties; at the other extreme it may consist of a handshake and a 'See you on Monday'. In such cases the court has to clarify the agreement by determining what the parties must be taken to have agreed.

Senior personnel may sign a contract specially drafted to include terms on confidentiality and restraint of trade. Other employees may sign a standard form contract, exchange letters with the new employer or simply agree terms orally at interview.

Each of these situations will form a valid contract of employment, subject to the requirements outlined below as to written particulars, as long as there is **agreement** on **essential terms** such as hours and wages. We will consider some of these essential terms in the following sections. Nor should it be forgotten that even prior to employment commencing the potential employer has legal obligations, for example not to discriminate in recruitment.

3.1 Requirement for written particulars

Within two months of the beginning of the employment the employer must give to an employee a written **statement of prescribed particulars** of his employment: s 1.

The statement should identify the following.

- The names of **employer** and **employee**
- The **date** on which employment began
- Whether any service with a previous employer forms part of the employee's **continuous period** of employment
- **Pay** - scale or rate and intervals at which paid
- **Hours** of work (including any specified 'normal working hours')
- Any **holiday** and **holiday pay** entitlement

- **Sick leave** and **sick pay** entitlement
- **Pensions** and pension **schemes**
- Length of **notice** of termination to be given on either side
- The **title** of the job which the employee is employed to do (or a brief job description)

A 'principal statement', which must include the first six items above and the title of the job, must be provided, but other particulars may be given by way of separate documents.

If the employee has a **written contract of employment** covering these points and has been given a copy it is not necessary to provide him with separate written particulars.

The written particulars must also contain details of **disciplinary procedures** and **grievance procedures** or reference to where they can be found. S35 Employment Act 2002.

If the employer fails to comply with these requirements the employee may apply to an employment tribunal for a declaration of what the terms should be: s 11. S38 Employment Act 2002 allows a tribunal to award compensation to an employee claiming unfair dismissal if the particulars are incomplete.

Question — Employee or independent contractor?

Charles saw a sign advertising vacancies at a local building site. He contacted the foreman and was told that he would be required but that, because work depended on the weather conditions, he would not be given an employment contract - he would be accountable for his own income tax and National Insurance. The foreman added that he would be provided with tools and that at the beginning of each day he would be told which site he would work on that day. Lateness or theft of materials would lead to his dismissal.

Is Charles an employee?

Answer

Charles is an employee. Even though he does not receive an employment contract the facts indicate a contract of service since he is controlled by the employer in that the latter provides tools, tells him where to work and reserves the right to dismiss him.

4 Common law duties

FAST FORWARD

The **employer** has an implied **duty at common law** to take **reasonable care** of his employees; he must select proper staff, materials and provide a safe system of working.
The **employee** has a duty to exercise **care and skill** in performance of his duties.

4.1 Employee's duties

The employee has a **fundamental duty of faithful service** to his employer. All other duties are features of this general duty.

> *Hivac Ltd v Park Royal Scientific Instruments Ltd 1946*
> *The facts:* In their spare time certain of the claimant's employees worked for the defendant company, which directly competed with the claimant.
>
> *Decision:* Even though the employees had not passed on any confidential information, they were still in breach of their duty of fidelity to the claimants.

The **implied** duties of the employee include the following.

- **Reasonable competence** to do his job.
- **Obedience** to the employer's instructions unless they require him to do an unlawful act or to expose himself to personal danger (not inherent in his work) or are instructions outside the employee's contract.

  Ottoman Bank Ltd v Chakarian 1930
  The facts: The defendant, an Armenian, was ordered by his employers to stay in Constantinople, where he had previously been sentenced to death.

  Decision: He was within his rights in refusing.

- **Duty to account for all money and property** received during the course of his employment.

  Boston Deep Sea Fishing and Ice Co v Ansell 1888
  The facts: The defendant, who was managing director of the claimant company, accepted personal commissions from suppliers on orders which he placed with them for goods supplied to the company. He was dismissed and the company sued to recover from him the commissions.

  Decision: The company was justified in dismissing the claimant and he must account to it for the commissions.

- **Reasonable care and skill** in the performance of his work: Lister v Romford Ice and Cold Storage Co 1957. What is reasonable depends on the degree of skill and experience which the employee professes to have.
- **Personal service** - the contract of employment is a personal one and so the employee may not delegate his duties without the employer's express or implied consent.
- The same duty of **fidelity** to an employer to whom he is seconded as to a **contractual employer**.

4.2 Employer's duties **6/02**

There is an overriding **duty of mutual trust and confidence** between the employer and the employee.

The employer usually also has the following duties at common law:

- To **pay remuneration** to employees. If there is no rate fixed by the parties, this duty is to pay **reasonable** remuneration. There is statutory provision for this, see section 5.
- To **indemnify the employee** against expenses and losses incurred in the course of employment.
- To take care of the employees' **health and safety** at work. This is also provided for in statute.
- To **select fit and competent fellow-employees**.
- To **provide work**, where
  - Employee is an apprentice
  - Employee is paid with reference to work done
  - The opportunity to work is the essence of the contract (for example, for actors)
  - There is work available to be done (subject to contractual terms to the contrary) **and** the relevant employee is a skilled worker who needs work to preserve his or her skills (*William Hill Organisation v Tucker 1998).*

The importance of these common law implied duties on both parties is that:

(a) **Breach of a legal duty**, if it is important enough, may entitle the injured party to treat the contract as **discharged** and to claim damages for breach of contract at common law, and

(b) In an employee's claim for compensation for unfair dismissal, the employee may argue that it was a case of **constructive dismissal** by the employer, or the employer may seek to justify his express dismissal of the employee by reference to his conduct. We shall discuss constructive dismissal in Chapter 24.

You should note also that an employer **does not have a duty** to provide a reference for an employee. It is a common misconception that he does. Neither is there a duty to protect an employee's property.

5 Statutory duties

FAST FORWARD

Statute implies terms into employment contracts, which may not usually be overridden, regarding pay, maternity leave and work-life balance generally, time off, health and safety and working time.

Various matters are implied into contracts of employment by statute. Some of them build upon the basic matters covered by common law above. Most of the employment statutes in this area implement European Directives on employment law issues. The employer has statutory duties in the following areas:

- Pay
- Time off work
- Maternity rights and the 'work-life balance'
- Health and safety
- Working time

5.1 Pay

There are two key pieces of legislation in relation to pay. These are the **Equal Pay Act 1970** and the **National Minimum Wage Act 1998**.

5.1.1 Equal Pay Act 1970

Under this Act, contractual **employment terms should be at least as favourable as those given to an employee of the opposite sex**. The Act covers terms such as sick pay, holiday pay and working hours, and it applies to all forms of full-time and part-time work.

Hayward v Cammell Laird Shipbuilders 1986
The facts: The House of Lords upheld the claim of a canteen cook to equal pay with painters, joiners and thermal insulation engineers employed in the same shipyard on the ground that her work was of equal value.

Decision: Overall the applicant was considered to be employed on work of equal value. Hayward's application was the first successful claim for equal pay for work of equal value.

A difference in pay which is connected with economic factors affecting the efficient carrying on of the employer's business or other activity may well be relevant: *Rainey v Greater Glasgow Health Board 1987.* Examples are as follows.

- Greater length of service is a material factor: *Capper Pass v Lawton 1977.*
- Working at different times of day is not a material factor: *Dugdale v Kraft Foods 1977.*
- A distinction in hourly pay between workers in London and those based in (the cheaper area of) Nottingham is based on a material factor: *NAAFI v Varley 1976.*

- 'Market forces' do not necessarily amount to a genuine material factor: *Ratcliffe & Others v North Yorkshire County Council 1995.*

5.1.2 National Minimum Wage Act 1998

A national minimum wage was introduced in the UK in 1999. The current hourly rate (from October 2004) is £4.85. For persons between the ages of 18 and 21, the rate is £4.10 and for 16-17 year olds it is £3.00.

5.1.3 Other matters

Employers are obliged to provide an itemised pay statement: s 8.

5.2 Time off work

In addition to the rights relating to maternity and parental leave discussed below, statute lists several occasions when an employee has a right to time off work.

(a) **Trade union officials** are entitled to time off on full pay at the employer's expense to enable them to carry out **trade union duties***:* ss 168-169 Trade Union and Labour Relations (Consolidation) Act 1992.

(b) An employee who has been given notice of dismissal for **redundancy** may have time off to look for work or to arrange training for other work.

(c) A member of a recognised independent **trade union** may have time off work (without statutory right to pay) for **trade union activities**, for example, attending a branch meeting: s 170 TULRCA 1992.

(d) Employees also have a duty to allow an employee to have reasonable time off to carry n out certain **public duties**, for example performing his duties as a magistrate. There is **no statutory provision** entitling an employee to time off for jury service, but prevention of a person from attending as a juror is contempt of court.

5.3 Maternity rights and the 'work-life balance'

A woman who is pregnant is given substantial rights under statute, including:

- A right to **time off work** for ante-natal care
- The right to **ordinary maternity leave**
- The right to **additional maternity leave**
- The right to **maternity pay**
- The right to **return to work** after maternity leave
- If dismissed, a claim for **unfair dismissal** (this will be discussed in Chapter 25)

Much recent employment legislation, including provisions introduced by the Employment Act 2002, has been concerned with the introduction of **family-friendly** employment policies. There has been a specific focus on the so-called **'work-life balance'**. The law has developed as a result in the areas of:

- **Maternity leave** and pay
- Paternity leave
- Rights of adoptive parents
- A right to request flexible working

5.3.1 Ante-natal care

An employee has a right not to be unreasonably refused time off for ante-natal care during working hours. She is also entitled to pay during such an absence. There is no minimum qualifying period, ss 55-57 Employment Rights Act 1996.

5.3.2 Maternity leave

Every woman is given the right to **ordinary maternity leave** which is **twenty-six weeks** long, subject to her satisfying conditions giving her employer notice of her intentions. A woman who has been continuously employed for 26 weeks has a right to **additional maternity leave**, which allows the employee a further period of **twenty-six weeks' leave**. This means that the total period of statutory maternity leave is 52 weeks.

An employee on **ordinary** maternity leave has the **right to return to work** in the job she had before her absence, with her seniority, pension and similar rights which she would have had if she had not been absent and on no less favourable terms than if she had not been absent: s 71.

An employee on **additional** maternity leave has the same rights, except if it is **not practicable** for her to return to the job she had before, she has the right to another job which is **suitable and appropriate** to her, on the same or better status, terms and conditions.

5.3.3 Maternity pay

Statutory maternity pay is paid during an employee's ordinary maternity leave. Additional maternity leave is unpaid. The employee must have at least 26 weeks of continuous employment and her average earnings must be above a certain level (otherwise she may be entitled to claim **maternity allowance** instead). SMP is paid at the following rate:

(a) For the first six weeks, 90% of salary,

(b) For the remainder of ordinary maternity leave, the lower of £100 per week or 90% of her average weekly earnings.

5.3.4 Paternity leave

New rights to paternity leave and pay are available to employees of children born on or after 6 April 2003. The employee claiming the right must:

- Be the biological father of the child or the mother's husband or partner;
- Have or expect to have responsibility for the child's upbringing;
- Have 26 weeks' continuous service.

Eligible employees will be entitled to take either one week or two consecutive weeks paid paternity leave. The leave must be completed within 56 days of the actual birth of the child.

Statutory Paternity Pay will be paid during the paternity leave. This will be paid at the lower of £100 per week or 90% of the employee's average weekly earnings. These rights are **in addition to** the existing parental leave provisions (see below) which allow up to 13 weeks of **unpaid** paternity leave for each child under 5 years old, provided that the employee has one year's continuous service.

5.3.5 Adoptive parents

The family-friendly employment policies introduced by the Employment Act 2002 extend to adoptive parents, who now have similar rights to those provided under the maternity provisions. There is a right to **statutory adoption leave** (SAL) and **statutory adoption pay** (SAP). Statutory adoption leave may consist of 26 weeks of ordinary adoption leave and 26 weeks of additional adoption leave.

Adoptive parents' rights extend to one of the adopting couple but not to both. The adopting parent must have 26 weeks of continuous employment. Leave is not available in cases of step family adoption, adoption by existing step parents or extended family adoption.

5.3.6 Flexible working

Since April 2003, employees have the right:

- To apply for a change in terms and conditions of employment in respect of hours, time and place of work and
- Not to be unreasonably refused.

To be eligible to apply for flexible working, the employee must:

- Have a child under six years of age (or under 18 if the child is disabled)
- Have been continuously employed for 26 weeks at the date of the application
- Have, or expect to have, responsibility for the child's upbringing
- Be making the application in order to care for the child and
- Not have made another application for flexible working in the previous 12 months

There is a detailed set of procedures for the submission of an application, the provision of a response by the employer and, if necessary, any subsequent appeal by the employee. If a request is granted, any changes are regarded as permanent contract changes. The employer may reasonably refuse a request on the grounds of:

- The burden of additional cost
- A detrimental effect on ability to meet customer demand
- An inability to re-organise the work amongst existing staff or to recruit additional staff
- A detrimental impact on quality or performance
- Insufficiency of work during the periods the employee proposes to work or
- Planned structural changes

The given business reasons may not be contested by the employee. The only grounds for complaint are either that the employer has failed to follow the procedures properly or that the decision to reject an application was based on incorrect facts. If the body to which a complaint is made (an employment tribunal or ACAS) upholds the complaint it may award compensation up to a maximum of 8 weeks' pay but can not order the employer to implement the request for flexible working.

5.3.7 Parental leave

Any employee with a year's continuous service who has responsibility for a child is entitled to unpaid parental leave to care for that child: s 7 Employment Relations Act 1999.

The period allowed is 13 weeks for each child born or adopted after 15 December 1999. The entitlement ceases after the child is 5 years old, or on the 5th anniversary of the child being adopted. If the child is disabled (entitled to disability allowance), the right ceases after the child's eighteenth birthday.

The leave may not be taken in periods of less than one week, unless the child is disabled.

5.4 Health and safety

The key legislation under which an employer has a duty to his employees with regard to health and safety is the Health and Safety at Work Act 1974, which has been augmented by subsequent regulations, notably the Health and Safety at Work Regulations 1999. This act makes it the duty of every employer to ensure the health, safety and welfare of his employees, as far as is practicable.

This general duty includes the following issues:

- Provide and maintain plant and systems of work which are safe and without risk
- Make arrangements to ensure safe use, handling, storage and transport of articles/substances
- Provide adequate information, instruction, training and supervision
- Maintain safe places of work and ensure that there is adequate access in and out
- Provide a safe and healthy working environment

5.4.1 Employment rights

The contract of employment contains an implied right not to be subjected to detriment by the employer on grounds of health and safety: s 44(1). Specifically, the employee has a right not to be subjected to detriment on the ground that he intended to or did:

- Carry out activities designated to him in connection with preventing/reducing health and safety risks at work
- Perform duties as a representative of workers on issues of health and safety
- Take part in consultation with the employer under the Health and Safety (Consultation with Employees) Regulations 1996
- Leave his place of work or refused to work in circumstances which he reasonably believed to be serious or imminent and he could not reasonably be expected to avert
- Take appropriate steps to protect himself or others from circumstances of danger which he believed to be serious and imminent

5.5 Working time

The Working Time Regulations 1998 provide broadly that a worker's **average working time in a seventeen week period,** (including overtime) shall **not exceed 48 hours for each 7 days period**, unless the worker has agreed in writing that this limit shall not apply.

The Regulations also give every worker the **right to paid annual leave**, which shall be a minimum of four weeks long. The employer may be able to specify when such holiday can or cannot be taken, but must give the employees notice of such occasions.

There are special rules relating to Sunday working.

6 Varying the terms of an employment contract

FAST FORWARD

A contract of employment can only be varied if the contract expressly gives that right, or if all parties consent to the variation.

It should be clear, from your earlier studies of general contract law, that a change in contract terms **can only be made with the consent of both parties** to the contract.

- Some terms are negotiated on a **collective** basis between employer and union(s).
- Some terms are negotiated **individually.**
- Some terms are implied by **statute.**

6.1 Varying terms without changing the contract

There may be circumstances in which an employer can vary the terms of an employment contract without actually needing to vary the contract itself. For example, there may be an **express term** in the contract which itself gives rights of variation, for example to allow a change in area of work.

Alternatively, an **implied term** may act to vary the contract.

(a) A sales representative may be required to take responsibility for such area as his employer considers necessary in order to meet changing market conditions: *Burnett v F A Hughes.*

(b) Terms may also be implied by custom, for example, where a steel erector is required at the request of his employer to change sites: *Stevenson v Teeside Bridge & Engineering Co Ltd 1971.*

6.2 Changing the existing contract

The existing contract can be changed by **consent**. Consent might be demonstrated by **oral agreement** to new terms, by the **signing** of a new statement of terms and conditions or by the employee showing acceptance by **working** under the new terms.

If an employer does not obtain willing agreement to a variation but the employer changes the contract anyway, the employee has a number of options.

- He may consent.
- He may stay in employment but make it clear by that he does not accept the variation.
- He may resign and claim constructive dismissal. (See Chapter 24.)

6.3 Signing a new contract

The third broad option open to the employer is to give contractual notice to the employee and then offer a new contract on the new terms. This opens the employer to a **potential claim** for unfair dismissal. It is generally best for the employer to obtain consent to vary the terms of an existing contract.

7 Continous employment

FAST FORWARD

Many rights given to employees under the **Employment Rights Act 1996** are only available if an employee has a specified period of **continuous employment**.

You may have noticed references to 'continuous employment' in the previous sections. Most of the employment protection discussed here and in the following two Chapters is given to an employee who has one year's continuous service.

Exam focus point

You learn that one year's continuous service is required to qualify for employment protection and then learn the **exceptions** to this rule which are pointed out for you where they are discussed.

There are provisions in statute for how the year's continuous service should be calculated, and what counts as service and what does not. **The basic rule is that a year is twelve calendar months.**

Certain weeks might not be taken into account in calculating continuous service, but they do not break the period of continuous service. This might be the case if the employee takes place in a strike, or is absent due to service in the armed forces.

If Ben was employed for 8 months and then was given leave to do some service in the armed services for 5 months, on his return to the employer he would have been employed for 13 calendar months.

However, until he completes another 4 months of service he will not be eligible for the employment protection given to those employees with a year's continuous service. Once he has completed those 4 months, the 8 months prior and the 4 months subsequent to the armed service will count as continuous service, despite being split by a period away from the employer.

7.1 Transfer of undertakings

Another factor that impacts on continuous service is when a business or undertaking is transferred by one person to another. Where the business is transferred, so that an employee works for a new employer, this change represents **no break in the continuous service of the employee** (Transfer of Undertaking Regulations 1981).

Chapter roundup

- It is important to distinguish between a **contract of service** (employment) and a **contract for services** (independent contractor). Each type of contract has different rules for taxation, health and safety provisions, protection of contract and vicarious liability in tort and contract.
- A contract of service is **distinguished** from a contract for services usually because the parties **express** the agreement to be one of service. This does not always mean that an employee will not be treated as an independent contractor by the court, however; much depends on the three tests.
  - Control test
  - Integration test
  - Economic reality test
- There are no particular legal rules relating to the commencement of employment - it is really **just like any other contract** in requiring offer and acceptance, consideration and intention to create legal relations.
- Most employers are required to give employees a **statement of prescribed particulars** relating to their employment within eight weeks of commencement unless the employee already has a written contract of employment to cover these particulars.
- **Express terms** agreed between the parties override terms implied by common law.
- The **employer** has an implied **duty at common law** to take **reasonable care** of his employees; he must select proper staff, materials and provide a safe system of working.
- The **employee** has a duty to exercise **care and skill** in performance of his duties.
- **Statute** implies terms into employment contracts, which may not usually be overridden, regarding pay, maternity leave and work-life balance generally, time off, health and safety and working time.
- A contract of employment can only be varied if the contract expressly gives that right, or if all parties consent to the variation.
- Many rights given to employees under the **Employment Rights Act 1996** are only available if an employee has a specified period of **continuous employment**.

Quick quiz

1 What tests are applied by the courts to answer these questions?

- Has the employer control over the way in which the employee performs his duties? (1) ....
- Is the skilled employee part of the employer's organisation? (2) ....
- Is the employee working on his own account? (3)....................

2 Is working for a number of different people an automatic sign of self employment?

True ☐

False ☐

3 Give five reasons why the distinction between employed and self employed workers is important.

4 A 'principal statement' must include the following (tick all that apply)

(a) Names of parties ☐

(b) Job title ☐

(c) Date employment began ☐

(d) Notice details ☐

(e) Details of continuous employment ☐

(f) Pay details ☐

(g) Pensions and pension scheme details ☐

(h) Holiday entitlement ☐

5 What is an employee's fundamental duty?

6 Which of these options are open to an employer who wishes to vary the terms of an employment contract?

(i) Sign a wholly new contract
(ii) Vary the terms without changing the contract
(iii) Change the existing contract

A (iii) only
B (i) and (ii) only
C (ii) and (iii) only
D (i), (ii) and (iii)

Answers to quick quiz

1. (1) control test
   (2) integration test
   (3) multiple (economic reality) test

2. No

3. Social security
   Taxation
   Employment protection
   Tortious acts
   Health and safety
   (also implied terms, VAT, rights in bankruptcy)

4. (a) (b) (c) (e) (f) (h)

5. Faithful service to his employer

6. D

Now try the question below from the Exam Question Bank

Number	Level	Marks	Time
Q24	Examination	10	18 mins

Termination of employment

Topic list	Syllabus reference
1 Termination by notice	11(b)
2 Termination of employment by breach of contract	11(b)
3 Wrongful dismissal	11(b)
4 Unfair dismissal	11(b)
5 Unfair dismissal – justification of dismissal	11(b)
6 Remedies for wrongful dismissal	11(b)
7 Remedies for unfair dismissal	11(b)
8 Redundancy	11(c)

Introduction

Chapter 23 provided an introduction to the contract of employment. In this chapter we consider how the contract is **terminated** when dismissal occurs, and the **remedies available** to the employee.

Under the general principles of the law of contract a contract may be terminated in the same ways as any contract as we learnt in Chapter 8.

There are two further circumstances which are extremely important in any study of employment law. These are termination by **notice** and termination by **dismissal**, and most of this chapter is about these two topics. Sections 1 and 2 lay the foundations for an understanding of unfair and wrongful dismissal.

Statutory references in this chapter are to the Employment Rights Act 1996 unless otherwise noted.

This topic could be examined in either Section A or B.

1 Termination by notice

A contract of employment may be terminated by **notice**. The following rules apply.

(a) The period of notice given must **not be less than the statutory minimum,** whatever the contract may specify.

(b) It **may be given without specific reason** for so doing, unless the contract requires otherwise.

(c) If the contract states that notice may **only be given in specific circumstances** then generally it may **not** be given for any other reason.

McClelland v Northern Ireland General Health Services Board 1957
The facts: The claimant's contract gave the employer a right to terminate his employment for misconduct or inefficiency.

Decision: There was no contractual right of termination for redundancy - it was a breach of contract to do so.

Although there is no breach of contract, termination by notice or non-renewal qualifies as 'dismissal' under the statutory code. This means that the employee may be entitled to compensation for unfair dismissal (see section 4).

Statute imposes a **minimum period of notice** of termination to be given on either side.

1.1 Minimum period of notice

FAST FORWARD

Where employment is **terminated by notice** the period given must **not be less** than the **statutory minimum**.

If an employer terminates the contract of employment by giving notice, the **minimum period of notice** to be given is determined by the employee's length of continuous service in the employer's service as follows: s 86.

(a) An employee who has been continuously employed for **one month or more** but less than one year is entitled to not less than **one week's** notice.

(b) An employee who has been continuously employed for **two years or more** but less than twelve years is entitled to **one week's notice for each year of continuous employment.**

(c) Any employee who has been employed for **twelve years** or more is entitled to not less than **twelve weeks'** notice.

If the **employee** gives notice, the minimum period required is **one week** if he has been employed for at least one month.

The notice must specify the **date of its expiry**. Either party may waive his entitlement to notice or accept a sum in lieu of notice.

The statutory rules on length of notice merely prescribe a **minimum**. If the contract provides for a longer period, notice must be given in accordance with the contract.

During the period of notice an employee is entitled to pay at a rate not less than the average of his earnings over the previous twelve weeks.

If the employee is **dismissed** in any way he may request his employer to give him a **written statement of the reasons** for his dismissal and **the employer must provide it** within fourteen days. The statement must

contain at the least a simple summary of the reasons for dismissal and can be used as **admissible evidence** before an employment tribunal: s 92.

Dismissal is the word used to describe termination of an employment contract by the employer. This term is used in several ways, which we shall investigate through the rest of this Chapter. Here are a few definitions relating to dismissal.

Key terms

Summary dismissal is where the employer dismisses the employee without notice. He may do this if the employee has committed a serious breach of contract.

Constructive dismissal is where the employer commits a breach of contract, thereby causing the employee to resign. By implication, this is also dismissal without notice.

Wrongful dismissal is a common law concept arising in specific circumstances (which are discussed in section 3. It gives the employee an action for breach of contract.

Unfair dismissal is a statutory concept introduced by employment protection legislation. As a rule, every employee has the right not to be unfairly dismissed: s 54.

Correspondingly, **fair dismissal** is a statutory concept where a person has been dismissed as a result of a fair reason under legislation. (Fair and unfair dismissal will be discussed in section 4.)

Exam focus point

Note that the distinction between wrongful and unfair dismissal depends not so much upon the nature of the dismissal, as on the **remedies available**.

2 Termination of employment by breach of contract 12/04

FAST FORWARD

Breach of the employment contract occurs where there is summary dismissal, constructive dismissal, inability on the employer's side to continue employment, or repudiation of the contract by the employee.

An employment contract is **terminated by breach in the following circumstances**.

- Summary dismissal
- Constructive dismissal
- Inability on the employer's behalf to continue
- Repudiation of the contract by the employee

The concepts of summary dismissal and constructive dismissal are both examples of dismissal without proper notice. A dismissal with proper notice is generally held to be lawful, unless it is shown to be wrongful or unfair.

However, under the ERA 1996, the reason for dismissal has to be determined in relation to both when the notice is given and when the employment is terminated.

2.1 Summary dismissal

Summary dismissal occurs where the employer dismisses the employee without notice. He may do this if the employee has committed a serious breach of contract and, if so, the employer incurs no liability.

If, however, he has **no sufficient justification** the employer is liable for **breach of contract** and the employee may claim a remedy for wrongful dismissal. Whether the employee's conduct justifies summary dismissal will vary according to the circumstances of the case.

Pepper v Webb 1969
The facts: A gardener was asked to put in some plants, but refused to do so, using vulgar language.

Decision: His summary dismissal was justified; he was in breach of contract for refusing to obey a lawful and reasonable order. He had a history of complaints against him for insolence.

Wilson v Racher 1974
The facts: A gardener swore at his employer using even choicer obscenities.

Decision: His action for wrongful dismissal succeeded, as the employer's own conduct had provoked the outburst. This was a solitary outburst following a history of diligence and competence.

2.2 Constructive dismissal 12/01, 6/02

Constructive dismissal occurs where the employer, although willing to continue the employment, repudiates some **essential term** of the contract, for example by the imposition of a complete change in the employee's duties, and the employee resigns. The employer is liable for breach of contract.

2.2.1 Establishing constructive dismissal

To establish constructive dismissal, an employee must show that:

- His employer has committed a serious breach of contract (a repudiatory breach).
- He left because of the breach.
- He has not 'waived' the breach, thereby affirming the contract.

Examples of breaches of contract which have lead to claims of constructive dismissal include the following.

- A reduction in pay: *Industrial Rubber Products v Gillon 1977*
- A complete change in the nature of the job: *Ford v Milthorn Toleman Ltd 1980*
- A failure to follow the prescribed disciplinary procedure: *Post Office v Strange 1981*
- A failure to provide a suitable working environment: *Waltons and Morse v Dorrington 1997*

The breach must be a serious one.

Western Excavating (ECC) Ltd v Sharp 1978
The facts: The defendant was suspended without pay for misconduct. This caused him financial difficulties, and so he applied for an advance against holiday pay but was refused. He then left and claimed for constructive dismissal.
Decision: The employers had not repudiated the contract and so there had been no dismissal.

2.3 Employer's inability to continue employment

If a personal employer dies, an employing firm of partners is dissolved, an employing company is compulsorily wound up, a receiver is appointed or the employee's place of employment is permanently closed, the employer may become unable to continue to employ the employee.

2.4 Repudiation of the contract by the employee

If the employee resigns or goes on strike or fails to perform the contract and to observe its conditions, that is breach of contract by him and the employer may dismiss him or treat the contract as discharged by the employee's breach.

3 Wrongful dismissal 6/05

Where the employer has **summarily dismissed** an employee without notice (as where the employer becomes insolvent), there may be a claim for **damages** at common law for **wrongful dismissal**.

An action for wrongful dismissal, since it derives from the employee's **common law** rights in contract, must be brought in the county court or the High Court. The claimant must show that he was **dismissed in breach of contract**, for example with less than the statutory minimum period of notice and that he has **as a result suffered loss**.

A dismissal will not be wrongful if it is **justified**.

3.1 Justification of dismissal

The following have been taken as justifiable circumstances.

(a) **Wilful disobedience** of a lawful order suffices if it amounts to wilful and serious defiance of authority.

(b) **Misconduct**, in connection with the business or outside it if it is sufficiently grave. For example, acceptance of a secret commission, disclosure of confidential information, assault on a fellow employee or even financial embarrassment of an employee in a position of trust (*Pearce v Foster 1886* - stockbroker's clerk who incurred heavy gambling losses).

(c) **Dishonesty**, where the employee is in a position of particular trust.

(d) **Incompetence or neglect**, insofar as the employee lacks or fails to use skill which he professes to have.

(e) **Gross negligence**, depending on the nature of the job.

(f) **Immorality**, only if it is likely to affect performance of duties or the reputation of the business.

(g) **Drunkenness**, only if it occurs in aggravated circumstances such as when driving a vehicle or a train, or is repeated: *Williams v Royal Institute of Chartered Surveyors 1997.*

4 Unfair dismissal 12/02, 6/03, 12/04, 6/05

FAST FORWARD

Certain employees have a right not to be **unfairly dismissed**. Breach of that right allows an employee to claim compensation from a tribunal. To claim for unfair dismissal, the employee must satisfy certain criteria.

Unfair dismissal is an extremely important element of employment protection legislation.

The remedies available following a successful action for **wrongful dismissal** are **limited to damages** compensating for the sum which would have been earned **if proper notice had been given.**

Legislation seeks to **widen the scope of protection** and **increase the range of remedies** available to an employee who has been unfairly dismissed. Under the terms of the **Employment Rights Act 1996**, the top rate of compensation for proven unfair dismissal is £63,100). This cap does not apply to those dismissed for 'whistleblowing', which falls under the Public Interest Disclosure Act 1998.

4.1 Scope

Every **included employee who qualifies** under the criteria (a) and (b) below has a statutory right not to be unfairly dismissed: s 94. Certain categories of employee are **excluded** from the statutory unfair dismissal code.

- Persons employed to work **outside Great Britain**
- Employees dismissed while taking **unofficial strike** or other industrial action
- Other categories, including members of the police

In order to obtain compensation or other remedies for unfair dismissal the employee must satisfy several criteria.

(a) Be **under the normal retiring age** applicable to his job or grade or under 65 if there is no normal age. The House of Lords has held (*Waite v Government Communications Headquarters 1983*) that the 'normal age' is to be determined by the employer's practice. If practice is altered while the employee is in service it is the 'reasonable expectation' at the time of retirement which determines the 'normal age' (*Hughes v Department of Health and Social Security 1985*).

(b) Have been **continuously employed for one year** whether full-time or part-time.

(c) Have been **dismissed.** This may have to be determined by the tribunal, for example if the employee resigned claiming constructive dismissal.

(d) Have been **unfairly** dismissed. Dismissal may be unfair even though it is not a breach of contract by the employer.

As noted in Chapter 23 there are some **exceptions** to the one year's continuous service qualification. These are:

- Where the matter concerns a **safety representative** being penalised for carrying out legitimate health and safety activities
- Where an employee is being **denied a statutory** right (for example an unlawful deduction from wages)
- Where the employee is **pregnant**

Exam focus point

You should learn these exceptions to the continuous service rule.

The **effective date** of **dismissal** is reckoned as follows.

- Where there is termination by notice, the date on which the notice expires
- Where there is termination without notice, the date on which the termination takes effect
- Where an employee's fixed term contract is not renewed, the date on which that term expires

4.2 Making a claim

There are four steps to making a claim for **compensation** for unfair dismissal.

Step 1 The **employee** must **apply to a tribunal** within **three months** of dismissal

Step 2 The **employee** must **show** that he is a **qualifying employee** and that he has in fact been **dismissed**.

Step 3 Then the **employer** must **demonstrate** (prove):

(i) What was the alleged **only or principal reason** for dismissal

(ii) That it was one of the reasons listed in s 96 (discussed in Section 5 below) or was otherwise a '**substantial reason** of a kind such as to be capable of justifying the dismissal of an employee' in this position.

Step 4 Then the tribunal must decide if the principal reason did in fact justify the dismissal and whether the employer acted reasonably in treating the reason as sufficient.

If the employer cannot show that the principal reason allegedly justifying the dismissal was one of the fair reasons given in statute (these are discussed in section 5), the dismissal is unfair.

Dismissal may be identified in three separate circumstances.

(a) **Actual dismissal** is usually fairly clear-cut and can be recognised from the words used by an employer.

(b) **Constructive dismissal**, as described earlier, involves a fundamental breach of the employment contract by the employer.

(c) **Expiry of a fixed-term contract** without renewal amounts to a dismissal.

The employee must show that he has in fact been dismissed. The courts often have to debate whether or not the use of abusive language by employers constitutes mere abuse or indicates dismissal.

4.3 The reason for dismissal

The fair reasons for dismissal are discussed in section 5. As noted above, if the principal reason for dismissal is not one of those fair reasons, then dismissal will be unfair.

However, even if the employer shows that he dismissed the employee for a reason which is recognised as capable of being sufficient, **a tribunal may still decide that the dismissal was unfair** if it considers that on the basis of **equity and the substantial merits** of the case **the employer acted unreasonably** in dismissing the employee: s 98.

4.3.1 Reasonableness of employer

The **employment tribunal** is required to review the circumstances and to decide whether it was reasonable to dismiss the employee for the reasons given.

Determining whether the employer has acted reasonably requires the tribunal to ask:

- Has the correct **procedure** been applied?
- Did the employer take all **circumstances** into consideration?
- What would any **reasonable employer** have done?

The employer does not act reasonably unless he **takes account of the relevant circumstances**. If an inexperienced employee is struggling to do his work, the employer is expected to help by advice or supervision in the hope that he may improve.

The emphasis placed on giving one or more warnings before dismissing is partly so that the employee may heed the warning and amend his conduct or his performance.

4.3.2 Disciplinary procedure

Since October 2004 there have been statutory rules for dealing with disciplinary and grievance procedures. These provisions form part of an employee's contract of employment.

The standard statutory procedure for dismissal (and disciplinary) cases sets out three steps.

- There must be a statement of the grounds for the action and an invitation to a meeting
- The nature of the meeting
- An appeal stage

Where dismissal has already taken place the employer must provide details of the grounds for the dismissal and permit the employee to appeal that decision.

These procedures (set out in the Employment Act 2002) have three general requirements

- The timing and location of any meeting must be reasonable
- The meeting must be conducted in such a way as to allow both the employer and the employee to explain their case
- If there is more than one meeting the employer should, if reasonably practicable, be represented by a more senior person then at the first meeting

All steps in the procedure should also be taken without unreasonable delay.

If either party fails to comply with the relevant procedures then neither party has to comply with the rest of the procedures. In addition s98A provides that a dismissal will **automatically** be unfair if the employer fails to comply with the procedures but the employer may still be able to prove the dismissal was reasonable if he can show he would have dismissed the employee even if the procedure had been followed.

4.3.3 Warnings

Except in the most flagrant cases it is **not reasonable for an employer to dismiss an employee without first warning him** that if he continues or repeats what has happened at least once he is likely to be dismissed.

> *Newman v T H White Motors 1972*
> *The facts:* An employee used foul language to a trainee. The employer asked him not to do so. When he persisted the employer dismissed him.
>
> *Decision:* This was an unreasonable and therefore unfair dismissal. The employer must make it clear to the employee that he risks dismissal if he persists.

4.3.4 Concluding on reasonableness

In reaching its conclusion on the issue of reasonableness, **the tribunal should not substitute what it would have done if placed in the employer's situation**. It is necessary to set the rights and interests of the employee against the interests of the employer's business and then decide whether **any reasonable employer could have come to a different conclusion**.

Unreasonableness and breach of contract by the employer must be distinguished. Some unreasonable conduct of the employer may be serious enough to amount to repudiation of the contract, and if the employee leaves he can claim for constructive dismissal by the employer.

If the employer acts unreasonably but in a manner which does not amount to repudiation of the contract, the employee who resigns terminates a contract by his own act and cannot claim constructive dismissal: *Western Excavating (ECC) Ltd v Sharp 1978.*

5 Unfair dismissal - Justification of dismissal 6/03

FAST FORWARD

Dismissal must be **justified** if it related to the employee's capability or qualifications, the employee's conduct, redundancy, legal prohibition or restriction on the employee's continued employment or some other substantial reason.

Dismissal is **automatically unfair** if it is on the grounds of trade union membership or activities, refusal to join a trade union, pregnancy, redundancy when others are retained, a criminal conviction which is 'spent' under the Rehabilitation of Offenders Act 1974 or race or sex.

5.1 Potentially fair reasons for dismissal

To be able to justify dismissal as fair dismissal the employer must show that his **principal reason** related to one of the following.

(a) The **capability or qualifications** of the employee for performing work of the kind which he was employed to do

(b) The **conduct** of the employee

(c) **Redundancy**

(d) **Legal prohibition** or restriction by which the employee could not lawfully continue to work in the position which he held (for example, if a doctor or a solicitor employed as such is struck off the relevant professional register or an employee loses his driving licence which he needs to be able to do his job)

(e) **Some other substantial reason** which justifies dismissal

5.1.1 Capability/qualifications

If the employer dismisses for want of capability on the part of the employee, the employer has to establish that fault.

- What does the contract require?
- What is the general standard of performance of his employees in this trade?
- What is the previous standard of performance of the dismissed employee himself?

If the employee is incompetent it must be of such a nature and quality as to justify dismissal - such as a shop manageress who left her shop dirty and untidy, who failed to maintain cash registers and who did not put stock away: *Lewis Shops Group Ltd v Wiggins 1973.*

'**Capability** is to be assessed by reference to skills, aptitude, health or any other physical or mental quality. '**Qualification'** means any academic or technical qualifications relevant to the position that the employee holds': s 98(3).

'Reasonableness' on the part of the employer is required, for example:

- **Consultation** with employee to determine areas of difficulty
- Allowing a **reasonable time** for improvement
- Providing **training** if necessary
- Considering **all alternatives** to dismissal

If the employer relies on **ill health** as the grounds of incapability there must be **proper medical evidence**. The employer is entitled to consider his own business needs. A reasonable procedure involves cautions, confrontation with records and the granting of a period for improvement.

> *International Sports Ltd v Thomson 1980*
> *The facts*: The employee had been away from work for around 25% of the time, suffering from a number of complaints all of which were certified by medical certificates. She received a number of warnings. Following a final warning and prior to dismissal the company consulted their medical adviser. As the illnesses were unrelated and unverifiable, he did not consider an examination worthwhile. She was dismissed.
>
> *Decision*: The dismissal was fair.

5.1.2 Misconduct

It is usual to apply the common law distinction between **gross misconduct** which justifies summary dismissal on the first occasion, for example, theft, and **ordinary misconduct** which is not usually sufficient grounds for dismissal unless it is persistent.

Assault on a fellow employee, conduct exposing others to danger (for example, smoking in an area prohibited for safety reasons), unpleasant behaviour towards customers and persistent absences from work have been treated as sufficient misconduct to justify dismissal.

5.1.3 Redundancy

If an employee is dismissed mainly or only on the ground of **redundancy**, he may claim remedies for unfair dismissal if he can show one of the following.

(a) There were one or more other employees in similar positions who might have been made redundant and that he was **selected for redundancy in breach of a customary arrangement or agreed procedure**.

(b) He was selected for a reason connected with **trade union membership**.

A redundancy selection procedure should be in conformity with **good industrial relations practice** which requires consultation and objective criteria of selection. The criteria set out by the EAT in *Williams v Compair Maxam Ltd 1982* have been accepted as standards of behaviour.

(a) The employer should give as much **warning** as possible of impending redundancies.

(b) The employer should **consult with the trade union** as to the best means of achieving the desired management result. In *Mugford v Midland Bank plc 1997* it was held that even when an employer has consulted a trade union over the selection criteria for redundancy, this does not release the employer from consulting the individual to be made redundant before a final decision is taken.

(c) It should be possible to check **criteria** for selection against such things as attendance records, efficiency at the job and length of service.

(d) The employer should ensure that the selection is made **fairly**.

(e) The employer should consider whether an **offer of alternative employment** can be made.

Redundancy is discussed further in section 8.

5.1.4 Other substantial reason

The category of **other substantial reason** permits the employer to rely on some factor which is unusual and likely to affect him adversely. An employer has justified dismissal on specific grounds.

(a) The employee was married to one of his competitors.

(b) The employee refused to accept a reorganisation, for example, a change of shift working, made in the interests of the business and with the agreement of a large majority of other employees.

5.1.5 Automatically fair reasons for dismissal

Other reasons are designated as being **automatically fair** by legislation.

- Taking part in **unofficial industrial action**
- Being a **threat to national security** (to be certified by the government)

An employee who strikes or refuses to work normally may be fairly dismissed unless the industrial action has been lawfully organised under the protection conferred by the Employment Relations Act 1999. Where dismissal results from a lock-out or a strike, the tribunal cannot deal with it as a case of alleged unfair dismissal unless victimisation is established.

5.1.6 Automatically unfair reasons for dismissal

Some reasons are automatically unfair (known as **'inadmissible reasons'**). Examples include:

- Pregnancy or other maternity-related grounds
- A spent conviction under the Rehabilitation of Offenders Act 1974
- Trade union membership or activities
- Dismissal on transfer of an undertaking (unless there are 'economic, technical or organisational reasons' justifying the dismissal)
- Taking steps to avert danger to health and safety at work
- Seeking to enforce rights relating to the national minimum wage
- Exercising rights under the Working Time Regulations 1998
- Refusing or opting out of Sunday working (in the retail sector)
- Making a protected disclosure order under the Public Interest Disclosure Act 1998.

Dismissal on grounds of pregnancy or pregnancy-related illness is automatically unfair, **regardless of length of service**. It amounts to **gender discrimination** contrary to EC Directive 76/207: *Webb v Emo Air Cargo (UK) Ltd 1994.* Sex discrimination is discussed further in Chapter 25.

5.2 Proving what was the reason for dismissal

The employer may be required to give to the employee a **written statement** of the **reason for dismissal**: s 92.

If an employee is dismissed for trying to **enforce his employment rights**, by for example asking for a written statement of particulars or an itemised pay statement, he may claim unfair dismissal **regardless of the length of service** and hours worked.

Question — **Wrongful and unfair dismissal**

What is the difference between wrongful dismissal and unfair dismissal?

Answer

Wrongful dismissal is a common law concept arising in specific circumstances and which gives the employee an action for breach of contract, for example where insufficient notice has been given.

Unfair dismissal is a statutory concept introduced by employment protection legislation. As a rule, every employee has the right not to be unfairly dismissed: s 54.Note that the distinction between wrongful and unfair dismissal depends not so much upon the nature of the dismissal, as on the remedies available.

6 Remedies for wrongful dismissal

Generally, the **only effective remedy available to a wrongfully dismissed employee is a claim for damages based on the loss of earnings**. The measure of damages is usually the **sum that would have been earned if proper notice had been given.**

As with any other case of compensation, the wronged party is expected to **mitigate** his loss by, say, seeking other employment.

Where breach of contract leaves the employer as the injured party, he may dismiss the employee and withhold wages. The employer may recover confidential papers, or apply for an injunction to enforce a valid restrictive covenant: *Thomas Marshall (Exporters) v Guinle 1978.*

Employment tribunals have jurisdiction to deal with wrongful dismissal cases, which formerly had to be heard in the civil courts.

7 Remedies for unfair dismissal

FAST FORWARD

Remedies for unfair dismissal include:

- Reinstatement
- Re-engagement
- Compensation

An employee who alleges unfair dismissal must present his complaint to an **employment tribunal** within three months of the effective date of termination. The dispute is referred to a Conciliation Officer and only comes before the tribunal if his efforts to promote a settlement fail.

7.1 Reinstatement

If unfair dismissal is established, the tribunal first considers the possibility of making an order for reinstatement.

Key term

Reinstatement is return to the same job without any break of continuity: s 114.

7.2 Re-engagement

The tribunal may alternatively order **re-engagement**. The new employment must be comparable with the old or otherwise suitable.

Key term

Re-engagement means that the employee is given new employment with the employer (or his successor or associate) on terms specified in the order.

In deciding whether to exercise these powers, the tribunal must take into account whether the complainant wishes to be reinstated and, whether it is practicable and just for the employer to comply. **Such orders are in fact very infrequent.**

The Employment Appeal Tribunal has ruled that an order for re-engagement should not be made if there has been a breakdown in confidence between the parties: *Wood Group Heavy Industrial Turbines Ltd v Crossan 1998* (employee dismissed following allegations of drug dealing on company premises and time-keeping offences).

7.3 Compensation

If the tribunal does not order reinstatement or re-engagement the tribunal may award **compensation**, which may be made in three stages as follows.

(a) A **basic award** calculated as follows. Those aged 41 and over receive one and a half weeks' pay (up to a current (from February 2004) maximum of £270 gross per week) for each year of service up to a maximum of 20 years. In other age groups the same provisions apply, except that the 22-40 age group receive one week's pay per year and the under 22 age group receive half a week's pay.

(b) A **compensatory award** (taking account of the basic award) for any additional loss of earnings, expenses and benefits on common law principles of damages for breach of contract: s 124. This is limited to £55,000 by the Employment Rights Act 1996.

(c) If the employer does not comply with an order for reinstatement or re-engagement and does not show that it was impracticable to do so a **punitive additional award** is made of between 26 and 52 weeks' pay (again subject to the £270 per week maximum).

The tribunal may reduce the amount of the award in any of the following circumstances.

- If the employee **contributed** in some way to his own dismissal: s 123(6)
- If he has **unreasonably refused** an offer of reinstatement
- If it is **just and equitable** to reduce the basic award by reason of some matter which occurred before dismissal: s 123(1)

Question **Non-renewal of fixed term contract**

Nick commences employment under a three-year contract with Equis Ltd on 1.8.X6. On 30.6.X9 he is given notice that the contract is not to be renewed. Assuming that he has a case, what claims may he bring against Equis Ltd?

Answer

For the purposes of the Act, dismissal occurs when a fixed term contract is not renewed even though such an eventuality is implicit in the fact that the agreement has a fixed term. Nick is therefore entitled to claim for redundancy pay and/or compensation for unfair dismissal if he can prove the requisite facts. However, non-renewal cannot give rise to a claim for wrongful dismissal, which is only possible when there has been summary dismissal or dismissal with less than the required period of notice.

8 Redundancy 12/02, 6/04, 6/05

An employee may claim a redundancy payment where he is

- Dismissed by his employer by reason of redundancy
- Laid off or kept on short time

8.1 What is redundancy?

Key term

A dismissal is treated as caused by **redundancy** if the only or main reason is that:

- The employer has ceased, or intends to cease, to carry on the business (or the local establishment of the business) in which the employee has been employed
- The requirements of that business for employees to carry on the work done by the employee have ceased or diminished (or are expected to): s 139 (1)

If the employee's contract requires him to work at other places than his present place of employment, and the employer **under the terms of the contract** requires him to move to a different place of work because there is no longer work at his present place of employment, that is not a case of redundancy, although in some cases it might be constructive dismissal.

The Court of Appeal has decided that the proper test for determining whether or not an employee is redundant is to see whether there has been a reduction of the employers' requirements for employees to work **at the place where the person concerned is employed**.

High Table Ltd v Horst and Others 1997
The facts: High Table Ltd, contract caterers, employed waitresses who had worked for several years at one company. The client company told High Table that the waitresses were no longer required, so they were dismissed by High Table on the grounds of redundancy. The waitresses, who had mobility clauses in their contracts, alleged unfair dismissal since High Table had not tried to re-employ them somewhere else.

Decision: The Court of Appeal ruled against them, saying that the place of work was at the client company premises and the dismissals were for genuine redundancy.

In considering whether the requirements of the business for staff have diminished, it is the **overall** position which must be considered. If for example A's job is abolished and A is moved into B's job and B is dismissed, that is a case of redundancy although B's job continues.

In *British Broadcasting Corporation v Farnworth 1998* a radio producer's fixed term contract was not renewed and the employer advertised for a radio producer with more experience. It was held by the EAT that the less experienced radio producer was indeed redundant as the requirement for her level of services had diminished.

If the employer reorganises his business or alters his methods so that the same work has to be done by different means which are beyond the capacity of the employee, that is not redundancy.

North Riding Garages v Butterwick 1967
The facts: A garage reorganised its working arrangements so that the workshop manager's duties included more administrative work . He was dismissed when it was found he could not perform these duties.

Decision: His claim for redundancy pay must fail since it was not a case of redundancy.

Vaux and Associated Breweries v Ward 1969
The facts: The owners of a public house renovated their premises and as part of the new image they dismissed the middle-aged barmaid and replaced her with a younger employee.

Decision: The claim for redundancy pay must fail since the same job still existed.

Exam focus point

Like unfair dismissal, redundancy is a favourite topic. Link your studies on redundancy and unfair dismissal to the material on remedies.

8.2 Exceptions to the right to redundancy payment

A person is excluded from having a right to redundancy payment where

- They do not fit the definition of 'employee' given in statute
- They are past the **normal retirement age** for the job
- They have not been **continuously employed** for **two** years
- They have been or could be dismissed for **misconduct**
- An offer to **renew the contract** is unreasonably **refused**
- Claim is made **out of time**

8.2.1 Misconduct of the employee

An employee who is dismissed for **misconduct** is **not entitled to redundancy pay** even though he may become redundant.

Sanders v Neale 1974
The facts: In the course of a dispute employees refused to work normally. The employer dismissed them and closed down his business. The employees claimed redundancy pay.

Decision: the claim must be dismissed since the employees had repudiated the contract before the employer's decision to close down made them redundant.

An employee can be dismissed for misconduct but still claim redundancy pay in the event of a strike.

- After receiving notice of termination of the contract from the employer
- After the employee has given notice claiming redundancy pay on account of lay-off or short time

8.2.2 Offer of further employment

The employer may offer a redundant employee **alternative** employment for the future. **If the employee then unreasonably refuses the offer, he loses his entitlement to redundancy pay**: s 141.

The offer must be of alternative employment **in the same capacity**, at the same place and on the same terms and conditions as the previous employment. It should not be perceived as being lower in status: *Cambridge District Co-operative Society v Ruse 1993*.

When there is a difference between the terms and conditions of a new contract and the previous contract, the employee is entitled to a **four week trial** period in the new employment. If either party terminates the new contract during the trial period, it is treated as a case of dismissal for redundancy at the expiry date of the previous employment. The employee can also still bring claims for unfair dismissal: *Trafalgar House Services Ltd v Carder 1997*.

8.3 Lay-off and short time

An employee's exact remuneration may depend on the employer providing work. He is 'laid off' in any week in which he earns nothing by reason of lack of work or he is 'kept on short time', which is any week in which he earns less than half a normal week's pay: s 86.

When an employee is **laid off** or **kept on short time** for four or more consecutive weeks, or six weeks in a period of thirteen weeks he **may claim redundancy** pay by giving notice to the employer of his intention to claim.

In addition to his notice of claim the employee must also give notice to the employer to terminate the contract of employment: s 150(1).

8.4 Calculation of redundancy pay

Redundancy pay is calculated on the same basis as the basic compensation for unfair dismissal.

Chapter roundup

- **Breach of the employment contract** occurs where there is **summary dismissal**, **constructive dismissal**, **inability** on the employer's side to **continue employment**, or **repudiation** of the contract by the employee.
- Where employment is **terminated by notice** the period given must **not be less** than the **statutory minimum**.
- If an employee is dismissed with **shorter notice** than the statutory or contractual requirements, or without notice when summary dismissal is unjustified, he can sue for wrongful dismissal.
- Certain employees have a right not to be **unfairly dismissed**. Breach of that right allows an employee to claim compensation from a tribunal. To claim for unfair dismissal, the employee must satisfy certain criteria.
- Dismissal must be **justified** if it related to the employee's capability or qualifications, the employee's conduct, redundancy, legal prohibition or restriction on the employee's continued employment or some other substantial reason.
- Dismissal is **automatically unfair** if it is on the grounds of trade union membership or activities, refusal to join a trade union, pregnancy, redundancy when others are retained, a criminal conviction which is 'spent' under the Rehabilitation of Offenders Act 1974 or race or sex.
- Even where the reason for dismissal is justified or automatically fair, the tribunal must also decide whether the employer acted **reasonably** in the circumstances.
- **Automatically fair** reasons are dismissal for striking (providing all strikers are dismissed), or being a threat to national security (to be certified by the Government).

  The only effective remedy available for wrongful dismissal is a claim for **damages** based on loss of earnings.
- Remedies for **unfair dismissal** include:
  - **Reinstatement**
  - **Re-engagement**
  - **Compensation**
- Dismissal is caused by **redundancy** when the employer has ceased to carry on the business in which the employee has been employed or the business no longer needs employees to carry on that work. In these circumstances, dismissal is **presumed** by the courts to he been for redundancy unless otherwise demonstrated.

Quick quiz

1 How much notice is an employee with 5 years' continuous service entitled to?

2 If an employer cannot continue with the employment contract because the company has gone into liquidation, does that constitute breach of contract?

Yes ☐

No ☐

3 Is summary dismissal ever justified? If so, when?

4 **Fill in the blanks** below, using the words in the box.

To claim (1) .... for unfair dismissal, three issues have to be considered.

- The employee must show that he is a (2) .... employee and that he has been (3) ....
- The (4) .... must show what was the (5) .... for dismissal
- Application has to be made to the (6) .... within (7) .... months of the dismissal

• qualifying	• dismissed	• employer
• reason	• three	• compensation
• employment tribunal		

5 Expiry of a fixed term contract without renewal amounts to a dismissal

True ☐

False ☐

6 Which of the following is *not* a question that a tribunal, when considering an employer's reasonableness in an unfair dismissal claim, will want to answer?

A What would a reasonable employer have done?
B Has the correct procedure been applied?
C Has any employee been dismissed in this way before?
D Did the employer take all circumstances into consideration?

7 Give an automatically fair reason for dismissal.

8 Which is the most frequent remedy awarded for unfair dismissal?

compensation
re-engagement
re-instalment

9 An employee is not entitled to redundancy if he resigns voluntarily.

True ☐

False ☐

Answers to quick quiz

1 5 weeks (1 week for each year's continuous service)

2 Yes

3 Yes, in cases of serious breach of contract by the employee

4 (1) compensation (2) qualifying (3) dismissed (4) employer (5) reason (6) employment tribunal (7) three

5 True

6 C

7 Being a threat to national security (alternatively, taking part in unofficial industrial action)

8 Compensation

9 True

Now try the question below from the Exam Question Bank

Number	Level	Marks	Time
Q25	Examination	20	36 mins

25

Discrimination at work

Topic list	Syllabus reference
1 What is discrimination?	11(d)
2 Sex discrimination	11(d)
3 Race discrimination	11(d)
4 Disability discrimination	11(d)
5 Victimisation and harassment	11(d)
6 Remedies for discrimination	11(d)
7 Other forms of discrimination	11(d)
8 Employment law and human rights	11(d)

Introduction

The issue of discrimination at work has given rise to several important pieces of legislation. Following a period of development of statutory regulation in the 1970s, addressing the principal areas of sex and race discrimination, there has been a flurry of activity in the last couple of years driven by changes in European law and broadening the scope of the law.

Discrimination usually consists of one or more of:

- Different treatment due to sex or race. (This also covers harassment.)
- Employees receiving different rates of pay for similar work on the grounds of sex. (See the earlier material on the Equal Pay Act 1970.)
- Disabled people receiving less favourable treatment than their not disabled work colleagues.
- People being treated differently due to membership of a trade union.

This chapter will set out the key areas of discrimination on the grounds of sex (or marital status), race and disability, as well as the newer areas of religion and sexual orientation.

There are two forms of discrimination, direct and indirect. You need to be aware of both kinds, and be able to interpret them in scenario questions.

Introduction (cont)

A person who feels they have been discriminated against at work may apply to an employment tribunal. The remedies that a tribunal may give in the even of discrimination being proven are:

- Compensation
- Recommendations of employer action
- Settlement (referral to a conciliation process)

The next area to be tackled, and which must be addressed by the UK by 2006, is age discrimination.

This topic could be examined in Part A or B. it could be examined in conjunction with unfair or wrongful dismissal (Chapter 24) or possibly the Human Rights Act 1998 (Chapter 3) which is referred to in this chapter.

1 What is Discrimination?

FAST FORWARD

There is legislation against discrimination on the following grounds:

- Sex
- Race
- Disability
- Religion or belief
- Sexual orientation

Key term

Discrimination is the practice of treating one or more members of a specified group in a manner that is unfair as compared to the treatment of other people who are not part of that group.

In recent years, extensive new legislation has been passed to broaden the coverage of the law as successive governments seek to prevent discrimination in the workplace. The key areas in which legislation has been passed are:

- Sex, including marital status and gender reassignment
- Race – some statutes relate to ethnic origins, others to colour or nationality
- Disability
- Religion
- Sexual orientation

These areas represent 'groups' in the definition above. Discrimination is behaving in a detrimental manner to people who fall within the groups.

Towards the end of this chapter, we examine forthcoming extensions to the anti-discrimination framework covering the issue of age discrimination.

Discrimination is a **comparison** issue. It is central to the concept of discrimination that one set of employees **is treated in an inferior manner to other employees.** It is not possible to claim discrimination by a bad employer, therefore, if he treats all employees as badly, regardless of what 'group' they are in. Discrimination is essentially a matter of **double standards.**

Within this definition, and across the various groups of people that are discriminated against, there are two forms of discrimination, direct and indirect.

1.1 Direct discrimination

FAST FORWARD

Discrimination on the grounds of race or sex may be direct or indirect.

Direct discrimination tends to be the most obvious type of discrimination.

Key term

> **Direct discrimination** is when an employee or prospective employee is treated less favourably because of their race, sex or disability.

Examples of such direct discrimination could be:

- The person being passed over for promotion
- A comparably qualified person not being given the job

In such cases, an employer cannot claim that there was no **intention** to discriminate. A tribunal will only consider the end effect.

1.2 Indirect discrimination

Indirect discrimination is a more complex form of discrimination. It occurs where, for example, an employer makes it impossible for a person with the correct qualifications to do a certain job by putting in place criteria which cannot be justified as a real requirement of the job.

Key term

> **Indirect discrimination** is more complex discrimination which arises through unjustifiable criteria for particular jobs which cause a group of employees to be unfairly treated in comparison to other employees.

A person claiming that they have suffered indirect discrimination must show that they have suffered as a result of it. Suffering as a result of direct discrimination is much easier to prove.

In some case, indirect discrimination is considered justifiable because of a genuine occupational reason, such as authenticity, for example, in a theme restaurant.

There is no provision in the law for indirect discrimination in the case of disability.

2 Sex discrimination

FAST FORWARD

> Sex discrimination is legislated against in the Sex Discrimination Act 1975, as updated by the Act of the same name in 1986.

2.1 Sex Discrimination Act 1975

This Act **prohibits discrimination on the grounds of gender** against any employee (or a person who is self-employed), male or female, in recruitment, promotion, training, benefits or dismissal.

The **Equal Opportunities Commission (EOC)** oversees the working of safeguards for ensuring equality of women with men.

The Act is based on the EU's 1976 Equal Treatment Directive. An amending directive was issued in 2002 to address a number of areas of potential discrimination in the workplace. Gender equality is now at the heart of the EU's social policy agenda.

2.1.1 Unlawful discriminatory practices

The following matters are unlawful:

- Publishing an advertisement which indicates an intention to discriminate unlawfully
- **Instructing another person** to do an act which amounts to unlawful discrimination
- **Sexual harassment** in the workplace. (An employer may have a defence if he took reasonable steps to prevent such behaviour)

A new definition of sexual harassment is introduced:

> "Sexual harassment shall be deemed to be discrimination on the grounds of sex at the workplace when an unwanted conduct related to sex takes place with the purpose or effect of affecting the dignity of a person and/or creating an intimidating, hostile, offensive or disturbing environment, in particular if a person's rejection of, or submission to, such conduct is used as a basis for a decision which affects that person."

Note that it is conduct relating to the sex of the victim that is relevant, including bullying, intimidation and threats. (The treatment complained of does not have to be sexual in nature). A single incident can constitute harassment, although it would more usually be identified from a repeated or recurring behaviour.

2.2 Direct discrimination

Direct discrimination arises where an employer treats an employee less favourably on the grounds of the employee's sex. The employee must then make a comparison between how she was treated and how a man would have been treated. This may be an actual or hypothetical situation.

The principles applicable in cases of direct discrimination have been helpfully summarised in *Law Society v Bahl (2003)*, as follows:

(i) The **onus lies on the claimant** to show discrimination in accordance with the normal standard of proof.

(i) **Discrimination need not be conscious**; there may be direct discrimination as a result in inbuilt and unrecognised prejudice of which the person discriminating is unaware.

(iii) The discriminatory reason need not be the sole or even the principal reason for the discrimination – it is enough that it is a **contributing cause** in the sense of being a 'significant influence'.

(iv) In determining whether there has been direct discrimination it is necessary in all save the most obvious cases for the tribunal to discover what was in the **mind of the alleged discriminator**. This will generally involve the tribunal in making appropriate inferences from the primary facts which it finds.

Unfavourable treatment of a **woman because she is pregnant** will automatically constitute direct sex discrimination. This includes discrimination by reason of her pregnancy or by reason of her taking maternity leave. Pregnancy-related illness is also included.

2.3 Indirect discrimination

The Sex Discrimination (Indirect Discrimination and Burden of Proof) Regulations 2001 amend the original version of indirect discrimination. The new test is whether a person applies to a woman a 'provision, criterion or practice' which he applies or would apply equally to a man, but –

(i) Which is such that it would be to the detriment of a considerably larger proportion of women than of men, and

(ii) Which he cannot show to be justifiable irrespective of the sex of the person to whom it is applied, and

(iii) Which is to her detriment.

There is no need, under the new definition, to show that a woman 'cannot comply' with some standard that can be identified as a 'requirement or condition'.

Illustration

You discriminate against a woman indirectly if you cause her a detriment by putting on obstacle in her path which she cannot personally overcome in practice and which is of such a nature that women generally are less likely than men to be able to overcome it, unless that obstacle can be justified irrespective of sex.

A policy may appear to be neutral but its effect may impact on more women than men (for example, a requirement for full-time working, which generally fewer women can do by reason of childcare commitments, so it would be indirectly discriminatory).

2.4 Burden of proof

Section 63A of the Sex Discrimination Act now applies the same burden of proof in sex discrimination cases as in race, religion and sexual orientation claims. Thus, an application must prove facts from which the tribunal **could** conclude that the employer had committed discrimination and the tribunal must then uphold the applicant's complaint unless the employer proves that his action was not discriminatory.

2.5 Exceptions to unlawful discrimination

The following do not constitute unlawful discrimination:

- **Special treatment** of women in relation to **pregnancy**
- Where a **genuine occupational qualification** or requirement is required for a particular employment.

Genuine occupational qualifications may include:

- Reason of **physiology** (excluding strength or stamina) or **authenticity** (say in the arts)
- To preserve **decency/privacy** (say in sanitary facilities or a private home)
- Where the job involves duties **abroad** and the **foreign laws and customs** are such that it would be impossible for a woman to do the job
- Where the **nature of the establishment** reasonably requires a man
- Where **personal services** promoting welfare of education can most effectively be provided by a man
- Where the job is one of two to be provided by a married couple

2.6 Victimisation

Victimisation arises when a person is discriminated against, not because of his or her gender, but because he or she has either brought proceedings under the Sex Discrimination Act or has alleged a breach of the Act.

2.7 Discrimination on the grounds of marital status

The Sex Discrimination Acts make it unlawful to discriminate against **married people** in any way, for example, if an employer believes that a single man will be able to devote more time to a job than a married man.

2.8 Gender reassignment

Under the Sex Discrimination (Gender Reassignment) Regulations 1999, it is unlawful to discriminate against anyone in the employment field on the grounds of gender reassignment.

3 Race discrimination

FAST FORWARD

Race discrimination is legislated against in the Race Relations Act 1976.

Discrimination on the grounds of race is prohibited by the Race Relations Act 1976, which also set up the Commission for Racial Equality (CRE).

The RRA has been subject to important amendments. In particular, the Race Relations Act (Amendment) Regulations 2003 introduced a range of changes. The changes provide:

- an extended definition of indirect discrimination applicable in cases where there is discrimination on the grounds of race, ethnic or national origin
- protection against harassment as a discrete wrong
- circumstances of genuine and determining occupational requirements.

New provision was also made with regard to the burden of proof in complaints made under the Act.

The Act's provisions are similar to the Sex Discrimination Act 1975, although there are fewer grounds to justify discrimination. As in the related legislation, there are four distinct ways in which discrimination may occur.

- Direct discrimination
- Discrimination by way of harassment
- Indirect discrimination
- Victimisation

3.1 Direct discrimination

A person discriminates against another by treating that other less favourably than another person. If discrimination is on racial grounds it is unlawful. Direct discrimination also includes racial *harassment*, the definition being similar to that applied in sex discrimination legislation. Racial *segregation* is unlawful direct discrimination, even where a segregated employee has the same access to promotion and training and the same pay and conditions as other employees.

3.2 Indirect discrimination

Indirect discrimination arises where an employer operates a policy which on the face of it has nothing to do with race but in practice the effect is to disadvantage ethnic minorities. This includes formal and informal practices and provisions.

3.3 Race

Racial discrimination includes discrimination on the basis of colour, race, nationality and ethnic or national origins.

3.4 Exceptions to unlawful discrimination

It is acceptable to discriminate on grounds of race if that is a 'genuine occupational requirement or qualification.'

The following are grounds to justify race discrimination.

- Authenticity in **entertainment, art or photography** is allowed – a black man to play Othello for instance.

- **Personal welfare services** – recruiting a Bangladeshi housing officer in a Bangladeshi area for example.
- Maintaining **ethnic authenticity** in a **bar or restaurant**.
- The Act applies only to establishments in Great Britain.
- Employment in private households is exempted from the provisions of the Act (with the exemption of victimisation).

3.4.1 Burden of proof

Amendments to the Race Relations Act in respect of proving a case of race discrimination have the following effect. The applicant must prove facts from which the tribunal **could** conclude that the employer had committed an act of discrimination and the tribunal must then uphold the applicant's complaint unless the employer proves that his action was not discriminatory.

3.5 Liability

Liability for race discrimination usually lies with the employer, although any employee who is found to have discriminated will also be liable. If, in discriminating, the employee was acting in the course of his employment, the employer will also be liable under the principle of vicarious liability.

3.6 Positive discrimination

Positive discrimination, the giving of preferential treatment to a particular racial group, counts as discrimination under the Act. However, some forms of *positive action* are permitted, for example encouraging a particular racial group to apply for particular work may be permitted.

4 Disability discrimination 12/01

FAST FORWARD

Disability discrimination is legislated against in the Disability Discrimination Act 1995.

The **Disability Discrimination Act 1995** gives disabled people similar rights to those already enjoyed in relation to sex and race.

The **Disability Rights Commission Act 1999** and has provided for the establishment of a **Disability Rights Commission**, which has the same powers as the Equal Opportunities Commission and the Commission for Racial Equality when determining whether unlawful discrimination has taken place.

Key term

Disability is defined by the Disability Discrimination Act as 'a physical or mental impairment which has a substantial and long-term adverse effect on the ability to carry out normal day-to-day activities'.

It is unlawful to discriminate against a disabled person in:

- The **arrangements made to determine to whom employment will be offered** and the **terms and conditions** in which it is offered
- The **opportunities given** for promotions, a transfer, training or receiving other benefit
- Refusing to offer such opportunities
- **Dismissing him or subjecting him to other detriment**

An employer discriminates against a disabled person if :

- He **treats him less favourably than others for reason of disability**, and
- He **cannot show** that the treatment in question is **justified**.

The employment sections of the Act do not apply to employers with less than 15 employees. In addition, certain Crown employees including prison officers, firefighters, police officers and members of the armed forces are excluded from protection under the Act.

4.1 Justification for discrimination

Less favourable treatment will only be justified if it is **both material** to the circumstances of the case and **substantial**. This will largely depend on the circumstances of the case.

However, less favourable treatment **cannot be justified** if the employer has failed to make **reasonable adjustments**.

4.1.1 Duty to make reasonable adjustments

Under the Disability Discrimination Act 1995, an employer has a duty to facilitate the employment of disabled people: s 6.

This requirement includes the need to take reasonable steps to so facilitate employment, that is, to make reasonable adjustments.

Illustration

The Act contains examples of such reasonable adjustments. They include (amongst other things):

- Adjustments to premises
- Allocating duties to other persons
- Transferring the disabled person to an existing vacancy
- Altering working hours
- Assigning the disabled person to a different place of work
- Allowing time off for rehabilitation

The Act originally made no specific reference to harassment of disabled employees. However, this is now covered by the Act.

Exam focus point

Discrimination at work is a very topical area and has been the subject of numerous decisions recently. Make sure you are up to date.

Question GOQs

There are various genuine occupational qualifications which do not constitute unlawful discrimination on the grounds of sex or race. Under those two headings, give examples.

Answer

Sex

Jobs abroad where it would be difficult for a woman to perform her duties

Decency

Exemptions such as:

- Ministers of religion
- Police
- Prison officers

Race

Authenticity in art

Personal welfare services

Authenticity in restaurants

5 Victimisation and harassment

Key terms

Victimisation is where a person discriminates against another (treats him less favourably than others) because the victimised person has performed a 'protected act' (see below).

Harassment is subjecting a person to torment by subjecting them to constant interference or intimidation. **However, this term is not defined by legislation.** This definition is a dictionary definition.

5.1 Protected acts

The following are 'protected acts' for the basis of the victimisation definition:

(a) Bringing proceedings under the:

- Sex Discrimination Act 1975
- Race Relations Act 1976
- Disability Discrimination Act 1995
- The new regulations on religion, belief and sexual orientation (see below)
- Equal Pay Act 1970
- Pensions Act 1995 (sections 62-65)

(b) Giving evidence or information in connection with proceedings brought by any person under the above Acts.

(c) Committing any act done with reference to the above Acts.

(d) Alleging that the discriminator or others have committed an Act which would amount to a contravention of, or permit a claim under, the above Acts.

An employer can be regarded as having subjected employees to racial harassment by allowing a third party to inflict racial abuse on them in circumstances in which he could have prevented the harassment or reduced the amount of it: *Burton and Another v De Vere Hotels 1996.*

6 Remedies for discrimination

FAST FORWARD

A person who feels they have been discriminated against may make a claim to an Employment Tribunal The remedies a tribunal will suggest in a discrimination case are:

- Compensation
- Recommendation of employer action
- Referral to ACAS

A person who believes that they have been discriminated against should make an application to an employment tribunal within **three months** of the discrimination taking place.

If the employment tribunal decide that discrimination has taken place, they can make the following orders.

(a) Compensation

(b) Recommendation that the employer take action to correct the situation or limit the damage done to the applicant.

(c) Appointment of an official from the Advisory, Conciliation and Arbitration Service (ACAS) to try and work out a settlement between the two parties.

There is no upper limit in sex, race and disability discrimination cases. In *Kirker v British Sugar 1997*, a partially sighted employee who was able to prove that his defective eyesight was the dominant factor in his selection for redundancy was awarded £100,000.

The Court of Appeal has decided that employment tribunals can award damages for personal injury caused by unlawful discrimination. In *Sheriff v Klyne Tugs (Lowestoft) Ltd 1999*, a ship's engineer had a nervous breakdown following racial abuse. The decision is significant because it means that it is no longer necessary to pursue the personal injury claim separately in the County Court.

The tribunal **cannot:**

- Force the employer to promote someone
- Insist the employer takes on a job applicant

7 Other forms of discrimination

FAST FORWARD

The law has been extended into further areas in which the individual is protected against discrimination in the workplace:

- The Employment Equality (Religion or Belief) Regulations 2003
- The Employment Equality (Sexual Orientation) Regulations 2003

7.1 Discrimination on grounds of religion or belief

The Employment Equality (Religion or Belief) Regulations 2003 are now in force. They cover all aspects of the employment relationship, including recruitment, pay, working conditions, training, promotion and dismissal.

The legislation follows the framework set out in earlier discrimination legislation. It outlaws the following:

- *Direct discrimination*: treating people less favourably than others because of their religion or beliefs.
- *Indirect discrimination*: applying a provision or practice which disadvantages people of a certain religion or belief and which is not objectively justifiable.

- *Victimisation*: treating people less favourably because of some action they have taken in connection with the new legislation.
- *Harassment*: indulging in unwarranted conduct that violates an individual's dignity or creates an intimidating or degrading environment.

7.2 Discrimination on grounds of sexual orientation

The Employment Equality (Sexual Orientation) Regulations 2003 outlaw discrimination on grounds of sexual orientation. This means that it will be unlawful to deny lesbian, gay or bisexual peoples jobs because of prejudice. These regulations came into effect in December 2003.

The legislation follows the framework set out above, and outlaws direct and indirect discrimination, harassment and victimisation.

7.3 Age discrimination

The new regulations described in the sections above have been issued in response to an EU directive on equal treatment in the workplace in 2000. One area remains to be addressed.

Discrimination on the grounds of **age** is due to be included in the scope of UK legislation by 2006 at the latest. As yet there are no relevant draft regulations.

8 Employment law and human rights

Employment law is one area where the potential impact of the Human Rights Act 1998 is perceived to be high. This will be assessed as cases come to court, but as yet there has been little impact.

Illustration

The following articles could have an impact on the relationship between employer and employee:

Article 4	Prohibition of slavery and forced labour
Article 5	Right to liberty and security
Article 6	Right to a fair trial
Article 8	Right to respect for private and family life
Article 9	Right to freedom of thought, conscience and religion
Article 10	Right to freedom of expression
Article 11	Right to freedom of assembly and association
Article 14	Right to freedom from discrimination

What it is vital to remember in this context is that it is **not possible for an individual to bring a claim against a private sector employee under the Human Rights Act 1998**.

This is because the Act provides that public authorities must act in a manner consistent with the Convention, not all employers.

However, **employment tribunals are public authorities**, so they have a duty to interpret existing employment law so that it is compatible with the Convention. They must also take into consideration the decisions made by the European Courts.

Question — Human Rights Act and employment law

Can you think of ways that the articles listed above might impact upon employment law?

Answer

The important thing to note in answering this question is that the impact will only be seen in the **interpretation of existing statute**. Hence under the Telecommunications (Lawful Business Practice) (Interception of Communications) Regulations 2000, monitoring a person's emails could be failing to comply with the privacy requirement in Article 8. Instituting a certain dress code could cause discrimination on the grounds of race, and contravene Article 10, freedom of expression. You may have thought of others.

Chapter roundup

- Discrimination is the practice of treating one or more members of a specified group that is unfair as compared to the treatment of other people who are not in the group.
- Discrimination on the following grounds has been legislated against.
  - Sex
  - Race
  - Disability
  - Religion or belief
  - Sexual orientation
- Discrimination on the grounds of race or sex may be direct or indirect.
- Sex discrimination is legislated against in the Sex Discrimination Act 1975, as updated by the Act of the same name in 1986.
- Race discrimination is legislated against in the Race Relations Act 1976.
- Disability discrimination is legislated against in the Disability Discrimination Act 1995.
- Victimisation and harassment are also forms of discrimination.
- A person who feels they have been discriminated against may make a claim to an Employment Tribunal
- The remedies a tribunal will suggest in a discrimination case are:
  - Compensation
  - Recommendation of employer action
  - Referral to ACAS
- The law has been extended into further areas in which the individual is protected against discrimination in the workplace:
  - The Employment Equality (Religion or Belief) Regulations 2003
  - The Employment Equality (Sexual Orientation) Regulations 2003
- Employment law is one area which could be severely impacted by the Human Rights Act 1998.

Quick quiz

1 Complete the definition, using the words given below.

.... is the practice or .... one or more member of a ....

in a manner that is .... as .... to the treatment of other who are not part of that group.

(1)	treating	(3)	discrimination	(5)	group
(2)	unfair	(4)	compared		

2 A disabled person can be indirectly discriminated against on the grounds of her disability.

True ☐

False ☐

3 Name three instances where sex is a genuine occupational qualification.

(1) ....

(2) ....

(3) ....

4 Name three justifications for race discrimination.

(1) ....

(2) ....

(3) ....

5 Failure by an employer to make reasonable adjustments to accommodate a disabled person without justification is classed as discrimination

True ☐

False ☐

6 (a) What are three orders an employment tribunal can make with regard to discrimination?

(1) ....

(2) ....

(3) ....

(b) What two things can a tribunal not do?

(1) ....

(2) ....

Answers to quick quiz

1 (3), (1), (5), (2), (4)

2 False. There is no indirect discrimination in the case of disability.

3 (1) Decency (ie attendant in female toilets)
(2) Exemptions such as ministers of religion
(3) Law and custom in a country **other than** UK.

4 (1) Authenticity – artistic
(2) Personal services
(3) Authenticity – restaurant

5 True

6 (a) (1) Compensation
(2) Recommendation re employer action
(3) Refer to ACAS

(b) (1) Force the employer to promote someone
(2) Insist the employer take on someone

Now try the question below from the Exam Question Bank

Number	Level	Marks	Time
Q26	Examination	10	18 mins

Exam question bank

1 County court and high court — 18 mins

Explain the importance of:

(a) The county court (4 marks)
(b) The High Court (4 marks)

in the system of civil justice.

(c) Briefly explain where appeals from the decisions of the county court and the High Court are heard. (2 marks)

(10 marks)

2 EU law — 18 mins

Article 189 of the Treaty of Rome provides that 'in order to carry out their task the Council and the Commission shall, in accordance with the provisions of this Treaty, make regulations, issue directives, take decisions, make recommendations or deliver opinions'.

Explain the effect of regulations, directives and decisions. What do you understand by the terms 'directly applicable' and 'direct effect'?

(10 marks)

3 Human Rights Act — 10 mins

Explain what effect the Human Rights Act 1998 has had on the rest of English Law.

4 Contract basics — 10 mins

Explain the difference between essential elements of a contract and matters which affect the validity of a contract.

5 Offer — 18 mins

Explain in relation to the law of contract:

(a) The rules relating to acceptance of an offer (5 marks)
(b) The rules relating to the revocation of an offer (5 marks)

(10 marks)

6 Advertisement — 36 mins

Data Ltd is a supplier of office equipment and accessories. On Monday, the company puts several 'Clearance sale' notices in its showroom. These read 'Clearance sale. Series III laser printers. Special price of £50 each to the first ten customers in the showroom on Tuesday morning.'

Clive, an accountant, sees the notices on Monday and decides to wait outside the showroom all night in order to be the first customer into the showroom. Half an hour before the showroom is due to open on Tuesday morning, the manager arrives to open up and tells Clive that the sale has been cancelled.

The company has also placed an advertisement in the local paper, which comes out on a Thursday. The advertisement reads 'Special offer. Latest Series V printers for sale. The first ten customers who reply enclosing cheque for £600 will receive one of these fabulous printers. Send in now.'

Alvin reads the advertisement and immediately writes out a cheque and sends it to Data Ltd. Later on Thursday he changes his mind and sends a fax to Data Ltd asking them to return his cheque and stating that he has cancelled his order. The cheque and order reach Data Ltd on Friday morning. The company cashes the cheque and refuses to refund the money to Alvin on the grounds that a valid and binding contract has been formed between them.

Advise Clive and Alvin. **(20 marks)**

7 Paint spraying equipment 36 mins

Graham is in practice as an accountant. He wishes to refurbish the exterior of his office premises and, to save money, decides to do it himself. He hires paint spraying equipment from Paint Supplies Ltd, signing a written contract which contains the following clause.

'Paint Supplies Ltd shall not be liable for any loss or damage, however caused, arising from use of the company's products.'

Graham puts the contract in his pocket without reading it.

While Graham is using the equipment it explodes, because of negligent maintenance by Paint Supplies Ltd. Paint is spread all over Graham's premises, and two clients leave him as a result, causing a considerable loss of earnings. Minor injuries are caused to Graham. Relying on the exclusion clause, Paint Supplies Ltd refuse to pay any compensation to Graham.

Advise Graham. **(20 marks)**

8 Restraint of trade 18 mins

A purchaser of a new business wishes to prevent the seller from setting up a rival business. He seeks your advice as to how he may protect himself by the inclusion of restraint terms in the contract of sale.

Advise him accordingly. **(10 marks)**

9 Remedies for breach 18 mins

Describe in outline the remedies which may be available to the injured party in relation to breaches of contract.

(10 marks)

10 Contractual remedies 36 mins

Richard is an accountant. He agreed with Simon, a garage proprietor, that he will assist Simon with his annual tax return if Simon will service his car for him. He also agreed with Thomas, a landscape gardener, that he will advise Thomas on the installation of a computerised financial management system if Thomas, in return, will carry out some landscaping work at the house of Richard's daughter, Ursula.

Richard assists Simon and advises Thomas, but both refuse to carry out their side of the agreements. Because his car has not been serviced Richard is late for an important meeting with a client after the car breaks down on the way to the meeting. As a result of this the client switches his work, worth some £5,000 per annum, to another accountant. Ursula is very anxious to have the landscaping work done on her garden and because Thomas has a reputation for doing good quality work she is keen that it is done by Thomas.

Advise Richard and Ursula as to the nature of the contractual remedies, if any, which may be available to them. **(20 marks)**

11 Agent's authority 36 mins

(a) 'An agent can only contract on behalf of his principal where he has express authority.'

Explain whether the above statement is true and if not, how an agent can act without express authority and still bind his principal in contract. (14 marks)

(b) Trevor agrees to sell a consignment of electrical goods to Albert. Albert accepts the goods on behalf of Philip even though he has no authority to do so. Trevor subsequently informs Albert that the goods are no longer available.

The following day Philip learns of Albert's transaction and agrees to take the goods.

Advise Trevor whether or not he will be liable under the contract. (6 marks)

(20 marks)

12 Separate legal personality 36 mins

(a) 'The principle of corporate legal personality is an important and basic fundamental of law in the United Kingdom.'

Briefly explain this statement. (5 marks)

(b) 'But there have been several departures from this rule where the court has lifted the corporate veil and looked at the realities of the situation.'

Which do you consider to have been some of the more important of such 'departures'? (5 marks)

(c) Until 20X0 Paul carried on a radio and television sales and incorporated the business, assigning the whole of its assets to the company known as Brightscreen Ltd. Payment was effected by the allotment to Paul and his wife of 3,000 fully paid £1 shares in Brightscreen Ltd. Paul continued to insure the assets of the business in his own name as he had done prior to the incorporation of Brightscreen Ltd. This year, the premises of Brightscreen Ltd were burgled and some £5,000 worth of audio equipment stole. Paul has made a claim on the policy but the insurance company refuses to meet his claim. Advise Paul. (10 marks)

(20 marks)

13 Pre-incorporation 18 mins

Explain how the law provides for the enforcement of contracts entered into on a company's behalf prior to the incorporation of a company.

(10 marks)

14 Alteration of objects **18 mins**

The main object of Train U Up is to provide training courses for office administrators and secretaries.

The directors have recently decided that it would be best to diversify the company's activities and start supplying computers, office equipment and stationery, using the contacts they have made on their courses.

It appears that approximately 75% of the company's shareholders support the change, although a minority will undoubtedly strongly oppose diversification.

Advise the directors.

(a) How the company's memorandum needs to be altered to enable diversification to occur. Describe the steps that will have to be followed to alter the memorandum. (6 marks)

(b) State the rights of the minority shareholders who oppose diversification. (4 marks)

(10 marks)

15 Section 14 **18 mins**

S 14(1) Companies Act 1985 provides as follows.

'Subject to the provisions of the Act, the memorandum and the articles when registered, blind the company and its members to the same extent as if they respectively had been signed and sealed by each member, and contained covenants on the part of each member to observe all the provisions of the memorandum and of the articles.'

(a) In your own words explain what this provision means. (3 marks)

(b) If the Articles contained a clause providing that any dispute between members and the company's management should be referred to arbitration, could a member insist that arbitration occur? (3 marks)

(c) Would a company secretary be able to enforce a clause in the articles which stated he should hold office for ten years if he were removed before the expiration of ten years? (4 marks)

(10 marks)

16 Kate **36 mins**

(a) Kate plc has adopted Table A articles of association. An extraordinary general meeting of the company has been properly convened. Two resolutions are proposed, namely the alteration of the objects clause and an increase in the company's authorised share capital. Both are expected to be passed as a matter of course. The meeting has been called for 8 pm on 17 March 20X7.

On the day of the meeting only one shareholder, Nick, has arrived on time. He has been appointed as a proxy by Alison, who cannot attend because her cat is ill.

Edmund arrives twenty minutes late. He is a director but not a shareholder. Nick suggests that he chairs the meeting but Edmund modestly declines. Five minutes later, at 8.25 pm, Kathryn and Roger arrive.

Bob, the company secretary, has held his position only a short time and has therefore asked your advice on the following points of procedure.

(i) A valid meeting has certain requirements. To what extent have those requirements been met in this particular case?

(ii) If Kathryn and Roger were to leave before the end of the meeting before all the business has been transacted, how would this affect the validity of the proceedings?

What advice would you give? (10 marks)

(b) Suppose that the shareholders of Kate plc wished to alter certain clauses in the memorandum of association. Could this be done by the company in general meeting, and if so, how? (10 marks)

(20 marks)

17 Officers — 18 mins

Ann is about to attend her first ever annual general meeting of Borg plc. The documentation for the meeting mentions various people, but Ann is not sure what their exact roles are within a public limited company.

Briefly explain to Ann the role and powers of the following:

(a) Chairman of the Board
(b) Managing Director
(c) Company Secretary **(10 marks)**

18 Happy — 36 mins

Your client, Happy, has been offered the managing directorship of Grumpy Ltd, with a 40% share holding in the company. The rest of the shares will be equally divided between Dopey and Sleepy, who at present hold all the shares and who will remain as directors of the company. Dopey and Sleepy are anxious to bring Happy into the company and are prepared to consider any conditions Happy may seek to impose, save that they are not willing to increase his share holding.

Advise Happy on any two methods by which he might seek to secure himself against dismissal from the managing directorship of Grumpy Ltd, and comment on the effectiveness of these methods.

(20 marks)

19 Wrongful trading — 18 mins

Explain the meaning and effect of 'wrongful trading' under S214 of the Insolvency Act 1986

(10 marks)

20 Issue of shares — 36 mins

(a) What are the limitations placed on the powers of a company to issue shares at a discount? Why are they necessary? (6 marks)

(b) Shares may be issued for a consideration other than cash. In what circumstances will the court treat such a transaction as an issue of shares at a discount? (6 marks)

(c) In an issue of shares for a consideration other than cash, a company may acquire an asset of much greater value than the nominal value of the shares. How must it treat, for accounting purposes, the 'profit' which accrues from such a transaction? (8 marks)

(20 marks)

21 Maintenance of capital — 36 mins

It is a fundamental principle of company law that a company should maintain its share capital.

You are required to explain how the following provisions of the Companies Act 1985 below help to achieve this objective:

(a) S 135: reduction of share capital (8 marks)
(b) S 263, s 264: payment of dividends (8 marks)
(c) S 142: serious losses of capital (4 marks)

(20 marks)

22 Loan capital — 18 mins

Explain the following terms in company law:

(a) A debenture (3 marks)
(b) A fixed charge (3 marks)
(c) A floating charge (4 marks)

(10 marks)

23 Insolvency — 36 mins

Compare the functions of an administrative receiver and an administrator explaining in particular:

(a) The legal grounds under which a company may be put into administrative receivership (6 marks)

(b) The legal grounds under which a company may be put into administration (6 marks)

(c) The legal position of secured creditors, preferential creditors and unsecured creditors under each system (8 marks)

(20 marks)

24 Employers' duties — 18 mins

What terms may be included in a contract of employment? Where might they be found?

(10 marks)

25 Redundancy and dismissal — 36 mins

Brian is the manager of a distribution warehouse which supplies a number of Do-It-Yourself stores. Following the introduction of a new computerised stock record system, Brian is dismissed, because he is unable to adapt to the new working practices. Brian has worked for the company for fifteen years.

As a result of the re-organisation three further employees are dismissed. John is dismissed because of his involvement in trade union activities. He has worked for the company for nine months. Peter is offered a job elsewhere within the company, some fifty miles away, which he refuses. Peter has been employed by the company for three years. Michael, who has been employed by the company for eighteen months, has been offered part-time working for three days per week. This he finds unacceptable and resigns.

Brian, Peter and Michael seek compensation for redundancy and in addition, Brian and John intend to make a claim for unfair dismissal.

You are required to advise Brian, John, Peter and Michael of their respective legal positions.

(20 marks)

26 Discrimination 18 mins

In recent cases heard before tribunals, substantial awards have been made for discrimination on the grounds of race or sex.

Explain briefly the main provisions of the respective legislation governing

(a) Sex discrimination (7 marks)
(b) Race discrimination (3 marks)
(10 marks)

27 Promises (20 marks) 36 mins

Explain whether Paul is required by the law of contract to fulfil his promises in the following situations:

(a) He promises to sell an expensive car to Arthur for £10.

(b) He returns home to find that his house windows have been cleaned by Bernard and he promises to pay Bernard £1 for his work.

(c) He agrees to pay Charles £100 for painting his house within three weeks and he later promises a further 310 if Charles finishes the job on time.

(d) He promises to deliver goods to David in return for a payment to him of £50 by Eric.

(e) He promises to release Frank from a debt of £500 if Frank pays him £400.

Approaching the answer

You should read the requirement through before working through and annotating the question as we have, so that you are aware what you are looking for.

Explain whether Paul is required by the law of contract to fulfil his promises in the following situations:

ther words, a valid tract been ned? This uld prompt to think:
greement
onsideration
ntention

Who is Arthur? Is there intention? Has he accepted?

£10 is not adequate consideration for an expensive car, but is it sufficient? Courts will not weigh up (Thomas) and some value is sufficient (Nestle).

(a) He promises to sell an expensive car to Arthur for £10. (4 marks)

(b) He returns home to find that his house windows have been cleaned by Bernard and he promises to pay Bernard £1 for his work. (4 marks)

First contract appears to be valid – all three elements present.

Consideration may be executory or executed, but it may not be past. Bernard's appears to be past – unless there was previous agreement– implied by service being carried out?

(c) He agrees to pay Charles £100 for painting his house within three weeks and he later promises a further £20 is Charles finishes the job on time. (4 marks)

Finishing job on time is an existing contractual obligation (Stilk). Therefore it is insufficient consideration for new promise of £20. But, courts taking new view? (Williams v Roffey Bros)

(d) He promises to deliver goods to David in return for a payment to him of £50 by Eric. (4 marks)

(e) He promises to release Frank from a debt of £500 if Frank pays him £400. (4 marks)

Part payment is no consideration (Foakes v Beer) However, consider exceptions – promissory estoppel?

Valid contract between Paul and Eric (all three elements present). David may or may not be able to enforce – 3P rights?

Answer plan

Then organise the things you have noticed and your points arising into a coherent answer plan. Not all the points you have noticed will necessarily have to go into your answer – you should spend a few minutes thinking them through and prioritising them.

In this case, as the scenarios are short, the points made above are probably sufficient answer plan. In a longer scenario question, the relevant factors might not all be in order in the question and this step would be more important.

28 Martin, Neil and Owen (20 marks) 36 mins

Martin, Neil and Owen were partners in a successful garage business. Two years ago they incorporated the business as Parking Ltd, each taking three of the nine issued shares of the company. Last year they were joined by Quentin who took one share in the company and was referred to as an associate, although in practice he was consulted on all management decisions.

This year there has been a major disagreement between Martin and Neil, on the one hand, and Owen and Quentin on the other. As a result Owen has been dismissed as a director by an ordinary resolution of the company and Quentin is no longer consulted on management issues. Owen and Quentin have set up a separate garage business and have attracted business from some of the former customers of the company.

Required

Advise Owen and Quentin whether either or both of them may be able to require Martin and Neil to purchase their shares in the company at a value determined by the court, with or without winding up Parking Ltd.

Approaching the answer

You should read through the requirement before working through and annotating the question as we have so that you are aware what things you are looking for.

Quasi partnership between M, N and O.

Martin, Neil and Owen were partners in a successful garage business. Two years ago they incorporated the business as Parking Ltd, each taking three of the nine issued shares of the company. Last year they were joined by Quentin who took one share in the company and was referred to as an associate, although in practice he was consulted on all management decisions.

Q is a minority shareholder (10%), but is consulted – shadow director? Usually majority shareholders – may just be courtesy.

Correct procedure – but unfairly prejudicial to quasi partner?

This year there has been a major disagreement between Martin and Neil, on the one hand, and Owen and Quentin on the other. As a result Owen has been dismissed as a director by an ordinary resolution of the company and Quentin is no longer consulted on management issues. Owen and Quentin have set up a separate garage business and have attracted business from some of the former customers of the company.

Unclear whether this is unfairly prejudicial, as Quentin is only a minority shareholder. Is he a quasi-partner? Not an original partner…

Relevance to the question? Could this prejudice any claim against Martin and Neil?

ırt order re chase of shares ilable under ı1, in reference ınfairly judicial conduct ler s459, so k for indicators JPC in scenario.

Required

Advise Owen and Quentin whether either or both of them may be able to require Martin and Neil to purchase their shares in the company at a value determined by the court, with or without winding up Parking Ltd.

Might be an option under Insolvency Act in relation to a just and equitable winding up – consider three cases, is very rare.

Answer plan

Then organise the things you have noticed and your points arising into a coherent answer plan. Not all the points you have noticed will have to go into your answer – you should spend a few minutes thinking them through and prioritising them.

In a law answer, you will need to jot down the law that is relevant to the points raised in the scenario, and note how the law applies so that you can draw a conclusion about Owen and Quentin's situation.

Relevant law

Two areas of law raised by the requirement – s459 CA 1985, unfairly prejudicial conduct and s22 IA 86, just and equitable winding up.

S459 most important provisions in this area. Discuss briefly. Common situations where conduct is unfairly prejudicial to a minority, or in a quasi-partnership (case: Ebrahimi).

Application

To Owen: Appears to be a quasi-partner. Similar to Ebrahimi and Re Bird Precision Bellows. Fact that his new business is now competing should not prejudice (LSE case).

To Quentin: Not as clear cut. Arguable that he was a director too. But up to the court to decide. Should try and show that all four people operated in a quasi-partnership – but he is new addition.

Court order

If application to the court is successful, the following could happen:

Could order that the affairs of the partnership be regulated a certain way in future, but

Court likely to judge for compulsory acquisition of shares at a fair price.

Winding up

Link to Ebrahimi, but s459 post-dates. In order to gain a winding up, you have to show that there is no other solution in the situation – here the shares can be purchased.

Conclusion

Owen's shares will be bought. Quentin's shares may be bought – the court will take a view.

This answer plan sets out the answer in the format you should use:

State the law

Explain the law

Apply the law

Conclude

However, you will note that you have to know the relevant area of law to apply to the facts in the first place. You have to learn the law thoroughly before you can tackle a question like this well.

Exam answer bank

1 County court and high court

Tutorial note. Do not be tempted to start writing about criminal law issues. Be clear about the court structure – the diagram in the Study Text should be in your memory, showing the routes of appeal.

(a) The **county court** is a court of original jurisdiction. It hears only civil cases, but deals with **virtually every type of civil matter** arising within the geographical area which it serves. In some types of case, its jurisdiction is concurrent with that of the High Court. It is involved in hearing the following, subject to limits applied in some categories.

- Contract and tort claims
- Equitable matters concerning trusts, mortgages and partnership dissolution
- Disputes concerning land
- Undefended matrimonial cases
- Probate matters
- Miscellaneous matters conferred by various statutes, for example the Consumer Credit Act 1974
- Some bankruptcy, company winding-up and admiralty cases

(b) The **High Court** also deals with civil cases at first instance. It is divided into **three divisions**. The **Queen's Bench Division** deals with common law matters, such as contract and tort. It also includes two specialist courts, dealing with Admiralty and Commercial matters. **The Chancery Division** of the High Court deals with equity matters such as trusts, bankruptcy and taxation, and also has a special Companies Court. The **Family Division** of the High Court deals with matrimonial and similar family cases. The Family Division also has a limited appellate function in that it hears some appeals on domestic matters from the magistrates' court.

Under the Woolf Reforms, cases are allocated either to the small claims track or the fast track or the multi-track, taking into account the financial value and complexity of the claim. Generally speaking, county courts hear small claims and fast track cases and the High Court hears multi-track cases.

Under the small claims track, cases are heard where the claim is for less than £5,000 (or £1,000 in the case of personal injury claims, claims for possession of land, housing disrepair claims and harassment claims). If the claim is for more than the stated amount, the parties may still elect to use the small claims track, subject to the court's approval. The small claims track is intended to permit litigants to conduct their case in person if they so wish as the procedure is less formal, cheaper and quicker than court proceedings. The arbitrator is usually the district judge or may be appointed by the parties.

Cases under £15,000 may be allocated to the 'fast track'. This is a strictly limited procedure, designed to enable cases to be brought to trial within a short but reasonable timescale. Costs are fixed and hearings are designed to last no longer than one day.

Finally, the multi-track approach is intended to provide a new and more flexible regime for the handling of claims over £15,000 in value. These are the cases that tend to be more complex. Soon after allocation of the case to the multi-track, a 'case management conference' will be held to encourage the parties to settle the dispute or to consider the merits of alternative dispute resolution. The trial judge sets a budget and a final timescale for the trial.

(c) From a decision of a county court there is a right of appeal to the **Civil Division of the Court of Appeal**. In bankruptcy cases an appeal goes to the Chancery Division of the High Court.

Appeals from the High Court in civil cases may also be made to the Court of Appeal (Civil Division) or alternatively (and unusually) to the House of Lords, under what is known as the **leapfrog**

procedure. For the leapfrog procedure to be followed, all parties and the House of Lords must give their consent to it and the case must involve a point of law of general public importance. Also, the point of law must already be the subject of an existing Court of Appeal decision.

The Civil Division of the Court of Appeal is presided over by the Master of the Rolls. Normally, three judges sit together, although in important cases five may sit.

2 EU law

Tutorial note. The UK has been part of the European community for over 30 years now and EU law is assuming increasing practical importance in the study and operation of English law. The Companies Act 1989, for instance, was occasioned by two EU Directives which the legislature was obliged to incorporate into the English system.

Regulations

Regulations (unless expressed to the contrary) **have effect as law** and operate throughout the European Union as soon as they are made. Direct law-making of this type is generally restricted to matters within the basic aims of the Treaty of Rome such as the establishment of a single unrestricted market in the EU territory in manufactured goods. There is no need in such cases to enact any UK Act of Parliament since the regulation is already legally binding. One consequence of this is that the UK courts are required to override UK legislation if it is inconsistent with an EU Regulation. A UK court would almost certainly seek a ruling from the European Court confirming the inconsistency before declaring UK legislation inconsistent (*R v Secretary, of State for Transport ex p Factortame Ltd 1990)*.

Directives

Directives are **statements of principle** to which the member states must, by their national law-making process, adapt their own law. For example, the several directives on company law require that company law of member states shall conform to certain principles, such as the law on prospectuses now contained in the Financial Services Act 1986.

Although directives are mainly statements of principle to be absorbed into national law by a national law-making process, it is sometimes permissible for an EU national in court proceedings to rely on the principles of a Directive: *Van Duyn v Home Office 1974*.

This means that a Directive (and a Decision) may have 'direct effect'. Only a directive which is unconditional and precise can have direct effect. Where a directive (or decision) has direct effect is only confers rights on an individual against the state or a state body and not (unlike a regulation) against other individuals. Where a directive (or decision) has direct effect, a UK court is required, as with a regulation, to override inconsistent UK legislation.

Decisions

Decisions are taken in Brussels to implement such objectives as the Common Agricultural Policy. A decision is **immediately binding** on the government or person to whom it is addressed.

Direct applicability

If law is made in Brussels with **immediate legal effect** in the EU area, it is said to be 'directly applicable' so that no national law-making is needed to introduce it into national law. A self-executing regulation is directly applicable.

Direct effect

EU law has 'direct effect' when an individual person can rely on it to **establish rights or obligations**. To that extent, direct effect and direct application overlap. But a regulation, for example, may be directly applicable without also having direct effect in terms of rights and obligations of citizens.

3 Human Rights Act

Tutorial note. This question is not exam standard. However it summarises all the things you need to know about the HRA98 and is a useful consolidation exercise.

The Human Rights Act 1998 enacts the rights set out in the European Convention on Human Rights into English law. The impact it has on English law is that **UK courts** are now **required to interpret UK law in a way that is compatible with the Convention**, as far as it is possible to do so. In practice, this has the following effects:

- The courts must interpret English law in a way that is compatible with the Convention so far as it is possible to do so.
- They must take into account judgements made by the European Court of Human Rights even though these judgements are not binding in UK courts.
- If a court feels that a provision of existing legislation is incompatible with the Convention, it must make a declaration of incompatibility.
- Any law declared incompatible in this way is still valid in domestic law until it is amended.
- A Minister of the Crown may make adjustments to the legislation to remove the incompatibility.
- Individuals and companies may now bring a case claiming infringement of human rights to the UK courts. Thereafter an appeal may be made to the European Court of Human Rights.

When presenting new legislation to Parliament, the person proposing the legislation must make a statement of compatibility with the Convention.

If the provisions of the bill are not compatible with the Convention, he must state so, but state that the government nevertheless wants to proceed with the legislation.

4 Contract basics

Tutorial note. Again, this question is not exam standard, but it is absolutely vital that you grasp the basics of contract, so it is useful for you to work through this question. Use the answer in your revision.

In order to be legally binding, a contract must contain three essential elements. The three essential elements are:

- Agreement (offer + acceptance)
- Intention to create legal relations
- Consideration

Without these three essential elements a contract is no more than an agreement, and does not have any legal weight or recourse.

There are also factors which will impact on the validity of a contract. The distinction between these factors and those above is that without essential elements, there is no contract (no legally binding agreement). Without the presence of validity factors, there is a contract, but it may be fundamentally flawed, and various results arise.

Examples of validity factors include **capacity** and **form**. Certain persons may not have the capacity to contract, for example persons suffering a mental incapacity. A company is restrained in its acts by its constitution. Certain contracts may be outside the scope of its capacity and hence void. Similarly, some contracts must be made in a certain form.

If these factors prove invalidity, a contract which exists (as it has the three essential elements above) may be declared void, voidable or unenforceable depending on the invalidating factor.

5 Offer

Tutorial note. This is a useful run through of the basics of 'offer'. This is an area you must be happy to both explain and apply in an exam as it is likely to be examined, and could be examined in either Part A or Part B.

(a) Valid acceptance of a valid offer is one of the essentials of a contract, the others being an intention to create legal relations and consideration.

The acceptance must be an unqualified agreement to the terms of the offer. If it in fact introduces new terms then it is a counter offer (which might then be accepted by the original offeror) and not an acceptance.

Thus in *Hyde v Wrench 1840*, where an offer was made to sell land for £1000 and the plaintiff made a counter offer of £950 but later sought to accept the original offer, it was held that the claimant's counter offer had terminated the original offer.

A response to an offer which is actually a request for further information will not constitute acceptance but it is **not** a counter offer, and acceptance made 'subject to contract' will not amount to a valid acceptance until the proposed formal contract has been signed.

The acceptance may be by express words or be inferred from conduct: *Brogden v Metropolitan Rly Co 1877*. In a unilateral contract (as in *Carlill v Carbolic Smoke Ball Co 1893*), performance of the act required by the offer or advertisement constitutes acceptance. There must be some act on the part of the offeree, however, as mere passive inaction is not capable of constituting acceptance: *Felthouse v Bindley 1862*. Acceptance of an offer may only be made by a person authorised to do so, usually the offeree or his authorised agent.

Generally speaking, acceptance must be communicated to the offeror before it can be effective, unless the offeror expressly waives the need for communication (as in Carlill's case). The offeror may stipulate the sole means of communication in which case only compliance with his or her terms will suffice.

If the offeror specifies a means of communication but does not make it absolutely compulsory, then acceptance by another means which is equally expeditious and does not disadvantage the offeror in any way will be sufficient: *Yates Building Co v R J Pulleyn and Sons (York) 1975*.

Communication of acceptance by post is subject to the postal rule established in *Adams v Lindsell* 1818. This provides that where the use of the post is in the contemplation of both parties and the acceptance is correctly addressed and stamped and is actually put in the post, then acceptance will be valid and effective once posted and it is irrelevant whether the offeror actually receives the letter. There is no need for the offer specifically to state that acceptance must be communicated by post – whether this was in the contemplation of the parties may be deduced from the circumstances, for example if the offer was itself made by post: *Household Fire and Carriage Accident Insurance Co v Grant 1879*.

Clearly if it is evident that the parties did not intend the postal rule to apply – for example where the offer requires 'notice in writing'– then the rule will be excluded: *Holwell Securities v Hughes 1974* (where it was held that the stipulation for 'notice in writing' meant that notice of acceptance actually had to be received by the offeror).

(b) The offeror may 'revoke' (or cancel) the offer at any time prior to acceptance: *Payne v Cave 1789* unless by a separate option agreement, for which consideration must have been given, he has agreed to keep the offer open for a certain period of time: *Routledge v Grant 1828*. Once accepted, an offer cannot be revoked.

Revocation may be made by an express statement to that effect or may be implied from an act of the offeror indicating that the offer is no longer in force (for example sale of the goods to a third party). Whatever form it takes, it is essential that the revocation is communicated to the offeree in order to be effective. Revocation of an offer may be communicated by the offeror or by any third party who is a sufficiently reliable informant: *Dickinson v Dodds 1876.*

While a postal acceptance of an offer is usually effective from the time of posting, a postal revocation of an offer does not take effect until received by the offeree (ie communicated to the offeree). Thus, where a letter of revocation of an offer crosses in the post with a letter of acceptance, a legally binding contract will have been formed from the time the letter of acceptance was posted: *Byrne v van Tienhoven 1880.*

Where an offer is intended to be accepted by conduct (a unilateral contract), it has been held that the offer cannot be revoked once the offeree has begun to perform the necessary act required to accept the contract

6 Advertisement

Tutorial note. The question here is whether or not the advertisements in each case constitute offers which are capable of acceptance, following the contrasting judgements in Carlill and Partridge v Crittenden. Consider the rules governing communication of acceptance, and the fact that an offer can be revoked legitimately at any time before acceptance. Refer to the postal rules governing acceptance when considering Alvin's case.

For a contract to be enforceable, there must be an agreement (generally offer and acceptance), there must be intent to create legal relations and the contract must be supported by consideration (or alternatively be under seal).

Offers and invitations to treat

An offer is made where a party (the offeror) makes express his willingness to enter into a binding agreement with another party (the offeree) on specified terms. An offer must be distinguished from an invitation to treat. An invitation to treat is an invitation to enter into negotiations which may or may not eventually lead to the making of an offer. A display of goods in a self-service shop is an invitation to treat: *Pharmaceutical Society of Great Britain v Boots Cash Chemists (Southern) Ltd 1952.*

The legal nature of an advertisement

An advertisement may constitute an offer or an invitation to treat. It is necessary to consider the intention with which it is made. If the words of the advertisement are clear and precise, the advertisement may constitute an offer: *Carlill v Carbolic Smoke Ball Co 1893*, where the defendants advertised that they would pay £100 to anyone who caught influenza while using their product. This was held to be an offer to the world at large capable of being accepted by anyone fulfilling the necessary conditions. This is distinguished from an advertisement of goods for sale, which is generally an invitation to treat, and not an offer for sale: *Partridge v Crittenden 1962*, where Partridge advertised the sale of bramblefinches; it was held that his conviction under the Protection of Birds Act 1954 for 'offering for sale' a bramblefinch could not stand. Similarly an advertisement of an auction is not an offer: *Harris v Nickerson 1873.*

Communication of acceptance of an offer

If the offeree wishes to accept the offer he must usually communicate this acceptance to the offeror. The offeror may stipulate a means of acceptance, in which case it would appear that a contract is formed only if acceptance is in the form specified. The general rule is that acceptance must be communicated to the offeror and that the contract is made when and where the acceptance is received: *Entores Ltd v Miles Far Eastern Corporation 1955*, although if post is the method of communication, acceptance is complete once the letter of acceptance is posted, even if it is lost in the post or delayed: *Household Fire Insurance Co v Grant 1879.*

An offer may be revoked at any time up to acceptance: *Payne v Cave 1789*. For revocation to be effective, it must be communicated to the offeree before he has accepted the offer: *Byrne v Van Tienhoven 1880*.

Clive's situation

The first matter to resolve here is the nature of the sales notices in the showroom. A display of goods in a shop window is usually held to be an invitation to treat. However, there are circumstances in which a display of a notice can constitute an offer. In *Thornton v Shoe Lane Parking Ltd 1971,* it was held that the display of a notice at the entrance to the car park constituted an offer. Similarly, in cases involving unilateral contract, such as an offer of a reward for information leading to the capture of a felon, or an offer of a reward for finding lost jewellery, it is accepted that the notice containing the offer constitutes a legal offer.

It is therefore likely that the showroom notices would be held by the court to be an offer.

As noted above, an offer can be revoked at any time before it has been accepted. The second matter which needs to be resolved is therefore whether or not the offer has been accepted before the company purports to revoke it on the following morning. There would appear to be two possibilities.

(a) Clive has *started* to accept the offer. In this case the company will be unable to revoke its offer. There is no clear-cut legal decision supporting this proposition, but it has been suggested *(obiter dicta)* that such a situation can arise. In this case, the company would be unable to revoke its offer and it must supply the sale goods.

(b) Clive has not accepted the offer because he has not complied with all its terms in that he did not actually get into the showroom. In this case, the company can revoke its offer and is not legally bound to supply the goods.

Alvin's situation

If the advertisement is to amount to an offer, it must manifest a clear intention on the part of the offeror to enter into a contract. The conclusion of the court will depend on whether it follows *Partridge* or *Carlill* and so either outcome is possible. The terms of the advertisement are fairly clear and so it is certainly possible that it could constitute an offer which is capable of being accepted by the offeree.

Alvin posts a letter of acceptance as required by the terms of the offer. Under the postal rule, such an acceptance is valid as soon as the letter is posted. This would result in a binding contract being formed and render the attempted revocation of acceptance ineffective. There is no direct English authority for this view, but it is supported by, for example, non-binding decisions of courts in New Zealand and South Africa.

It can be argued that the postal rule was developed in order to protect the position of the offeree who accepts an offer in the intended manner, by ensuring that he does not suffer loss in the event of a delay in the postal deliveries. If this view is taken, it would be inequitable for the offeror to turn the postal rule round and use it for his own advantage. Under these circumstances, Alvin could argue that no binding contract had been formed.

7 Paint spraying equipment

Tutorial note. Exclusion clauses are covered both by statutory rules and case law. Refer to both when constructing your answer, and the courts' approach when faced with exclusion clauses.

There are three key issues to be determined. Firstly, Paint Supplies Ltd must demonstrate that the clause upon which they intend to rely has been properly *incorporated* into the contract with Graham. Secondly, the courts will *interpret* the clause. Thirdly, the courts will consider whether the *Unfair Contract Terms Act 1977* limits the effects of the clause in any way.

Incorporation of exclusion clause

If a party to a business transaction introduces a clause into his contracts expressly restricting his liability for losses he must ensure that the clause is incorporated into the contracts in accordance with common law rules.

The customer must be aware of the clauses at the time when the contract is made, ie when each party enters into the agreement: *Olley v Marlborough Court 1949*. If the existence of the clause is indicated at the time of the contract being made, this may be adequate notice: *Thompson v LMS Railway 1930*).

If the supplier has previously dealt with customers on the basis of the contract including the clause, he may be able to show incorporation by this past use: *Spurling v Bradshaw 1956*. However in a consumer contract (where there have not been 'consistent' dealings) he will have to show that the customers were actually aware of and had agreed to the clause: *Hollier v Rambler Motors 1972*.

In a written signed contract it is usually considered that the person signing is bound by the terms of that contract (*L'Estrange v Graucob 1934*) although this will not be the case if that person has been given a misleading explanation of the terms: *Curtis v Chemical Cleaning Co 1951*.

Interpretation of exclusion clause

Even if incorporation is shown it is then a question of interpretation as to whether the clause is drawn widely enough to cover the type of liability alleged: *Photo Productions v Securicor Transport 1980*.

In deciding what an exclusion clause means, the courts interpret any ambiguity against the person at fault who relies on the exclusion. This is known as the *contra proferentem* rule ('against the person relying on it').

In the case of *Hollier v Rambler Motors 1972,* the court decided that the disclaimer of liability could be interpreted to apply (i) only to accidental fire damage or (ii) to fire damage caused in any way including negligence. It should therefore be interpreted against the garage in the narrower sense of (i) so that it did *not* give exemption from fire damage due to negligence. If a person wishes successfully to exclude or limit liability for loss caused by negligence the courts require that the word 'negligence', or an accepted synonym for it, should be included in the clause: *Alderslade v Hendon Laundry 1945*.

Unfair Contract Terms Act 1977

There are also statutory limitations on exclusion clauses in consumer contracts imposed by the Unfair Contract Terms Act 1977. In general the Act applied to clauses inserted into agreements by commercial concerns or businesses. It renders void any clause purporting to exclude liability for death or personal injury arising from negligence. In a contract for the provision of services to the consumer, a term excluding liability for certain breaches of contract is void except insofar as it is subject to a test of reasonableness. This attacks those clauses which purport to allow either no performance or a performance substantially different from that agreed.

The Act also controls the use of clauses which attempt to exclude liability for negligence not causing death or personal injury. Exclusion from liability for other types of damage is permitted only as far as the clause is reasonable (s 2).

The clause must be fair and reasonable in all the circumstances which were or ought to have been known by the parties when the contract was made: *Walker v Boyle 1981*. There are some guidelines as to factors in the Act; these include the relative bargaining power of the parties, the resources of the supplier to meet liability if it arises and how far he could insure himself against it.

Paint Supplies Ltd and Graham

Graham has signed a written hire contract which contains the exclusion clauses at the time of signing. There is no evidence that he has been given a misleading explanation of its effect, nor that there have been past dealings between the parties. It is therefore probable that the courts will hold the clause to be properly incorporated.

As regards interpretation, it is probable that negligence is covered by such a clause, and that liability for negligence is therefore excluded.

Finally, there is the issue of UCTA 1977. This will allow Graham to sue the company in respect of his injuries, as personal injuries caused by negligence cannot be excluded. In respect of the financial losses, the courts will consider the matters described above, including the relative bargaining power of the parties and the existence of any inducements to accept the contract terms provided, of course, the loss is not too remote a consequence of the breach.

8 Restraint of trade

Tutorial note. Restraint of trade is specifically mentioned on the syllabus so it is an important aspect of contract law for your exam. It could be examined in conjunction with terms of a contract, or in connection with Employment Law issues.

As a general rule, contracts in restraint of trade are void under the common law and clauses imposing restraint of trade in otherwise valid contracts can be struck out without rendering the whole contract void.

The law generally seeks not to uphold restrictions on freedom of trade although it does allow the imposition of clauses of this type where three factors are satisfied:

- The person seeking to impose the restriction must have a legitimate interest to protect
- The limitation must be no more than is necessary to protect the legitimate interests in question
- The clause must not be against the public interest

A purchaser of the goodwill of a business is entitled to protect what he has bought by imposing restrictions to prevent the vendor doing business with his old customers or clients. However, the restraint must protect the business sold and it must not be excessive.

In *British Reinforced Concrete Engineering Co v Schelff 1921,* S carried on a small local business of making one type of road reinforcement. The purchaser of the business carried on business throughout the UK in making a range of road reinforcements. S had undertaken not to compete with the purchaser in the sale or manufacture of road reinforcements.

It was held that the restraint was void since it was drawn too widely to protect the purchaser from any competition by S. In buying the business of S, the purchaser was only entitled to protect what he had bought, ie a local business making one type of product and not the entire range produced by the purchaser in the UK.

In *Allied Dunbar (Frank Weisinger) Ltd v Frank Weisinger 1987,* the defendant had sold his business to A, for a sum which included £386,000 as consideration for F, a financial consultant who had built up his successful business from scratch, not to be employed in a similar capacity for 2 years.

The restraint was held to be valid, since it had been agreed after equal negotiation, paid for and was reasonable in itself. The courts will not allow 'protection of goodwill' to be a smokescreen for simple restraint of competition. It must actually exist (*Vancouver Malt & Sake Brewing Co Ltd v Vancouver Breweries Ltd 1934*).

9 Remedies for breach

Tutorial note. Focus your attention on damages as the main remedy, and the principles relating to it, such as remoteness and measure of damages.

Damages

Damages are a **common law** remedy intended to restore the wronged party to the position he would have been in if the contract had been performed but not to put him in a better or more profitable position. This is sometimes referred to as protecting the **expectation interest** of the claimant.

The claimant's expectation loss may be defined as the loss of what the claimant would have received had the contract been properly performed. A claimant may alternatively seek to have his **reliance interest** protected; this refers to the position he would have been in had he not relied on the contract. Because they compensate for wasted expenditure, damages for reliance loss cannot be awarded if they would put the claimant in a better position than he would attain under protection of his expectation interest. A defendant may defeat a claim for wasted expenditure by showing that the claimant has made a bad bargain: *CCC Films (London) Ltd v Impact Quadrant Films Ltd 1985*.

Measurement of financial loss may be made with reference to the **available market** rule. Thus if a buyer refuses to take delivery of goods which he has contracted to buy, and the seller sues for loss of profit on the transaction, the existence of a market in which there is an excess of supply over demand will lead to a successful claim (as in *Thompson Ltd v Robinson (Gunmaker) Ltd 1955*), whereas if there is an excess of demand over supply, only nominal damages will be payable (*Charter v Sullivan 1957*). Damages will be awarded only in respect of **reasonably foreseeable** loss, not damage which is too **remote**: *Hadley v Baxendale 1854*).

The amount of damages payable is usually quantified as a **financial loss**, based on the **actual loss** suffered, although some types of **non financial loss** are recoverable, for example personal injuries or distress caused by a holiday failing to match the brochure's promises: *Jarvis v Swan Tours 1973*.

In some cases the cost of putting the claimant in the position he would have been in had the contract been performed may be extremely large relative to the actual loss suffered. In such cases the court **may** restrict the amount of damages.

For example, in the case of *Ruxley Electronics and Construction Ltd v Forsyth 1995*, contractors built a swimming pool which was shallower than the contractually specified depth. The householder claimed damages based on the cost of digging up the pool and constructing a new one. The court held that such a course of action was out of all proportion to the benefit of such rectification and instead awarded a lesser sum as compensation for the loss of a pleasurable amenity.

The claimant must take reasonable steps to **mitigate his loss** or he may not receive his full losses: *Payzu v Saunders 1919*. This means that he must take reasonable steps to put himself in as good a position as if the contract had been performed. For example, where goods are not delivered the buyer must take steps to buy the same goods from elsewhere as cheaply as possible. He does not have to take discreditable or risky measures to mitigate his loss: *Pilkington v Wood 1953*.

Liquidated damages

The parties to a contract may seek to avoid complicated calculations of loss and disputes as to damages by providing a formula for the calculation of such damages in the contract itself, for example a daily rate of payment in the event of late completion or late delivery of goods. This is called **liquidated damages**. This must be contrasted with a **penalty clause** in a contract. Here the clause operates to impose a penalty on the person in breach, with no attempt to link the payment to the other party's losses.

The distinction is important. A liquidated damages clause will be upheld by the court in the event of breach. If, however, the arrangement is not a genuine attempt to anticipate the appropriate level of damages it will not be enforceable (*Ford Motor Co (England) Ltd v Armstrong 1915*) and certainly any term which amounts to a penalty clause will be **void**. In determining whether the clause in question is a penalty clause or a liquidated damages provision the courts will look to see if the cause represents a genuine pre-estimate of loss: *Dunlop Pneumatic Tyre Co Ltd v New Garage & Motor Co Ltd 1915*. If so, the clause will be upheld, even if the actual loss is greater or smaller.

Action for the price

If the breach of contract is one party's failure to pay the contractually agreed sum, the other party should bring a personal **action for the price** against the party in breach provided property in the goods has passed to him and (generally speaking) provided that any sums due after an anticipatory breach will only be recoverable where he affirms the contract.

10 Contractual remedies

Tutorial note. It is clear that both of the contracts have been breached, so the real requirement of the question is a discussion of the remedies available in the two situations.

The giving of a promise as consideration for the making of a promise by another is executory consideration and is good enough to create a binding contract.

Richard and Simon

Richard carries out his side of the bargain but Simon does not perform his promised tasks. Simon is in breach of contract and Richard has a remedy against him. There are a number of remedies available for breach of contract; in this case the most useful would be an award of damages. The object of the award is to restore Richard to the position he would have been in had Simon performed his obligations. Two points require consideration: remoteness of damage and measure of damages.

It is necessary first to determine the extent to which Simon caused the loss complained of, which is that Richard lost his valuable client because his car was not serviced, and also that he did not receive payment for his work on Simon's tax return. In *Hadley v Baxendale 1854* it was held that the plaintiff may recover in respect of loss which arises naturally from the breach or for any damage which the parties might reasonably have supposed to be the probable results of the breach. This rule was reiterated in *Victoria Laundry v Newman Industries 1949*; the former test applies only to that damage which is reasonably foreseeable and special knowledge is required before abnormal damages can be claimed.

Applying these principles to this case, Simon is responsible for any damage which might arise in the natural course of things following his failure to fix the car (a stricter rule in contract than in tort: *The Heron II 1969*). This might cover physical damage to the car. Provided that this type of damage is foreseeable it seems that it is not too remote and Simon will be liable to the full extent of any consequential damage.

It is not clear whether there is liability for the lost client. If Simon was aware of the special circumstances making this loss foreseeable (that is, that Richard was due for an important meeting) then he is liable for that £5,000 loss. There is no indication that this is the case, and it seems unlikely that Richard can recover the £5,000.

Richard and Thomas

The second contract is made between Thomas and Richard but for the benefit of Ursula. Under the doctrine of privity of contract only Richard, as the person providing consideration, can sue on the contract: *Tweddle v Atkinson 1861*. If Richard can show that he is party in some representative capacity (say as Ursula's agent or trustee) then Ursula may be judged to be a party to the contract and be able to sue, but this does not seem to be the case here.

Alternatively, if, as here, the contract purports to confer a benefit on a person who is not a party to that contract, the third party, Ursula, may be able to rely on the Contract (Rights of Third parties) Act 1999.

Since the object of damages is to restore the person to the position he would have been in had the contract been performed there is a problem because Richard has suffered no physical or financial loss. The only damage is Ursula's disappointment, which may be foreseeable but is not suffered by Richard. A person cannot usually recover damages for the loss suffered by a third party.

Richard's alternative is to sue for an order for specific performance. This is preferable as Ursula would then have her garden landscaped as envisaged. As an equitable remedy, specific performance is granted only when damages would not be a sufficient remedy. However, the courts do not award this remedy where performance is likely to take some time, such as in this case with a contract for personal service. It is thus unlikely that the court would be prepared to order specific performance.

Conclusion

In the case of Simon, Richard can possibly recover the costs of repairing the car, but loss of the client is unlikely to attract an award unless there is evidence of special knowledge by Simon. The award for Thomas' breach is unlikely to exceed nominal damages in recognition of the fact of the breach; although specific performance would be most favoured by Richard and Ursula, it is rare that such an award would be made in the case of a contract for personal service. In both cases it is likely that Richard could seek restitution for the amount of work he has performed by means of a *quantum meruit* claim.

11 Agent's authority

Tutorial note. This question tests agent's authority in essay and in problem form.

(a) In order to be valid and binding on the principal and third party, a contract entered into by an agent must be entered into within the bounds of the agent's authority. However, it is not true to say that 'an agent can only contract on behalf of his principal where he has express authority'. Express authority is the most straightforward instance but there are several other circumstances where an agent can bind his principal in contract. That authority can be actual authority, whether express or implied, or ostensible authority. Agency may also arise by operation of law, most significantly agency of necessity, in which case also an agent can act without express authority and still bind his principal in contract. There are also a number of very specific circumstances where an agent can bind his principal without express authority as a consequence of statutory provisions (eg Disposal of Uncollected Goods Act 1952).

Actual authority is the extent of authority which it is agreed, between the principal and agent, the agent shall have to enter into contracts on the principal's behalf. It may be authority explicitly given to the agent to enter into a particular contract ('express authority') in which case the precise scope and extent of the authority will depend on the proper construction of the written document in which the appointment or conferring of authority is contained or on the evidence supporting an oral giving of actual express authority. Alternatively, actual authority may be implied.

(i) 'Implied incidental authority' will be deemed to exist where it is reasonable to suppose that the principal also gave the agent authority to enter into transactions which are necessarily incidental or subordinate to the matter of the express authority, eg the authority to advertise goods when the agent is expressly authorised to sell them.

(ii) 'Implied customary authority' is that which an agent shall be deemed to have by reason of his operating in a particular market or business. Thus in *Dingle v Hare 1859* an agent was held to have implied customary authority to supply a warranty when selling manure because it was customary to do so.

(iii) 'Implied usual authority' is that which an agent shall be deemed to have by reason of his occupying a particular position or engaging in a particular trade. Thus in *Howard v Sheward 1866* an agent was held to have implied usual authority when he gave a warranty as to the soundness of a horse he was selling because it was normal practice for an agent to give assurances of this kind.

In cases of implied authority, the third party who contracts with the agent is entitled to assume that the agent has implied authority unless he knows to the contrary. As between the agent and the principal however, the extent of the authority depends entirely on authority expressly given. In *Watteau v Fenwick 1893*, the principal was held to be bound by a contract entered into by his agent with implied usual authority (as a hotel manager, he bought cigars on credit) even though the third party did not know that the agent, as the other contracting party, was the agent of the principal (he had previously been the owner of the hotel (the principal's position).

'Ostensible' or 'apparent' authority is that which the principal represents to other parties he has given to his agent. Although matters of ostensible authority and implied usual authority often appear to be co-extensive, it is the conduct of the principal (expressly or by inference) which creates ostensible authority. The matter of authority might be something which is usual or customary for the agent but equally it might be something exceptional or additional to the agent's actual authority (for example where partners allow one of their number to exercise a greater authority than is normally implied in the case of a partner, they represent that he has that wider authority and they will be bound by acts entered into him acting under that authority. There need not be a pre-existing agency relationship. Ostensible authority is actually a form of estoppel which, as with any estoppel (this is often termed 'agency by estoppel') requires a representation which is relied upon thereby causing an alteration in the position of the representee: *Rama Corp v Proved Tin and General Investments Ltd 1952*.

The representation may be express or implied from previous dealings or implied from conduct. Thus in *Summers v Salomon 1957*, where the defendant regularly paid for goods ordered by his nephew-employee from the claimant and the nephew disappeared having misappropriated goods obtained in the defendant's name, it was held that the defendant was liable on the basis of previous dealings amounting to a representation that he would pay for the goods ordered as previously and that the nephew was acting as his general agent. The representation cannot be made by the agent who is claiming ostensible authority but must be made either by the principal or by another agent acting on his behalf: *Armagas Ltd v Mundogas SA, The Ocean Frost 1985*. It must be one of fact and not of law and it must be made to the third party. It is essential that there be a causal link between reliance on the representation (which must be proved) and the alteration in the representee's position. If the third party knew that the agent had no authority or did not believe him to have, he cannot claim agency by estoppel: *Overbrooke Estates Ltd v Glencombe Properties Ltd 1974*. Unless the alteration of position also causes damage or detriment, any damages awarded will be minimal although, strictly speaking, it is not necessary to show that reliance resulted in such damage or detriment.

The principle of agency of necessity applies when a principal entrusts his goods to the possession of his agent for some particular purpose (eg shipment abroad), and while the agent has possession of the goods, some emergency arises in which action must be taken to protect the goods. The emergency must require immediate action to protect the goods, in circumstances where it is impossible to communicate with the principal to receive his instructions in time. If these conditions are satisfied, the principal is bound by any contract made by the agent on his behalf to protect his interests; an agency of necessity has arisen. There must, however, have been an existing contract between the parties (eg the contract of carriage), the action must have been taken *bona fide* by the agent to protect the interests of the principal and must have been reasonable and prudent in all the circumstances: *Great Northern Railway v Swaffield 1874*.

Another instance occurs where a mercantile agent, who has implied authority to enter into certain transactions and has possession of the relevant goods with the principal's consent, then enters into such a transaction in the ordinary course of his business but without express authority (the third party being unaware of his authority having been exceeded). In those circumstances, he binds the principal.

(b) When an agent makes a contract on the principal's behalf at a time when he had no authority to do so, it is open to the principal to ratify that contract, when it will be treated as the principal's contract from the time it was made. There are some strict conditions for the exercise of this right however. The principal must have existed at the time when the contract was made (*Kelner v Baxter 1866*) and he must have the legal capacity to make the contract himself, both when the contract was made and at the time of the purported ratification (*Bird v Brown 1850*). An unnamed principal should be capable of being ascertained, or identified, at the time that the unauthorised actions occurred *Watson v Swann 1862*. It is also necessary for the agent to make it clear that he is acting as agent for the principal, or that the principal is a party to the contract *Keighley Maxsted v Durant 1900*. An undisclosed principal cannot ratify.

The principal must ratify within a reasonable time of the agent making the contract (*Portuguese Consolidated Copper Mines Ltd 1890*) and he must also ratify the whole contract by some positive act of ratification. This may be by express words but conduct implying ratification will also suffice (for instance retaining goods sold under the agent's contract). Finally the principal must know of the terms of the contract or must be prepared to ratify whatever the agent has agreed: *The Bonita 1861*.

Once ratification has taken place the principal may sue or be sued by the third party, the agent no longer has any liability to the third party nor liability for exceeding his authority and the principal is liable to pay the agent reasonable remuneration.

Under the law of contract, an offer may be revoked at any time up to acceptance. However, in an agency situation such as this, this creates the slightly strange result that the third party is bound as soon as the agent accepts his offer, while the principal is not bound unless and until he ratifies. In *Bolton Partners v Lambert 1889*, an agent agreed to buy a house on his principal's behalf without authority. The vendor tried to revoke his offer but the principal swiftly ratified his agent's actions and it was held that the third party was bound by the effective retrospective ratification. However, restrictions have been developed on this rule which, alone, produces a harsh result for the third party. Thus ratification must take place within a reasonable time so as to minimise uncertainty (*Metropolitan Asylums Board Mangers v Kingham & Sons 1890*), the third party's offer may be made expressly subject to ratification (*Watson v Davies 1931*) and if the third party commits a breach of contract after the agent's acceptance but before ratification, he will not be liable to the principal (*Kidderminster Corpn v Hardwick 1873*).

In this case, Trevor's offer was not made subject to ratification. Therefore, unless Trevor can show that Philip's ratification on the following day was not within a reasonable time, he will be bound by the contract. This will be a question of fact.

12 Separate legal personality

Tutorial note. Note in (b) that examples of circumstances where the veil of incorporation is lifted derive from statute and case law.

(a) This principle was authoritatively confirmed by the House of Lords in its judgement in *Salomon v Salomon & Co Ltd 1897*. In that case a sole trader had transferred his business to a company of which he was the sole owner and part of the purchase price was outstanding as a secured debt. It was held that even in these circumstances the shareholder and the company were different persons so that one could be a creditor of the other. The same principle was applied in *Lee v Lee's Air Farming Ltd* 1961 where the company was the employer of its sole owner and managing director.

As a consequence of this principle a sole owner has no **insurable interest** in the assets of a company which are the property of the company alone: *Macaura v Northern Assurance Co Ltd*

1925. The company's debts are its liabilities. Shareholders therefore as different persons from the company may have a limited liability only to contribute to the capital of the company.

Another consequence is that a shareholder has a transferable form of property in his shares in the company and a change of shareholders does not affect the continued existence of the company which is said to have **perpetual succession**.

A company must, as an artificial person, have **directors** to manage its affairs but shareholders are not automatically directors nor are they agents of the company. In all these respects a company is entirely different from a partnership.

(b) The distinction made between a company and its members or directors is the **'veil of incorporation'**. Exceptions are made by '**lifting the veil** of incorporation', or treating the company as identified with some other persons.

Some of these exceptions are statutory. For instance, if statutory rules on **minimum membership** or the correct use of the **company name** are infringed those in default become liable for debts of the company: s 24.

Other statutory examples are:

(i) Directors are made liable for debts where there has been fraudulent trading or wrongful trading.

(ii) Directors may be liable for third party's loss where a public company has traded without a s 117 certificate.

Exceptions are also made when the distinction between a company and its members is used for **fraudulent purposes** or to **evade legal obligations**. *Gilford Motor Co Ltd v Horne 1933*, or where it is used to **disguise nationality**: *Daimler Co Ltd v Continental Tyre and Rubber Co Ltd 1916.*

A different group of exceptions recognises that if a holding company and its subsidiaries effectively carry on a **single business** the 'economic reality' of the situation may require that they should be treated as one entity: *DHN Food Distributors Ltd v Tower Hamlets LBC 1976.*

However *Adams v Cape Industries 1990* limited the use of this exception to cases where a contract or statute explicitly laid down that group members were to be treated as a single entity. The *Adams* case reinforced the general principle that a holding company and its subsidiaries were separate legal entities.

(c) It is a principle of insurance law that the insured must have an interest in the property insured. If that is not so the policy is void. Paul has no insurable interest in the assets of the business and so his claim must fail. The facts of the question are based on *Macaura's* case mentioned above.

13 Pre-incorporation

Tutorial note. You were required to explain how pre-incorporation contracts can be enforced: a general essay on contracts or on ultra vires was not required. You needed to state that the company could not be a party, simply to show that there is a legal difficulty which needs a solution, but you should then have concentrated on who can be liable.

Remember pre-incorporation contracts cannot be ratified when a company is incorporated; evidence of a new contract is required.

A company can **never ratify a contract** made on its behalf **before** it was **incorporated**. Since it did not exist when the pre-incorporation contract was made, it cannot be made a party to it. This principle applies to both rights and obligations.

Where contracts are entered into in the name of a company prior to the incorporation of the company, the **company** will **not** be **bound** by them. Where a person purportedly contracts in the name of or as agent for a company before its incorporation that **person** will be **personally liable** (s 36) unless there is agreement to the contrary.

In *Natal Land and Colonisation Co v Pauline Colliery Syndicate 1904* it was held that a company could not enforce an option granted to it before it existed. In *Re English & Colonial Produce Co Ltd 1908*, a solicitor could not recover his charges; the company had no obligation to pay since the contract was made before the company was formed.

Need for novation

Once the company is incorporated there must be novation for a pre-incorporation contract to be enforced. This means that a **new contract** is **made** with the same subject matter, or the terms of the contract modified to the extent that it constitutes a new offer: *Howard v Patent Ivory Manufacturing Co 1888.*

Acknowledgement of the pre-incorporation contract by performance or accepting benefits will not count as **novation**: *Re Northumberland Avenue Hotel Co Ltd 1886.* **Re-negotiation** of **payment terms** will however count as making a **new contract**: *Howard v Patent Ivory Manufacturing Co 1888.*

Problems of promoters

The problems of pre-incorporation contracts particularly apply to promoters. A **promoter** is 'one who undertakes to form a company with reference to a given project and to set it going and who takes the necessary steps to accomplish that purpose': *Twycross v Grant 1877.* It is therefore a promoter who enters into pre-incorporation contracts.

A promoter **cannot enter** into **a contract** to be paid for expenses incurred before incorporation, such as drafting legal documents, because the company does not possess legal capacity. However, he can generally arrange that the first directors, of whom he may be one, should reimburse him or pay the bills.

Although a company is not liable on a pre-incorporation contract the **promoter** may nevertheless incur **personal liability** both at common law and statute. In *Kelner v Baxter 1866* it was held that promoters who signed a contract on behalf of a company which had not at that time been incorporated were liable on the contract.

Liability is now determined by s 36 above, as illustrated by *Phonogram Ltd v Lane 1981.* In the latter case, a sum was advanced to a company which was never subsequently incorporated. Under what is now s 36 (4) that the promoter was held personally liable for repayment of the sum.

Avoidance of promoter liability

Promoters can avoid liability by buying a company **off-the-shelf**. Even though the promoter contracts on the company's behalf before it is bought, the company can ratify the terms of the existing contract (ie novation is not required) if it existed at the time. This applies even if it existed under a different name: *Oshkosh B'Gosh Inc v Dan Marbel Inc Ltd 1989.* The promoter must though hold himself as an agent for the company.

Personal liability may also be avoided where a company is formed to take over an existing business. There are various ways in which this can be done.

(a) The **contract for sale** does **not** become **operative** until the **company** is **formed**. The company's objects and articles allow the promoters (as the first directors) to enter into the contract

(b) If a contract has to be made prior to incorporation, the **promoters** should **state** in it that their **personal liability** is to **cease** if the **company offers** to enter a **new contract** (thus fulfilling the novation requirement), which is however on identical terms. The objects and articles should again allow for this.

(c) The **promoters** can declare themselves **trustees** for the company (it is possible to have an unborn beneficiary of a trust). The objects and articles need again to allow the directors to enter into the contract.

14 Alteration of objects

Tutorial note. Questions about the objects clause are likely to reflect the important practical matters, particularly the ability to have a widely drafted objects clause and the procedures for changing objects.

(a) Because of the extent of the diversification, the company should **alter** its **objects** clause. A company can now alter its objects for any reason whatsoever, and, by taking advantage of s 3A provide that 'the object of the company is to carry on business as a **general commercial company**'.

To carry out the proposed alterations, the directors must call an **extraordinary general meeting**, or place the matters on the agenda of the annual general meeting. Both the name and the objects clause may be altered by **special resolution** (75% majority of votes cast).

The company must **deliver** to the **registrar** of companies a signed copy of the **resolution** by which the alteration is made (s 380) and a **copy** of the **altered memorandum** itself. This must be done within 15 days of making the alteration. The registrar gives notice of receiving it in the *London Gazette*: s 711. The company cannot rely on the alteration against a person ignorant of it if this notification procedure is not observed.

(b) S 5 provides a procedure for a dissenting minority to apply to the court to modify an otherwise valid alteration of the objects clause. The conditions are that:

(i) Application to the court must be **made within 21 days** from the passing of the special resolution to alter the objects.

(ii) The applicants must **hold** in aggregate **at least 15 per cent** of the **issued share capital** or 15 per cent of any class of shares. They must not originally have voted in favour of the alteration, nor consented to it.

The court may do any one of the following:

(i) Confirm the resolution to alter the objects clause (possibly subject to certain conditions)

(ii) Cancel the alteration

(iii) Adjourn the proceedings to allow the majority shareholders the opportunity of purchasing the shares of the dissenting minority

(iv) Provide for the purchase by the company of the dissenting minority's shares and for the consequent reduction of the company's capital

15 Section 14

Tutorial note. S14 is an important aspect of the Articles. You must understand that members are bound to each other and the company in their roles as members only. The articles could be examined in conjunction with directors and/or minority protection. Alternatively, a part A, 'explain, compare and contrast with the memorandum' question could come up.

(a) The effect of s 14 Companies Act 1985 is that, without obtaining from a new member any express agreement to that effect, the memorandum and articles of the company are a **binding agreement** between the member and the company.

A member must comply with the obligations imposed on him in relation to his shares. The company on its side must permit him to exercise his member's rights to vote (*Pender v Lushington 1877*) or to receive a dividend.

The articles, if so expressed, may also constitute a contract between members: *Rayfield v Hands 1960.*

(b) This issue arose in *Hickman v Kent or Romney Marsh Sheep Breeders Association 1915*. The article is only effective, however, insofar as the matter to be submitted to arbitration is a **membership matter**. A dispute between a company and a director in that capacity would not have to go to arbitration under an article in this form: *Re Beattie v E C F Beattie 1938.*

(c) As stated in (b) the memorandum and articles are a binding contract under s 14 only in respect of the rights and obligations of members in that capacity. The issue raised by this part of the question is based on the facts of *Eley v Positive Life Assurance Co 1875*, where the articles provided that the company should always employ Eley as its solicitor and he was also a member of the company. He was unable to enforce the article against the company since it did **not** relate to his position as a **member** but to his professional services.

If, however, the secretary was claiming **remuneration** at a rate **stated** in the **articles** for services already given to the company he could probably rely on this statement as **evidence** of the **terms** agreed between him and the company apart from the articles. This was the position when a director claimed fees for services already given: he was entitled to the rate stated in the articles: *Re New British Iron Co ex p Beckwith 1898.*

16 Kate

Tutorial note. Part (a) requires knowledge of Table A. Remember the rules about notice cover time period, who should receive the notice, and what the notice should contain.

A quorum cannot be less than two (except in single member private companies). The articles can prescribe a higher quorum, and can also allow a meeting that has started to continue if a quorum ceases to be present.

Note in (b) the different procedures for altering different parts of the memorandum.

(a) (i) In order to be validly constituted, a meeting must satisfy the following requirements.

(1) Proper notice must be given.
(2) A quorum must be present.
(3) A chairman must preside.

Proper notice

This is an extraordinary general meeting at which a special resolution is to be passed. As a result **21 clear days notice** must have been given unless this requirement has been waived by a majority of members holding at least 95% of the issued shares carrying voting rights (or between 90% and 95% where an appropriate elective resolution has been passed: s 369). 21 'clear days' notice means that the day of receipt of the notice and the day of the meeting are excluded.

The notice must have been given to **all members** entitled to receive it having a registered addresses in the UK (although accidental omission will not invalidate the proceedings) and must have been delivered personally or by post or other delivery to their registered addresses. Notice need not have been given to members who are not entitled to attend and vote at the meeting.

The notice must have contained **adequate information** concerning the date, time, venue and description of the meeting and the business to be conducted so that the members will understand what is to be done at the meeting.

If the meeting has been called as a result of a requisition by members (rather than by the directors) then additional requirements, especially concerning the date of the meeting will need to have been satisfied: s 368.

On the given facts, it is stated that the meeting has been properly convened which implies that all requirements as to notice have been satisfied.

Quorum

The requirement for a quorum to be present is that at least two persons need to attend a meeting of members and that they must be entitled to vote (Table A). They might be proxies or authorised representatives rather than shareholders. So one member plus another member's proxy will be sufficient but one member who is also another's proxy will not be sufficient: *Re Sanitary Carbon Co 1877*. Normally the quorum must be present within the first half-hour of the meeting.

A quorum is present from 8.25 pm when Kathryn and Roger arrive, meaning that at least 2 members are present. This is within the first half hour of the meeting. Nick's presence even being also a proxy for Alison is not sufficient, nor is Edmund's arrival at 8.20 pm since he is not a shareholding member of the company.

Chairman

A meeting must be presided over by a chairman who will usually be the chairman of the board of directors but may be another director chosen by the board or (in the last resort) a member chosen by the members present.

The one director present is not prepared to act as chairman but Nick, Kathryn and Roger are entitled and should elect one of themselves as chairman.

(ii) If Kathryn and Roger were to leave the meeting before business was completed this would leave the meeting **inquorate** for the reasons outlined above. Table A, Article 40, provides in these circumstances for automatic and compulsory adjournment of the inquorate meeting. Usually the meeting is re-called for the same time, day and place in the following week but with power to the directors to fix some other date, time and place. The meeting must stop – as being inquorate – once Kathryn and Roger leave.

(b) There are various clauses contained in a company's memorandum of association. However, it is possible to alter each clause and the type of resolution required in each case are described below. In each case, a printed copy of the altered memorandum must be submitted to the registrar: s 18(1)

(i) **The company name**. This clause may be altered and the name changed by passing a special resolution to that effect. This requires a majority of **75%** of votes cast. It is necessary to ensure that the new name complies with the provisions of sections 25-31 CA 1985. In order to be effective the company must **give notice** in the prescribed form to the Registrar of Companies of the resolution to change the company name and obtain a new certificate of incorporation evidencing the new name: s 28.

(ii) **The country of origin**. This clause states the country in which the registered office is situate, eg England and Wales or Scotland. It is not possible for a company to alter this clause.

(iii) **The objects of the company**. This clause can be altered by the company in general meeting passing a special resolution to that effect and the alteration can now be made for any reason whatsoever: s 4(1). Again such a resolution requires a **75%** majority. Although the alteration can be made for any reason whatsoever, it is worth noting that s 5 provides that a dissenting minority (holding at least 15% of the issued share capital) may apply to the court within 21 days of such resolution to state its objection and apply for modification of the alteration: s 6.

(iv) **The limited liability of members**. Where a company is limited by shares, the company in general meeting may pass a resolution providing that in future the company will have unlimited liability. Such a resolution requires the **unanimous consent** of all members. In addition, a certificate from the Registrar of Companies must also be obtained to evidence and effect such a change.

(v) **Public company clause**. If there is a clause which identifies a public company, this may be removed by the company passing a special resolution to that effect **(75%** majority). This will make the company a private company. There is a right of objection to the court and re-registration again is needed.

(vi) **The authorised capital**. This may be altered by the company in general meeting by **whatever resolution** the company's **articles prescribe**. Normally this will be an ordinary resolution (as in Table A) which requires a simple majority of all votes. Particulars of such a resolution must be filed with the Registrar of Companies.

(vii) **Optional clauses**. Generally, a company may pass a special resolution (75% majority) to effect an alteration of any additional clauses which appear in the memorandum and which are not compulsory: s 17. However this is subject to certain restrictions.

(1) A dissenting minority may apply to the court (in the same way as in an alteration of the objects clause).

(2) Any specified alteration procedure must be followed.

(3) An express prohibition on alteration of the clause will exclude the general power.

(4) A court order will be needed where the clause is included as a result of a previous court order.

(5) No alteration can compel any member to subscribe for additional shares nor increase his liability in respect of existing shares.

17 Officers

Tutorial note. It is important that you are aware of the key officers in a company and their role. This could be examined in Part A in a similar question to this, or in a longer question in connection with agency or directors' duties.

A **director** is someone (whether or not he is called a director) who takes part in making decisions affecting the company by attendance at meetings of the board of directors. Every company must have one or more directors to manage its affairs. Directors are given certain powers which they are obliged to exercise in performance of their duties and in accordance with certain standards.

(a) The **chairman** is the director appointed by his fellow directors (who may also remove him) who chairs board meetings. He will usually also preside at general meetings of the company. The chairman has no carrying vote unless given one by the articles. His duties are to maintain order and to deal with the agenda in a methodical way so that the business of the meeting can be properly transacted.

(b) The directors may also appoint one of their members to be **managing director**, provided the articles provide for such appointment. A managing director has apparent authority to make business contracts on behalf of the company. His actual authority is whatever authority is given to him by the board.

(c) Every company is required to have a **company secretary** among its officers. The directors of a public company must ensure that he is **suitably qualified**. The Companies Acts do not clearly define the general duties of a company secretary. As a minimum, the secretary will be responsible for making the arrangements incidental to meetings of the board of directors and for maintaining the statutory registers.

He will **convene board meetings**, issue the agenda, collect and prepare papers for submission to the meeting, attend meetings and draft minutes, communicate decisions to staff or third parties as required by the meeting. He will enter in the **register transfers of shares** and prepare share certificates for issue. He will prepare the notices, returns and other documents for delivery to the registrar of companies from time to time.

Depending on the size of the company, the secretary may also act as the **general administrator** and **head office manager**, dealing with staff matters, office equipment and pensions as well as being responsible for the company's correspondence. In the absence of a finance director or chief accountant, the secretary may also have duties regarding the company's accounts and taxation aspects.

The Cadbury Report 1992 stated that the company secretary will also have a primary responsibility for the **statement of compliance with the Combined Code of Best Practice** in the report, for providing information to non-executive directors and for preparing a formal schedule of matters reserved for the board's decision.

With regard to the **powers** of a company secretary, the courts have applied the general principles of agency law to the general nature of a company secretary's duties, at the same time recognising the broader administrative duties of today's typical company secretary. In *Panorama Developments (Guildford) Ltd v Fidelis Furnishing Fabrics Ltd 1971*, it was held that the secretary had apparent authority to enter into contracts such as the one in that case, namely ordering cars from a car hire firm for the use of the company's customers, but that the secretary would be unlikely to have apparent authority to enter into commercial contracts for the sale and purchase of trade goods since that would not be the normal duty of a company secretary.

18 Happy

Tutorial note. The key points in this area are:

(a) The right of shareholders to remove directors under s 303

(b) The ways in which a director can legally prevent removal (weighted voting rights, shareholders' agreement)

(c) The fact that a separate contract with the director cannot *in law* prevent a director being removed under s 303. The point about damages is a *practical* point the company will need to consider.

The risk to which H is exposed is that the other shareholders have 60 per cent of the votes and can carry an **ordinary resolution** to remove H from the office of director: s 303. If H ceases to be a director he also ceases to be managing director since the former is a necessary qualification for the latter.

'Bushell v Faith' clause

H could safeguard his position by securing the agreement of the other shareholders to a provision being inserted in the articles to the effect that on any resolution for his removal his 40 per cent of the shares should carry a majority of the total votes which could be cast. He could thus defeat the resolution. This device was used and upheld by the House of Lords in *Bushell v Faith 1969. S* 303 requires that an ordinary resolution shall be passed. It does not prohibit **weighted voting rights** even if they are provided for the purpose of frustrating the statutory power of removal.

If H uses this method he could prevent any alteration of the articles by special resolution which would remove his weighted voting rights. H will have 40 per cent of the votes in normal circumstances and this suffices to enable him to block a special resolution for which a three quarters majority of votes cast is required.

H cannot effectually prevent his removal by requiring that he shall be employed under a service contract which assures him of a long period of service. The statutory **power to remove** a director **overrides** any **contract**.

Shareholders' agreement

H might also enter into a shareholders' agreement with the other two shareholders by which the latter would undertake to use their votes to retain him in office as a director. The court would probably grant an injunction to restrain them from voting for the removal of H contrary to the terms of the agreement. There is no legal objection to a shareholder committing himself to vote in a particular way at general meetings (though a director may not fetter the exercise of his powers as a director).

S 319

Any agreement which the company cannot terminate without penalty within 5 years is subject to s 319. Unless it is approved in general meeting (which may well be possible in this case) the agreement is, in spite of its express terms, terminable without penalty on reasonable notice.

A long-term service agreement, if approved under s 319, can still be overridden by removal under s 303. However H would in that case be entitled to **damages** related to loss of earnings over the unexpired period of the contract: *Southern Foundries (1926) Ltd v Shirlaw 1940.* It would be costly to the company to dismiss him, if it had to pay a large sum in damages. That factor would be a disincentive to the other shareholders. But H could not by this means prevent them using their control of the company, so he could not obtain an injunction to restrain the company from removing him under s 303, if it was willing to pay the price.

19 Wrongful trading

Tutorial note. Wrongful trading is an important aspect of your studies about directors and it has obvious links to insolvency. It could be examined in a 20 mark scenario question combining your knowledge about directors' duties with your understanding of the legal situation arising in insolvency.

The offence of wrongful trading was introduced to make it easier for creditors to make **negligent directors liable for company debts since**, before this provision, they were required to prove fraud which was very difficult. The assets available for distribution in a winding up may be significantly increased by directors' contributions ordered under this statutory provision.

Under s 214 Insolvency Act 1986, in the case of an insolvent company, where the liquidator can show that the directors **knew**, or **should have known**, that there was **no reasonable prospect** that the **company could have avoided going into insolvent liquidation**, and that the **directors did not take sufficient steps to minimise the potential loss to creditors**, the directors will be liable for wrongful trading. (The element of real dishonesty needed for liability for fraudulent trading under s 213 need not be shown).

An **objective test** will be applied, namely whether a reasonably diligent person with the general knowledge, skill and experience that might reasonably be expected of a person carrying out that particular director's duties would have concluded that the company could not avoid insolvent liquidation. A director cannot claim lack of knowledge where it results from failing to comply with Companies Acts requirements, such as preparation of accounts: *Re Produce Marketing Consortium 1989.*

In the event of liability, the court could require the directors to contribute to the assets of the company in an amount determined by the court. The extent of liability will be assessed in the light of all relevant circumstances of the case, but will not be low or nominal merely because there is no fraud *Re Produce Marketing*). s727 CA, which provides relief in proceedings for negligence or breach of duty or trust to directors who acted honestly and reasonably, is not available as a defence to proceedings under s214 *Halls v David and Another 1989.*

20 Issue of shares

Tutorial note. This question is about issue of shares at a discount, **not** reduction of capital.

In (b) the distinction between what a public and private company can accept is very important.

(a) It is a basic principle of English company law that every share of a limited company shall have a **nominal value.** A member of a limited company has limited liability, so he need contribute no more for his shares than the amount agreed at the time of allotment. However in **the interests of creditors** of the company a member may not be allotted his shares in return for a consideration which is of less value than the nominal value of the shares: s 100.

If that rule is broken the member is required to pay in cash whatever additional amount is necessary to make up the total consideration received by the company to an amount equal to the nominal value: *Ooregum Gold Mining Co of India v Roper 1892.*

Any company may allot shares at **par** (at a price equal to the nominal value) and pay underwriting commission or brokerage in connection with the issue. In such cases the net proceeds are less than the nominal value. But the amount of underwriting commission and brokerage is restricted: s 97 (2)(a).

(b) When a private company allots shares for a non-cash consideration the court will not usually enquire whether that consideration is of equal value to the nominal value of the shares: *Re Wragg 1897.* This is because the value of an asset to the company is a matter of business judgement. But even a private company may **not** openly **breach** the prohibition against **issue of shares** at a **discount**, for example by allotting shares for past services: *Re Eddystone Marine insurance Co 1893.*

A public company is now subject to various statutory rules.

(i) It may **not agree to accept** even **future services** as consideration for the allotment of shares: s 99(2).

(ii) If it allots shares to acquire property the **property** must be **valued** by or under arrangements made by a person qualified to be auditor of the company: s 103. If the procedure is not correctly followed the allottee (or subsequent holder of the shares other than a purchaser for value) may have to pay cash for the shares. This valuation requirement does not however apply to a take-over bid by which Company A allots shares and acquires shares of Company B as consideration for its shares.

Non-cash consideration may **not** be **accepted** as payment for shares if an **undertaking** contained in such consideration is to be, or may be, **performed more than five years** after the allotment: s 102. This rule relates to a property or business promised in return for shares.

(c) If a company receives consideration other than cash of greater value than the shares which it allots the **surplus** must be **credited** to **share premium account** since s 130 refers to the issue of shares at a premium for cash or otherwise: *Henry Head & Co v Ropner Holdings 1952.* But where the premium obtained represents undistributed profits of the company whose shares are acquired by a take-over it may be permissible to follow **merger accounting practice** with the result that the surplus is not credited to share premium account: ss 131 – 134.

21 Maintenance of capital

Tutorial note. Note the extra conditions that apply to public companies.

(a) A limited company is permitted **without restriction** to cancel unissued shares and in that way to reduce its **authorised share capital**. That change does not alter its financial position.

If a limited company with a share capital wishes to **reduce** its **issued share capital** (and incidentally its authorised capital of which the issued capital is part) it may do so provided that it:

(i) Has **power** to do so in its articles
(ii) **Passes** a **special resolution**
(iii) Obtains confirmation of the reduction from the court s 135

Requirement (i) is simply a matter of procedure. Articles (Table A Article 34) usually contain the necessary power. If not, the company in general meeting would first pass a special resolution to alter the articles appropriately and then proceed, as the second item on the agenda of the meeting, to pass a special resolution to reduce the capital.

There are three basic methods of reducing share capital specified in s 135(2):

(i) **Extinguish** or **reduce liability** on partly-paid shares

(ii) **Cancel paid up share capital** which has been lost or which is no longer represented by available assets

(iii) **Pay off part** of the **paid up share capital** out of surplus assets

Although these are the methods specified in s 135, they are not the only possibilities.

If method (i) or (iii) is used (or is part of a more complex scheme to reduce capital) creditors must be invited to object, and their consent must be granted. An alternative is that they are paid off, which will allow the court to approve the reduction. These requirements, along with other court procedures, are contained in s 136.

It should be remembered that public companies are subject to a **minimum capital requirement**, currently of **£50,000**: s 11. This means that any public company wishing to reduce its capital below this figure will only be allowed to do so by the court if it re-registers as a private company, which is not subject to the minimum capital requirement. This situation is, of course, relatively rare.

(b) Dividends may only be paid by a company out of profits available for the purpose: s 263. There is now a detailed code of statutory rules which determines what are distributable profits. This statutory code replaces much of the confused and uncertain case-law which previously applied. The **profits** which may be **distributed** as dividend are **accumulated realised profits**, so far as not previously utilised by distribution or capitalisation, **less accumulated realised losses**, so far as not previously written off in a reduction or reorganisation of capital duly made.

The word 'accumulated' requires that any losses of previous years must be included in reckoning the current distributable surplus.

The word 'realised' presents more difficulties. It clearly prevents the distribution of an increase in the value of a retained asset resulting from revaluation. However, it does not prevent a company from transferring to profit and loss account, for example, profit earned on an uncompleted contract, if it is 'in accordance with generally accepted accounting principles. Sch 4 para 36A requires that:

'it shall be stated whether the accounts have been prepared in accordance with applicable accounting standards and particulars of any material departure from those standards and the reasons for it shall be given.'

There is no mention here of realised profits and so it would seem that there is now no statutory guidance on this point. Nevertheless, in view of the authority of SSAPs and FRSs, it is unlikely that profits determined in accordance with SSAPs and FRSs would be considered unrealised. A realised capital loss will reduce realised profits.

The above rules on distributable profits apply to all companies, private or public. A public company is subject to an additional rule (s 264) which may diminish but cannot increase its distributable profit as determined under the above rules.

A **public company** may **only make** a **distribution** if its **net assets** are, at the time, **not less** than the **aggregate of its called-up share capital and undistributable reserves**. The dividend which it may pay is limited to such amount as will leave its net assets at not less than that aggregate amount.

(c) If the **net assets** of a **public company** are **half or less** of the **amount of its called up share capital** there must be an extraordinary general meeting: s 142.

The duty to call the meeting arises as soon as any of the directors comes to know that the financial situation is as described above. It does not appear that the directors have any duty to make enquiries and they are not deemed to know what they might have known but did not, in fact, know. It is not stated how the net value of the company is to be determined (a 'going concern' valuation of assets might well be inappropriate).

When the directors' duty arises they must issue a notice to convene a meeting within **28 days** of becoming aware of the need to do so. The meeting must be convened for a date within **56 days** of their coming to know the relevant facts.

The directors have no obligation to lay a report or proposals before the meeting though in practice they would be wise to take the initiative in doing so.

The purpose of this procedure is to enable shareholders to consider 'whether any, and if so what, measures should be taken to deal with the situation'. One incidental result might well be to alert the company's creditors to the deterioration in its situation and so precipitate the financial crisis in its affairs. Often the measure taken is to reduce capital.

22 Loan capital

Tutorial note. This question is typical of the sort of question you could expect to see on loan capital in the exam and is therefore very good practice.

Remember also that you could be faced with a 20 mark question combining this sort of knowledge with your knowledge of the relevant procedures when a company gets into difficulty and fails to pay its debts.

(a) A debenture is a **written acknowledgement** of a debt (s744 CA 1985), ie any document which states the terms on which a company has borrowed money.

A debenture **often creates a fixed or floating charge** over the company's assets as security for the loan (though a document relating to an unsecured loan is still a debenture in company law).

A debenture can be a **single debenture** (typically a bank's standard form debenture for a secured loan or overdraft facility) or a **series of debentures** (by which a global sum is raised and which normally rank *pari passu*). A public company may offer its debentures to the public by means of a prospectus which is an offer to issue its debenture stock.

The debenture almost invariably gives the debentureholder, in specified circumstances of default by the company, power to appoint a **receiver**. The receiver will have suitable powers of management and disposal of the charged assets and shall be an agent of the company. A receiver may be appointed pursuant to a fixed or floating charge to enforce the security for the benefit of the secured creditor by whom he is appointed. For floating charges registered since 15 September 2003, the shareholder may no longer appoint an administrative receiver. The course of action under the Enterprise Act 2002 is to appoint an administrator, whose principal objective is company rescue as a going concern.

Any type of charge gives to the holder a **priority** claim to payment of what is owing to him out of the value of the property which is subject to that charge. The ranking of that priority will depend on the types and times of creation of all relevant charges. Most types of charge must be **registered** within 21 days with the registrar of companies (ss 395-399). A company is also obliged to keep a copy of documents creating charges and a register of other charges at its registered office (s.406).

(b) A fixed or specific charge attaches to the **relevant asset** as soon as the charge is created, for example a charge over named property given as security for a loan to the owner of the property. If the company does need to dispose of the charged asset, it will either repay the secured debt out of the sale proceeds so that the charge is discharged or dispose of the asset subject to the charge.

A fixed charge may be **legal** or **equitable** and over land or other company assets, from buildings and chattels to book debts. A charge by way of legal mortgage must be created by deed under s.85LPA1925. Holders of fixed charges, properly created and registered, rank in priority to subsequent claimants against the company's charged assets.

A holder of a fixed charge might opt to sell the charged assets to enforce his security quickly or he might appoint a receiver where, for example, the property has a substantial income (eg an office block) and it appears to be a more appropriate means of enforcement. Any excess of the proceeds over the amount of the debt goes to pay off other company debts. If there is a shortfall then the debentureholder becomes an unsecured creditor for the amount outstanding.

(c) **No particular form of wording is required to create a floating charge**. The nature of a floating charge was summarised in *Re Yorkshire Woolcombers Association Ltd 1903* as a charge on a class of assets of a company, present and future, which class is, in the ordinary course of the company's business, changing from time to time and until the holder enforces the charge the company may carry on business and deal with the assets charged.

If the **company retains the right to deal** with the charged assets during the ordinary course of business until the charge crystallises, then that charge is a 'floating charge'. The charge will not attach to the assets on creation of the charge but rather on **crystallisation** of the charge, at which point the floating charge becomes a fixed charge. Crystallisation will occur on the happening of any of the events specified in the charge, such as the liquidation of the company or the cessation of its business: *Re Woodroffes (Musical Instruments) Ltd 1986*. A floating charge over 'the undertaking and assets' of a company applies to fixed as well as to current assets.

A receiver who was appointed under a floating charge (registered prior to 15 September 2003) which extends over 'the whole or substantially the whole' of the company's property is called an administrative receiver (s 29 IA86). He must be a qualified insolvency practitioner and will be responsible for management of the company's business. He has extensive statutory powers including the power to borrow money and give security and to sell the company's property.

An administrator appointed under a floating charge (since 15 September 2003) has three hierarchical objectives:

(i) Company rescue
(ii) Some better result for the creditors than would be obtained under an immediate winding-up
(iii) Only if neither of these is possible, a realisation of property.

Whether or not the parties label a charge as 'fixed' or 'floating' will not be conclusive. For example a charge which covers present and future book debts, whatever it is called by the parties, will be floating if the company is allowed to deal with money collected from debtors without notifying the chargee and fixed if the money must be paid to the chargee, for example in reduction of an overdraft (*Siebe Gorman & Co Ltd v Barclays Bank Ltd 1979*).

A fixed charge will rank in priority to a floating charge even if it was created after the floating charge since it attaches to the property at the time of creation rather than at the time of crystallisation (except where a floating charge contains an express prohibition on the creation of subsequent fixed charges (a negative pledge clause) and a subsequent chargee has actual notice of such prohibition).

23 Insolvency

Tutorial note. Candidates often confuse the roles of an administrative receiver, administrator and liquidator. It is important to be able to distinguish between them.

The Insolvency Act 1986 provides for appointment in respect of a company's affairs of an administrate receiver (s 33) or an administrator (s 13). Their methods of appointment and functions are markedly different.

An **administrative receiver** is appointed by a lender who has security by means of a floating charge over the whole of the assets of the company where the charge was registered prior to 15 September 2003. There is no application to the court involved. The appointment is made by the lender when there is a breach of the lending agreement such as non payment of interest or principal. The appointment can be made immediately after the breach occurs and normally within a matter of hours.

The purpose of a receiver is primarily to recover any amounts outstanding to the lender as quickly as possible. In law an administrative receiver also has obligations to other creditors including preferential and unsecured creditors. He will often seek to sell the business as a going concern in order to obtain the best price for the assets. Any surplus after repayment of the lender will go to the other creditors in order of priority.

An **administrator** is appointed by the court by the terms of an administration order. The function of the administrator is to initiate one of the rescue procedures identified in the Insolvency Act whilst enjoying the protection of the court from hostile creditors.

This may involve:

- Disposing of all or some of the assets
- A reorganisation of capital, or
- Another arrangement conducive to the continuation of the business.

Administration has wider scope than receivership, as receivers are most concerned with the interests of the creditors who appoint them. Administrators can also deal with certain matters such as past transactions and retention of title clauses which receivers cannot challenge.

(a) The legal grounds under which a company may be put into administrative receivership are also wholly contractual, the only exception being a residual power for the court to act if there is some doubt about the terms of the lending agreement. The lending agreement, often termed a debenture, will specific the circumstances under which a receiver may be appointed. These usually include default on payment of interests when due or repayment after a period of notice.

In addition failure to maintain certain financial ratios or net asset values are common trigger points. Finally other incidents of insolvency such as being unable to pay its debts when due, winding up, appointment of any other receiver under a separate charge from that held by the lender or petition for an administration order will normally trigger the appointment of an administrative receiver.

(b) Administration was introduced by the Insolvency Act 1986. It can only be achieved by order of the court following the submission of a petition intended to achieve one of the hierarchical purposes set out in s 8(3) as follows.

- Company rescue, first and foremost
- A more advantageous realisation of the company's assets than could be achieved by a winding up
- A realisation of property in order to make a distribution to secured and/or preferential creditors.

(c) **Secured creditors**

In receiverships anyone holding a fixed charge over the company's assets is entitled to be paid first out of the proceeds of sale subject only to a prior claim for the costs of realisation.

The position in an administration is somewhat different. On the presentation to the court of a petition for an administration order, notice must be given to anyone who could appoint a receiver by virtue of the security they hold or to a receiver already in existence. During the period after presentation of the petition and before its hearing no steps may be taken to enforce any security over the company's property without the permission of the court.

A creditor seeking leave from the court to enforce the security must show that refusal would result in undue hardship: *Re Atlantic Computer Systems plc 1992.*

An order cannot be granted however if a receiver is already in place without the consent of the floating charge holder. The petitioner must therefore convince the holder of the charge that administration would be more beneficial than receivership. This is a purely commercial decision.

Preferential creditors

Preferential creditors are paid next in a receivership from any surplus from the disposal of the charged assets. By contrast in an administration, there is effectively a moratorium on the company's debts. Most importantly, while the administration order is in place, no winding up or proceedings for the recovery or enforcement of debts can take place.

This means that the position of preferential creditors is weakened during administration. This is one of the benefits of administration for the company since it means that a preferential creditor cannot force the company into liquidation whilst rescue is being attempted.

Unsecured creditors

Under both systems unsecured creditors rank after secured and preferential creditors in terms of repayment, although a certain part of the company's assets is to be ring-fenced for them under the Enterprise Act 2002. (This provision is not yet in force.) In a receivership they will have no say in the matter until a liquidator is appointed. In an administration however the unsecured creditors are entitled to vote on any proposals that the administrator presents and to form a committee to advise the administrator.

Since the proposals must be presented within three months of the administration order being granted, this means that at least matters are being dealt with more expeditiously than in a liquidation following receivership which may take years to resolve.

24 Employer's duties

Tutorial note. This question is a useful run through the main issues relating to an employment contract.

Terms

The terms to be included will be found in a number of sources.

Express terms need not be set out in writing but within eight weeks of an employee commencing employment (presuming he works more than 8 hours a week), his employer must give him certain written particulars of his employment covering such things as salary, hours of work, sick pay, holidays, notice and so on: s 1 Employment Rights Act 1996. Terms outlining the disciplinary and grievance procedure must also be notified. This will not be necessary if, as is usual, the written particulars refer the employee to some other written notice of the terms, usually included in an employee handbook, wall notices and other documents.

An employee is also entitled periodically to receive a pay statement itemising gross pay and deductions.

Many terms are inserted through **collective agreements** made between employer and union or employee representatives. They are not legally binding, as the individual employee is not a party to the agreement, but in fact are observed by both parties to the contract and thus become part of the individual employment contract. Terms may also be implied by reference to an employer's customary practice with his workforce. Examples are wage-rates and working hours.

Other terms are inserted **by operation of law**. Case law has led to certain terms being implied into contracts such as the employee's duty to carry out his work in good faith (*Boston Deep Sea Fishing & Ice Co v Ansell 1888*) and the employer's duty to provide work to a person specifically employed to do that work: *Collier v Sunday Referee Publishing Co 1940*.

A more important source is the extensive **legislation** on employment which imposes a number of requirements on the parties as to the terms of employment. An employee has rights to engage in union duties and activities (ss 168-170 TULRCA 1992), and he will be protected from discrimination on the grounds of race or sex (Equal Pay Act 1970, Sex Discrimination Acts 1975 and 1986, Race Relations Act 1976). The 1996 Act gives important rights as to dismissal and redundancy and to minimum periods of notice. Statute also allows time off from main duties to find work if an employee is about to be made redundant.

The employer has a duty to provide a safe system of working, to select proper staff and to provide adequate materials. These common law duties are supplemented by the extensive statutory requirements of the Health and Safety at Work Act 1974 and the Occupiers' Liability Acts.

Duties

The **implied duties** owed by an employer to his employee will be governed both by common law and statute, subject to any express agreement between the parties to the contrary, assuming that such agreement is not contrary either to law or public policy.

The common law implies several terms into the contract of employment, all of which are fundamental to the relationship. First, the employer has a duty to take reasonable care for the **safety** of the worker. Thus, he must provide competent staff, safe premises and equipment and a safe system of work. This term is also governed by statute and the employer must comply with those regulations too.

In the unlikely circumstances of there being no agreement as to remuneration, the rate of **remuneration must be reasonable**. However, statute largely governs the method and rate of payment.

In certain circumstances, the common law will imply a duty to **provide work**. Employees protected include those paid on a piecework or commission basis and those whose earning power and reputation is founded on active occupation; such workers would include actors and journalists: *Collier v Sunday Referee*

Publishing Co Ltd 1940. Further, if an employee is appointed to a particular post, there will be an implied duty not to remove the employee from that post or to abolish it.

The employee is also entitled to **reasonable management**, so that arbitrary and inconsiderate action may constitute a breach of contract.

Where no specific period of notice has been agreed, the employer has an implied common law duty to give **reasonable notice** in the event of a dismissal. Whether the period of notice given is reasonable will depend on the particular circumstances of the employment. This term is also governed by statute which provides a minimum period of notice which cannot be varied by agreement.

If an employee properly incurs **expenses** in the performance of his duties, the employer has a common law duty to **reimburse** him. The employee must also be indemnified against liability for any unlawful act, provided that he has no knowledge that the act is unlawful.

There are many terms implied by **statute** into the employer/employee relationship. It would be impractical to attempt to deal with more than a selection of these terms.

The most fundamental include the **anti-discriminatory provisions**. These relate to trade union membership and activities, gender and race. They also apply to equal pay for men and women working in comparable posts. The provisions are generally designed to regulate the advertisement of posts and the selection for appointments, promotions and dismissal, although some situations must of necessity be excluded.

For example, in the case of selection for appointment, the requirement of decency may necessitate single-sex workers, or there may be a genuine occupational qualification such as the necessity that an actress play the part of Joan of Arc.

The employer must in certain circumstances allow his employee **time off work**. This would include time to attend for ante-natal and other maternity care and to perform duties for local government or as a magistrate. In some cases the employee will be paid for the time spent away from work.

Finally, there are statutory provisions regulating the **termination of employment**; that is, redundancy and unfair dismissal. These provisions are too complex to be discussed in the context of this question, but, basically, they protect the worker in circumstances where the employment is terminated through no fault of his own.

25 Redundancy and dismissal

Tutorial note. Your statutory references should be mainly to the Employment Rights Act 1996. The compensation payable is subject to a maximum which is in addition to the basic award.

Brian

Brian has been dismissed because he has been unable to adapt to new works practices, not by reason of redundancy. In any event it is not redundancy where an employer alters his methods of work so that the same work has to be done by different means which are beyond the capability of an employee: *North Riding Garages v Butterwick 1967.* He has been employed by the company for 15 years. He proposes to make a claim for unfair dismissal.

Unfair dismissal is a statutory concept contained in the Employment Rights Act 1996. An action may be brought by an employee who satisfies the statutory criteria. First he must be below the normal retirement age for that job (determined by normal employment practice: *Waite v GCHQ 1983*). Secondly, he must have been continuously employed for at least one year either full time or part time. Thirdly, the employee must have been dismissed, either by the employer bringing the contract to an end (with or without notice) or where a fixed term contract ends and is not renewed or where there is a constructive dismissal. Finally the dismissal must have been unfair. The employee does not have to prove this; it is for the employer to show that it was not by giving a good reason. Even if he does, the tribunal may still decide that the dismissal was unfair.

Unfair dismissal may arise if the employer does not act reasonably, by following correct procedures, by taking all circumstances into account and by doing what a reasonable employer would have done. Some reasons for dismissal are automatically unfair eg dismissal for trade union membership or because of pregnancy.

To defeat a claim for unfair dismissal the employer must show his main or sole reason for the dismissal which must be either one of those listed in the 1996 Act as being automatically fair (eg redundancy, employee's conduct or legal restrictions) or must be some other substantial reason which justifies dismissal (eg a refusal to accept changed work practices agreed by a majority of the workforce).

Brian has been dismissed for being incapable of performing his job with the new working practices. Such alleged incapability will be judged with reference to the requirement of the contract, the work standards achieved by employees generally and by the employee in question. Even if the employer proves an acceptable reason for dismissal, he must also show (and the test applied is an objective one) that he acted reasonably in dismissing the employee.

He must have applied the correct disciplinary procedure (for example by giving warnings in the case of all but the most serious misconduct, or consulting the appropriate employee representatives when considering redundancies). He must have taken account of all the relevant circumstances. This means that he must take previous conduct into account before dismissing for misconduct, or must offer help to an employee who has difficulties with his work before dismissing on grounds of incapacity.

Evidence of an employer's reasonable conduct in this regard would be consultation with the employee to determine the areas of difficulty, allowing a reasonable time for improvement, providing training if necessary and considering all alternatives to dismissal.

It is clear in this case that whatever the extent of Brian's incapability, the employer has not acted reasonably in simply dismissing him. His dismissal is therefore unfair and Brian's claim should succeed. He must apply to the employment tribunal within 3 months of his dismissal.

Once unfair dismissal is established, an employment tribunal may first consider reinstatement (ie a return to the same job without any break in the continuity of employment) or re-engagement (which is a different but comparable job with the same employer). Practical considerations and all other relevant factors, including the employee's wishes will be taken into account. Compensation is the most usual award. This consists of a basic award, calculated on age, length of service (up to 20 years) and weekly wage. There may also be a compensatory award for additional losses calculated on ordinary principles of breach of contract (up to a limit of £55,000) which should represent the amount which the tribunal considers to be just and equitable in all the circumstances: s 123.

He does not have a claim for redundancy (see *North Riding Garages* case referred to above).

John

John has been dismissed because of his involvement in TU activities and has worked for the company for 9 months. He intends to make a claim for unfair dismissal.

Under s 152 TULRCA 92 a dismissal is automatically unfair if it is on account of an employee's membership (actual or proposed) of an independent TU or his taking part at an appropriate time (outside work hours or within those hours at an agreed time) in the activities of such a TU or refusal to be a member of a TU. Under s 154, where dismissal is for TU membership, neither the condition of continuous service nor the age limit applies.

Peter

Peter is offered alternative employment 50 miles away and refuses. He has worked for the company for 3 years.

There will be no breach of contract and no claim for redundancy if there is an appropriate mobility clause in Peter's contract which entitles the company to require him to work at this alternative site. Peter's dismissal would appear to be on the grounds of redundancy following the reorganisation at the warehouse.

The law relating to redundancy is found in the Employment Rights Act 1996. An employee has a right to a redundancy payment (as compensation) in the event that he is dismissed because of redundancy, that is where the only or main reason for the dismissal is that (a) the employer has ceased or intends to cease carrying on the business in which the employee has been employed or at the local establishment where the employee has been employed or (b) his requirements of that business for employees to carry on the work done by the employee have ceased or diminished.

The onus is on the employee to show that he was dismissed and then on the employer to show that the dismissal was for some reason other than redundancy. It is open to the employer to offer a redundant employee alternative employment, which offer must be made before the old employment comes to an end and must take effect within 4 weeks thereafter. If the employee unreasonably refuses the offer, he loses his entitlement to a redundancy payment. The alternative employment must be in the same capacity, at the same place and on the same terms and conditions as the old employment or, if it differs in any of those respects, must constitute suitable employment in relation to the employee. In this case the alternative employment offered to Peter is 50 miles away. Whether or not that is reasonable will be a question of fact. (It seems likely that it would not be regarded as reasonable.)

Where an employee has been dismissed because of redundancy, he will (as with a claim for unfair dismissal) be entitled to a redundancy payment if he is under the normal retirement age for the business (or 65 where no age is specified) and has been continually employed for 2 years or more. Redundancy pay is calculated as follows: 1.5 weeks pay for each complete year of employment during which the employee was aged 41 or more, 1 week's pay for each year where he was aged between 22 and 40 and 0.5 week's pay for each year where he was aged between 18 and 21. Peter qualifies for redundancy pay (provided the offer of alternative employment is unreasonable) and should claim within 6 months following his dismissal. If his claim is disputed by the employer, he should refer it to an employment tribunal.

Michael

Michael has been dismissed for reasons of redundancy and therefore is not entitled to claim unfair dismissal. He does not qualify to claim a redundancy payment as he has only worked for the company for 18 months and so it is not necessary to consider whether the offer of alternative part time work is reasonable. He has been constructively dismissed provided he can show that his resignation was as a result of the employer's breach of contract and that he has not waived the breach, for example by delaying too long before resigning. The unilateral imposition of a change in the employee's terms and conditions, such as changing a full time job to a part time one, amounts to a repudiatory breach. He is however entitled to claim damages at common law for breach of contract.

26 Discrimination

Tutorial note. New cases on sex and racial discrimination are being heard all the time so you should keep up to date in this topical area.

(a) The Sex Discrimination Act 1975 restricts on an employer's ability to discriminate on grounds of sex when choosing a new employee. The Act prevents discrimination on grounds of gender; it applies equally to male and female employees. Many cases involve female employees – in such cases a woman is discriminated against if a person treats her less favourably than he would a man or if he sets conditions which men are more able to meet than women. This amounts to direct discrimination.

The Act forbids discrimination in the recruitment, promotion training, benefits or dismissal of employees. Some guidance is given in the question of recruitment by a Code of Practice drawn up under the Act in 1985, which recommends that employers should clearly state that they have a regularly monitored equal opportunities policy and that they should also encourage applications from either sex in recruitment advertising.

Indirect discrimination is also forbidden. This would include the imposition of criteria which are more easily met by one sex, such as age limits. For example, in *Price v Civil Service 1978* it was held that the imposition of an age limit for appointment to a particular civil service grade discriminated indirectly against women who had taken a career break to have children.

The Act allows some discrimination in specific circumstances. If the employment of a person of one sex is a 'genuine occupational requirement or qualification' (GOQ), discrimination may be acceptable. Some occupations are outside the scope of the Act, for example prison officers. It is illegal to employ women in certain occupations, for example as underground workers in mines. Finally some derogations are allowed if there is a sufficiently good reason, for example a female attendant in a ladies' lavatory.

The Equal Pay Act 1970 imposes the requirement on an employer that the conditions under which he employs female workers must be at least as favourable as those available to male employees. This requirement has been interpreted as meaning that an employee must receive equal pay for work of equal value.

Under the Act, an equality clause is implied into every woman's contract of employment where the woman is employed on like work with a man, on work rated as equivalent with that of a man or on work of equal value to that of a man in the same employment. The clause acts as follows.

(i) If any term of the woman's contract is or becomes less favourable to the woman than a term of a similar kind in the contract under which the man is employed, that term of the woman's contract shall be treated as so modified as not to be less favourable.

(ii) If at any time the woman's contract does not include a term corresponding to a term benefiting the man included in his contract, the woman's contract shall be treated as including such a term.

The employer must show that the reason for the difference is a genuine material factor other than sex. Examples are as follows:

(i) Greater length of service is a material factor: *Capper Pass v Lawton 1977*.

(ii) Working at different times of day is not a material factor: *Dugdale v Kraft Foods 1977*.

(iii) 'Market forces' do not necessarily amount to a genuine material factor: *Ratcliffe & Others v North Yorkshire County Council 1995*.

(b) Discrimination on the grounds of race is similarly prohibited by the Race Relations Act 1976. The Commission for Racial Equality was set up to supervise the law in this area. The provisions of the Act are broadly in line with the provisions of the Sex Discrimination Act. Again, there are grounds on which discrimination may be justified.

(i) Authenticity in art entertainment or photography

(ii) Personal services ie where a local authority employee such as a housing officer might be required to be of the same ethnic origin as the community in which he works

(iii) Maintaining ethnic authenticity in a place of work such as a restaurant

An employee may complain to an industrial tribunal if he feels that his rights have been infringed by discrimination.

There is no upper limit on compensation in discrimination claims. It is important to remember that once the applicant has proved facts from which the tribunal could conclude that the employer had discriminated in some way, then it must uphold the application's complaint unless the employer can prove his action was not discriminatory.

27 Promises

Tutorial note. This question was not exam standard. However, it is a useful question to attempt. It gives you practice spotting the relevant issues in deciding whether a contract has been formed (this question concentrates on consideration). This will be a vital skill if the same requirement is given to you on a longer scenario question in Part B of the question paper. You should expect that one of the 20 mark questions is likely to be on contract law.

In this question, you had five scenarios to consider. Seeing that the requirement was on whether a contract had been formed, you should have had the three essential elements of contract in your mind and soon spotted that these scenarios were concerned with consideration.

When you spot an issue in a scenario, you must remember to **state the law** which it relates to, **explain that law** and then **apply it** in the scenario. Notice how the answer given below follows that pattern in each part.

We have included a brief introduction stating the general requirements for a valid contract to be formed so that this information is not repeated in each section of the requirement. If you feel that such an introduction is required in a question, make sure that you keep it as brief as possible. You do not want to cover issues that should be used in answering the specific questions in this introduction and risk not being given credit for it.

Introduction

In order for a contract to have been formed, three essential elements must be present. These three elements are valid agreement (offer + acceptance), valid consideration and a valid intention to be bound in legal relations. In the absence of specific information about intention in this question, we have assumed that intention in valid in each case.

(a) **Arthur**

In this situation, Paul has promised to sell an expensive car to Arthur for £10. The values of the car and the £10 are not comparable.

Consideration must have some economic value but it need not be of an equal value to that of the promise given. This is the law of contract that states that **consideration must be sufficient but need not be adequate**.

The case *Thomas v Thomas 1842* illustrates how the courts will not weigh up the comparative values of consideration. It is up to the parties to strike a bargain.

The case *Chappell and Co v Nestle Co 1960* decided that if the consideration had some kind of identifiable value, then it was sufficient.

In this case, although Paul has made an astonishingly bad bargain, it appears that **he is bound** by his promise.

(b) **Bernard**

In this situation, Bernard has provided a service for Paul, and Paul appears to have subsequently agreed to pay Bernard £1 for it.

On the basis of the points made above, this consideration would appear to be sufficient, but it may be invalid.

Consideration may be **executory** (a promise in return for a promise) or **executed** (an act or forbearance in return for a promise). However, it may not be **past**. A promise to pay for what has already been done is **generally insufficient** to make the promise binding: *Re McArdle*.

There are some exceptions to the above rule, notably the exception when debts are settled by a bill of exchange. However, the exceptions do not appear to apply in this case.

If Bernard, unprompted by Paul, has cleaned Paul's windows then this act is past and **does not form consideration** for a promise Paul has later made to pay him £1. Paul is therefore **not bound**.

However, if Bernard is a professional window-cleaner and there is an **ongoing agreement** between them (this is implied by the fact that the service has been provided) then **Paul would be bound**.

(c) **Charles**

The initial contract in this scenario is valid.

However, a promisee's performance of **existing obligations** which already bind him under a contract with the promisor is no consideration for a further promise: *Stilk v Myrick 1809*.

Charles has given Paul no additional consideration for the promise of the extra £20.

However, the courts' view appears to have changed in recent times on this issue. In *Williams v Roffey Bros and Nicholls (Contractors) Ltd 1990*, as it was decided that both parties derived benefit from the additional promise, the further promise was valid.

If Paul gets **some additional benefit** from the further contract then the promise may be binding.

(d) **Eric**

There appears to be a **valid contract between Paul and Eric** as they have given consideration to each other. Paul has promised to make a delivery, albeit to a third party, and Eric has promised money.

David is involved in the contract as a third party to whom the goods are to be delivered. Ordinarily, **David** would assume no rights under the contract as he is **not a direct party** to the contract: *Tweddle v Atkinson 1861*.

However, **David may have enforceable rights** under the Contracts (Rights of Third Parties) Act 1999.

(e) **Frank**

In this situation, Paul has promised to release Frank from part of his debt to him.

Acceptance of part payment of an existing debt is no consideration for a promise to forgo the balance: *Foakes v Beer 1884*.

However, there is an exception to this rule if the promise is given with the intention that the other party should act on it and he does act on it, and cannot be restored to his original position in the event of the promise being withdrawn. This is called the doctrine of **promissory estoppel**.

Insufficient detail is given in the question to determine whether Paul has made the promise with such intention and whether this doctrine applies.

However, it is **unlikely that it does apply**, so in the absence of further information, it would appear that **Paul is not bound** by his promise to accept part payment for Frank's debt.

28 Martin, Neil and Owen

Tutorial note. The terms of the question mean restriction to the two statutory remedies, s 459 and compulsory winding up.

The question is quite a tough one since you not only have to know the rules but apply them to a case where the decision would not be straightforward.

With these questions, you should state the law, explaining its effects, and apply the law to the problem detailing any uncertainties. Your answer should conclude by giving advice as required by the question.

The key points in the answer are:

(a) Why a s 459 action might be brought (discrimination against a minority, exclusion of partners)
(b) The court taking into account the conduct of the parties
(c) The court being able to make whatever order it sees fit under s 461 (generally, as here, purchase of the minority's shares)
(d) Compulsory winding up is likely to be used rarely, since the petitioner must show no other remedy is available (the *Ebrahimi* case was settled before the current s 459 came into force, and arguably Ebrahimi could use s 459 today)

Owen and Quentin's complaint is that Owen has been dismissed from the board of directors and Quentin is no longer consulted on management matters by Martin and Neil who have a 60% majority in the company. There are two main actions which Owen and Quentin might consider taking against the majority.

S 459 action

State both the key examples of unfairly prejudicial conduct

S 459 provides that a member of a company may petition the court for an order on the grounds that the company's affairs have been or are being conducted in a manner which is **unfairly prejudicial** to the interests of the members generally or some part of the members, including the applicant.

Most commonly such actions are brought in cases of complaints of discrimination against a minority or exclusion of a 'partner' from participating in the management of a **'quasi-partnership'** company. Application can be made in respect of a particular act or omission (such as the removal of Owen from the board) as well as ongoing conduct (such as failing to consult Quentin as previously).

State and explain the law

The applicant is not required to show bad faith or intentional discrimination by the majority but must show that he is prejudiced as a member and not, for example, as an employee or unpaid creditor.

In considering a case, the court will take account of all relevant facts and surrounding circumstances. It will also have regard to the conduct of the parties, thus in *R A Noble & Sons (Clothing) Ltd 1983*, the applicant's complaint that he had been excluded from discussion of management matters was considered to have resulted largely from his own lack of interest and his case was dismissed.

Apply the law to both their situations

Owen's position

As far as Owen is concerned, the case of *Ebrahimi v Westbourne Galleries Ltd 1973* is particularly relevant. Here, in very similar circumstances the complainant, Ebrahimi, was removed from the board of directors.

It was held that the past relationship between Ebrahimi and another director made it unjust or inequitable that he should be removed and the court ordered that the company be wound up.

Draw out the difference between Owen's history with the business and Quentin being new

More particularly, as a case brought under s 459, in *Re Bird Precision Bellows Ltd 1985*, again very similar facts, the removal from the board of the applicant was held to be unfairly prejudicial conduct and the claim was allowed.

However, one of the factors to be taken into account would be Owen's operating a competing business but in *Re London School of Electronics Ltd 1985* an ousted director who was also running a competing business still succeeded in his action brought under s 459. In the light of these cases it would seem that Owen could succeed in obtaining a court order (discussed below) under s 459.

Quentin's position

In the case of Quentin, although he was not a founder member as were Martin Neil and Owen and held fewer shares than those three, he was consulted on management decisions as if he were a director, despite his 'associate' title. In view of this, it might be argued that he too was a partner in a quasi-partnership company and as such had a legitimate expectation that he would continue to participate in management: *Re A Company 1986*. In *O'Neill v Phillips 1999* the House of Lords stressed that where an action is in compliance with company law that action will not be unfairly prejudicial unless there has been some breach of the terms on which the parties agreed that the affairs of the company would be conducted.

State that this is not clear cut and would be for the court to decide on the facts

However, the evidence is weaker in the case of Quentin than of Owen and it might be argued that no longer consulting a 10% minority shareholder who is operating a competing business is not unfairly prejudicial to him in the same way as ousting a director from the board. Quentin would be advised to endeavour to illustrate to the court that the four members had indeed operated Parking Ltd as a quasi-partnership company. This seems unlikely to succeed in the light of *O'Neill v Phillips*.

Court order

Following a successful application, the court may make such **order** as it **thinks fit** for giving relief in respect of the matters complained of: s 461. For example, the court might make an order regulating the future conduct of the company's affairs.

Of particular relevance here, the court might make an order for the **purchase** of the **applicant's shares** by other members or by the company. Thus the court might order that Owen's shares – and possibly Quentin's shares – be purchased by Martin and/or Neil provided the petition presented states that this particular relief is being sought.

It is likely that such an order would provide for the shares to be purchased at a **'fair price'** which may be determined by the court. In particular, it has been held that the value should be calculated on the basis of the shares' worth before being diminished by the controlling shareholders' conduct: *SCWS v Meyer 1958* and no allowance should be made on the basis that the shares are a minority holding only and do not give control: *Re Bird Precision Bellows 1985*.

Compulsory winding up

The second action which Owen and Quentin might consider is to petition the court under s 122 IA 1986 for a winding up of Parking Ltd on the ground that it is **just and equitable** to do so. This remedy is commonly sought by a member who is dissatisfied or in total disagreement with the directors or controlling shareholders.

Review the case for a comparison. Ebrahimi is similar, but remember that s459 has been introduced after this case

However, a petitioner must show more than dissatisfaction in order to persuade the court that it is just and equitable to wind the company up since **winding up is a very drastic step** which a court will not order lightly. In particular it must be shown that **no other remedy is available** (s 125 (2)).

So whereas a winding up might be ordered where the only or main object of a company can no longer be achieved because the **company's substructure has gone** (*Re German Date Coffee Co 1882*) or where there is **complete deadlock in the management of its affairs** (*Re Yenidje Tobacco Co Ltd 1916*), it will not be ordered where the problem can be resolved by, for example, an order for the purchase of the petitioners' shares.

Thus, in *Re A Company 1983*, on facts similar to the *Ebrahimi* case, it was held that an order for winding up, which **can only be made in the absence of other remedies** was not applicable where it was appropriate to give an order for the purchase of the petitioner's shares.

Conclusion

You must draw a conclusion as you have been asked to advise the parties

It is **unlikely that a court would order the winding up of Parking Ltd since the purchase of Owen's and Quentin's shares by Martin and Neil would seem to resolve the problem** between the parties. Also it might seem inequitable to put Parking Ltd into liquidation but at the same time allow the rival company to continue in business. The court could make such an order, setting out terms as it thinks fit, in the case of either a s 459 application or s 122 IA 1986 petition. Quentin might consider pursuing both courses of action in case he should face difficulties in evidencing unfairly prejudicial conduct, provided he can make out a *prima facie* case under s 122 IA 1986.

List of cases and index

Note: Key Terms and their page references are given in **bold.**

Review Form & Free Prize Draw – Paper 2.2 Corporate and Business Law (6/05)

All original review forms from the entire BPP range, completed with genuine comments, will be entered into one of two draws on 31 January 2006 and 31 July 2006. The names on the first four forms picked out on each occasion will be sent a cheque for £50.

Name: ______________________ **Address:** ______________________

How have you used this Interactive Text?
(Tick one box only)

- ☐ Home study (book only)
- ☐ On a course: college ______________
- ☐ With 'correspondence' package
- ☐ Other ______________

Why did you decide to purchase this Interactive Text? *(Tick one box only)*

- ☐ Have used BPP Texts in the past
- ☐ Recommendation by friend/colleague
- ☐ Recommendation by a lecturer at college
- ☐ Saw advertising
- ☐ Saw information on BPP website
- ☐ Other ______________

During the past six months do you recall seeing/receiving any of the following?
(Tick as many boxes as are relevant)

- ☐ Our advertisement in *ACCA Student Accountant*
- ☐ Our advertisement in *Pass*
- ☐ Our advertisement in *PQ*
- ☐ Our brochure with a letter through the post
- ☐ Our website www.bpp.com

Which (if any) aspects of our advertising do you find useful?
(Tick as many boxes as are relevant)

- ☐ Prices and publication dates of new editions
- ☐ Information on Text content
- ☐ Facility to order books off-the-page
- ☐ None of the above

Which BPP products have you used?

Text	☑	*Success CD*	☐	*Learn Online*	☐
Kit	☐	*i-Learn*	☐	*Home Study Package*	☐
Passcard	☐	*i-Pass*	☐	*Home Study PLUS*	☐

Your ratings, comments and suggestions would be appreciated on the following areas.

	Very useful	*Useful*	*Not useful*
Introductory section (Key study steps, personal study)	☐	☐	☐
Chapter introductions	☐	☐	☐
Key terms	☐	☐	☐
Quality of explanations	☐	☐	☐
Case studies and other examples	☐	☐	☐
Exam focus points	☐	☐	☐
Questions and answers in each chapter	☐	☐	☐
Fast forwards and chapter roundups	☐	☐	☐
Quick quizzes	☐	☐	☐
Question Bank	☐	☐	☐
Answer Bank	☐	☐	☐
Index	☐	☐	☐
Icons	☐	☐	☐

Overall opinion of this Study Text *Excellent* ☐ *Good* ☐ *Adequate* ☐ *Poor* ☐

Do you intend to continue using BPP products? *Yes* ☐ *No* ☐

The BPP author of this edition can be e-mailed at: pippariley@bpp.com

Please return this form to: Nick Weller, ACCA Publishing Manager, BPP Professional Education, FREEPOST, London, W12 8BR

Review Form & Free Prize Draw (continued)

Please note any further comments and suggestions/errors below

Free Prize Draw Rules

1. Closing date for 31 January 2006 draw is 31 December 2005. Closing date for 31 July 2006 draw is 30 June 2006.
2. Restricted to entries with UK and Eire addresses only. BPP employees, their families and business associates are excluded.
3. No purchase necessary. Entry forms are available upon request from BPP Professional Education. No more than one entry per title, per person. Draw restricted to persons aged 16 and over.
4. Winners will be notified by post and receive their cheques not later than 6 weeks after the relevant draw date.
5. The decision of the promoter in all matters is final and binding. No correspondence will be entered into.

ACCA Order

To BPP Professional Education, Aldine Place, London W12 8AW
Tel: 020 8740 2211 Fax: 020 8740 1184
email: publishing@bpp.com website: www.bpp.com
Order online www.bpp.com/mybpp

Mr/Mrs/Ms (Full name)

Daytime delivery address

Postcode

Daytime Tel Date of exam (month/year) Scots law variant Y / N

Occasionally we may wish to email you relevant offers and information about courses and products.
Please tick to opt into this service.

	6/05 Texts	1/05 Kits	1/05 Passcards	Success CDs	7/05 i-Learn	7/05 i-Pass	Learn Online
PART 1							
1.1 Preparing Financial Statements (UK)	£26.00	£12.95	£9.95	£14.95	£40.00	£30.00	£100
1.2 Financial Information for Management	£26.00	£12.95	£9.95	£14.95	£40.00	£30.00	£100
1.3 Managing People	£26.00	£12.95	£9.95	£14.95	£40.00	£30.00	£100
PART 2							
2.1 Information Systems	£26.00	£12.95	£9.95	£14.95	£40.00	£30.00	£100
2.2 Corporate and Business Law (UK)**	£26.00	£12.95	£9.95	£14.95	£40.00	£30.00	£100
2.3 Business Taxation FA2004 (12/05 exams)	£24.95 (8/04)	£12.95	£9.95	£14.95	£34.95 (8/04)	£24.95 (8/04)	£100
2.3 Business Taxation FA2005	£26.00 †	£12.95	£9.95	£14.95	£40.00 (9/05)	£30.00 (9/05)	£100
2.4 Financial Management and Control	£26.00	£12.95	£9.95	£14.95	£40.00	£30.00	£100
2.5 Financial Reporting (UK)	£26.00 (7/05)	£12.95	£9.95	£14.95	£40.00	£30.00	£100
2.6 Audit and Internal Review (UK)	£26.00	£12.95	£9.95	£14.95	£40.00	£30.00	£100
PART 3						**8/04**	
3.1 Audit and Assurance Services (UK)	£26.00	£12.95	£9.95	£14.95		£30.00 (4/05)	£60
3.2 Advanced Taxation FA2004 (12/05 exams)	£24.95	£12.95	£9.95	£14.95		£24.95	£60
3.2 Advanced Taxation FA2005	£26.00 †	£12.95	£9.95	£14.95		£30.00 (9/05)	£60
3.3 Performance Management	£26.00	£12.95	£9.95	£14.95		£24.95	£60
3.4 Business Information Management	£26.00	£12.95	£9.95	£14.95		£24.95	£60
3.5 Strategic Business Planning and Devt	£26.00	£12.95	£9.95	£14.95		£24.95	£60
3.6 Advanced Corporate Reporting (UK)	£26.00 (7/05)	£12.95	£9.95	£14.95		£24.95	£60
3.7 Strategic Financial Management	£26.00	£12.95	£9.95	£14.95		£24.95	£60
INTERNATIONAL STREAM						**7/05**	
1.1 Preparing Financial Statements (Int'l)	£26.00	£12.95	£9.95		£40.00	£30.00	£100
2.2 Corporate and Business Law (Global)	£26.00	£12.95	£9.95				
2.5 Financial Reporting (Int'l)	£26.00	£12.95	£9.95		£40.00	£30.00	£100
2.6 Audit and Internal Review (Int'l)	£26.00	£12.95	£9.95		£40.00	£30.00	£100
3.1 Audit and Assurance Services (Int'l)	£26.00	£12.95	£9.95			£30.00	£60
3.6 Advanced Corporate Reporting (Int'l)	£26.00	£12.95	£9.95		£40.00 (12/05)	£30.00	£60
Success in Your Research and Analysis Project - Tutorial Text (10/05)	£26.00						
Learning to Learn Accountancy (7/02)	£9.95						
Business Maths and English (6/04)	£9.95						

SUBTOTAL £

†(**8/05** for 6/06 & 12/06 exams. New edition Kit, Passcard, i-Learn and i-Pass available in 2006)

POSTAGE & PACKING

Study Texts/Kits

	First	*Each extra*	*Online*	
UK	£5.00	£2.00	£2.00	£
EU*	£6.00	£4.00	£4.00	£
Non EU	£20.00	£10.00	£10.00	£

Passcards/Success CDs/i-Learn/i-Pass

	First	*Each extra*	*Online*	
UK	£2.00	£1.00	£1.00	£
EU*	£3.00	£2.00	£2.00	£
Non EU	£8.00	£8.00	£8.00	£

Learning to Learn Accountancy/Business Maths and English

	Each	*Online*	
UK	£3.00	£2.00	£
EU*	£6.00	£4.00	£
Non EU	£20.00	£10.00	£

Grand Total (incl. Postage)

I enclose a cheque for £
(Cheques to *BPP Professional Education*)

Or charge to Visa/Mastercard/Switch

Card Number

Expiry date Start Date

Issue Number (Switch Only)

Signature

We aim to deliver to all UK addresses inside 5 working days; a signature will be required. Orders to all EU addresses should be delivered within 6 working days. All other orders to overseas addresses should be delivered within 8 working days. *EU includes the Republic of Ireland and the Channel Islands. **For Scots law variant students, a free **Scots Law Supplement** is available with the 2.2 Text. Please indicate in the name and address section if this applies to you.

ACCA Order

To BPP Professional Education, Aldine Place, London W12 8AW

Tel: 020 8740 2211 Fax: 020 8740 1184

email: publishing@bpp.com website: www.bpp.com

Order online www.bpp.com/mybpp

Mr/Mrs/Ms (Full name)

Daytime delivery address

Postcode

Daytime Tel Date of exam (month/year) Scots law variant Y / N

	Home Study Package*	Home Study PLUS*	Success CDs	7/05 i-Learn	Learn Online
PART 1					
1.1 Preparing Financial Statements UK	£115.00 ☐	£180.00 ☐	£14.95 ☐	£40.00 ☐	£100.00 ☐
1.2 Financial Information for Management	£115.00 ☐	£180.00 ☐	£14.95 ☐	£40.00 ☐	£100.00 ☐
1.3 Managing People	£115.00 ☐	£180.00 ☐	£14.95 ☐	£40.00 ☐	£100.00 ☐
PART 2					
2.1 Information Systems	£115.00 ☐	£180.00 ☐	£14.95 ☐	£40.00 ☐	£100.00 ☐
2.2 Corporate and Business Law UK***	£115.00 ☐	£180.00 ☐	£14.95 ☐	£40.00 ☐	£100.00 ☐
2.3 Business Taxation FA2004 (12/05 exams)	£115.00 ☐	£180.00 ☐	£14.95 ☐	£34.95 ☐ (8/04)	£100.00 ☐
2.3 Business Taxation FA2005 (2006 exams)	£115.00 ☐	£180.00 ☐	£14.95 ☐	£40.00 ☐ (9/05)	£100.00 ☐
2.4 Financial Management and Control	£115.00 ☐	£180.00 ☐	£14.95 ☐	£40.00 ☐	£100.00 ☐
2.5 Financial Reporting UK	£115.00 ☐	£180.00 ☐	£14.95 ☐	£40.00 ☐	£100.00 ☐
2.6 Audit and Internal Review UK	£115.00 ☐	£180.00 ☐	£14.95 ☐	£40.00 ☐	£100.00 ☐
PART 3					
3.1 Audit and Assurance Services UK	£115.00 ☐	£150.00 ☐	£14.95 ☐		£60.00 ☐
3.2 Advanced Taxation FA2004 (12/05 exams)	£115.00 ☐	£150.00 ☐	£14.95 ☐		£60.00 ☐
3.2 Advanced Taxation FA2005 (2006 exams)	£115.00 ☐	£150.00 ☐	£14.95 ☐		£60.00 ☐
3.3 Performance Management	£115.00 ☐	£150.00 ☐	£14.95 ☐		£60.00 ☐
3.4 Business Information Management	£115.00 ☐	£150.00 ☐	£14.95 ☐		£60.00 ☐
3.5 Strategic Business Planning and Development	£115.00 ☐	£150.00 ☐	£14.95 ☐		£60.00 ☐
3.6 Advanced Corporate Reporting UK	£115.00 ☐	£150.00 ☐	£14.95 ☐		£60.00 ☐
3.7 Strategic Financial Management	£115.00 ☐	£150.00 ☐	£14.95 ☐		£60.00 ☐
INTERNATIONAL STREAM					
1.1 Preparing Financial Statements (Int'l)	£115.00 ☐	£180.00 ☐		£40.00 ☐	£100.00 ☐
2.2 Corporate and Business Law (Global)	£115.00 ☐				
2.5 Financial Reporting (Int'l)	£115.00 ☐	£180.00 ☐		£40.00 ☐	£100.00 ☐
2.6 Audit and Internal Review (Int'l)	£115.00 ☐	£180.00 ☐		£40.00 ☐	£100.00 ☐
3.1 Audit and Assurance Services (Int'l)	£115.00 ☐	£150.00 ☐			£60.00 ☐
3.6 Advanced Corporate Reporting (Int'l)	£115.00 ☐	£150.00 ☐		£40.00 ☐ (12/05)	£60.00 ☐
Success in Your Research and Analysis Project - Tutorial Text (10/05)	£26.00 ☐				
Learning to Learn Accountancy (7/02)	Free/£9.95 ☐				
Business Maths and English (6/04)	Free/£9.95 ☐				

SUBTOTAL £

Occasionally we may wish to email you relevant offers and information about courses and products.
Please tick to opt into this service. ☐

POSTAGE & PACKING

Home Study Packages

	First	*Each extra*	*Each*	
UK	£6.00	£6.00	-	£
EU**	-	-	£15.00	£
Non EU	-	-	£50.00	£

Success CDs/i-Learn

	First	*Each extra*	*Online*	
UK	£2.00	£1.00	£1.00	£
EU**	£3.00	£2.00	£2.00	£
Non EU	£8.00	£8.00	£8.00	£

Learning to Learn Accountancy/Business Maths and English/Success in Your Research and Analysis Project

	Each	*Online*	
UK	£3.00†	£2.00	£
EU**	£6.00	£4.00	£
Non EU	£20.00	£10.00	£

(†£5.00 Success in Your Research and Analysis Project)

Postage and packing not charged on free copy ordered with Home Study Course.

Grand Total (incl. Postage)

I enclose a cheque for £
(Cheques to *BPP Professional Education*)

Or charge to Visa/Mastercard/Switch

Card Number

Expiry date Start Date

Issue Number (Switch Only)

Signature

We aim to deliver to all UK addresses inside 5 working days; a signature will be required. Orders to all EU addresses should be delivered within 6 working days. All other orders should be delivered within 8 working days. *Home Study Courses include Texts, Kits, Passcards and i-Pass (i-Pass not available for 2.2 Global and 3.1 International). You can also order one free copy of either Learning to Learn Accountancy or Business Maths and English per Home Study course, to a maximum of one of each per person. **EU includes the Republic of Ireland and the Channel Islands. ***For Scots law variant students, a free **Scots Law Supplement** is available with the 2.2 Text.